Econometric Theory and Practice

This book is a collection of essays written in honor of Professor Peter C. B. Phillips of Yale University by some of his former students. The essays analyze several state-of-the-art issues in econometrics, all of which Professor Phillips has directly influenced through his seminal scholarly contribution and remarkable achievements as a teacher. The essays are organized to cover topics in higher-order asymptotics, deficient instruments, nonstationarity, least absolute deviation (LAD) and quantile regression, and nonstationary panels. These topics span both theoretical and applied approaches and are intended for use by professionals and advanced graduate students.

Dean Corbae is Rex A. and Dorothy B. Sebastian Centennial Professor in Business Administration at the University of Texas at Austin. He is an Associate Editor of the *International Economic Review* as well as *Economic Theory*. Professor Corbae's research interests include applied time series analysis in macroeconomics and international finance.

Steven N. Durlauf is the Kenneth J. Arrow Professor of Economics at the University of Wisconsin, Madison. He is a former Director of the Economics Program at the Santa Fe Institute. A Fellow of the Econometric Society, Professor Durlauf is coeditor of the *Journal of Applied Econometrics*. His research interests include income inequality, economic growth, and applied econometrics.

Bruce E. Hansen is Professor of Economics at the University of Wisconsin, Madison. He is a coeditor of *Econometric Theory* and Associate Editor of *Econometrica*. Professor Hansen is a Fellow of the Econometric Society and the *Journal of Econometrics*. He has published widely in the leading econometrics journals.

Econometric Theory and Practice

Frontiers of Analysis and Applied Research

Edited by

DEAN CORBAE

University of Texas at Austin

STEVEN N. DURLAUF

University of Wisconsin at Madison

BRUCE E. HANSEN

University of Wisconsin at Madison

CAMBRIDGE
UNIVERSITY PRESS

CAMBRIDGE UNIVERSITY PRESS
Cambridge, New York, Melbourne, Madrid, Cape Town, Singapore,
São Paulo, Delhi, Dubai, Tokyo, Mexico City

Cambridge University Press
32 Avenue of the Americas, New York, NY 10013-2473, USA

www.cambridge.org
Information on this title: www.cambridge.org/9780521184304

First published 2006
First paperback edition 2010

A catalog record for this publication is available from the British Library

Library of Congress Cataloging in Publication data

Econometric theory and practice: frontiers of analysis and applied research /
edited by P. Dean Corbae, Steven N. Durlauf, Bruce E. Hansen.
p. cm.
A collection of essays written in honor of Prof. Peter C. B. Phillips of Yale University.
Includes bibliographical references and index.
ISBN-13: 978-0-521-80723-4 (hardback)
ISBN-10: 0-521-80723-9 (hardback)
1. Econometrics. I. Phillips, P. C. B. II. Corbae, Dean. III. Durlauf, Steven N.
IV. Hansen, Bruce E., 1962– V. Title.
HB139.E285 2006
330′.01′5195 – dc22 2005014249

ISBN 978-0-521-80723-4 Hardback
ISBN 978-0-521-18430-4 Paperback

Contents

Preface

In Praise of a Remarkable Teacher

This volume presents a selection of papers offered to Professor Peter C. B. Phillips by a set of his past students. The collection is somewhat unusual in that it is not offered on the occasion of his reaching a particular venerable age or having decided to retire but rather in recognition of his extraordinary and continuing achievements as a teacher and mentor.

Peter Phillips is universally recognized as one of the great econometricians in the history of our profession. His work on finite sample theory, asymptotic expansions, nonstationary and long-memory time series, and the interface of Bayesian and frequentist methods, to name only a subset of the areas of his scholarship, evidences an extraordinary combination of mathematical analysis of the highest order as well as a level of creativity and insight reflecting that touch of genius apparent in even the most casual interactions with Peter. His more-than-170 published research articles and 30 current working papers attest to a coupling of brilliance with incredible energy.

It is all the more remarkable, then, that Peter has been one of the truly great teachers of aspiring economists. In the last 23 years, he has been a primary advisor to no fewer than 45 graduate students. His students have obtained positions throughout the world and at many of the leading research institutions. Peter's indirect contributions to economics via this college of econometricians would by itself earn him a distinguished place in the annals of scholarship.

Simple numbers cannot describe the reasons so many students have been attracted to Peter as an advisor. One reason is intellectual. Working with Peter has represented, at each stage of his career, an opportunity to participate in an important current research program. In this regard, Peter is well known for his incredible generosity in integrating students into his current research program – usually by making them coauthors. Such an experience can be both exhilarating and occasionally terrifying for a graduate student, for coauthorship with a scholar of Peter's depth demands that one work at one's absolute intellectual peak. Yet this "ordeal by fire" has for many of us remained one of the best memories of our careers, let alone of graduate school. A second reason is personal. Peter is in every respect an extraordinarily dedicated and caring advisor. He is a champion of all of his students, regardless of ability or success, and any student who works with him knows that it is the beginning of a lifetime commitment. A third reason combines both the scholarly and the personal: Peter embodies that love of discovery that makes the vagaries of academic life worthwhile. Not only is he able to promote that same love of discovery in his students, but he has also instilled in us a deep concern for maintaining the highest intellectual and professional standards. It will come as no surprise that many of Peter's students have themselves been exceptionally active teachers and advisors, reflecting his many gifts.

It is, therefore, with the deepest affection and respect that we present these essays to Peter C. B. Phillips as a reflection of our appreciation. As a one-time student of the classics, Peter will appreciate that it is he we have in mind when we say *magister dixit.*

Contributors

Jushan Bai
Boston College

John C. Chao
University of Maryland

Yoosoon Chang
Rice University

In Choi
Hong Kong University of Science and Technology

Dean Corbae
University of Texas at Austin

Bruce E. Hansen
University of Wisconsin

Douglas J. Hodgson
University of Quebec at Montreal

Yuichi Kitamura
Yale University

Roger Koenker
University of Illinois at Urbana–Champaign

Guido M. Kuersteiner
Boston University

Charles R. Nelson
University of Washington

Sam Ouliaris
International Monetary Fund and
National University of Singapore

Joon Y. Park
Rice University

Pierre Perron
Boston University

Richard Startz
University of Washington

Norman R. Swanson
Rutgers University

Yoon-Jae Whang
Korea University

Zhijie Xiao
Boston College

Eric Zivot
University of Washington

Introduction

The thirteen essays: in this volume have been written by the students of Professor Peter C. B. Phillips to recognize, honor, and demonstrate his impact on the practice of econometrics. These writings span parts of Phillips' seminal and enormous research program. His students have continued to work in the areas he helped initiate.

The first section of essays deals with higher-order asymptotics. In "Edgeworth Expansions for the Wald and GMM Statistics for Nonlinear Restrictions," Hansen derives an Edgeworth expansion for the generalized method of moments (GMM) distance statistic for a real-valued, nonlinear restriction on a normal linear regression. He also provides a refinement of the Edgeworth expansion for the Wald statistic derived by Park and Phillips (1988) and shows that the leading coefficient is the same in these two expansions. This establishes that, to the order of approximation of the Edgeworth expansion, the GMM distance statistic has a better approximation to the chi-square distribution than does the Wald statistic. Finally, the essay updates the Monte Carlo simulation of Gregory and Veall (1985) to include both heteroskedasticity-robust covariance matrix estimation and the GMM distance statistic. He finds that if the robust covariance matrix is calculated under the null, the GMM statistic has near-perfect finite sample Type I error in his experiments – even in sample sizes as small as $n = 20$.

In "Moment Selection and Bias Reduction for GMM in Conditionally Heteroskedastic Models," Guido Kuerstiener extends his previous work on GMM estimators for autoregressive moving average (ARMA) models with martingale difference errors to a class with conditionally heteroskedastic innovations. In contrast to standard results for two-stage least squares (TSLS), in which adding more instruments affects the bias of the GMM estimator, the higher-order analysis provided by Kuerstiener reveals that the dimension of the instrument space does not affect the higher-order mean-squared error under a given set of assumptions provided the number of instruments is not too large. Informing the difference is the way he implements the instrumental variables (IV) estimator; the presence of the parametric component is responsible for the good bias properties.

The second set of essays considers deficient instruments. In "Specification Tests with Instrumental Variables and Rank Deficiency," Yuichi Kitamura studies problems associated with two commonly used misspecification testing procedures in linear models when there is moment matrix rank deficiency. His chapter makes extensive use of invariance properties of orthogonal groups of matrices, which were previously shown by Phillips (1989) to be extremely useful in studying rank deficiency problems.[1] Using these tools, Kitamura is able to study a unified rank deficiency problem allowing him to tie together a "partial identification" problem in which the correlation matrix between the regressors and the instruments satisfies a reduced rank condition as well as the power problem under certain moment conditions in GMM misspecification tests identified by Newey (1985). His theoretical results imply that an applied researcher may find his model passes IV misspecification tests in the partially identified case even when the model is misspecified because the rejection probability of standard tests is below their nominal size asymptotically.

John Chao and Norman Swanson analyze conditions under which various single-equation estimators are asymptotically normal in a simultaneous-equations framework with many weak instruments. In "Asymptotic Normality of Single-Equation Estimators for the Case with a Large Number of Weak Instruments," the authors consider the case in which instrument weakness is such that the rate of growth of the concentration parameter r_n is slower than the rate of growth of the number of instruments K_n but such that $\frac{\sqrt{K_n}}{r_n} \to 0$ as $n \to \infty$. They show how the asymptotic variances of various estimators are different from the case in which r_n is assumed to grow at the same or faster rate than K_n.

Because standard IV estimation techniques are well known to give spuriously small standard errors in the presence of weak instruments, Eric Zivot analyzes the inference problem on individual coefficients in the IV regression model with multiple, endogenous, right-hand-side variables and weak instruments. His essay, "Inference in Weakly Identified Instrumental Variables Regression" extends the previous work of Choi and Phillips (1992) to allow for weak instruments.[2] Zivot evaluates existing techniques for performing inference on individual coefficients using Staiger and Stock's (1997) weak instrument asymptotics and performs extensive finite sample analyses using Monte Carlo simulations. He shows that the only asymptotically valid tests for individual coefficients are based on projections of asymptotically valid tests for

[1] Phillips, P. C. B. (1989) "Partially identified econometric models," *Econometric Theory*, Vol. 5, pp. 181–240.

[2] Choi, I. and P. C. B. Phillips (1992) "Asymptotic and finite sample distribution theory for IV estimators and tests in partially identified structural equations," *Journal of Econometrics*, Vol. 51, pp. 113–50.

all coefficients and that Kleibergen's (2002) concentrated K statistic has quite good size and power behavior relative to other methods.

The third group of essays deals with nonstationarity. In "Extracting Cycles from Nonstationary Data," Dean Corbae and Sam Ouliaris develop a frequency-domain filter to extract the cyclical component of a series that easily handles stochastic and deterministic trends based on earlier work with P. C. B. Phillips (2002).[3] They assess its goodness-of-fit properties relative to the known cyclical component as well as some popular time-domain filters such as the Hodrick–Prescott filter. They apply the filter to U.S. real GDP data and also analyze the cyclical properties of the price level.

In "Nonstationary Nonlinearity: An Outlook for New Opportunities," Joon Park introduces basic tools to deal with nonstationary nonlinearity and uses them to study three different topics associated with data generation, regression analysis, and stochastic volatility. In the first case, Park studies non-linear transformations of random walks, which can generate stationary long memory as well as bounded nonstationarity. An example of such a transformation is policy intervention in the case of target zone exchange rate regimes. In the second case, he considers parametric nonlinear and nonparametric cointegration methods, shows that convergence rates are dramatically reduced in the nonparametric case, and suggests a new two-step, partial parametric approach to estimation and inference. Finally, Park studies a stochastic volatility model in which conditional variance is given by a nonlinear function of a random walk and shows that such models may generate samples with volatility clustering and leptokurticity, which are commonly observed in financial time series.

Jushan Bai and Pierre Perron provide Monte Carlo evidence on the size and power of tests for linear models with multiple structural changes that they developed in earlier papers (1998, 1999), the coverage rates of confidence intervals for break dates, and the relative merits of methods to select the number of breaks in their chapter "Multiple Structural Change Models: A Simulation Analysis." Their simulations cover a wide variety of data-generation processes, and their findings provide a series of suggestions for the applied researcher. Among other things, they show the following: (i) If serial correlation, heterogeneity in the data or errors across segments, or all of these are allowed, trimming the errors will help avoid size problems; (ii) Selecting break points using the Bayesian information criterion (BIC) works well when breaks are present but less so when there is serial correlation; (iii) A strategy for using sequential procedures suggested in their earlier work has good size and power properties; and (iv) Correcting for heterogeneity in the distribution of the data or the errors and for serial correlation improves the power of structural break tests and the accuracy in selecting the number of breaks.

[3] Corbae, D., S. Ouliaris, P. C. B. Phillips (2002) "Band spectral regression with trending data," *Econometrica*, 70, 2002, pp. 1067–1109.

The fourth section provides new developments in LAD and quantile regression. To analyze financial variables that tend to be characterized by distributions having thick tails, Douglas Hodgson studies estimation methods in the presence of possibly non-Gaussian disturbances in cointegrating regressions in his essay "On Efficient, Robust, and Adaptive Estimation in Cointegrated Models." Estimators (robust LAD and M-estimators) that downweight outlying observations in cointegrating regressions were developed earlier by Phillips' (1995), but such estimators were not asymptotically efficient.[4] To handle this, Hodgson explicitly parameterizes short-run dynamics as a general VARMA process and develops an adaptive estimator that allows for thick tails of unknown form in the density, showing it to be asymptotically equivalent to a full-information maximum likelihood (FIML) estimator. Hodgson also considers the implications for estimation when the thick tails are generated by conditional heteroskedacity and conducts a Monte Carlo study to assess alternative estimators' small sample properties.

In "Testing Stationarity Using M-Estimation," Roger Koenker and Zhijie Xiao study a general test of stationarity that has power against a wide range of alternatives based on M-estimators. Their results extend previous unit root tests based on M-estimation with least-squares detrending by such authors as Phillips (1995) to the case in which the detrending itself is based on M-estimation.[5] To obtain distribution free tests, the authors consider a martingale transformation on the partial sum process, which yields consistency. The authors discuss various implementations of the test and compare size and power of the text with conventional stationarity tests in finite samples via a series of Monte Carlos. The authors conclude with an application of their test to macroeconomic variables from the Nelson–Plosser dataset.

In "Consistent Specification Testing for Quantile Regression Models," Yoon-Jae Whang introduces specification tests for linear quantile regression models applicable to cases with dependent observations. The tests he considers are generalizations of the Kolmogorov–Smirnov and Cramer–von Mises tests of goodness of fit, which can be applied to stationary time series as well as cross sections. The tests are consistent against all alternatives to the null hypothesis, powerful against $1/\sqrt{N}$ alternatives, independent of any smoothing parameters, and simple to compute. Although the asymptotic null distributions are case dependent, Whang suggests a simple subsampling procedure to calculate critical values. Monte Carlo experiments show that his test has good finite sample performance relative to those in Zheng (1978).

The fifth topic area develops unit root tests for nonstationary panels with cross-sectional correlation. In "Combination Unit Root Tests for

[4] Phillips, P.C.B. (1995) "Robust nonstationary regression," *Econometric Theory*, 11, pp. 912–51.

[5] Phillips, P.C.B. (1995) "Robust nonstationary regression," *Econometric Theory*, 11, pp. 912–51.

Cross-Sectionally Correlated Panels," In Choi proposes a test statistic that combines p-values from the augmented Dickey–Fuller test applied to each time series whose nonstochastic trend components and cross-sectional correlations are eliminated by GLS-based detrending derived from Elliott, Rothenberg, and Stock (1996) and the conventional cross-sectional demeaning for panel data.[6] These combination tests have a standard, normal, limiting distribution, and Monte Carlo evidence points to good size and power properties. He applies these tests to the real GDP data for a panel of 23 OECD countries and finds evidence for the presence of a unit root.

In "Nonlinear IV Panel Unit Root Tests," Yoosoon Chang shows that if nonlinear transformations of lagged levels by an integrable function are used as instruments, the t-ratio based on the usual IV estimator for the autoregressive coefficient in an augmented Dickey–Fuller-type regression yields asymptotically normal unit root tests for each cross section. More importantly, the nonlinear IV t-ratios from different cross sections are asymptotically independent even when the cross sections are dependent, provided they are not cointegrated.

[6] Elliott, G., T. J. Rothenberg, and J. H. Stock (1996) "Efficient tests for autoregressive time series with a unit root," *Econometrica*, 64, pp. 813–36.

PART ONE

HIGHER-ORDER ASYMPTOTICS

ONE

Edgeworth Expansions for the Wald and GMM Statistics for Nonlinear Restrictions

Bruce E. Hansen*

1.1 INTRODUCTION

The Wald test is a popular test of statistical hypotheses largely because it is simple to compute. There are many reasons, however, to believe that the Wald test is generically a poor choice as a test of nonlinear hypothesis. One reason frequently mentioned is that the Wald statistic is not invariant to the algebraic formulation of the hypothesis. Gregory and Veall (1985) and Lafontaine and White (1986) showed in Monte Carlo simulations the potentially large consequences of alternative algebraic formulations. Park and Phillips (1988) formalized this finding by showing that the coefficients of the Edgeworth expansion of the Wald statistic depend on the formulation.

Separately, Newey and West (1987) proposed a distance generalized method of moments (GMM) statistic for nonlinear hypotheses. In the context of linear regression, their statistic is simply the GMM criterion function evaluated at the restricted estimates. When the hypothesis is a linear restriction on the parameters, their test corresponds to the Wald statistic. When the hypothesis is nonlinear, the two statistics differ. A striking feature of the GMM distance statistic is that it is invariant to the algebraic formulation of the hypothesis. (The invariance follows directly from its definition in terms of the criterion function.) The GMM distance statistic also has the advantage of being robust to heteroskedasticity (if a heteroskedasticity-consistent covariance matrix is used to define the GMM criterion). This is in contrast to the likelihood ratio statistic, which is invariant to formulation of the hypothesis but is not robust to heteroskedasticity. For a pedagogical description of this statistic, see section 9.2 of Newey and McFadden (1994).

Little is known, however, about the finite sample behavior of the GMM statistic. This chapter attempts to fill this gap by providing an Edgeworth

* This research was supported by a grant from the National Science Foundation. I thank Yuichi Kitamura and Ken West for helpful comments and discussions.

expansion for the GMM statistic in the leading case considered by Park and Phillips (1988). We use the explicit matrix approach to Edgeworth expansions initiated by Park and Phillips (1988) and push their approach one step further by using explicit matrix formulas for all our expressions. The advantage of this approach is that we are able to calculate greatly simplified expressions for our Edgeworth expansions, which enable us to make direct comparisons between statistics.

We rederive the Park–Phillips Edgeworth expansion for the Wald statistic along with that for the GMM statistic. We find the striking result that the Edgeworth expansion for the GMM statistic is a strict simplification of that for the Wald statistic. Thus the chi-square approximation for the GMM statistic is as good as that for any algebraic formulation of the Wald statistic – at least up to the level of the Edgeworth expansion approximation.

Gregory and Veall (1985) provided dramatic simulation evidence that two alternative formulations of the same hypothesis lead to very different finite sample behavior of the Wald statistic. We update their experiment and contrast the performance of the Wald statistics with the GMM statistic. We also compare the performance of the tests when heteroskedasticity-robust covariance matrices and GMM weight matrices are used. The simulations show that, if the GMM statistic is computed with a weight matrix calculated under the alternative hypothesis, its performance is nearly identical to the Gregory–Veall "good" form of the Wald statistic, whereas if the GMM statistic is computed with the weight matrix calculated under the null hypothesis, the size distortion virtually disappears. The results show that, even in samples as small as $n = 20$, test statistics can be made robust to unknown heteroskedasticity without any loss of control over Type I error.

The chapter is organized as follows. Section 1.2 states the model and test statistics. Section 1.3 describes alternative methods to calculate the covariance matrix of the estimates and the weight matrix for GMM estimation. Section 1.4 presents our main results. Section 1.5 is a Monte Carlo simulation. A brief conclusion follows in Section 1.6. Appendix A is a restatement of the Park–Phillips (1988) Edgeworth expansion (for reference). Appendix B contains the proof of Theorem 1.1 (the Edgeworth expansion for the Wald statistic). Appendix C contains the proof of Theorem 1.2 (the Edgeworth expansion for the GMM statistic).

A Gauss program that calculates the GMM statistics described in this chapter can be downloaded from my Web page <www.ssc.wisc.edu/~bhansen>.

1.2 LINEAR REGRESSION WITH NONLINEAR HYPOTHESES

The model is a linear regression

$$y_i = x_i'\beta + e_i$$
$$E(x_i e_i) = 0,$$

$i = 1, \ldots, n$, where x_i and β are each $k \times 1$. Let β_0 denote the true value of β.

The goal is to test the nonlinear hypothesis

$$H_0 : g(\beta) = 0 \qquad (1)$$
$$H_1 : g(\beta) \neq 0,$$

where $g : R^k \to R$. We are interested in testing H_0 against H_1.

Let

$$\hat{\beta} = (X'X)^{-1}(X'Y)$$

be the ordinary least squares (OLS) estimator of β, and let

$$V_n = (X'X)^{-1}\Omega_n(X'X)^{-1} \qquad (2)$$

be an estimator of the covariance matrix of $\hat{\beta}$, where Ω_n is an estimate of $nE\left(x_i x_i' e_i^2\right)$. We discuss specific choices below.

A common test statistic for H_0 is the Wald statistic

$$W = n\, g(\hat{\beta})' \left(\hat{G}' V_n \hat{G}\right)^{-1} g(\hat{\beta})$$
$$\hat{G} = \frac{\partial}{\partial \beta} g(\hat{\beta}).$$

The strengths of the Wald statistic are that it is easy to compute but asymptotically χ_1^2 under H_0 and very general conditions. A major weakness, however, is that the statistic is not invariant to the formulation of the hypothesis g.

A less commonly applied test of H_0 is the GMM distance statistic introduced by Newey and West (1987) and discussed in Newey and McFadden (1994, Section 9.2). This statistic is defined as the difference in the GMM criterion evaluated at estimates calculated under the null and alternative and constructed with the same efficient weight matrix. For the regression model, the GMM criterion function is

$$J(\beta) = (Y - X\beta)'\, X\Omega_n^{-1} X'\,(Y - X\beta),$$

where Ω_n again is an estimate of $nE\left(x_i x_i' e_i^2\right)$.

The unrestricted GMM estimator minimizes $J(\beta)$ over $\beta \in R^k$, that is,

$$\hat{\beta} = \underset{\beta \in R^k}{\text{argmin}}\ J(\beta)$$
$$= (X'X)^{-1}(X'Y),$$

and is identical to the OLS estimator. Note that $J(\hat{\beta}) = 0$.

The restricted GMM estimator minimizes $J(\beta)$ subject to constraint (1):

$$\tilde{\beta} = \underset{g(\beta)=0}{\text{argmin}}\ J(\beta). \qquad (3)$$

When $g(\beta)$ is nonlinear, a closed-form expression for $\tilde{\beta}$ does not exist. However, in general $\tilde{\beta}$ is quite simple to calculate because the criterion $J(\beta)$ is quadratic in β. Minimizing a quadratic function subject to a nonlinear constraint is a straightforward numerical optimization problem.

The Newey–West GMM distance test statistic is the difference in the criterion function evaluated at the two estimates:

$$DM = J(\tilde{\beta}) - J(\hat{\beta})$$
$$= \min_{g(\beta)=0} (Y - X\beta)' X\Omega_n^{-1} X' (Y - X\beta). \qquad (4)$$

The statistic (4) has several wonderful advantages over the Wald statistic. Primarily, it is invariant to the formulation of the hypothesis (1). This is because the parameter space $\{\beta : g(\beta) = 0\}$ is invariant to its algebraic formulation. The lack of invariance is a major problem with implementation of the Wald statistic when g is nonlinear. In the special case in which g is linear, however, the two statistics are numerically identical (if the same Ω_n is used).

A by-product of the computation of the test statistic (4) is the restricted estimate $\tilde{\beta}$. For reference, an estimate of the covariance matrix for $\tilde{\beta}$ can be calculated as

$$\tilde{V}_n = V_n - V_n\hat{G}\left(\hat{G}' V_n \hat{G}\right)^{-1} \hat{G}' V_n,$$

where V_n is defined in (2). (For a derivation, See Section 9.1 of Newey and McFadden, 1994).

1.3 CHOICE OF VARIANCE AND WEIGHT MATRIX

The statistics depend on the choice of Ω_n. The Wald statistic is typically calculated from the unrestricted estimates $\hat{\beta}$. One choice for Ω_n is the Eicker–White estimator

$$\hat{\Omega}_n = \sum_{i=1}^{n} x_i x_i' \hat{e}_i^2 \qquad (5)$$
$$\hat{e}_i = y_i - x_i'\hat{\beta},$$

For this is asymptotically valid for the specified model without additional auxiliary assumptions. An alternative choice is the OLS estimator

$$\hat{\Omega}_n^0 = X' X \hat{\sigma}^2 \qquad (6)$$
$$\hat{\sigma}^2 = \frac{1}{n-k} \sum_{i=1}^{n} \hat{e}_i^2,$$

which is valid under the conditional homoskedasticity assumption $E\left(e_i^2 \mid x_i\right) = \sigma^2$.

The GMM statistic (4) may also be computed setting Ω_n to equal either $\hat{\Omega}_n$ or $\hat{\Omega}_n^0$, the latter being valid only under the assumption of homoskedasticity. These choices correspond to computing the weight matrix under the alternative hypothesis because they are computed from the unrestricted estimates. Another choice is to compute the weight matrix from estimates obtained under the null hypothesis. This requires iterated GMM. The first step sets Ω_n to equal (5) or (6) and calculates the first-step estimator $\tilde{\beta}$ as in (3). In the second step we calculate

$$\tilde{\Omega}_n = \sum_{i=1}^{n} x_i x_i' \tilde{e}_i^2$$
$$\tilde{e}_i = y_i - x_i' \tilde{\beta}$$

for the general case, or

$$\tilde{\Omega}_n^0 = X' X \tilde{\sigma}^2,$$
$$\tilde{\sigma}^2 = \frac{1}{n-k+1} \sum_{i=1}^{n} \tilde{e}_i^2$$

under the homoskedasticity assumption. Then, if one sets $\Omega_n = \tilde{\Omega}_n$ or $\Omega_n = \tilde{\Omega}_n^0$, (3) and (4) are recomputed as a second-step minimization.

Newey and West (1987) and Newey and McFadden (1994) do not provide any guidance about whether the weight matrix should be computed under the null ($\tilde{\Omega}_n$) or alternative ($\hat{\Omega}_n$). Because $\tilde{\Omega}_n$ is computed from the restricted estimates, we would expect it to be a more efficient estimator under the null hypothesis and thus to provide better finite-sample Type I error approximations at the cost of a somewhat greater computational burden and an uncertain effect on the power of the test.

1.4 EDGEWORTH EXPANSIONS

Park and Phillips (1988) used an Edgeworth expansion to show that the noninvariance of the Wald statistic to the formulation of (1) is responsible for the poor size properties of the Wald statistic. Our goal in this section is to use the same Edgeworth expansion argument to show that the GMM statistic has an Edgeworth approximation to the chi-square distribution superior to that of the Wald statistic and thus should be expected to have better size properties.

Following Park and Phillips (1988), we derive our expansions under the assumptions that $e \mid X \sim N(0, I_n)$ and $X'X = nI_k$ and that this knowledge has been used to simplify the statistics; thus, $\Omega_n = nI_n$. Although this assumption is not relevant for applications, it places the focus on the nonlinearity. Under these conditions, if g were linear, then both W and DM would have exact χ_1^2 distributions; thus, the divergence from the χ_1^2 is due only to the nonlinearity of g.

On the assumption that $g(\beta)$ is three-times continuously differentiable, define

$$\underset{k\times 1}{G(\beta)} = \frac{\partial}{\partial\beta}g(\beta),$$
$$\underset{k\times k}{D(\beta)} = \frac{\partial^2}{\partial\beta\partial\beta'}g(\beta), \text{ and}$$
$$\underset{k\times k^2}{C(\beta)} = \frac{\partial}{\partial\beta}\left((\text{vec}\, D(\beta))'\right),$$

where vec (A) stacks the columns of the matrix A. Let $G = G(\beta_0)$, $D = D(\beta_0)$, and $C = C(\beta_0)$.

Define the projection matrices

$$P = G(G'G)^{-1}G'$$
$$\overline{P} = I - P.$$

Note that these are defined if $G'G > 0$ (which holds when rank$(G) = 1$), which is a standard condition for hypothesis testing.

Let F_W denote the cumulative distribution function (CDF) of W, let F_{DM} denote that of DM, and let F denote the CDF of the χ_1^2 distribution.

Theorem 1.1 *The asymptotic expansion of W as $n \to \infty$ is given by*

$$F_W(x) = F\left(x - n^{-1}\left(G'G\right)^{-1}\left(\alpha_1 x + \alpha_2 x^2 + \alpha_3 x^3\right)\right) + o(n^{-1}), \tag{7}$$

where

$$\alpha_1 = -\frac{1}{2}\,\text{tr}\left(\overline{P}D\overline{P}D\right) + \frac{1}{4}\left(\text{tr}\left(\overline{P}D\right)\right)^2,$$

$$\alpha_2 = \frac{3}{2}\left(\text{tr}\,(PD)\right)^2 - \text{tr}\,(PDD) - \frac{1}{2}\,\text{tr}\,(D)\,\text{tr}\,(PD) - \frac{2}{3}\,\text{tr}\,(PC \otimes G),$$

and

$$\alpha_3 = \frac{1}{4}\left(\text{tr}\,(PD)\right)^2.$$

Theorem 1.2 *The asymptotic expansion of DM as $n \to \infty$ is given by*

$$F_{DM}(x) = F\left(x - n^{-1}\left(G'G\right)^{-1}\alpha_1 x\right) + o(n^{-1}), \tag{8}$$

where α_1 is defined in Theorem 1.

The Edgeworth expansion (7) for W was derived by Park and Phillips (1988). The main difference is that our expression (7) provides a much more compact set of expressions for the coefficients $\alpha_1, \alpha_2, \alpha_3$, which allows a direct comparison with the expansion for the GMM statistic. The Edgeworth expansion (8) for DM appears to be new.

There are several striking implications of Theorems 1.1 and 1.2.

First, the expansion for the GMM statistic is a strict simplification of that for the Wald statistic. The Wald statistic is approximately chi-square after a cubic transformation. The GMM statistic is approximately chi-square after a linear transformation, and the linear term is identical to that for the Wald statistic. Thus, up to order $o(n^{-1})$, the expansion for the GMM statistic is less distorted from the chi-square than is that for the Wald statistic.

Second, the expansion (8) shows that the CDF of $(1 - n^{-1}(G'G)^{-1}\alpha_1)^{-1} DM$ is $F(x) + o(n^{-1})$, and thus only a scale adjustment is necessary to achieve an $o(n^{-1})$ approximation to the chi-square distribution. This is a necessary condition for a statistic to be Bartlett correctable.

Third, because DM is invariant to the formulation of (1), so is its distribution F_{DM}, and hence, so is its Edgeworth expansion. It follows that the coefficient α_1 is invariant to the formulation of (1). This is also the leading term in the Edgeworth expansion for W. It follows that the Wald statistic's noninvariance to the formulation (1) appears in the Edgeworth expansion (7) only through the higher-order coefficients α_2 and α_3. This generalizes the finding of Park and Phillips (1988), who found that α_1 was invariant to the formulation (1) in their examples. Indeed, the invariance of α_1 to the formulation of (1) is generally true.

1.5 GREGORY–VEALL EXAMPLE

We illustrate the size performance of the GMM distance test in a replication of the Gregory–Veall (1985) experiment. The model is

$$y_i = \beta_0 + \beta_1 x_{1i} + \beta_2 x_{2i} + e_i$$

with $\beta_1\beta_2 = 1$ and $E(e_i \mid x_i) = 0$. In our experiments, we generate x_{1i}, x_{2i}, and e_i as mutually independent, indepent and identically distributed (iid), $N(0, 1)$ variables. We consider two formulations of the Wald statistic based on the hypotheses

$$H_0^A : \beta_1 - \frac{1}{\beta_2} = 0$$

and

$$H_0^B : \beta_1\beta_2 - 1 = 0.$$

Let W^A and W^B denote the Wald statistics corresponding to these two formulations of the null hypothesis. Although Gregory–Veall only examined the behavior of the Wald statistic constructed with a conventional covariance matrix

Table 1.1 *Percentage Rejections at the 5% Asymptotic Level (Tests Constructed Using Homoskedastic Covariance Matrix)*

Case	Test	$n = 20$	$n = 30$	$n = 50$	$n = 100$	$n = 500$
$\beta_1 = 10,\ \beta_2 = 0.1$	W^A	.372	.317	.257	.189	.105
	W^B	.066	.059	.055	.052	.051
	DM^{alt}	.066	.059	.056	.052	.051
	DM^{null}	.039	.042	.046	.048	.050
$\beta_1 = 5,\ \beta_2 = 0.2$	W^A	.222	.183	.145	.115	.069
	W^B	.065	.061	.055	.053	.049
	DM^{alt}	.065	.061	.055	.053	.050
	DM^{null}	.038	.044	.046	.049	.049
$\beta_1 = 2,\ \beta_2 = 0.5$	W^A	.091	.082	.071	.059	.049
	W^B	.065	.058	.055	.052	.052
	DM^{alt}	.067	.059	.056	.053	.052
	DM^{null}	.040	.043	.046	.048	.051
$\beta_1 = 1,\ \beta_2 = 1$	W^A	.047	.043	.045	.046	.049
	W^B	.078	.069	.062	.055	.051
	DM^{alt}	.065	.060	.056	.052	.050
	DM^{null}	.039	.043	.046	.047	.049

estimate, we also consider the performance of the Wald and GMM statistics constructed with Eicker–White covariance matrix estimates.

As shown by Park and Phillips (1988), the expansion of the W^A statistic has coefficients α_2 and α_3, which are very large, especially when β_2 is small; yet, the expansion of the W^B statistic has coefficients α_2 and α_3, which are quite small, predicting that the W^A statistic will have larger size distortions than the W^B statistic.

We also consider the GMM statistic, which is invariant to the formulation H_0^A and H_0^B. Let DM^{alt} denote this statistic if the weight matrix is calculated using the unrestricted estimates (the alternative hypothesis), and let DM^{null} denote the statistic if the weight matrix is calculated using the restricted estimates (the null hypothesis).

We calculate the finite sample size (Type I error) of asymptotic 5% tests, using a selection of parameter values and sample sizes from $n = 20$ to $n = 500$, from 100,000 Monte Carlo replications.[2] The results are presented in Tables 1.1 and 1.2. As predicted by our theory, the W^A statistic has substantial size distortion when β_2 is small even if the sample size is quite large regardless of the method to compute the covariance matrix. The size distortions of the W^B and DM^{alt} statistics are quite similar and quite modest in comparison to the W^A statistic. In addition, the size distortions of W^B and DM^{alt} are insensitive to the true value of the parameters. If the homoskedastic covariance

[2] The standard error for the estimated rejection frequencies is about .0007.

Table 1.2 *Percentage Rejections at the 5% Asymptotic Level (Tests Constructed Using Eicker–White Covariance Matrix)*

Case	Test	$n = 20$	$n = 30$	$n = 50$	$n = 100$	$n = 500$
$\beta_1 = 10,\ \beta_2 = 0.1$	W^A	.410	.342	.270	.198	.107
	W^B	.024	.097	.078	.064	.052
	DM^{alt}	.125	.097	.078	.064	.052
	DM^{null}	.051	.050	.051	.051	.050
$\beta_1 = 5,\ \beta_2 = 0.2$	W^A	.258	.204	.158	.121	.073
	W^B	.122	.095	.077	.064	.053
	DM^{alt}	.123	.096	.078	.064	.053
	DM^{null}	.049	.050	.050	.051	.051
$\beta_1 = 2,\ \beta_2 = 0.5$	W^A	.124	.104	.084	.064	.051
	W^B	.123	.096	.079	.062	.052
	DM^{alt}	.124	.098	.079	.063	.052
	DM^{null}	.051	.050	.051	.049	.050
$\beta_1 = 1,\ \beta_2 = 1$	W^A	.094	.077	.065	.058	.051
	W^B	.133	.104	.083	.067	.052
	DM^{alt}	.123	.096	.077	.064	.052
	DM^{null}	.049	.049	.049	.050	.049

matrix estimate is used, these tests have minimal size distortion (because the true error is indeed homoskedastic) but have moderate size distortion if the heteroskedasticity-robust covariance matrix estimate is used.

The performance of the DM^{null} statistic is stunning. Regardless of the parameterization, sample size, or covariance matrix estimation method, the Type I error is excellent. If the heteroskedasticity-robust covariance matrix estimator is used, the estimated Type I error ranges from 4.9 to 5.1%, which is not statistically different from the nominal 5.0% level. Thus, the robust DM^{null} statistic has dramatically better size performance than the robust W^B statistic or the robust DM^{alt} statistic.

1.6 CONCLUSION

We have extended the explicit matrix approach to Edgeworth expansions developed by Park and Phillips (1988), extended their Edgeworth expansion for the Wald statistic, and developed a new Edgeworth expansion for the GMM statistic. The major limitation of our results is that they are calculated for the restrictive setting of a normal regression with known error variance. Variance estimation would dramatically complicate the expansions. It would be quite desirable to relax this restriction in future work.

Our simulation reports near-perfect performance of the statistic DM^{null}. A theoretical explanation of this finding would be an important avenue for future research.

APPENDIX A: THE PARK–PHILLIPS EXPANSION

For coherence, we repeat here a summary of the Edgeworth expansion of Park and Phillips (1988). Let K_{12} be the commutation matrix such that $K_{12}\operatorname{vec} A = \operatorname{vec}(A')$ if A is $k \times k^2$, K_{21} be the commutation matrix such that $K_{21}\operatorname{vec} A = \operatorname{vec}(A')$ if A is $k^2 \times k$, and $H = I + K_{12} + K_{21}$.

The following result is a restatement of Theorem 2.4 of Park and Phillips (1988) for the case $r = 1$ (in their notation). We use the result $(\operatorname{vec} P)(\operatorname{vec} P)' = P \otimes P$ and a few other minor algebraic simplifications.

Theorem A.1 *For a statistic S that has the asymptotic expansion*

$$S = \frac{(G'm)^2 + n^{-1/2}u(m) + n^{-1}v(m)}{G'G} + O_p(n^{-3/2}),$$

where

$$u(m) = J'(m \otimes m \otimes m),$$
$$v(m) = \operatorname{tr}[L(mm' \otimes mm')]$$

for some $k^3 \times 1$ vector J and $k^2 \times k^2$ matrix L, the asymptotic expansion of the distribution function $F_S(x)$ of S is given by

$$F_S(x) = F\left(x - n^{-1}(G'G)^{-1}\left(\alpha_0 + \alpha_1 x + \alpha_2 x^2 + \alpha_3 x^3\right)\right) + o(n^{-1}),$$

where

$$\alpha_0 = \frac{1}{4}(4a_0 - b_1), \tag{9}$$
$$\alpha_1 = \frac{1}{4}(4a_1 + b_1 - b_2), \tag{10}$$
$$\alpha_2 = \frac{1}{12}(4a_2 + b_2 - b_3), \tag{11}$$
$$\alpha_3 = \frac{1}{60}b_3, \tag{12}$$

and

$$a_0 = \operatorname{tr}\left\{(\overline{P} \otimes \overline{P})\, L(I + K)\right\} + (\operatorname{vec}\overline{P})'\, L(\operatorname{vec}\overline{P}), \tag{13}$$
$$a_1 = \operatorname{tr}\left\{((P \otimes \overline{P}) + (\overline{P} \otimes P))\, L(I + K)\right\} + (\operatorname{vec} P)'\, L(\operatorname{vec}\overline{P}) + (\operatorname{vec}\overline{P})'\, L(\operatorname{vec} P) \tag{14}$$
$$a_2 = 2\operatorname{tr}\left\{(P \otimes P)\, L\right\} + \operatorname{tr}\left\{(P \otimes P)\, LK\right\}, \tag{15}$$

$$b_1 = (G'G)^{-1} J'\Big\{H(P \otimes \overline{P} \otimes \overline{P})H + H\left(P \otimes (\operatorname{vec}\overline{P})(\operatorname{vec}\overline{P})'\right)H + 2H\left(\overline{P} \otimes (\operatorname{vec} P)(\operatorname{vec}\overline{P})'\right)H + (P \otimes K(\overline{P} \otimes \overline{P})) + 2(\overline{P} \otimes K(P \otimes \overline{P})) + 2(K(P \otimes \overline{P}) \otimes \overline{P}) \tag{16}$$

$$+\left(K\left(\overline{P}\otimes\overline{P}\right)\otimes P\right)+K_{12}\left(P\otimes K\left(\overline{P}\otimes\overline{P}\right)\right)K_{21}$$
$$+\,2K_{12}\left(\overline{P}\otimes K\left(P\otimes\overline{P}\right)\right)K_{21}\Big\}\,J,$$

$$\begin{aligned} b_2 = (G'G)^{-1}J'\{&2H\left(\overline{P}\otimes P\otimes P\right)H \\ &+2H\left(P\otimes\left(\operatorname{vec}\overline{P}\right)(\operatorname{vec}P)'\right)H+\left(\overline{P}\otimes K\left(P\otimes P\right)\right) \\ &+2\left(P\otimes K\left(\overline{P}\otimes P\right)\right)+2\left(K\left(\overline{P}\otimes P\right)\otimes P\right) \\ &+\left(K\left(P\otimes P\right)\otimes\overline{P}\right)+K_{12}\left(\overline{P}\otimes K\left(P\otimes P\right)\right)K_{21} \\ &+2K_{12}\left(P\otimes K\left(\overline{P}\otimes P\right)\right)K_{21}\}\,J, \end{aligned} \tag{17}$$

$$\begin{aligned} b_3 = (G'G)^{-1}J'\{&H(P\otimes P\otimes P)+H(P\otimes P\otimes P)H+(P\otimes K(P\otimes P)) \\ &+(K(P\otimes P)\otimes P)+K_{12}(P\otimes K(P\otimes P))K_{21}\}\,J. \end{aligned} \tag{18}$$

APPENDIX B: PROOF OF THEOREM 1.1

B.1 A VECTOR-VALUED THIRD-ORDER TAYLOR EXPANSION

Our Edgeworth expansions will involve third-order Taylor series expansions. To facilitate our explicit matrix formulation, the following algebraic development will be helpful.

Lemma B.1 *If $g : R^k \to R$ is three times continuously differentiable, then*

$$g(\beta_0+\delta)=g(\beta_0)+G'\delta+\frac{1}{2}\delta'D\delta+\frac{1}{6}\delta'C\left(\delta\otimes\delta\right)+O\left(|\delta|^4\right),$$

where G, D, and C are defined in Section 1.3.

Proof. Note that, for any δ,

$$\delta'\frac{\partial}{\partial\beta_j}D(\beta_0)\delta=\frac{\partial}{\partial\beta_j}\left(\operatorname{vec}D(\beta_0)\right)'\left(\delta\otimes\delta\right),$$

and so

$$\sum_{j=1}^{k}\delta_j\frac{\partial}{\partial\beta_j}\left(\operatorname{vec}D(\beta_0)\right)'\left(\delta\otimes\delta\right)=\delta'C\left(\delta\otimes\delta\right).$$

Thus, a third-order Taylor expansion of $g(\beta_0+\delta)$ about $\delta=0$ yields

$$\begin{aligned} g(\beta_0+\delta)&=g(\beta_0)+G'\delta+\frac{1}{2}\delta'D\delta+\frac{1}{6}\delta'\sum_{j=1}^{k}\frac{\partial}{\partial\beta_j}D(\beta_0)\delta\delta_j+O\left(|\delta|^4\right) \\ &=g(\beta_0)+G'\delta+\frac{1}{2}\delta'D\delta+\frac{1}{6}\delta'C\left(\delta\otimes\delta\right)+O\left(|\delta|^4\right), \end{aligned}$$

as stated. ∎

Let K be the commutation matrix such that for any $k \times k$ matrix A, $K \operatorname{vec} A = \operatorname{vec}(A')$. Note that $K' = K$. The matrix D is symmetric, so that $\operatorname{vec} D = \operatorname{vec}(D')$, and

$$K \operatorname{vec} D = \operatorname{vec} D. \tag{19}$$

A similar set of properties hold for C. The following facts are useful:

Lemma B.2

1. $CK = C$;
2. $\operatorname{vec} C = \operatorname{vec}(C')$.
3. *For any* $k \times k$ *matrix* B *and* $k \times 1$ *vector* a,

$$\operatorname{tr}[K(BC \otimes a)] = \operatorname{tr}[a \otimes BC] = \operatorname{tr}[BC \otimes a] = \operatorname{tr}[BC(I_k \otimes a)].$$

Proof. Let

$$C_j = \frac{\partial}{\partial \beta_j} D(\beta_0)$$

and

$$\begin{aligned} c_j &= \operatorname{vec} C_j \\ &= \frac{\partial}{\partial \beta_j} \operatorname{vec} D(\beta_0). \end{aligned}$$

Note that c_j is the j'th column of C'. Because $K \operatorname{vec} D(\beta) = \operatorname{vec} D(\beta)$, it follows that

$$K c_j = \frac{\partial}{\partial \beta_j} K \operatorname{vec} D(\beta_0) = \frac{\partial}{\partial \beta_j} \operatorname{vec} D(\beta_0) = c_j.$$

Hence, $KC' = C'$ and $CK = C$, establishing Part 1.

Also, we see that

$$\begin{aligned} C_j &= \frac{\partial}{\partial \beta} \frac{\partial^2}{\partial \beta_j \partial \beta'} g(\beta_0) \\ &= \frac{\partial}{\partial \beta} d_j(\beta_0)', \end{aligned}$$

where $d_j(\beta)$ is the j'th column of $D(\beta)$. Hence,

$$C = [C_1 \; C_2 \cdots C_k].$$

Thus,

$$\operatorname{vec} C = \begin{pmatrix} \operatorname{vec} C_1 \\ \operatorname{vec} C_2 \\ \vdots \\ \operatorname{vec} C_k \end{pmatrix} = \begin{pmatrix} c_1 \\ c_2 \\ \vdots \\ c_k \end{pmatrix}.$$

But, given that c_j is the j'th column of C',

$$\mathrm{vec}\,(C') = \begin{pmatrix} c_1 \\ c_2 \\ \vdots \\ c_k \end{pmatrix}.$$

We conclude, therefore, that $\mathrm{vec}\, C = \mathrm{vec}\,(C')$, establishing Part 2.

For Part 3, the equality $\mathrm{tr}\,[K\,(BC \otimes a)] = \mathrm{tr}\,[a \otimes BC]$ is taken from Magnus and Neudecker (1988, Chapter 3, Theorem 9). Then, because $C = CK$,

$$\begin{aligned} \mathrm{tr}\,(a \otimes BC) &= \mathrm{tr}\,(a \otimes BCK) = \mathrm{tr}\,((a \otimes BC)\,K) = \mathrm{tr}\,(K\,(a \otimes BC)) \\ &= \mathrm{tr}\,(BC \otimes a)\,, \end{aligned}$$

establishing Part 3.

For Part 4,

$$\mathrm{tr}\,[BC\,(I_k \otimes a)] = \mathrm{tr}\,[(I_k \otimes a)\,BC] = \mathrm{tr}\,[(I_k \otimes a)\,(BC \otimes 1)] = \mathrm{tr}\,[BC \otimes a]\,.$$

■

B.2 EXPANSION FOR THE WALD STATISTIC

Let

$$\psi(\beta) = (G(\beta)'G(\beta))^{-1}$$

so that $\left(\hat{G}'\hat{G}\right)^{-1} = \psi(\hat{\beta})$.

First, note that

$$\frac{\partial}{\partial \beta}\psi(\beta) = -2\,(G(\beta)'G(\beta))^{-2}\,D(\beta)G(\beta).$$

Second, because

$$\begin{aligned} \left(\frac{\partial}{\partial \beta'}D(\beta_0)G\right)' &= \frac{\partial}{\partial \beta}G'D(\beta_0) \\ &= \frac{\partial}{\partial \beta}\,\mathrm{vec}(G'D)' \\ &= \frac{\partial}{\partial \beta}\,\mathrm{vec}(D)'\,(I \otimes G) \\ &= C\,(I \otimes G)\,, \end{aligned}$$

it follows that

$$\begin{aligned} \frac{\partial^2}{\partial \beta \partial \beta'}\psi(\beta_0) &= -2(G'G)^{-2}DD + 8(G'G)^{-3}DGG'D - 2(G'G)^{-2}C\,(I \otimes G) \\ &= 2(G'G)^{-2}\,[-DD + 4DPD - C\,(I \otimes G)]\,. \end{aligned}$$

Hence,

$$\psi(\hat{\beta}) = \frac{1}{G'G}\left(1 - n^{-1/2}2(G'G)^{-1}G'Dm \right. \tag{20}$$
$$\left. + n^{-1}(G'G)^{-1}m'[-DD + 4DPD - C(I \otimes G)]m\right) + O_p(n^{-3/2}).$$

Under the assumptions, we have

$$\begin{aligned} W &= n\, g(\hat{\beta})' \left(\hat{G}'\hat{G}\right)^{-1} g(\hat{\beta}) \\ &= \left(\sqrt{n}g(\hat{\beta})\right)^2 \psi(\hat{\beta}). \end{aligned}$$

Let

$$m = \sqrt{n}\,(\hat{\beta} - \beta) = n^{-1/2}X'e \sim N(0, I)\,.$$

By Lemma 1,

$$\sqrt{n}g(\hat{\beta}) = G'm + n^{-1/2}m'Dm + n^{-1}\frac{1}{6}m'C(m \otimes m) + O_p(n^{-3/2}).$$

Hence,

$$\left(\sqrt{n}g(\hat{\beta})\right)^2 = (G'm)^2 + n^{-1/2}m'Gm'Dm$$
$$+ n^{-1}\left[\frac{1}{4}(m'Dm)^2 + \frac{1}{3}m'Gm'C(m \otimes m)\right] + O_p(n^{-3/2}). \tag{21}$$

Putting (21) and (20) together, we obtain the asymptotic expansion

$$W = \frac{(G'm)^2 + n^{-1/2}u + n^{-1}v}{G'G} + O_p(n^{-3/2}),$$

where

$$u = m'Gm'Dm - 2m'PmG'Dm$$

and

$$v = (\tfrac{1}{4}(m'Dm)^2 + \tfrac{1}{3}m'Gm'C(m \otimes m) - 2m'Dmm'PDm$$
$$+ m'Pmm'[-DD + 4DPD - C(I \otimes G)]m.$$

Because

$$m'am'Dm = \left(a' \otimes (\mathrm{vec}\, A)'\right)(m \otimes m \otimes m)\,,$$

we can write $u = J'(m \otimes m \otimes m)$, where

$$\begin{aligned} J &= (G \otimes \mathrm{vec}\, D) - 2\,(G \otimes G \otimes DG)\,(G'G)^{-1} \\ &= G \otimes (\mathrm{vec}\, D - 2\,\mathrm{vec}\,(DP)) \\ &= G \otimes \mathrm{vec}\left(D\left(\overline{P} - P\right)\right) \\ &= \left(G \otimes \left(\overline{P} - P\right) \otimes I\right) \mathrm{vec}\, D. \end{aligned}$$

Similarly, because

$$\begin{aligned} m'Am\, m'Bm &= (m \otimes m)' (\operatorname{vec} A)' (\operatorname{vec} B)' (m \otimes m) \\ &= \operatorname{tr}\left[\left((\operatorname{vec} A)(\operatorname{vec} B)'\right)(m \otimes m)(m \otimes m)'\right] \\ &= \operatorname{tr}\left[\left((\operatorname{vec} A)(\operatorname{vec} B)'\right)(mm' \otimes mm')\right], \end{aligned}$$

and, by Magnus and Neudecker (1988, Chapter 2), Theorem 3,

$$\begin{aligned} m'am'A(m \otimes m) &= (m \otimes m)' (A' \otimes a) \operatorname{vec}(mm') \\ &= \operatorname{tr}\left[(A' \otimes a)(mm' \otimes mm')\right], \end{aligned}$$

it follows that $v = \operatorname{tr}[L(mm' \otimes mm')]$, where

$$\begin{aligned} L = \frac{1}{4} & (\operatorname{vec} D)(\operatorname{vec} D)' - 2(\operatorname{vec} PD)(\operatorname{vec} D)' - (\operatorname{vec} P)(\operatorname{vec} DD)' \\ & + 4(\operatorname{vec} P)(\operatorname{vec} DPD)' - (\operatorname{vec} P)(\operatorname{vec}(C(I \otimes G)))' + \frac{1}{3}(C \otimes G). \end{aligned}$$

This expansion is equivalent to equation (7) of Park and Phillips (1988) but is in a different algebraic form. The preceding expression turns out to be more convenient for evaluation of the coefficients of the Edgeworth expansion. Using Theorem A.1 in Appendix A, one can find the coefficients of the expansion (7) by explicit calculation of the coefficients $a_0, a_1, a_2, b_1, b_2, b_3$ from the expressions for J and L.

B.3 CALCULATION OF a_0

First, because $\left(\overline{P} \otimes \overline{P}\right) \operatorname{vec} P = \operatorname{vec} \overline{P} P \overline{P} = 0$ and $\left(\overline{P} \otimes \overline{P}\right) \operatorname{vec} PD = \operatorname{vec} \overline{P} P D \overline{P} = 0$, then

$$\left(\overline{P} \otimes \overline{P}\right) L = \frac{1}{4}\left(\operatorname{vec}\left(\overline{P} D \overline{P}\right)\right)(\operatorname{vec} D)'.$$

Using (19) and the fact that $\operatorname{vec} A' \operatorname{vec} B = \operatorname{tr}(A'B)$, we find that

$$\begin{aligned} \operatorname{tr}\left\{\left(\overline{P} \otimes \overline{P}\right) L(I+K)\right\} &= \frac{1}{4} \operatorname{tr}\left\{\left(\operatorname{vec}\left(\overline{P} D \overline{P}\right)\right)(\operatorname{vec} D)'(I+K)\right\} \\ &= \frac{1}{2} \operatorname{tr}\left\{\left(\operatorname{vec}\left(\overline{P} D \overline{P}\right)\right)(\operatorname{vec} D)'\right\} \\ &= \frac{1}{2} \operatorname{tr}\left(D \overline{P} D \overline{P}\right). \end{aligned}$$

Second, because $\left(\operatorname{vec} \overline{P}\right)' (\operatorname{vec} P)' = \operatorname{tr}\left(\overline{P} P\right) = 0$, $\left(\operatorname{vec} \overline{P}\right)' (\operatorname{vec} PD) = \operatorname{tr}\left(\overline{P} P D\right) = 0$, and

$$0 = \operatorname{vec}\left(G' \overline{P} C\right) = (C' \otimes G') \operatorname{vec}\left(\overline{P}\right),$$

it follows that

$$\begin{aligned}(\operatorname{vec}\overline{P})' L(\operatorname{vec}\overline{P}) &= \frac{1}{4}(\operatorname{vec}\overline{P})'(\operatorname{vec}D)(\operatorname{vec}D)'(\operatorname{vec}\overline{P})' \\ &\quad + \frac{1}{3}(\operatorname{vec}\overline{P})' C(I\otimes G)(\operatorname{vec}\overline{P}) \\ &= \frac{1}{4}\left(\operatorname{tr}\left(D\overline{P}\right)\right)^2.\end{aligned}$$

Summing these terms, we see that (13) equals

$$a_0 = \frac{1}{2}\operatorname{tr}\left(D\overline{P}D\overline{P}\right) + \frac{1}{4}\left(\operatorname{tr}\left(D\overline{P}\right)\right)^2. \qquad (22)$$

B.4 CALCULATION OF a_1

First,

$$\operatorname{tr}\left[\left(P\otimes\overline{P}\right)L(I+K)\right] = \frac{1}{4}\operatorname{tr}\left[\left(\operatorname{vec}\overline{P}DP\right)(\operatorname{vec}D)'(I+K)\right] = \frac{1}{2}\operatorname{tr}\left(D\overline{P}DP\right).$$

Second, using Lemma 2, Part 3, we obtain

$$\begin{aligned}&\operatorname{tr}\left[\left(\overline{P}\otimes P\right)L(I+K)\right] \\ &= \operatorname{tr}\left\{\left[-\frac{7}{4}\left(\operatorname{vec}PD\overline{P}\right)(\operatorname{vec}D)' + \frac{1}{3}\left(\overline{P}C\otimes G\right)\right](I+K)\right\} \\ &= -\frac{7}{2}\operatorname{tr}\left(D\overline{P}DP\right) + \frac{2}{3}\operatorname{tr}\left(\overline{P}C\otimes G\right).\end{aligned}$$

Third, using the fact that $\operatorname{tr}(P) = 1$, and Lemma 2, Part 4, we see that

$$\begin{aligned}(\operatorname{vec}P)' L(\operatorname{vec}\overline{P}) &= \frac{1}{4}\operatorname{tr}(DP)\operatorname{tr}\left(D\overline{P}\right) - 2\operatorname{tr}(DP)\operatorname{tr}\left(D\overline{P}\right) - \operatorname{tr}(P)\operatorname{tr}\left(DD\overline{P}\right) \\ &\quad + 4\operatorname{tr}(P)\operatorname{tr}\left(DPD\overline{P}\right) - \operatorname{tr}(P)\operatorname{tr}\left(\overline{P}C(I\otimes G)\right) \\ &\quad + \frac{1}{3}(\operatorname{vec}P)'(C\otimes G)\left(\operatorname{vec}\overline{P}\right) \\ &= -\frac{7}{4}\operatorname{tr}(DP)\operatorname{tr}\left(D\overline{P}\right) - \operatorname{tr}\left(DD\overline{P}\right) + 4\operatorname{tr}\left(DPD\overline{P}\right) \\ &\quad - \frac{2}{3}\operatorname{tr}\left(\overline{P}C\otimes G\right).\end{aligned}$$

The final equality uses Lemma B.2, Part 3 and the fact that $K\operatorname{vec}P = \operatorname{vec}P$, $\operatorname{vec}(C') = \operatorname{vec}C$. Magnus and Neudecker (1988, Theorem 3, Chapter 2) and Lemma B.2, Part 3 imply that

$$\begin{aligned}(\operatorname{vec}P)'(C\otimes G)\left(\operatorname{vec}\overline{P}\right) &= (\operatorname{vec}P)' K(C\otimes G)\left(\operatorname{vec}\overline{P}\right) \\ &= (\operatorname{vec}P)'(G\otimes C)\left(\operatorname{vec}\overline{P}\right) \\ &= (\operatorname{vec}(C'PG))'\left(\operatorname{vec}\overline{P}\right)\end{aligned}$$

$$
\begin{aligned}
&= (\operatorname{vec}(C'))' (G \otimes I \otimes I) \left(\operatorname{vec} \overline{P}\right) \\
&= (\operatorname{vec} C)' ((G \otimes I) \otimes I) \left(\operatorname{vec} \overline{P}\right) \\
&= \operatorname{tr}\left[\overline{P} C (G \otimes I)\right] \\
&= \operatorname{tr}\left[\left(1 \otimes \overline{P} C\right) (G \otimes I)\right] \\
&= \operatorname{tr}\left(G \otimes \overline{P} C\right) \\
&= \operatorname{tr}\left(\overline{P} C \otimes G\right).
\end{aligned}
$$

Fourth,

$$
\begin{aligned}
\left(\operatorname{vec} \overline{P}\right)' L (\operatorname{vec} P) &= \frac{1}{4} \operatorname{tr}\left(D\overline{P}\right) \operatorname{tr}(DP) + \frac{1}{3} \left(\operatorname{vec} \overline{P}\right)' (C \otimes G) (\operatorname{vec} P) \\
&= \frac{1}{4} \operatorname{tr}\left(D\overline{P}\right) \operatorname{tr}(DP).
\end{aligned}
$$

Summing these three terms, we find that (14) equals

$$
\begin{aligned}
a_1 &= -\frac{3}{2} \operatorname{tr}(DP) \operatorname{tr}\left(D\overline{P}\right) + \operatorname{tr}\left(DPD\overline{P}\right) - \operatorname{tr}\left(DD\overline{P}\right) \\
&= -\frac{3}{2} \operatorname{tr}(DP) \operatorname{tr}\left(D\overline{P}\right) - \operatorname{tr}\left(D\overline{P}D\overline{P}\right).
\end{aligned} \tag{23}
$$

B.5 CALCULATION OF a_2

Observe that

$$
\begin{aligned}
(P \otimes P) L = & \frac{1}{4} (\operatorname{vec} PDP) (\operatorname{vec} D)' - 2 (\operatorname{vec} PDP) (\operatorname{vec} D)' \\
& - (\operatorname{vec} P) (\operatorname{vec} DD)' + 4 (\operatorname{vec} P) (\operatorname{vec} DPD)' \\
& - (\operatorname{vec} P) (\operatorname{vec}(C (I \otimes G)))' + \frac{1}{3} (PC \otimes G).
\end{aligned}
$$

Hence, using Lemma B.2, Part 3, we see that (15) equals

$$
\begin{aligned}
a_2 = & \, 3 \left\{ -\frac{7}{4} \operatorname{tr}(DPDP) - \operatorname{tr}(DDP) + 4 \operatorname{tr}(DPDP) - \operatorname{tr}(PC \otimes G) \right\} \\
& + \frac{2}{3} \operatorname{tr}(PC \otimes G) + \frac{1}{3} \operatorname{tr}(G \otimes PC) \\
= & \, \frac{27}{4} (\operatorname{tr}(DP))^2 - 3 \operatorname{tr}(DDP) - 2 \operatorname{tr}(PC \otimes G),
\end{aligned} \tag{24}
$$

where the final equality uses the fact that $\operatorname{tr}(DPDP) = (\operatorname{tr}(DP))^2$ because P has rank one.

B.6 CALCULATION OF b_1

First, observe that

$$K_{12}J = \left(I \otimes G \otimes \left(\overline{P} - P\right)\right) \operatorname{vec} D,$$
$$K_{21}J = \left(\left(\overline{P} - P\right) \otimes I \otimes G\right) \operatorname{vec} D.$$

Second, observe that

$$\left(\left(\overline{P} - P\right) \otimes I\right) \operatorname{vec} \overline{P} = \operatorname{vec} \overline{P}$$

and

$$\left(\left(\overline{P} - P\right) \otimes I\right) \operatorname{vec} P = - \operatorname{vec} P.$$

Using the facts that J lies in the span of $(G \otimes I \otimes I)$, $K_{12}J$ lies in the span of $(I \otimes G \otimes I)$, and $K_{21}J$ lies in the span of $(I \otimes I \otimes G)$, we see that (16) equals

$$\begin{aligned} b_1 &= (G'G)^{-1} \left\{ J' \left(P \otimes \overline{P} \otimes \overline{P}\right) J + J' \left(P \otimes \left(\operatorname{vec} \overline{P}\right) \left(\operatorname{vec} \overline{P}\right)'\right) J \right. \\ &\quad \left. + J' \left(P \otimes K \left(\overline{P} \otimes \overline{P}\right)\right) J \right\} \\ &= 2 \operatorname{vec} D' \left(\overline{P} \otimes \overline{P}\right) \operatorname{vec} D' + \operatorname{vec} D' \left(\operatorname{vec} \overline{P}\right) \left(\operatorname{vec} \overline{P}\right)' \operatorname{vec} D \\ &= 2 \operatorname{tr} \left(\overline{P} D \overline{P} D\right) + \left(\operatorname{tr} \left(\overline{P} D\right)\right)^2. \end{aligned} \tag{25}$$

B.7 CALCULATION OF b_2

Using similar reasoning, we find that (17) equals

$$\begin{aligned} b_2 &= (G'G)^{-1} \left\{ 2 \left(K_{12}J + K_{21}J\right)' \left(\overline{P} \otimes P \otimes P\right) \left(K_{12}J + K_{21}J\right) \right. \\ &\quad + 2J' \left(P \otimes \left(\operatorname{vec} \overline{P}\right) \left(\operatorname{vec} P\right)'\right) HJ + 2J' \left(P \otimes K \left(\overline{P} \otimes P\right)\right) J \\ &\quad \left. + J' \left(K \left(P \otimes P\right) \otimes \overline{P}\right) J + J' K_{12} \left(\overline{P} \otimes K \left(P \otimes P\right)\right) K_{21} J \right\}. \end{aligned}$$

We take the terms on the right-hand side in turn. First, because

$$P \otimes G = (G'G)^{-1} (GG' \otimes G) = (G'G)^{-1} (G \otimes GG') = G \otimes P,$$

then

$$\left(\overline{P} \otimes P \otimes P\right) \left(K_{12}J + K_{21}J\right) = \left[- \left(\overline{P} \otimes G \otimes P\right) + \left(\overline{P} \otimes P \otimes G\right) \right] \operatorname{vec} D = 0.$$

Second,

$$\begin{aligned} J' \left(P \otimes \left(\operatorname{vec} \overline{P}\right) \left(\operatorname{vec} P\right)'\right) HJ &= \operatorname{vec} D' \left(G' \otimes \left(\operatorname{vec} \overline{P}\right) \left(\operatorname{vec} P\right)'\right) HJ \\ &= -3(G'G) \left(\operatorname{vec} D\right)' \operatorname{vec} \overline{P} \left(\operatorname{vec} P\right)' \operatorname{vec} D \\ &= -3(G'G) \operatorname{tr} \left(\overline{P} D\right) \operatorname{tr} \left(P D\right). \end{aligned}$$

Third,

$$J'\left(P \otimes K\left(\overline{P} \otimes P\right)\right) J = -G'G \operatorname{vec} D' \left(P \otimes \overline{P}\right) \operatorname{vec} D$$
$$= -G'G \operatorname{tr}\left(\overline{P} D P D\right).$$

Fourth,

$$J'\left(K\left(P \otimes P\right) \otimes \overline{P}\right) J = G'G \operatorname{vec} D' \left(P \otimes \overline{P}\right) \operatorname{vec} D = G'G \operatorname{tr}\left(\overline{P} D P D\right).$$

Fifth,

$$J' K_{12}\left(\overline{P} \otimes K\left(P \otimes P\right)\right) K_{21} J = G'G \operatorname{tr}\left(\overline{P} D P D\right).$$

Hence,

$$b_2 = -6 \operatorname{tr}\left(\overline{P} D\right) \operatorname{tr}\left(P D\right). \tag{26}$$

B.8 CALCULATION OF b_3

First, (18) equals

$$\begin{aligned} b_3 = (G'G)^{-1} \{ & J'H\left(P \otimes P \otimes P\right) J + J'H\left(P \otimes P \otimes P\right) HJ \\ & + J'\left(P \otimes K\left(P \otimes P\right)\right) J + J'\left(K\left(P \otimes P\right) \otimes P\right) J \\ & + J' K_{12}\left(P \otimes K\left(P \otimes P\right)\right) K_{21} J \}. \end{aligned} \tag{27}$$

Next, note that

$$\left(P \otimes P \otimes P\right) J = -\left(G \otimes P \otimes P\right) \operatorname{vec} D$$

and

$$\begin{aligned} \left(P \otimes P \otimes P\right) HJ &= -\left[\left(G \otimes P \otimes P\right) + \left(P \otimes G \otimes P\right) + \left(P \otimes P \otimes G\right)\right] \operatorname{vec} D \\ &= -3\left(G \otimes P \otimes P\right) \operatorname{vec} D \end{aligned}$$

because $G \otimes P = P \otimes G$. Thus, the first term in (27) is

$$\begin{aligned} J'H\left(P \otimes P \otimes P\right) J &= 3(G'G) \operatorname{vec} D' \left(P \otimes P\right) \operatorname{vec} D \\ &= 3(G'G) \operatorname{tr}\left(P D P D\right) \\ &= 3(G'G) \left(\operatorname{tr}\left(P D\right)\right)^2, \end{aligned}$$

the last equality, because the rank of PD is one. Similarly, the second term is

$$J'H\left(P \otimes P \otimes P\right) HJ = 9(G'G) \left(\operatorname{tr}\left(P D\right)\right)^2.$$

The third, fourth, and fifth terms are similar:

$$\begin{aligned} & J'\left(P \otimes K\left(P \otimes P\right)\right) J + J'\left(K\left(P \otimes P\right) \otimes P\right) J \\ & \quad + J' K_{12}\left(P \otimes K\left(P \otimes P\right)\right) K_{21} J = 3(G'G) \left(\operatorname{tr}\left(P D\right)\right)^2. \end{aligned}$$

Hence,

$$b_3 = 15 (\mathrm{tr}(PD))^2 . \tag{28}$$

B.9 CALCULATION OF FINAL COEFFICIENTS

We now can calculate the coefficients α_0 through α_3 for the expansion of the Wald statistic's distribution. From (9), (22), and (25), we have

$$\alpha_0 = \frac{1}{4}(4a_0 - b_1) = \frac{1}{2}\mathrm{tr}\left(D\overline{P}D\overline{P}\right) + \frac{1}{4}\left(\mathrm{tr}\left(D\overline{P}\right)\right)^2 - \frac{1}{2}\mathrm{tr}\left(\overline{P}D\overline{P}D\right) - \frac{1}{4}\left(\mathrm{tr}\left(\overline{P}D\right)\right)^2 = 0.$$

From (10), (23), (25), and (26), we have

$$\begin{aligned}\alpha_1 &= \frac{1}{4}(4a_1 + b_1 - b_2) \\ &= -\frac{3}{2}\mathrm{tr}(DP)\,\mathrm{tr}\left(D\overline{P}\right) - \mathrm{tr}\left(D\overline{P}D\overline{P}\right) + \frac{1}{2}\mathrm{tr}\left(\overline{P}D\overline{P}D\right) \\ &\quad + \frac{1}{4}\left(\mathrm{tr}\left(\overline{P}D\right)\right)^2 + \frac{3}{2}\mathrm{tr}\left(\overline{P}D\right)\mathrm{tr}(PD) \\ &= -\frac{1}{2}\mathrm{tr}\left(\overline{P}D\overline{P}D\right) + \frac{1}{4}\left(\mathrm{tr}\left(\overline{P}D\right)\right)^2 .\end{aligned}$$

From (11), (24), (26), and (28),

$$\begin{aligned}\alpha_2 &= \frac{1}{12}(4a_2 + b_2 - b_3) \\ &= \frac{9}{4}(\mathrm{tr}(DP))^2 - \mathrm{tr}(DDP) - \frac{2}{3}\mathrm{tr}(PC \otimes G) \\ &\quad - \frac{1}{2}\mathrm{tr}\left(\overline{P}D\right)\mathrm{tr}(PD) - \frac{5}{4}(\mathrm{tr}(PD))^2 \\ &= (\mathrm{tr}(DP))^2 - \mathrm{tr}(PDD) - \frac{2}{3}\mathrm{tr}(PC \otimes G) - \frac{1}{2}\mathrm{tr}((I - P)D)\,\mathrm{tr}(PD) \\ &= \frac{3}{2}(\mathrm{tr}(DP))^2 - \mathrm{tr}(PDD) - \frac{2}{3}\mathrm{tr}(PC \otimes G) - \frac{1}{2}\mathrm{tr}(D)\,\mathrm{tr}(PD).\end{aligned}$$

From (12) and (28), it follows that

$$\alpha_3 = \frac{1}{60}b_3 = \frac{1}{4}(\mathrm{tr}(PD))^2 ,$$

completing the proof of Theorem 1.1.

APPENDIX C: PROOF OF THEOREM 1.2

C.1 EXPANSION FOR GMM STATISTIC

In the simplified setting for the theorem, $\tilde{\beta} = \text{argmin}_{g(\beta)=0} J(\beta)$, where

$$J(\beta) = n^{-1}(Y - X\beta)' XX' (Y - X\beta).$$

Newey and McFadden (1994) established that $\tilde{\beta} \to_p \beta_0$ (Theorem 9.1) and that $\tilde{q} = \sqrt{n}\left(\tilde{\beta} - \beta_0\right) = O_p(1)$ (p. 2219). Thus, with probability that tends to one as $n \to \infty$, $\tilde{\beta}$ lies in the interior of the parameter space and there exists a Lagrange multiplier $\tilde{\lambda}$ such that

$$0 = -\tilde{m} + \tilde{G}\tilde{\lambda}, \tag{29}$$

where $\tilde{m} = n^{-1/2}X'\left(Y - X\tilde{\beta}\right)$ and $\tilde{G} = G(\tilde{\beta})$. Hence, we can write $\tilde{\lambda} = \left(G'\tilde{G}\right)^{-1} G'\tilde{m}$ and

$$\tilde{m} = \tilde{G}\left(G'\tilde{G}\right)^{-1} G'\tilde{m}. \tag{30}$$

Expanding $\tilde{G} = G(\tilde{\beta})$ about β_0, and using the fact that $\tilde{q} = O_p(1)$, we see

$$\tilde{G} = G + n^{-1/2} D\tilde{q} = G + O_p(n^{-1/2}). \tag{31}$$

Equations (30) and (31) combine to yield $\tilde{m} = P\tilde{m} + O_p(n^{-1/2})$, or

$$\overline{P}\tilde{m} = O_p(n^{-1/2}). \tag{32}$$

From Lemma B.1 evaluated at $\tilde{\beta}$, and noting that $g(\tilde{\beta}) = g(\beta_0) = 0$, we have

$$0 = G'\tilde{q} + n^{-1/2}\frac{1}{2}\tilde{q}'D\tilde{q} + n^{-1}\frac{1}{6}\tilde{q}'C\left(\tilde{q} \otimes \tilde{q}\right) + O_p\left(n^{-3/2}\right). \tag{33}$$

One implication of (33) is that $G'\tilde{q} = O_p(n^{-1/2})$, and hence $P\tilde{q} = O_p(n^{-1/2})$. Thus, because $\tilde{q} = m - \tilde{m}$,

$$\begin{aligned}\tilde{q} &= \overline{P}\tilde{q} + O_p(n^{-1/2}) \\ &= \overline{P}m - \overline{P}\tilde{m} + O_p(n^{-1/2}) \\ &= \overline{P}m + O_p(n^{-1/2}),\end{aligned}$$

where the last equality is (32). We have established that

$$\tilde{q} = \overline{P}m + O_p(n^{-1/2}). \tag{34}$$

Our next task is to obtain an expansion of the form $\tilde{q} = \overline{P}m + n^{-1/2}q_1 + O_p(n^{-1})$. Applying (34) to (31), we find

$$\tilde{G} = G + n^{-1/2}D\overline{P}m + O_p(n^{-1}).$$

Thus,

$$\begin{aligned}
&\tilde{G}\left(G'\tilde{G}\right)^{-1} \\
&= G\left(G'G\right)^{-1} + n^{-1/2}\left[\left(G'G\right)^{-1} D\overline{P}m - G\left(G'G\right)^{-2} G'D\overline{P}m\right] + O_p(n^{-1}) \\
&= G\left(G'G\right)^{-1} + n^{-1/2}\left(G'G\right)^{-1}\overline{P}D\overline{P}m + O_p(n^{-1}). \qquad (35)
\end{aligned}$$

Applying $\tilde{m} = m - \tilde{q}$ to (33), we find that

$$G'\tilde{m} = G'm + n^{-1/2}\frac{1}{2}\tilde{q}'D\tilde{q} + n^{-1}\frac{1}{6}\tilde{q}'C\left(\tilde{q}\otimes\tilde{q}\right) + O_p\left(n^{-3/2}\right). \qquad (36)$$

Combined with (34), this implies

$$G'\tilde{m} = G'm + n^{-1/2}\frac{1}{2}m'\overline{P}D\overline{P}m + O_p(n^{-1}). \qquad (37)$$

Thus, (30), (35), and (37) combine as

$$\begin{aligned}
\tilde{m} &= G\left(G'G\right)^{-1} G'\tilde{m} + n^{-1/2}\left(G'G\right)^{-1}\left[G'm\overline{P}D\overline{P}m + \frac{1}{2}Gm'\overline{P}D\overline{P}m\right] \\
&\quad + O_p(n^{-1}).
\end{aligned}$$

This implies

$$\tilde{q} = \overline{P}m - n^{-1/2}\left(G'G\right)^{-1}\left[G'm\overline{P}D\overline{P}m + \frac{1}{2}Gm'\overline{P}D\overline{P}m\right] + O_p(n^{-1}) \qquad (38)$$

as desired.

From (30), we have the representation for the test statistic

$$\begin{aligned}
DM &= \tilde{m}'\tilde{m} \\
&= \tilde{m}'G\left(\tilde{G}'G\right)^{-1}\tilde{G}'\tilde{G}\left(G'\tilde{G}\right)^{-1}G'\tilde{m} \\
&= \left(\tilde{m}'G\right)^2\ \Psi(\tilde{\beta}) \qquad (39)
\end{aligned}$$

where

$$\Psi(\beta) = \frac{G(\beta)'G(\beta)}{\left(G'G(\beta)\right)^2}.$$

We proceed by developing expansions for $(G'\tilde{m})^2$ and $\Psi(\tilde{\beta})$, each to the order $O_p(n^{-3/2})$.

We first take $(G'\tilde{m})^2$. Equation (36) combined with (38) yields

$$G'\tilde{m} = G'm + n^{-1/2}\frac{1}{2}m'\overline{P}D\overline{P}m + n^{-1}\Upsilon + O_p\left(n^{-3/2}\right),$$

where

$$\Upsilon = -\left(G'G\right)^{-1}m'\overline{P}D\left[G'm\overline{P}D\overline{P}m + \frac{1}{2}Gm'\overline{P}D\overline{P}m\right] + \frac{1}{6}m'\overline{P}C\left(\overline{P}m\otimes\overline{P}m\right).$$

Thus,

$$(G'\tilde{m})^2 = (G'm)^2 + n^{-1/2}G'mm'\overline{P}D\overline{P}m + n^{-1}\left[\frac{1}{4}\left(m'\overline{P}D\overline{P}m\right)^2 + 2G'm\Upsilon\right] + O_p\left(n^{-3/2}\right). \quad (40)$$

Second, consider $\Psi(\tilde{\beta})$. Note that

$$\frac{\partial}{\partial\beta}\Psi(\beta) = \frac{2}{(G'G(\beta))^2}D(\beta)G(\beta) - \frac{2G(\beta)'G(\beta)}{(G'G(\beta))^3}D(\beta)G(\beta),$$

and so

$$\begin{aligned}\frac{\partial}{\partial\beta}\Psi(\beta_0) &= \frac{2}{(G'G)^2}DG - \frac{2G'G}{(G'G)^3}DG.\\ &= 0.\end{aligned}$$

We also calculate that

$$\begin{aligned}\frac{\partial^2}{\partial\beta\partial\beta'}\Psi(\beta_0) &= \frac{2}{(G'G)^2}DD - \frac{2}{(G'G)^3}DGG'H\\ &= \frac{2}{(G'G)}D\overline{P}D.\end{aligned}$$

Thus, a second-order Taylor expansion yields

$$\begin{aligned}\Psi(\tilde{\beta}) &= \Psi(\beta_0) + n^{-1/2}\frac{\partial}{\partial\beta}\Psi(\beta_0)\tilde{q} + n^{-1}\frac{1}{2}\tilde{q}'\frac{\partial^2}{\partial\beta\partial\beta'}\Psi(\beta_0)\tilde{q} + O_p(n^{-3/2})\\ &= (G'G)^{-1}\left\{1 + n^{-1}(G'G)^{-1}m'\overline{P}D\overline{P}D\overline{P}m\right\} + O_p(n^{-3/2}). \quad (41)\end{aligned}$$

Combining (39), (40), and (41), we find that

$$DM = \frac{(G'm)^2 + n^{-1/2}u + n^{-1}v}{G'G} + O_p(n^{-3/2}),$$

where

$$u = G'mm'\overline{P}D\overline{P}m$$

and

$$\begin{aligned}v &= \frac{1}{4}\left(m'\overline{P}D\overline{P}m\right)^2 + 2G'm\Upsilon + (G'm)^2(G'G)^{-1}m'\overline{P}D\overline{P}D\overline{P}m\\ &= \frac{1}{4}\left(m'\overline{P}D\overline{P}m\right)^2 - m'Pmm'\overline{P}D\overline{P}D\overline{P}m\\ &\quad - m'PD\overline{P}mm'\overline{P}D\overline{P}m + G'm\frac{1}{3}m'\overline{P}C\left(\overline{P}m\otimes\overline{P}m\right).\end{aligned}$$

We can write $u = J'(m\otimes m\otimes m)$, where

$$J = \left(G\otimes\overline{P}\otimes\overline{P}\right)\operatorname{vec} D,$$

and $v = \operatorname{tr}[L(mm' \otimes mm')]$, where

$$L = \frac{1}{4}(\overline{P} \otimes \overline{P})(\operatorname{vec} D)(\operatorname{vec} D)'(\overline{P} \otimes \overline{P}) - (\operatorname{vec} P)(\operatorname{vec} D\overline{P}D)'(\overline{P} \otimes \overline{P})$$
$$- (\overline{P} \otimes P)(\operatorname{vec} D)(\operatorname{vec} D)'(\overline{P} \otimes \overline{P}) + \frac{1}{3}(\overline{P}C(\overline{P} \otimes \overline{P})) \otimes G.$$

Using Theorem A.1 in Appendix A, we see that the coefficients of the expansion (8) are found by calculation of the coefficients $a_0, a_1, a_2, b_1, b_2, b_3$ from the preceding expressions for J and L. We calculate each explicitly.

C.2 CALCULATION OF a_0

First,

$$(\overline{P} \otimes \overline{P})L = \frac{1}{4}(\overline{P} \otimes \overline{P})(\operatorname{vec} D)(\operatorname{vec} D)'(\overline{P} \otimes \overline{P}),$$

and so

$$\operatorname{tr}\{(\overline{P} \otimes \overline{P})L(I+K)\} = \frac{1}{2}(\operatorname{vec} D)'(\overline{P} \otimes \overline{P})(\operatorname{vec} D) = \frac{1}{2}\operatorname{tr}(\overline{P}D\overline{P}D).$$

Second,

$$(\operatorname{vec}\overline{P})' L(\operatorname{vec}\overline{P}) = \frac{1}{4}(\operatorname{vec}\overline{P})'(\operatorname{vec} D)(\operatorname{vec} D)'(\operatorname{vec}\overline{P}) = \frac{1}{4}(\operatorname{tr}(\overline{P}D))^2..$$

Summing these terms, we see that (13) equals

$$a_0 = \frac{1}{2}\operatorname{tr}(\overline{P}D\overline{P}D) + \frac{1}{4}(\operatorname{tr}(\overline{P}D))^2. \tag{42}$$

C.3 CALCULATION OF a_1

First,

$$(P \otimes \overline{P})L + (\overline{P} \otimes P)L = -(\overline{P} \otimes P)(\operatorname{vec} D)(\operatorname{vec} D)'(\overline{P} \otimes \overline{P})$$
$$+ \frac{1}{3}(\overline{P}C(\overline{P} \otimes \overline{P})) \otimes G,$$

and so

$$\operatorname{tr}\{((P \otimes \overline{P}) + (\overline{P} \otimes P))L(I+K)\}$$
$$= -2(\operatorname{vec} PD\overline{P})'(\operatorname{vec}\overline{P}D\overline{P}) + \frac{1}{3}\operatorname{tr}\{(\overline{P}C(\overline{P} \otimes \overline{P})) \otimes G\}$$
$$+ \frac{1}{3}\operatorname{tr}\{G \otimes (\overline{P}C(\overline{P} \otimes \overline{P}))\}$$
$$= \frac{1}{3}\operatorname{tr}\{(\overline{P}C \otimes G)(\overline{P} \otimes \overline{P})\} + \frac{1}{3}\operatorname{tr}\{(G \otimes \overline{P}C)(\overline{P} \otimes \overline{P})\}$$

$$= \frac{1}{3}\operatorname{tr}\left\{\left(\overline{P}\otimes\overline{P}\right)\left(\overline{P}C\otimes G\right)\right\} + \frac{1}{3}\operatorname{tr}\left\{\left(\overline{P}\otimes\overline{P}\right)\left(G\otimes\overline{P}C\right)\right\}$$
$$= 0.$$

Second,

$$\begin{aligned}
&(\operatorname{vec} P)' L\left(\operatorname{vec}\overline{P}\right)\\
&\quad= -\left(\operatorname{vec} D\overline{P}D\right)'\left(\operatorname{vec}\overline{P}\right) + \frac{1}{3}(\operatorname{vec} P)'\left(\left(\overline{P}C\left(\overline{P}\otimes\overline{P}\right)\right)\otimes G\right)\left(\operatorname{vec}\overline{P}\right)\\
&\quad= -\operatorname{tr}\left(\overline{P}D\overline{P}D\right) + \frac{1}{3}(\operatorname{vec} P)'\left(\overline{P}C\otimes G\right)\left(\operatorname{vec}\overline{P}\right)\\
&\quad= -\operatorname{tr}\left(\overline{P}D\overline{P}D\right) + \frac{1}{3}\left(\operatorname{vec} G'P\overline{P}C\right)'\left(\operatorname{vec}\overline{P}\right)\\
&\quad= -\operatorname{tr}\left(\overline{P}D\overline{P}D\right).
\end{aligned}$$

Third,

$$\begin{aligned}
\left(\operatorname{vec}\overline{P}\right)' L(\operatorname{vec} P) &= \frac{1}{3}\left(\operatorname{vec}\overline{P}\right)'\left(\left(\overline{P}C\left(\overline{P}\otimes\overline{P}\right)\right)\otimes G\right)(\operatorname{vec} P)\\
&= \frac{1}{3}\left(\operatorname{vec}\overline{P}\right)'\left(\overline{P}C\otimes G\right)\left(\overline{P}\otimes\overline{P}\right)(\operatorname{vec} P)\\
&= 0.
\end{aligned}$$

Summing these terms, we see that (14) equals

$$a_1 = -\operatorname{tr}\left(\overline{P}D\overline{P}D\right). \tag{43}$$

C.4 CALCULATION OF a_2

Note that

$$(P\otimes P)\, L = -(\operatorname{vec} P)\left(\operatorname{vec} D\overline{P}D\right)'\left(\overline{P}\otimes\overline{P}\right),$$

and so

$$a_2 = 2\operatorname{tr}\left\{(P\otimes P)\, L\right\} + \operatorname{tr}\left\{(P\otimes P)\, LK\right\} = -3\operatorname{tr}\left\{P\overline{P}D\overline{P}D\overline{P}\right\} = 0. \tag{44}$$

C.5 CALCULATION OF b_1, b_2, b_3

First, observe that

$$\begin{aligned}
\left(P\otimes\overline{P}\otimes\overline{P}\right) HJ &= \left(G\otimes\overline{P}\otimes\overline{P}\right)\operatorname{vec} D,\\
\left(P\otimes K\left(\overline{P}\otimes\overline{P}\right)\right) J &= \left(G\otimes\overline{P}\otimes\overline{P}\right)\operatorname{vec} D,\\
K_{21}J &= \left(\overline{P}\otimes\overline{P}\otimes G\right)\operatorname{vec} D.
\end{aligned}$$

Thus, (16) equals

$$b_1 = (G'G)^{-1} (\text{vec}\, D)' \left\{2G'G\left(\overline{P} \otimes \overline{P}\right) + G'G\left(\text{vec}\, \overline{P}\right)\left(\text{vec}\, \overline{P}\right)'\right\} \text{vec}\, D$$
$$= 2\,\text{tr}\left(\overline{P}D\overline{P}D\right) + \left(\text{tr}\left(\overline{P}D\right)\right)^2. \quad (45)$$

By simple projection calculations, it is straightforward to calculate that $b_2 = 0$ and $b_3 = 0$.

C.6 CALCULATION OF FINAL COEFFICIENTS

We now can calculate the coefficients α_0 through α_3 for the expansion of the distribution of the GMM statistic. From (9), (42), and (45), we have

$$\begin{aligned}\alpha_0 &= \frac{1}{4}(4a_0 - b_1) \\ &= \frac{1}{2}\,\text{tr}\left(\overline{P}D\overline{P}D\right) + \frac{1}{4}\left(\text{tr}\left(\overline{P}D\right)\right)^2 - \left(\frac{1}{2}\,\text{tr}\left(\overline{P}D\overline{P}D\right) + \frac{1}{4}\left(\text{tr}\left(\overline{P}D\right)\right)^2\right) \\ &= 0.\end{aligned}$$

From (10), (43), (45), and $b_2 = 0$, we have

$$\begin{aligned}\alpha_1 &= \frac{1}{4}(4a_1 + b_1 - b_2) \\ &= -\,\text{tr}\left(\overline{P}D\overline{P}D\right) + \frac{1}{2}\,\text{tr}\left(\overline{P}D\overline{P}D\right) + \frac{1}{4}\left(\text{tr}\left(\overline{P}D\right)\right)^2 \\ &= -\frac{1}{2}\,\text{tr}\left(\overline{P}D\overline{P}D\right) + \frac{1}{4}\left(\text{tr}\left(\overline{P}D\right)\right)^2.\end{aligned}$$

From (11), $a_2 = 0$, $b_2 = 0$, and $b_3 = 0$, we obtain

$$\alpha_2 = \frac{1}{12}(4a_2 + b_2 - b_3) = 0.$$

From (12) and $b_3 = 0$, we determine that

$$\alpha_3 = \frac{1}{60} b_3 = 0,$$

completing the proof of Theorem 1.2.

References

Gregory, A. and M. Veall (1985). "On formulating Wald tests of nonlinear restrictions," *Econometrica*, 53, 1465–1468.

Lafontaine, F. and K. J. White (1986). "Obtaining any Wald statistic you want," *Economics Letters*, 21, 35–40.

Magnus, J. R. and H. Neudecker (1988). *Matrix Differential Calculus with Applications in Statistics and Econometrics*, New York: John Wiley and Sons.

Newey, W. K. and D. L. McFadden (1994). "Large sample estimation and hypothesis testing," *Handbook of Econometrics, Vol. IV*, R. F. Engle and D. L McFadden, eds., 2113–2245. New York: Elsevier.

Newey, W. K. and K. D. West (1987). "Hypothesis testing with efficient method of moments estimation," *International Economic Review*, 28, 777–787.

Park, J. Y. and P. C. B. Phillips (1988). "On the formulation of Wald tests of nonlinear restrictions," *Econometrica*, 56, 1065–1083.

TWO

Moment Selection and Bias Reduction for GMM in Conditionally Heteroskedastic Models

Guido M. Kuersteiner*

2.1 INTRODUCTION

Generalized method of moments (GMM) estimators are one of the main tools for analyzing models of financial markets. Estimation of these models is often motivated by exploiting Euler equations for optimal investment and consumption decisions. This leads to a set of conditional moment restrictions that can be used to set up a GMM estimator. Rational expectations hypotheses imply that the estimation equation is augmented by an error that satisfies a martingale difference sequence property or, in other words, that is orthogonal to the information set of the agent.

Although the informational structure of rational choice models implies lack of correlation between the innovation and elements of the information set of the agent, it does not imply a particular structure for the correlation pattern of nonlinear functions of the innovations. In fact, an enormous empirical literature has documented correlations between squared residuals and other nonlinear functions of the innovation process.

In the context of GMM estimation, this lack of restrictions on the higher order moments of data and innovations complicates estimation of the optimal weight matrix and correct standard errors for the parameter estimates. Newey and West (1987), Andrews (1991), and Andrews and Monahan (1992) address the issue of consistent covariance matrix estimation in the presence of conditionally heteroskedastic and autocorrelated errors, whereas White (1980) considers the conditionally heteroskedastic case without autocorrelation. Andrews (1991) and Andrews and Monahan (1992) develop automated bandwidth selection procedures that minimize the asymptotic mean-squared error (MSE) of the estimated covariance matrix. Such bandwidth selection rules are not directly applicable to the estimation of the optimal weight matrix in the GMM problem. Xiao and Phillips (1998) obtain optimal data-dependent

* Financial support from NSF grant SES-0095132 is gratefully acknowledged.

bandwidth rules for the weight matrix in a regression model with serially correlated but homoskedastic errors.

Efficiency properties of GMM estimators in the context of conditionally heteroskedastic errors have been analyzed by Hansen (1985), Bates and White (1990), and Newey (1990). More recently Kuersteiner (1997) and Guo and Phillips (1997) have constructed GMM estimators based on a linear set of instruments in a time series context that allows for general forms of conditional heteroskedasticity. In Kuersteiner (1997), a fully feasible, efficient GMM estimator in a more restricted class of problems is analyzed. In the context of an autoregressive model, additional restrictions on the fourth-order moments of the innovation sequence are used to construct an estimator free of truncation or bandwidth parameters. This is achieved by exploiting the parametric structure and moment restrictions in a way that essentially reduces the infinite-dimensional instrument problem to a finite-dimensional one.

In Kuersteiner (2001), consistency and asymptotic normality of a GMM estimator for autoregressive moving average (ARMA) models with martingale difference errors are analyzed. The higher-order analysis provided in this chapter reveals that the dimension of the instrument space does not affect the higher order bias – at least under certain assumptions about the way the estimator is constructed and some restrictions on the innovation process as discussed in Kuersteiner (2002a). This contrasts with the usual result for two-stage least squares (TSLS), where adding more instruments primarily affects the bias of the estimator. The reason for this difference lies in the way the instrumental variables (IV) estimator is implemented here. Although the weight matrix is truly infinite dimensional there is still a parametric component in the construction of the optimal instrument. The presence of the parametric component is responsible for the good bias properties of these alternative IV procedures.

The problem of selecting the right number of instruments has been analyzed by Donald and Newey (2001) in the context of a cross-sectional regression. Kuersteiner (2002b) extends their approach to a time series context and proposes a moment selection criterion for the GMM estimator. Kuersteiner (2002b) also shows that a new kernel weighting method reduces the asymptotic higher-order bias and mean-squared error of the estimator. In the context of covariance stationary time series processes, kernel weighting has intuitive appeal because it exploits an approximate natural ordering of the instruments implied by the summability properties of the autocovariance function of stationary processes.

In this chapter, we propose to apply the moment selection criterion to the problem of efficient GMM estimation of univariate time series models with general martingale difference errors similar to the ones studied in Kuersteiner (2001). We analyze the second-order asymptotic properties of standard GMM estimators by means of an approximation to the asymptotic MSE.

We also show that the particular implementation strategy used in Kuersteiner (2001) eliminates part of the higher order bias term that depends on the number of instruments. The higher order analysis also confirms findings in Kuersteiner (2002a) that the higher order bias of the estimator essentially is independent of the number of instruments within a certain range.

2.2 MODEL AND ESTIMATORS

We consider the problem of estimating the parameters of a univariate time series model of the form

$$y_t = \phi(1)\mu + \phi_1 y_{t-1} + \cdots + \phi_p y_{t-p} + \varepsilon_t - \theta_1 \varepsilon_{t-1} \cdots - \theta_q \varepsilon_{t-q}, \tag{1}$$

where the innovations ε_t are a martingale difference sequence with $E|\varepsilon_t|^{12} < \infty$. We define the lag polynomials $\phi(L) = 1 - \phi_1 L - \cdots - \phi_p L^p$ and $\theta(L) = 1 - \theta_1 L - \cdots - \theta_q L^q$, where L is the lag operator. The vector of parameters determining (1) is defined as $\beta = (\phi_1, \ldots, \phi_p, \theta_1, \ldots, \theta_q)$. We allow for special cases of (1) where $q = 0$. Here we consider estimation of $\phi = (\phi_1, \ldots, \phi_p)$, whereas the moving average part of the model is treated as a nuisance parameter. Estimators for this model were proposed by Hayashi and Sims (1983), Stoica, Soderstrom, and Friedlander (1985), Hansen and Singleton (1996), and Kuersteiner (2002b).

The martingale difference property of ε_t imposes restrictions on the fourth-order moments. These restrictions can be conveniently summarized by defining the following function:

$$\sigma(s, r) = \begin{cases} E\left(\varepsilon_t^2 \varepsilon_{t-|s|} \varepsilon_{t-|r|}\right) & r \neq s \\ E\left(\varepsilon_t^2 \varepsilon_{t-s}^2\right) - \sigma^4 & r = s \end{cases} \quad \text{for } r, s \in \{0, \pm 1, \pm 2, \ldots\}. \tag{2}$$

It should be emphasized that $\sigma(s, r)$ is equal to the fourth-order cumulant for $s, r > 0$. Also, we define

$$\alpha_{s,r} = \begin{cases} \sigma(s, r) & \text{if } s \neq r \\ \sigma(r, r) + \sigma^4 & \text{if } s = r \end{cases}. \tag{3}$$

We assume that we have a probability space $(\Omega, \mathcal{F}, P)$ with a filtration $\mathcal{F}_t$ of increasing σ-fields such that $\mathcal{F}_t \subseteq \mathcal{F}_{t+1} \subseteq \mathcal{F}\ \forall t$. The doubly infinite sequence of random variables $\{\varepsilon_t\}_{t=-\infty}^{\infty}$ generates the filtration $\mathcal{F}_t$ such that $\mathcal{F}_t = \sigma(\varepsilon_t, \varepsilon_{t-1}, \ldots)$. The assumptions on $\{\varepsilon_t\}_{t=-\infty}^{\infty}$ are summarized as follows:

Condition 2.1 *(i) ε_t is strictly stationary and ergodic, (ii) $E(\varepsilon_t \mid \mathcal{F}_{t-1}) = 0$ almost surely, (iii) $E(\varepsilon_t^2) = \sigma^2 > 0$, (iv) $\sum_{r=1}^{\infty} \sum_{s=1}^{\infty} |\sigma(s, r)| = B < \infty$, (v) $E(\varepsilon_t^2 \varepsilon_{t-s}^2) \neq 0$ for all s.*

Remark 2.1 Assumption 2.1(iii) rules out degenerate distributions. A consequence of the martingale assumption (i) is that, in general, terms of the form

$E\left(\varepsilon_t^2\varepsilon_{t-s}\varepsilon_{t-r}\right)$ are nonzero for $s \neq r \neq 0$ and depend on s for $s = r \neq 0$. Assumption (iv) limits the dependence in higher moments by imposing a summability condition on the fourth cumulants. The assumption is needed to prove invertibility of the infinite-dimensional weight matrix of the optimal GMM estimator. Assumption (v) together with $\sum_{s=1}^{\infty} \left|\sigma(s,s)\right| < \infty$ implied by (iv) ensures that $E\left(\varepsilon_t^2\varepsilon_{t-s}^2\right) > \underline{\alpha}$ uniformly in s.

For the higher order expansions in the next section we need additional moment restrictions in the form of summability conditions on higher order cumulants. Such conditions are common in the literature on optimal weight matrix estimation as, for example, in Andrews (1991). We first define the higher order cumulants. Let $\xi = (\xi_1, \ldots, \xi_k) \in \mathbb{R}^k$ and $\varepsilon = (\varepsilon_{t_1}, \ldots, \varepsilon_{t_k})$; then, $\phi_{t_1,\ldots,t_k}(\xi) \equiv E\left(e^{i\xi'\varepsilon}\right)$ is the joint characteristic function with corresponding cumulant generating function $\ln \phi_{j_1,\ldots j_k,t_1,\ldots,t_k}(\xi)$. The joint vth order cross-cumulant is

$$\mathrm{cum}_{v_1,\ldots,v_k}(\varepsilon_{t_1}, \ldots, \varepsilon_{t_k}) \equiv \frac{\partial^{v_1+\cdots+v_k}}{\partial\xi_1^{v_1}\cdots\partial\xi_k^{v_k}} \ln \phi_{j_1,\ldots j_k,t_1,\ldots,t_k}(\xi)\bigg|_{\xi=0}, \tag{4}$$

where v_i are nonnegative integers $v_1 + \cdots + v_k = v$. When $v_1, \ldots, v_k = 1$, the shorthand notation $\mathrm{cum}(\varepsilon_{t_1}, \ldots, \varepsilon_{t_k})$ for $\mathrm{cum}_{1,\ldots,1}(\varepsilon_{t_1}, \ldots, \varepsilon_{t_k})$ is used.

Condition 2.2 *For* $\mathrm{cum}(\varepsilon_{t_1}, \ldots, \varepsilon_{t_k})$ *defined in (4) with* $E\left|\varepsilon_t\right|^{12} < \infty$,

$$\sum_{t_1,\ldots,t_{k-1}=-\infty}^{\infty} \left|1 + t_k\right| \left|\mathrm{cum}(\varepsilon_{t_1}, \ldots, \varepsilon_{t_k})\right| < \infty \text{ for } k = 2, 3, \ldots, 12.$$

To guarantee identification of the parameters $\phi = (\phi_1, \ldots, \phi_p)$, we impose restrictions on the parameter space Θ. These restrictions ensure the existence of a stationary solution to (1) and guarantee that the autoregressive and moving average parts of the model do not cancel out.

Condition 2.3 *Let* $C(\beta, L) = \theta(L)/\phi(L)$. *The parameter space* $\Theta \subset int\Theta_0$, *where* Θ_0 *is a subset of* $\mathbb{R}^d$ *defined by* $\Theta_0 = \{\beta \in \mathbb{R}^d \mid \phi(\zeta) \neq 0$ *for* $|\zeta| \leq 1$, $\theta(\zeta) \neq 0$ *for* $|\zeta| \leq 1, \theta(\zeta), \phi(\zeta)$ *have no common zeros,* $\theta_q \neq 0$ *or* $\phi_p \neq 0\}$. *Assume that* Θ *is compact in* $\mathbb{R}^d$.

GMM estimation of (1) exploits moment conditions of the form

$$E(\phi_0(L)(y_{t+q} - \mu_y)y_{t-j}) = 0 \text{ for all } j > 0.$$

Note that this representation is valid for the pure AR(p) case as well as for the case in which the moving average part is treated as a nuisance parameter. It is convenient to collect the instruments $y_{t-1}, y_{t-2}, \ldots$ in a vector $z_{t,n}^* = (y_{t-1}, y_{t-2}, \ldots y_{t-n})'$. In practice such an instrument vector is not available.

We introduce the observable instrument $z_{t,M} = S_M(t)\left(z^*_{t,M} - \mathbf{1}_M \otimes \mu_y\right)$, where $S_M(t) = \operatorname{diag}(\{t > 1 + p + q\}, \ldots, \{t > M + p + q\})$, $\{.\}$ is the indicator function and $\mathbf{1}_M = (1, \ldots, 1)'$ is an $M \times 1$ vector. Also define $\bar{z}_{t,M} = S_M(t)\left(z^*_{t,M} - \mathbf{1}_M \otimes \bar{y}\right)$ with $\bar{y} = n^{-1}\sum_{t=1}^n y_t$. An efficient GMM estimator with instruments $z_{t,M}$ is then obtained by weighting the moment conditions by a weight matrix Ω_M.

When $q = 0$, then $\Omega_M = n^{-1}\sum_{t,s=1}^n E\varepsilon_t\varepsilon_s z_{t,M}z'_{s,M}$. From the martingale property of the innovations this expression simplifies to

$$\Omega_M = n^{-1}\sum_{t=1}^n E\varepsilon_t^2 z_{t,M}z'_{t,M} = n^{-1}\sum_{t=1}^n S_M(t)\tilde{\Omega}_M S_M(t)$$

with $\tilde{\Omega}_M = E\varepsilon_t^2 z^*_{t,M}z^{*'}_{t,M}$, which is independent of t owing to the stationarity of ε_t. In fact, for M fixed, $\Omega_M \to \tilde{\Omega}_M$ as $n \to \infty$.

For the case in which $q > 0$ the instruments need to be adjusted for the potential presence of moving average terms. The optimal weight matrix is now given by

$$\Omega_M = n^{-1}\sum_{j=-q}^{q}\sum_{t=q+1}^{n-q} Eu_{t+q}u_{t+q-j}z_{t,M}z'_{t-j,M}$$

with $u_t = \theta(L)\varepsilon_t$.

The weight matrix Ω_M can be estimated if a consistent first-stage estimate $\tilde{\phi}$ is available. Then $\hat{u}_t = y_t - \tilde{\phi}_1 y_{t-1} - \cdots - \tilde{\phi}_p y_{t-p}$, and the sample average

$$\hat{\Omega}_M = n^{-1}\sum_{j=-q}^{q}\sum_{t=q+1}^{n-q} \hat{u}_{t+q}\hat{u}_{t+q-j}z_{t,M}z'_{t-j,M} \tag{5}$$

is a consistent estimate of Ω_M for any M fixed. Note that $\hat{\Omega}_M$ is not necessarily positive definite, which does not matter for estimation purposes. For hypothesis testing and the construction of confidence intervals, $\hat{\Omega}_M$, however, needs to be replaced by a positive definite alternative.

Letting $X = [x_{\max(q,p)+1} - \bar{x}, \ldots, x_n - \bar{x}]'$ with $x_t = [y_{t-1} - \bar{y}, \ldots, y_{t-p} - \bar{y}]'$ and $Z_M = \left[\bar{z}_{\max(0,p-q)+1,M}, \ldots, \bar{z}_{n-q,M}\right]'$, we find that the GMM estimator can now be written as a TSLS estimator

$$\hat{\phi}_{n,M} = \left(X'Z_M\hat{\Omega}_M^{-1}Z'_MX\right)^{-1} X'Z_M\hat{\Omega}_M^{-1}Z'_MY,$$

where $Y = \left[y_{\max(q,p)+1} - \bar{y}, \ldots, y_n - \bar{y}\right]$. The higher order properties of this estimator were analyzed in a multivariate context in Kuersteiner (2002b) under the additional assumption that ε_t is conditionally homoskedastic. Here we extend the analysis of that paper to the heteroskedastic case. Under the assumption of homoskedasticity it can also be shown that a bias correction based on higher order approximations can be implemented. As will be shown later, such a correction is no longer feasible in the heteroskedastic case. To overcome this problem we consider an alternative formulation of the GMM estimator first proposed in Kuersteiner (1997).

The idea behind the alternative estimator is to replace $n^{-1}X'Z_M$ by the population moments. These population moments depend on the underlying parameters in a way that allows estimating them at parametric or nearly parametric rates. Note that $En^{-1}X'Z_M \approx P_M$, where $P_M = [b_1, \ldots, b_M]$ with the lth element of b_k given by $[b_k]_l = \int_{-\pi}^{\pi} f_y(\lambda)e^{i\lambda(k+q-l)}d\lambda$, where $f_y(\lambda)$ is the spectral density of y_t. We assume that b_k can be estimated sufficiently well by estimators $\hat{b}_k$.

Condition 2.4 *Let $\hat{b}_k$ be an estimator of b_k such that* $\sup \left\|\hat{b}_k - b_k\right\| / \|c_k\| = O_p(n^{-1/2}(\log n)^{1/2})$, *where c_k is a nonstochastic sequence such that* $\sum_{k=0}^{\infty} \|c_k\| < \infty$.

Such an assumption can be justified, for example, if a parametric model for $f_y(\lambda)$ is available, which would be the case when $q = 0$, or, if one uses, an autoregressive approximation for $f_y(\lambda)$, as in Berk (1974) and Lewis and Reinsel (1985). Kuersteiner (2002b) used such an approximation in a nuisance parameter estimation problem. We write $\hat{P}_M = [\hat{b}_1, \ldots, \hat{b}_M]$. One can then define the alternative estimator based on $\hat{Q}'_M = \hat{P}_M \hat{\Omega}_M^{-1} Z'_M$ by

$$\hat{\phi}^{+}_{n,M} = \left(\hat{Q}'_M X\right)^{-1} \hat{Q}'_M Y.$$

Using a parametric estimate for P_M essentially removes the higher order bias typically associated with standard TSLS procedures in which the bias is explained by the correlation between $X'Z_M$ and $Z'_M\varepsilon$.

When Ω_n^{-1} is a diagonal matrix, $q = 0$, and $M = n$, then $\hat{\phi}^{+}_{n,M}$ corresponds to the estimator analyzed in Kuersteiner (1997, 2002a). It is shown there that, under some conditions, the estimator is first-order asymptotically equivalent to an infeasible optimal IV estimator.

An alternative to implementing the estimator $\hat{\phi}^{+}_{n,M}$ can be obtained by defining an approximation to the optimal weight matrix Ω_M as

$$\Omega^{*}_{n,M} = \begin{bmatrix} \Omega_M & 0 \\ 0 & \sigma^4 I_{n-M} \end{bmatrix}.$$

It is shown in Kuersteiner (2001) that, as $n,\ M \to \infty$, the matrix $\Omega^{*}_{n,M}$ converges to Ω_M in an appropriate operator norm on the space of square summable sequences. The inverse of $\Omega^{*}_{n,M}$ is given by $\operatorname{diag}\left(\Omega_M^{-1}, \sigma^{-4}I\right)$. Feasible versions of this estimator are formulated in the same manner as before by replacing Ω_M by an estimate $\hat{\Omega}_M$ and P_M by an estimate $\hat{P}_M$. Note that, by assumption, P_M can be estimated $\sqrt{n/\log n}$-consistently independent of the dimension M. The estimator $\hat{\beta}^{*}_{n,M}$ is then obtained from $Q^{*\prime}_M = \hat{P}_n \hat{\Omega}^{*-1}_{n,M} Z'_n$ by

$$\hat{\phi}^{*}_{n,M} = \left(Q^{*\prime}_M X\right)^{-1} Q^{*\prime}_M Y.$$

For the purpose of this chapter we will not consider this version of the estimator further and focus attention instead on $\hat{\phi}_{n,M}$ and $\hat{\phi}^{+}_{n,M}$.

2.3 SECOND-ORDER ASYMPTOTIC APPROXIMATION

Approximations are developed around the optimal infeasible version of the estimators. These can be obtained by letting $z_{t,\infty} = (y_{t-1}, y_{t-2}, \ldots.)$ and defining the optimal weight matrix

$$\Omega = \sum_{j=-q}^{q} Eu_{t+q}u_{t+q-j}z_{t,\infty}z'_{t-j,\infty}.$$

In the terminology developed in Kuersteiner (2001), Ω defines an invertible operator on an l^2 space. It follows that $P'\Omega^{-1} \in l^2$ for $P' = [b_1, b_2, \ldots.]$, which has rows that are in l^2. This implies that $q_t^{\infty} = P'\Omega^{-1}z_{t,\infty}$ exists almost surely, is stationary, and has finite second moments.

We impose the following additional conditions on Ω and Ω^{-1}:

Condition 2.5 *Let $\omega_{i,j}$ be the i, jth element of Ω and let $\vartheta_{i,j}$ be the i, jth element of Ω^{-1}. Assume that $\omega_{i,j} = g_{\omega}(i-j) + o\left(\lambda_{\omega}^{|i-j|}\right)$ and $\vartheta_{i,j} = g_{\vartheta}(i-j) + o(\lambda_{\vartheta}^{|i-j|})$ for some constants $\lambda_{\omega}, \lambda_{\vartheta} \in (0,1)$ and functions g_{ω} and g_{ϑ} such that $g_{.}(M) = O(\lambda_{.}^{M})$.*

Condition 2.5 imposes exponential rates of decay on the off-diagonal elements of Ω and Ω^{-1}. Such rates are typically satisfied for linear process models such as the ARMA class but also hold for the higher cross moments of generalized autoregressive conditional heteroskedasticity (GARCH)-type processes.

If we let $D = P'\Omega^{-1}P$, an infeasible efficient estimator for ϕ can be written as $\sqrt{n}(\hat{\phi} - \phi) = D^{-1}d_0$, where $d_0 = n^{-1/2}\sum_t u_{t+q}z_{t,\infty}$, and it follows from results in Kuersteiner (2001) that $D^{-1}d_0 \to N(0, D^{-1})$.

The bandwidth parameter M is chosen such that the approximate MSE of the estimator $\hat{\phi}_{n,M}$ is minimized. We use the Nagar (1959) type of approximation to the MSE applied in Donald and Newey (2001). Let $\hat{\phi}_{n,M}$ be stochastically approximated by $b_{n,M}$ such that $n^{1/2}(\hat{\phi}_{n,M} - \phi) = b_{n,M} + r_{n,M}$, where $r_{n,M}$ is an error term. Define the approximate MSE $\varphi_n(M, \ell, k(.))$ of $\hat{\beta}_{n,M}$ as in Donald and Newey (2001) such that

$$\operatorname{tr} D^{1/2} E\left(b_{n,M}b'_{n,M}\right) D^{1/2\prime} = 1 + \varphi_n(M) + R_{n,M}$$

and require that the error terms $r_{n,M}$ and $R_{n,M}$ satisfy

$$\frac{\left\|r_{n,M}\right\|^2 + R_{n,M}}{\varphi_n(M, \ell, k(.))} = o_p(1) \text{ as } M \to \infty, n \to \infty, M/\sqrt{n} \to 0. \qquad (6)$$

The stochastic expansion $b_{n,M}$ of $\hat{\phi}_{n,M}$ is obtained by a second-order Taylor approximation of $\hat{D}_M^{-1}$ around D^{-1}, which leads to

$$\sqrt{n}(\hat{\phi}_{n,M} - \phi) = D^{-1}[I + (\hat{D}_M - D)D^{-1} + (\hat{D}_M - D)D^{-1}(\hat{D}_M - D)D^{-1}]\hat{d}_M + o_p(M/\sqrt{n}).$$

The expansion is valid as long as $M/\sqrt{n} \to 0$. We decompose the expansion into $\hat{D}_M - D = H_1 + \cdots + H_k$ and $\hat{d}_n = d_0 + d_1 + \cdots + d_g$ such that

$$\sqrt{n}(\hat{\phi}_{n,M} - \phi) = D^{-1}\sum_i d_i + D^{-1}\sum_i\sum_j H_i D^{-1} d_j + o_p(M/\sqrt{n}).$$

We now denote by $\sqrt{n}\,(b_{n,M} - \phi)$ all the terms $D^{-1}d_i$ and $D^{-1}H_i D^{-1}d_j$ that depend on M and are largest in probability. The next proposition gives an expression for the asymptotic MSE using the largest-in-probability terms depending on M and n.

Proposition 2.1 *Suppose Conditions (2.1), (2.2), (2.3), and (2.5) hold. Let* $\Gamma_{t-s}^{ux} = Eu_t x_s$, $\Gamma_{t-s}^{yy} = \operatorname{cov}(y_t, y_s)$ *and let* $\mathcal{A}_2 = \lim_n \sqrt{n}/M E d_7$ *where* d_7 *is defined in (26). Define*

$$\mathcal{A}_1 = \mathcal{A}_2 + \lim_{M\to\infty} M^{-1} \sum_{j_1,j_2=1}^{M} \sum_{j_3=-\infty}^{\infty} \vartheta_{j_1,j_2} \Gamma_{j_3}^{yy} \Gamma_{-j_1+j_2-j_3}^{ux}. \tag{7}$$

Let $\mathcal{A} = \operatorname{tr}(D^{-1/2}\mathcal{A}_1'\mathcal{A}_1 D^{-1/2})$ *and* $\sigma_M = \operatorname{tr}\left(D^{-1/2} P_M' \Omega_M^{-1} P_M D^{-1/2}\right)$. *Then for* M *such that* $M \to \infty$, $n/M^2(\sigma_M - p) \to \mathcal{B}_1/\kappa$ *with* $0 < \kappa < \infty$ *and* $0 < \mathcal{B}_1 < \infty$

$$\lim_n n/M^2 \varphi_n(M) = \mathcal{A} + \mathcal{B}_1/\kappa.$$

Proposition (2.1) shows that, unlike the homoskedastic case analyzed in Kuersteiner (2002b), the bias term $\mathcal{A}_1$ is of a fairly complicated form, which makes estimation of this constant more challenging. On the other hand, it is well known (see for example Hannan and Deistler, 1988, p. 307) that, if $p - \sigma_M = O(\lambda^{2M})$ for some $\lambda \in (0,1)$, then an equivalent criterion for selecting M can be based on

$$\min_M \frac{M^2}{n} - \log\left|P_M'\Omega_M^{-1}P_M\right|.$$

This approach was previously proposed by Kuersteiner (2002b). Note that $\left(P_M'\Omega_M^{-1}P_M\right)^{-1}$ is the asymptotic variance covariance matrix of the GMM estimator based on M instruments. To implement the criterion, the matrix $P_M'\Omega_M^{-1}P_M$ needs to be replaced by an estimator. In the present context of heteroskedastic innovations of unknown functional form, this is more difficult than in the case analyzed in Kuersteiner (2002b) in which a linear process could be used to approximate the relevant variance–covariance terms. Here a less parametric procedure is required, but the details are beyond the scope of this chapter.

Besides selection of M, one is typically also interested in correcting the bias of TSLS estimators. The complexity of the bias expression suggests that bias correction is more difficult to achieve under heteroskedasticity. The higher order analysis of the alternative estimator $\hat{\phi}^{+}_{n,M}$ reveals that part of the higher order bias can be eliminated by fitting a parametric model to the instrument-regressor covariance.

We let $\hat{\phi}^{+}_{n,M}$ be stochastically approximated by $b^{+}_{n,M}$ such that $n^{1/2}(\hat{\beta}_{n,M} - \beta) = b^{+}_{n,M} + r^{+}_{n,M}$, where $r^{+}_{n,M}$ is an error term. Then

$$\operatorname{tr}\left(D^{1/2} E\left(b^{+}_{n,M} b^{+\prime}_{n,M}\right) D^{1/2\prime}\right) = 1 + \varphi^{+}_{n}(M) + R^{+}_{n,M}.$$

We require, moreover, that the error terms $r^{+}_{n,M}$ and $R^{+}_{n,M}$ satisfy the same restrictions as before. The approximate MSE $\varphi^{+}_{n}(M)$ then is obtained as follows.

Proposition 2.2 *Suppose Conditions (2.1), (2.2), (2.3), (2.4), and (2.5) hold. If $M/\sqrt{n} \to 0$, then*

$$\lim_{n} \sqrt{n}/M E b^{+}_{n,M} = \mathcal{A}_2.$$

and

$$\lim_{n} n/M^2 \varphi_n(M) = \mathcal{B}_1/\kappa.$$

The result is promising because it shows that the alternative formulation of the GMM estimator successfully removes part of the largest order bias term and thus can be seen as an alternative to the bias correction methods developed in Kuersteiner (2002b). Those bias correction methods are difficult to implement in the case of heteroskedastic errors. Inspection of the proof of Proposition 2.2 shows that under the conditions of Kuersteiner (2002a), where estimated residuals are used as instruments, the bias $\mathcal{A}_2 = 0$. In this case the alternative estimator $\hat{\phi}^{+}_{n,M}$ successfully removes all of the higher order bias.

2.4 CONCLUSIONS

We have provided a higher order asymptotic analysis of estimators for the autoregressive parameters in ARMA models when the innovations are general martingale difference sequences. Instrumental variable estimators based on instruments that are linear in the observations are frequently used to estimate such models. First-order asymptotic efficiency requires that the number of instruments tend to infinity. In practice, such a rule can not be directly implemented owing to limitations of sample size. More importantly, standard

2SLS procedures suffer from significant small sample bias. This bias increases with the number of instruments.

Here it is shown that under certain conditions parametric estimation of the sample correlation between instruments and regressors essentially eliminates the instrument-induced bias.

It is also shown that even the effects of more instruments increasing higher order variance terms of the estimators are eliminated by using the alternative formulations of the GMM estimator. It thus turns out that the usual trade-off between efficiency and bias in selecting moments can be eliminated under the conditions studied here at least as long as the number of instruments is not too large.

APPENDIX A: PROOF

Lemma A.1 *Let $\hat{\Omega}_M$ be defined in (5) and $\sqrt{n}(\tilde{\phi} - \phi) = O_p(1)$. Let $M \to \infty$ such that $M/n^{1/2} \to 0$. Then $\|\hat{\Omega}_M - \Omega_M\| = O_p(M/n^{1/2})$.*

Proof. Let $v_t = u_{t+q}(z_{t,M} - \mathbf{1}_M\mu_y)$, $\bar{v}_t = u_{t+q}\bar{z}_{t,M}$, and $\hat{v}_t = \hat{u}_{t+q}\bar{z}_{t,M}$, where $\hat{u}_{t+q} - u_{t+q} = (\phi - \tilde{\phi})' Y_{t+q} + \mu - \bar{y}$ with $Y_t = (y_t, \ldots, y_{t-p+1})'$. Then $\hat{v}_t - \bar{v}_t = \left((\phi - \tilde{\phi})' Y_{t+q} + \mu - \bar{y}\right)(z_{t,M} - \mathbf{1}_M\bar{y})$. Let $\check{\Omega}_M = \sum_{j=-q}^{q} n^{-1} \sum_{t=q}^{n-q} \bar{v}_t\bar{v}_{t-j}'$. Note that

$$\begin{aligned} \|\hat{\Omega}_M - \Omega_M\| &\leq \|\hat{\Omega}_M - \check{\Omega}_M\| + \|\check{\Omega}_M - \Omega_M\| \\ &\leq \|\hat{\Omega}_M - \check{\Omega}_M\| + \textstyle\sum_{j=-q}^{q} \left\|n^{-1} \sum_{t=q}^{n-q} \left(\bar{v}_t\bar{v}_{t-j}' - Ev_tv_{t-j}'\right)\right\|. \end{aligned}$$

Let $\check{\Omega}_M(j) = n^{-1}\sum_{t=q}^{n-q} \bar{v}_t\bar{v}_{t-j}'$ with $\Omega_M(j) = Ev_tv_{t-j}'$. Let $v_{t,j} = u_{t+q}(y_{t-j} - \mu_y)$ and let r_1, r_2 be defined as $r_1 = \max(i+1, j+l+1)$ and $r_2 = \min(n, n+j)$. Define a typical element of $\check{\Omega}_M(l)$ as $\hat{\omega}_{ij}(l) = n^{-1}\sum_{t=r_1}^{r_2} \bar{v}_{t,i}\bar{v}_{t-l,j}$ and $\omega_{i,k}(j) = Ev_{t,i}v_{t-j,k}$. Next note that

$$\left\|n^{-1}\textstyle\sum_{t=q}^{n-q}\left(\bar{v}_t\bar{v}_{t-j}' - Ev_tv_{t-j}'\right)\right\|^2 = \sum_{i,j=1}^{M} \left\|\hat{\omega}_{i,j}(l) - \omega_{i,j}(l)\right\|^2.$$

Then, let $\check{\omega}_{i,j}(l) = n^{-1}\sum_{t=r_1}^{r_2} v_{t,i}v_{t-l,j}$ such that

$$\begin{aligned} \|\hat{\omega}_{i,j}(l) - \check{\omega}_{i,j}(l)\| \leq{}& \|\bar{y} - \mu_y\| \left\|n^{-1}\textstyle\sum_{t=r_1}^{r_2} u_{t+q}u_{t+q-l}(y_{t-j-l} - \bar{y})\right\| \\ &+ \|\bar{y} - \mu_y\| \left\|n^{-1}\textstyle\sum_{t=r_1}^{r_2} u_{t+q}u_{t+q-l}(y_{t-i} - \bar{y})\right\| \\ &+ \left\|(\bar{y} - \mu_y)(\bar{y} - \mu_y)'\right\|. \end{aligned}$$

Use the bound

$$\begin{aligned} \left\|n^{-1}\textstyle\sum_{t=q}^{n-q} u_{t+q}u_{t+q-l}(y_{t-j-l} - \bar{y})\right\| \leq{}& \|\bar{y} - \mu_y\| \left\|n^{-1}\textstyle\sum_{t=r_1}^{r_2} u_{t+q}u_{t+q-l}\right\| \\ &+ \left\|n^{-1}\textstyle\sum_{t=r_1}^{r_2} u_{t+q}u_{t+q-l}(y_{t-j-l} - \mu)\right\| \end{aligned}$$

to evaluate $E\left\|\hat{\omega}_{i,j}(l)-\check{\omega}_{i,j}(l)\right\|^2$. By repeated application of the Cauchy–Schwarz inequality it follows that this expectation depends on products of $\left(E\left\|\bar{y}-\mu_y\right\|^4\right)^{1/2}=O(n^{-1})$, $\left(E\left\|n^{-1}\sum_{t=r_1}^{r_2}u_{t+q}u_{t+q-l}\right\|^2\right)^{1/2}=O(1)$. Using these results it can be shown that $E\left\|\hat{\omega}_{i,j}(l)-\check{\omega}_{i,j}(l)\right\|^2=O(n^{-2})$ uniformly in i, j, l. This implies that $E\left\|\check{\Omega}_M(l)-\Omega_M(l)\right\|^2=\sum_{i,j=1}^{M}E\left\|\check{\omega}_{i,j}(l)-\omega_{i,j}(l)\right\|^2+o(M/n^{3/2})$ as long as $M/n^{1/2}\to 0$. Also note that

$$\check{\omega}_{i,j}(l)=n^{-1}\sum_{t=r_1}^{r_2}\bar{\omega}_{t,j,l,i}+\frac{r_2-r_1}{n}Ev_{t,i}v_{t-l,j}$$

with $\bar{\omega}_{t,j,i,l}=v_{t,i}v_{t-l,j}-Ev_{t,i}v_{t-l,j}$. Now

$$\begin{aligned}\left\|\check{\omega}_{i,j}(l)-\omega_{i,j}(l)\right\|^2&\le\left\|n^{-1}\sum_{t=r_1}^{r_2}\bar{\omega}_{t,j,i,l}\right\|^2+\left(\frac{2M}{n}\right)^2\left\|Ev_{t,i}v_{t-l,j}\right\|^2\\&\quad+4\frac{M}{n}\left\|Ev_{t,i}v_{t-l,j}\right\|\left\|n^{-1}\sum_{t=r_1}^{r_2}\bar{\omega}_{t,j,i,l}\right\|.\end{aligned}$$

For $Ev_{t,i}v_{t-l,j}=\gamma_l^{vv(i,j)}$ it follows that

$$\begin{aligned}E\left\|n^{-1}\sum_{t=r_1}^{r_2}\bar{\omega}_{t,j,i,l}\right\|^2&\le n^{-2}\sum_{t,s=r_1}^{r_2}E\bar{\omega}_{t,j,i,l}\bar{\omega}_{s,j,i,l}\\&=n^{-2}\sum_{t,s=r_1}^{r_2}\left[\gamma_{t-s}^{vv(i,i)}\gamma_{t-s}^{vv(j,j)}+\gamma_{t-l+s}^{vv(i,j)}\gamma_{s-t+l}^{vv(i,j)}+\mathcal{K}_4^4\right]\\&=O(n^{-1})\end{aligned}$$

uniformly in i and j. Thus, $\sum_{i,j=1}^{M}E\left\|n^{-1}\sum_{t=r_1}^{r_2}\bar{\omega}_{t,j,i,l}\right\|^2=O(M^2/n)$, whereas $\left(\frac{2M}{n}\right)^2\sum_{i,j=1}^{M}\left\|\gamma_l^{vv(i,j)}\right\|^2=O(M^3/n^2)=o(M/n)$ and $\frac{M}{n}\sum_{i,j=1}^{M}\left\|\gamma_l^{vv(i,j)}\right\|$ $E\left\|n^{-1}\sum_{t=r_1}^{r_2}\bar{\omega}_{t,j,i,l}\right\|=O(M^2/n^{3/2})=o(M/n)$. Taken together these calculations show that $\sum_{i,j=1}^{M}E\left\|\check{\omega}_{i,j}(l)-\omega_{i,j}(l)\right\|^2=O(M^2/n)$ and $\left(E\left\|\check{\Omega}_M-\Omega_M\right\|^2\right)^{1/2}=O(M/n^{1/2})$. Next consider $\left\|\hat{\Omega}_M-\tilde{\Omega}_M\right\|$, where

$$\begin{aligned}\left\|\hat{\Omega}_M-\check{\Omega}_M\right\|&\le\sum_{j=-q}^{q}n^{-1}\sum_{t=q}^{n-q}\left\|(\hat{v}_t-\bar{v}_t)\bar{v}_{t-j}'\right\|\\&\quad+\left\|(\hat{v}_t-\bar{v}_t)(\hat{v}_{t-j}-\bar{v}_{t-j})'\right\|+\left\|\bar{v}_t(\bar{v}_{t-j}-\hat{v}_{t-j})'\right\|\\&\le\sum_{j=-q}^{q}n^{-1}\sum_{t=q}^{n-q}2\left(\left\|\phi-\tilde{\phi}\right\|\left\|Y_{t-1}\right\|+\left\|\mu-\bar{y}\right\|\right)\left\|u_{t+q-j}\bar{z}_{t,M}\bar{z}_{t-j,M}'\right\|\\&\quad+\left(\left\|\phi-\tilde{\phi}\right\|+\left\|\mu-\bar{y}\right\|\right)^2\sum_{j=-q}^{q}n^{-1}\sum_{t=q}^{n-q}\left\|\bar{z}_{t,M}\bar{z}_{t-j,M}'\right\|\end{aligned}$$

and by similar arguments, as before, $n^{-1}\sum_{t=q}^{n-q}\left\|Y_{t-1}\right\|\left\|u_{t+q-j}\bar{z}_{t,M}\bar{z}_{t-j,M}'\right\|=O_p(M)$ and $\left\|\phi-\tilde{\phi}\right\|$, $\left\|\mu-\bar{y}\right\|$ are $O_p(n^{-1/2})$. This establishes the result. ■

Lemma A.2 *Let d_5 be as defined in (24) and d_7 as defined in (26).*

$$E(d_5+d_7)(d_5+d_7)' = M^2/n\mathcal{A}_1'\mathcal{A}_1 + o(M^2/n),$$

where $\mathcal{A}_1$ is defined in (7).

Proof. Let $v_{t,j} = u_{t+q}\,(y_{t-j}-\mu_y)$, $w_{t,i} = (x_{t+q}-\mu_x)(y_{t-i}-\mu_y)$, and $\Gamma_i^{xy} = Ew_{t,i}$ with $\Gamma_{-i}^{yx} = Ew_{t,i}'$ and let $\breve{w}_{t,i} = w_{t,i} - \Gamma_i^{xy}$. We only consider the largest order term

$$d_{51} = n^{-3/2}\sum_{j_1,j_2=1}^{M}\sum_{t=1+j_1}^{n-q}\breve{w}_{t,j_1}\vartheta_{j_1,j_2}^{M}\sum_{t=1}^{n}v_{t,j_2}$$

where $\breve{w}_{t,j_1} = w_{t,j_1} - \Gamma_{j_1}^{xy}$. We have for any $\ell \in \mathbb{R}^p$ with $\|\ell\| < \infty$,

$$\begin{aligned}E\ell' d_{51}d_{51}'\ell = \frac{1}{n^3}\sum_{j_1,\ldots,j_4}^{M}\sum_{t_1,t_2 s_1,s_2}^{n-q}&\{\vartheta_{j_1,j_2}^{M}E(v_{t_1,j_2}\breve{w}_{s_1,j_1}')\ell\ell' E(\breve{w}_{s_2,j_4}v_{t_2,j_3})\vartheta_{j_3,j_4}^{M}\\ &+\left[\vartheta_{j_1,j_2}^{M\prime}E(v_{t_1,j_2}\ell'\breve{w}_{s_2,j_4})\vartheta_{j_3,j_4}^{M}E(v_{t_2,j_3}\ell'\breve{w}_{s_1,j_1})\right]\\ &+\left[\vartheta_{j_1,j_2}^{M\prime}E(v_{t_1,j_2}v_{t_2,j_3})\vartheta_{j_3,j_4}^{M}E(\breve{w}_{s_1,j_1}'\ell\ell'\breve{w}_{s_2,j_4})\right]\} + \ell'\mathcal{K}_8\ell,\end{aligned}$$

where the matrix of eighth-order cumulant terms $\mathcal{K}_8$ contains elements of the form

$$\frac{1}{n^3}\sum_{j_1,\ldots,j_4}^{M}\sum_{t_1,t_2 s_1,s_2}^{n-q}\operatorname{cum}^*\left(y_{t_1-j_1},y_{t_1-i_1},y_{t_2-j_2},y_{t_2-i_2},y_{s_2-j_3},y_{s_1-j_4},u_{s_2+q},u_{s_1+q}\right),$$

which are of lower order owing to Assumption (2.2). The first term can be written as

$$\frac{1}{n^3}\sum_{j_1,j_2}^{M}\sum_{t_1,s_1}^{n-q}\vartheta_{j_1,j_2}^{M}E\left(v_{t_1,j_2}\breve{w}_{s_1,j_1}'\right)\ell\ell'\sum_{j_3,j_4}^{M}\sum_{t_2,s_2}E\left(\breve{w}_{s_2,j_4}v_{t_2,j_3}\right)\vartheta_{j_3,j_4}^{M},$$

where

$$Ev_{t_1,j_2}\breve{w}_{s_1,j_1}' = \Gamma_{s_1-t_1-j_1+j_2}^{yy}\Gamma_{t_1-s_1}^{ux\prime} + \Gamma_{t_1-s_1+j_1}^{yu}\Gamma_{t_1-s_1-j_2}^{yx} + \mathcal{K}_4^1 \tag{8}$$

with $\mathcal{K}_4^1$ being a term of fourth-order cumulants. Focusing on the first term, we find

$$\begin{aligned}&\frac{1}{nM}\sum_{t_1,s_1}^{n-q}\sum_{j_1,j_2}^{M}\vartheta_{j_1,j_2}^{M}\Gamma_{s_1-t_1-j_1+j_2}^{yy}\Gamma_{t_1-s_1}^{ux'}\\ &=\int_{-\pi}^{\pi}\int_{-\pi}^{\pi}\frac{1}{M}\sum_{j_1,j_2}^{M}\vartheta_{j_1,j_2}^{M}f_y(\lambda)f_{ux'}(\mu)e^{i\lambda(-j_1+j_2)}n^{-1}\sum_{t_1,s_1}e^{i(\mu-\lambda)(t_1-s_1)}d\lambda d\mu,\end{aligned}$$

where $K_n(\lambda) = (2\pi)^{-1}n^{-1}\sum_{t_1,s_1}e^{i\lambda(t_1-s_1)}$ is the Fejer kernel (see Brockwell and Davis, 1991, p. 70). Let $\eta_M(\lambda) = \frac{1}{M}\sum_{j_1,j_2}^{M}\vartheta_{j_1,j_2}^{M}e^{i\lambda(-j_1+j_2)}$. Note that $\|\eta_M(\lambda)\| \le \frac{1}{M}\sum_{j_1,j_2}^{M}\left\|\vartheta_{j_1,j_2}^{M\prime}\right\| < \infty$ for all n such that $\eta_M(\lambda)\to\eta(\lambda)$ for some function $\eta(\lambda)$. Then

$$\left\| \int_{-\pi}^{\pi} \eta_M(\mu-\lambda) K_n(\lambda) d\lambda - \eta(\mu) \right\| \leq \left\| \int_{-\pi}^{\pi} (\eta_M(\mu-\lambda) - \eta(\mu-\lambda))\, K_n(\lambda) d\lambda \right\| + \left\| \int_{-\pi}^{\pi} \eta(\mu-\lambda) K_n(\lambda) d\lambda - \eta(\mu) \right\| \leq \epsilon_1 + \epsilon_2,$$

where $\left\| \int_{-\pi}^{\pi} (\eta_M(\mu-\lambda) - \eta(\mu-\lambda))\, K_n(\lambda) d\lambda \right\| \leq \sup_\mu \left\| \eta_M(\mu) - \eta(\mu) \right\| \times \int_{-\pi}^{\pi} K_n(\lambda) d\lambda \leq \epsilon_1$ for M large enough by uniform convergence of $\eta_M(\lambda)$ and $\left\| \int_{-\pi}^{\pi} \eta(\mu-\lambda) K_n(\lambda) d\lambda - \eta(\mu) \right\| \leq \epsilon_2$ for n large enough by Theorem 2.11.1 of Brockwell and Davis (1991). It follows that

$$\int_{-\pi}^{\pi} \int_{-\pi}^{\pi} 2\pi\ \eta_M(\lambda) f_y(\lambda) f_{ux'}(\mu) K_n(\lambda-\mu) d\lambda d\mu \to 2\pi \int_{-\pi}^{\pi} \eta(\lambda) f_y(\lambda) f_{ux'}(\lambda) d\lambda.$$

The terms involving $\Gamma^{uy}_{t_1-s_1+j_1} \Gamma^{yx}_{t_1-s_1-j_2}$ and $\mathcal{K}_4^1$ in (8) go to zero by the same arguments as in Parzen (1957, p. 341) because, for some constant c such that $\sup_{j_1,j_2,M} \left| \vartheta^M_{j_1,j_2} \right| < c$,

$$\left\| \frac{1}{nM} \sum_{t_1,s_1} \sum^{M}_{j_1,j_2} \vartheta^M_{j_1,j_2} \Gamma^{uy}_{t_1-s_1+j_1} \Gamma^{yx}_{t_1-s_1-j_2} \right\| \leq \frac{c}{nM} \sum_{t_1,s_1} \sum^{M}_{j_1,j_2} \left\| \Gamma^{uy}_{t_1-s_1+j_1} \Gamma^{yx}_{t_1-s_1-j_2} \right\|$$

and the cumulant term is of lower order. Next turn to

$$\begin{aligned} &\vartheta^M_{j_1,j_2} E(v_{t_1,j_2} \ell' \bar{w}_{s_2,j_4}) \vartheta^M_{j_3,j_4} E(v_{t_2,j_3} \ell' \bar{w}_{s_1,j_1}) \\ &= \vartheta^M_{j_1,j_2} (\ell' \Gamma^{ux}_{t_1-s_2} \Gamma^{yy}_{t_1-s_2-j_2+j_4} + \Gamma^{uy}_{t_1-s_2+j_4} \ell' \Gamma^{xy}_{s_2-t_1+j_2} \\ &\quad + \mathcal{K}_4) \vartheta^M_{j_3,j_4} (\ell' \Gamma^{ux}_{t_2-s_1} \Gamma^{yy}_{t_2-s_1-j_3+j_1} + \Gamma^{uy}_{t_2-s_1+j_1} \ell' \Gamma^{xy}_{s_1-t_2+j_3} + \mathcal{K}_4) \end{aligned}$$

for some fourth-order cumulant term $\mathcal{K}_4$, where, for a typical term in this product, we have

$$\begin{aligned} &\left\| \sum_{j_1,j_2,j_3,j_4} \vartheta^M_{j_1,j_2} \ell' \sum_{h_1} \left[(1 - \tfrac{|h_1|}{n}) \Gamma^{ux}_{h_1} \Gamma^{yy}_{h_1-j_2+j_4} \right] \vartheta^M_{j_3,j_4} \sum_{h_2} (1 - \tfrac{|h_2|}{n}) \Gamma^{uy}_{h_2+j_1} \ell' \Gamma^{xy}_{h_2+j_3} \right\| \\ &\leq \sum_{j_1,j_2,j_3,j_4} \left\| \vartheta^M_{j_1,j_2} \right\| \left\| \ell' \sum_{h_1} \left[(1 - \tfrac{|h_1|}{n}) \Gamma^{ux}_{h_1} \Gamma^{yy}_{h_1-j_2+j_4} \right] \right\| \left\| \vartheta^M_{j_3,j_4} \right\| \\ &\quad \times \left\| \sum_{h_2} (1 - \tfrac{|h_2|}{n}) \Gamma^{uy}_{h_2+j_1} \ell' \Gamma^{xy}_{h_2+j_3} \right\| = O(1). \end{aligned}$$

Similar arguments show that the remaining terms of $E\ell d_5 d_5' \ell$ are all $O(M/n)$. Terms involving d_7 can be analyzed in the same way.

Lemma A.3 *Let H_1 be defined as in (11). Then*

$$H_1 = O(\lambda^{2M})$$

for some $\lambda \in (0, 1)$.

Proof. Let $\vartheta_{i,j}^M$ be the i, jth element of Ω_M^{-1}. Let $[\Omega^{-1}]_M$ be the upper $pM \times pM$ block of the infinite-dimensional matrix Ω^{-1}. We partition Ω as

$$\Omega = \begin{bmatrix} \Omega_{11} & \Omega_{12} \\ \Omega_{21} & \Omega_{22} \end{bmatrix}$$

such that $\Omega_{11} = \Omega_M$ and, correspondingly, $P = [P_1', P_2']'$ with $P_M = P_1$. Then

$$\begin{aligned} & P_M'\Omega_M^{-1}P_M - P'\Omega^{-1}P \\ & = P_M'\left(\Omega_M^{-1} - [\Omega^{-1}]_M\right)P_M + P_M'[\Omega^{-1}]_M\Omega_{12}\Omega_{22}^{-1}P_2 \\ & \quad + P_2'\Omega_{22}^{-1}\Omega_{21}[\Omega^{-1}]_M P_M - P_2'\left(\Omega_{22}^{-1} + \Omega_{22}^{-1}\Omega_{21}[\Omega^{-1}]_M\Omega_{12}\Omega_{22}^{-1}\right)P_2 \\ & = P_M'\left(\Omega_M^{-1} - [\Omega^{-1}]_M\right)P_M \\ & \quad + \sum_{j_1,j_2=1}^{M}\sum_{j_3,j_4=1}^{\infty}\Gamma_{j_1}^{xy}\vartheta_{j_1,j_2}\omega_{j_2,j_3+M}\vartheta_{j_3+M,j_4+M}\Gamma_{-j_4-M}^{yx} \\ & \quad + \sum_{j_1,j_2=1}^{\infty}\sum_{j_3,j_4=1}^{M}\Gamma_{j_1+M}^{xy}\vartheta_{j_1+M,j_2+M}\omega_{j_2+M,j_3}\vartheta_{j_3,j_4}\Gamma_{-j_4}^{yx} \\ & \quad - \sum_{j_1,j_2=1}^{\infty}\Gamma_{j_1+M}^{xy}\vartheta_{j_1+M,j_2+M}\Gamma_{-j_2-M}^{yx}. \end{aligned}$$

From Kuersteiner (2002b) it follows that $\Gamma_{j_1+M}^{xy} = g_\Gamma(j_1 + M) + o(\lambda_\Gamma^M)$ for some function $g_\Gamma(M) = O(\lambda_\Gamma^M)$ and some $\lambda_\Gamma \in (0, 1)$, and by Condition (2.5) $\omega_{j_2+M,j_3} = g_\omega(j_3 - j_2 - M) + o(\lambda_\omega^M)$, where $g_\omega(M) = O(\lambda_\omega^M)$ for some $\lambda_\omega \in (0, 1)$ and $\vartheta_{j_1+M,j_2+M} = g_\vartheta(j_1 - j_2) + o(\lambda_\vartheta^{|j_1-j_2|})$. Substituting these expressions then leads to

$$\begin{aligned} H_{11} & = P_M'\left(\Omega_M^{-1} - [\Omega^{-1}]_M\right)P_M + O(\lambda^M\sum_{j_1,\ldots,j_4=1}^{\infty} \\ & \quad \times [g_\Gamma(j_1)g_\vartheta(j_1 - j_2)g_\Gamma(j_3 - j_2 - M)g_\vartheta(j_3 - j_4)g_\Gamma(j_4)]) \\ & \quad - O(\lambda^{2M}\sum_{j_1,j_2=1}^{\infty}g_\Gamma(j_1)g_\vartheta(j_1 - j_2)g_\Gamma(j_2)) + o(\lambda^{2M}). \end{aligned}$$

Here, $\lambda = \max(\lambda_\Gamma, \lambda_\omega, \lambda_\vartheta) + \varepsilon$ for some $\varepsilon > 0$ and the first sum in the previous display is of order $O(\lambda^M)$. For $P_M'\left(\Omega_M^{-1} - [\Omega^{-1}]_M\right)P_M$ note that, by the partitioned inverse formula $[\Omega^{-1}]_M = \left(\Omega_{11} - \Omega_{12}\Omega_{22}^{-1}\Omega_{21}\right)^{-1}$, where we have used the partition of Ω with $\Omega_{11} = \Omega_M$ and the remaining matrices Ω_{ij} defined conformingly. Then, by the same arguments as before,

$$\begin{aligned} & P_M'\left(\Omega_M^{-1} - [\Omega^{-1}]_M\right)P_M \\ & = P_M'[\Omega^{-1}]_M\left(\Omega_{12}\Omega_{22}^{-1}\Omega_{21}\right)\Omega_M^{-1}P_M \end{aligned}$$

$$= \sum_{j_1,j_2,j_5,j_6=1}^{M} \sum_{j_3,j_4=1}^{\infty} \Gamma_{j_1}^{xy} \vartheta_{j_1,j_2}^{M} (\omega_{j_2,j_3+M} \vartheta_{j_3,j_4} \omega_{j_4+M,j5}) \vartheta_{j_5,j_6} \Gamma_{-j_6}^{yx}$$

$$= \sum_{j_1,\ldots,j_6=1}^{\infty} \Gamma_{j_1}^{xy} \vartheta_{j_1,j_2} (\omega_{j_2,j_3+M} \vartheta_{j_3,j_4} \omega_{j_4+M,j5}) \vartheta_{j_5,j_6} \Gamma_{-j_6}^{yx} + o(\lambda^{2M})$$

such that

$$\left\| P_M' \left(\Omega_M^{-1} - [\Omega^{-1}]_M \right) P_M \right\|$$

$$= O\left(\sum_{j_1,\ldots,j_6=1}^{\infty} g_\Gamma(j_1) g_\vartheta(j_1 - j_2) g_\Gamma(j_3 - j_2 - M) g_\vartheta \right.$$

$$\left. \times (j_3 - j_4) g_\Gamma(j_4 - j_5 - M) g_\vartheta(j_6 - j_5) g_\Gamma(j_6) \right) + o(\lambda^{2M}).$$

The last sum is $O(\lambda^{2M})$ by Condition 2.5. ■

Proof of Proposition 2.1. For the purpose of this proof and to maintain the same notation with Kuersteiner (2002b) we redefine $\hat{P}_M$ as $\hat{P}_M' = n^{-1} X' Z_M$. Consider a second-order Taylor approximation of $\hat{D}_M^{-1}$ around D^{-1} such that, for $\hat{d}_M = \hat{P}_M' \hat{\Omega}_M^{-1} n^{-1/2} \sum_{t=1}^{n-q} u_{t+q} \bar{z}_{t,M}$,

$$\sqrt{n}(\hat{\phi}_{n,M} - \phi) = D^{-1}[I - (\hat{D}_M - D)D^{-1} + (\hat{D}_M - D)D^{-1}(\hat{D}_M - D)D^{-1}]\hat{d}_M + o_p(M/\sqrt{n}), \tag{9}$$

where for $M/n^{1/2} \to 0$ the error term is $o_p(M/\sqrt{n})$ by the Taylor theorem and because $\det D \neq 0$, $\hat{D}_M - D = O_p(M/n^{1/2})$, and $\hat{d}_M = O_p(M/n^{1/2})$, as shown in equations (10)–(28). We decompose the expansion into $\hat{D}_M - D = H_1 + \cdots + H_4$, where $H_1 = P_M' \Omega_M^{-1} P_M - P' \Omega^{-1} P$, $H_2 = \hat{P}_M' \Omega_M^{-1} \hat{P}_M - P_M' \Omega_M^{-1} P_M$, $H_3 = -\hat{P}_M' \Omega_M^{-1} (\hat{\Omega}_M - \Omega_M) \Omega_M^{-1} \hat{P}_M$, and H_4 is defined in (20). Also, $\hat{d}_M = d_0 + d_1 + \cdots + d_9$ with d_i defined in (21)–(28) such that $\sqrt{n}(\beta_{n,M} - \beta) = b_{n,M} + o_p(M/\sqrt{n})$ with

$$b_{n,M} = D^{-1} \sum_{i=0}^{9} d_i - D^{-1} \sum_{i=1}^{4} \sum_{j=0}^{9} H_i D^{-1} d_j.$$

The terms H_3 and H_4 contain a Taylor series expansion of $\hat{\Omega}_M^{-1}$ around Ω_M^{-1} given by

$$\hat{\Omega}_M^{-1} = \Omega_M^{-1} - \Omega_M^{-1}(\hat{\Omega}_M - \Omega_M)\Omega_M^{-1} + B + o_p(\|\hat{\Omega}_M - \Omega_M\|^2), \tag{10}$$

where B has typical element k, l given by $\text{vec}(\hat{\Omega}_M - \Omega_M)' \frac{\partial^2 \vartheta_{kl}}{\partial \,\text{vec}\,\Omega \partial \,\text{vec}\,\Omega'} \text{vec}(\hat{\Omega}_M - \Omega_M)$. The term $o_p(\|\hat{\Omega}_M - \Omega_M\|^2) = o_p(1)$ by Lemma (A.1). By

Lemma (A.3),

$$H_1 \equiv P_M' \Omega_M^{-1} P_M - P' \Omega^{-1} P = O(\lambda^{2M}) \tag{11}$$

for some $\lambda \in (0, 1)$, where $\equiv$ means "equal by definition." From the proofs in Kuersteiner (2002b), the term $H_2 = H_{211} + H_{212} + H_{221} + H_{222}$ is analyzed to be

$$H_{211} \equiv -\left(\hat{P}_M - \check{P}_M\right)' \Omega_M^{-1} (\hat{P}_M - \check{P}_M) = O_p(M/n) \tag{12}$$
$$H_{212} \equiv \hat{P}_M' \Omega_M^{-1} (\hat{P}_M - \check{P}_M) + (\hat{P}_M - \check{P}_M)' \Omega_M^{-1} \hat{P}_M = O_p(n^{-1/2}) \tag{13}$$
$$H_{221} \equiv -\left(\check{P}_M - P_M\right)' \Omega_M^{-1} \left(\check{P}_M - P_M\right) = O_p(M/n) \tag{14}$$
$$H_{222} \equiv \check{P}_M' \Omega_M^{-1} (\check{P}_M - P_M) + (\check{P}_M - P_M)' \Omega_M^{-1} \check{P}_M = O_p(M/n^{1/2}), \tag{15}$$

where $\hat{P}_M$ is defined as $\hat{P}_M = n^{-1} Z_M' X$ and $\check{P}_M' = \left[\check{\Gamma}_1^{xy}, \ldots, \check{\Gamma}_M^{xy}\right]$ with $\check{\Gamma}_j^{xy} = n^{-1} \sum_{t=1+j+p-q}^{n-q} \check{w}_{t,j}'$.

Using Lemma (A.1) it follows by the same arguments as in Kuersteiner (2002b) that $H_3 = H_{31} + H_{32} + H_{33} + H_{34}$ is

$$H_{31} \equiv (\hat{P}_M - P_M)' \Omega_M^{-1} (\hat{\Omega}_M - \Omega_M) \Omega_M^{-1} (\hat{P}_M - P_M) = o_p(M/n), \tag{16}$$
$$H_{32} \equiv -\hat{P}_M' \Omega_M^{-1} (\hat{\Omega}_M - \Omega_M) \Omega_M^{-1} (\hat{P}_M - P_M) = o_p(M/n), \tag{17}$$
$$H_{33} \equiv -(\hat{P}_M - P_M)' \Omega_M^{-1} (\hat{\Omega}_M - \Omega_M) \Omega_M^{-1} \hat{P}_M = o_p(M/n), \tag{18}$$
$$H_{34} \equiv -P_M' \Omega_M^{-1} (\hat{\Omega}_M - \Omega_M) \Omega_M^{-1} P_M = O_p(n^{-1/2}), \tag{19}$$

and H_4, which is a remainder term defined as

$$H_4 \equiv \hat{P}_M' (\hat{\Omega}_M^{-1} - \Omega_M^{-1} + \Omega_M^{-1} (\hat{\Omega}_M - \Omega_M) \Omega_M^{-1}) \hat{P}_M = o_p(M/n). \tag{20}$$

Next we turn to the analysis of $\hat{d}_M$, which is decomposed as $\hat{d}_k = \sum_j^9 d_j$. Define

$$V_M = \left[n^{-1/2} \sum_t v_{t,1}', \ldots, n^{-1/2} \sum_t v_{t,M}' \right]'$$

with $V \equiv V_\infty$ such that it follows from the results in Kuersteiner (2002b) that

$$d_0 \equiv P' \Omega^{-1} V = O_p(1) \tag{21}$$
$$d_1 \equiv P_M' \Omega_M^{-1} V_M - P' \Omega^{-1} V = O_p(\lambda^M) \tag{22}$$
$$d_4 \equiv \left(\hat{P}_M - \check{P}_M\right)' \Omega_M^{-1} V_M = O_p(M/n) \tag{23}$$
$$d_5 \equiv \left(\check{P}_M - P_M\right)' \Omega_M^{-1} V_M = O_p(M/n^{1/2}) \tag{24}$$
$$d_6 \equiv \left(\hat{P}_M - P_M\right)' \Omega_M^{-1} (\Omega_M - \hat{\Omega}_M) \Omega_M^{-1} V_M = O_p(M/n) \tag{25}$$
$$d_7 \equiv P_M' \Omega_M^{-1} (\Omega_M - \hat{\Omega}_M) \Omega_M^{-1} V_M = O_p(M/n^{1/2}) \tag{26}$$
$$d_8 \equiv \hat{P}_M' B V_M + o_p(M/n) = O_p(M/n) \tag{27}$$
$$d_9 \equiv n^{-1/2} \sum_t \varepsilon_t \hat{P}_M' \hat{\Omega}_M^{-1} \left[\mathbf{1}_M \otimes (\bar{y} - \mu_y)\right] = O_p(M/n^{3/2}). \tag{28}$$

The terms H_1, H_{222}, d_0, d_1, and d_5 are largest in probability. In Kuersteiner (2002b) it is shown that $Ed_0d_0'D^{-1}H_1 = Ed_1d_0'$ such that these terms cancel out. The largest term remaining is therefore $Ed_1d_1' = -H_1 + o\left(\lambda^{2M}\right)$. The largest term growing with M is $E(d_5 + d_7)(d_5 + d_7)' = O(M^2/n)$.

We only need to consider the terms $A_n = Ed_5d_5'$ and $B_n = Ed_1d_1'$. Because for all $n \geq 1$ we have $A_n \geq 0$ and $B_n \geq 0$, it follows that $\liminf_n A_n \geq 0$ and $\liminf_n B_n \geq 0$.

From Lemma (A.2) it follows that

$$ED^{-1/2}(d_5 + d_7)(d_5 + d_7)'D'^{-1/2} = M^2/nD^{-1/2}A_1'A_1D^{-1/2} + o(M^2/n)$$

and $E \operatorname{tr} D^{-1/2}d_1d_1D^{-1/2} = p - \sigma_M + o\left(\lambda^{2M}\right)$. ∎

Proof of Proposition 2.2. We use the same decomposition as in (9) taking into account that now the elements of P and corresponding estimates of them are in terms of the parameters b_k. We note that $D = P'\Omega^{-1}P = \sum_{k,j=1}^{\infty} b_kb_j'\vartheta_{kj}$, where ϑ_{kj} is the k, jth element of Ω^{-1} and $D = H_1 + H_2 + H_3$, where $H_1 = -\sum_{k,j=M+1}^{\infty} b_kb_j'\vartheta_{kj} + 2\sum_{k=1}^{M}\sum_{j=M+1}^{\infty} b_kb_l'\vartheta_{kl} = O(\lambda^{2M})$ by Lemma (A.3). Let $H_2 = H_{21} + H_{22}$, where $H_{21} = \sum_{l,j=1}^{M}\left(b_l - \hat{b}_l\right)\vartheta_{lj}b_j'$ and $H_{22} = \sum_{l,j=1}^{M}\hat{b}_l\vartheta_{lj}(b_j' - \hat{\Gamma}_j^{yx})$, where the matrix $\hat{\Gamma}_j^{yx}$ is defined as

$$\hat{\Gamma}_j^{yx} = n^{-1}\sum_{t=1+j+p-q}^{n-q}(y_{t-j} - \bar{y})(x_{t+q} - \bar{x})'.$$

The term H_{21} is bounded by

$$H_{21} \leq \sup_l \left\|b_l - \hat{b}_l\right\| / \|c_l\| \sum_{l,j=1}^{M} \|c_l\| \left\|\vartheta_{lj}\right\| \left\|b_j'\right\| = O_p(n^{-1/2}(\log n)^{1/2}).$$

Next, for any $\epsilon > 0$,

$$\begin{aligned}
P(\|H_{22}\| > \epsilon) &\leq P\left(\sum_{l,j=1}^{M} \|\hat{b}_l\| \left\|\vartheta_{lj}\right\| \left\|b_j' - \hat{\Gamma}_j^{yx}\right\| > \epsilon\right) \\
&\leq P\left(\sum_{l,j=1}^{M} \|b_l\| \left\|\vartheta_{lj}\right\| \left\|b_j' - \hat{\Gamma}_j^{yx}\right\| > \epsilon\right) \\
&\quad + P\left(\sup_l \left\|b_l - \hat{b}_l\right\| / \|c_l\| \sum_{l,j=1}^{M} \|c_l\| \left\|\vartheta_{lj}\right\| \left\|b_j' - \hat{\Gamma}_j^{yx}\right\| > \epsilon\right).
\end{aligned}$$

Let $\check{\Gamma}_j^{yx} = n^{-1}\sum_{t=1+j+p+q}^{n-q}(y_{t-j} - \mu_y)(x_{t+q} - \mu_x)'$ such that

$$E\left\|\hat{\Gamma}_j^{yx} - \check{\Gamma}_j^{yx}\right\|^2 = O(n^{-1})$$

uniformly in j by results in Kuersteiner (2002b). This implies that $\sum_{l,j=1}^{n} \|b_l\| \left\|\vartheta_{lj}\right\| \left\|\hat{\Gamma}_j^{yx} - \check{\Gamma}_j^{yx}\right\| = O_p(n^{-1/2})$.

Next note that $E\left[b_j' - \check{\Gamma}_j^{yx}\right] = (j+p)/nb_j'$. We now bound

$$\sum_{l,j=1}^{M} \|b_l\| \left\|\vartheta_{lj}\right\| \left\|b_j' - \check{\Gamma}_j^{yx}\right\|$$
$$\leq \sum_{l,j=1}^{n} \|b_l\| \left\|\vartheta_{lj}\right\| \left(\left\|\check{\Gamma}_j^{yx} - E\check{\Gamma}_j^{yx}\right\| + (j+p)/n \left\|b_j\right\|\right),$$

where

$$E\left\|\check{\Gamma}_j^{yx} - E\check{\Gamma}_j^{yx}\right\|^2 = n^{-2} \sum_{t,s=1+j+p-q}^{n-q} tr(\gamma_y(t-s)\Gamma_{s-t}^{xx} + \Gamma_{t-s-q-j}^{yx}\Gamma_{s-t+j+q}^{yx'}$$
$$+\operatorname{cum}(y_{t-j}, y_{s-j}, x_{t+q}, x_{s+q})) = O(n^{-1}),$$

which establishes $\sum_{l,j=1}^{M} \|b_l\| \left\|\vartheta_{lj}\right\| \left\|b_j' - \check{\Gamma}_j^{yx}\right\| = O_p(n^{-1/2})$. We have shown that $H_{22} = O_p(n^{-1/2}(\log n)^{1/2})$.

Next we consider the decomposition of $H_3 = -n^{-1}\hat{P}_n\Omega_M^{-1}(\hat{\Omega}_M - \Omega_M)\Omega_M^{-1}Z_M'X$. Then

$$H_3 = H_{31} + H_{32}$$
$$= \sum_{l,j=1}^{M}\sum_{h,i=1}^{M} \hat{b}_l\vartheta_{lj}(\hat{\omega}_{j,h} - \omega_{j,h})\vartheta_{h,i}(\hat{\Gamma}_i^{yx} - b_i')$$
$$+ \sum_{l,j=1}^{M}\sum_{h,i=1}^{M} \hat{b}_l\vartheta_{lj}(\hat{\omega}_{j,h} - \omega_{j,h})\vartheta_{h,i}b_i'.$$

Using the properties of $\hat{b}_l$ we find that

$$\|H_{32}\| \leq \sup_l \left\|b_l - \hat{b}_l\right\| / \|c_l\| \sum_{h,j=1}^{M} \textstyle\sum_{l=1}^{M} \|c_l\| \left\|\vartheta_{lj}\right\| \left\|\hat{\omega}_{j,h} - \omega_{j,h}\right\| \left\|a_h^{\prime n}\right\|,$$

where $a_j^n = \sum_{l=1}^{n} b_l\vartheta_{lj}$. By Lemma (A.1) it follows that $H_{32} = O_p(n^{-1}(\log n)^{1/2})$. For H_{31}, note that as before we decompose $\hat{\Gamma}_i^{yx} - b_i' = \hat{\Gamma}_i^{yx} - \check{\Gamma}_i^{yx} + \check{\Gamma}_i^{yx} - b_i'$. It then follows that

$$\|H_{31}\| = \textstyle\sum_{l,j=1}^{M}\sum_{h,i=1}^{M} \left\|\hat{b}_l\right\| \left\|\vartheta_{lj}\right\| \left\|\hat{\omega}_{j,h} - \omega_{j,h}\right\| \left\|\vartheta_{h,i}\right\| \left\|\hat{\Gamma}_i^{yx} - \check{\Gamma}_i^{yx}\right\|$$
$$+\textstyle\sum_{l,j=1}^{M}\sum_{h,i=1}^{M} \left\|\hat{b}_l\right\| \left\|\vartheta_{lj}\right\| \left\|\hat{\omega}_{j,h} - \omega_{j,h}\right\| \left\|\vartheta_{h,i}\right\| \left\|\check{\Gamma}_i^{yx} - b_i'\right\|. \quad (29)$$

For the first term note that

$$\textstyle\sum_{l,j=1}^{M}\sum_{h,i=1}^{M} \left\|\hat{b}_l\right\| \left\|\vartheta_{lj}\right\| \left\|\hat{\omega}_{j,h} - \omega_{j,h}\right\| \left\|\vartheta_{h,i}\right\| \left\|\hat{\Gamma}_i^{yx} - \check{\Gamma}_i^{yx}\right\|$$
$$\leq \sup_l \left\|b_l - \hat{b}_l\right\| / \|c_l\| \textstyle\sum_{l,j=1}^{M}\sum_{h,i=1}^{M} \|c_l\| \left\|\vartheta_{lj}\right\| \left\|\hat{\omega}_{j,h} - \omega_{j,h}\right\| \left\|\vartheta_{h,i}\right\|$$
$$\times \left\|\hat{\Gamma}_i^{yx} - \check{\Gamma}_i^{yx}\right\| + \textstyle\sum_{l,j=1}^{M}\sum_{h,i=1}^{M} \|b_l\| \left\|\vartheta_{lj}\right\| \left\|\hat{\omega}_{j,h} - \omega_{j,h}\right\| \left\|\vartheta_{h,i}\right\| \left\|\hat{\Gamma}_i^{yx} - \check{\Gamma}_i^{yx}\right\|$$
$$= O_p(n^{-1}(\log n)^{1/2})$$

because $\sum_{l,j=1}^{M}\sum_{h,i=1}^{M}\|c_l\|\left\|\vartheta_{lj}\right\|\left\|\hat{\omega}_{j,h}-\omega_{j,h}\right\|\left\|\vartheta_{h,i}\right\|\left\|\hat{\Gamma}_i^{yx}-\check{\Gamma}_i^{yx}\right\|=O_p(1/n)$. The same arguments also establish that the second term in H_{31} is $O_p(n^{-1/2}(\log n)^{1/2})$ such that $H_{31}=O_p(n^{-1/2}(\log n)^{1/2})$.

Next we turn to the analysis of $\hat{d}_M$. From arguments similar to Kuersteiner (2002b) it follows that $d_0=n^{-1/2}\sum_{t=1}^{n}\sum_{j_1,j_2=1}^{\infty}b_{j_1}\vartheta_{j_1,j_2}v_{t,j_2}=O_p(1)$ with $v_{t,j_2}=u_{t+q}(y_{t-j_2}-\mu_y)$ and $\lim_n Ed_0d_0'=D$. From Lemma (A.3) and Kuersteiner (2002b) it follows that $d_1=O_p(\lambda^M)$. Next turn to

$$d_5=n^{-1/2}\sum_{t=1}^{n}\sum_{j_1,j_2=1}^{M}\left(\hat{b}_{j_1}-b_{j_1}\right)\vartheta_{j_1,j_2}v_{t,j_2},$$

where

$$\|d_5\|\leq\sup_l\left\|b_l-\hat{b}_l\right\|/\|c_l\|\sum_{j_1,j_2=1}^{M}\left\|c_{j_1}\right\|\left\|\vartheta_{j_1j_2}\right\|\left\|n^{-1/2}\sum_{t=1}^{n}v_{t,j_2}\right\|$$

and $E\left\|n^{-1/2}\sum_{t=1}^{n}v_{t,j_2}\right\|^2=O(1)$ and $\sum_{j_1,j_2=1}^{M}\left\|\vartheta_{j_1j_2}\right\|=O(M)$ such that $\|d_5\|=O_p(n^{-1/2}(\log n)^{1/2})$. Next consider

$$d_6=n^{-1/2}\sum_{t=1}^{n}\sum_{j_1,\ldots,j_4=1}^{M}\left(\hat{b}_{j_1}-b_{j_1}\right)\vartheta_{j_1,j_2}(\hat{\omega}_{j_2,j_3}-\omega_{j_2,j_3})\vartheta_{j_3,j_4}v_{t,j_4},$$

which, by the previous argument, can be bounded by

$$\begin{aligned}\|d_6\|\leq\sup_l\left\|b_l-\hat{b}_l\right\|/\|c_l\|&\sum_{j_1,\ldots,j_4=1}^{M}\left\|c_{j_1}\right\|\left\|\vartheta_{j_1j_2}\right\|\left\|\hat{\omega}_{j_2,j_3}\right.\\&\left.-\omega_{j_2,j_3}\right\|\left|\vartheta_{j_3,j_4}\right|\left\|n^{-1/2}\sum_{t=1}^{n}v_{t,j_4}\right\|\\=O_p(n^{-1/2}(\log n)^{1/2})&\end{aligned}$$

from $E\left\|n^{-1/2}\sum_{t=1}^{n}v_{t,j}\right\|^2=\left(1-\frac{j}{n}\right)Eu_{t+q}^2y_{t-j}^2=O(1)$ uniformly in j and $E\left\|\hat{\omega}_{j_2,j_3}-\omega_{j_2,j_3}\right\|^2=O(n^{-1})$. The term $d_7=n^{-1/2}\sum_{t=1}^{n}\sum_{j_1,\ldots,j_4=1}^{n}b_{j_1}\vartheta_{j_1,j_2}(\hat{\omega}_{j_2,j_3}-\omega_{j_2,j_3})\vartheta_{j_3,j_4}v_{t,j_4}=O_p(M/n^{1/2})$ by similar arguments. It also follows by the same arguments that d_8 and d_9 are of smaller order. The arguments presented show that the only terms depending on M are H_1, d_1 and d_7. The result then follows from the argument in the proof of Proposition (2.1). ■

References

Andrews, D. W. (1991). "Heteroskedasticity and autocorrelation consistent covariance matrix estimation," *Econometrica*, 59(3), 817–858.

Andrews, D. W. and J. Monahan (1992). "An improved heteroskedasticity and autocorrelation consistent covariance matrix estimator," *Econometrica*, 60(4), 953–966.

Bates, C. and H. White (1990). "Efficient instrumental variables estimation of systems of implicit heterogeneous nonlinear dynamic equations with nonspherical errors," in *Dynamic Econometric Modeling*, E. B. W. Barnett and H. White (eds.), pp. 3–25. New York: Cambridge University Press.

Berk, K. N. (1974). "Consistent autoregressive spectral estimates," *Annals of Statistics*, 2(3), 489–502.

Brockwell, P. J. and R. A. Davis (1991). *Time Series: Theory and Methods*. New York: Springer–Verlag, Inc., 2nd ed.

Donald, S. G. and W. K. Newey (2001). "Choosing the number of instruments," *Econometrica*, 69(5), 1161–1191.

Guo, B. and P. C. Phillips (1997). "Efficient estimation of second moment parameters in the ARCH model," manuscript, Yale University.

Hannan, E. J. and M. Deistler (1988). *The Statistical Theory of Linear Systems*. New York: John Wiley.

Hansen, L. P. (1985). "A method for calculating bounds on the asymptotic covariance matrices of generalized method of moments estimators," *Journal of Econometrics*, 30(1), 203–238.

Hansen, L. P. and K. J. Singleton (1996). "Efficient estimation of linear asset-pricing models with moving average errors," *Journal of Business and Economic Statistics*, 14(1), 53–68.

Hayashi, F. and C. Sims (1983). "Nearly efficient estimation of time series models with predetermined, but not exogenous, instruments," *Econometrica*, 51(3), 783–798.

Kuersteiner, G. M. (1997). "Efficient inference in time series models with conditional heterogeneity," Ph.D. thesis, Yale University.

Kuersteiner, G. M. (2001). "Optimal instrumental variables estimation for ARMA models," *Journal of Econometrics*, 104(2), 359–405.

Kuersteiner, G. M. (2002a). "Efficient IV estimation for autoregressive models with conditional heteroskedasticity," *Econometric Theory*, 18(3), 547–583.

Kuersteiner, G. M. (2002b). "Rate-adaptive GMM estimators for linear time series models," manuscript.

Lewis, R. and G. Reinsel (1985). "Prediction of multivariate time series by autoregressive model fitting," *Journal of Multivariate Analysis*, 16(3), 393–411.

Nagar, A. L. (1959). "The bias and moment matrix of the general k-class estimators of the parameters in simultaneous equations," *Econometrica*, 27(4), 575–595.

Newey, W. K. (1990). "Efficient instrumental variables estimation of nonlinear models," *Econometrica*, 58(4), 809–837.

Newey, W. K. and K. D. West (1987). "A simple, positive semi-definite, heteroskedasticity and autocorrelation consistent covariance matrix," *Econometrica*, 55(3), 703–708.

Parzen, E. (1957). "On consistent estimates of the spectrum of a stationary time series," *Annals of Mathematical Statistics*, 28(2), 329–348.

Stoica, P., T. Söderström, and B. Friedlander (1985). "Optimal instrumental variable estimates of the AR parameters of an ARMA process," *IEEE Transactions on Automatic Control*, 30(9), 1066–1074.

White, H. (1980). "A heteroskedasticity-consistent covariance matrix estimator and a direct test for heteroskedasticity," *Econometrica*, 48(4), 817–838.

Xiao, Z. and P. C. Phillips (1998). "Higher order approximations for frequency domain time series regression," *Journal of Econometrics*, 86(2), 297–336.

PART TWO

IV SPECIFICATION TESTS

THREE

Specification Tests with Instrumental Variables and Rank Deficiency

Yuichi Kitamura*

3.1 INTRODUCTION

This chapter studies some problems concerning two commonly used instrumental variable (IV)-based misspecification tests in linear models. One is Sargan's (1958, 1959) test of overidentifying restrictions, and the other is the Durbin–Hausman–Wu test based on the ordinary least squares – instrumental variables estimator (OLS–IV) contrasts. What causes these problems is the potential rank deficiency of a certain moment matrix. This chapter extensively uses orthogonal groups of matrices and their invariance properties to investigate these issues. As shown in Phillips' (1989a) treatment of "partially identified models," coordinate rotations by orthogonal matrices are useful in studying a rank deficiency problem. Moreover, the theory of group invariance often simplifies derivations of seemingly complicated distributions as exemplified by a series of papers by Phillips (1984; 1985a,b; 1986a,b; 1989b).

It has been recognized that some IV-based misspecification tests can fail to detect misspecification in certain cases. Newey (1985) provides a unified framework for misspecification tests based on the generalized method of moments (GMM) and points out a potential failure of such tests. That is, if the departure from the moment condition is in certain directions, the GMM misspecification tests have no power. See also Tauchen (1986) and Holly (1982). Because IV estimators are special cases of GMM, this potential failure clearly applies to some misspecification testing procedures based on (linear) IV estimators such as Sargan's test.

There is another potential problem in misspecification testing with instrumental variables. If the "relevance condition" – the correlation matrix between the regressors and the instruments should be full rank – fails to hold, the conventional asymptotic distribution theory is no longer valid. Phillips (1989a)

* I acknowledge financial support from the Alfred P. Sloan Foundation Research Fellowship and the National Science Foundation via grants SES-9905247 and SES-0214081.

uses the term "partial identification" for the case in which the full-rank condition is replaced by a reduced-rank condition. He develops a complete asymptotic theory of IV estimators and the IV-based Wald test under partial identification (see also Choi and Phillips 1992). In a recent paper, Han and Schmidt (2001) consider the case of irrelevant instruments in which the instruments are uncorrelated with the regressors. They obtain an explicit form of the density of the asymptotic distribution of the two-stage least-squares (TSLS) estimator and show that the mean of the distribution is identical to the probability limit of OLS.

Our investigation is related to the papers cited above; note, however, that (i) we focus on specification testing, and (ii) we study a unified rank-deficiency problem that allows us to tie together the partial identification problem and Newey's type problem. As we will see, applications of coordinate rotations, as used effectively by Phillips (1989a), reveal a fundamental mathematical structure that lies behind these seemingly disparate problems. Although some results have been obtained for each of the two problems, the asymptotic distribution results obtained in this chapter are new. Also, this is likely to be the first publication that treats the two problems at the same time in a unified manner. We consider potential rank deficiency of a certain "augmented" moment matrix (see Section 3.2) to develop a unified theory of these problems.[1]

An interesting outcome of our investigation is that it allows us to characterize the asymptotic distributions of the test statistics under rank deficiency by what may be called the "nominal degree of overidentification" and the "actual degree of underidentification" of the model (see Remark 3.5 in Section 3.3). For example, various stochastic dominance relations emerge depending on these two "degrees of identification."

[1] This chapter considers problems associated with "exact" rank deficiency. Phillips' (1989a) investigation of partially identified IV regression models, for example, involves a matrix that is "exactly" rank deficient. On the other hand, it would be interesting to consider asymptotics of the two IV specification tests when the augmented moment matrix is "nearly" rank deficient. In Section 3.2 we multiply the augmented moment matrix by an orthogonal matrix to extract a sub-matrix that consists of zeros. Staiger and Stock's (1997) analysis of the "weak instrument" problem (see also Stock & Wright 2000 and Kleibergen 2002) suggests that we can, for example, replace the submatrix of zeros with a matrix of constants multiplied by the square root of the sample size. Such a specification would include "near partial identification" (as recently considered by Guggenburger 2002) and "near Newey's type power failure" as special cases. It would be also useful to consider these two simultaneously, as we do here. Asymptotics under this type of assumption would be expressed as functionals of Gaussian processes. Though this is not a problem theoretically, the resulting distributions need to be evaluated through simulations. Under our "exact" rank-deficiency assumption we obtain asymptotic results that are interpretable without simulations. We also obtain useful characterizations of the asymptotic distributions in terms of two "degrees of identification," as defined in Remark 3.5. This is possible with powerful tools such as group invariance theory as used by Phillips (1989a) for analysis of an "exact" rank deficiency problem.

The first IV test we consider is Sargan's test for overidentifying restrictions. Typically Sargan's test is interpreted as a test of orthogonality between the regressors and the instruments. Hansen (1982) showed that Sargan's test can be extended to general nonlinear GMM in a time series context. Hansen's overidentifying restrictions test, sometimes called the J-test, is treated in standard textbooks (e.g., Hayashi 2000). An advantage of Hansen's J-test is that it allows for conditional heteroskedasticity and time series dependence in a natural manner.[2] Qin and Lawless (1994) also propose a test of overidentifying restrictions based on Owen's (2001) empirical likelihood (see also Kitamura 1997 and Guggenberger 2002). Kitamura and Stutzer (1997) propose a statistic termed the "κ-statistic" for overidentifying restrictions, using their "information theoretic" estimator. Kitamura (2001) further shows that the empirical likelihood-based test enjoys an important advantage of being "most powerful" in the sense of large deviations (this is sometimes referred to as a Generalized Neyman–Pearson [GNP] optimality property). This chapter focuses on Sargan's test partly because its structure yields informative nonstandard asymptotics. It is widely used in the literature as well: as Arellano (2002) puts it, "it is a standard complement when reporting IV estimates."

The second test investigated in this chapter is the Durbin–Hausman–Wu statistic based on the IV–OLS contrast. This statistic is often used as a criterion to determine the exogeneity property of the regressors; see, for example, Godfrey (1988) or Davidson and MacKinnon (2004) for further discussion.

The rest of the chapter is organized as follows. The model, notation, and test statistics are defined in Section 3.2. Section 3.3 reports results for the overidentifying restrictions test. Section 3.4 discusses the Durbin–Hausman–Wu test followed by concluding remarks in Section 3.5.

3.2 MODEL, TEST STATISTICS, AND ASSUMPTIONS

We consider the linear model

$$y_i = b_0' x_i + u_i, i = 1, \ldots, n,$$

where b_0 is an $m \times 1$ vector of parameters, x_i an $m \times 1$ random vector, and u_i a disturbance term. Let z_i denote a $q \times 1$ vector of instrumental variables with $q \geq m$. The researcher observes (x_i', y_i, z_i'), $i = 1, \ldots, n$. We assume random sampling (across i) throughout the chapter. We maintain that the regressor and the disturbance term are possibly correlated; therefore, the instrumental variable estimator is used to deal with the problem of endogeneity.

[2] Kitamura and Phillips (1997) developed a version of overidentifying restrictions test in which (some of) the regressors and instruments are possibly nonstationary; such cases are beyond the scope of this chapter.

The IV estimation relies on the orthogonality condition

$$E[z_i u_i] = 0. \tag{1}$$

Define $M_{xz} = E[x_i z_i'] < \infty$ and $M_{zz} = E[z_i z_i'] < \infty$. Conventional IV estimation theory assumes that M_{xz} is of full row rank, that is,

$$\operatorname{rank}(M_{xz}) = m, \tag{2}$$

and M_{zz} is nonsingular. Let $y = (y_1, \ldots, y_n)'$, $X = (x_1, \ldots, x_n)'$, and $Z = (z_1, \ldots, z_n)'$. The usual two-stage least-squares (2SLS) estimator is given by

$$\hat{b} = (X' P_Z X)^{-1} X' P_Z y, \tag{3}$$

where $P_Z = Z(Z'Z)^{-1}Z'$. $\hat{b}$ is $n^{1/2}$-consistent, and with an additional condition of conditional homoskedasticity, $E[u_i^2|z_i] = \sigma_u^2 < \infty$, it is efficient; $\sqrt{n}(\hat{b} - b_0)$ is asymptotically normal distributed with mean 0 and variance $\sigma_u^2(M_{xz}M_{zz}^{-1}M_{xz}')^{-1}$.

Now consider the case in which (2) no longer holds, that is,

$$\operatorname{rank}(M_{xz}) < m. \tag{4}$$

Such rank deficiency means a failure of identification; therefore, the IV estimator (3) is not consistent – at least for a subset of b_0. In Phillips' (1989a) terminology, b_0 is "partially identified" if $0 < \operatorname{rank}(M_{xz}) < m$, and it is "totally unidentified" if $\operatorname{rank}(M_{xz}) = 0$. The pdf of the asymptotic distribution of $\hat{b}$ with rank deficiency can be found in Phillips (1989a). The lack of correlation between (a subset of) the instruments and the regressors is clearly a special case of (4).

Let us now introduce the test statistics considered in the chapter. The first is the overidentifying restrictions test proposed by Sargan (1957,1958) and extended by Hansen (1982). This test is often regarded as a test of the orthogonality condition (1). To be more specific, define Sargan's statistic, when the parameter is estimated by (3), as

$$\tau_n = \hat{u}' P_Z \hat{u} / \hat{\sigma}_u^2, \tag{5}$$

where $\hat{u} = y - X\hat{b}$, $\hat{\sigma}_u^2 = \hat{u}'\hat{u}/(n - m)$. This statistic is important for two reasons. First, as mentioned before, many empirical researchers rely on this method to test the model adequacy. Second, Newey (1985) shows that this statistic covers a large class of misspecification test statistics.

If the full-rank condition (2) and the other regularity conditions hold, it is straightforward to see that τ_n converges weakly to a chi-squared distributed random variable with $q - m$ degrees of freedom under the null hypothesis (1). Under a sequence of local alternatives ($E[z_i u_i] = d_n$, where $d_n = n^{-1/2} d$ and d is in $\mathbf{R}^q$), the statistic converges to a noncentral chi-square random variable with $q - m$ degrees of freedom with the noncentrality parameter

$$d' M_{zz}^{-1/2}(I - P_{M_{zz}^{-1/2} M_{zx}}) M_{zz}^{-1/2} d / \sigma_u^2.$$

Let $sp(M_{zx})$ denote the span of the columns of M_{zx}. The preceding expression of the noncentrality parameter implies that the test fails to be consistent if deviations from the null are in $sp(M_{zx})$ (see Newey 1985).

The second statistic considered is the Durbin–Hausman–Wu statistic based on the OLS–IV contrast:

$$h_n = (\hat{b} - \tilde{b})'[(X'P_Z X)^{-1} - (X'X)^{-1}]^{-1}(\hat{b} - \tilde{b})/\sigma_u^2, \tag{6}$$

where $\tilde{b}$ denotes the OLS estimator $(X'X)^{-1}X'y$. This is sometimes called an exogeneity test statistic and is interpreted as a test of the orthogonality between the regressors and the error term. Under the full-rank condition (2), the asymptotic distribution of this statistic is chi-square with m degrees of freedom if the "exogeneity condition" for the regressors holds. Under the local alternative $E[x_i u_i] = c_n$, with $c_n = n^{-1/2}c \in \mathbf{R}^m$, h_n is asymptotically noncentral chi-square distributed with the noncentrality parameter

$$c' M_{xx}^{-1}[(M_{xz} M_{zz}^{-1} M_{zx})^{-1} - M_{xx}^{-1}]^{-1} M_{xx}^{-1} c/\sigma_u^2.$$

Unlike τ_n, this test is consistent no matter in which direction the alternative lies because the degrees of freedom of the test and the dimension of the alternative coincide.

As noted in Section 3.1, there are some cases in which these misspecification tests can "fail." First, the rank deficiency (4) would invalidate both tests, as we will discuss in Sections 3.3 and 3.4 in detail. Second, Newey's result shows that the test based on τ_n has no power in certain directions. To consider these two failures in a unified setup, let w_i denote $(u_i, x_i')'$ and define the "augmented" moment matrix

$$M_{wz} = [m_{zu} \vdots M_{zx}]',$$

where $m_{zu} = E[z_i u_i]$. It is the property of this matrix that determines the nature of the asymptotic theory considered here. If $m_{zu} \in sp(M_{zx})$, clearly M_{wz} is not of full-row rank. Equation (4) also implies a rank deficiency in M_{wz}. Of course, both deficiencies can occur simultaneously. Therefore, it would be useful to consider the following case instead of (4):

$$\text{rank}(M_{wz}) = \bar{m}_1 \leq \bar{m}, \bar{m} = m + 1.$$

This implies that there exists an $\bar{m} \times \bar{m}$ orthogonal matrix $H = [H_1 \vdots H_2]$ such that

$$H_1' M_{wz} = M_{1z}$$

is of full-row rank (rank $\bar{m}_1$), and

$$H_2' M_{wz} = 0,$$

where H_1 is $\bar{m} \times \bar{m}_1$, H_2 is $\bar{m} \times \bar{m}_2$ and $\bar{m}_1 + \bar{m}_2 = \bar{m}$. Because H_2 is unique up to right-side multiplications by $\bar{m}_2 \times \bar{m}_2$ orthogonal matrices, without loss of generality we assume that the first row of H_2 consists of zeros except for the first element; otherwise, we can apply the first step of the Householder transformation to sweep out nonzero elements. The first element may or may not be zero. The following four cases are possible:

$$H_2 = \begin{pmatrix} \psi_2 & 0 \\ \phi_2 & G_2 \end{pmatrix}, \tag{7}$$

$$H_2 = \begin{pmatrix} \psi_2 \\ \phi_2 \end{pmatrix}, \tag{8}$$

$$H_2 = \begin{pmatrix} 0 \\ G_2 \end{pmatrix}, \tag{9}$$

or

$$\bar{m}_2 = 0, \tag{10}$$

where $\phi_2 \in \mathbf{R}^m$. G_2 is a $m \times m_2$ matrix whose columns are orthonormal. Therefore, there exists an $m \times m_1$ matrix G_1 such that $G = [G_1 \vdots G_2]$ is an $m \times m$ orthogonal matrix. The matrix G corresponds to the orthogonal matrix used in Phillips (1989a) in the study of estimable components and nonestimable components of the IV estimator of structural equations in simultaneous equation systems.

Our asymptotic results depends on the preceding four cases of H_2. In what follows we classify our asymptotic results according to the form of H_2:

- Equation (8):
  τ_n is asymptotically χ^2_{q-m}. If, in addition, $\phi_2 = 0$ (thus $\psi_2 = 1$), this corresponds to the standard "null distribution" case, whereas if $\phi_2 \neq 0$, τ_n has a flat power function corresponding to the power failure considered by Newey and others.
- Equation (7) or (9):
  M_{xz} is deficient ($m_2 \geq 1$) in both cases, and thus some elements of b_0 are not identified. Whether the first column $(\psi_2, \phi_2')'$ is present (7) or not (9), our asymptotic theory is non-standard. Equation (7) corresponds to (8) above (the "standard distribution" case, which includes the power failure of τ_n), though here the lack of full identification gives rise to nonstandard asymptotics. As we demonstrate in Section 3.4, the asymptotic property of h_n depends on m_2.
- Equation (10):
  No rank deficiency in M_{wz}. τ_n diverges, and a violation of the orthogonality condition is detected with probability approaching one.

We use the representations (7)–(10) of H_2 extensively. Define

$$w_{1i} = H_1' w_i, \quad w_{2i} = H_2' w_i, \quad x_{1i} = G_1' x_i, \quad x_{2i} = G_2' x_i,$$

and

$$v_i = [\psi_2, \phi_2']w_i.$$

Let $M_{z1} = E[z_i w_{1_i}]$. Assume it is finite and of rank $\bar{m}_1$. Also assume that M_{zz} is finite and nonsingular. Finally, assume $E[w_{2i} w_{2i}' | z_i] = \Sigma$, almost surely, with Σ positive definite and partitioned as

$$\Sigma = \begin{pmatrix} \sigma_v^2 & \Sigma_{v2} \\ \Sigma_{2v} & \Sigma_{22} \end{pmatrix}.$$

Define $C_n = Z(Z'Z)^{-1/2}$, $D_{1n} = C_n' X_1$, $D_{2n} = C_n' X_2$, and $\eta_n = C_n' v$, where $v = (v_1, \ldots, v_n)'$, $X_1 = (x_{11}, \ldots, x_{1n})'$, and $X_2 = (x_{21}, \ldots, x_{2n})'$. Also let $W_2 = (w_{21}, \ldots, w_{2n})'$. By the definition of w_{2i}, we have $E[w_{2i} \otimes z_i] = 0$. Therefore, the preceding assumptions imply the following:

$$C_n' W_2 = [\eta_n \vdots D_{2n}] \xrightarrow{\mathcal{L}} [\eta \vdots D_2], \tag{11}$$

where $[\eta \vdots D_2]' \sim N(0, \Sigma \otimes I_q)$ and

$$\begin{aligned} n^{-1/2} D_{1n} &\xrightarrow{p} M_{zz}^{-1/2} M_{z1} \\ &\equiv D_1. \end{aligned}$$

3.3 OVERIDENTIFYING RESTRICTIONS TEST (SARGAN'S TEST)

When a rank deficiency is present, the test based on τ_n can fail. First, the case $\psi_2 \neq 0$ is analyzed followed by the case $\psi_2 = 0$.

3.3.1 Case (1): $\psi_2 \neq 0$

In terms of the form of H_2 in the previous section, (7) and (8) fall into this category. This case includes the situation in which the orthogonality condition (1) holds, but M_{xz} may not be of full-row rank. However, even if (1) fails, so that $E[z_i u_i] = m_{zu} \neq 0$, this case still applies when $m_{zu} \in \text{sp}(M_{zx})$ whereas the rank condition on M_{xz} may be violated.

Before analyzing τ_n, we start with the analysis of a modified statistic τ_n^*, in which the estimated variance $\hat{\sigma}_u^2$ in (5) is replaced by the constant $\psi_2^{-2}\sigma_{v\cdot 2}^2$, where $\sigma_{v\cdot 2}^2 = \sigma_v^2 - \Sigma_{v2}\Sigma_{22}^{-1}\Sigma_{2v}$:

$$\tau_n^* = \hat{u}' P_Z \hat{u} / (\psi_2^{-2}\sigma_{v\cdot 2}^2).$$

Of course, $\sigma_{v\cdot 2}^2$ can be interpreted as the conditional variance of v_i given x_{2i} under normality. The following theorem establishes the large sample property of τ_n^*. Note that m_2 may or may not be zero at this point.

Lemma 3.1 *If $\psi_2 \neq 0$,*

$$\tau_n^* \xrightarrow{\mathcal{L}} \chi^2_{q-m}.$$

Proof. Writing $v = \psi_2 u + X\phi_2$, we notice that

$$\begin{aligned}\hat{u} &= [I_n - X(X'P_Z X)^{-1}X'P_Z]u \\ &= \psi_2^{-1}[I_n - X(X'P_z X)^{-1}X'P_Z]v.\end{aligned}$$

Then,

$$\begin{aligned}\tau_n^* &= \psi_2^{-2}v'[I_n - P_Z X(X'P_Z X)^{-1}X]P_Z[I_n - X(X'P_Z X)^{-1}X'P_Z]v/(\psi_2^{-2}\sigma^2_{v\cdot 2}) \\ &= v'C_n[I_q - P_{C_n'X}]C_n'v/\sigma^2_{v\cdot 2} \\ &= \eta_n'[I_q - P_{C_n'XG}]\eta_n/\sigma^2_{v\cdot 2} \\ &= \eta_n'[I_q - P_{[D_{1n},D_{2n}]}]\eta_n/\sigma^2_{v\cdot 2}.\end{aligned}$$

Note that $P_{[D_{1n},D_{2n}]} = P_{D_{2n}} + P_{\bar{D}_{1n}} = P_{D_{2n}} + P_{n^{-1/2}\bar{D}_{1n}}$, where $\bar{D}_{1n} = (I_q - P_{D_{2n}})\,D_{1n}$. By the continuous mapping theorem (CMT),

$$\begin{aligned}\tau_n^* &\xrightarrow{\mathcal{L}} \eta'\,[I_q - P_{D_2} - P_{\bar{D}_1}]\eta/\sigma^2_{v\cdot 2} \\ &= [\eta - D_2\gamma]'[I_q - P_{[D_1,D_2]}][\eta_n - D_2\gamma]/\sigma^2_{v\cdot 2} \\ &\equiv \tau^*,\end{aligned}$$

Although the preceding expression holds for any $m_2 \times 1$ vector γ, it is convenient to let $\gamma = \Sigma_{22}^{-1}\Sigma_{2v}$ ($\equiv \Upsilon$, for instance). Because $[\eta - D_2\Upsilon \vdots D_2]' \sim N(0, diag(\sigma^2_{v\cdot 2}, \Sigma_{22}) \otimes I_q)$ (see eq. (11)), $\eta - D_2\Upsilon$ and D_2 are independent. Therefore, $[\eta - D_2\Upsilon]'[I_q - P_{[D_1,D_2]}][\eta - D_2\Upsilon] \sim \sigma^2_{v\cdot 2}\chi^2_{q-m}$ conditional on D_2. Given that this distribution does not depend on D_2, it is also the unconditional distribution. The conclusion follows. ∎

Remark 3.1 This lemma shows the interesting fact that, after an appropriate scaling, the numerator of the overidentifying restrictions test statistic converges weakly to a chi-square distributed random variable with $q - m$ degrees of freedom just as in the standard case even if a rank deficiency is present. It is also possible to obtain the exact distribution of τ_n^* under stronger assumptions. If $\{(u_i, x_i')\}_{i=1}^n$ is independent and identically distributed (iid) normal and independent of $\{z_i\}_{i=1}^n$, τ_n^* is χ^2_{q-m} in finite samples. To see this, write τ_n^* as a quadratic form of u and notice that u can be replaced by $u - X\Upsilon$, which is independent of Z and X. The conditioning argument, as in the proof, shows the finite sample result. When the block G_2 is not present, or when there is no endogeneity in the regressors, the conditional variance can be replaced by the unconditional one; however, the factor ψ_2^2 remains necessary in general.

With the preceding result in hand we now derive the asymptotic distribution of τ_n. In what follows, we use the symbol "$\stackrel{\mathcal{L}}{=}$" to signify equality in probability law.

Theorem 3.1 *If* $\psi_2 \neq 0$,

$$\tau_n \stackrel{\mathcal{L}}{\to} \tau,$$

where $\tau \stackrel{\mathcal{L}}{=} \chi^2_{q-m} \cdot$ *Beta* $\left(\frac{q-m+1}{2}, \frac{m_2}{2}\right)$ *and* χ^2_{q-m} *and Beta* $\left(\frac{q-m+1}{2}, \frac{m_2}{2}\right)$ *are independent.*

Proof. Using the coordinate rotation by G, write

$$\begin{aligned} G'(X'P_ZX)^{-1}G &= (G'X'P_ZXG)^{-1} \\ &= \begin{pmatrix} D'_{1n}D_{1n} & D'_{1n}D_{2n} \\ D'_{2n}D_{1n} & D'_{2n}D_{2n} \end{pmatrix}^{-1} \\ &= S \\ &\equiv \begin{pmatrix} S_{11} & S_{12} \\ S_{21} & S_{22} \end{pmatrix}, \end{aligned} \tag{12}$$

where $S_{11} = [D'_{1n}Q_{2n}D_{1n}]^{-1}$, $S_{12} = -(D'_{1n}D_{1n})^{-1}D'_{1n}D_{2n}[D'_{2n}Q_{1n}D_{2n}]^{-1}$, $S_{22} = [D'_{2n}Q_{1n}D_{2n}]^{-1}$, $S_{21} = S'_{12}$, $Q_{1n} = I - P_{D_{1n}}$, and $Q_{2n} = I - P_{D_{2n}}$. There exists a $q \times (q - m_1)$ matrix $D_{1\perp}$ such that $\mathrm{sp}(D_{1\perp}) = \mathrm{sp}(D_1)^{\perp}$ and $D'_{1\perp}D_{1\perp} = I_{q-m_1}$. Then $D_{1\perp}D'_{1\perp} = Q_1$ and

$$\begin{aligned} D'_{2n}Q_{1n}D_{2n} &\stackrel{\mathcal{L}}{\to} D'_2Q_1D_2 \\ &= D'_2D_{1\perp}D'_{1\perp}D_2 \\ &\sim W_{m_2}(q - m_1, \Sigma_{22}) \end{aligned} \tag{13}$$

because $D'_2D_{1\perp} \sim N(0, \Sigma_{22} \otimes I_{q-m_1})$ (the preceding notation for the Wishart distribution is standard; see Muirhead 1982). Noting that $(D'_{1n}D_{1n})^{-1}$ is $O_p(n^{-1})$, we find that S_{11}, S_{12}, and S_{22} are, respectively, $O_p(n^{-1})$, $O_p(n^{-1/2})$, and $O_p(1)$. Similarly,

$$G'X'P_Z[v - X_2\Upsilon] = \begin{pmatrix} O_p(n^{1/2}) \\ D'_{2n}[\eta_n - D_{2n}\Upsilon]. \end{pmatrix}$$

Then

$$G'(X'P_ZX)^{-1}X'P_Z[v - X_2\Upsilon] = \begin{pmatrix} O_p(n^{-1/2}) \\ (D'_{2n}Q_{1n}D_{2n})^{-1}D'_{2n}Q_{1n}[\eta_n - D_{2n}\Upsilon] \end{pmatrix}$$

and

$$G'X'[v - X_2\Upsilon] = \begin{pmatrix} O_p(n) \\ O_p(n^{1/2}) \end{pmatrix}.$$

By (12),

$$\begin{aligned}\hat{\sigma}_u^2 &= n^{-1}u'(I - P_Z X(X'P_Z X)^{-1}X')(I - X(X'P_Z X)^{-1}X'P_Z)u \\ &= n^{-1}\psi_2^{-2}[v - X_2\Upsilon]'(I - P_Z X(X'P_Z X)^{-1}X') \\ &\quad \times (I - X(X'P_Z X)^{-1})X'P_Z)[v - X_2\Upsilon] \\ &= G_{1n} + G_{2n} + G_{2n}' + G_{3n},\end{aligned}$$

where

$$G_{1n} = n^{-1}\psi_2^{-2}[v - X_2\Upsilon]'[v - X_2\Upsilon] \xrightarrow{p} \psi_2^{-2}\sigma_{v\cdot 2}^2, \tag{14}$$

$$\begin{aligned}G_{2n} &= -n^{-1}\psi_2^{-2}[v - X_2\Upsilon]'XGG'(X'P_Z X)^{-1}GG'X'P_Z[v - X_2\Upsilon] \\ &= O_p(n^{-1/2}),\end{aligned} \tag{15}$$

and

$$\begin{aligned}G_{3n} &= -n^{-1}\psi_2^{-2}[v - X_2\Upsilon]'P_Z XGG'(X'P_Z X)^{-1} \\ &\quad \times GG'X'XGG'(X'P_Z X)^{-1}GG'X'P_Z[v - X_2\Upsilon] \\ &= \psi_2^{-2}[\eta_n - D_{2n}\Upsilon]'Q_{1n}D_{2n}(D_{2n}'Q_{1n}D_{2n})^{-1}(n^{-1}X_2'X_2) \\ &\quad \times (D_{2n}'Q_{1n}D_{2n})^{-1}D_{2n}'Q_{D_{1n}}[\eta_n - D_{2n}\Upsilon] + O_p(n^{-1/2}) \\ &\xrightarrow{\mathcal{L}} \psi_2^{-2}[\eta - D_2\Upsilon]'Q_1 D_2(D_2'Q_1 D_2)^{-1}\Sigma_{22}(D_2'Q_1 D_2)^{-1}D_2'Q_1[\eta - D_2\Upsilon] \\ &\equiv G_3.\end{aligned} \tag{16}$$

Clearly, the joint convergence to the two random variables $(I_q - P_{[D_1,D_2]}) \times [\eta - D_2\Upsilon]$ in τ^* and $(D_2'Q_1 D_2)^{-1}D_2'Q_1[\eta - D_2\Upsilon]$ in G_3 applies, and they are normal conditional on D_2. Moreover,

$$\begin{aligned}&E\left[(I_q - P_{[D_1,D_2]})[\eta - D_2\Upsilon][\eta - D_2\Upsilon]'Q_1 D_2(D_2'Q_1 D_2)^{-1}|D_2\right] \\ &= \sigma_{v\cdot 2}^2(I_q - P_{[D_1,D_2]})Q_1 D_2'(D_2'Q_1 D_2)^{-1} \\ &= 0,\end{aligned}$$

and so the two random variables are independent conditional on D_2. However, in the proof of Lemma 3.1 we have seen that the pdf of τ^* conditional on D_2 does not depend on D_2. Now we make use of the following proposition:

Proposition 3.1 *Let X, Y, and Z be three random variables. If X and Y are independent conditional on Z, and X and Z are (unconditionally) independent, then X and Y are (unconditionally) independent.*

The proof of this proposition is trivial and omitted. By the proposition, τ^* and $(D_2'Q_1 D_2)^{-1}D_2'Q_1[\eta - D_2\Upsilon]$ are (unconditionally) independent and so are τ^* and G_3.

Finally, we derive the distribution of G_3. By the independence of D_2 and $[\eta - D_2\Upsilon]$, $(D_2'Q_1 D_2)^{-1/2}D_2'Q_1[\eta - D_2\Upsilon] \sim N(0, \sigma_{v\cdot 2}^2 I_{m_2})$ conditional on D_2. This distribution does not depend on D_2; hence, it is the unconditional distribution. Moreover, this normal random variable is independent of D_2 (and $D_2' Q_1 D_2$). The latter is, by (13), a Wishart matrix. G_3 can be written as

$$G_3 = \psi^{-2}[\eta - D_2\Upsilon]' Q_1 \underline{D}_2(\underline{D}_2' Q_1 \underline{D}_2)^{-1/2}(\underline{D}_2' Q_1 \underline{D}_2)^{-1}(\underline{D}_2' Q_1 \underline{D}_2)^{-1/2} \times \underline{D}_2 Q_1[\eta - D_2\Upsilon],$$

where $\underline{D}_2 = D_2\Sigma_{22}^{-1/2}$, and by Theorem 3.2.12 of Muirhead (1982),

$$\psi_2^{-2}[\eta - D_2\Upsilon]' Q_1 \underline{D}_2(\underline{D}_2' Q_1 \underline{D}_2)^{-1/2}(\underline{D}_2' Q_1 \underline{D}_2)^{-1/2} \underline{D}_2 Q_1[\eta - D_2\Upsilon]/G_3 \sim \chi^2_{q-m+1}, \tag{17}$$

which is independent of the normal random variable $(\underline{D}_2' Q_1 \underline{D}_2)^{-1/2} \underline{D}_2 Q_1 [\eta - D_2\Upsilon]$. Noting that the numerator of (3.6) is distributed as $\psi_2^{-2}\sigma^2_{v\cdot 2}\chi^2_{m_2}$, we conclude that

$$G_3 \overset{\mathcal{L}}{=} \psi^{-2}\sigma^2_{v\cdot 2} \cdot \frac{\chi^2_{m_2}}{\chi^2_{q-m+1}}, \tag{18}$$

where the numerator and the denominator are independent. By (14)–(16) and (18),

$$\hat{\sigma}_u^2 \overset{\mathcal{L}}{\to} \psi_2^{-2}\sigma^2_{v\cdot 2} \cdot \frac{\chi^2_{q-m+1} + \chi^2_{m_2}}{\chi^2_{q-m+1}}, \tag{19}$$

or $\psi_2^{-2}\sigma^2_{v\cdot 2}/\sigma_u^2$ converges to a *Beta* $\left(\frac{q-m+1}{2}, \frac{m_2}{2}\right)$ distributed random variate in distribution. The independence of τ^* and G_3 shows the independence result stated in the theorem. ■

Remark 3.2 The theorem shows the effect of a rank deficiency caused by, for example, the use of "irrelevant" instruments. In such cases, because the support of the beta distribution is (0, 1), this theorem shows that the asymptotic distribution function of the overidentifying restrictions test statistic τ_n is first-order stochastically dominated by the chi-square distribution function with $q - m$ degrees of freedom, which is the distribution used in practice under the assumption of no rank deficiency. The true size of the test is therefore smaller than standard theory predicts (asymptotically). The expression for the limiting random variate derived in the theorem is convenient because it does not include nuisance parameters such as covariances. The limiting variate can be written as $\chi^2_{q-m}(1 + \chi^2_{m_2}/\chi^2_{q-m+1})^{-1}$, and the independence property holds; therefore, roughly speaking, the discrepancy between χ^2_{q-m} and τ becomes large when m_2 is large relative to $q - m + 1$.

Note that the standard asymptotic results obtained under the null and Newey's type failure are special cases of Case (1) with $m_2 = 0$; $\phi_2 = 0$ in the former, and $\phi_2 \neq 0$ in the latter. In both cases the limiting distribution is χ^2_{q-m}, which corresponds to the limiting distribution of τ with $m_2 = 0$.

Remark 3.3 The independence property established in Theorem 3.1 enables us to obtain the pdf of the limiting distribution of τ_n as shown in the appendix:

$$pdf(\tau) = \frac{\Gamma\left(\frac{q-m_1+1}{2}\right)}{2^{\frac{q-m}{2}}\Gamma\left(\frac{q-m}{2}\right)\Gamma\left(\frac{q-m+1}{2}\right)} e^{\frac{-\tau}{2}}\tau^{\frac{q-m}{2}-1}\Psi\left(\frac{m_2}{2},\frac{1}{2},\frac{\tau}{2}\right), 0 \le \tau.$$

Here $\Psi(\cdot,\cdot,\cdot)$ denotes a confluent hypergeometric function.[3] Tables for confluent hypergeometric functions can be found in, for example, Slater (1970).

The numerical evaluation of the $pdf(\tau)$ is easy when the degree of rank deficiency is $m_2 = 1$ because $\Psi\left(1/2, 1/2, z^2\right) = 2\sqrt{\pi}e^{z^2}(1-\Phi(2^{1/2}z))$, where $\Phi(\cdot)$ denotes the standard normal distribution function. (See Magnus, Oberhettinger and Soni 1966.) The pdf becomes

$$\frac{\Gamma\left(\frac{q-m+2}{2}\right)}{\Gamma\left(\frac{q-m}{2}\right)\Gamma\left(\frac{q-m+1}{2}\right)}\left(\frac{\tau}{2}\right)^{\frac{q-m}{2}-1}\left(1-\Phi\left(\sqrt{\tau}\right)\right), 0 \le \tau.$$

Because standard computer packages include $\Phi(\cdot)$ as a builtin function, this can be calculated easily.

3.3.2 Case (2): $\psi_2 = 0$ and $m_2 > 0$

This case means that H_2 takes the form (9). In this case, coordinates in $\mathbf{R}^{m_1}$ for the rows of H_1 can be rotated as we did for H_2, and thus

$$H_1 = \begin{pmatrix} \psi_1 & 0 \\ \phi_1 & G_1 \end{pmatrix},$$

where ψ_1 is a scalar. The vector $m_{zu} = E[z_i u_i]$ has at least one nonzero element and is not in $\mathrm{sp}(M_{zx})$. Nevertheless, the overidentifying restrictions test is not consistent owing to the presence of G_2 (or, equivalently, owing to the violation of the full-rank condition (2)). If M_{xz} were assumed to be of full-row rank as in conventional analysis, considering local departures from the null would be appropriate. However, the test is not consistent here, and nonlocal "alternatives" are allowed.

The derivation of the asymptotic distribution of τ_n is quite different from Case (1). First, the numerator $\hat{u}'P_Z\hat{u}$ and the denominator $\hat{\sigma}_u^2$ are of order n; they were stochastically bounded in Case (1). Second, they jointly converge weakly to random variates that are not independent after scaling by the factor of n^{-1}. Despite this difficulty, we can obtain the following simple asymptotic distribution, which provides useful insights when compared with the results in Case (1).

[3] $\Psi(a, c, z)$ is a solution to the confluent hypergeometric equation $z\frac{d^2w}{dz^2} + (c-z)\frac{dw}{dz} - aw = 0$. Another confluent hypergeometric function is the generalized hypergeometric function ${}_1F_1$, (see, for example, Magnus, Oberhettinger, and Soni 1966), which is often used in multivariate analysis.

Theorem 3.2 *If $\psi_2 = 0$ and $m_2 > 0$,*

$$\tau_n \xrightarrow{\mathcal{L}} \tau_\delta,$$

where $\tau_\delta = \chi^2_{q-m} \cdot IB\left(\frac{m_2}{2}, \frac{q-m+1}{2}\right)$ and χ^2_{q-m} and $IB\left(\frac{m_2}{2}, \frac{q-m+1}{2}\right)$ are independent. $IB(a, b)$ denotes the inverted Beta distribution (see, for example, p.375 of Zellner 1971), whose pdf is $\frac{1}{Beta(a,b)} \frac{u^{b-1}}{(1+u)^{a+b}}$, $0 \leq u$.

Proof. Let $\upsilon = \psi_1 u - X\phi_1$. This corresponds to the definition of υ in Case (1); however, here υ is not orthogonal to the instrumental variables. Also let $\delta_n = (Z'Z)^{-1/2}Z'\upsilon (= C_n'\upsilon)$ and $\delta = M_{zz}^{-1/2} m_{z\upsilon}$, where $m_{z\upsilon}$ is the first column of M_{z1}. Write $\tau_n = J_{1n}/J_{2n}$, where $J_{1n} = n^{-1}\hat{u}' P_Z \hat{u}$ and $J_{2n} = n^{-1}\hat{\sigma}_u^2$.

First we consider J_{2n}. Using the definition similar to (14)–(16), we decompose J_{2n}. Note that J_{2n} can be expressed in terms of υ owing to the projection property of $[I_n - X(X'P_Z X)^{-1}X'P_Z]$. Let

$$\begin{aligned} J_{2n} &= n^{-2}\psi_1^{-2}\upsilon'[I_n - P_Z X(X'P_Z X)^{-1}X']P_Z[I_i - X(X'P_Z X)^{-1}X'P_Z]\upsilon \\ &= K_{1n} + K_{2n} + K_{2n}' + K_{3n}, \end{aligned}$$

where

$$K_{1n} = n^{-2}\psi_1^{-2}\upsilon'\upsilon = O_p(n^{-1}). \tag{20}$$

Note that

$$\begin{aligned} &n^{-1/2}G'(X'P_Z X)^{-1}X'P_Z\upsilon \\ &= \begin{pmatrix} O_p(n^{-1}) & O_p(n^{-1/2}) \\ S_{21} & S_{22} \end{pmatrix} \begin{pmatrix} n^{1/2} \times (n^{-1/2}D_{1n}') \\ 1 \times D_{2n}' \end{pmatrix} (n^{-1/2}\delta_n) \\ &= \begin{pmatrix} O_p(n^{-1/2}) \\ (D_{2n}'Q_{1n}D_{2n})^{-1}D_{2n}Q_{1n} \end{pmatrix} n^{-1/2}\delta_n = \begin{pmatrix} O_p(n^{-1/2}) \\ O_p(1) \end{pmatrix}. \end{aligned}$$

Therefore

$$\begin{aligned} K_{2n} &= -n^{-2}\psi_1^{-2}\upsilon'XGG'(X'P_Z X)^{-1}GG'X'P_Z\upsilon \\ &= (n^{-1}\upsilon'XG)\begin{pmatrix} O_p(n^{-1}) \\ O_p(n^{-1/2}) \end{pmatrix} \\ &= O_p(n^{-1/2}), \end{aligned} \tag{21}$$

and

$$\begin{aligned} K_{3n} &= -n^{-2}\psi_1^{-2}\upsilon'P_Z XGG'(X'P_Z X)^{-1}GG'X'XGG'(X'P_Z X)^{-1}GG'X'P_Z\upsilon \\ &= \psi_1^{-2}[n^{-1/2}\delta_n]'Q_{1n}D_{2n}(D_{2n}'Q_{1n}D_{2n})^{-1}(n^{-1}X_2'X_2) \\ &\quad \times (D_{2n}'Q_{1n}D_{2n})^{-1}D_{2n}'Q_{D_{1n}}[n^{-1/2}\delta_n] + O_p(n^{-1/2}) \\ &\xrightarrow{\mathcal{L}} \psi_1^{-2}\delta'Q_1 D_2(D_2'Q_1 D_2)^{-1}\Sigma_{22}(D_2'Q_1 D_2)^{-1}D_2 Q_1\delta \\ &= \psi_1^{-2}\delta'D_{1\perp}D_{1\perp}'\underline{D}_2(\underline{D}_2'D_{1\perp}D_{1\perp}'\underline{D}_2)^{-2}\underline{D}_2 D_{1\perp}D_{1\perp}'\delta. \end{aligned} \tag{22}$$

Define $\Lambda = D'_{1\perp}\underline{D}_2(\underline{D}'_2 D_{1\perp} D'_{1\perp}\underline{D}_2)^{-1/2}$ and $A = (\underline{D}'_2 D_{1\perp} D_{1\perp}\underline{D}_2)^{1/2}$ so that $D'_{1\perp}\underline{D}_2 = \Lambda A$. Notice that $\Lambda \in \mathbf{V}_{q-m_1,m_2}$, where $\mathbf{V}_{q-m_1,m_2}$ denotes the Stiefel manifold consisting of $(q-m_1)\times m_2$ matrices whose columns form an orthonormal set in $\mathbf{R}^{m_2}$. Recall that $\underline{D}'_2 D_{1\perp}$ is distributed as $N(0, I_{m_2}\otimes I_{q-m_1})$; therefore, $D'_{1\perp}D_2 \stackrel{\mathcal{L}}{=} \Gamma D'_{1\perp}D_2$ for any Γ in $\mathbf{O}(q-m_1)$, the group of $(q-m_1)\times(q-m_1)$ orthogonal matrices. (Such a property is sometimes called left $\mathbf{O}(q-m_1)$-invariance.) By Proposition 7.4 of Eaton (1983), Λ and A are independent, and Λ has a uniform (and left $\mathbf{O}(q-m_1)$-invariant) distribution on $\mathbf{V}_{q-m_1,m_2}$.

By (20)–(22),

$$\begin{aligned} J_{2n} &\stackrel{\mathcal{L}}{\to} \psi_1^{-2}\delta' D_{1\perp}D'_{1\perp}\underline{D}_2(\underline{D}'_2 D_{1\perp}D'_{1\perp}\underline{D}_2)^{-2}\underline{D}_2 D_{1\perp}D'_{1\perp}\delta \\ &= \psi_1^{-2}\delta' D_{1\perp}\Lambda(\underline{D}'_2 D_{1\perp}D'_{1\perp}\underline{D}_2)^{-1}D'_{1\perp}\Lambda'\delta \\ &\equiv J_2. \end{aligned}$$

By (13) in the proof of Theorem 3.1, $(\underline{D}'_2 D_{1\perp}D'_{1\perp}\underline{D}_2)^{-1} \sim W_{m_2}^{-1}(q-m_1, I_{m_2})$, which denotes the inverse Wishart distribution. It follows from Theorem 3.2.12 of Muirhead (1982) that $\psi_1^{-2}\delta' D_{1\perp}\Lambda\Lambda' D'_{1\perp}\delta/J_2$ is a chi-squared distributed random variable that has $(q-m_1+1)-m_2 = q-m+1$ degrees of freedom and is independent of $\Lambda' D_{1\perp}\delta$. This (indirectly) determines the asymptotic distribution of J_{2n}.

Next we turn to J_{1n}. Using the results in the proof of Theorem 3.1 it is straightforward to show

$$\begin{aligned} J_{1n} &= n^{-1}\psi_1^{-2}\delta'_n[I_q - P_{D_n}]\delta_n \\ &\stackrel{\mathcal{L}}{\to} \psi_1^{-2}\delta'[I_q - P_{D_1} - P_{\bar{D}_2}]\delta \\ &= \psi_1^{-2}\delta' Q_1\delta - \psi_1^{-2}\delta' D_{1\perp}D'_{1\perp}D_2(D'_2 D_{1\perp}D'_{1\perp}D_2)^{-1}D'_2 D_{1\perp}D'_{1\perp}\delta \\ &= \psi_1^{-2}\delta' D_{1\perp}[I_q - \Lambda\Lambda']D'_{1\perp}\delta \\ &\equiv J_1. \end{aligned}$$

Finally, we consider the limiting distribution of $\tau_n = J_{1n}/J_{2n}$. Observe that the preceding two convergence results hold jointly: $(J_{1n}, J_{2n}) \stackrel{\mathcal{L}}{\to} (J_1, J_2)$. Therefore, $\tau_n \stackrel{\mathcal{L}}{\to} J_1/J_2$ by the CMT. Define $\tau_\delta = J_1/J_2$ and write

$$\tau_\delta = \frac{J_1}{\psi_1^{-2}\delta' D_{1\perp}\Lambda\Lambda' D'_{1\perp}\delta} \times \frac{\psi_1^{-2}\delta' D_{1\perp}\Lambda\Lambda' D'_{1\perp}\delta}{J_2}, \tag{23}$$

where, as we have seen, the second factor is χ^2_{q-m+1} and independent of $\Lambda' D_{1\perp}\delta$. Because the first factor only depends on $\Lambda' D_{1\perp}\delta$, the first factor and the second factor are independent. Let Ξ be a matrix distributed according to the Haar (probability) measure on $\mathbf{O}(q-m_1)$ (i.e., Ξ is in $\mathbf{O}(q-m_1)$ and $\Xi \stackrel{\mathcal{L}}{=} \Gamma\Xi$ for any Γ in $\mathbf{O}(q-m_1)$) and independent of Λ. The following results hold for the first factor in (23):

$$\frac{J_1}{\psi_1^{-2}\delta' D_{1\perp}\Lambda\Lambda' D_{1\perp}'\delta} \overset{\mathcal{L}}{=} \frac{\delta_*' D_{1\perp}(I_{q-m_1} - \Xi\Lambda\Lambda'\Xi')D_{1\perp}'\delta_*}{\delta_*' D_{1\perp}\Xi\Lambda\Lambda'\Xi' D_{1\perp}'\delta_*}$$
$$= \frac{\delta_*' D_{1\perp}\Xi(I_{q-m_1} - \Lambda\Lambda')\Xi' D_{1\perp}'\delta_*}{\delta_*' D_{1\perp}\Xi\Lambda\Lambda'\Xi' D_{1\perp}'\delta_*},$$

where $\delta_* = \delta/\|\delta\|$ ($\|\cdot\|$ denotes the Euclidean norm of $\cdot$). The first line follows from the left $\mathbf{O}(q-m_1)$-invariance of Λ. Obviously $\Xi' D_{1\perp}'\delta_* \in \mathbf{V}_{1,q-m_1}$, the unit sphere in $\mathbf{R}^{q-m_1}$, and by the $\mathbf{O}(q-m_1)$-invariance of Ξ, it is uniformly distributed on $\mathbf{V}_{1,q-m_1}$. Consequently, we can find a $(q-m_1)\times 1$ random vector $\varepsilon \sim N(0, I_{q-m_1})$ such that $\varepsilon/\|\varepsilon\| = \Xi' D_{1\perp}'\delta_*$. By construction, ε and Λ are independent. Thus,

$$\frac{J_1}{\psi_1^{-2}\delta' D_{1\perp}\Lambda\Lambda' D_{1\perp}'\delta} \overset{\mathcal{L}}{=} \frac{\varepsilon'(I_{q-m_1} - \Lambda\Lambda')\varepsilon}{\varepsilon'\Lambda\Lambda'\varepsilon}$$
$$\overset{\mathcal{L}}{=} \frac{\chi^2_{q-m}}{\chi^2_{m_2}},$$

where χ^2_{q-m} and $\chi^2_{m_2}$ in the last line are independent. The last line follows from the following argument: Notice that $\Lambda\Lambda'$ is the projection onto $\mathrm{sp}(\underline{D}_2' D_{1\perp})$. Because $D_2' D_{1\perp} \sim N(0, I_{m_2}\otimes I_{q-m_1})$ and $q-m_1 \geq m_2$, $\mathrm{rank}(\underline{D}_2' D_{1\perp}) = m_2$ with probability one. Therefore, conditional on $D_2' D_{1\perp}$, an application of Cochrane's theorem shows that the random variable in the first line is equal to the ratio of two independent chi-square random variables with the stated degrees of freedom in distribution. Because this distribution does not depend on the conditioning variable $D_2' D_{1\perp}$, this is an unconditional distribution. It follows that $\tau_\delta \overset{\mathcal{L}}{=} \frac{\chi^2_{q-m}\chi^2_{q-m+1}}{\chi^2_{m_2}}$, where the three chi-square distributed random variables are mutually independent. Given that the distribution of the ratio of two independent random variables, χ^2_b and χ^2_a, is $IB(a/2, b/2)$, the conclusion follows. ∎

Remark 3.4 As shown above, if rank deficiency in M_{zx} is present, the overidentifying restrictions test statistic τ_n does not diverge but converges to a nonstandard distribution as the sample size goes to infinity; therefore, the test is not consistent. An interesting fact is that the asymptotic distribution under the "alternative" $E[z_i u_i] = m_{zu} \neq 0$ does not depend on the deviation m_{zu}. It means that the (nonlocal) power function is entirely flat. This makes our result easy to interpret; other nuisance parameters do not appear in the asymptotic distribution as in Theorem 3.1. The density of τ_δ is

$$pdf(\tau_\delta)$$
$$= \frac{\Gamma\left(\frac{q-m_1+1}{2}\right)\Gamma\left(\frac{q-m_1}{2}\right)}{\Gamma\left(\frac{q-m}{2}\right)\Gamma\left(\frac{m_2}{2}\right)\Gamma\left(\frac{q-m+1}{2}\right)}\left(\frac{\tau_\delta}{2}\right)^{\frac{q-m}{2}}\tau_\delta^{-1}\Psi\left(\frac{q-m_1}{2},\frac{1}{2},\frac{\tau_\delta}{2}\right), 0 \leq \tau_\delta.$$

See the appendix for the derivation.

Remark 3.5 Let us now summarize and discuss some implications of asymptotic results with respect to the overidentifying restrictions test statistic τ_n. We can write the results in Theorem 3.1 and Theorem 3.2 in a comparable way such as

$$\tau \stackrel{\mathcal{L}}{=} \frac{\chi^2_{q-m}\chi^2_{q-m+1}}{\chi^2_{q-m+1} + \chi^2_{m_2}} \tag{24}$$

and

$$\tau_\delta \stackrel{\mathcal{L}}{=} \frac{\chi^2_{q-m}\chi^2_{q-m+1}}{\chi^2_{m_2}}. \tag{25}$$

It might be useful to call $q - m$ the *nominal degree of overidentification* because it simply counts the number of overidentification restrictions and implies little about actual identification. Similarly, one may call m_2 the *actual degree of underidentification* because m_2 components of b_0 are not identifiable. Equations (24) and (25) suggest these two "degrees of identification" characterize the limiting behavior of the overidentifying restrictions test statistic τ_n. We note the following:

- As seen before, the distribution of the proper χ^2_{q-m} first-order stochastically dominates the distribution of τ. If the actual degree of underidentification is sufficiently large relative to the nominal degree of overidentification, or more precisely, if $q - m \geq m_2$, (24) implies that the distribution of χ^2_{q-m} first-order stochastically dominates that of τ_δ as well.
- As seen in (24), even if the vector of departure from the null is not in $\mathrm{sp}(M_{zx})$, the overidentifying restrictions test would have very weak power against such an alternative; it is lower than the nominal size (based on the proper χ^2_{q-m} distribution) asymptotically if $q - m \geq m_2$.
- The distribution of τ_δ first-order stochastically dominates that of τ, and the difference of the two increases as the nominal degree of overidentification $q - m$ increases relative to the actual degree of underidentification m_2.
- In the case in which the nominal degree of overidentification is very large relative to the actual degree of underidentification $\mathrm{rank}(M_{zx})$, (24) suggests that the distribution of τ is close to the proper χ^2_{q-m}; therefore, the size distortion would be mild. From (25) we see that the distribution of τ_δ will be shifted to the right in such a case. This suggests the possibility that the departure from the orthogonality condition in certain directions might be detected with reasonable power if the "relative" degree of underidentification is very small.[4]

[4] In fact, when the degree of rank deficiency is small, the endogeneity is very strong ($\sigma^2_{v\cdot 2}$ is very small), or both, the overidentifying restrictions tests may overreject the null in certain "near-rank deficient" cases; the reader is referred to Staiger and Stock (1997) for the analysis of the overidentifying restrictions tests with "weak instruments."

- Intuitively the last statement may sound reasonable, though we need to be careful about this interpretation of our results. Consider the following strategy: add new instruments that are poor when the original instruments are also suspected to be poor. Although this process brings the limiting distribution "close" to the proper chi-square distribution, it may not be recommended because the power of chi-square tests is decreasing in the degrees of freedom. Also, in the next section we will see that, if M_{zx} is totally deficient, the cumulative distribution of the Durbin–Hausman–Wu test based on the OLS–IV contrast is always first-order stochastically dominated by the proper chi-square distribution in large samples no matter how large the nominal degree of overidentification is relative to the actual degree of underidentification. Thus, the preceding intuition needs to be applied with some caution.

3.4 DURBIN–HAUSMAN–WU TEST

This section discusses the second misspecification test introduced in Section 3.2. The test, based on h_n in (6), is a special case of the well-known specification testing procedure proposed by Hausman (1978). For earlier tests based on the same idea, see Durbin (1954) and Wu (1973). The feature of this statistic h_n is that, unlike τ_n, any (local) departure from the moment condition that is being tested ($E[x_i u_i] = 0$, in this case) leads to noncentrality. This is manifested in the fact that the degrees of freedom of the test m and the dimension of the vector $E[x_i u_i]$ are equal. As will be seen in what follows, the asymptotic behavior of h_n when the moment matrix M_{zx} is not full-row rank is quite different from that of τ_n.

In this section the instrument admissibility condition $E[z_i u_i] = 0$ is maintained, and so the matrix H_2 always can be written as

$$\begin{pmatrix} 1 & 0 \\ 0 & G_2 \end{pmatrix},$$

that is, $(\psi_2, \phi_2')' = (1, 0, \ldots, 0)$. Consequently, Case (2) in the previous section does not arise here.

If $m_2 = m$ (i.e., if there is no identifiable component in b_0), then the next theorem shows that the test based on h_n is not consistent. If $1 \leq m_1 < m$, however, h_n diverges to infinity as n grows if the null hypothesis $E[x_i u_i] = 0$ does not hold. It is therefore necessary to consider local alternatives to obtain meaningful power results if $m_2 < m$ even though M_{xz} (or M_{wz}) is deficient. This differs from our previous results on Sargan's test, which fails to be consistent whenever M_{wx} is deficient, and its behavior under global alternatives is of interest.

To be more specific, consider the following parameterization: for a constant $c \in \mathbf{R}$, let $E[x_i u_i] = c_n$, where $c_n = n^{-1/2} c$ if $m_2 < m$ and $c_n = c$ if $m_2 = m$. Accordingly, the covariance Σ_{u2} and the coefficient vector Υ need to be indexed by n if $m_2 < m$, though we suppress their dependence on n for notational simplicity. Also assume that $M_{xx} = E[x_i x_i']$ is finite and of full rank and $E(u_i^2|x_i, z_i) = \sigma_u^2$ almost surely. Finally, define the partitioned matrix $\{M_{i,j}\} = G' M_{xx} G$, $i, j = 1, 2$, which is partitioned conformably with x_{1i} and x_{2i}. If these conditions hold in addition to the assumptions stated in Section 3.2, we have the next theorem. Note that part (a) of the theorem with the total lack of identification is not a special case of the partial identification results in part (b) because the deviation c_n is global in the former and local in the latter. The definition of the random matrix S in the theorem is given in (12).

Theorem 3.3 *(a) If $m_2 = m$, then*

$$h_n \xrightarrow{\mathcal{L}} h,$$

where $h \stackrel{\mathcal{L}}{=} \frac{\chi_m^2 \chi_{q-m+1}^2}{\chi_m^2 + \chi_{q-m+1}^2}$, and χ_m^2 and χ_{q-m+1}^2 are independent.

(b) If $1 \le m_2 < m$, then

$$h_n \xrightarrow{\mathcal{L}} h_1 h_2,$$

where $h_1 \stackrel{\mathcal{L}}{=} \chi_m^2(\lambda^2)$ with

$$\lambda^2 = c' M_{xx}^{-1} G \begin{pmatrix} I_{m_1} & 0 \\ 0 & 0 \end{pmatrix} \left[S - \begin{pmatrix} M_{11\cdot 2}^{-1} & 0 \\ 0 & 0 \end{pmatrix} \right]^{-1} \begin{pmatrix} I_{m_1} & 0 \\ 0 & 0 \end{pmatrix} G' M_{xx}^{-1} c / \sigma_u^2$$

conditional on D_2 and $h_2 \stackrel{\mathcal{L}}{=} \frac{\chi_{q-m+1}^2}{\chi_{m_2}^2 + \chi_{q-m+1}^2}$, where $\chi_{m_2}^2$ and χ_{q-m+1}^2 are independent.

Proof. First consider part (b). Let $\Delta_n = diag(n^{-1/2} \cdot I_{m_1}, I_{m_2})$. The regularity conditions imply the following convergence results

$$\Delta_n G' [(X' P_Z X)^{-1} - (X'X)^{-1}]^{-1} G \Delta_n \xrightarrow{\mathcal{L}} \left[S - \begin{pmatrix} M_{11\cdot 2}^{-1} & 0 \\ 0 & 0 \end{pmatrix} \right]^{-1}, \tag{26}$$

$$\Delta_n^{-1} G' [\hat{b} - \tilde{b}] \xrightarrow{\mathcal{L}} \begin{pmatrix} (D_1' Q_2 D_1)^{-1} D_1 Q_2 \eta \\ (D_2' Q_1 D_2)^{-1} D_2' Q_1 \eta \end{pmatrix} - \begin{pmatrix} E \\ 0 \end{pmatrix}, \tag{27}$$

where the random variable E is defined by the following convergence relation:

$$n^{1/2} (X_1' (I - P_{X_2}) X_1)^{-1} X_1' (I - P_{X_2}) u \xrightarrow{\mathcal{L}} E.$$

Note E is asymptotically normal:

$$E \sim N([I_{m_1}, 0] G' M_{xx} c, \sigma_u^2 M_{11\cdot 2}).$$

The first term on the right-hand side of (27) is normal with mean zero and variance $\sigma_u^2 S$, conditional on D_2. It is straightforward to check that the covariance between E and $(D_1' Q_2 D_1)^{-1} D_1' Q_2 \eta$ is $(\sigma_u^2 M_{11\cdot 2})^{-1}$ conditional on D_2. Therefore, the right-hand side of (26) (divided by σ_u^2) is the inverse of the covariance matrix of the limiting random variable in (27) conditional on D_2. This implies that the numerator of h_n divided by σ_u^2 converges weakly to a random variable, which is chi-square distributed with m degrees of freedom and noncentrality parameter

$$c' M_{xx}^{-1} G \begin{pmatrix} I_{m_1} & 0 \\ 0 & 0 \end{pmatrix} \left[S - \begin{pmatrix} M_{11\cdot 2}^{-1} & 0 \\ 0 & 0 \end{pmatrix} \right]^{-1} \begin{pmatrix} I_{m_1} & 0 \\ 0 & 0 \end{pmatrix} G' M_{xx}^{-1} c / \sigma_u^2$$

conditional on D_2. The limiting distribution of $\hat{\sigma}_u^2$ is derived in the proof of Theorem 3.1 (see Equation (19)). Recall, $(\psi_2, \phi_2')' = (1, 0, \ldots, 0)$. Therefore, $u_i = v_i$ and $\psi^{-2}\sigma_{v\cdot 2}^2 \to \sigma_u^2$ as $n \to \infty$ (recall our local parameterization), and $\hat{\sigma}_u^2$ converges to $\sigma_u^2(\chi_{q-m+1}^2 + \chi_{m_2}^2)/\chi_{q-m+1}^2$ in distribution. The convergence results for h_n and $\hat{\sigma}^2$ hold jointly, and the result follows.

Next consider part (a). Noting that $\Upsilon = \Sigma_{u2}\Sigma_{22}^{-1} = c'\Sigma_{22}^{-1}$, we obtain

$$\begin{aligned}
[\hat{b} - \tilde{b}] &= (X'P_Z X)^{-1} X'P_Z[u - X_2\Upsilon] - (X'X)^{-1}X'[u - X_2\Upsilon] \\
&= (D_{2n}'D_{2n})^{-1} D_{2n}'[\eta_n - D_{2n}\Upsilon] + O_p(n^{-1/2}) \\
&\xrightarrow{\mathcal{L}} (D_2'D_2)^{-1} D_2'[\eta - D_2\Upsilon].
\end{aligned}$$

Also notice that

$$[(X'P_Z X)^{-1} - (X'X)^{-1}]^{-1} \xrightarrow{\mathcal{L}} D_2'D_2.$$

Thus, the numerator of h_n weakly converges to

$$[\eta - D_2\Upsilon]' D_2 (D_2'D_2)^{-1} D_2'[\eta - D_2\Upsilon] \equiv h_a.$$

Notice that $\sigma_{u\cdot 2}^{-1}(D_2'D_2)^{-1/2} D_2[\eta - D_2\Upsilon]$ is $N(0, I_m)$ conditional on D_2. Because this does not depend on D_2, it is also the unconditional distribution. Therefore, $\sigma_{u\cdot 2}^{-2}h_a$ is chi-square distributed with m degrees of freedom. The estimated variance $\hat{\sigma}_u^2$ converges to $\sigma_{u\cdot 2}^2(\chi_{q-m+1}^2 + \chi_m^2)/\chi_{q-m+1}^2$ in distribution, where χ_{q-m+1}^2 and $\chi_{m_2}^2$ are independent. Moreover, the numerator of (17) in the proof of Theorem 3.1 shows that the chi-squared random variable χ_m^2 that appears in h_a is in fact the same as the one in the limit of $\hat{\sigma}_u^2$. The conclusion follows. ∎

Remark 3.6 The preceding result implies the possibility of downward size distortion of the h_n-test when $m_2 \geq 1$, that is, when rank deficiency of M_{xz} is present. Also, if M_{xz} is totally deficient (i.e., if $m_2 = m$), the problem associated with h_n becomes serious. The limiting distribution of h_n is always first-order stochastically dominated by the central χ_m^2, distribution which is used as a criterion even if the exogeneity of the regressors is violated. This dominance is caused by the fact that $\hat{\sigma}_u^2/\sigma_{u\cdot 2}^2$ converges to a random variable whose support is $(1, \infty)$. Because in this case the limit does not depend on the departure from the null, the asymptotic (nonlocal) power is always smaller than the size of the test if the researcher is not aware of rank deficiency. With our terminology introduced in Remark 3.5, we see that this effect is substantial when the actual degree of underidentification m_2 (in this case it coincides with m) is large relative to the nominal degree of overidentification $q - m$ as a direct result of the theorem. Unlike the case of τ_n, even if the nominal degree of overidentification $q - m$ is sufficiently larger than the actual degree of underidentification, still the distribution of h is biased toward underrejection. As long as M_{xz} is totally deficient, the asymptotic distribution of χ^2_{q-m} always first-order stochastically dominates that of h_n, and thus the power of the test exceeds the size asymptotically. This makes a good contrast with our results in Section 3.3 on the overidentifying restrictions test.

Remark 3.7 The pdf of h for the totally deficient case is

$$\left[\Gamma\left(\frac{q-m+1}{2}\right)\Gamma\left(\frac{m}{2}\right)\right]^{-1}\left(\frac{h}{2}\right)^{(q+1)/2} e^{-h}$$
$$\times \int_0^\infty g^{-m/2-1}(g+1)^{(q+1)/2} e^{-1/2h(g+1/g)} dg,$$

where $0 \leq h$. (See the appendix for the derivation.)

3.5 CONCLUSION

The theoretical results on the overidentifying restrictions test obtained in Sections 3.3 can be summarized as follows. When the rank condition of the moment matrix between the regressors and the instruments fails, (1) the limiting probability of rejecting the null hypothesis correctly is smaller than the size of the test if significance levels are chosen ignoring such a failure; (2) this is true when overidentifying restrictions are violated but Newey's type failure occurs; and (3) in the remaining case in which Newey's type failure does not occur, the limiting distribution is different, but still the test is not consistent and the (nonlocal) power of the test is possibly smaller than the size. These effects of rank deficiency become strong when the actual degree of underidentification is large relative to the nominal degree of overidentification.

The asymptotics of the Durbin–Hausman–Wu test based on the OLS–IV contrast when the preceding rank condition fails were considered in Section 3.4. Again, the test can be biased toward the overacceptance. For example, when the rank of the moment matrix between the regressors and the instruments is zero, the test is not consistent and the limiting rejection probability is smaller than the size whether the null hypothesis (no endogeneity in the regressors) holds or not.

One of the implications of our result is that using irrelevant instruments (i.e., instruments that are uncorrelated with the regressors) potentially distorts specification analysis based on the two testing procedure in a serious manner. Suppose, for example, the researcher's list of instrumental variables includes many irrelevant ones (but not enough relevant ones) and thus that the model is only partially identified. Then our Theorem 3.2 shows that the rejection probability of Sargan's test is below its nominal size asymptotically even when the orthogonality condition is violated. Likewise, our Theorem 3.3 shows that if all the instruments are irrelevant, then the Durbin–Hausman–Wu test suffers from a similar problem, and the testing result would spuriously support the conclusion that the OLS is valid. In both cases, using irrelevant instruments can therefore lead to spurious acceptances of model specifications that are actually misspecified.

APPENDIX

Derivation of the PDF of τ. Consider $z \sim \chi^2_{q-m}$ and $v \sim Beta\left(\frac{q-m+1}{2}, \frac{m_2}{2}\right)$. We use the transformation $(z, v) \to (\tau, w)$, where $\tau = zv$, $w = (1-v)/v$, $0 \le \tau$, and $0 \le w$. Noting that the Jacobian is $(w+1)^{-1}$, we simply integrate the joint density of (τ, w) with respect to w. Let $C = \left[2^{\frac{q-m}{2}}\Gamma\left(\frac{q-m}{2}\right) Beta\left(\frac{q-m+1}{2}, \frac{m_2}{2}\right)\right]^{-1}$. Then the pdf of τ is

$$C \cdot \int_0^\infty [\tau(w+1)]^{\frac{q-m}{2}-1} e^{-\frac{\tau(w+1)}{2}} (w+1)^{-\frac{q-m+1}{2}+1} (w+1)^{1-\frac{m_2}{2}} w^{\frac{m_2}{2}-1} (w+1)^{-1} dw$$

$$= C \cdot \tau^{\frac{q-m}{2}-1} e^{-\frac{\tau}{2}} \int_0^\infty e^{-\frac{\tau w}{2}} w^{\frac{m_2}{2}-1} (w+1)^{-\frac{m_2+1}{2}} dw$$

$$= C \cdot \Gamma\left(\frac{m_2}{2}\right) \tau^{\frac{q-m+1}{2}} e^{-\frac{\tau}{2}} \Psi\left(\frac{m_2}{2}, \frac{1}{2}, \frac{\tau}{2}\right)$$

and the desired result follows. The last equality follows from an integral representation of the confluent hypergeometric function $\Psi(a, c, z)$ for $Re\ a > 0$ and $Re\ c > 0$ (see p. 277 of Magnus, Oberhettinger, and Soni 1966). ■

Derivation of the PDF of τ_δ. Let $z \sim \chi^2_{q-m}$ and $\lambda \sim IB\left(\frac{m_2}{2}, \frac{q-m+1}{2}\right)$. Use the transformation $(z, \lambda) \to (\tau_\delta, \omega)$, where $\tau_\delta = z\lambda$, $\omega = \lambda^{-1}$, $0 \le \tau_\delta$, and $0 \le \omega$. (The Jacobian is ω^{-1}.) We need to integrate the joint density of (τ_δ, ω) with respect to ω. Let C denote the same function defined in the derivation of the pdf of τ. Then the pdf of τ_δ is

$$C \cdot \int_0^\infty (\tau_\delta \omega)^{\frac{q-m}{2}-1} e^{-\frac{\tau_\delta \omega}{2}} \omega^{-\frac{q-m-1}{2}} (\omega+1)^{-\frac{q-m_1+1}{2}} \omega^{\frac{q-m_1+1}{2}} \omega^{-1} d\omega$$

$$= C \cdot \tau_\delta^{\frac{q-m}{2}-1} \int_0^\infty e^{-\frac{\tau_\delta \omega}{2}} \omega^{\frac{q-m_1}{2}-1} (\omega+1)^{\frac{1}{2}-\left(\frac{q-m_1}{2}\right)-1} d\omega$$

$$= C \cdot \Gamma\left(\frac{q-m_1}{2}\right) \tau_\delta^{\frac{q-m}{2}-1} \Psi\left(\frac{q-m_1}{2}, \frac{1}{2}, \frac{\tau_\delta}{2}\right),$$

and we obtain the desired result. ■

Derivation of the PDF of h when $m_2 - m$. Let $z \sim \chi^2_{q-m+1}$ and $\zeta \sim \chi^2_m$, where z and ζ are independent. Use the transformation $(z, \zeta) \to (h, g)$, where $h = \frac{z\zeta}{z+\zeta}$ and $g = \zeta/z$ with $0 \leq z$ and $0 \leq \zeta$. Thus, the Jacobian is $h(g+1)^2/g^2$. By integrating the joint pdf of (h, g) with respect to g, we obtain the result. ∎

References

Arellano, M. (2002). "Sargan's instrumental variables estimation and the generalized method of moments," *Journal of Business and Economic Statistics*, 20, 50–59.

Choi, I. and P. C. B. Phillips (1992). "Asymptotic and finite sample distribution theory for IV estimators and tests in partially identified structural equations," *Journal of Econometrics*, 51, 113–150.

Davidson, R. and J. G. MacKinnon (2004). Econometric Theory and Methods. Oxford: Oxford University Press.

Durbin, J. (1954). "Errors in Variables," *Review of the International Statistical Institute*, 22, 23–32.

Eaton, M. L. (1983). Multivariate Statistics: A Vector Space Approach. New York: Wiley.

Eaton, M. L. (1989). Group Invariance Applications in Statistics, IMS Regional Conference Series in Probability and Statistics, Vol. 1.

Godfrey, L. G. (1988). Misspecification Tests in Econometrics, Cambridge: Cambridge University Press.

Guggenburger, P. (2002). "Generalized empirical likelihood tests under partial, weak, and strong identification," Yale University, mimeo.

Han, C. and P. Schmidt (2001). "The asymptotic distribution of the instrumental variable estimators when the instruments are not correlated with the regressions," *Economic Letters* 74, 61–66.

Hansen, L. P. (1982). "Large sample properties of generalized method of moments estimators," *Econometrica*, 50, 1029–1054.

Hausman, J. A. (1978). "Specification tests in econometrics," *Econometrica*, 46, 1251–1271.

Hayashi, F. (2000). Econometrics. Princeton: Princeton University Press.

Holly, A. (1982). "A remark on Hausman's specification test," *Econometrica*, 50, 749–759.

Kitamura, Y. (1997). "Empirical likelihood methods with dependent processes," *Annals of Statistics*, 25, 2084–2102.

Kitamura, Y. (2001). "Asymptotic optimality of empirical likelihood for testing moment restrictions," *Econometrica*, 69, 1661–1672.

Kitamura, Y. and P. C. B. Phillips (1997). "Fully modified IV, GIVE and GMM estimation with possibly non-stationary regressors and instruments," *Journal of Econometrics* 80, 85–123.

Kitamura, Y. and M. Stutzer (1997). "An information-theoretic alternative to generalized method of moments estimation," *Econometrica*, 65, 861–874.

Kleibergen, F. (2002). "Pivotal statistics for testing structural parameters in instrumental variables regression," *Econometrica*, 70, 1781–1805.

Magnus, W., F. Oberhettinger, and R. P. Soni (1966). Formulas and Theorems for Special Functions of Mathematical Physics, New York: Springer–Verlag.

Muirhead, R. (1982). Aspects of Multivariate Statistical Theory, New York: Wiley.

Newey, W. K. (1985). "Generalized method of moments specification testing," *Journal of Econometrics*, 29, 229–256.

Owen, A. (2001). Empirical Likelihood. New York: Chapman and Hall.

Phillips, P. C. B. (1984). "The exact distribution of LIML: I," *International Economic Review*, 25, 249–261.

Phillips, P. C. B. (1985a). "The exact distribution of LIML: II," *International Economic Review*, 26, 21–36.

Phillips, P. C. B. (1985b). "The exact distribution of the SUR estimator," *Econometrica*, 53, 745–756.

Phillips, P. C. B. (1986a). "The exact distribution of the Wald statistic," *Econometrica*, 54, 881–895.

Phillips, P. C. B. (1986b). "The distribution of FIML in the leading case," *International Economic Review*, 27, 239–243.

Phillips, P. C. B. (1989a). "Partially identified econometric models," *Econometric Theory*, 5, 181–240.

Phillips, P. C. B. (1989b). "Spherical matrix distributions and Cauchy quotients," *Statistics and Probability Letters*, 8, 51–53.

Qin, J. and J. Lawless (1994). "Empirical likelihood and general estimating equations," *Annals of Statistics*, 22, 300–325.

Sargan, J. D. (1958). "The estimation of economic relationships using instrumental variables," *Econometrica*, 26, 393–415.

Sargan, J. D. (1959). "The estimation of relationships with autocorrelated residuals by the use of instrumental variables," *Journal of the Royal Statistical Society*, Series B 21, 91–105.

Slater, L. J. (1970), "Confluent hypergeometric functions," Chapter 13 of Handbook of Mathematical Functions, edited by M. Abramowitz and I.A. Stegun, New York: Dover.

Staiger, D. and J. H. Stock (1997). "Instrumental variables regression with weak instruments," *Econometrica*, 65, 557–586.

Stock, J. and J. Wright (2000). "GMM with weak identification," *Econometrica*, 68, 1055–1096.

Tauchen, G. (1981). "Statistical properties of generalized method-of-moments estimators of structural parameters obtained from financial market data," *Journal of Business and Economic Statistics*, 4, 397–416.

Wu, D. (1973). "Alternative tests of independence between stochastic regressors and disturbances," *Econometrica*, 41, 733–750.

Zeller (1971). *An Introduction to Bajgesian Inference in Econometrics*. New York: Wiley.

FOUR

Asymptotic Normality of Single-Equation Estimators for the Case with a Large Number of Weak Instruments*

John C. Chao and Norman R. Swanson

4.1 INTRODUCTION

Among Peter C. B. Phillips's many contributions to econometrics are two papers exploring the theoretical properties of conventional econometric procedures in models that suffer from a lack of identification. These papers, Phillips (1989) and Choi and Phillips (1992), were the first to derive both finite sample and asymptotic distributions of the instrumental variables (IV) estimator in a simultaneous equations system with identification failure. One of the key findings of Phillips (1989) and Choi and Phillips (1992) is that, when the model is underidentified, the IV estimator is inconsistent and converges to a random variable, reflecting the fact that even in the limit the estimation uncertainty does not go away owing to the lack of identification.

Since the work of Phillips and Choi and Phillips, research on econometric models with identification problems has intensified, and the area is currently one of the most active ones in econometrics. In particular, econometricians have become interested in the case in which the model is weakly identified (or nearly unidentified), which, in the context of an IV regression, translates to the case in which the instruments are only weakly correlated with the endogenous explanatory variables. Indeed, in recent years, it has become popular to model weak instruments using the local-to-zero asymptotic framework of Staiger and Stock (1997), which takes the coefficients of the instruments in the first-stage regression to be in an $n^{-\frac{1}{2}}$ shrinking neighborhood of the origin, where n denotes the sample size.[1] An essential feature of the Staiger–Stock local-to-zero device is that it keeps the so-called concentration parameter from diverging as the sample size approaches infinity, and thus, under their framework, conventional k-class estimators, such as the two-stage least squares (2SLS) and the

[1] Other interesting papers making use of the local-to-zero setup include Wang and Zivot (1998) and Kleibergen (2002).

* The authors thank Dean Corbae for several helpful comments and suggestions.

limited information maximum likelihood (LIML) estimator, exhibit asymptotic behavior similar to that occurring in the underidentified case – at least when the number of instruments is held fixed as the sample size is allowed to approach infinity. Specifically, under the Staiger–Stock local-to-zero framework, conventional k-estimators can be shown to be inconsistent and, in fact, converge weakly to nonstandard distributions.

Recently, Chao and Swanson (2002) argue that there may be benefits to using a large number of instruments when the available instruments are of poor quality. In particular, they show that, by allowing the number of instruments to increase to infinity with the sample size, the growth of the concentration parameter may be accelerated sufficiently so that consistent estimation may become achievable even when all available instruments are weak in the local-to-zero sense. In this case, the choice of estimator becomes important, for not all estimators are equally susceptible to instrument weakness. Along these lines, Chao and Swanson show that single-equation estimators satisfying certain conditions, such as the LIML estimator and the jackknife instrumental variables estimators (JIVE), are consistent even when instrument weakness is such that the rate at which the concentration parameter grows, denoted by r_n, is slower than the rate of expansion of the number of instruments, denoted by K_n, so long as $\frac{\sqrt{K_n}}{r_n} \to 0$ as $n \to \infty$[2]. On the other hand, the 2SLS estimator is only consistent if r_n approaches infinity faster than K_n.[3] In addition, asymptotic distributions for various k-class estimators in the case in which r_n approaches infinity at the same rate as K_n (i.e., $\frac{K_n}{r_n} \to \alpha$ for $0 < \alpha < \infty$) have now been derived by Stock and Yogo (2003a). Overall, the work of Chao and Swanson (2002) and Stock and Yogo (2003a) can be viewed as adding to the many instrument asymptotic results of Morimune (1983), Bekker (1994), Angrist and Krueger (1995), Donald and Newey (2001), and Hahn, Hausman, and Kuersteiner (2001) by considering a weakly identified IV regression model with a local-to-zero structure.

The purpose of this chapter is to extend the results presented in Chao and Swanson (2002) and in Stock and Yogo (2003a) further. Precisely, we extend the asymptotic normality results obtained by Stock and Yogo (2003a) for LIML, Fuller's modified LIML (FLIML, henceforth), and the bias-adjusted two-stage least-squares (B2SLS) estimators to the case in which instrument weakness is such that the rate of growth of the concentration parameter r_n is slower than the rate of growth of the number of instruments K_n but such that $\frac{\sqrt{K_n}}{r_n} \to 0$ as $n \to \infty$. Thus, we obtain asymptotic normality results in situations

[2] One version of the JIVE estimator was introduced by Phillips and Hale (1977). Other versions of JIVE have since been introduced and studied independently by Angrist, Imbens, and Krueger (1999) and Blomquist and Dahlberg (1999).

[3] Note, however, that, in a fascinating recent paper, Phillips and Han (2003) show that, in models with an intercept term, some linear combination of the structural coefficient may be consistently estimable even if the instruments are completely irrelevant.

with weaker instruments than has been assumed in other papers using the many instruments setup. The rate of convergence in our case is shown to be $\frac{r_n}{\sqrt{K_n}}$, which is slower than the rate of convergence to normality obtained by other authors and reflects our assumption of weaker instruments. Formulas for the asymptotic variances of the estimators are also shown to be different from those obtained under assumptions of stronger instruments, that is, cases in which r_n is assumed to grow at the same rate or at a faster rate than K_n. An additional finding of this chapter is that, for the case studied here, both the LIML and the FLIML estimators can be shown to be asymptotically more efficient than the B2SLS estimator – not just for the case in which the error distribution is assumed to be Gaussian but for all error distributions that lie within the elliptical family.

The rest of the chapter proceeds as follows. Section 4.2 sets up the model and discusses our asumptions. Section 4.3 presents the main results and briefly comments on the implications of these results. Concluding remarks are given in Section 4.4, and all proofs are gathered in two appendixes. The following notation is used in the remainder of the chapter: $Tr(\cdot)$ denotes the trace of a matrix, " > 0" denotes positive definiteness when applied to matrices, $\underline{\lim}_{n\to\infty} a_n$ denotes the limit inferior of the sequence $\{a_n\}$, and $\overline{\lim}_{n\to\infty} a_n$ denotes the limit superior of the sequence $\{a_n\}$. In addition, $P_X = X(X'X)^{-1}X'$ denotes the matrix that projects orthogonally onto the range space of X and $M_X = I - P_X$.

4.2 MODEL AND ASSUMPTIONS

Consider the two-equation simultaneous equations model (SEM)

$$y_{1n} = y_{2n}\beta + X_n\gamma + u_n, \tag{1}$$

$$y_{2n} = Z_n\pi + X_n\varphi + v_n, \tag{2}$$

where y_{1n} and y_{2n} are $n \times 1$ vectors of observations on the two endogenous variables of the system, X_n is an $n \times J$ matrix of observations on the J exogenous variables included in the structural equation (1), Z_n is an $n \times K_n$ matrix of observations on the K_n instrumental variables, or exogenous variables excluded from the structural equation (1), and u_n and v_n are $n \times 1$ vectors of random disturbances.[4] Further, let $\eta_i = (u_i, v_i)'$, where u_i and v_i are the ith component of the random vectors u_n and v_n, respectively. The following assumptions are used in the sequel.

[4] Although we only study the case with one endogenous explanatory variable, generalization to the case with an arbitrary number of endogenous explanatory variables is straightforward. We do not pursue this generalization here because it complicates notation but does not change the qualitative features of our results.

Assumption 4.1 $\pi = \pi_n = \frac{c_n}{b_n}$ for some sequence of positive real numbers $\{b_n\}$, nondecreasing in n, and for some sequence of nonrandom, $K_n \times 1$ parameter vectors $\{c_n\}$.

Assumption 4.2 Let $\{\overline{Z}_{i,n} : i = 1, \ldots, n;\ n \geq 1\}$ be a triangular array of R^{K_n+J}-valued random variables, where $\overline{Z}_{i,n} = (Z'_{i,n}, X'_{i,n})'$ with $Z'_{i,n}$ and $X'_{i,n}$ denoting the ith row of the matrices Z_n and X_n, respectively. Moreover, suppose that

(a) $K_n \to \infty$ as $n \to \infty$ such that $\frac{K_n}{n} \to \alpha$ for some constant α satisfying $0 \leq \alpha < 1$.

(b) Let $m_{1n} \nearrow \infty$ as $n \to \infty$, and suppose that there exist constants $\underline{D}_\lambda$ and $\overline{D}_\lambda$, with $0 < \underline{D}_\lambda \leq \overline{D}_\lambda < \infty$, such that

$$\underline{D}_\lambda \leq \varliminf_{n\to\infty} \lambda_{\min}\left(\frac{\overline{Z}'_n \overline{Z}_n}{m_{1n}}\right) \text{ almost surely} \tag{3}$$

and

$$\varlimsup_{n\to\infty} \lambda_{\max}\left(\frac{\overline{Z}'_n \overline{Z}_n}{m_{1n}}\right) \leq \overline{D}_\lambda \text{ almost surely,} \tag{4}$$

where $\overline{Z}_n = (Z_n\ X_n)$.

(c) There exists a sequence of positive real numbers $\{m_{2n}\}$, nondecreasing in n, and constants $\underline{D}_c$ and $\overline{D}_c$, with $0 < \underline{D}_c \leq \overline{D}_c < \infty$, such that

$$\underline{D}_c \leq \varliminf_{n\to\infty}\left(\frac{c'_n c_n}{m_{2n}}\right) \tag{5}$$

and

$$\varlimsup_{n\to\infty}\left(\frac{c'_n c_n}{m_{2n}}\right) \leq \overline{D}_c. \tag{6}$$

Assumption 4.3 $\overline{Z}_n$ and η_i are independent for all i and n.

Assumption 4.4

(a) $\eta_i \equiv i.i.d.(0, \Sigma)$, where $\Sigma > 0$, and partition Σ conformably with $(u_i, v_i)'$ as $\Sigma = \begin{pmatrix} \sigma_{uu} & \sigma_{vu} \\ \sigma_{vu} & \sigma_{vv} \end{pmatrix}$.

(b) There exists some constant D_η with $0 < D_\eta < \infty$ such that $\max\{E(u_i^8), E(v_i^8)\} \leq D_\eta$.

(c) $E(u_i^3) = E(v_i^3) = E(u_i^2 v_i) = E(u_i v_i^2) = 0$.

Assumption 4.5 Define the ratio $r_n = \frac{m_{1n} m_{2n}}{b_n^2}$. Suppose that, as $n \to \infty$, $r_n \to \infty$ such that $\frac{r_n}{K_n} \to 0$ but $\frac{\sqrt{K_n}}{r_n} \to 0$.

Remark 4.2.1 (i) Assumptions 4.1 and 4.2 are the same as corresponding assumptions that were made in Chao and Swanson (2002). As explained in that paper, these assumptions imply that there exists a positive integer N such that, for all $n \geq N, 0 < \underline{D}_\lambda \underline{D}_c \leq \frac{\pi_n' Z_n' M_{X_n} Z_n \pi_n}{r_n} \leq \overline{D}_\lambda \overline{D}_c < \infty$ with probability one, and thus the concentration parameter $\pi_n' Z_n' M_{X_n} Z_n \pi_n$ grows at the rate $r_n = \frac{m_{1n} m_{2n}}{b_n^2}$.

(ii) Assumption 4.4(c) imposes a certain symmetry on the distribution of the disturbances of the simultaneous equations model given by equations (1) and (2). Similar conditions have also been assumed in the paper by Koenker and Machado (1999), which examines the asymptotic properties of a GMM estimator as the number of moment conditions goes to infinity with the sample size. Note also that our Assumption 4.4 is satisfied by all distributions within the elliptical family having finite eighth moments.

(iii) Assumption 4.5 focuses attention on the case in which the concentration parameter grows at a slower rate than the number of instruments K_n but at a faster rate than $\sqrt{K_n}$. To the best of our knowledge, this is a case for which the asymptotic normality of various IV estimators, such as LIML, FLIML, and B2SLS, has not been established previously. In particular, earlier papers by Morimune (1983) and Bekker (1994) studied the case in which $r_n \sim n$, that is, the case in which the concentration parameter diverges at the same rate as the sample size; thus, those papers consider situations in which the concentration parameter either grows at the same rate as K_n (if $\frac{K_n}{n} \to \alpha$ for some constant α such that $0 < \alpha < 1$) or at a faster rate than K_n (if $\frac{K_n}{n} \to 0$). In addition, as part of a larger paper on choosing the number of instruments using (asymptotic) mean-square error formulas of various IV estimators, Donald and Newey (2001) present proof of the asymptotic normality of LIML in a many-instruments setup when $r_n \sim n$. Finally, a recent paper by Stock and Yogo (2003a), which derives the limiting distributions of LIML, FLIML, and B2SLS within a many-weak-instruments framework, also considers a case different from ours, for these authors assume that r_n and K_n grow at the same rate. Because the concentration parameter is a natural measure of instrument weakness, as pointed out by Phillips (1983), Rothenberg (1983), Stock and Yogo (2003b), and others, our analysis here can be viewed as considering cases in which the instruments are weaker than those investigated by other authors using a many-instruments asymptotic framework. As we will show in the next section, the case we study here is also interesting because the weaker instruments lead to rates of convergence and asymptotic variances that are different vis-à-vis those obtained by assuming faster growth of the concentration parameter relative to K_n.

(iv) Note that our assumptions involve a trade-off of conditions relative to Donald and Newey (2001) and Stock and Yogo (2003a). In particular, we do not make i.i.d. assumptions on the triangular array of exogenous variables $\overline{Z}_{i,n}$. Thus, our assumptions on the exogenous variables are weaker than those made in Donald and Newey (2001) and Stock and Yogo (2003a). On the other hand, we make more stringent assumptions on the moments of the error distributions.

In addition to the symmetry condition discussed in Remark 4.2.1(ii) above, our Assumption 4.4(b) require the error distributions to possess finite eighth moments, whereas Donald and Newey (2001) and Stock and Yogo (2003a) only assume finite fourth moments. Finally, our Assumption 4.2(a) imposes a less stringent condition on the rate of increase of the number of instruments relative to Donald and Newey (2001) and Stock and Yogo (2003a). Although Donald and Newey (2001) require that $\frac{K_n}{n} \to 0$ as $n \to \infty$ in deriving their asymptotic normality result for LIML and Stock and Yogo (2003a) require that $\frac{K_n^2}{n} \to 0$, we require only that $\frac{K_n}{n} \to \alpha$ with $0 \leq \alpha < 1$, and thus the results of this chapter will hold with K_n growing either at the same rate as n or at a slower rate relative to n.

4.3 ASYMPTOTIC NORMALITY OF SINGLE-EQUATION ESTIMATORS

We focus our analysis on the following three estimators:

1. Limited infomation maximum likelihood (LIML) estimator

$$\widehat{\beta}_{\text{LIML},n} = \left(y_{2n}' M_{X_n} y_{2n} - \widehat{\lambda}_{\text{LIML},n} y_{2n}' M_{\overline{Z}_n} y_{2n}\right)^{-1} \times \left(y_{2n}' M_{X_n} y_{1n} - \widehat{\lambda}_{\text{LIML},n} y_{2n}' M_{\overline{Z}_n} y_{1n}\right), \tag{7}$$

where $\widehat{\lambda}_{\text{LIML},n}$ is the smallest root of the determinantal equation

$$\det\left\{\begin{pmatrix} y_{1n}' M_{X_n} y_{1n} & y_{1n}' M_{X_n} y_{2n} \\ y_{2n}' M_{X_n} y_{1n} & y_{2n}' M_{X_n} y_{2n} \end{pmatrix} - \lambda_n \begin{pmatrix} y_{1n}' M_{\overline{Z}_n} y_{1n} & y_{1n}' M_{\overline{Z}_n} y_{2n} \\ y_{2n}' M_{\overline{Z}_n} y_{1n} & y_{2n}' M_{\overline{Z}_n} y_{2n} \end{pmatrix}\right\} = 0 \tag{8}$$

2. Fuller's modified LIML (FLIML) estimator:

$$\widehat{\beta}_{\text{FLIML},n} = \left(y_{2n}' M_{X_n} y_{2n} - \widehat{k}_{\text{FLIML},n} y_{2n}' M_{\overline{Z}_n} y_{2n}\right)^{-1} \times \left(y_{2n}' M_{X_n} y_{1n} - \widehat{k}_{\text{FLIML},n} y_{2n}' M_{\overline{Z}_n} y_{1n}\right), \tag{9}$$

where $\widehat{k}_{\text{FLIML},n} = \widehat{\lambda}_{\text{LIML},n} - \frac{a}{n-K_n-J}$ for some positive constant a.

3. Bias-corrected two-stage least-squares (B2SLS) estimator:

$$\widehat{\beta}_{\text{B2SLS},n} = \left(y_{2n}' M_{X_n} y_{2n} - \left(\frac{n}{n - K_n + 2}\right) y_{2n}' M_{\overline{Z}_n} y_{2n}\right)^{-1} \times \left(y_{2n}' M_{X_n} y_{1n} - \left(\frac{n}{n - K_n + 2}\right) y_{2n}' M_{\overline{Z}_n} y_{1n}\right). \tag{10}$$

All three of these estimators are, of course, special cases of the k-class estimator defined by

$$\widehat{\beta}_{k,n} = \left(y_{2n}' M_{X_n} y_{2n} - k y_{2n}' M_{\overline{Z}_n} y_{2n}\right)^{-1} \left(y_{2n}' M_{X_n} y_{1n} - k y_{2n}' M_{\overline{Z}_n} y_{1n}\right). \tag{11}$$

These three estimators are three of the most well-known k-class estimators, and the asymptotic properties of one or more of these estimators have been studied previously in the many-instruments context by Morimune (1983), Bekker

(1994), Donald and Newey (2001), and Stock and Yogo (2003a). As discussed in the introduction, however, the purpose of this paper is to derive the asymptotic distributions of these estimators in the case in which the instruments are weaker than assumed in these earlier papers.

The following theorems present the main asymptotic results of this paper:

Theorem 4.3.1 (LIML) *Let $\widehat{\beta}_{\text{LIML},n}$ be as defined in eq. (7) above. Then, under assumptions 4.1–4.5,*

$$\left(\frac{\Psi_n}{\sigma_{L,n}}\right)\left(\widehat{\beta}_{\text{LIML},n}-\beta_0\right)\xrightarrow{d}N(0,1)\quad \text{as } n\to\infty,$$

where $\Psi_n = b_n^{-2}c_n' Z_n' M_{X_n} Z_n c_n$, where

$$\begin{aligned}\sigma_{L,n}^2 =& \left[E\left(u_j^2v_j^2\right)-\sigma_{uv}^2\right]\sum_{j=1}^{n}E\left(g_{jj,n}^2\right)+\frac{\sigma_{uv}^2}{\sigma_{uu}^2}\left[E\left(u_j^4\right)-\sigma_{uu}^2\right]\sum_{j=1}^{n}E\left(g_{jj,n}^2\right)\\ &-2\frac{\sigma_{uv}}{\sigma_{uu}}\left[E\left(u_j^3v_j\right)-\sigma_{uu}\sigma_{uv}\right]\sum_{j=1}^{n}E\left(g_{jj,n}^2\right)\\ &+2\left(\sigma_{uu}\sigma_{vv}-\sigma_{uv}^2\right)\sum_{1\le i<j\le n}E\left(g_{ij,n}^2\right),\end{aligned}\tag{12}$$

and where $g_{jj,n}$ and $g_{ij,n}$ denote, respectively, the jth *diagonal element and the (i, j)th element of the matrix $G_n = P_{\overline{Z}_n} - P_{X_n} - \left(\frac{K_n}{n-K_n-J}\right)M_{\overline{Z}_n}$.*

Theorem 4.3.2 (FLIML) *Let $\widehat{\beta}_{\text{FLIML},n}$ be as defined in eq. (9) above. Then, under Assumptions 4.1–4.5,*

$$\left(\frac{\Psi_n}{\sigma_{L,n}}\right)\left(\widehat{\beta}_{\text{FLIML},n}-\beta_0\right)\xrightarrow{d}N(0,1)\quad \text{as } n\to\infty,$$

where Ψ_n and $\sigma_{L,n}$ are as defined in Theorem 4.3.1 above.

Theorem 4.3.3 (B2SLS) *Let $\widehat{\beta}_{\text{B2SLS},n}$ be as defined in eq. (10) above. Then, under Assumptions 4.1–4.5,*

$$\left(\frac{\Psi_n}{\sigma_{B,n}}\right)\left(\widehat{\beta}_{\text{B2SLS},n}-\beta_0\right)\xrightarrow{d}N(0,1)\quad \text{as } n\to\infty,$$

where Ψ_n is as defined in Theorem 4.3.1 and where

$$\sigma_{B,n}^2=\left[E\left(u_j^2v_j^2\right)-\sigma_{uv}^2\right]\sum_{j=1}^{n}E\left(g_{jj,n}^2\right)+2\left(\sigma_{uu}\sigma_{vv}+\sigma_{uv}^2\right)\sum_{1\le i<j\le n}E\left(g_{ij,n}^2\right)\tag{13}$$

with $g_{jj,n}$ and $g_{ij,n}$ defined as in Theorem 4.3.1.

Remark 4.3.2 (i) Note that Lemma A.3 part (b) in the appendix shows that $\sigma_{L,n}^2$ and $\sigma_{B,n}^2$ grow at the same rate as K_n as $n \to \infty$. If we make the additional assumptions that, as $n \to \infty$, $\overline{\Psi}_n = r_n^{-1}\Psi_n \overset{a.s.}{\to} \overline{\Psi}$, $K_n^{-1}\sigma_{L,n}^2 \to \sigma_L^2$, and $K_n^{-1}\sigma_{B,n}^2 \to \sigma_B^2$ for positive constants $\overline{\Psi}$, σ_L^2, and σ_B^2, then the asymptotic normality results given in Theorems 4.3.1–4.3.3 can be restated as

$$\frac{r_n}{\sqrt{K_n}}\left(\widehat{\beta}_{\text{LIML},n} - \beta_0\right) \overset{d}{\to} N\left(0, \sigma_L^2\overline{\Psi}^{-2}\right),$$
$$\frac{r_n}{\sqrt{K_n}}\left(\widehat{\beta}_{\text{FLIML},n} - \beta_0\right) \overset{d}{\to} N\left(0, \sigma_L^2\overline{\Psi}^{-2}\right),$$
$$\frac{r_n}{\sqrt{K_n}}\left(\widehat{\beta}_{\text{B2SLS},n} - \beta_0\right) \overset{d}{\to} N\left(0, \sigma_B^2\overline{\Psi}^{-2}\right).$$

Interestingly, under Assumption 4.5, $\widehat{\beta}_{\text{LIML},n}$, $\widehat{\beta}_{\text{FLIML},n}$, and $\widehat{\beta}_{\text{B2SLS},n}$ are all consistent, but the rate of convergence is $\frac{r_n}{\sqrt{K_n}}$, which depends both on the rate of growth of the concentration parameter r_n and on the rate of increase of the number of instruments. Note further that, under Assumptions 4.2(a) and 4.5, $\frac{r_n}{\sqrt{K_n}} = o\left(\sqrt{n}\right)$, and thus this rate of convergence is slower than the usual $\sqrt{n}$ rate of convergence. This slower rate of convergence, in turn, reflects the fact that here we are studying the case in which the instruments are weaker than that under the conventional strong identification case in which the concentration parameter grows at the rate n.

(ii) It is of interest to compare briefly the results we obtained here under Assumption 4.5 with results that occur in cases in which r_n is assumed to grow at the same rate or at a faster rate than K_n. Such a comparison illuminates the differences between our results and those obtained by other authors employing a many-instruments setup.

To begin, note that, in general, it can be shown that the three estimators studied here have the generic (asymptotic) representation

$$\frac{\Psi_n}{\sigma_{\cdot,n}}\left(\widehat{\beta} - \beta_0\right) = \frac{f_n'u_n + d_1 v_n' G_n u_n + d_2 u_n' G_n u_n}{\sigma_{\cdot,n}} + o_p(1), \tag{14}$$

where

$$d_2 = \begin{cases} -\frac{\sigma_{uv}}{\sigma_{uu}} & \text{for } \widehat{\beta}_{\text{LIML},n}, \widehat{\beta}_{\text{FLIML},n} \\ 0 & \text{for } \widehat{\beta}_{\text{B2SLS},n} \end{cases},$$

where

$$\sigma_{\cdot,n}^2 = \begin{cases} \sigma_{L,n}^2 + \sigma_{uu}E\left(f_n'f_n\right) & \text{for } \widehat{\beta}_{\text{LIML},n}, \widehat{\beta}_{\text{FLIML},n} \\ \sigma_{B,n}^2 + \sigma_{uu}E\left(f_n'f_n\right) & \text{for } \widehat{\beta}_{\text{B2SLS},n} \end{cases}$$

with $\sigma_{L,n}^2$ and $\sigma_{B,n}^2$ as defined in expressions (12) and (13) above, and where $\Psi_n = \frac{c_n' Z_n' M_{X_n} Z_n c_n}{b_n^2}$, $f_n = b_n^{-1} M_{X_n} Z_n c_n$, and $d_1 = 1$ for all three estimators. Under Assumption 4.5, $\frac{f_n' u_n}{\sigma_{\cdot,n}} = o_p(1)$, and thus the asymptotic distributions of the estimators depend only on the bilinear part of (14), that is,

$$\frac{\Psi_n}{\sigma_{\cdot,n}}\left(\widehat{\beta}-\beta_0\right)=\frac{d_1 v_n' G_n u_n + d_2 u_n' G_n u_n}{\sigma_{\cdot,n}}+o_p(1).$$

It is of interest first to compare our case with the case studied recently by Stock and Yogo (2003a), which assumes that r_n grows at the same rate as K_n. In the Stock–Yogo case, the asymptotic distributions of LIML, FLIML, and B2SLS depend on both the linear part, $\frac{f_n' u_n}{\sigma_{\cdot,n}}$ and the bilinear part $\frac{d_1 v_n' G_n u_n + d_2 u_n' G_n u_n}{\sigma_{\cdot,n}}$. Thus, the general form of the asymptotic variance for these estimators in the Stock–Yogo case is different from that obtained in Theorems 4.3.1–4.3.3 and in Remark 4.3.2(i) above, for the asymptotic variance in their case also depends on contribution from the linear component. In addition, Stock and Yogo (2003a) find the rate of convergence in their case to be $\sqrt{K_n}$. This is the same as our rate of convergence of $\frac{r_n}{\sqrt{K_n}}$ in the case in which $r_n \sim K_n$. However, for $r_n = o(K_n)$, our rate of convergence is slower than theirs, reflecting the fact that we treat a case with weaker instruments.

It should be noted that earlier papers by Morimune (1983) and Bekker (1994) have also examined the case in which the concentration parameter grows at the same rate as the number of instruments, but those papers differ from Stock and Yogo (2003a) and also from this chapter in that they assume r_n and K_n to grow at the same rate as the sample size n. Hence, the situation studied in those papers might be better characterized as one with strong, as opposed to weak, instruments.

Finally, in the case in which r_n grows faster than K_n,

$$\frac{d_1 v_n' G_n u_n + d_2 u_n' G_n u_n}{\sigma_{\cdot,n}} = o_p(1),$$

and the asymptotic distributions depend only on the linear part $\frac{f_n' u_n}{\sigma_{\cdot,n}}$ and not on the bilinear component at all. Thus, the general form of the asymptotic variance of LIML, FLIML, and B2SLS in this case is also qualitatively different from the one we derived under Assumption 4.5. The case in which r_n grows faster than K_n is one that has been well studied in the literature. In particular, as discussed in Remark 4.2.1(iii), Donald and Newey (2001) derive asymptotic normality results for LIML under the assumptions that $r_n \sim n$ and $\frac{K_n}{n} \to 0$ as $n \to \infty$. Note also that the case in which r_n grows faster than K_n includes the conventional case with full identification and $\sqrt{n}$ convergence of estimators to asymptotic normal distributions because the conventional setup can be obtained by assuming $r_n \sim n$ and taking K_n to be fixed for all n.

(iii) Note further that Theorems 4.3.1–4.3.3 show that LIML and FLIML are asymptotically equivalent. However, the B2SLS estimator is not asymptotically equivalent to LIML or FLIML. Indeed, the following result shows that if the distribution of the disturbances of the simultaneous equations system (1)–(2) are taken to belong to the family of elliptical distributions with finite eighth moments, then LIML and FLIML can be shown to be asymptotically more efficient than B2SLS.

Theorem 4.3.4 *Suppose that Assumptions 4.1–4.5 hold. Suppose, in addition, that* $\eta_i \sim E_2(0, \Xi)$, *where* $\Xi = \tau \Sigma$ *for some positive constant* τ *and* $E_2(0, \Xi)$ *is as defined in Definition A.1 of Appendix A with* $m = 2$. *Then, there exists a positive integer* N *such that, for all* $n \geq N$,

$$\sigma^2_{B,n} > \sigma^2_{L,n}. \tag{15}$$

Note that when the error distribution is Gaussian, LIML and FLIML have interpretations as maximum likelihood (ML) estimators and so one would expect LIML and FLIML to be more efficient than B2SLS within a many-weak-instruments asymptotic framework. However, our result shows that even when the errors are non-Gaussian but lie within the elliptical family, in which case LIML and FLIML do not have strict interpretations as ML estimators, these estimators are still asymptotically more efficient than B2SLS within the local-to-zero, many instruments framework studied here. This result is consistent with the asymptotic mean square error results obtained by Donald and Newey (2001) for these estimators under the assumption of i.i.d. instruments. With regard to the relative efficiency of LIML vis-à-vis the B2SLS estimator, our results might be viewed as extending the work of Donald and Newey (2001) both to the case with weaker instruments and to the case in which the instruments are possibly not i.i.d.

(iv) Another well-known k-class estimator is the (unadjusted) two-stage least squares (2SLS) estimator. However, we did not derive the asymptotic distribution of this estimator here because, as shown in Chao and Swanson (2002), the 2SLS estimator is inconsistent under Assumption 4.5. More specifically, part (a) of Theorem 3.4 of Chao and Swanson (2002) shows that, when $\frac{r_n}{K_n} \to 0$ as $n \to \infty$,

$$\widehat{\beta}_{2SLS,n} \xrightarrow{p} \beta_0 + \frac{\sigma_{vu}}{\sigma_{vv}}.$$

Note further that, as shown in Chao and Swanson (2003), $\beta_0 + \frac{\sigma_{vu}}{\sigma_{vv}}$ is also the probability limit of the ordinary least-squares (OLS) estimator in a local-to-zero framework, and thus the $2SLS$ and the OLS estimators have the same asymptotic bias in the case in which the concentration parameter grows at a slower rate than the number of instruments. Hence, under Assumption 4.5, both $2SLS$ and OLS are asymptotically deficient relative to the three estimators studied in this chapter.

4.4 CONCLUDING REMARKS

We have derived the limiting distributions of the LIML, FLIML, and B2SLS estimators in a many-weak-instruments setup in which the concentration parameter is assumed to grow at a slower rate than the number of instruments K_n but at a faster rate than $\sqrt{K_n}$. Thus, we have obtained asymptotic normality results for these estimators in situations with weaker instruments than in previous papers that use the many-instruments asymptotic framework. In our context, both the rate of convergence and the form of the variance of the limiting distributions are different than for cases in which the instruments are stronger, that is cases in which the instruments grow at the same rate or at a faster rate than K_n. In addition, in contrast to the conventional full-identification case in which all three estimators are asymptotically equivalent, we find that the B2SLS estimator is not asymptotically equivalent to LIML and FLIML under the weak instruments scenario studied here. In particular, we show that LIML and FLIML are asymptotically more efficient than B2SLS if the distribution of the disturbances of the underlying instrumental variables regression model is assumed to belong to the elliptical family.

APPENDIX A

In this appendix, we collect some definitions and preliminary lemmas that will be used to prove our main results.

Definition A.1 The $m \times 1$ random vector X is said to have an elliptical distribution with parameters μ $(m \times 1)$ and Ξ $(m \times m)$ if its density function is of the form

$$k_m \left(\det \Xi\right)^{-\frac{1}{2}} h\left((x-\mu)' \,\Xi^{-1} (x-\mu)\right) \tag{16}$$

for some normalizing constant k_m and some function $h(\cdot)$, where Ξ is positive definite. (**Note:** A similar definition appears in Muirhead 1982, p. 34.)

Lemma A.1 *Let*

$$G_n = P_{\overline{Z}_n} - P_{X_n} - \left(\frac{K_n}{n-K_n-J}\right) M_{\overline{Z}_n} \tag{17}$$

and let $g_{jj,n}$ and $g_{ij,n}$ denote, respectively, the jth diagonal element and the (i,j)th off-diagonal element of the matrix G_n. Then, under Assumptions 4.2(a) and 4.2(b), the following statements hold as $n \to \infty$:

(a) $Tr(G_n^4) = O_{a.s.}(K_n)$

(b) $\sum_{i=1}^{n}\sum_{j=1}^{n} g_{ij,n}^4 = O_{a.s.}(K_n)$,

(c) $\sum_{1 \le i \le n}\left[\sum_{1 \le j < k \le n} g_{ij,n}^2 g_{ik,n}^2\right] = O_{a.s.}(K_n)$,

(d) $\sum_{1 \le i < j \le n} g_{ii,n}^2 g_{ij,n}^2 = O_{a.s.}(K_n)$,

(e) $\sum_{1 \le i < j \le n} g_{jj,n}^2 g_{ij,n}^2 = O_{a.s.}(K_n)$,

(f) $\sum_{1\leq i<j<k\leq n} g_{ij,n}^2 g_{ik,n}^2 = O_{a.s.}(K_n)$,

(g) $\sum_{1\leq i<j<k\leq n} g_{ij,n}^2 g_{jk,n}^2 = O_{a.s.}(K_n)$,

(h) $\sum_{1\leq i<j<k\leq n} g_{ik,n}^2 g_{jk,n}^2 = O_{a.s.}(K_n)$,

(i) $Tr(G_n^2) = O_{a.s.}(K_n)$,

(j) $\sum_{j=1}^{n} g_{jj,n}^2 = O_{a.s.}(K_n)$,

(k) $\sum_{1\leq i<j\leq n} g_{ij,n}^2 = O_{a.s.}(K_n)$.

Proof of Lemma A.1: To show part (a), note that, by direct calculation,

$$G_n^4 = P_{\overline{Z}_n} - P_{X_n} + \left(\frac{K_n}{n-K_n-J}\right)^4 M_{\overline{Z}_n},$$

where $P_{\overline{Z}_n}$ and P_{X_n}, and thus G_n^4, are well defined with probability one for n sufficiently large given Assumption 4.2(b). It follows that, with probability one for n sufficiently large,

$$\frac{1}{K_n} Tr\left(G_n^4\right) = \frac{1}{K_n}\left[Tr\left(P_{\overline{Z}_n} - P_{X_n}\right) + \left(\frac{K_n}{n-K_n-J}\right)^4 Tr\left(M_{\overline{Z}_n}\right)\right]$$
$$= 1 + \frac{K_n^3}{(n-K_n-J)^3},$$

and thus $Tr\left(G_n^4\right) = O_{a.s.}(K_n)$ as required.

To show (b), note that, for n sufficiently large with probability one, we have

$$Tr(G_n^4) = \sum_{1\leq i\leq n}\left(\sum_{1\leq j\leq n} g_{ij,n}^2\right)^2 + \sum_{1\leq i<j\leq n}\left(\sum_{1\leq k\leq n} g_{ki,n}g_{kj,n}\right)^2$$
$$+ \sum_{1\leq j<i\leq n}\left(\sum_{1\leq k\leq n} g_{ki,n}g_{kj,n}\right)^2$$
$$\geq \sum_{1\leq i\leq n}\left(\sum_{1\leq j\leq n} g_{ij,n}^2\right)^2$$
$$\geq \sum_{i=1}^{n}\sum_{j=1}^{n} g_{ij,n}^4,$$

where $g_{ij,n}$ denotes the (i,j)th element of G_n. It follows from the result given in part (a) that

$$O_{a.s.}(K_n) = Tr(G_n^4) \geq \sum_{i=1}^{n}\sum_{j=1}^{n} g_{ij,n}^4.$$

Similarly, for part (c), we have, for n sufficiently large with probability one, that

$$Tr(G_n^4) \geq \sum_{1\leq i\leq n}\left(\sum_{1\leq j\leq n} g_{ij,n}^2\right)^2$$
$$\geq 2\sum_{1\leq i\leq n}\left[\sum_{1\leq j<k\leq n} g_{ij,n}^2 g_{ik,n}^2\right],$$

and so again the result given in part (a) implies that

$$O_{a.s.}(K_n) = \frac{1}{2}Tr(G_n^4) \geq \sum_{1\leq i\leq n}\left[\sum_{1\leq j<k\leq n} g_{ij,n}^2 g_{ik,n}^2\right].$$

To show parts (d)–(h), we note that part (c) of this lemma implies that

$$\begin{aligned} &O_{a.s.}(K_n)\\ &= \sum_{1\leq i\leq n}\left[\sum_{1\leq j<k\leq n} g_{ij,n}^2 g_{ik,n}^2\right]\\ &= 2\left\{\sum_{1\leq i<j<k\leq n} g_{ij,n}^2 g_{ik,n}^2 + \sum_{1\leq i<j\leq n} g_{ii,n}^2 g_{ij,n}^2 + \sum_{1\leq i<j<k\leq n} g_{ij,n}^2 g_{jk,n}^2\right.\\ &\quad\left. + \sum_{1\leq i<j\leq n} g_{jj,n}^2 g_{ij,n}^2 + \sum_{1\leq i<j<k\leq n} g_{ik,n}^2 g_{jk,n}^2\right\}. \end{aligned} \tag{18}$$

The results stated in parts (d)–(h) then follow directly from the expression on the right-hand side of the last equality in (18) because each term of the sum constituting that expression is nonnegative.

The proofs for parts (i)–(k) are very similar to the proofs for parts (a)–(h) if we note

$$G_n^2 = P_{\overline{Z}_n} - P_{X_n} + \left(\frac{K_n}{n-K_n-J}\right)^2 M_{\overline{Z}_n}.$$

Hence, to avoid redundancy, we omit these proofs. ■

Lemma A.2 *Let G_n and $g_{jj,n}$ and $g_{ij,n}$ be as defined in Lemma A.1. Then, under Assumptions 4.2(a) and 4.2(b), as $n\to\infty$,* $\sum_{1\leq i<j\leq n}\left(E\left(g_{ij,n}^2\right)\right)^2 = O(K_n)$ *and* $\sum_{1\leq i<j<k\leq n} E\left(g_{ij,n}^2\right)E\left(g_{ik,n}^2\right) = O(K_n)$.

Proof of Lemma A.2: To proceed, note that part (a) of Lemma A.1 implies that

$$O(K_n) = E\left[Tr\left(G_n^4\right)\right]$$
$$\geq E\left[\sum_{1\leq i\leq n}\left(\sum_{1\leq j\leq n} g_{ij,n}^2\right)^2\right]$$

$$\geq \sum_{i=1}^{n}\left(\sum_{j=1}^{n} E\left(g_{ij,n}^2\right)\right)^2$$

$$\geq \sum_{1\leq i<j\leq n}\left(E\left(g_{ij,n}^2\right)\right)^2 + \sum_{1\leq i<j<k\leq n} E\left(g_{ij,n}^2\right)E\left(g_{ik,n}^2\right), \quad (19)$$

where the second inequality above follows from application of Jensen's inequality. The desired result follows immediately from (19) by noting that both $\sum_{1\leq i<j\leq n}\left(E\left(g_{ij,n}^2\right)\right)^2$ and $\sum_{1\leq i<j<k\leq n} E\left(g_{ij,n}^2\right)E\left(g_{ik,n}^2\right)$ are nonnegative, and thus they cannot be of an order greater than K_n. ■

Lemma A.3 *Define the bilinear form*

$$W_n = d_1 v_n' G_n u_n + d_2 u_n' G_n u_n, \quad (20)$$

where d_1 and d_2 are constants and G_n is as defined in (17). Let $\sigma_{W_n}^2$ denote the variance of W_n. Suppose Assumptions 4.2–4.4 hold; then,

$$\text{(a) } \sigma_{W_n}^2 = \sum_{j=1}^{n} d_1^2 E\left(g_{jj,n}^2\right)\left[E\left(u_j^2 v_j^2\right) - \sigma_{uv}^2\right] + \sum_{j=1}^{n} d_2^2 E\left(g_{jj,n}^2\right)\left[E\left(u_j^4\right) - \sigma_{uu}^2\right]$$
$$+ 2\left\{\sum_{j=1}^{n} d_1 d_2 E\left(g_{jj,n}^2\right)\left[E\left(u_j^3 v_j\right) - \sigma_{uu}\sigma_{uv}\right]\right\}$$
$$+ 2\left\{\sum_{1\leq i<j\leq n} d_1^2 E\left(g_{ij,n}^2\right)\left(\sigma_{uu}\sigma_{vv} + \sigma_{uv}^2\right)\right.$$
$$\left. + 2\sum_{1\leq i<j\leq n} d_2^2 E\left(g_{ij,n}^2\right)\sigma_{uu}^2 + 4\sum_{1\leq i<j\leq n} d_1 d_2 E\left(g_{ij,n}^2\right)\sigma_{uu}\sigma_{uv}\right\}$$

(b) $\sigma_{W_n}^2 \asymp K_n$,

where $g_{jj,n}$ and $g_{ij,n}$ denote, respectively, the jth diagonal element and the (i, j)th off-diagonal element of the matrix G_n and where, for two sequences x_n and y_n, the notation "$x_n \asymp y_n$" means that x_n is of the same order as y_n, that is, $x_n \asymp y_n$ if and only if $x_n = O(y_n)$ and $y_n = O(x_n)$.

Proof of Lemma A.3: To show part (a), note that we can write $W_n = \sum_{j=1}^{n} W_{jn}$, where

$$W_{jn} = d_1 g_{jj,n}\left(u_j v_j - \sigma_{uv}\right) + \sum_{1\leq i<j} d_1 g_{ij,n}\left(v_i u_j + v_j u_i\right)$$
$$+ d_2 g_{jj,n}\left(u_j^2 - \sigma_{uu}\right) + 2\sum_{1\leq i<j} d_2 g_{ij,n} u_i u_j \quad (21)$$

and where expression (21) has made use of the fact that G_n is a symmetric matrix. Moreover, given that $\eta_i = (u_i, v_i)$ is an independent sequence by Assumption 4.4(a), it is easy to see that $\sigma_{W_n}^2 = \sum_{j=1}^{n} E\left(W_{jn}^2\right)$. It follows by straightforward calculation that

$$\sigma^2_{W_n} = \sum_{j=1}^{n} d_1^2 E\left(g^2_{jj,n}\right)\left[E\left(u_j^2 v_j^2\right) - \sigma^2_{uv}\right] + \sum_{j=1}^{n} d_2^2 E\left(g^2_{jj,n}\right)\left[E\left(u_j^4\right) - \sigma^2_{uu}\right]$$
$$+2\left\{\sum_{j=1}^{n} d_1 d_2 E\left(g^2_{jj,n}\right)\left[E\left(u_j^3 v_j\right) - \sigma_{uu}\sigma_{uv}\right]\right\}$$
$$+2\left\{\sum_{1\le i<j\le n} d_1^2 E\left(g^2_{ij,n}\right)\left(\sigma_{uu}\sigma_{vv} + \sigma^2_{uv}\right) + 2\sum_{1\le i<j\le n} d_2^2 E\left(g^2_{ij,n}\right)\sigma^2_{uu}\right.$$
$$\left. + 4\sum_{1\le i<j\le n} d_1 d_2 E\left(g^2_{ij,n}\right)\sigma_{uu}\sigma_{uv}\right\} \tag{22}$$

as required.

To show part (b), we first show that $\sigma^2_{W_n}$ is at most of order K_n. To show this, note that

$$\sigma^2_{W_n} = \left\{\sum_{j=1}^{n} d_1^2 E\left(g^2_{jj,n}\right)\left[E\left(u_j^2 v_j^2\right) - \sigma^2_{uv}\right] + \sum_{j=1}^{n} d_2^2 E\left(g^2_{jj,n}\right)\left[E\left(u_j^4\right) - \sigma^2_{uu}\right]\right\}$$
$$2\sum_{j=1}^{n} d_1 d_2 E\left(g^2_{jj,n}\right)\left[E\left(u_j^3 v_j\right) - \sigma_{uu}\sigma_{uv}\right]$$
$$+2\left\{\sum_{1\le i<j\le n} d_1^2 E\left(g^2_{ij,n}\right)\left(\sigma_{uu}\sigma_{vv} + \sigma^2_{uv}\right) + 2\sum_{1\le i<j\le n} d_2^2 E\left(g^2_{ij,n}\right)\sigma^2_{uu}\right.$$
$$\left. + 4\sum_{1\le i<j\le n} d_1 d_2 E\left(g^2_{ij,n}\right)\sigma_{uu}\sigma_{uv}\right\}$$
$$\le 2\left(d_1^2 + d_2^2 + 2d_1 d_2\right) D_\eta^{\frac{1}{2}} \sum_{j=1}^{n} E\left(g^2_{jj,n}\right)$$
$$+4\left(d_1^2 + 2d_2^2 + 4d_1 d_2\right) D_\eta^{\frac{1}{2}} \sum_{1\le i<j\le n} E\left(g^2_{ij,n}\right)$$
$$= O\left(K_n\right), \tag{23}$$

where the last equality is implied by parts (j) and (k) of Lemma A.1.

Next, we show that $\sigma^2_{W_n}$ is not of an order lower than K_n. To proceed, note that

$$\sigma^2_{W_n} = \varpi_1^2\left(\sum_{j=1}^{n} E\left[g^2_{jj,n}\right]\right) + 2\varpi_2^2\left(\sum_{1\le i<j\le n} E\left[g^2_{ij,n}\right]\right)$$
$$\ge \varpi_*^2\left(\sum_{i=1}^{n}\sum_{j=1}^{n} E\left[g^2_{ij,n}\right]\right)$$

$$= \varpi_*^2 E\left[Tr\left(G_n^2\right)\right]$$
$$= \varpi_*^2 \left(K_n + \frac{K_n^2}{n - K_n - J}\right), \tag{24}$$

where $\varpi_1^2 = E\left(d_2\left[u_j v_j - \sigma_{uv}\right] + d_3\left[u_j^2 - \sigma_{uu}\right]\right)^2$, $\varpi_2^2 = E(d_2\left[u_j v_i + u_i v_j\right] + d_3 u_i u_j)^2$, and $\varpi_*^2 = \min\left\{\varpi_1^2, \varpi_2^2\right\}$ and where the last equality follows from direct calculation. The desired result follows immediately from expressions (23) and (24) given Assumption 4.2(a). ■

Lemma A.4 *Let G_n be as defined in (17) above and let $g_{jj,n}$ and $g_{ij,n}$ denote, respectively, the jth diagonal element and the (i, j)th off-diagonal element of the matrix G_n. Then, under Assumptions 4.2–4.4 as $n \to \infty$,*

$$\frac{1}{K_n^2} \sum_{1 \le i < j < k < l \le n} E\left(g_{ik,n} g_{jk,n} g_{il,n} g_{jl,n}\right) = o(1). \tag{25}$$

Proof of Lemma A.4: We will prove this lemma in two steps. First, we will show that

$$\frac{1}{K_n^2} \sum_{1 \le i < j < k < l \le n} \left[g_{ik,n} g_{jk,n} g_{il,n} g_{jl,n} + g_{ij,n} g_{jk,n} g_{il,n} g_{kl,n} + g_{ij,n} g_{ik,n} g_{jl,n} g_{kl,n}\right]$$
$$= o_{a.s}(1). \tag{26}$$

We will then use (26) to show the desired result (25). To proceed, first define

$$\overline{G}_n = G_n - dg\left(G_n\right),$$

where $dg\left(G_n\right) = \mathrm{diag}\left(g_{11,n}, \ldots, g_{nn,n}\right)$, that is, $dg\left(G_n\right)$ is an $n \times n$ diagonal matrix whose diagonal elements are the same as that of G_n. Now, note that, by direct calculation, we obtain

$$Tr(\overline{G}_n^4) = \sum_{1 \le i \le n} \left(\sum_{j \ne i} g_{ij,n}^2\right)^2 + 2 \sum_{1 \le i < j \le n} \left(\sum_{k \ne i, k \ne j} g_{ki,n} g_{kj,n}\right)^2$$
$$= 2 \sum_{1 \le i < j \le n} g_{ij,n}^4$$
$$+ 4 \sum_{1 \le i < j < k \le n} \left[g_{ik,n}^2 g_{jk,n}^2 + g_{ij,n}^2 g_{ik,n}^2 + g_{ij,n}^2 g_{jk,n}^2\right]$$
$$+ 8 \sum_{1 \le i < j < k < l \le n} \left[g_{ik,n} g_{jk,n} g_{il,n} g_{jl,n} + g_{ij,n} g_{jk,n} g_{il,n} g_{kl,n}\right.$$
$$\left. + g_{ij,n} g_{ik,n} g_{jl,n} g_{kl,n}\right], \tag{27}$$

where $P_{\overline{Z}_n}$ and P_{X_n}, and, thus $\overline{G}_n$ and $\overline{G}_n^4$, are each well defined with probability one for n sufficiently large in light of Assumption 4.2(b). Now, let

$\lambda_{1,n} \leq \lambda_{2,n} \leq \cdots \leq \lambda_{n,n}$ be the eigenvalues of the matrix $\overline{G}_n$ and note that

$$Tr(\overline{G}_n^4) = \sum_{i=1}^{n} \lambda_{i,n}^4. \tag{28}$$

Next, observe that part (b) and parts (f)–(h) of Lemma A.1 imply that

$$\frac{1}{K_n^2} \sum_{1 \leq j < k \leq n} g_{jk,n}^4 = O_{a.s.}\left(K_n^{-1}\right), \tag{29}$$

$$\frac{1}{K_n^2} \sum_{1 \leq i < j < k \leq n} \left[g_{ik,n}^2 g_{jk,n}^2 + g_{ij,n}^2 g_{jk,n}^2 + g_{ij,n}^2 g_{ik,n}^2\right] = O_{a.s.}\left(K_n^{-1}\right). \tag{30}$$

It follows from eqs. (27)–(30) that showing that

$$\frac{1}{K_n^2} \sum_{1 \leq i < j < k < l \leq n} \left[g_{ik,n} g_{jk,n} g_{il,n} g_{jl,n} + g_{ij,n} g_{jk,n} g_{il,n} g_{kl,n} + g_{ij,n} g_{ik,n} g_{jl,n} g_{kl,n}\right]$$
$$= o_{a.s.}(1), \quad \text{as } n \to \infty,$$

is equivalent to showing that

$$\frac{1}{K_n^2} \sum_{i=1}^{n} \lambda_{i,n}^4 = o_{a.s.}(1) \quad \text{as } n \to \infty. \tag{31}$$

To show (31), we first note that, for each n,

$$\lambda_{n,n}^4 \leq \sum_{i=1}^{n} \lambda_{i,n}^4 \leq \lambda_{n,n}^2 \left(\sum_{i=1}^{n} \lambda_{i,n}^2\right) \tag{32}$$

and

$$\begin{aligned}
\frac{1}{K_n} \sum_{i=1}^{n} \lambda_{i,n}^2 &= \frac{1}{K_n} Tr\left(\overline{G}_n^2\right) \\
&\leq \frac{1}{K_n} \sum_{i=1}^{n} \sum_{j=1}^{n} g_{ij,n}^2 \\
&= \frac{1}{K_n} Tr\left(G_n^2 - dg\left(G_n\right) G_n - G_n dg\left(G_n\right) + \left[dg\left(G_n\right)\right]^2\right) \\
&= \frac{1}{K_n} Tr\left(G_n^2 - \left[dg\left(G_n\right)\right]^2\right) \\
&= \frac{1}{K_n} \left\{ Tr\left[P_{\overline{Z}_n} - P_{X_n} + \left(\frac{K_n}{n - K_n - J}\right)^2 M_{\overline{Z}_n}\right] \right. \\
&\quad \left. + \sum_{j=1}^{n} \left[\left(\frac{n - J}{n - K_n - J}\right) p_{jj,n}^{\overline{Z}} - p_{jj,n}^{X} - \left(\frac{K_n}{n - K_n - J}\right)\right]^2 \right\} \\
&\leq \frac{1}{K_n} \left\{ Tr\left[P_{\overline{Z}_n} - P_{X_n} + \left(\frac{K_n}{n - K_n - J}\right)^2 M_{\overline{Z}_n}\right] \right.
\end{aligned}$$

$$+\left(\frac{n-J}{n-K_n-J}\right)^2\sum_{j=1}^{n}\left(p_{jj.n}^{\overline{Z}}\right)^2\Bigg\}$$

$$\leq \frac{1}{K_n}\left\{K_n+\frac{K_n^2}{n-K_n-J}+\left(\frac{n-J}{n-K_n-J}\right)^2 K_n\right\}$$

$$=1+\left(\frac{n-J}{n-K_n-J}\right)^2+\frac{K_n}{n-K_n-J}, \tag{33}$$

where $p_{jj,n}^{\overline{Z}}$ and $p_{jj,n}^{X}$ are the jth diagonal elements of the projection matrices $P_{\overline{Z}_n}$ and P_{X_n}, follow from Assumption 4.2(a) that $\frac{1}{K_n}\sum_{i=1}^{n}\lambda_{i,n}^2=O_{a.s.}(1)$. Hence, to show (31), we need to show that

$$\frac{1}{K_n}\lambda_{n,n}^2=o_{a.s.}(1) \quad \text{as } n\rightarrow\infty. \tag{34}$$

To show (34), we proceed as follows: let x_n be any $n\times 1$ vector such that $\|x_n\|=1$ and let $x_{j,n}$ denote the jth element of x_n. Now, consider the quadratic form

$$\begin{aligned} x_n'\overline{G}_n^2x_n &= x_n'G_n^2x_n - x_n'\left[dg\left(G_n\right)G_n\right]x_n \\ &\quad - x_n'\left[G_n dg\left(G_n\right)\right]x_n + x_n'\left[dg\left(G_n\right)\right]^2 x_n \\ &\leq x_n'G_n^2x_n + \left|x_n'\left[dg\left(G_n\right)G_n\right]x_n\right| \\ &\quad + \left|x_n'\left[G_n dg\left(G_n\right)\right]x_n\right| + x_n'\left[dg\left(G_n\right)\right]^2 x_n. \end{aligned} \tag{35}$$

Note that, for n sufficiently large so that $P_{\overline{Z}_n}$ and P_{X_n} are well defined with probability one, we have that

$$\begin{aligned} x_n'\left[dg\left(G_n\right)\right]^2 x_n &= \sum_{j=1}^{n}\left[\left(\frac{n-J}{n-K_n-J}\right)p_{jj,n}^{\overline{Z}}-p_{jj,n}^{X}-\left(\frac{K_n}{n-K_n-J}\right)\right]^2 x_{j,n}^2 \\ &\leq \left(\frac{n-J}{n-K_n-J}\right)^2\sum_{i=1}^{n}x_{j,n}^2 \\ &= \left(\frac{n-J}{n-K_n-J}\right)^2 x_n'x_n \\ &= \left(\frac{n-J}{n-K_n-J}\right)^2, \end{aligned} \tag{36}$$

where the inequality above follows from the fact that $0\leq p_{jj,n}^{\overline{Z}}\leq 1$, $0\leq p_{jj,n}^{X}\leq 1$, and $\left(\frac{K_n}{n-K_n-J}\right)>0$, and note that

$$\begin{aligned} x_n'G_n^2x_n &\leq x_n'P_{\overline{Z}_n}x_n + x_n'P_{X_n}x_n + \left(\frac{K_n}{n-K_n-J}\right)^2 x_n'M_{\overline{Z}_n}x_n \\ &\leq 2+\left(\frac{K_n}{n-K_n-J}\right)^2, \end{aligned} \tag{37}$$

where inequality the follows from the Rayleigh quotient by making use of the fact that $\lambda_{\max}(P_{\overline{Z}_n}) = \lambda_{\max}(P_{X_n}) = \lambda_{\max}(M_{\overline{Z}_n}) = 1$ because $P_{\overline{Z}_n}$, P_{X_n}, and $M_{\overline{Z}_n}$ are idempotent matrices. (See pages 203 and 204 of Magnus and Neudecker 1988, for a statement of the Rayleigh quotient.) It then follows from the Cauchy–Schwarz inequality that

$$\left|x_n'\left[dg(G_n)G_n\right]x_n\right| \leq \sqrt{x_n'\left[dg(G_n)\right]^2 x_n}\sqrt{x_n'G_n^2x_n}$$
$$= \left(\frac{n-J}{n-K_n-J}\right)\sqrt{2+\left(\frac{K_n}{n-K_n-J}\right)^2}. \quad (38)$$

Define

$$\Delta_n = \left(\frac{n-J}{n-K_n-J}\right)^2 + 2 + \left(\frac{K_n}{n-K_n-J}\right)^2$$
$$+ 2\left(\frac{n-J}{n-K_n-J}\right)\sqrt{2+\left(\frac{K_n}{n-K_n-J}\right)^2}$$

and note that, for n sufficiently large so that $\overline{G}_n$ is well defined with probability one, expressions (36), (37), and (38) imply that $x_n'\overline{G}_n^2 x_n \leq \Delta_n$ for any $n \times 1$ vector x_n such that $\|x_n\| = 1$. Moreover, because Assumption 2(a) implies that

$$\Delta_n \to 2 + \left(\frac{1}{1-\alpha}\right)^2 + \left(\frac{\alpha}{1-\alpha}\right)^2 + 2\left(\frac{1}{1-\alpha}\right)\sqrt{2+\left(\frac{\alpha}{1-\alpha}\right)^2}$$
$$< \infty,$$

and thus there exist a positive constant $\overline{\Delta}_\alpha$ and a positive integer N such that, for all $n \geq N$,

$$\Delta_n \leq \overline{\Delta}_\alpha < \infty.$$

It then follows that, for all $n \geq N$,

$$\lambda_{n,n}^2 = \max_{x_n:\|x_n\|=1} x_n'\overline{G}_n^2 x_n \leq \Delta_n \leq \overline{\Delta}_\alpha < \infty$$

with probability one, from which (34) and thus (26) follow immediately as $K_n \to \infty$.

Next, we show that (26) implies the desired result (25). To proceed, first define

$$\zeta_{1n} = \sum_{1\leq i<j<k\leq n} g_{ik,n}g_{jk,n}\left(v_iv_j\sigma_{uu} + u_iv_j\sigma_{uv} + v_iu_j\sigma_{uv} + u_iu_j\sigma_{vv}\right)$$

and note that

$$E\left(\zeta_{1n}^2\right) = \left(2\sigma_{uu}^2\sigma_{vv}^2 + 12\sigma_{uu}\sigma_{vv}\sigma_{uv}^2 + 2\sigma_{uv}^4\right)\left[\sum_{1\leq i<j<k\leq n} E\left(g_{ik,n}^2g_{jk,n}^2\right)\right.$$
$$\left. + 2\sum_{1\leq i<j<k<l\leq n} E\left(g_{ik,n}g_{jk,n}g_{il,n}g_{jl,n}\right)\right].$$

Because part (h) of Lemma A.1 implies that $\frac{1}{K_n^2} \sum_{1 \leq i < j < k \leq n} E\left(g_{ik,n}^2 g_{jk,n}^2\right) = o(1)$, it follows, given Assumption 4, that

$$\frac{1}{K_n^2} \sum_{1 \leq i < j < k < l \leq n} E\left(g_{ik,n} g_{jk,n} g_{il,n} g_{jl,n}\right) = o(1) \tag{39}$$

if and only if

$$\frac{1}{K_n^2} E\left(\zeta_{1n}^2\right) = o(1). \tag{40}$$

To show eq. (40), further define

$$\begin{aligned}
\zeta_{2n} = & \sum_{1 \leq i < j < k \leq n} \left[g_{ik,n} g_{jk,n}\left(v_i v_j \sigma_{uu} + u_i v_j \sigma_{uv} + v_i u_j \sigma_{uv} + u_i u_j \sigma_{vv}\right)\right. \\
& + g_{ij,n} g_{jk,n}\left(v_i v_k \sigma_{uu} + u_i v_k \sigma_{uv} + v_i u_k \sigma_{uv} + u_i u_k \sigma_{vv}\right) \\
& \left. + g_{ij,n} g_{ik,n}\left(v_j v_k \sigma_{uu} + u_j v_k \sigma_{uv} + v_j u_k \sigma_{uv} + u_j u_k \sigma_{vv}\right)\right], \\
\zeta_{3n} = & \sum_{1 \leq i < j < k \leq n} \left[g_{ij,n} g_{jk,n}\left(v_i v_k \sigma_{uu} + u_i v_k \sigma_{uv} + v_i u_k \sigma_{uv} + u_i u_k \sigma_{vv}\right)\right. \\
& \left. + g_{ij,n} g_{ik,n}\left(v_j v_k \sigma_{uu} + u_j v_k \sigma_{uv} + v_j u_k \sigma_{uv} + u_j u_k \sigma_{vv}\right)\right]
\end{aligned}$$

and note that $\zeta_{1n} = \zeta_{2n} - \zeta_{3n}$; thus,

$$E\left(\zeta_{1n}^2\right) = E\left(\zeta_{2n}^2\right) + E\left(\zeta_{3n}^2\right) - 2E\left(\zeta_{2n}\zeta_{3n}\right). \tag{41}$$

By direct calculation, we obtain

$$E\left(\zeta_{2n}^2\right) = \mathcal{T}_1 + 4\mathcal{T}_2,$$

where

$$\begin{aligned}
\mathcal{T}_1 = & \left(2\sigma_{uu}^2 \sigma_{vv}^2 + 12\sigma_{uu}\sigma_{vv}\sigma_{uv}^2 + 2\sigma_{uv}^4\right) \\
& \times \sum_{1 \leq i < j < k \leq n} E\left[g_{ik,n}^2 g_{jk,n}^2 + g_{ij,n}^2 g_{jk,n}^2 + g_{ij,n}^2 g_{ik,n}^2\right],
\end{aligned}$$

$$\begin{aligned}
\mathcal{T}_2 = & \left(2\sigma_{uu}^2 \sigma_{vv}^2 + 12\sigma_{uu}\sigma_{vv}\sigma_{uv}^2 + 2\sigma_{uv}^4\right) \left[\sum_{1 \leq i < j < k < l \leq n} E\left(g_{ik,n} g_{il,n} g_{jk,n} g_{jl,n}\right)\right. \\
& + \sum_{1 \leq i < j < k < l \leq n} E\left(g_{ij,n} g_{il,n} g_{jk,n} g_{kl,n}\right) \\
& \left. + \sum_{1 \leq i < j < k < l \leq n} E\left(g_{ij,n} g_{ik,n} g_{jl,n} g_{kl,n}\right)\right],
\end{aligned}$$

and

$$E\left(\zeta_{3n}^2\right) = \mathcal{T}_3 + 2\mathcal{T}_2,$$

where

$$\mathcal{T}_3 = \left(2\sigma_{uu}^2\sigma_{vv}^2 + 12\sigma_{uu}\sigma_{vv}\sigma_{uv}^2 + 2\sigma_{uv}^4\right) \sum_{1\leq i<j<k\leq n} E\left[g_{ij,n}^2 g_{jk,n}^2 + g_{ij,n}^2 g_{ik,n}^2\right].$$

Next, observe that Assumption 4.4 and Lemma A.1 parts (f)–(h) imply that $K_n^{-2}\mathcal{T}_1 = o(1)$ and $K_n^{-2}\mathcal{T}_3 = o(1)$. In addition, (26) implies that

$$\frac{1}{K_n^2} \sum_{1\leq i<j<k<l\leq n} [E(g_{ik,n}g_{jk,n}g_{il,n}g_{jl,n}) + E(g_{ij,n}g_{jk,n}g_{il,n}g_{kl,n}) + E(g_{ij,n}g_{ik,n}g_{jl,n}g_{kl,n})] = o(1),$$

and thus $K_n^{-2}\mathcal{T}_2 = o(1)$ given Assumption 4.4. It follows that

$$K_n^{-2}E\left(\zeta_{2n}^2\right) \to 0, \tag{42}$$

$$K_n^{-2}E\left(\zeta_{3n}^2\right) \to 0. \tag{43}$$

The Jensen and Cauchy–Schwartz inequalities then imply that, as $n \to \infty$,

$$K_n^{-2}\left|E(\zeta_{2n}\zeta_{3n})\right| \leq K_n^{-2}E\left|\zeta_{2n}\zeta_{3n}\right| \leq \sqrt{K_n^{-2}E\left(\zeta_{2n}^2\right)}\sqrt{K_n^{-2}E\left(\zeta_{3n}^2\right)} \to 0. \tag{44}$$

$K_n^{-2}E\left(\zeta_{1n}^2\right) \to 0$ then follows as a direct consequence of (42), (43), and (44) in view of eq. (41). ■

Lemma A.5 *Under Assumptions 4.1–4.5,* $b_n^{-1}K_n^{-\frac{1}{2}}c_n'Z_n'M_{X_n}u_n \xrightarrow{p} 0$ *as* $n \to \infty$.

Proof of Lemma A.5: We will show that $b_n^{-1}K_n^{-\frac{1}{2}}c_n'Z_n'M_{X_n}u_n$ goes to zero in a mean-square sense. To proceed, note that Assumptions 4.1–4.5 and the law of iterated expectations imply that

$$E\left[\frac{c_n'Z_n'M_{X_n}u_n}{b_n\sqrt{K_n}}\right] = E_{\overline{Z}_n}\left[\frac{c_n'Z_n'M_{X_n}E(u_n|\overline{Z}_n)}{b_n\sqrt{K_n}}\right] = E_{\overline{Z}_n}\left[\frac{c_n'Z_n'M_{X_n}E(u_n)}{b_n\sqrt{K_n}}\right] = 0 \tag{45}$$

$$\begin{aligned} E\left[\left(\frac{c_n'Z_n'M_{X_n}u_n}{b_n\sqrt{K_n}}\right)^2\right] &= E_{\overline{Z}_n}\left[\frac{c_n'Z_n'M_{X_n}E(u_nu_n'|\overline{Z}_n)M_{X_n}Z_nc_n}{b_n^2K_n}\right] \\ &= E_{\overline{Z}_n}\left[\frac{c_n'Z_n'M_{X_n}E(u_nu_n')M_{X_n}Z_nc_n}{b_n^2K_n}\right] \\ &= \sigma_{uu}\left(\frac{r_n}{K_n}\right)E_{\overline{Z}_n}\left[\frac{c_n'Z_n'M_{X_n}Z_nc_n}{b_n^2r_n}\right] \\ &= O\left(\frac{r_n}{K_n}\right) \\ &= o(1) \end{aligned} \tag{46}$$

given that $\frac{r_n}{K_n} \to 0$ as $n \to \infty$, where the expectation $E_{\overline{Z}_n}\left[\frac{c_n' Z_n' M_{X_n} Z_n c_n}{b_n^2 r_n}\right]$ exists for n sufficiently large in light of Assumptions 4.2. The desired result follows immediately from (45) and (46). ∎

Lemma A.6 (Gänsler and Stute 1977) *Let $\left\{X_{i,n}, \mathcal{F}_{i,n},\ 1 \le i \le l_n, n \ge 1\right\}$ be a square, integrable, martingale difference array. Also, let $l_n \nearrow \infty$ as $n \to \infty$ and suppose that, for all $\varepsilon > 0$,*

$$\sum_{i=1}^{l_n} E\left[X_{i,n}^2 \mathbf{I}\left(\left|X_{i,n}\right| > \varepsilon\right) \mid \mathcal{F}_{i-1,n}\right] \stackrel{P}{\to} 0 \tag{C.1}$$

and

$$\sum_{i=1}^{l_n} E\left[X_{i,n}^2 \mid \mathcal{F}_{i-1,n}\right] \stackrel{P}{\to} 1. \tag{C.2}$$

Then, $\sum_{i=1}^{l_n} X_{i,n} \stackrel{d}{\to} N(0,1)$.

Proof of Lemma A.6: See Gänsler and Stute (1977). ∎

Remark Note that, as discussed in Kelejian and Prucha (2001), a sufficient condition for condition (C.1) is the following:

Condition C.1

$$\sum_{j=1}^{k_n} E\left\{E\left[\left|X_{j,n}\right|^{2+\delta} \mid \mathcal{F}_{j-1,n}\right]\right\} \to 0$$

for some $\delta > 0$.

Because condition C.1′ is easier to verify in our case, in the proofs that follow we will be verifying condition C.1′ instead of condition C.1 for the case $\delta = 2$.

Lemma A.7 *Let W_n be as defined in (20) and let $\sigma_{W_n}^2$ be the variance of W_n with explicit formula given in expression (22). Define*

$$B_n = \sigma_{W_n}^{-1} W_n. \tag{47}$$

Then, under Assumptions 4.2–4.4,

$$B_n \stackrel{d}{\to} N(0,1) \quad \text{as } n \to \infty.$$

Proof of Lemma A.7: The proof of this lemma involves verifying conditions C.1′ and C.2, which jointly imply the central limit theorem given in Lemma A.6. As discussed in the Remark above, we will verify condition C.1′ rather than condition C.1. The proof is thus divided into two parts: In Part I, we check condition C.1′ and, in Part II, we check condition C.2. ■

I. Checking Condition C.1

As in the proof of Lemma A.2, we can write $W_n = \sum_{j=1}^n W_{jn}$, where W_{jn} is as defined in (21). To verify condition C.1′ for $\delta = 2$, we need to show that $\sum_{j=1}^n E\left\{\left(\sigma_{W_n}^{-1} W_{jn}\right)^4\right\} \to 0$ as $n \to \infty$. In light of Lemma A.3 Part (b), this is equivalent to showing that $K_n^{-2} \sum_{j=1}^n E\left(W_{jn}^4\right) \to 0$ as $n \to \infty$. To proceed, note that direct calculation yields the following expression for the fourth moment of W_{jn}

$$E\left(W_{jn}^4\right) = \sum_{i=1}^{8} \mathcal{E}_{ij,n},$$

where

$$\begin{aligned}
\mathcal{E}_{1j,n} &= d_1^4 E\left(g_{jj,n}^4\right) E\left(u_j v_j - \sigma_{uv}\right)^4 \\
&\quad + 6 d_1^2 d_2^2 E\left(g_{jj,n}^4\right) E\left[\left(u_j^2 - \sigma_{uu}\right)^2 \left(u_j v_j - \sigma_{uv}\right)^2\right] \\
&\quad + d_2^4 E\left(g_{jj,n}^4\right) E\left(u_j^2 - \sigma_{uu}\right)^4 \\
&\quad + 4 d_1^3 d_2 E\left(g_{jj,n}^4\right) E\left[\left(u_j v_j - \sigma_{uv}\right)^3 \left(u_j^2 - \sigma_{uu}\right)\right] \\
&\quad + 4 d_1 d_2^3 E\left(g_{jj,n}^4\right) E\left[\left(u_j v_j - \sigma_{uv}\right) \left(u_j^2 - \sigma_{uu}\right)^3\right],
\end{aligned}$$

$$\begin{aligned}
\mathcal{E}_{2j,n} = 4 \Bigg\{ & \sum_{1 \le i < j} d_1^4 E\left(g_{jj,n}^2 g_{ij,n}^2\right) E\left[\left(u_j v_j - \sigma_{uv}\right)^2 \left(v_i u_j + v_j u_i\right)^2\right] \\
& + 4 \sum_{1 \le i < j} d_2^4 E\left(g_{jj,n}^2 g_{ij,n}^2\right) E\left[u_i^2 u_j^2 \left(u_j^2 - \sigma_{uu}\right)^2\right] \\
& + 4 \sum_{1 \le i < j} d_1^2 d_2^2 E\left(g_{jj,n}^2 g_{ij,n}^2\right) E\left[u_i^2 u_j^2 \left(u_j v_j - \sigma_{uv}\right)^2\right] \\
& + \sum_{1 \le i < j} d_1^2 d_2^2 E\left(g_{jj,n}^2 g_{ij,n}^2\right) E\left[\left(u_j^2 - \sigma_{uu}\right)^2 \left(v_i u_j + v_j u_i\right)^2\right] \Bigg\}
\end{aligned}$$

$$\begin{aligned}
\mathcal{E}_{3j,n} = 4 \Bigg\{ & 4 \sum_{1 \le i < j} d_1^2 d_2^2 E\left(g_{jj,n}^2 g_{ij,n}^2\right) E\left[u_i u_j \left(u_j^2 - \sigma_{uu}\right) \left(u_j v_j - \sigma_{uv}\right) \right. \\
& \left. \times \left(v_i u_j + v_j u_i\right)\right] \\
& + 2 \sum_{1 \le i < j} d_1^3 d_2 E\left(g_{jj,n}^2 g_{ij,n}^2\right) E\left[u_i u_j \left(u_j v_j - \sigma_{uv}\right)^2 \left(v_i u_j + v_j u_i\right)\right]
\end{aligned}$$

$$+ \sum_{1\le i<j} d_1^3 d_2 E\left(g_{jj,n}^2 g_{ij,n}^2\right) E\left[\left(u_j^2-\sigma_{uu}\right)\left(u_j v_j-\sigma_{uv}\right)\left(v_i u_j+v_j u_i\right)^2\right]$$
$$+4 \sum_{1\le i<j} d_1 d_2^3 E\left(g_{jj,n}^2 g_{ij,n}^2\right) E\left[u_i^2 u_j^2\left(u_j^2-\sigma_{uu}\right)\left(u_j v_j-\sigma_{uv}\right)\right]$$
$$+2 \sum_{1\le i<j} d_1 d_2^3 E\left(g_{jj,n}^2 g_{ij,n}^2\right) E\left[u_i u_j\left(u_j^2-\sigma_{uu}\right)^2\left(v_i u_j+v_j u_i\right)\right]$$
$$+2 \sum_{1\le i<j} d_1^2 d_2^2 E\left(g_{jj,n}^2 g_{ij,n}^2\right) E\left[u_i u_j\left(u_j v_j-\sigma_{uv}\right)\right.$$
$$\left.\times\left(u_j^2-\sigma_{uu}\right)\left(v_i u_j+v_j u_i\right)\right]\Bigg\}$$

$$\begin{aligned}
\mathcal{E}_{4j,n} = {} & \sum_{1\le i<j} d_1^4 E\left(g_{ij,n}^4\right) E\left[\left(v_i u_j+v_j u_i\right)^4\right] \\
& +96 \sum_{1\le h<i<j} d_2^4 E\left(g_{hj,n}^2 g_{ij,n}^2\right) \sigma_{uu}^2 E\left(u_j^4\right) \\
& +6 \sum_{1\le h<i<j} d_1^4 E\left(g_{hj,n}^2 g_{ij,n}^2\right) E\left[\left(v_h u_j+v_j u_h\right)^2\left(v_i u_j+v_j u_i\right)^2\right] \\
& +16 \sum_{1\le i<j} d_2^4 E\left(g_{ij,n}^4\right) E\left(u_i^4\right) E\left(u_j^4\right) \\
& +16 \sum_{1\le i<j} d_1^2 d_2^2 E\left(g_{ij,n}^4\right) E\left[u_i^2 u_j^2\left(v_i u_j+v_j u_i\right)^2\right] \\
& +32 \sum_{1\le h<i<j} d_1^2 d_2^2 E\left(g_{hj,n}^2 g_{ij,n}^2\right) E\left[u_h u_i u_j^2\left(v_h u_j+v_j u_h\right)\left(v_i u_j+v_j u_i\right)\right] \\
& +16 \sum_{1\le h<i<j} d_1^2 d_2^2 E\left(g_{hj,n}^2 g_{ij,n}^2\right) E\left[u_i^2 u_j^2\left(v_h u_j+v_j u_h\right)^2\right] \\
& +16 \sum_{1\le h<i<j} d_1^2 d_2^2 E\left(g_{hj,n}^2 g_{ij,n}^2\right) E\left[u_h^2 u_j^2\left(v_i u_j+v_j u_i\right)^2\right]
\end{aligned}$$

$$\begin{aligned}
\mathcal{E}_{5j,n} = {} & 8 \sum_{1\le i<j} d_1^2 d_2^2 E\left(g_{ij,n}^4\right) E\left[u_i^2 u_j^2\left(v_i u_j+v_j u_i\right)^2\right] \\
& +8 \sum_{1\le h<i<j} d_1^2 d_2^2 E\left(g_{hj,n}^2 g_{ij,n}^2\right) E\left[u_h^2 u_j^2\left(v_i u_j+v_j u_i\right)^2\right] \\
& +8 \sum_{1\le h<i<j} d_1^2 d_2^2 E\left(g_{hj,n}^2 g_{ij,n}^2\right) E\left[u_i^2 u_j^2\left(v_h u_j+v_j u_h\right)^2\right] \\
& +8 \sum_{1\le i<j} d_1^3 d_2 E\left(g_{ij,n}^4\right) E\left[u_i u_j\left(v_i u_j+v_j u_i\right)^3\right] \\
& +32 \sum_{1\le i<j} d_1 d_2^3 E\left(g_{ij,n}^4\right) E\left[u_i^3 u_j^3\left(v_i u_j+v_j u_i\right)\right]
\end{aligned}$$

$$+8 \sum_{1\leq h<i<j} d_1^3 d_2 E\left(g_{hj,n}^2 g_{ij,n}^2\right) E\left[u_i u_j \left(v_i u_j + v_j u_i\right)\left(v_h u_j + v_j u_h\right)^2\right]$$
$$+8 \sum_{1\leq h<i<j} d_1^3 d_2 E\left(g_{hj,n}^2 g_{ij,n}^2\right) E\left[u_h u_j \left(v_i u_j + v_j u_i\right)^2\left(v_h u_j + v_j u_h\right)\right]$$
$$+96 \sum_{1\leq h<i<j} d_1 d_2^3 E\left(g_{hj,n}^2 g_{ij,n}^2\right) E\left[u_h u_i^2 u_j^3 \left(v_h u_j + v_j u_h\right)\right]$$
$$+96 \sum_{1\leq h<i<j} d_1 d_2^3 E\left(g_{hj,n}^2 g_{ij,n}^2\right) E\left[u_h^2 u_i u_j^3 \left(v_i u_j + v_j u_i\right)\right]$$
$$+32 \sum_{1\leq h<i<j} d_1^2 d_2^2 E\left(g_{hj,n}^2 g_{ij,n}^2\right) E\left[u_j^2 u_i \left(v_i u_j + v_j u_i\right) u_h \left(v_h u_j + v_j u_h\right)\right]$$
$$+16 \sum_{1\leq h<i<j} d_1^3 d_2 E\left(g_{hj,n}^2 g_{ij,n}^2\right) E\left[u_i u_j \left(v_i u_j + v_j u_i\right)\left(v_h u_j + v_j u_h\right)^2\right]$$
$$+16 \sum_{1\leq h<i<j} d_1^3 d_2 E\left(g_{hj,n}^2 g_{ij,n}^2\right) E\left[u_h u_j \left(v_i u_j + v_j u_i\right)^2\left(v_h u_j + v_j u_h\right)\right]$$
$$+32 \sum_{1\leq h<i<j} d_1^2 d_2^2 E\left(g_{hj,n}^2 g_{ij,n}^2\right) E\left[u_h u_i u_j^2 \left(v_i u_j + v_j u_i\right)\left(v_h u_j + v_j u_h\right)\right]$$

$$\begin{aligned}\mathcal{E}_{6j,n} = 2\Bigg\{ &\sum_{1\leq i<j} d_1^4 E\left(g_{jj,n}^2 g_{ij,n}^2\right) E\left[\left(u_j v_j - \sigma_{uv}\right)^2 \left(v_i u_j + v_j u_i\right)^2\right] \\ &+ \sum_{1\leq i<j} d_1^2 d_2^2 E\left(g_{jj,n}^2 g_{ij,n}^2\right) E\left[\left(u_j^2 - \sigma_{uu}\right)^2 \left(v_i u_j + v_j u_i\right)^2\right] \\ &+2 \sum_{1\leq i<j} d_1^3 d_2 E\left(g_{jj,n}^2 g_{ij,n}^2\right) E\left[\left(u_j v_j - \sigma_{uv}\right)\left(u_j^2 - \sigma_{uu}\right)\left(v_i u_j + v_j u_i\right)^2\right]\Bigg\}\end{aligned}$$

$$\begin{aligned}\mathcal{E}_{7j,n} = 8\Bigg\{ &\sum_{1\leq i<j} d_2^4 E\left(g_{jj,n}^2 g_{ij,n}^2\right) \sigma_{uu} E\left[u_j^2 \left(u_j^2 - \sigma_{uu}\right)^2\right] \\ &+ \sum_{1\leq i<j} d_1^2 d_2^2 E\left(g_{jj,n}^2 g_{ij,n}^2\right) \sigma_{uu} E\left[u_j^2 \left(u_j v_j - \sigma_{uv}\right)^2\right] \\ &+ 2 \sum_{1\leq i<j} d_1 d_2^3 E\left(g_{jj,n}^2 g_{ij,n}^2\right) \sigma_{uu} E\left[u_j^2 \left(u_j v_j - \sigma_{uv}\right)\left(u_j^2 - \sigma_{uu}\right)\right]\Bigg\}\end{aligned}$$

$$\begin{aligned}\mathcal{E}_{8j,n} = 8\Bigg\{ &\sum_{1\leq i<j} d_1^3 d_2 E\left(g_{jj,n}^2 g_{ij,n}^2\right) E\left[u_i u_j \left(u_j v_j - \sigma_{uv}\right)^2 \left(v_i u_j + v_j u_i\right)\right] \\ &+ \sum_{1\leq i<j} d_1 d_2^3 E\left(g_{jj,n}^2 g_{ij,n}^2\right) E\left[u_i u_j \left(u_j^2 - \sigma_{uu}\right)^2 \left(v_i u_j + v_j u_i\right)\right]\end{aligned}$$

$$+ 2 \sum_{1 \leq i < j} d_1^2 d_2^2 E\left(g_{jj,n}^2 g_{ij,n}^2\right) E\left[u_i u_j \left(u_j v_j - \sigma_{uv}\right)\right.$$

$$\left.\left. \times \left(u_j^2 - \sigma_{uu}\right)\left(v_i u_j + v_j u_i\right)\right]\right\}.$$

Now, making use of Lemma A.1 and Assumptions 4.3 and 4.4, we see that

$$\frac{1}{K_n^2}\sum_{j=1}^{n}\left|\mathcal{E}_{1j,n}\right| \leq 14 D_\eta \frac{1}{K_n^2}\sum_{j=1}^{n} E\left(g_{jj,n}^4\right) = o(1), \tag{48}$$

$$\frac{1}{K_n^2}\sum_{j=1}^{n}\left|\mathcal{E}_{2j,n}\right| \leq 16\sqrt{14} D_\eta \left(d_1^4 + d_2^4 + 2d_1^2 d_2^2\right) \frac{1}{K_n^2}\sum_{1 \leq i < j \leq n} E\left(g_{jj,n}^2 g_{ij,n}^2\right) = o(1), \tag{49}$$

$$\begin{aligned}\frac{1}{K_n^2}\sum_{j=1}^{n}\left|\mathcal{E}_{3j,n}\right| \leq\ & 16\sqrt{14} D_\eta \left(3d_1^2 d_2^2 + 2d_1^3 d_2 + d_1 d_2^3\right) \frac{1}{K_n^2}\sum_{1 \leq i < j \leq n} E\left(g_{jj,n}^2 g_{ij,n}^2\right) \\ & + 16\sqrt{2}\,(14)^{\frac{1}{4}}\, D_\eta^{\frac{7}{8}} d_1 d_2^3 \frac{1}{K_n^2}\sum_{1 \leq i < j \leq n} E\left(g_{jj,n}^2 g_{ij,n}^2\right) \\ =\ & o(1),\end{aligned} \tag{50}$$

$$\begin{aligned}\frac{1}{K_n^2}\sum_{j=1}^{n}\left|\mathcal{E}_{4j,n}\right| \leq\ & 16 D_\eta \left(d_1^4 + d_2^4 + 4d_1^2 d_2^2\right) \frac{1}{K_n^2}\sum_{1 \leq i < j \leq n} E\left(g_{ij,n}^4\right) \\ & + 32 D_\eta \left(3d_1^4 + 3d_2^4 + 8d_1^2 d_2^2\right) \frac{1}{K_n^2}\sum_{1 \leq h < i < j \leq n} E\left(g_{hj,n}^2 g_{ij,n}^2\right) \\ =\ & o(1),\end{aligned} \tag{51}$$

$$\begin{aligned}\frac{1}{K_n^2}\sum_{j=1}^{n}\left|\mathcal{E}_{5j,n}\right| \leq\ & 32 D_\eta \left(d_1^2 d_2^2 + 2d_1^3 d_2 + 2d_1 d_2^3\right) \frac{1}{K_n^2}\sum_{1 \leq i < j \leq n} E\left(g_{ij,n}^4\right) \\ & + 64 D_\eta \left(5d_1^2 d_2^2 + 6d_1^3 d_2 + 3d_1 d_2^3\right) \frac{1}{K_n^2}\sum_{1 \leq h < i < j \leq n} E\left(g_{hj,n}^2 g_{ij,n}^2\right) \\ =\ & o(1),\end{aligned} \tag{52}$$

$$\frac{1}{K_n^2}\sum_{j=1}^{n}\left|\mathcal{E}_{6j,n}\right| \leq 8\sqrt{14} D_\eta \left(d_1^4 + d_1^2 d_2^2 + 2d_1^3 d_2\right) \frac{1}{K_n^2}\sum_{1 \leq i < j \leq n} E\left(g_{jj,n}^2 g_{ij,n}^2\right) = o(1), \tag{53}$$

$$\frac{1}{K_n^2}\sum_{j=1}^{n}\left|\mathcal{E}_{7j,n}\right| \leq 8D_\eta\left(\sqrt{14}d_2^4+\sqrt{14}d_1^2d_2^2+4d_1d_2^3\right)\frac{1}{K_n^2}\sum_{1\leq i<j\leq n}E\left(g_{jj,n}^2g_{ij,n}^2\right)$$
$$= o(1), \tag{54}$$

$$\frac{1}{K_n^2}\sum_{j=1}^{n}\left|\mathcal{E}_{8j,n}\right| \leq 16\sqrt{14}D_\eta\left(d_1^3d_2+d_1d_2^3+2d_1^2d_2^2\right)\frac{1}{K_n^2}\sum_{1\leq i<j\leq n}E\left(g_{jj,n}^2g_{ij,n}^2\right)$$
$$= o(1), \tag{55}$$

where the inequalities in expressions (48)–(55) are obtained by repeated applications of the Cauchy–Schwartz and the triangle inequalities. From expressions (48)–(55), it follows immediately that

$$\frac{1}{K_n^2}\sum_{j=1}^{n}E\left(W_{jn}^4\right) \leq \sum_{i=1}^{8}\left(\frac{1}{K_n^2}\sum_{j=1}^{n}\left|\mathcal{E}_{ij,n}\right|\right).$$
$$= o(1) \text{ as } n\to\infty. \tag{56}$$

II. Checking Condition C.2

First define

$$B_{jn} = \sigma_{W_n}^{-1}W_{jn},$$

where W_{jn} and $\sigma_{W_n}^2$ are as defined in expressions (21) and (22), respectively. Now, consider the σ-fields $\mathcal{F}_{j,n} = \sigma\left(\eta_1,\ldots,\eta_j,\overline{Z}_n\right), i = 1,\ldots,n$ and take $\mathcal{F}_{0,n}$ to be the trivial σ-field. It follows by construction that $\mathcal{F}_{j-1,n}\subseteq\mathcal{F}_{j,n}$. Moreover, note that W_{jn} is $\mathcal{F}_{j,n}$-measurable and straightforward calculation shows that $E\left(W_{jn}\mid\mathcal{F}_{j-1,n}\right)=0$; thus, $\left\{W_{jn},\mathcal{F}_{j,n},1\leq j\leq n,n\geq 1\right\}$ forms a martingale difference array.

Hence, to verify Condition C.2, we need to show

$$\sum_{j=1}^{n}E\left[B_{j,n}^2\mid\mathcal{F}_{j-1,n}\right]\xrightarrow{P}1,\quad \text{as } n\to\infty, \tag{57}$$

or, alternatively,

$$\sum_{j=1}^{n}\left(\frac{E\left[W_{j,n}^2\mid\mathcal{F}_{j-1,n}\right]-E\left[W_{j,n}^2\right]}{\sigma_{W_n}^2}\right)\xrightarrow{P}0,\quad \text{as } n\to\infty. \tag{58}$$

Expression (58), in turn, is implied by

$$\frac{1}{K_n^2}E\left(\sum_{j=1}^{n}\left\{E\left[W_{j,n}^2\mid\mathcal{F}_{j-1,n}\right]-E\left[W_{j,n}^2\right]\right\}\right)^2\to 0,\quad \text{as } n\to\infty \tag{59}$$

in light of the result we obtained in part (b) of Lemma A.3. To show (59), we proceed by noting that

$$\begin{aligned}
&\sum_{j=1}^{n}\left(E\left[W_{j,n}^2 \mid \mathcal{F}_{j-1,n}\right]-E\left[W_{j,n}^2\right]\right)\\
&\quad=\sum_{1\le i<j\le n} d_1^2\left[\sigma_{uu}\left(g_{ij,n}^2 v_i^2-E\left(g_{ij,n}^2\right)\sigma_{vv}\right)+2\sigma_{uv}\left(g_{ij,n}^2 u_i v_i-E\left(g_{ij,n}^2\right)\sigma_{uv}\right)\right.\\
&\qquad\left.+\sigma_{vv}\left(g_{ij,n}^2 u_i^2-E\left(g_{ij,n}^2\right)\sigma_{uu}\right)\right]+4\sum_{1\le i<j\le n} d_2^2\sigma_{uu}\left(g_{ij,n}^2 u_i^2-E\left(g_{ij,n}^2\right)\sigma_{uu}\right)\\
&\qquad+2\sum_{1\le h<i<j\le n} d_1^2 g_{hj,n}g_{ij,n}\left[\sigma_{uu}v_h v_i+\sigma_{uv}u_h v_i+\sigma_{uv}u_i v_h+\sigma_{vv}u_h u_i\right]\\
&\qquad+8\sum_{1\le h<i<j\le n} d_2^2 g_{hj,n}g_{ij,n}\sigma_{uu}u_h u_i\\
&\qquad+4\sum_{1\le i<j\le n} d_1 d_2\left[\sigma_{uu}\left(g_{ij,n}^2 u_i v_i-E\left(g_{ij,n}^2\right)\sigma_{uv}\right)\right.\\
&\qquad\left.+\sigma_{uv}\left(g_{ij,n}^2 u_i^2-E\left(g_{ij,n}^2\right)\sigma_{uu}\right)\right]\\
&\qquad+4\sum_{1\le h<i<j\le n} d_1 d_2 g_{hj,n}g_{ij,n}\left[\sigma_{uu}v_h u_i+\sigma_{uv}u_h u_i\right]\\
&\qquad+4\sum_{1\le h<i<j\le n} d_1 d_2 g_{hj,n}g_{ij,n}\left[\sigma_{uu}u_h v_i+\sigma_{uv}u_h u_i\right]
\end{aligned}$$

Further calculations yield

$$\frac{1}{K_n^2}E\left(\sum_{j=1}^{n}\left\{E\left[W_{j,n}^2 \mid \mathcal{F}_{j-1,n}\right]-E\left[W_{j,n}^2\right]\right\}\right)^2=\frac{1}{K_n^2}\sum_{i=1}^{4}\mathcal{A}_{i,n},$$

where

$$\begin{aligned}
\mathcal{A}_{1,n}=&\sum_{1\le i<j\le n} d_1^4 E\left(g_{ij,n}^4\right)\left[\sigma_{uu}^2 E\left(v_i^4\right)+4\sigma_{uv}^2 E\left(u_i^2 v_i^2\right)+\sigma_{vv}^2 E\left(u_i^4\right)\right.\\
&\left.+4\sigma_{uu}\sigma_{uv}E\left(u_i v_i^3\right)+2\sigma_{uu}\sigma_{vv}E\left(u_i^2 v_i^2\right)+4\sigma_{vv}\sigma_{uv}E\left(u_i^3 v_i\right)\right]\\
&-4\sum_{1\le i<j\le n} d_1^4\left(E\left(g_{ij,n}^2\right)\right)^2\left[\sigma_{uu}^2\sigma_{vv}^2+\sigma_{uv}^4+2\sigma_{uu}\sigma_{vv}\sigma_{uv}^2\right]\\
&+16\sum_{1\le i<j\le n} d_2^4\left[E\left(g_{ij,n}^4\right)\sigma_{uu}^2 E\left(u_i^4\right)-\left(E\left(g_{ij,n}^2\right)\right)^2\sigma_{uu}^4\right]\\
&+8\sum_{1\le h<i<j\le n} d_1^4 E\left(g_{hj,n}^2 g_{ij,n}^2\right)\left[\sigma_{uu}^2\sigma_{vv}^2+6\sigma_{uv}^2\sigma_{uu}\sigma_{vv}+\sigma_{uv}^4\right]\\
&+64\sum_{1\le h<i<j\le n} d_2^4 E\left(g_{hj,n}^2 g_{ij,n}^2\right)\sigma_{uu}^4\\
&+16\sum_{1\le i<j\le n} d_1^2 d_2^2 E\left(g_{ij,n}^4\right)\left[\sigma_{uu}^2 E\left(u_i^2 v_i^2\right)\right.
\end{aligned}$$

$$+ \sigma_{uv}^2 E\left(u_i^4\right) + 2\sigma_{uu}\sigma_{uv} E\left(u_i^3 v_i\right)\Big] - 64 \sum_{1\le i<j\le n} d_1^2 d_2^2 \left(E\left(g_{ij,n}^2\right)\right)^2 \sigma_{uu}^2 \sigma_{uv}^2$$

$$+ 32 \sum_{1\le h<i<j\le n} d_1^2 d_2^2 E\left(g_{hj,n}^2 g_{ij,n}^2\right)\left[\sigma_{uu}^3\sigma_{vv} + 3\sigma_{uu}^2\sigma_{uv}^2\right]$$

$$\mathcal{A}_{2,n} = 2\Bigg\{ \sum_{1\le i<j<k\le n} d_1^4 E\left(g_{ij,n}^2 g_{ik,n}^2\right)\Big[\sigma_{uu}^2 E\left(v_i^4\right) + 4\sigma_{uv}^2 E\left(u_i^2 v_i^2\right) + \sigma_{vv}^2 E\left(u_i^4\right)$$

$$+ 4\sigma_{uu}\sigma_{uv} E\left(u_i v_i^3\right) + 2\sigma_{uu}\sigma_{vv} E\left(u_i^2 v_i^2\right) + 4\sigma_{vv}\sigma_{uv} E\left(u_i^3 v_i\right)\Big]\Big\}$$

$$- 4 \sum_{1\le i<j<k\le n} d_1^4 E\left(g_{ij,n}^2\right) E\left(g_{ik,n}^2\right)\left[\sigma_{uu}^2\sigma_{vv}^2 + \sigma_{uv}^4 + 2\sigma_{uu}\sigma_{vv}\sigma_{uv}^2\right]$$

$$+ 16 \sum_{1\le i<j<k\le n} d_2^4\left[E\left(g_{ij,n}^2 g_{ik,n}^2\right)\sigma_{uu}^2 E\left(u_i^4\right) - E\left(g_{ij,n}^2\right) E\left(g_{ik,n}^2\right)\sigma_{uu}^4\right]$$

$$+ 8 \sum_{1\le h<i<j<k\le n} d_1^4 E\left(g_{hj,n} g_{ij,n} g_{hk,n} g_{ik,n}\right)\left[\sigma_{uu}^2\sigma_{vv}^2 + 6\sigma_{uv}^2\sigma_{uu}\sigma_{vv} + \sigma_{uv}^4\right]$$

$$+ 64 \sum_{1\le h<i<j<k\le n} d_2^4 E\left(g_{hj,n} g_{ij,n} g_{hk,n} g_{ik,n}\right)\sigma_{uu}^4$$

$$+ 16 \sum_{1\le i<j<k\le n} d_1^2 d_2^2 E\left(g_{ij,n}^2 g_{ik,n}^2\right)\Big[\sigma_{uu}^2 E\left(u_i^2 v_i^2\right) + \sigma_{uv}^2 E\left(u_i^4\right)$$

$$+ 2\sigma_{uu}\sigma_{uv} E\left(u_i^3 v_i\right)\Big] - 64 \sum_{1\le i<j<k\le n} d_1^2 d_2^2 E\left(g_{ij,n}^2\right) E\left(g_{ik,n}^2\right)\sigma_{uu}^2\sigma_{uv}^2$$

$$+ 32 \sum_{1\le h<i<j<k\le n} d_1^2 d_2^2 E\left(g_{hj,n} g_{ij,n} g_{hk,n} g_{ik,n}\right)\left[\sigma_{uu}^3\sigma_{vv} + 3\sigma_{uu}^2\sigma_{uv}^2\right]\Bigg\}$$

$$\mathcal{A}_{3,n} = 2\Bigg\{ \sum_{1\le i<j\le n} d_1^2 d_2^2 E\left(g_{ij,n}^4\right)\Big[\sigma_{uu}^2 E\left(u_i^2 v_i^2\right) + 2\sigma_{uu}\sigma_{uv} E\left(u_i^3 v_i\right)$$

$$+ \sigma_{uu}\sigma_{vv} E\left(u_i^4\right)\Big] - 2 \sum_{1\le i<j\le n} d_1^2 d_2^2 \left(E\left(g_{ij,n}^2\right)\right)^2\left[\sigma_{uu}^3\sigma_{vv} + \sigma_{uu}^2\sigma_{uv}^2\right]$$

$$+ 4 \sum_{1\le i<j\le n} d_1^3 d_2 E\left(g_{ij,n}^4\right)\Big[\sigma_{uu}^2 E\left(u_i v_i^3\right) + 3\sigma_{uu}\sigma_{uv} E\left(u_i^2 v_i^2\right)$$

$$+ 2\sigma_{uv}^2 E\left(u_i^3 v_i\right) + \sigma_{uu}\sigma_{vv} E\left(u_i^3 v_i\right) + \sigma_{vv}\sigma_{uv} E\left(u_i^4\right)\Big]$$

$$- 16 \sum_{1\le i<j\le n} d_1^3 d_2 \left(E\left(g_{ij,n}^2\right)\right)^2\left[\sigma_{uu}^2\sigma_{vv}\sigma_{uv} + \sigma_{uu}\sigma_{uv}^3\right]$$

$$+ 16 \sum_{1\le i<j\le n} d_1 d_2^3 E\left(g_{ij,n}^4\right)\left[\sigma_{uu}^2 E\left(u_i^3 v_i\right) + \sigma_{uu}\sigma_{uv} E\left(u_i^4\right)\right]$$

$$- 32 \sum_{1\le i<j\le n} d_1 d_2^3 \left(E\left(g_{ij,n}^2\right)\right)^2 \sigma_{uu}^3\sigma_{uv}$$

$$+ 16 \sum_{1\le h<i<j\le n} d_1^2 d_2^2 E\left(g_{hj,n}^2 g_{ij,n}^2\right)\left[3\sigma_{uu}^2\sigma_{uv}^2 + \sigma_{uu}^3\sigma_{vv}\right]$$

$$+ 64 \sum_{1 \le h < i < j \le n} d_1^3 d_2 E\left(g_{hj,n}^2 g_{ij,n}^2\right)\left[\sigma_{uu}^2 \sigma_{vv} \sigma_{uv} + \sigma_{uu} \sigma_{uv}^3\right]$$
$$+ 128 \sum_{1 \le h < i < j \le n} d_1 d_2^3 E\left(g_{hj,n}^2 g_{ij,n}^2\right) \sigma_{uu}^3 \sigma_{uv}$$
$$\left. + 64 \sum_{1 \le h < i < j \le n} d_1 d_2^3 E\left(g_{hj,n}^2 g_{ij,n}^2\right) \sigma_{uu}^2 \sigma_{uv}^2 \right\}$$

$$\mathcal{A}_{4,n} = 4 \left\{ \sum_{1 \le i < j < k \le n} d_1^2 d_2^2 E\left(g_{ij,n}^2 g_{ik,n}^2\right)\left[\sigma_{uu}^2 E\left(u_i^2 v_i^2\right)\right.\right.$$
$$\left. + 2\sigma_{uu}\sigma_{uv} E\left(u_i^3 v_i\right) + \sigma_{uu}\sigma_{vv} E\left(u_i^4\right)\right]$$
$$- 2 \sum_{1 \le i < j < k \le n} d_1^2 d_2^2 E\left(g_{ij,n}^2\right) E\left(g_{ik,n}^2\right)\left[\sigma_{uu}^3 \sigma_{vv} + \sigma_{uu}^2 \sigma_{uv}^2\right]$$
$$+ 4 \sum_{1 \le i < j < k \le n} d_1^3 d_2 E\left(g_{ij,n}^2 g_{ik,n}^2\right)\left[\sigma_{uu}^2 E\left(u_i v_i^3\right) + 3\sigma_{uu}\sigma_{uv} E\left(u_i^2 v_i^2\right)\right.$$
$$\left. + 2\sigma_{uv}^2 E\left(u_i^3 v_i\right) + \sigma_{uu}\sigma_{vv} E\left(u_i^3 v_i\right) + \sigma_{vv}\sigma_{uv} E\left(u_i^4\right)\right]$$
$$- 16 \sum_{1 \le i < j < k \le n} d_1^3 d_2 E\left(g_{ij,n}^2\right) E\left(g_{ik,n}^2\right)\left[\sigma_{uu}^2 \sigma_{vv} \sigma_{uv} + \sigma_{uu} \sigma_{uv}^3\right]$$
$$+ 16 \sum_{1 \le i < j < k \le n} d_1 d_2^3 E\left(g_{ij,n}^2 g_{ik,n}^2\right)\left[\sigma_{uu}^2 E\left(u_i^3 v_i\right) + \sigma_{uu}\sigma_{uv} E\left(u_i^4\right)\right]$$
$$- 32 \sum_{1 \le i < j < k \le n} d_1 d_2^3 E\left(g_{ij,n}^2\right) E\left(g_{ik,n}^2\right) \sigma_{uu}^2 \sigma_{uu} \sigma_{uv}$$
$$+ 16 \sum_{1 \le h < i < j < k \le n} d_1^2 d_2^2 E\left(g_{hj,n} g_{ij,n} g_{hk,n} g_{ik,n}\right)\left[3\sigma_{uu}^2 \sigma_{uv}^2 + \sigma_{uu}^3 \sigma_{vv}\right]$$
$$+ 64 \sum_{1 \le h < i < j < k \le n} d_1^3 d_2 E\left(g_{hj,n} g_{ij,n} g_{hk,n} g_{ik,n}\right)\left[\sigma_{uu}^2 \sigma_{vv} \sigma_{uv} + \sigma_{uu} \sigma_{uv}^3\right]$$
$$+ 128 \sum_{1 \le h < i < j < k \le n} d_1 d_2^3 E\left(g_{hj,n} g_{ij,n} g_{hk,n} g_{ik,n}\right) \sigma_{uu}^3 \sigma_{uv}$$
$$\left. + 64 \sum_{1 \le h < i < j < k \le n} d_1 d_2^3 E\left(g_{hj,n} g_{ij,n} g_{hk,n} g_{ik,n}\right) \sigma_{uu}^2 \sigma_{uv}^2 \right\}.$$

Again, making use of Lemma A.1 and Assumptions 4.3 and 4.4, we see that

$$\frac{1}{K_n^2}\left|\mathcal{A}_{1,n}\right| \le 16\left(d_1^4 + d_2^4 + 4d_1^2 d_2^2\right) D_\eta \frac{1}{K_n^2} \sum_{1 \le i < j \le n} E\left(g_{ij,n}^4\right)$$
$$+ 16\left(d_1^4 + d_2^4 + 4d_1^2 d_2^2\right) D_\eta \frac{1}{K_n^2} \sum_{1 \le i < j \le n} \left(E\left(g_{ij,n}^2\right)\right)^2$$
$$+ 64\left(d_1^4 + d_2^4 + 2d_1^2 d_2^2\right) D_\eta \frac{1}{K_n^2} \sum_{1 \le h < i < j \le n} E\left(g_{hj,n}^2 g_{ij,n}^2\right)$$
$$= O\left(K_n^{-1}\right) = o(1), \tag{60}$$

$$
\begin{aligned}
&\frac{1}{K_n^2}\left|\mathcal{A}_{2,n}\right| \\
&\quad \leq 32\left(d_1^4+d_2^4+4d_1^2d_2^2\right)D_\eta\frac{1}{K_n^2}\sum_{1\leq i<j<k\leq n}E\left(g_{ij,n}^2g_{ik,n}^2\right) \\
&\qquad +32\left(d_1^4+d_2^4+4d_1^2d_2^2\right)D_\eta\frac{1}{K_n^2}\sum_{1\leq i<j<k\leq n}E\left(g_{ij,n}^2\right)E\left(g_{ik,n}^2\right) \\
&\qquad +128\left(d_1^4+d_2^4+2d_1^2d_2^2\right)D_\eta\frac{1}{K_n^2}\sum_{1\leq h<i<j<k\leq n}E\left(g_{hj,n}g_{ij,n}g_{hk,n}g_{ik,n}\right) \\
&\quad = o(1), \qquad (61)
\end{aligned}
$$

$$
\begin{aligned}
\frac{1}{K_n^2}\left|\mathcal{A}_{3,n}\right| &\leq 8\left(d_1^2d_2^2+8d_1^3d_2+8d_1d_2^3\right)D_\eta\frac{1}{K_n^2}\sum_{1\leq i<j\leq n}E\left(g_{ij,n}^4\right) \\
&\quad +8\left(d_1^2d_2^2+8d_1^3d_2+8d_1d_2^3\right)D_\eta\frac{1}{K_n^2}\sum_{1\leq i<j\leq n}\left(E\left(g_{ij,n}^2\right)\right)^2 \\
&\quad +128\left(d_1^2d_2^2+2d_1^3d_2+3d_1d_2^3\right)D_\eta\frac{1}{K_n^2}\sum_{1\leq h<i<j\leq n}E\left(g_{hj,n}^2g_{ij,n}^2\right) \\
&= O\left(K_n^{-1}\right)=o(1), \qquad (62)
\end{aligned}
$$

$$
\begin{aligned}
&\frac{1}{K_n^2}\left|\mathcal{A}_{4,n}\right| \\
&\leq 16\left(d_1^2d_2^2+8d_1^3d_2+8d_1d_2^3\right)D_\eta\frac{1}{K_n^2}\sum_{1\leq i<j<k\leq n}E\left(g_{ij,n}^2g_{ik,n}^2\right) \\
&\quad +16\left(d_1^2d_2^2+8d_1^3d_2+8d_1d_2^3\right)D_\eta\frac{1}{K_n^2}\sum_{1\leq i<j<k\leq n}E\left(g_{ij,n}^2\right)E\left(g_{ik,n}^2\right) \\
&\quad +256\left(d_1^2d_2^2+2d_1^3d_2+3d_1d_2^3\right)D_\eta\frac{1}{K_n^2}\sum_{1\leq h<i<j<k\leq n}E\left(g_{hj,n}g_{ij,n}g_{hk,n}g_{ik,n}\right) \\
&= o(1), \qquad (63)
\end{aligned}
$$

where the inequalities in expressions (60)–(63) have been obtained by repeated applications of the Cauchy–Schwartz and the triangle inequalities. Then (59) follows directly from expressions (60)–(63). ■

Lemma A.8 *Under assumptions, let $\widehat{\lambda}_{\mathrm{LIML},n}$ be the smallest root of the determinantal equation given by (8). Then, under Assumptions 4.1–4.5,*

$$
\widehat{\lambda}_{\mathrm{LIML},n}=\frac{n-J}{n-K_n-J}+\left(\frac{\sqrt{K_n}}{n-K_n-J}\right)\frac{s_{uu}^G}{\sigma_{uu}}+o_p\left(\frac{\sqrt{K_n}}{n-K_n-J}\right),
$$

where $s_{uu}^G=\frac{u_n'G_nu_n}{\sqrt{K_n}}$ and G_n is defined in (17) above.

Proof of Lemma A.8: To proceed, note first that, by definition, $\widehat{\lambda}_{\text{LIML},n}$ is the smallest root of the determinantal equation

$$\det\left\{\begin{pmatrix} y_{1n}'M_{X_n}y_{1n} & y_{1n}'M_{X_n}y_{2n} \\ y_{2n}'M_{X_n}y_{1n} & y_{2n}'M_{X_n}y_{2n}\end{pmatrix} - \lambda_n\begin{pmatrix} y_{1n}'M_{\overline{Z}_n}y_{1n} & y_{1n}'M_{\overline{Z}_n}y_{2n} \\ y_{2n}'M_{\overline{Z}_n}y_{1n} & y_{2n}'M_{\overline{Z}_n}y_{2n}\end{pmatrix}\right\} = 0 \quad (64)$$

or, in more succinct notation,

$$\det\left\{Y_n'M_{X_n}Y_n - \lambda_n Y_n'M_{\overline{Z}_n}Y_n\right\} = 0, \quad (65)$$

where $Y_n = [y_{1n}, y_{2n}]$ and where the elements of the determinantal equation are all well defined with probability one for n sufficiently large as a consequence of Assumption 4.2. Now, define $\Upsilon = \begin{pmatrix} 1 & 0 \\ -\beta_0 & 1\end{pmatrix}$ and note that the smallest root of eq. (64) is the same as the smallest root of the equation

$$\det\left\{\Upsilon'Y_n'M_{X_n}Y_n\Upsilon - \lambda_n\Upsilon'Y_n'M_{\overline{Z}_n}Y_n\Upsilon\right\} = 0, \quad (66)$$

where

$$\begin{aligned}\Upsilon'Y_n'M_{X_n}Y_n\Upsilon &= \begin{pmatrix} 1 & -\beta_0 \\ 0 & 1\end{pmatrix}\begin{pmatrix} y_{1n}'M_{X_n}y_{1n} & y_{1n}'M_{X_n}y_{2n} \\ y_{2n}'M_{X_n}y_{1n} & y_{2n}'M_{X_n}y_{2n}\end{pmatrix}\begin{pmatrix} 1 & 0 \\ -\beta_0 & 1\end{pmatrix} \\ &= \begin{pmatrix} u_n'M_{X_n}u_n & u_n'M_{X_n}y_{2n} \\ y_{2n}'M_{X_n}u_n & y_{2n}'M_{X_n}y_{2n}\end{pmatrix} \end{aligned} \quad (67)$$

and

$$\Upsilon'Y_n'M_{\overline{Z}_n}Y_n\Upsilon = \begin{pmatrix} u_n'M_{\overline{Z}_n}u_n & u_n'M_{\overline{Z}_n}v_n \\ v_n'M_{\overline{Z}_n}u_n & v_n'M_{\overline{Z}_n}v_n\end{pmatrix}. \quad (68)$$

Now, let $\lambda_n = \frac{n-J}{n-K_n-J} + \frac{\tau_n r_n}{n-K_n-J}$ and rewrite (66) as

$$\begin{aligned}\det&\left\{\begin{pmatrix} u_n'M_{X_n}u_n & u_n'M_{X_n}y_{2n} \\ y_{2n}'M_{X_n}u_n & y_{2n}'M_{X_n}y_{2n}\end{pmatrix} - \left(\frac{n-J}{n-K_n-J}\right)\begin{pmatrix} u_n'M_{\overline{Z}_n}u_n & u_n'M_{\overline{Z}_n}v_n \\ v_n'M_{\overline{Z}_n}u_n & v_n'M_{\overline{Z}_n}v_n\end{pmatrix}\right. \\ &\left. - \tau_n\begin{pmatrix} \frac{r_n u_n'M_{\overline{Z}_n}u_n}{n-K_n-J} & \frac{r_n u_n'M_{\overline{Z}_n}v_n}{n-K_n-J} \\ \frac{r_n v_n'M_{\overline{Z}_n}u_n}{n-K_n-J} & \frac{r_n v_n'M_{\overline{Z}_n}v_n}{n-K_n-J}\end{pmatrix}\right\} = 0, \end{aligned} \quad (69)$$

which, in turn, can be shown, by straightforward manipulation, to be equivalent to the determinantal equation

$$\begin{aligned}\det&\left\{\begin{pmatrix} u_n'G_nu_n & \frac{u_n'M_{X_n}Z_nc_n}{b_n} + u_n'G_nv_n \\ \frac{c_n'Z_n'M_{X_n}u_n}{b_n} + v_n'G_nu_n & \frac{c_n'Z_n'M_{X_n}Z_nc_n}{b_n^2} + \frac{c_n'Z_n'M_{X_n}v_n}{b_n} + \frac{v_n'M_{X_n}Z_nc_n}{b_n} + v_n'G_nv_n\end{pmatrix}\right. \\ &\left. - \tau_n\begin{pmatrix} \frac{r_n u_n'M_{\overline{Z}_n}u_n}{n-K_n-J} & \frac{r_n u_n'M_{\overline{Z}_n}v_n}{n-K_n-J} \\ \frac{r_n v_n'M_{\overline{Z}_n}u_n}{n-K_n-J} & \frac{r_n v_n'M_{\overline{Z}_n}v_n}{n-K_n-J}\end{pmatrix}\right\} = 0. \end{aligned} \quad (70)$$

Moreover, it is apparent that $\widehat{\lambda}_{\text{LIML},n}$, the smallest root of eq. (64), is related to $\widehat{\tau}_{\text{LIML},n}$, the smallest root of (70), by the equation

$$\widehat{\lambda}_{\text{LIML},n} = \frac{n-J}{n-K_n-J} + \frac{\widehat{\tau}_{\text{LIML},n} r_n}{n-K_n-J}. \tag{71}$$

Furthermore, note that $\widehat{\tau}_{\text{LIML},n}$ is also the smallest root of the determinantal equation

$$\det\left\{\begin{pmatrix} \frac{u_n' G_n u_n}{r_n} & \frac{u_n' M_{X_n} Z_n c_n}{b_n r_n} + \frac{u_n' G_n v_n}{r_n} \\ \frac{c_n' Z_n' M_{X_n} u_n}{b_n r_n} + \frac{v_n' G_n u_n}{r_n} & \frac{c_n' Z_n' M_{X_n} Z_n c_n}{b_n^2 r_n} + \frac{c_n' Z_n' M_{X_n} v_n}{b_n r_n} + \frac{v_n' M_{X_n} Z_n c_n}{b_n r_n} + \frac{v_n' G_n v_n}{r_n} \end{pmatrix} \right.$$
$$\left. - \tau_n \begin{pmatrix} \frac{u_n' M_{\bar{Z}_n} u_n}{n-K_n-J} & \frac{u_n' M_{\bar{Z}_n} v_n}{n-K_n-J} \\ \frac{v_n' Q_{\bar{Z}_n} u_n}{n-K_n-J} & \frac{v_n' M_{\bar{Z}_n} v_n}{n-K_n-J} \end{pmatrix} \right\} = 0. \tag{72}$$

Now, rewrite (72) as follows

$$\det\left\{\begin{pmatrix} \frac{\sqrt{K_n}}{r_n} s_{uu}^G & \frac{1}{\sqrt{r_n}} x_{cu} + \frac{\sqrt{K_n}}{r_n} s_{uv}^G \\ \frac{1}{\sqrt{r_n}} x_{cu} + \frac{\sqrt{K_n}}{r_n} s_{uv}^G & \Psi_n + \frac{2}{\sqrt{r_n}} x_{cv} + \frac{\sqrt{K_n}}{r_n} s_{vv}^G \end{pmatrix} \right.$$
$$\left. - \tau_n \begin{pmatrix} \sigma_{uu} + \frac{1}{\sqrt{n^*}} s_{uu}^M & \sigma_{uv} + \frac{1}{\sqrt{n^*}} s_{uv}^M \\ \sigma_{uv} + \frac{1}{\sqrt{n^*}} s_{uv}^M & \sigma_{vv} + \frac{1}{\sqrt{n^*}} s_{vv}^M \end{pmatrix} \right\} = 0, \tag{73}$$

where $n^* = n - K_n - J$, $s_{uu}^G = \frac{u_n' G_n u_n}{\sqrt{K_n}}$, $s_{uv}^G = \frac{u_n' G_n v_n}{\sqrt{K_n}}$, $s_{vv}^G = \frac{v_n' G_n v_n}{\sqrt{K_n}}$, $x_{cu} = \frac{c_n' Z_n' M_{X_n} u_n}{b_n \sqrt{r_n}}$, $x_{cv} = \frac{c_n' Z_n' M_{X_n} v_n}{b_n \sqrt{r_n}}$, $s_{uu}^M = \sqrt{n^*}\left[\frac{u_n' M_{\bar{Z}_n} u_n}{n^*} - \sigma_{uu}\right]$, $s_{uv}^M = \sqrt{n^*}\left[\frac{u_n' M_{\bar{Z}_n} v_n}{n^*} - \sigma_{uv}\right]$, and $s_{vv}^M = \sqrt{n^*}\left[\frac{v_n' M_{\bar{Z}_n} v_n}{n^*} - \sigma_{vv}\right]$. Next, using arguments similar to those used to derive results in Lemmas A1 and A2 of Chao and Swanson (2002) and also using Theorem 4.5 of White (1984), we can, after ignoring lower order terms, write

$$\det\left\{\begin{pmatrix} \frac{\sqrt{K_n}}{r_n} s_{uu}^G & \frac{\sqrt{K_n}}{r_n} s_{uv}^G + o_p\left(\frac{\sqrt{K_n}}{r_n}\right) \\ \frac{\sqrt{K_n}}{r_n} s_{uv}^G + o_p\left(\frac{\sqrt{K_n}}{r_n}\right) & \Psi_n + \frac{\sqrt{K_n}}{r_n} s_{vv}^G + o_p\left(\frac{\sqrt{K_n}}{r_n}\right) \end{pmatrix} \right.$$
$$\left. - \tau_n \begin{pmatrix} \sigma_{uu} + O_p\left(\frac{1}{\sqrt{n^*}}\right) & \sigma_{uv} + O_p\left(\frac{1}{\sqrt{n^*}}\right) \\ \sigma_{uv} + O_p\left(\frac{1}{\sqrt{n^*}}\right) & \sigma_{vv} + O_p\left(\frac{1}{\sqrt{n^*}}\right) \end{pmatrix} \right\} = 0. \tag{74}$$

Explicit calculation of the determinant yields

$$\left(\frac{\sqrt{K_n}}{r_n} s_{uu}^G - \tau_n \left[\sigma_{uu} + O_p\left(\frac{1}{\sqrt{n^*}}\right)\right]\right)$$
$$\times \left(\Psi_n + \frac{\sqrt{K_n}}{r_n} s_{vv}^G + o_p\left(\frac{\sqrt{K_n}}{r_n}\right) - \tau_n \left[\sigma_{vv} + O_p\left(\frac{1}{\sqrt{n^*}}\right)\right]\right)$$

$$
- \left(\frac{\sqrt{K_n}}{r_n} s_{uv}^G + o_p\left(\frac{\sqrt{K_n}}{r_n}\right) - \tau_n \left[\sigma_{uv} + O_p\left(\frac{1}{\sqrt{n^*}}\right) \right] \right)^2
$$

$$
= 0,
$$

and thus by rearranging terms, we obtain, up to terms of order $O_p\left(K_n^{\frac{1}{2}} r_n^{-1}\right)$, the quadratic relationship

$$
\begin{aligned}
&\left(\sigma_{uu}\sigma_{vv} - \sigma_{uv}^2 + O_p\left(\frac{1}{\sqrt{n^*}}\right) \right) \tau_n^2 \\
&\quad - \left(\sigma_{uu}\Psi_n + \frac{\sqrt{K_n}}{r_n} s_{vv}^G \sigma_{uu} + \frac{\sqrt{K_n}}{r_n} s_{uu}^G \sigma_{vv} - 2\frac{\sqrt{K_n}}{r_n} s_{uv}^G \sigma_{uv} + o_p\left(\frac{\sqrt{K_n}}{r_n}\right) \right) \tau_n \\
&\quad + \frac{\sqrt{K_n}}{r_n} s_{uu}^G \Psi_n + O_p\left(\frac{K_n}{r_n^2}\right) \\
&= 0.
\end{aligned}
$$

It follows from the quadratic formula that

$$
\begin{aligned}
&\widehat{\tau}_{\text{LIML},n} \\
&= \left[2 \left(\sigma_{uu}\sigma_{vv} - \sigma_{uv}^2 + O_p\left(\frac{1}{\sqrt{n^*}}\right) \right) \right]^{-1} \\
&\quad \times \left\{ \left(\sigma_{uu}\Psi_n + \frac{\sqrt{K_n}}{r_n} s_{vv}^G \sigma_{uu} + \frac{\sqrt{K_n}}{r_n} s_{uu}^G \sigma_{vv} - 2\frac{\sqrt{K_n}}{r_n} s_{uv}^G \sigma_{uv} + o_p\left(\frac{\sqrt{K_n}}{r_n}\right) \right) \right. \\
&\quad - \left[\left(\sigma_{uu}\Psi_n + \frac{\sqrt{K_n}}{r_n} s_{vv}^G \sigma_{uu} + \frac{\sqrt{K_n}}{r_n} s_{uu}^G \sigma_{vv} - 2\frac{\sqrt{K_n}}{r_n} s_{uv}^G \sigma_{uv} + o_p\left(\frac{\sqrt{K_n}}{r_n}\right) \right)^2 \right. \\
&\quad \left. \left. - 4 \left(\sigma_{uu}\sigma_{vv} - \sigma_{uv}^2 + O_p\left(\frac{1}{\sqrt{n^*}}\right) \right) \left(\frac{\sqrt{K_n}}{r_n} s_{uu}^G \Psi_n + O_p\left(\frac{K_n}{r_n^2}\right) \right) \right]^{\frac{1}{2}} \right\} \\
&= \left[2 \left(\sigma_{uu}\sigma_{vv} - \sigma_{uv}^2 + O_p\left(\frac{1}{\sqrt{n^*}}\right) \right) \right]^{-1} \\
&\quad \times \left\{ \left(\sigma_{uu}\Psi_n + \frac{\sqrt{K_n}}{r_n} \left[s_{vv}^G \sigma_{uu} + s_{uu}^G \sigma_{vv} - 2 s_{uv}^G \sigma_{uv} \right] + o_p\left(\frac{\sqrt{K_n}}{r_n}\right) \right) \right. \\
&\quad - \left[\sigma_{uu}\Psi_n \left(\sigma_{uu}\Psi_n + 2\frac{\sqrt{K_n}}{r_n} \left[s_{vv}^G \sigma_{uu} - s_{uu}^G \sigma_{vv} - 2 s_{uv}^G \sigma_{uv} + 2 s_{uu}^G \frac{\sigma_{uv}^2}{\sigma_{uu}} \right] \right) \right. \\
&\quad \left. \left. + o_p\left(\frac{\sqrt{K_n}}{r_n}\right) \right]^{\frac{1}{2}} \right\}. \qquad (75)
\end{aligned}
$$

Now, focusing on the square-root function

$$\mathcal{R}_{1n} = \left[\sigma_{uu}\Psi_n\left(\sigma_{uu}\Psi_n + 2\frac{\sqrt{K_n}}{r_n}\left[s^G_{vv}\sigma_{uu} - s^G_{uu}\sigma_{vv} - 2s^G_{uv}\sigma_{uv} + 2s^G_{uu}\frac{\sigma^2_{uv}}{\sigma_{uu}}\right]\right) + o_p\left(\frac{\sqrt{K_n}}{r_n}\right)\right]^{\frac{1}{2}},$$

we note that we can expand $\mathcal{R}_{1n}$ as a power series as follows:

$$\mathcal{R}_{1n} = \sigma_{uu}\Psi_n\left(1 + \frac{\sqrt{K_n}}{r_n}\sigma^{-1}_{uu}\Psi^{-1}_n\left[s^G_{vv}\sigma_{uu} - s^G_{uu}\sigma_{vv} - 2s^G_{uv}\sigma_{uv} + 2s^G_{uu}\frac{\sigma^2_{uv}}{\sigma_{uu}}\right] + o_p\left(\frac{\sqrt{K_n}}{r_n}\right)\right). \tag{76}$$

Inserting (76) into (75), we obtain, after minor manipulations,

$$\begin{aligned}\widehat{\tau}_{\mathrm{LIML},n} &= \left[2\left(\sigma_{uu}\sigma_{vv} - \sigma^2_{uv}\right)\right]^{-1}\left(1 + O_p\left(\frac{1}{\sqrt{n^*}}\right)\right) \\ &\quad \times \left\{2\frac{\sqrt{K_n}}{r_n}\left[s^G_{uu}\sigma_{vv} - s^G_{uu}\frac{\sigma^2_{uv}}{\sigma_{uu}}\right] + o_p\left(\frac{\sqrt{K_n}}{r_n}\right)\right\} \\ &= \frac{\sqrt{K_n}}{r_n}\frac{s^G_{uu}}{\sigma_{uu}}\left(1 + o_p(1)\right).\end{aligned} \tag{77}$$

The desired result follows immediately by substituting (77) into (71). ■

APPENDIX B

This appendix contains proofs of the main theorems of this chapter.

Proof of Theorem 4.3.1: By the usual regression algebra, we can write

$$\begin{aligned}\widehat{\beta}_{\mathrm{LIML},n} - \beta_0 &= \left(y'_{2n}\left[P_{\overline{Z}_n} - P_{X_n} - \widetilde{\lambda}_{\mathrm{LIML},n}M_{\overline{Z}_n}\right]y_{2n}\right)^{-1} \\ &\quad \times \left(y'_{2n}\left[P_{\overline{Z}_n} - P_{X_n} - \widetilde{\lambda}_{\mathrm{LIML},n}M_{\overline{Z}_n}\right]u_n\right),\end{aligned}$$

and thus

$$\begin{aligned}\frac{\Psi_n}{\sigma_{L,n}}\left(\widehat{\beta}_{\mathrm{LIML},n} - \beta_0\right) &= \left(\frac{\Psi_n}{r_n}\right)\left(\frac{y'_{2n}\left[P_{\overline{Z}_n} - P_{X_n} - \widetilde{\lambda}_{\mathrm{LIML},n}M_{\overline{Z}_n}\right]y_{2n}}{r_n}\right)^{-1} \\ &\quad \times \left(\frac{y'_{2n}\left[P_{\overline{Z}_n} - P_{X_n} - \widetilde{\lambda}_{\mathrm{LIML},n}M_{\overline{Z}_n}\right]u_n}{\sigma_{L,n}}\right),\end{aligned} \tag{78}$$

where the inverse in (78) exists in probability as $n \to \infty$ in the sense of White (1984) given our assumptions, as will be shown in expression (81). (See page 24 of White 1984 for a definition of "existence in probability.") To derive the limiting distribution of (78), first write

$$\begin{aligned}
&\frac{y_{2n}'\left[P_{\overline{Z}_n} - P_{X_n} - \widetilde{\lambda}_{\text{LIML},n} M_{\overline{Z}_n}\right] u_n}{\sigma_{L,n}} \\
&= \frac{y_{2n}'\left[P_{\overline{Z}_n} - P_{X_n} - \left(\widehat{\lambda}_{\text{LIML},n} - 1\right) M_{\overline{Z}_n}\right] u_n}{\sigma_{L,n}} \\
&= \left(\frac{\sqrt{K_n}}{\sigma_{L,n}}\right) \frac{c_n' Z_n' M_{X_n} u_n}{b_n \sqrt{K_n}} + \frac{v_n'\left[P_{\overline{Z}_n} - P_{X_n} - \left(\widehat{\lambda}_{\text{LIML},n} - 1\right) M_{\overline{Z}_n}\right] u_n}{\sigma_{L,n}},
\end{aligned}$$

where the first equality above follows from the definition of $\widetilde{\lambda}_{\text{LIML},n}$. It then follows from Lemmas A.5 and A.8 that

$$\begin{aligned}
&\frac{y_{2n}'\left[P_{\overline{Z}_n} - P_{X_n} - \widetilde{\lambda}_{\text{LIML},n} M_{\overline{Z}_n}\right] u_n}{\sigma_{L,n}} \\
&= \left(\frac{\sqrt{K_n}}{\sigma_{L,n}}\right) \frac{c_n' Z_n' M_{X_n} u_n}{b_n \sqrt{K_n}} + \frac{v_n' G_n u_n}{\sigma_{L,n}} - \frac{u_n' G_n u_n}{\sigma_{L,n}} \sigma_{uu}^{-1} \left(\frac{v_n' M_{\overline{Z}_n} u_n}{n - K_n - J}\right) + o_p(1) \\
&= \left(\frac{\sqrt{K_n}}{\sigma_{L,n}}\right) \left(\sqrt{\frac{r_n}{K_n}}\right) \frac{c_n' Z_n' M_{X_n} u_n}{b_n \sqrt{r_n}} + \frac{v_n' G_n u_n}{\sigma_{L,n}} - \frac{\sigma_{uv}}{\sigma_{uu}} \frac{u_n' G_n u_n}{\sigma_{L,n}} + o_p(1) \\
&= \frac{v_n' G_n u_n}{\sigma_{L,n}} - \frac{\sigma_{uv}}{\sigma_{uu}} \frac{u_n' G_n u_n}{\sigma_{L,n}} + o_p(1), \qquad (79)
\end{aligned}$$

where $G_n = P_{\overline{Z}_n} - P_{X_n} - \left(\frac{K_n}{n-K_n-J}\right) M_{\overline{Z}_n}$, for which the second equality above from part (d) of Lemma A2 of Chao and Swanson (2002), which shows that $\frac{v_n' M_{\overline{Z}_n} u_n}{n-K_n-J} \xrightarrow{p} \sigma_{uv}$, and the last equality above follows from arguments similar to those given in part (e) of Lemma A1 of Chao and Swanson (2002), which can be used to show that $\frac{c_n' Z_n' M_{X_n} u_n}{b_n \sqrt{r_n}} = O_p(1)$, and from part (d) of Lemma A2 of Chao and Swanson (2002). Note also that, by setting $d_1 = 1$ and $d_2 = -\frac{\sigma_{uv}}{\sigma_{uu}}$ in the general formula (22), we deduce that

$$\begin{aligned}
\sigma_{L,n}^2 &= \left[E\left(u_j^2 v_j^2\right) - \sigma_{uv}^2\right] \sum_{j=1}^{n} E\left(g_{jj,n}^2\right) + \frac{\sigma_{uv}^2}{\sigma_{uu}^2}\left[E\left(u_j^4\right) - \sigma_{uu}^2\right] \sum_{j=1}^{n} E\left(g_{jj,n}^2\right) \\
&\quad - 2\left\{\frac{\sigma_{uv}}{\sigma_{uu}}\left[E\left(u_j^3 v_j\right) - \sigma_{uu}\sigma_{uv}\right] \sum_{j=1}^{n} E\left(g_{jj,n}^2\right)\right\} \\
&\quad + 2\left(\sigma_{uu}\sigma_{vv} - \sigma_{uv}^2\right) \sum_{1 \le i < j \le n} E\left(g_{ij,n}^2\right)
\end{aligned}$$

is the variance of the bilinear form $v_n' G_n u_n - \frac{\sigma_{uv}}{\sigma_{uu}} u_n' G_n u_n$. It follows from Lemma A.7 above that, as $n \to \infty$,

$$\frac{y_{2n}'\left[P_{\overline{Z}_n} - P_{X_n} - \widetilde{\lambda}_{\mathrm{LIML},n} M_{\overline{Z}_n}\right] u_n}{\sigma_{L,n}} = \frac{v_n' G_n u_n}{\sigma_{L,n}} - \frac{\sigma_{uv}}{\sigma_{uu}} \frac{u_n' G_n u_n}{\sigma_{L,n}} + o_p(1) \xrightarrow{d} N(0,1). \tag{80}$$

Note further that

$$\begin{aligned}
\frac{y_{2n}'\left[P_{\overline{Z}_n} - P_{X_n} - \widetilde{\lambda}_{\mathrm{LIML},n} M_{\overline{Z}_n}\right] y_{2n}}{r_n}
&= \frac{c_n' Z_n' M_{X_n} Z_n c_n}{b_n^2 r_n} + 2\frac{c_n' Z_n' M_{X_n} v_n}{b_n r_n} + \frac{v_n'\left[P_{\overline{Z}_n} - P_{X_n} - \widetilde{\lambda}_{\mathrm{LIML},n} M_{\overline{Z}_n}\right] v_n}{r_n} \\
&= \frac{c_n' Z_n' M_{X_n} Z_n c_n}{b_n^2 r_n} + 2\frac{c_n' Z_n' M_{X_n} v_n}{b_n r_n} \\
&\quad + \frac{v_n'\left[P_{\overline{Z}_n} - P_{X_n} - \left(\frac{K_n}{n-K_n-J}\right) M_{\overline{Z}_n}\right] v_n}{r_n} + o_p(1) \\
&= \overline{\Psi}_n + o_p(1),
\end{aligned} \tag{81}$$

where $\overline{\Psi}_n = r_n^{-1}\Psi_n$ is nonsingular with probability one for n sufficiently large given Assumption 4.2, where the second equality above follows from Theorem 3.3 of Chao and Swanson (2002), and where the third equality follows from parts (c) and (f) of Lemma A.1. Equations (80) and (81) imply that

$$\begin{aligned}
\left(\frac{\Psi_n}{\sigma_{L,n}}\right)\left(\widehat{\beta}_{\mathrm{LIML},n} - \beta_0\right) &= \overline{\Psi}_n \left(\frac{y_{2n}'\left[P_{\overline{Z}_n} - P_{X_n} - \widetilde{\lambda}_{\mathrm{LIML},n} M_{\overline{Z}_n}\right] y_{2n}}{r_n}\right)^{-1} \\
&\quad \times \left(\frac{y_{2n}'\left[P_{\overline{Z}_n} - P_{X_n} - \widetilde{\lambda}_{\mathrm{LIML},n} M_{\overline{Z}_n}\right] u_n}{\sigma_{L,n}}\right) \\
&= \frac{v_n' G_n u_n}{\sigma_{L,n}} - \frac{\sigma_{uv}}{\sigma_{uu}} \frac{u_n' G_n u_n}{\sigma_{L,n}} + o_p(1),
\end{aligned}$$

and thus

$$\left(\frac{\Psi_n}{\sigma_{L,n}}\right)\left(\widehat{\beta}_{\mathrm{LIML},n} - \beta_0\right) \xrightarrow{d} N(0,1) \text{ as } n \to \infty$$

as required.

Proof of Theorem 4.3.2: By the usual regression algebra, we can write

$$\begin{aligned}
\widehat{\beta}_{\mathrm{FLIML},n} - \beta_0 &= \left(y_{2n}'\left[M_{X_n} - \widehat{k}_{\mathrm{FLIML},n} M_{\overline{Z}_n}\right] y_{2n}\right)^{-1} \\
&\quad \times \left(y_{2n}'\left[M_{X_n} - \widehat{k}_{\mathrm{FLIML},n} M_{\overline{Z}_n}\right] u_n\right)
\end{aligned}$$

$$= \left(y_{2n}' \left[P_{\overline{Z}_n} - P_{X_n} - \left(\widehat{\lambda}_{\text{LIML},n} - 1 - \frac{a}{n - K_n - J} \right) M_{\overline{Z}_n} \right] y_{2n} \right)^{-1}$$
$$\left(y_{2n}' \left[P_{\overline{Z}_n} - P_{X_n} - \left(\widehat{\lambda}_{\text{LIML},n} - 1 - \frac{a}{n - K_n - J} \right) M_{\overline{Z}_n} \right] u_n \right), \tag{82}$$

where again the inverse in (82) exists in probability as $n \to \infty$ in the sense of White (1984) given our assumptions, as will be shown in expression (84). Note that the second equality above follows from the fact that $\widehat{k}_{\text{FLIML},n} = \widehat{\lambda}_{\text{LIML},n} - \frac{a}{n-K_n-J}$ by definition. It follows from calculations similar to those used to derive expressions (79) and (81) above that

$$\frac{y_{2n}' \left[P_{\overline{Z}_n} - P_{X_n} - \left(\widehat{\lambda}_{\text{LIML},n} - 1 - \frac{a}{n-K_n-J} \right) M_{\overline{Z}_n} \right] u_n}{\sigma_{L,n}}$$
$$= \left(\frac{\sqrt{K_n}}{\sigma_{L,n}} \right) \frac{c_n' Z_n' M_{X_n} u_n}{b_n \sqrt{K_n}} + \frac{v_n' G_n u_n}{\sigma_{L,n}}$$
$$- \frac{u_n' G_n u_n}{\sigma_{L,n}} \sigma_{uu}^{-1} \left(\frac{v_n' M_{\overline{Z}_n} u_n}{n - K_n - J} \right) + \frac{a}{\sigma_{L,n}} \left(\frac{v_n' M_{\overline{Z}_n} u_n}{n - K_n - J} \right) + o_p(1)$$
$$= \frac{v_n' G_n u_n}{\sigma_{L,n}} - \frac{\sigma_{uv}}{\sigma_{uu}} \frac{u_n' G_n u_n}{\sigma_{L,n}} + o_p(1) \tag{83}$$

and

$$\frac{y_{2n}' \left[P_{\overline{Z}_n} - P_{X_n} - \left(\widehat{\lambda}_{\text{LIML},n} - 1 - \frac{a}{n-K_n-J} \right) M_{\overline{Z}_n} \right] y_{2n}}{r_n}$$
$$= \frac{c_n' Z_n' M_{X_n} Z_n c_n}{b_n^2 r_n} + 2 \frac{c_n' Z_n' M_{X_n} v_n}{b_n r_n}$$
$$+ \frac{v_n' \left[P_{\overline{Z}_n} - P_{X_n} - \left(\widehat{\lambda}_{\text{LIML},n} - 1 \right) M_{\overline{Z}_n} \right] v_n}{r_n}$$
$$+ \frac{a}{r_n} \left(\frac{v_n' M_{\overline{Z}_n} v_n}{n - K_n - J} \right)$$
$$= \overline{\Psi}_n + o_p(1), \tag{84}$$

where $\overline{\Psi}_n$ is nonsingular with probability one for n sufficiently large given Assumption 4.2. It follows immediately from (83) and (84) that

$$\left(\frac{\Psi_n}{\sigma_{L,n}} \right) \left(\widehat{\beta}_{\text{FLIML},n} - \beta_0 \right) \xrightarrow{d} N(0,1) \ \text{ as } n \to \infty$$

as required.

Proof of Theorem 4.3.3: To proceed, note first that, using the usual regression algebra, we can write

$$\widehat{\beta}_{\text{B2SLS},n} - \beta_0 = \left(y_{2n}' \left[P_{\overline{Z}_n} - P_{X_n} - \left(\frac{K_n - 2}{n - K_n + 2} \right) M_{\overline{Z}_n} \right] y_{2n} \right)^{-1} \times \left(y_{2n}' \left[P_{\overline{Z}_n} - P_{X_n} - \left(\frac{K_n - 2}{n - K_n + 2} \right) M_{\overline{Z}_n} \right] u_n \right),$$

and thus

$$\left(\frac{\Psi_n}{\sigma_{B,n}} \right) (\widehat{\beta}_{\text{B2SLS},n} - \beta_0) = \left(\frac{\Psi_n}{r_n} \right) \left(\frac{y_{2n}' \left[P_{\overline{Z}_n} - P_{X_n} - \left(\frac{K_n-2}{n-K_n+2} \right) M_{\overline{Z}_n} \right] y_{2n}}{r_n} \right)^{-1} \times \left(\frac{y_{2n}' \left[P_{\overline{Z}_n} - P_{X_n} - \left(\frac{K_n-2}{n-K_n+2} \right) M_{\overline{Z}_n} \right] u_n}{\sigma_{B,n}} \right), \quad (85)$$

where the inverse in (85) exists in probability as $n \to \infty$ in the sense of White (1984) given our assumptions, as will be shown in expression (89). Next, note that

$$\frac{K_n - 2}{n - K_n + 2} = \left(\frac{K_n}{n - K_n - J} \right) \left(\frac{n - K_n - J}{n - K_n + 2} \right) \left(\frac{K_n - 2}{K_n} \right) = \left(\frac{K_n}{n - K_n - J} \right) (1 + O(K_n^{-1})). \quad (86)$$

To derive the limiting distribution of (85), we write

$$\begin{aligned}
&\frac{y_{2n}' \left[P_{\overline{Z}_n} - P_{X_n} - \left(\frac{K_n-2}{n-K_n+2} \right) M_{\overline{Z}_n} \right] u_n}{\sigma_{B,n}} \\
&= \left(\frac{\sqrt{K_n}}{\sigma_{B,n}} \right) \frac{y_{2n}' \left[P_{\overline{Z}_n} - P_{X_n} - \left(\frac{K_n-2}{n-K_n+2} \right) M_{\overline{Z}_n} \right] u_n}{\sqrt{K_n}} \\
&= \left(\frac{\sqrt{K_n}}{\sigma_{B,n}} \right) \left(\sqrt{\frac{r_n}{K_n}} \right) \frac{c_n' Z_n' M_{X_n} u_n}{b_n \sqrt{r_n}} \\
&\quad + \frac{v_n' \left[P_{\overline{Z}_n} - P_{X_n} - \left(\frac{K_n-2}{n-K_n+2} \right) M_{\overline{Z}_n} \right] u_n}{\sigma_{B,n}} \\
&= \left(\frac{\sqrt{K_n}}{\sigma_{B,n}} \right) \left(\sqrt{\frac{r_n}{K_n}} \right) \frac{c_n' Z_n' M_{X_n} u_n}{b_n \sqrt{r_n}} \\
&\quad + \frac{v_n' \left[P_{\overline{Z}_n} - P_{X_n} - \left(\frac{K_n}{n-K_n-J} \right) M_{\overline{Z}_n} \right] u_n}{\sigma_{B,n}} \\
&\quad - 2 \left(\frac{1}{n - K_n - J} \right) \frac{v_n' M_{\overline{Z}_n} u_n}{\sigma_{B,n}} + O_p \left(\frac{\sqrt{K_n}}{n} \right)
\end{aligned}$$

$$= \frac{v_n'\left[P_{\overline{Z}_n} - P_{X_n} - \left(\frac{K_n}{n-K_n-J}\right)M_{\overline{Z}_n}\right]u_n}{\sigma_{B,n}} + O_p\left(\sqrt{\frac{r_n}{K_n}}\right), \tag{87}$$

where the fourth equality above follows from arguments similar to those given in part (e) of Lemma A1 of Chao and Swanson (2002), which can be used to show that $\frac{c_n' Z_n' M_{X_n} u_n}{b_n \sqrt{r_n}} = O_p(1)$, and from part (d) of Lemma A2 of Chao and Swanson (2002), which shows that $\frac{v_n' M_{\overline{Z}_n} u_n}{n-K_n-J} \xrightarrow{p} \sigma_{uv}$; thus,

$$\left(\frac{1}{n-K_n-J}\right)\frac{v_n' M_{\overline{Z}_n} u_n}{\sigma_{B,n}} = \left(\frac{\sqrt{K_n}}{\sigma_{B,n}}\right)\left(\frac{1}{\sqrt{K_n}}\right)\frac{v_n' M_{\overline{Z}_n} u_n}{n-K_n-J} = O_p\left(K_n^{-\frac{1}{2}}\right)$$

given Lemma A.3 part (b). Note also that, by setting $d_1 = 1$ and $d_2 = 0$ in the general formula (22), we deduce that

$$\sigma_{B,n}^2 = \left[E\left(u_j^2 v_j^2\right) - \sigma_{uv}^2\right]\sum_{j=1}^{n} E\left(g_{jj,n}^2\right) + 2\left(\sigma_{uu}\sigma_{vv} + \sigma_{uv}^2\right)\sum_{1 \le i < j \le n} E\left(g_{ij,n}^2\right)$$

is the variance of the bilinear form $v_n' G_n u_n$. It follows from Lemma A.7 above that, as $n \to \infty$,

$$\frac{y_{2n}'\left[P_{\overline{Z}_n} - P_{X_n} - \left(\frac{K_n-2}{n-K_n+2}\right)M_{\overline{Z}_n}\right]u_n}{\sigma_{B,n}} = \frac{v_n' G_n u_n}{\sigma_{B,n}} + o_p(1) \xrightarrow{d} N(0,1), \tag{88}$$

where $G_n = P_{\overline{Z}_n} - P_{X_n} - \left(\frac{K_n}{n-K_n-J}\right)M_{\overline{Z}_n}$. Moreover, note that

$$\begin{aligned}
&\frac{y_{2n}'\left[P_{\overline{Z}_n} - P_{X_n} - \left(\frac{K_n-2}{n-K_n+2}\right)M_{\overline{Z}_n}\right]y_{2n}}{r_n} \\
&= \frac{c_n' Z_n' M_{X_n} Z_n c_n}{b_n^2 r_n} + 2\frac{c_n' Z_n' M_{X_n} v_n}{b_n r_n} \\
&\quad + \frac{v_n'\left[P_{\overline{Z}_n} - P_{X_n} - \left(\frac{K_n-2}{n-K_n+2}\right)M_{\overline{Z}_n}\right]v_n}{r_n} \\
&= \frac{c_n' Z_n' M_{X_n} Z_n c_n}{b_n^2 r_n} + 2\frac{c_n' Z_n' M_{X_n} v_n}{b_n r_n} \\
&\quad + \frac{v_n'\left[P_{\overline{Z}_n} - P_{X_n} - \left(\frac{K_n}{n-K_n-J}\right)M_{\overline{Z}_n}\right]v_n}{r_n} \\
&\quad - 2\left(\frac{1}{n-K_n-J}\right)\frac{v_n' M_{\overline{Z}_n} u_n}{\sigma_{B,n}} + O_p\left(\frac{\sqrt{K_n}}{n}\right) \\
&= \overline{\Psi}_n + o_p(1),
\end{aligned} \tag{89}$$

where $\overline{\Psi}_n = r_n^{-1}\Psi_n$ is nonsingular with probability one for n sufficiently large given Assumption 4.2 and where the third equality follows from parts (a), (c), and (f) of Lemma A1 of Chao and Swanson (2002) and from the fact that

$$\left(\frac{1}{n-K_n-J}\right)\frac{v_n' M_{\overline{Z}_n} v_n}{\sigma_{B,n}} = \left(\frac{\sqrt{K_n}}{\sigma_{B,n}}\right)\left(\frac{1}{\sqrt{K_n}}\right)\frac{v_n' M_{\overline{Z}_n} v_n}{n-K_n-J} = O_p\left(K_n^{-\frac{1}{2}}\right).$$

Using arguments similar to those given to prove part (e) of Lemma A2 of Chao and Swanson (2002), we note that (88) and (89) imply that

$$\begin{aligned}\left(\frac{\Psi_n}{\sigma_{B,n}}\right)\left(\widehat{\beta}_{\mathrm{B2SLS},n} - \beta_0\right) &= \overline{\Psi}_n \left(\frac{y_{2n}'\left[P_{\overline{Z}_n} - P_{X_n} - \left(\frac{K_n-2}{n-K_n+2}\right) M_{\overline{Z}_n}\right] y_{2n}}{r_n}\right)^{-1} \\ &\quad\times \left(\frac{y_{2n}'\left[P_{\overline{Z}_n} - P_{X_n} - \left(\frac{K_n-2}{n-K_n+2}\right) M_{\overline{Z}_n}\right] u_n}{\sigma_{B,n}}\right) \\ &= \frac{v_n' G_n u_n}{\sigma_{B,n}} + o_p(1);\end{aligned}$$

thus,

$$\left(\frac{\Psi_n}{\sigma_{B,n}}\right)\left(\widehat{\beta}_{\mathrm{B2SLS},n} - \beta_0\right) \xrightarrow{d} N(0,1) \text{ as } n \to \infty$$

as required.

Proof of Theorem 4.3.4: Making use of expressions (12) and (13), we see that

$$\begin{aligned}\sigma_{B,n}^2 - \sigma_{L,n}^2 &= 2\frac{\sigma_{uv}}{\sigma_{uu}}\left[E\left(u_j^3 v_j\right) - \sigma_{uu}\sigma_{uv}\right]\sum_{j=1}^{n} E\left(g_{jj,n}^2\right) + 4\sigma_{uv}^2 \sum_{1\le i<j\le n} E\left(g_{ij,n}^2\right) \\ &\quad - \frac{\sigma_{uv}^2}{\sigma_{uu}^2}\left[E\left(u_j^4\right) - \sigma_{uu}^2\right]\sum_{j=1}^{n} E\left(g_{jj,n}^2\right).\end{aligned} \tag{90}$$

Because by assumption, η_i is $E_2\left(0.\Xi\right)$, we have, as a result of special properties of elliptical distributions, that

$$E\left(u_j^4\right) = 3\left(\kappa+1\right)\sigma_{uu}^2,$$
$$E\left(u_j^3 v_j\right) = 3\left(\kappa+1\right)\sigma_{uu}\sigma_{uv},$$

where κ here denotes the kurtosis parameter of an elliptical distribution as defined in Muirhead (1982, p. 41). It follows that we can rewrite (90) as

$$\sigma_{B,n}^2 - \sigma_{L,n}^2 = \left(3\kappa+2\right)\sigma_{uv}^2\sum_{j=1}^{n} E\left(g_{jj,n}^2\right) + 4\sigma_{uv}^2\sum_{1\le i<j\le n} E\left(g_{ij,n}^2\right).$$

Moreover, Bentler and Berkane (1986) show that the kurtosis parameter κ for a m-variate continuous elliptical distribution with real positive definite covariance matrix $\Sigma = \tau\,\Xi$ must be greater than $-2/(m+2)$. Setting $m = 2$, we have that

$$\begin{aligned}\sigma_{B,n}^2 - \sigma_{L,n}^2 &= (3\kappa + 2)\,\sigma_{uv}^2 \sum_{j=1}^{n} E\left(g_{jj,n}^2\right) + 4\sigma_{uv}^2 \sum_{1\le i<j\le n} E\left(g_{ij,n}^2\right)\\ &> \frac{1}{2}\sigma_{uv}^2 \sum_{j=1}^{n} E\left(g_{jj,n}^2\right) + +4\sigma_{uv}^2 \sum_{1\le i<j\le n} E\left(g_{ij,n}^2\right)\\ &> 0\end{aligned}$$

as required.

References

Angrist, J. D., G. W. Imbens, and A. Krueger (1999). "Jackknife instrumental variables estimation," *Journal of Applied Econometrics*, 14, 57–67.

Angrist, J. D. and A. B. Krueger (1995). "Split-sample instrumental variables estimates of the return to schooling," *Journal of Business and Economic Statistics*, 13, 225–235.

Bekker, P. A. (1994). "Alternative approximations to the distributions of instrumental variable estimators," *Econometrica*, 62, 657–681.

Bentler, P. M. and M. Berkane (1986). "Greatest lower bound to the elliptical theory kurtosis parameter," *Biometrika*, 73, 240–241.

Blomquist, S. and M. Dahlberg (1999). "Small sample properties of LIML and Jackknife IV Estimators: Experiments with Weak Instruments," *Journal of Applied Econometrics* 14, 69–88.

Chao, J. C. and N. R. Swanson (2002). "Consistent estimation with a large number of weak instruments," unpublished manuscript, University of Maryland.

Chao, J. C. and N. R. Swanson (2003). "Alternative approximations of the bias and MSE of the IV Estimator under weak identification with an application to bias correction," unpublished manuscript, University of Maryland.

Choi, I. and P. C. B. Phillips (1992). "Asymptotic and finite sample distribution theory for IV estimators and tests in partially identified structural equations," *Journal of Econometrics*, 51, 113–150.

Donald, S. G. and W. K. Newey (2001). "Choosing the number of instruments," *Econometrica*, 69, 1161–1191.

Fuller, W. A. (1977). "Some properties of a modification of the limited information estimator," *Econometrica*, 45, 939–953.

Gänsler, P. and W. Stute (1977). *Wahrscheinlichkeitstheorie* (Springer–Verlag, New York).

Hahn, J., J. Hausman, and G. Kuersteiner (2002). "Estimation with weak instruments: accuracy and higher order MSE approximations," unpublished working paper, MIT.

Kelejian, H. H. and I. R. Prucha (2001). "On the asymptotic distribution of the moran I test statistic with applications," *Journal of Econometrics*, 104, 219–57.

Kleibergen, F. (2002). "Pivotal statistics for testing structural parameters in instrumental variables regression," *Econometrica*, 70, 1781–1803.

Koenker, R. and J. A. F. Machado (1999). "GMM inference when the number of moment conditions is large," *Journal of Econometrics*, 93, 327–344.

Magnus, J. R. and H. Neudecker (1988). *Matrix Differential Calculus with Applications in Statistics and Econometrics* (John Wiley & Sons, New York).

Morimune, K. (1983). "Approximate distributions of k-class estimators when the degree of overidentifiability is large compared with the sample size," *Econometrica*, 51, 821–841.

Muirhead, R. J. (1982). *Aspects of Multivariate Statistical Theory* (John Wiley & Sons, New York).

Phillips, G. D. A. and C. Hale (1977). "The bias of instrumental variable estimators of simultaneous equation systems," *International Economic Review*, 18, 219–228.

Phillips, P. C. B. (1983). "Small sample distribution theory in econometric models of simultaneous equations," in Z. Griliches and M. D. Intriligator, eds., *Handbook of Econometrics, Vol. I* (North Holland, Amsterdam).

Phillips, P. C. B. (1989). "Partially identified econometric models," *Econometric Theory*, 5, 181–240.

Phillips, P. C. B. and C. Han (2003). "IV Estimation with irrelevant instruments," working paper, Yale University.

Rothenberg, T. J. (1983). "Asymptotic properties of some estimators in structural models," in S. Karlin, T. Amemiya, and L. Goodman, eds., *Studies in Econometrics, Time Series, and Multivariate Statistics* (Academic Press, San Diego).

Staiger, D. and J. H. Stock (1997). "Instrumental variables regression with weak instruments." *Econometrica*, 65, 557–586.

Stock, J. H. and M. Yogo (2003a). "Asymptotic distributions of instrumental variables statistics with many weak instruments," working paper, Harvard University.

Stock, J. H. and M. Yogo (2003b). "Testing for Weak Instruments in Linear IV Regression," working paper, Harvard University.

Wang, J. and E. Zivot (1998). "Inference on structural parameters in instrumental variables regressions with weak instruments," *Econometrica*, 66, 1389–1404.

White, H. (1984). *Asymptotic Theory for Econometricians* (Academic Press, San Diego).

FIVE

Improved Inference in Weakly Identified Instrumental Variables Regression

Eric Zivot, Richard Startz, and Charles R. Nelson*

5.1 INTRODUCTION

It is now well known that standard asymptotic inference techniques for instrumental variable (IV) estimation may perform very poorly in the presence of weak instruments. In some circumstances, the failure is of the worst kind: false results are accompanied by reported confidence intervals that lend an appearance of great precision. That point estimates of coefficients do a poor job of telling us the true values of those coefficients is probably irremediable. After all, if an equation is poorly identified, then the data do not tell us much about the parameters of the system. In this chapter we uncover test statistics and related confidence intervals that work quite well in the sense that they lead to reasonably accurate inference when instruments are poor and that are essentially identical to the usual asymptotic IV test statistics and confidence intervals when the instruments are good. This kind of performance under weak and strong identification, respectively, is important because it discourages practitioners' natural tendency to cling to traditional methods that may give (spuriously) tight confidence bounds and erroneous inference.

Most of the previous research on inference in IV regression models with weak instruments has concentrated on the simple model with a single right-hand-side, or included, endogenous variable. Unfortunately, when we consider the more general IV regression model with multiple included endogenous variables, many of the results for the single included endogenous variable model do not apply for individual structural coefficients in the more general model. The fundamental issue is that when a true null is specified for the complete parameter vector, then estimation under the null can give a consistent estimate of the error variance, whereas specification of a null on an individual

* Support from NSF grant SBR-9711301 is gratefully acknowledged.

coefficient does not. In this chapter, we concentrate our analysis on the problem of making valid inference on individual structural coefficients in the IV regression model with multiple included endogenous variables and weak instruments. Our approach is similar in spirit to that taken by Choi and Phillips (1992), who considered finite sample and asymptotic inference in partially identified structural equations. We extend the framework of Choi and Phillips to allow for weak instruments, and we consider nonstandard methods for inference on structural coefficients. We consider cases for which instruments are weak for all structural coefficients and cases for which instruments are weak for some coefficients but not others. We also consider the case for which instruments are weak for individual coefficients but strong for a linear combination of the structural coefficients. We utilize the weak instrument asymptotic framework of Staiger and Stock (1997) to analyze the asymptotic behavior of estimators and test statistics for individual structural coefficients. We also evaluate the finite sample performance of various estimators and test statistics through an extensive set of Monte Carlo experiments.

The plan of the chapter is as follows. After a review of the recent literature on estimation and inference in IV regression models with weak instruments, we present the standard IV regression model for the case of two right-hand-side endogenous variables to set notation. Next we present the standard identification conditions and establish cases of partial identification and weak instruments. We then survey estimation and inference methods in IV regression, paying particular attention to estimation and inference on individual structural parameters. Following this, we summarize the asymptotic behavior of various estimators and test statistics under a variety of weak instrument cases. We then appraise the finite sample performance of various statistics through an extensive set of Monte Carlo simulations. We conclude with a brief summary, recommendations for empirical practice, and suggestions for future research.

5.2 A BRIEF REVIEW OF THE LITERATURE

A series of recent papers have examined the distribution of the instrumental variable estimator under weak identification and the related issue of the performance of the traditional asymptotic tests. These papers include Bekker (1994); Blomquist and Dahlberg (1999); Bound, Jaeger, and Baker (1995); Choi and Phillips (1992); Hahn and Hausman (2002); Hahn and Inuoe (2002); Hall, Rudebusch, and Wilcox (1996); Chamberlain and Imbens (2004); Kleibergen (2000, 2002); Kleibergen and Zivot (2003); Maddala and Jeong (1992); Moreira (2003); Nelson and Startz (1990a, b); Phillips (1989); Staiger and Stock (1997); Stock, Wright, and Yogo (2002); Stock and Yogo (2004); Wang and Zivot (1998); Wong (1999); and Zivot, Startz, and Nelson (1998). Dufour (1997) gave general results for obtaining correct probability levels with weak identification. In particular, Dufour showed that for a test of nominal size α to be valid under weak identification, the confidence intervals implied by the test statistic must be unbounded at least $1 - \alpha$ percent of the time.

Half a century ago, Anderson and Rubin (1949) described the Anderson–Rubin (AR) statistic, which under normality provides an exact small-sample test of a hypothesis that specifies values for every element of the structural parameter vector β. Zivot, Startz, and Nelson (1998) showed how to use the AR statistic to construct confidence regions in the case of a single endogenous variable and provided improved statistics for maximum likelihood and generalized method of moments (GMM) estimates based on degrees-of-freedom-corrected LR and LM tests. Wang and Zivot (1998) provided an asymptotic justification using the Staiger and Stock (1997) local-to-zero asymptotics for these results. Recently, Kleibergen (2002) and Moreira (2003) have proposed asymptotically similar LM tests that have better power than the AR test and the likelihood ratio (LR) and Lagrange multiplier (LM) tests studied by Wang and Zivot (1998).

The analysis in most of the papers above is limited to inference in the case of a single, endogenous, right-hand-side variable or to hypotheses specifying values for the entire vector of coefficients; here we deal with inference on individual coefficients in a model with two right-hand-side variables extending the results of Choi and Phillips (1992) to the case of weak instruments. We note, however, that Dufour (1997), Wang and Zivot (1998), and Dufour and Jasiak (2000) describe the use of numerical projections of joint test statistics to obtain confidence sets for individual elements β but do not study these methods in the presence of weak instruments. As a practical matter, using the projection procedure in general requires complicated numerical maximization. Recently, Taamouti (2001) and Dufour and Taamouti (2003) provided a limited set of results for analytically obtaining projection-based confidence sets for individual structural coefficients based on certain types of test statistics.

Stock and Wright (2000) provide a general procedure for inference on structural parameters estimated by GMM with weak instruments, which for the linear single-equations model is based on two-stage least-squares (TSLS) or limited information maximum likelihood (LIML) estimates. If some endogenous variables are well identified, Stock and Wright suggest concentrating out the well-identified parameters and using an AR-type statistic for the remaining weakly identified parameters. However, Stock and Wright point out that using their method of "construction of asymptotically valid confidence intervals for subvectors... is somewhat... difficult," but that an asymptotically conservative confidence interval can be found by projecting out parameters as suggested in Dufour (1997). Kleibergen (2000) has provided an alternative to Stock and Wright's concentrated AR statistic in the linear IV model, and a more general alternative in the GMM context is provided in Kleibergen (2002). The statistics proposed by Stock and Wright and Kleibergen require partial identification to be asymptotically valid. We evaluate these statistics in a general framework in which partial identification is a special case.

5.3 THE IV REGRESSION MODEL

We begin with the classic statements about IV regression in an identified linear model in the process defining notation.

5.3.1 Structure and Reduced Form

Consider the structural linear equation with k right-hand-side variables[1]

$$\begin{aligned}\underset{(n\times 1)}{\mathbf{y}} &= \underset{(n\times k)}{\mathbf{X}}\underset{(k\times 1)}{\beta} + \underset{(n\times 1)}{\mathbf{u}} \\ &= \underset{(n\times 1)}{\mathbf{X}_i}\underset{(1\times 1)}{\beta_i} + \underset{(n\times(k-1))}{\mathbf{X}_{\text{-}i}}\underset{((k-1)\times 1)}{\beta_{\text{-}i}} + \underset{(n\times 1)}{\mathbf{u}}, \end{aligned} \tag{1}$$

where $\mathbf{X}_i$ is the ith column of $\mathbf{X}$, $\mathbf{X}_{\text{-}i}$ is the remainder of $\mathbf{X}$, and $\mathbf{u}$ is a random error vector. Our focus will be on making inference on the scalar parameter β_i using instrumental variables regression when the variables in $\mathbf{X}$ are endogenous (i.e., correlated with the error term $\mathbf{u}$.) The reduced form of the model consists of the population regression of $\mathbf{y}$ and each column of $\mathbf{X}$ on all q of the exogenous instruments in the matrix $\mathbf{Z}$:

$$\underset{(n\times 1)}{\mathbf{y}} = \underset{(n\times q)}{\mathbf{Z}}\underset{(q\times 1)}{\theta} + \underset{(n\times 1)}{\mathbf{v}} \tag{2}$$

$$\underset{(n\times k)}{\mathbf{X}} = \underset{(n\times q)}{\mathbf{Z}}\underset{(q\times k)}{\Gamma} + \underset{(n\times k)}{\mathbf{V}}. \tag{3}$$

The corresponding reduced-form equations for the endogenous variables $\mathbf{X}_i$ and $\mathbf{X}_{\text{-}i}$ are

$$\underset{(n\times 1)}{\mathbf{X}_i} = \underset{(n\times q)}{\mathbf{Z}}\underset{(q\times 1)}{\Gamma_i} + \underset{(n\times 1)}{\mathbf{V}_i} \tag{4}$$

$$\underset{(n\times(k-1))}{\mathbf{X}_{\text{-}i}} = \underset{(n\times q)}{\mathbf{Z}}\underset{(q\times(k-1))}{\Gamma_{\text{-}i}} + \underset{(n\times(k-1))}{\mathbf{V}_{\text{-}i}}. \tag{5}$$

The model described in equations (1)–(3) is traditionally called the linear IV regression model.

5.3.2 Assumptions

Let $\xrightarrow{p}$ denote convergence in probability and $\xrightarrow{d}$ denote convergence in distribution. We make the following high-level assumptions that impose rather weak moment conditions on the exogenous variables and error terms:

Assumption 5.1

1. $\mathbf{Z}$ has full-column rank q and is uncorrelated with $\mathbf{u}$ and $\mathbf{V}$.
2. $E[\mathbf{Z}_t\mathbf{Z}_t'] = \mathbf{M} > 0$, where $\mathbf{Z}_t$ denotes the tth observation on $\mathbf{Z}$.

[1] For notational brevity we omit any included exogenous variables. The model with included exogenous variables has the same form as the model without included exogenous variables by using the Frisch–Waugh–Lovell theorem and interpreting all data matrices as residuals from the projection on the included exogenous variables.

3. The error terms u_t, and $\mathbf{V}_t$ are assumed to have mean zero and to be serially uncorrelated and homoskedastic with positive definite covariance matrix

$$\boldsymbol{\Sigma} = \text{var}\begin{pmatrix} u_t \\ \mathbf{V}_t \end{pmatrix} = \begin{pmatrix} \sigma_{uu} & \boldsymbol{\Sigma}'_{\mathbf{V}u} \\ \boldsymbol{\Sigma}_{\mathbf{V}u} & \boldsymbol{\Sigma}_{\mathbf{VV}} \end{pmatrix}.$$

4. $(n^{-1}\mathbf{u}'\mathbf{u}, n^{-1}\mathbf{V}'\mathbf{u}, , n^{-1}\mathbf{V}'\mathbf{V}) \xrightarrow{p} (\sigma_{uu}, \boldsymbol{\Sigma}_{\mathbf{V}u}, \boldsymbol{\Sigma}_{\mathbf{VV}})$
5. $n^{-1}\mathbf{Z}'\mathbf{Z} \xrightarrow{p} \mathbf{M}$
6. $(n^{-1/2}\mathbf{Z}'\mathbf{u}, n^{-1/2}\mathbf{Z}'\mathbf{V}) \xrightarrow{d} (\boldsymbol{\Psi}_{Zu}, \boldsymbol{\Psi}_{ZV})$, where $\boldsymbol{\Psi} = (\boldsymbol{\Psi}'_{Zu}, \text{vec}(\boldsymbol{\Psi}_{ZV})')'$ is distributed as $N(0, \boldsymbol{\Sigma} \otimes \mathbf{M})$.

5.3.3 IV Estimation

The vector $\boldsymbol{\beta}$ is commonly estimated by the IV method (equivalently the TSLS or GMM method). The IV estimator is

$$\hat{\boldsymbol{\beta}}_{\text{IV}} = (\mathbf{X}'\mathbf{P_Z}\mathbf{X})^{-1}\mathbf{X}'\mathbf{P_Z}\mathbf{y} = (\hat{\mathbf{X}}'\hat{\mathbf{X}})^{-1}\hat{\mathbf{X}}'\mathbf{y}, \tag{6}$$

where $\mathbf{P_Z} = \mathbf{Z}(\mathbf{Z}'\mathbf{Z})^{-1}\mathbf{Z}'$ and $\hat{\mathbf{X}} = \mathbf{P_Z}\mathbf{X}$. Using standard partitioned regression techniques, we may express the IV estimator of β_i as

$$\hat{\beta}_{i,\text{IV}} = (\hat{\mathbf{X}}'_i\hat{\mathbf{Q}}_{\text{-}i}\hat{\mathbf{X}}_i)^{-1}\hat{\mathbf{X}}'_i\hat{\mathbf{Q}}_{\text{-}i}\mathbf{y}, \tag{7}$$

where $\hat{\mathbf{X}}_i = \mathbf{P}_Z\mathbf{X}_i$, $\hat{\mathbf{X}}_{\text{-}i} = \mathbf{P}_Z\mathbf{X}_{\text{-}i}$, and $\hat{\mathbf{Q}}_{\text{-}i} = \mathbf{I}_q - \mathbf{P}_{\hat{\mathbf{X}}_{\text{-}i}}$.

Given that Assumption 5.1 and the traditional rank and order conditions hold, $\sqrt{n}(\hat{\boldsymbol{\beta}}_{\text{IV}} - \boldsymbol{\beta}) \xrightarrow{d} N(\boldsymbol{\beta}, \sigma_{uu}\mathbf{H})$, where $\mathbf{H} = (\boldsymbol{\Gamma}'\mathbf{M}\boldsymbol{\Gamma})^{-1}$. A consistent estimate of the asymptotic variance $\sigma_{uu}\mathbf{H}$ is given by $n\hat{\sigma}_{uu,\text{IV}}\hat{\mathbf{H}}$, where $\hat{\sigma}_{uu,\text{IV}} = n^{-1}(\mathbf{y} - \mathbf{X}\hat{\boldsymbol{\beta}}_{\text{IV}})'(\mathbf{y} - \mathbf{X}\hat{\boldsymbol{\beta}}_{\text{IV}})$ and $\hat{\mathbf{H}} = (\mathbf{X}'\mathbf{P_Z}\mathbf{X})^{-1}$. Similarly, $\sqrt{n}(\hat{\beta}_{i,\text{IV}} - \beta_i) \xrightarrow{d} N(0, \sigma_{uu}H_{ii})$, where, given the partitioning in (1), $H_{ii} = \left\{\boldsymbol{\Gamma}'_i\left[\mathbf{M} - \mathbf{M}\boldsymbol{\Gamma}_{\text{-}i}(\boldsymbol{\Gamma}'_{\text{-}i}\mathbf{M}\boldsymbol{\Gamma}_{\text{-}i})^{-1}\boldsymbol{\Gamma}'_{\text{-}i}\mathbf{M}\right]\boldsymbol{\Gamma}_i\right\}^{-1}$ is the first diagonal element of $\mathbf{H}$. A consistent estimate of the asymptotic variance $\sigma_{uu}H_{ii}$ is given by $n\hat{\sigma}_{uu,\text{IV}}\hat{H}_{ii}$, where $\hat{H}_{ii} = (\hat{\mathbf{X}}'_i\hat{\mathbf{Q}}_{\text{-}i}\hat{\mathbf{X}}_i)^{-1}$ is the first diagonal element of $\hat{\mathbf{H}}$.

The asymptotic variance of $\hat{\boldsymbol{\beta}}_{\text{IV}}$ is finite provided the rank condition for identification holds (see Davidson and MacKinnon 1993, chapter 18). Equivalently, $\mathbf{H}$ and H_{ii} exist if the rank condition holds. For our purposes, β_i is identified in the full model (1)–(3) if H_{ii} exists, unidentified if H_{ii} does not exist, and is weakly identified if H_{ii} is "nearly infinite."[2] Because H_{ii} is a scalar, we can alternatively characterize the identifiability of β_i by examining

$$H_{ii}^{-1} = \boldsymbol{\Gamma}'_i\left(\mathbf{M} - \mathbf{M}\boldsymbol{\Gamma}_{\text{-}i}(\boldsymbol{\Gamma}'_{\text{-}i}\mathbf{M}\boldsymbol{\Gamma}_{\text{-}i})^{-1}\boldsymbol{\Gamma}'_{\text{-}i}\mathbf{M}\right)\boldsymbol{\Gamma}_i.$$

Notice that $H_{ii}^{-1} = 0$ if $\boldsymbol{\Gamma}_i = \mathbf{0}$ or if $\boldsymbol{\Gamma}_i = \boldsymbol{\Gamma}_{\text{-}i}\mathbf{a}$ for some nonzero $(k-1) \times 1$ vector $\mathbf{a}$. In the former case, β_i is not identified but $\boldsymbol{\beta}_{\text{-}i}$ is identified provided

[2] A formal characterization of weak identification based on Staiger and Stock's (1997) weak instrument asymptotics is given in Section 5.6.

$\boldsymbol{\Gamma}_{\neg i}$ has full rank. In the latter case, both β_i and $\beta_{\neg i}$ are not separately identified, but the linear combination $\alpha = \mathbf{a}\beta_i + \beta_{\neg i}$ is identified.[3]

The reduced-form coefficients are appropriately estimated by least squares, $\hat{\theta} = (\mathbf{Z}'\mathbf{Z})^{-1}\mathbf{Z}'\mathbf{y}$, $\hat{\boldsymbol{\Gamma}}_i = (\mathbf{Z}'\mathbf{Z})^{-1}\mathbf{Z}'\mathbf{X}_i$, $\hat{\boldsymbol{\Gamma}}_{\neg i} = (\mathbf{Z}'\mathbf{Z})^{-1}\mathbf{Z}'\mathbf{X}_{\neg i}$ and $\hat{\boldsymbol{\Gamma}} = (\mathbf{Z}'\mathbf{Z})^{-1}\mathbf{Z}'\mathbf{X}$. For the construction of the S-statistic in the next section, it is useful to note that $\hat{\beta}_{\mathrm{IV}}$ and $\hat{\mathbf{H}}$ can be written in terms of the estimated reduced-form parameters and the instruments $\mathbf{Z}$:

$$\hat{\beta}_{\mathrm{IV}} = (\hat{\boldsymbol{\Gamma}}'\mathbf{Z}'\mathbf{Z}\hat{\boldsymbol{\Gamma}})^{-1}\hat{\boldsymbol{\Gamma}}'\mathbf{Z}'\mathbf{Z}\hat{\theta}$$
$$\hat{\mathbf{H}} = (\hat{\boldsymbol{\Gamma}}'\mathbf{Z}'\mathbf{Z}\hat{\boldsymbol{\Gamma}})^{-1}.$$

Because we need the covariance matrix of the estimated reduced-form coefficients, it is convenient to think of the reduced form as a system of seemingly unrelated regressions:

$$\mathrm{vec}(\mathbf{y}, \mathbf{X}_i, \mathbf{X}_{\neg i}) = (\mathbf{I} \otimes \mathbf{Z})\mathrm{vec}(\boldsymbol{\theta}, \boldsymbol{\Gamma}_i, \boldsymbol{\Gamma}_{\neg i}) + \mathrm{vec}(\mathbf{v}, \mathbf{V}_i, \mathbf{V}_{\neg i}). \tag{8}$$

Define $\boldsymbol{\lambda}$ to be the $q \cdot (k+1) \times 1$ column vector of reduced form parameters in (8) and $\hat{\boldsymbol{\lambda}}$ to be the corresponding least-squares coefficients. Then, under assumption 1 $\sqrt{n}(\hat{\boldsymbol{\lambda}} - \boldsymbol{\lambda}) \xrightarrow{d} N(\mathbf{0}, \boldsymbol{\Sigma}_r \otimes \mathbf{M}^{-1})$, where $\boldsymbol{\Sigma}_r = \mathrm{var}((v_t, V_{it}, \mathbf{V}'_{\neg it})')$. A consistent estimate of the asymptotic covariance of $\hat{\boldsymbol{\lambda}}$ is given by $\hat{\boldsymbol{\Sigma}}_r \otimes (\mathbf{Z}'\mathbf{Z})^{-1}$, where $\hat{\boldsymbol{\Sigma}}_r = n^{-1}\sum_{t=1}^{n}(v_t, V_{it}, \mathbf{V}'_{\neg it})'(v_t, V_{it}, \mathbf{V}'_{\neg it})$.

5.4 TESTS FOR INDIVIDUAL COEFFICIENTS

Several statistics have been proposed for making inference on individual structural coefficients in the IV regression model that are robust, in some sense, to weak instruments. Some of these methods are based on the IV estimator, and some are based on the LIML estimator. In this section, we briefly describe these statistics and introduce some new statistics.

5.4.1 Traditional IV Asymptotic *t*-statistic

Suppose we wish to test $H_0 : \beta_i = \beta_i^0$ based on traditional IV estimation. Standard practice is to use the asymptotic t-statistic

$$t_{\mathrm{IV}}(\beta_i^0) = \frac{\hat{\beta}_{i,\mathrm{IV}} - \beta_i^0}{\mathrm{SE}(\hat{\beta}_{i,\mathrm{IV}})}, \tag{9}$$

where $\mathrm{SE}(\hat{\beta}_{i,\mathrm{IV}}) = \sqrt{\hat{\sigma}_{uu,\mathrm{IV}}\hat{H}_{ii}}$, and $\hat{\sigma}_{uu,\mathrm{IV}} = n^{-1}(\mathbf{y} - \mathbf{X}\hat{\beta}_{\mathrm{IV}})'(\mathbf{y} - \mathbf{X}\hat{\beta}_{\mathrm{IV}})$.

[3] We note that $H_{ii}^{-1} = \hat{\mathbf{X}}_i'\hat{\mathbf{Q}}_{-i}\hat{\mathbf{X}}_i$ is closely related to Shea's partial R^2 statistic for testing instrument relevance (see Shea 1997). Specifically, a little algebra, which is implicit in Shea's paper, shows that the numerator of Shea's partial R^2 is equal to H_{ii}^{-1}. Consequently, Shea's partial R^2 will be close to zero whenever H_{ii}^{-1} is close to zero.

5.4.2 LIML t and LR statistics

The LIML estimator of β maximizes the log-likelihood function concentrated with respect to $\mathbf{\Gamma}$ and $\mathbf{\Sigma}$, that is,

$$L^c(\beta) = -n\ln(2\pi) - \frac{n}{2}\ln k(\beta) - \frac{n}{2}\ln|\mathbf{Y}\mathbf{Q}_{\mathbf{Z}}'\mathbf{Y}|, \qquad (10)$$

where $\mathbf{Y} = [\mathbf{y}\ \mathbf{X}]$ and

$$k(\beta) = \frac{(\mathbf{y}-\mathbf{X}\beta)'(\mathbf{y}-\mathbf{X}\beta)}{(\mathbf{y}-\mathbf{X}\beta)'\mathbf{Q}_{\mathbf{Z}}(\mathbf{y}-\mathbf{X}\beta)}.$$

The LIML estimator of β equivalently minimizes $k(\beta)$, and the minimized value, $k(\widehat{\beta}_{\mathrm{LIML}}) = \widehat{k}_{\mathrm{LIML}}$, can be shown to be the smallest root of the determinantal equation $|\mathbf{Y}'\mathbf{Q}_{\mathbf{X}}\mathbf{Y} - k\mathbf{Y}'\mathbf{Q}_{\mathbf{Z}}\mathbf{Y}|$. The LIML estimator is usually expressed as the k-class estimator

$$\widehat{\beta}_{\mathrm{LIML}} = \left[\mathbf{X}'(\mathbf{I}_n - \widehat{k}_{\mathrm{LIML}}\mathbf{Q}_{\mathbf{Z}})\mathbf{X}\right]^{-1}\left[\mathbf{X}'(\mathbf{I}_n - \widehat{k}_{\mathrm{LIML}}\mathbf{Q}_{\mathbf{Z}})\mathbf{y}\right].$$

For testing $\beta_i = \beta_i^0$, the LIML *t-ratio* is

$$t_{\mathrm{LIML}}(\beta_i^0) = \frac{\hat{\beta}_{i,\mathrm{LIML}} - \beta_i^0}{\widehat{SE}(\hat{\beta}_{i,\mathrm{LIML}})}, \qquad (11)$$

where $\widehat{SE}(\hat{\beta}_{\mathrm{LIML}}) = \sqrt{\widehat{\mathrm{var}}(\hat{\beta}_{i,\mathrm{LIML}})} = \sqrt{\hat{\sigma}_{uu,\mathrm{LIML}} \cdot \left[\mathbf{X}'(\mathbf{I}_n - \widehat{k}_{\mathrm{LIML}}\mathbf{Q}_{\mathbf{Z}})\mathbf{X}\right]_{ii}^{-1}}$. The LR statistic is

$$\mathrm{LR}_{\mathrm{LIML}}(\beta_i^0) = n\ln(\widetilde{k}_{\mathrm{LIML}}(\beta_i^0)) - n\ln(\widehat{k}_{\mathrm{LIML}}), \qquad (12)$$

where $\widetilde{k}_{\mathrm{LIML}}(\beta_i^0)$ is computed from the concentrated log-likelihood function imposing the restriction $\beta_i = \beta_i^0$, and $\widehat{k}_{\mathrm{LIML}}$ is computed from the unconstrained log-likelihood function (10). The restricted LIML estimator of $\beta_{\text{-}i}$, $\tilde{\beta}_{\mathrm{LIML},\text{-}i}(\beta_i^0)$, minimizes the restricted variance ratio

$$k(\beta_{\text{-}i}) = \frac{(\mathbf{y} - \mathbf{X}_i\beta_i^0 - \mathbf{X}_{\text{-}i}\beta_{\text{-}i})'(\mathbf{y} - \mathbf{X}_i\beta_i^0 - \mathbf{X}_{\text{-}i}\beta_{\text{-}i})}{(\mathbf{y} - \mathbf{X}_i\beta_i^0 - \mathbf{X}_{\text{-}i}\beta_{\text{-}i})'\mathbf{Q}_{\mathbf{Z}}(\mathbf{y} - \mathbf{X}_i\beta_i^0 - \mathbf{X}_{\text{-}i}\beta_{\text{-}i})}. \qquad (13)$$

5.4.3 The S-statistic and Modified t-statistics

Consider forming a test statistic for $H_0 : \beta_i = \beta_i^0$ such that it will be close to zero either if the estimated deviation from the truth is small or if the evidence for identification is weak by forming

$$\hat{\Psi}_i = \hat{\Delta}_i(\hat{\beta}_{i,\mathrm{IV}} - \beta_i^0), \qquad (14)$$

where

$$\hat{\Delta}_i = \sqrt{\hat{H}_{ii}^{-1}} \qquad (15)$$

measures the identification of β_i. Recall that $\Delta_i > 0$ is necessary for the rank condition to hold and for β_i to be identified in the IV regression model. If β_i is weakly identified, then $\hat{\Delta}_i$, and therefore $\hat{\Psi}_i$ will be close to zero and we will be unable to reject the hypothesized value β_i^0 appropriately.

To derive a formal test statistic from (14), it is useful to write $\hat{\Psi}_i$ explicitly as a function of $\mathbf{Z}$, β_i^0 and the estimated reduced-form parameters $\hat{\mathbf{\Gamma}}$ and $\hat{\boldsymbol{\theta}}$:

$$\hat{\Psi}_i(\hat{\mathbf{\Gamma}}, \hat{\boldsymbol{\theta}}; \mathbf{Z}; \beta_i^0) = \sqrt{(\hat{\mathbf{\Gamma}}'\mathbf{Z}'\mathbf{Z}\hat{\mathbf{\Gamma}})_{ii}^{-1}} \left\{ \left[(\hat{\mathbf{\Gamma}}'\mathbf{Z}'\mathbf{Z}\hat{\mathbf{\Gamma}})^{-1}\hat{\mathbf{\Gamma}}'\mathbf{Z}'\mathbf{Z}\hat{\boldsymbol{\theta}} \right]_i - \beta_i^0 \right\}.$$

To normalize $\hat{\Psi}_i$, we require an estimate of the asymptotic variance, $\hat{\sigma}^2_{\hat{\Psi}_i}$. Because the estimated reduced form parameters are asymptotically normal, we can compute $\hat{\sigma}^2_{\hat{\Psi}_i}$ by the usual Taylor series approximation (delta method):

$$\hat{\sigma}^2_{\hat{\Psi}_i} = \frac{\partial \hat{\Psi}_i}{\partial \hat{\boldsymbol{\lambda}}'} \widehat{\text{var}}(\hat{\boldsymbol{\lambda}}) \frac{\partial \hat{\Psi}_i}{\partial \hat{\boldsymbol{\lambda}}}. \tag{16}$$

The partial derivatives $\frac{\partial \hat{\Psi}_i}{\partial \hat{\boldsymbol{\lambda}}}$ used in computing $\hat{\sigma}^2_{\hat{\Psi}_i}$ may be conveniently calculated by the numerical delta method, and $\widehat{\text{var}}(\hat{\boldsymbol{\lambda}}) = \hat{\mathbf{\Sigma}}_r \otimes (\mathbf{Z}'\mathbf{Z})^{-1}$ follows immediately from the reduced-form estimates. The S-statistic for testing $H_0 : \beta_i = \beta_i^0$ is then defined as the ratio[4]

$$\mathrm{S}(\beta_i^0) \equiv \frac{\hat{\Psi}_i}{\sqrt{\hat{\sigma}^2_{\hat{\Psi}_i}}}. \tag{17}$$

It is readily seen that the square of the S-statistic, $\mathrm{S}^2(\beta_i^0)$, is a Wald statistic based on a nonlinear function of the reduced-form parameters $\boldsymbol{\lambda}$ and β_i^0.

Zivot et al. (1998) have emphasized that a problem with the use of TSLS or LIML t-ratios in the presence of weak instruments is that the estimate of the structural error variance σ_{uu} is inconsistent. The S-statistic may be thought of as a t-statistic that is more robust to the presence of weak instruments by utilizing a better estimate of σ_{uu}. To see this, note that (9) may be reexpressed as

$$t_{\mathrm{IV}}(\beta_i^0) = \frac{(\hat{\beta}_{i,\mathrm{IV}} - \beta_i^0)\,\hat{\Delta}_i}{\sqrt{\hat{\sigma}_{uu,\mathrm{IV}}}} = \frac{\hat{\Psi}_i}{\sqrt{\hat{\sigma}_{uu,\mathrm{IV}}}}.$$

The variance estimate (16) is now seen to be an estimate of the structural error variance σ_{uu} using the reduced-form estimates $\hat{\boldsymbol{\lambda}}$ and β_i^0.

Modified versions of the IV and LIML t-statistics that are more robust to the presence of weak instruments may also be constructed by utilizing a better estimate of σ_{uu} as follows. The IV and LIML t-ratio for testing $\beta_i = \beta_i^0$ $(i = 1, 2)$ has the form

$$t_j(\beta_i^0) = \frac{(\hat{\beta}_{i,j} - \beta_i^0)\,\hat{\Delta}_{i,j}}{\sqrt{\hat{\sigma}_{uu,j}}}, \quad j = \mathrm{IV}, \mathrm{LIML},$$

[4] The S-statistic takes its name from its creator, Dick Startz.

where $\hat{\Delta}_{i,\mathrm{IV}} = \sqrt{\hat{H}_{ii}^{-1}}$ and $\hat{\Delta}_{i,\mathrm{LIML}} = \sqrt{[\mathbf{X}'(\mathbf{I}_n - \widehat{k}_{\mathrm{LIML}}\mathbf{Q}_\mathbf{Z})\mathbf{X}]_{ii}}$. Instead of computing an estimate of σ_{uu} using the unrestricted estimate of $\boldsymbol{\beta}$, we can utilize $\beta_i = \beta_i^0$ $(i = 1, 2)$ and compute a restricted residual variance estimate

$$\tilde{\sigma}_{uu,j}(\beta_i^0) = n^{-1}\left[\mathbf{y} - \mathbf{X}_i\beta_i^0 - \mathbf{X}_{\text{-}i}\tilde{\beta}_{\text{-}i,j}(\beta_i^0)\right]'\left[\mathbf{y} - \mathbf{X}_i\beta_i^0 - \mathbf{X}_{\text{-}i}\tilde{\beta}_{\text{-}i,j}(\beta_i^0)\right], \quad j = \mathrm{IV}, \mathrm{LIML}, \tag{18}$$

where $\tilde{\beta}_{\text{-}i,j}(\beta_i^0)$ denotes either the IV or LIML estimate of $\beta_{\text{-}i}$ imposing $\beta_i = \beta_i^0$. The restricted LIML estimate minimizes (13), and the restricted IV estimate is

$$\tilde{\beta}_{\text{-}i,\mathrm{IV}}(\beta_i^0) = (\mathbf{X}_{\text{-}i}'\mathbf{P}_\mathbf{Z}\mathbf{X}_{\text{-}i})^{-1}\mathbf{X}_{\text{-}i}'\mathbf{P}_\mathbf{Z}(\mathbf{y} - \mathbf{X}_i\beta_i^0). \tag{19}$$

The modified IV and LIML t-statistics are then

$$\tilde{t}_j(\beta_i^0) = \frac{\left(\hat{\beta}_{i,j} - \beta_i^0\right)\hat{\Delta}_{i,j}}{\sqrt{\tilde{\sigma}_{uu,j}(\beta_i^0)}}, \quad j = \mathrm{IV}, \mathrm{LIML}. \tag{20}$$

5.4.4 Concentrated AR statistic

Stock and Wright (2000) have considered a concentrated AR-type statistic for testing $H_0 : \beta_i = \beta_i^0$ in a GMM framework. In the linear IV regression, this statistic has the form

$$\mathrm{AR}(\beta_i^0) = \frac{[\mathbf{y} - \mathbf{X}_i\beta_i^0 - \mathbf{X}_{\text{-}i}\tilde{\beta}_{\text{-}i}(\beta_i^0)]'\mathbf{P}_\mathbf{Z}[\mathbf{y} - \mathbf{X}_i\beta_i^0 - \mathbf{X}_{\text{-}i}\tilde{\beta}_{\text{-}i}(\beta_i^0)]}{[\mathbf{y} - \mathbf{X}_{\text{-}i}\beta_i^0 - \mathbf{X}_{\text{-}i}\tilde{\beta}_{\text{-}i}(\beta_i^0)]'\mathbf{Q}_\mathbf{Z}[\mathbf{y} - \mathbf{X}_i\beta_i^0 - \mathbf{X}_{\text{-}i}\tilde{\beta}_{\text{-}i}(\beta_i^0)]\,/(n-k)}, \tag{21}$$

where $\tilde{\beta}_{\text{-}i}(\beta_i^0)$ denotes either the IV or LIML estimate of $\beta_{\text{-}i}$ imposing $\beta_i = \beta_i^0$. The restricted LIML estimate minimizes (13), whereas the restricted IV estimate has the analytic form (19). When $\tilde{\beta}_{\text{-}i}(\beta_i^0) = \tilde{\beta}_{\text{-}i,\mathrm{IV}}(\beta_i^0)$, we use $\mathrm{AR}_{\mathrm{IV}}(\beta_i^0)$; when $\tilde{\beta}_{\text{-}i}(\beta_i^0) = \tilde{\beta}_{\text{-}i,\mathrm{LIML}}(\beta_i^0)$, we use $\mathrm{AR}_{\mathrm{LIML}}\left(\beta_i^0\right)$.

5.4.5 Concentrated K statistic

Kleibergen (2000) has proposed a concentrated version of his joint K-statistic (see Kleibergen 2002 for details) for testing the individual hypothesis $H_0 : \beta_i = \beta_i^0$, which has the form

$$K(\beta_i^0) = \frac{(\mathbf{y} - \mathbf{X}_i\beta_i^0 - \mathbf{X}_{\text{-}i}\tilde{\beta}_{\text{-}i,\mathrm{LIML}}(\beta_i^0))'\mathbf{P}_{\mathbf{W}(\beta_i^0)}(\mathbf{y} - \mathbf{X}_i\beta_i^0 - \mathbf{X}_{\text{-}i}\tilde{\beta}_{\text{-}i,\mathrm{LIML}}(\beta_i^0))}{(\mathbf{y} - \mathbf{X}_i\beta_i^0 - \mathbf{X}_{\text{-}i}\tilde{\beta}_{\text{-}i,\mathrm{LIML}}(\beta_i^0))'\mathbf{Q}_\mathbf{Z}(\mathbf{y} - \mathbf{X}_i\beta_i^0 - \mathbf{X}_{\text{-}i}\tilde{\beta}_{\text{-}i,\mathrm{LIML}}(\beta_i^0))/(n-k)}, \tag{22}$$

where $\tilde{\beta}_{\neg i,\mathrm{LIML}}(\beta_i^0)$ is the LIML estimate of $\beta_{\neg i}$ imposing $\beta_i = \beta_i^0$,

$$\begin{aligned}
\mathbf{W}(\beta_i^0) &= [\mathbf{Q}_{\mathbf{Z}\tilde{\Gamma}_{\mathrm{LIML},\neg i}(\beta_i^0)} - \mathbf{Q}_Z](\mathbf{X}_i - \mathbf{H}(\beta_i^0)\mathbf{S}_{22}(\beta_i^0)^{-1}\mathbf{S}_{21}(\beta_i^0)),\\
\mathbf{H}(\beta_i^0) &= (\mathbf{X}_2\ \mathbf{y} - \mathbf{X}_i\beta_i^0),\\
\mathbf{S}_{22}(\beta_i^0) &= \frac{1}{n-q}\mathbf{H}(\beta_i^0)'\mathbf{Q}_Z\mathbf{H}(\beta_i^0),\\
\mathbf{S}_{21}(\beta_i^0) &= \frac{1}{n-q}\mathbf{H}(\beta_i^0)'\mathbf{Q}_Z\mathbf{X}_1,
\end{aligned}$$

and $\tilde{\boldsymbol{\Gamma}}_{\mathrm{LIML},\neg i}(\beta_i^0)$ is the LIML estimate of $\boldsymbol{\Gamma}_{\neg i}$ imposing $\beta_i = \beta_i^0$.

5.4.6 Projected AR statistic

Let $\boldsymbol{\beta} = (\beta_i, \boldsymbol{\beta}_{\neg i}')'$ and consider testing the hypotheses

$$H_0 : \boldsymbol{\beta} = \boldsymbol{\beta}^0$$

using the AR statistic

$$\mathrm{AR}(\boldsymbol{\beta}^0) = \frac{(\mathbf{y} - \mathbf{X}\boldsymbol{\beta}^0)'\mathbf{P}_\mathbf{Z}(\mathbf{y} - \mathbf{X}\boldsymbol{\beta}^0)/k}{(\mathbf{y} - \mathbf{X}\boldsymbol{\beta}^0)'\mathbf{Q}_\mathbf{Z}(\mathbf{y} - \mathbf{X}\boldsymbol{\beta}^0)/(n-k)}. \tag{23}$$

If the errors are normally distributed, Anderson and Rubin (1949) showed that (23) is distributed $F_{k,n-k}$ in finite samples under the null. This result holds regardless of the quality of the instruments. More generally, Staiger and Stock (1997) showed that (23) is asymptotically $\chi^2(q)$ under their weak instrument framework. A confidence set for $\boldsymbol{\beta}$ with level $1-\alpha$ can be obtained by inverting $\mathrm{AR}(\boldsymbol{\beta}^0)$, giving

$$C_{\boldsymbol{\beta}}(\alpha) = \{\boldsymbol{\beta}^0 : \mathrm{AR}(\boldsymbol{\beta}^0) \le \chi_\alpha^2(q)\}, \tag{24}$$

where $\chi_\alpha^2(q)$ is the $1-\alpha$ quantile of the chi-square distribution with q degrees of freedom.

If we are interested in making inference on β_i or some function of $\boldsymbol{\beta}$, for instance $\eta = g(\boldsymbol{\beta})$, then a Scheffe-type projection method as described in Dufour (1997), Wang and Zivot (1998), and Dufour and Jasiak (2001) can be employed to make valid inference. They show that a confidence set defined by

$$C_\eta(\alpha) = \{\eta_0 : \eta_0 = g(\boldsymbol{\beta}) \text{ for some } \boldsymbol{\beta} \in C_{\boldsymbol{\beta}}(\alpha)\}$$

has asymptotic coverage probability at least $1-\alpha$. If $g(\boldsymbol{\beta}) = \beta_i$, the set $C_\eta(\alpha)$ is simply the projection of $C_{\boldsymbol{\beta}}(\alpha)$ on the β_i axis. Taamouti (2001) and Dufour and Taamouti (2003) have given an analytic formula for computing projection-based confidence sets for linear functions $g(\boldsymbol{\beta}) = \mathbf{w}'\boldsymbol{\beta}$ based on (24).

5.5 ASYMPTOTIC PROPERTIES UNDER WEAK INSTRUMENTS

In this section, we evaluate the asymptotic properties under weak instruments of a subset of the competing statistics for making inference on individual coefficients in the IV regression. To simplify the asymptotic analysis, we restrict our attention to the IV regression model (1)–(3) with two right-hand-side endogenous variables so that $\boldsymbol{\beta} = (\beta_1, \beta_2)'$.

5.5.1 Weak Instrument Cases

We follow Staiger and Stock (1997) and Wang and Zivot (1998) and characterize weak instruments using a local-to-zero framework. With multiple endogenous variables, the characterization of weak instruments becomes a bit complicated because the instruments $\mathbf{Z}$ may be weak for the coefficients on all of the endogenous variables or for only a subset of the coefficients. Therefore, we consider the following weak instrument (WI) cases:

1. Weak Instrument Case I: $\boldsymbol{\Gamma} = [\boldsymbol{\Gamma}_1, \boldsymbol{\Gamma}_2] = n^{-1/2}\mathbf{G}$, where $\mathbf{G}$ is a fixed $q \times 2$ matrix of full rank. This case is considered by Staiger and Stock (1997) and Wang and Zivot (1998) and specifies that instruments are weak for both structural coefficients.
2. Weak Instrument Case II: $\boldsymbol{\Gamma}_1 = n^{-1/2}\mathbf{g}_1$, where $\mathbf{g}_1$ is a fixed $q \times 1$ vector and $\boldsymbol{\Gamma}_2$ is a nonzero fixed $q \times 1$ vector linearly independent of $\boldsymbol{\Gamma}_1$. This case specifies that instruments are weak for β_1 but not for β_2.
3. Weak Instrument Case III: $\boldsymbol{\Gamma}_1 = a\boldsymbol{\Gamma}_2 + n^{-1/2}\mathbf{g}_1$, where a is a nonzero scalar, $\mathbf{g}_1$ is a fixed $q \times 1$ vector, and $\boldsymbol{\Gamma}_2$ is a nonzero fixed $q \times 1$ vector linearly independent of $\mathbf{g}_1$. This case specifies that instruments are weak for both structural coefficients except for the linear combination $\alpha = a\beta_1 + \beta_2$.

5.5.2 Standardized Variables

The asymptotic distributions of various estimators and test statistics under the weak instrument cases defined above depend on nuisance parameters measuring the degree of endogeneity of $\mathbf{X}_1$ and $\mathbf{X}_2$, standardized multivariate normal random vectors, and standardized measures of the quality of the instruments $\mathbf{Z}$. Endogeneity is measured using the simple correlation coefficients

$$\rho_{u1} = \sigma_{u1}/(\sigma_{uu}\sigma_{11})^{1/2}, \ \rho_{u2} = \sigma_{u2}/(\sigma_{uu}\sigma_{22})^{1/2}, \rho_{12} = \sigma_{12}/(\sigma_{11}\sigma_{22})^{1/2},$$

where σ_{11}, σ_{12}, and σ_{22} are the unique elements of $\boldsymbol{\Sigma}_{VV}$. The weak instrument asymptotic distributions are functions of the standardized random vectors

$$\mathbf{z}_u = \mathbf{M}^{-1/2}\boldsymbol{\Psi}_{\mathbf{Z}u}/\sigma_{uu}^{1/2}$$
$$\mathbf{z}_1 = \mathbf{M}^{-1/2}\boldsymbol{\Psi}_{\mathbf{Z}1}/\sigma_{11}^{1/2}$$
$$\mathbf{z}_2 = \mathbf{M}^{-1/2}\boldsymbol{\Psi}_{\mathbf{Z}2}/\sigma_{22}^{1/2}$$

with $\mathbf{Z_V} = [z_1, \mathbf{z}_2]$ such that[5]

$$\begin{pmatrix} \mathbf{z}_u \\ \text{vec}(\mathbf{Z}_V) \end{pmatrix} \sim N(0, \mathbf{R} \otimes \mathbf{I}_q), \ \mathbf{R} = \begin{pmatrix} 1 & \rho_{u1} & \rho_{u2} \\ \rho_{u1} & 1 & \rho_{12} \\ \rho_{u2} & \rho_{12} & 1 \end{pmatrix}.$$

Staiger and Stock (1997) used an alternative standardization such that $\rho_{12} = 0$.

Additionally, define

$$\underset{(2\times 2)}{\underline{\boldsymbol{\Lambda}}} = \mathbf{M}^{1/2}\mathbf{G}\boldsymbol{\Sigma}_{\mathbf{VV}}^{-1/2} = [\underline{\boldsymbol{\lambda}_1}, \underline{\boldsymbol{\lambda}_2}],$$

and for $i = 1, 2$

$$\begin{aligned} \boldsymbol{\lambda}_i &= \mathbf{M}^{1/2}\mathbf{g}_i/\sigma_{ii}^{1/2} \\ \eta_i &= (\boldsymbol{\lambda}_i + \mathbf{z}_i)'(\boldsymbol{\lambda}_i + \mathbf{z}_i) \\ \xi_i &= (\boldsymbol{\lambda}_i + \mathbf{z}_i)'\mathbf{z}_u. \end{aligned}$$

The matrix $\underline{\boldsymbol{\Lambda}}'\underline{\boldsymbol{\Lambda}}/q$ is related to the noncentrality parameter of the limiting chi-square distribution of the Wald statistic for testing $\boldsymbol{\Gamma} = \mathbf{0}$ in (3) and measures the global quality of the instruments. The scalars $\boldsymbol{\lambda}_i'\boldsymbol{\lambda}_i/q$ $(i = 1, 2)$ are related to the noncentrality parameter of the limiting chi-square distribution of the Wald statistics for testing $\boldsymbol{\Gamma}_i = \mathbf{0}$ in (4) and measure the quality of the instruments for β_i.

5.5.3 Asymptotics Under Weak Instrument Case I

The appendix gives the convergence results for sample moments under weak instrument case I that are used in deriving the following results. In the following, "$\Rightarrow$" denotes convergence under the Staiger–Stock weak instrument asymptotics.

Theorem 5.1 *Under Assumption 5.1 and weak instrument case I, the following results hold jointly as $n \to \infty$:*

1. $$\hat{\beta}_{i,\text{IV}} - \beta_i \Rightarrow \left(\frac{\sigma_{uu}}{\sigma_{ii}}\right)^{1/2} \frac{(\boldsymbol{\lambda}_i + \mathbf{z}_i)'\mathbf{Q}_{\lambda_{\sim i}+z_{\sim i}}\mathbf{z}_u}{(\boldsymbol{\lambda}_i + \mathbf{z}_i)'\mathbf{Q}_{\lambda_{\sim i}+z_{\sim i}}(\boldsymbol{\lambda}_i + \mathbf{z}_i)} = \beta_i^*, \ i = 1, 2,$$

   where $\mathbf{Q}_{\lambda_{\sim i}+z_{\sim i}} = \mathbf{I}_q - \mathbf{P}_{\lambda_{\sim i}+z_{\sim i}}$ is a random idempotent matrix of rank $q - 1$ with probability 1.
2. Under the null hypothesis $H_0 : \beta_i = \beta_i^0$ $(i = 1, 2)$

   $$\tilde{\beta}_{\sim i,\text{IV}}(\beta_i^0) - \beta_{\sim i} \Rightarrow \left(\frac{\sigma_{uu}}{\sigma_{\sim i\sim i}}\right)^{1/2} \eta_{\sim i}^{-1}\xi_{\sim i} = \beta_{\sim i}^*(\beta_i^0)$$

[5] The correlation coefficients in the matrix **R** are not unrestricted. An analysis of the Choleski decomposition of **R** will spell out the necessary restrictions.

$$\tilde{\sigma}_{uu}(\beta_i^0) \Rightarrow \sigma_{uu}\left\{1 + \omega_{\tilde{i}}^*(\beta_i^0)\right\},$$

where $\omega_{\tilde{i}}^*(\beta_i^0) = \beta_{\tilde{i}}^*(\beta_i^0)^2\left(\frac{\sigma_{\tilde{i}\tilde{i}}}{\sigma_{uu}}\right) - 2\beta_{\tilde{i}}^*(\beta_i^0)\left(\frac{\sigma_{u\tilde{i}}}{\sigma_{\tilde{i}\tilde{i}}}\right).$

Proof. The proof follows directly from the results of Lemma A.1 in Appendix A. ∎

Result 1, first derived by Staiger and Stock (1997), shows that the IV estimate of β_i is inconsistent and converges to a random variable whose distribution depends on nuisance parameters that cannot be consistently estimated. Result 2 shows that the restricted IV estimate, $\tilde{\beta}_{\tilde{i},\mathrm{IV}}(\beta_i^0)$, is inconsistent and converges to the random variable $\beta_{\tilde{i}}^*(\beta_i^0)$ that depends on unknown nuisance parameters. As a result, the restricted residual variance estimate, $\tilde{\sigma}_{uu}(\beta_i^0)$, is also inconsistent and converges to a random variable.[6] Because the denominators of the asymptotic-t, S, modified-t, AR, and K statistics depend on restricted estimates of σ_{uu}, the inconsistency of $\tilde{\sigma}_{uu}(\beta_i^0)$ introduces a random variable like $\omega_{\tilde{i}}^*(\beta_i^0)$ into the limiting distributions of these test statistics. For example, if one uses Lemma A.1 from Appendix A, it is straightforward to show that

$$\mathrm{AR}(\beta_i^0) \Rightarrow \frac{\mathbf{z}_u'\mathbf{Q}_{\lambda_{\tilde{i}}+z_{\tilde{i}}}\mathbf{z}_u}{1 + \omega_{\tilde{i}}^*(\beta_i^0)}.$$

The results of Theorem 5.1 indicate that, if instruments are weak for all structural coefficients, asymptotically valid inference cannot be made using any of the proposed test statistics. However, asymptotically valid, but conservative, confidence sets for individual coefficients may be computed using the Dufour–Taamouti projection-AR sets. If instruments are very weak, these sets will be unbounded with probability close to the stated coverage probability.

5.5.4 Asymptotics Under Weak Instrument Case II

Most of the asymptotic results for estimators and test statistics to date have been based on weak instrument case I. In this section we provide some asymptotic results for a subset of the estimators and test statistics under weak instrument case II.

Theorem 5.2 *Under Assumption 5.1 and weak instrument case II, the following results hold as $n \to \infty$.*

Part 1.

(a) $\hat{\beta}_{1,\mathrm{IV}} - \beta_1 \Rightarrow \left(\frac{\sigma_{uu}}{\sigma_{11}}\right)^{1/2} \frac{(\boldsymbol{\lambda}_1+\mathbf{z}_1)'\mathbf{Q}_{\mathbf{M}^{1/2}\boldsymbol{\Gamma}_2}\mathbf{z}_u}{(\boldsymbol{\lambda}_1+\mathbf{z}_1)'\mathbf{Q}_{\mathbf{M}^{1/2}\boldsymbol{\Gamma}_2}(\boldsymbol{\lambda}_1+\mathbf{z}_1)} = \beta_1^{\dagger},$

[6] Similar results may be shown to hold for the LIML estimates.

(b) $\sqrt{n}(\hat{\beta}_{2,\mathrm{IV}} - \beta_2) \Rightarrow \sigma_{uu}^{1/2} \cdot \frac{\mathbf{\Gamma}_2'\mathbf{M}^{1/2\prime}\mathbf{Q}_{\boldsymbol{\lambda}_1+\mathbf{z}_1}\mathbf{z}_u}{\mathbf{\Gamma}_2'\mathbf{M}^{1/2\prime}\mathbf{Q}_{\boldsymbol{\lambda}_1+\mathbf{z}_1}\mathbf{M}^{1/2}\mathbf{\Gamma}_2}$, and

(c) $\hat{\sigma}_{uu,\mathrm{IV}} \Rightarrow \sigma_{uu}\{1 + \omega_1^\dagger\}$,

where $\mathbf{Q}_{\mathbf{M}^{1/2}\mathbf{\Gamma}_2}$ is an idempotent matrix with rank $q-1$, $\mathbf{Q}_{\boldsymbol{\lambda}_1+\mathbf{z}_1}$ is a random idempotent matrix of rank $q-1$ w.p.1, and $\omega_1^\dagger = \left(\beta_1^\dagger\right)^2\left(\frac{\sigma_{11}}{\sigma_{uu}}\right) - 2\beta_1^\dagger\left(\frac{\sigma_{u1}}{\sigma_{uu}}\right)$.

Part 2. Under the null hypothesis $H_0 : \beta_1 = \beta_1^0$

(d) $t_{\mathrm{IV}}(\beta_1^0)^2 \Rightarrow (1+\omega_1^\dagger)^{-1}\mathbf{z}_u'\mathbf{P}_{\mathbf{A}}\mathbf{z}_u$,

(e) $\tilde{\beta}_{2,j}(\beta_1^0) \Rightarrow \beta_2$, $j = \mathrm{IV}, \mathrm{LIML}$,

(f) $\sqrt{n}(\tilde{\beta}_{2,j}(\beta_1^0) - \beta_2) \Rightarrow N(0, \sigma_{uu}(\mathbf{\Gamma}_2'\mathbf{M}\mathbf{\Gamma}_2)^{-1})$, $j = \mathrm{IV}, \mathrm{LIML}$,

(g) $\tilde{\sigma}_{uu,j}(\beta_1^0) \Rightarrow \sigma_{uu}$, $j = \mathrm{IV}, \mathrm{LIML}$,

(h) $\mathrm{LR}_{\mathrm{LIML}}(\beta_1^0) \Rightarrow \mathbf{z}_u'\mathbf{Q}_{\mathbf{M}^{1/2}\mathbf{\Gamma}_2}\mathbf{z}_u \sim \chi^2(1)$ for $q = 2$; $\mathrm{LR}_{\mathrm{LIML}}(\beta_1^0) \Rightarrow \mathbf{z}_u'\mathbf{Q}_{\mathbf{M}^{1/2}\mathbf{\Gamma}_2}\mathbf{z}_u - k^*_{\mathrm{LIML}} < \chi^2(q-1)$ for $q > 2$,

(i) $\mathrm{S}^2(\beta_1^0)$, $\tilde{t}_{\mathrm{IV}}(\beta_1^0)^2 \Rightarrow \mathbf{z}_u'\mathbf{P}_{\mathbf{A}}\mathbf{z}_u < \mathbf{z}_u'\mathbf{Q}_{\mathbf{M}^{1/2}\mathbf{\Gamma}_2}\mathbf{z}_u \sim \chi^2(q-1)$,

(j) $\mathrm{AR}_j(\beta_1^0) \Rightarrow \mathbf{z}_u'\mathbf{Q}_{\mathbf{M}^{1/2}\mathbf{\Gamma}_2}\mathbf{z}_u \sim \chi^2(q-1)$, $j = \mathrm{IV}, \mathrm{LIML}$, and

(k) $\mathrm{K}(\beta_1^0) \Rightarrow \chi^2(1)$,

where $\mathbf{A} = \mathbf{Q}_{\mathbf{M}^{1/2}\mathbf{\Gamma}_2}(\boldsymbol{\lambda}_1 + \mathbf{z}_1)$.

Part 3. Under the null hypothesis $H_0 : \beta_2 = \beta_2^0$

(l) $t_{\mathrm{IV}}(\beta_2^0)^2 \Rightarrow (1+\omega_1^\dagger)^{-1}\mathbf{z}_u'\mathbf{P}_{\mathbf{B}}\mathbf{z}_u$,

(m) $\tilde{\beta}_{1,\mathrm{IV}}(\beta_2^0) - \beta_1 \Rightarrow \left(\frac{\sigma_{uu}}{\sigma_{11}}\right)^{1/2}\eta_1^{-1}\xi_1 = \beta_1^*(\beta_2^0)$, and

(n) $\tilde{\sigma}_{uu}(\beta_2^0) \Rightarrow \sigma_{uu}\left\{1 + \omega_1^*(\beta_2^0)\right\}$,

where $\mathbf{B} = \mathbf{Q}_{\boldsymbol{\lambda}_1+\mathbf{z}_1}\mathbf{M}^{1/2}\mathbf{\Gamma}_2$, and $\omega_1^*(\beta_2^0) = \left(\beta_1^*(\beta_2^0)\right)^2\left(\frac{\sigma_{11}}{\sigma_{uu}}\right) - 2\beta_1^*(\beta_2^0)\left(\frac{\sigma_{u1}}{\sigma_{uu}}\right)$.

Proof. The proof follows directly from the results of Lemma A.2 in the Appendix A. ■

Part 1 of the theorem shows that if instruments are weak for β_1 but not for β_2, then $\hat{\beta}_{1,\mathrm{IV}}$ is not consistent for β_1, but $\hat{\beta}_{2,\mathrm{IV}}$ is consistent for β_2. This corresponds to the result from Choi and Phillips (1992) for the partially identified model. Owing to the inconsistency of $\hat{\beta}_{1,\mathrm{IV}}$, the IV estimate of the residual error variance is inconsistent and converges to a random variable. The asymptotic distribution of $\hat{\beta}_{1,\mathrm{IV}}$ is a ratio of quadratic forms in correlated normal random vectors and is similar to the result established by Staiger and Stock (1997). When β_1 is totally unidentified, the limiting distribution reduces to the expression given in part (b) of Corollary 3.1 of Choi and Phillips (1992). The limiting distribution of $\hat{\beta}_{2,\mathrm{IV}}$ is not normal but may be expressed as a mixture-normal distribution using arguments from Staiger and Stock (1997). Conditional on $\mathbf{z}_1$, the asymptotic distribution of $\hat{\beta}_{2,\mathrm{IV}}$ is normal with mean zero and variance

$$\sigma_{uu}\left(\mathbf{\Gamma}_2'\mathbf{M}^{1/2\prime}\mathbf{Q}_{\boldsymbol{\lambda}_1+\mathbf{z}_1}\mathbf{M}^{1/2}\mathbf{\Gamma}_2\right)^{-1}.$$

When β_1 is totally unidentified, the limiting distribution reduces to the expression given in part (a) of Corollary 3.1 of Choi and Phillips (1992). As instruments become stronger, the limiting distribution of $\hat{\beta}_{2,\text{IV}}$ approaches its usual asymptotic normal distribution.

Part 2 shows Staiger and Stock's (1997) result that standard inference based on the IV t-statistic is not valid for β_1 because its limiting distribution depends on nuisance parameters that cannot be consistently estimated. However, valid inference may be performed on β_1 using the other statistics because their limiting distributions are either pivotal or boundedly pivotal. The main reason for this is that the residual error variance σ_{uu} may be consistently estimated when $\beta_1 = \beta_1^0$ and instruments are strong for β_2. When $q = 2$, $S^2(\beta_1^0)$, $\tilde{t}_{\text{IV}}(\beta_1^0)^2$, and $\text{LR}(\beta_1^0)$ have limiting $\chi^2(1)$ distributions, whereas when $q > 2$ the limiting distributions of these statistics are bounded from above by a $\chi^2(q-1)$ distribution. These results suggest that the usual normal critical values may be used to evaluate the S-statistic and modified t-statistics only for the case $q = 2$. The limiting distributions of $\text{AR}_{\text{IV}}(\beta_1^0)$, $\text{AR}_{\text{LIML}}(\beta_1^0)$ are $\chi^2(q-1)$, as suggested by the results of Stock and Wright (2000). Because the limiting distribution of Kleibergen's $\text{K}(\beta_1^0)$ statistic is $\chi^2(1)$, it has an apparent power advantage when q is large over the other statistics whose limiting distributions are $\chi^2(q-1)$ or are bounded by $\chi^2(q-1)$. The Monte Carlo results in Section 5.8, however, show that no statistic dominates in terms of power.

Part 3 of the theorem implies, surprisingly, that no method, except for the projection AR confidence sets, provides valid inference for β_2. This is because, under the null $\beta_2 = \beta_2^0$, we cannot remove the effects of weak instruments for β_1 on the distributions of the test statistics. For example, using straightforward calculations, it can be shown that the denominator of $\text{AR}_{\text{IV}}(\beta_2^0)$ converges to $\sigma_{uu}\left\{1 + \omega_1^*(\beta_2^0)\right\}$ instead of σ_{uu}. In effect, because we cannot consistently estimate σ_{uu} when $\beta_2 = \beta_2^0$ and instruments are weak for β_1, we cannot get asymptotically pivotal statistics for testing $\beta_2 = \beta_2^0$. If $\hat{\sigma}_{uu}$ is a consistent estimator of σ_{uu}, then straightforward conditioning arguments may be used to show that $t_{\text{IV}}(\beta_2^0) \Rightarrow N(0, 1)$ so that valid inference on β_2 may be performed using standard methods. Interestingly, the Monte Carlo results of Section 5.8 suggest that the $\chi^2(q-1)$ distribution is a good approximation to the distribution of $\text{AR}_{\text{LIML}}(\beta_2^0)$ and the $\chi^2(1)$ distribution is a good approximation to the distribution of $\text{K}(\beta_2^0)$.

5.6 ASYMPTOTICS UNDER WEAK INSTRUMENT CASE III

Under weak instrument case III, instruments are weak for β_1 and β_2 individually but are strong for the linear combination $\alpha = a\beta_1 + \beta_2$. To determine the limiting distributions of β_1, β_2 and α, we follow Choi and Phillips (1992) and consider a rotation of the IV regression model (1) to isolate the identified and weakly identified coefficients. Define

$$\tilde{\mathbf{X}}_1 = \mathbf{X}_1 - a\mathbf{X}_2.$$

Then the rotated IV regression model is

$$\begin{aligned}\mathbf{y} &= \tilde{\mathbf{X}}_1\beta_1 + \mathbf{X}_2\alpha + \mathbf{u}\\ \tilde{\mathbf{X}}_1 &= \mathbf{Z}\tilde{\boldsymbol{\Gamma}}_1 + \tilde{\mathbf{v}}_1\\ \mathbf{X}_2 &= \mathbf{Z}\boldsymbol{\Gamma}_2 + \mathbf{v}_2,\end{aligned}$$

where $\tilde{\boldsymbol{\Gamma}}_1 = \boldsymbol{\Gamma}_1 - a\boldsymbol{\Gamma}_2$ and $\tilde{\mathbf{v}}_1 = \mathbf{v}_1 - a\mathbf{v}_2$ and β_1 is weakly identified and α well identified. Under weak instrument case III, the analysis of the rotated IV regression model is identical to analysis of the unrotated model under weak instrument case II because $\tilde{\boldsymbol{\Gamma}}_1 = a\boldsymbol{\Gamma}_2 + n^{-1/2}\mathbf{g}_1 - a\boldsymbol{\Gamma}_2 = n^{-1/2}\mathbf{g}_1$ and $\boldsymbol{\Gamma}_2 \neq 0$. In particular, the TSLS estimate of β_1 is inconsistent and the TSLS estimate of α is consistent but asymptotically biased.

5.7 CONFIDENCE REGIONS

An asymptotically valid confidence set for the scalar β_i with level $1-\alpha$ based on inverting the statistic $T(\beta_i^0)$ is defined by

$$C_{\beta_i}(\alpha) = \{\beta_i^0 : T(\beta_i^0) \leq c_\alpha\}, \tag{25}$$

where c_α is the $1-\alpha$ quantile of the limiting distribution of $T(\beta_i^0)$. Computing the set (25) requires finding the values of β_i^0 such that $T(\beta_i^0) < c_\alpha$. In general, this process requires a numerical search. However, utilizing the insights of Dufour (1997); Zivot, Startz, and Nelson (1998); and Dufour and Jasiak (2001), we find that if the inequality $T(\beta_i^0) \leq c_\alpha$ may be rewritten as a quadratic inequality

$$a\left(\beta_i^0\right)^2 + b\beta_i^0 + c \leq 0, \tag{26}$$

where values of a, b, and c depend on the data and c_α, then the confidence regions defined by (25) have convenient closed-form expressions and may take one of four shapes: a familiar connected interval of the form $(\beta_i^L, \beta_i^H;\ ^L =$ lower, $^H =$ upper) the union of two rays $(-\infty, \beta_i^L) \cup (\beta_i^H, \infty)$, the entire real line, or the empty set. In Appendix B, we show that the inequality $T(\beta_i^0) \leq c_\alpha$ may be expressed in the form (26) for $\mathrm{S}(\beta_i^0)^2$, $\tilde{t}_{1,\mathrm{IV}}(\beta_1^0)^2$, and $\mathrm{AR}_{\mathrm{IV}}(\beta_i^0)$ but not for $\mathrm{AR}_{\mathrm{LIML}}(\beta_i^0)$, $\mathrm{LR}(\beta_i^0)$, and $\mathrm{K}(\beta_i^0)$. Consequently, easy-to-compute analytic formulas for the confidence sets based on the former set of statistics are readily available.

Figure 5.1 illustrates the shapes of typical confidence sets based on inverting the statistics $t_{\mathrm{IV}}(\beta_i^0)^2$, $\mathrm{S}(\beta_i^0)^2$, $\mathrm{AR}_{\mathrm{LIML}}(\beta_i^0)$, $\mathrm{LR}(\beta_i^0)$, and $\mathrm{K}(\beta_i^0)$ in the presence

Table 5.1 *95-Percent Confidence Sets from Simulated Data*

	Weak Instruments		Good Instruments	
	β_1	β_2	β_1	β_2
t^2_{IV}	[1.52, 1.80]	[1.00, 1.12]	[1.12, 1.44]	[1.00, 1.24]
S^2_1	[1.39, 1.80]	[0.99, 1, 14]	[1.08, 1.42]	[0.99, 1.26]
S^2_4	[1.00, 1.87]	[0.95, 1.20]	[0.89, 1.48]	[0.92, 1.36]
LR_1	[0.76, 1.62]	[1.00, 1.30]	[0.92, 1.32]	[1.00, 1.32]
LR_4	$[-\infty, 1.70]$	[0.92, 2.22]	[0.68, 1.40]	[0.90, 1.46]
K	$[0.76, 1.62] \cup [2.00, 2.06]$	[1.00, 1.30]	$[0.94, 1.32] \cup [1.84, 2.18]$	[1.00, 1.32]
$\mathrm{AR}_{\mathrm{LIML}}$	$\emptyset$	$\emptyset$	$\emptyset$	$\emptyset$
$\mathrm{AR}_{\mathrm{proj}}$	[1.17, 1.56]	[1.03, 1.18]	[1.07, 1.27]	[1.07, 1.23]

Notes: S^2_1 and LR_1 are computed using $\chi^2_{.05}(1)$; S^2_4 and LR_4 are computed using $\chi^2_{.05}(4)$

of weak and good instruments.[7] The plot of $\mathrm{AR}_{\mathrm{IV}}(\beta_i^0)$ is almost identical to $\mathrm{AR}_{\mathrm{LIML}}(\beta_i^0)$ and so is omitted. The top panel of Figure 5.1 shows plots of these statistics as functions of β_i^0 for a particular Monte Carlo realization of the IV regression model (1)–(3) with $k = 2$ and $q = 5$ in which $\beta_1 = 1$ is weakly identified and highly endogenous and $\beta_2 = 1$ is well identified and minimally endogenous. The bottom panel of Figure 5.1 shows plots of the statistics for a Monte Carlo realization in which both β_1 and β_2 are well identified.[8] Ninety-five-percent confidence intervals are the values of β_i^0 such that the test statistic in question lies below the appropriate critical value. These confidence intervals are summarized in Table 5.1 along with the projection-based confidence set determined from the joint AR statistic (23). On the basis of the asymptotic results in the previous section, $c_{.05} = \chi^2_{.05}(1) = 3.84$ is the appropriate critical value for $\mathrm{K}(\beta_1)$ and, potentially for $\mathrm{S}^2(\beta_1^0)$ and $\mathrm{LR}(\beta_1^0)$ as well. This critical value is the lower horizontal line on the plots. The critical value $c_{.05}(4) = \chi^2_{.05}(4) = 9.481$ is appropriate for $\mathrm{AR}_{\mathrm{LIML}}(\beta_1^0)$ and serves as a conservative critical value for $\mathrm{S}^2(\beta_1^0)$ and $\mathrm{LR}(\beta_1^0)$. This value is the upper horizontal line on the plots. There is no valid critical value for $t_{\mathrm{IV}}(\beta_1^0)^2$. For the statistics testing $\beta_2 = 1$, the chi-square critical values are not correct.[9] However, for illustrative purposes, these critical values are used when forming the confidence sets.

Consider first the plots of the statistics as functions of β_1 for the weak instrument case given in the upper left panel of Figure 5.1. The $t_{\mathrm{IV}}(\beta_1^0)^2$ statistic

[7] The confidence sets for the modified t-statistics are almost identical to those for the S-statistic and so are omitted.

[8] In particular, for the top panel, the design is as described in Section 5.8 for weak instrument case II with $\gamma_{11} = 0.2236$ and $\gamma_{22} = 1.1180$. For the bottom panel, $\gamma_{11} = \gamma_{22} = 1.1180$. For both panels, $\rho_{u1} = 0.99$ and $\rho_{u2} = 0.1$.

[9] The Monte Carlo results in the next section indicate that the chi-square critical values often produce reasonable results.

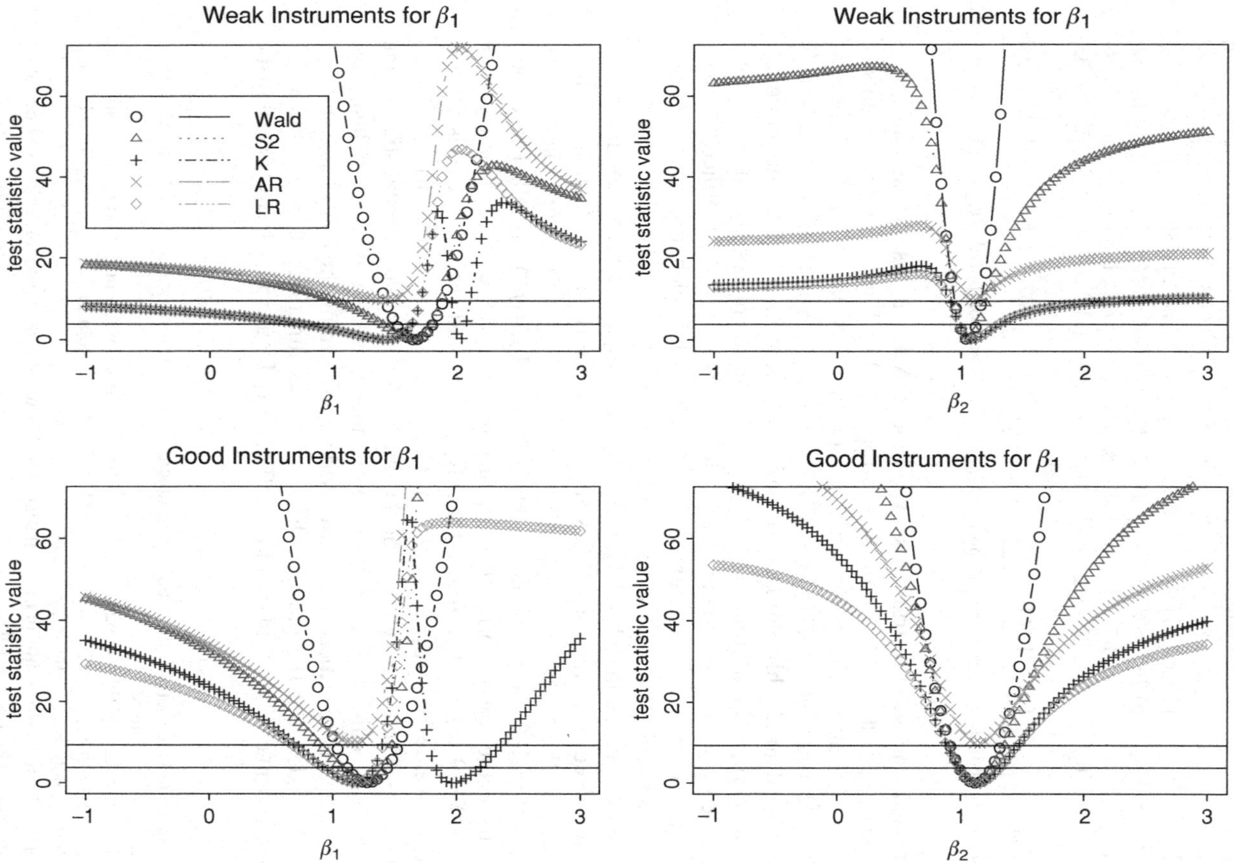

Figure 5.1. Test statistic values as a function of β_i^0 from Monte Carlo realization under weak instrument case II.

plots as a parabola and the incorrect 95 percent confidence region is a reasonably tight closed interval around $\hat{\beta}_{1,\mathrm{IV}} = 1.66$, (1.52, 1.80) – a region that excludes the true value. The shapes of the other statistics are generally similar to each other but display some important differences. All statistics eventually asymptotically approach a finite value. $\mathrm{AR}_{\mathrm{LIML}}(\beta_1)$ always lies above the critical value 9.481 and so produces an empty confidence set. This results from the data's rejecting the overidentifying restrictions when one imposes $\beta_1 = 1$. Unlike the $\mathrm{AR}_{\mathrm{LIML}}(\beta_1)$ set, the projected-AR confidence set is a closed interval but excludes $\beta_1 = 1$. The statistics $\mathrm{LR}(\beta_1^0)$ and $\mathrm{K}(\beta_1^0)$ follow each other very closely except for a region around $\beta_1^0 = 2$. In fact $\mathrm{K}(\beta_1^0)$ drops to zero at the point where $\mathrm{AR}_{\mathrm{LIML}}(\beta_1)$ attains its maximum value – a phenomenon noted by Kleibergen (2000). As a result, the 95-percent confidence set based on $\mathrm{K}(\beta_1^0)$ consists of two disconnected intervals with the true value $\beta_1 = 1$ contained in the first interval. The statistics $\mathrm{LR}(\beta_1^0)$ and $\mathrm{S}^2(\beta_1^0)$ behave similarly. Both statistics produce closed confidence sets using the $\chi^2(1)$ critical value with $\beta_1 = 1$ covered by the LR set but not by the S^2 set. When the conservative $\chi^2(4)$ critical value is used, the lower limit of the LR set becomes unbounded, whereas the S^2 remains closed. With the $\chi^2(4)$ critical value, the S^2 set contains $\beta_1 = 1$.

Next, consider the statistics for testing $\beta_1 = 1$ when instruments are good for both coefficients. All confidence sets except for those based on $\mathrm{AR}_{\mathrm{LIML}}(\beta_1^0)$ and $\mathrm{K}(\beta_1^0)$ are closed, and the right endpoints of the sets are similar. Owing to the high degree of endogeneity of X_1, the $t_{\mathrm{IV}}(\beta_1^0)^2$ confidence set still excludes $\beta_1 = 1$. However, $\beta_1 = 1$ is covered by the LR and K confidence sets using the $\chi^2(1)$ critical value and is covered by the S^2 confidence set using the $\chi^2(4)$ critical value.

Now consider the test statistics as functions of β_2. For both weak and good instruments of β_1, all confidence sets, except those based on $\mathrm{AR}_{\mathrm{LIML}}(\beta_2^0)$, are closed. The $\mathrm{AR}_{\mathrm{LIML}}$ set for β_2^0 is empty, and the projection AR set does not cover the value $\beta_2 = 1$. The remaining sets are very similar to each other and cover the true value $\beta_2 = 1$. The sets based on $t_{\mathrm{IV}}(\beta_1^0)^2$ and $\mathrm{S}^2(\beta_2^0)$ using the $\chi^2(1)$ critical value are very similar and have the smallest width. The sets based on $\mathrm{LR}(\beta_2^0)$ and $\mathrm{K}(\beta_2^0)$ using the $\chi^2(1)$ critical value are essentially identical.

5.8 FINITE SAMPLE PROPERTIES UNDER WEAK INSTRUMENTS

In this section, we evaluate the finite sample properties of the competing statistics for making inference on individual structural coefficients using a comprehensive set of Monte Carlo experiments. Several authors have considered Monte Carlo designs for IV regressions with weak instruments. The main papers are Choi and Phillips (1992); Hall, Rudebusch, and Wilcox (1997); Shea (1997); Staiger and Stock (1997); Zivot, Startz, and Nelson (1998); Dufour and Khalaf (1998); Blomquist and Dahlberg (1999); Flores-Lagunes (2000); Kleibergen (2000, 2002); Taamouti (2001); and Hahn and Inuoe (2002). Most of the Monte Carlo studies that have focused on the performance of estimation and inference methods in the presence of weak instruments are based on designs with a single right-hand-side endogenous variable. Choi and Phillips (1992), Flores-Lagunes (2000), and Kleibergen (2000) have considered designs with two right-hand-side endogenous variables, and the results from these papers indicate that it may be misleading to extrapolate the results from the one-variable case to the multiple-variable case. Much more work is needed in the multiple right-hand-side variable case, and we provide the most comprehensive study to date.

5.8.1 Monte Carlo Designs for Multiple Endogenous Variables

The Staiger–Stock weak instrument asymptotics show that the distributions of IV estimators and test statistics depend on three key nuisance parameters: (1) the degree of endogeneity as measured by the correlation coefficients ρ_{u1}, ρ_{u2}, and ρ_{12}; (2) the number of instruments, q; and (3) the relevance of the instruments as measured by $\underline{\mathbf{\Lambda}}'\underline{\mathbf{\Lambda}}/q$. Instruments are irrelevant when $\underline{\mathbf{\Lambda}}'\underline{\mathbf{\Lambda}}/q = \mathbf{0}$. For one right-hand-side endogenous variable, Staiger and Stock's simulation experiments reveal that instruments are essentially weak when $0 < \underline{\mathbf{\Lambda}}'\underline{\mathbf{\Lambda}}/q < 10$. Instruments become reasonably good when $\underline{\mathbf{\Lambda}}'\underline{\mathbf{\Lambda}}/q > 10$. In the multiple right-hand-side endogenous variable case, $\underline{\mathbf{\Lambda}}'\underline{\mathbf{\Lambda}}/q$ is a matrix, and weak instruments are characterized by the minimum eigenvalue of $\underline{\mathbf{\Lambda}}'\underline{\mathbf{\Lambda}}/q$. In addition, Staiger and Stock show that with weak instruments the performance of standard inference methods is the worst in models with many irrelevant instruments (large value of q and $\mathbf{\Gamma} \approx \mathbf{0}$) and very high degrees of endogeneity.

The data-generating process (DGP) for our experiments is similar to the designs in Flores-Lagunes (2000) and has the form

$$\begin{aligned}
\mathbf{y} &= \mathbf{X}_1\beta_1 + \mathbf{X}_2\beta_2 + \mathbf{u} \\
\mathbf{X}_1 &= \mathbf{Z}_1\gamma_{11} + \mathbf{Z}_2\gamma_{12} + \mathbf{Z}_3\mathbf{\Gamma}_{13} + \mathbf{v}_1 \\
\mathbf{X}_2 &= \mathbf{Z}_1\gamma_{21} + \mathbf{Z}_2\gamma_{22} + \mathbf{Z}_3\mathbf{\Gamma}_{23} + \mathbf{v}_2,
\end{aligned}$$

where $\beta_1 = \beta_2 = 1$, $\mathbf{\Gamma}_{13} = \mathbf{\Gamma}_{23} = \mathbf{0}$, and the covariates are generated following[10]

$$\mathbf{Z}_t = (Z_{1t}, Z_{2t}, \mathbf{Z}'_{3t})' \sim \text{iid } N(\mathbf{0}, \mathbf{I}_q)$$

$$\begin{bmatrix} u_t \\ v_{1t} \\ v_{2t} \end{bmatrix} \sim \text{iid } N\left(\begin{pmatrix} 0 \\ 0 \\ 0 \end{pmatrix}, \begin{pmatrix} 1 & \rho_{u1} & \rho_{u2} \\ \rho_{u1} & 1 & 0 \\ \rho_{u2} & 0 & 1 \end{pmatrix} \right).$$

The $q - 2$ variables in $\mathbf{Z}_3$ are superfluous instruments because their coefficient values in the reduced-form equations are zero. The main difference from the Flores-Lagunes designs is that the instruments are mutually uncorrelated

10 The correlation coefficients must satisfy $\rho^2_{ue_1} + \rho^2_{ue_2} < 1$ for the error covariance matrix to be positive definite.

with unit variances. In this design,

$$\begin{aligned}\mathbf{\Sigma_{VV}} &= \mathbf{I}_2, \mathbf{Q} = \mathbf{I}_q, \boldsymbol{\lambda} = \mathbf{C} = \boldsymbol{\Gamma}/\sqrt{n}\\ \rho &= \Sigma_{Vu} = (\rho_{u1}, \rho_{u2})'\\ \underline{\boldsymbol{\Lambda}}'\underline{\boldsymbol{\Lambda}} &= \mathbf{C}'\mathbf{C} = \mathbf{n}\boldsymbol{\Gamma}'\boldsymbol{\Gamma}.\end{aligned}$$

We set $n = 100$ and consider cases for which $\rho = (0.5, 0.5)', (0.1, 0.99)', (0.99, 0.1)'$. Because $\rho_{12} = 0$, the degree of overall endogeneity is measured by $\rho'\rho = \rho_{u1}^2 + \rho_{u2}^2$. In the first two cases, $\mathbf{X}_1$ and $\mathbf{X}_2$ are moderately endogenous; in the third case, $\mathbf{X}_1$ is mildly endogenous and $\mathbf{X}_2$ is strongly endogenous; in the fourth case, $\mathbf{X}_1$ is strongly endogenous and $\mathbf{X}_2$ is mildly endogenous.

We consider the following parameterizations for weak instrument cases I and II:

- Weak Instrument Case I (Staiger–Stock): $\gamma_{12} = \gamma_{21} = 0$. Set γ_{11} and γ_{22} such that

$$\underline{\boldsymbol{\Lambda}}'\underline{\boldsymbol{\Lambda}}/q = \left(\frac{n}{q}\right)\begin{pmatrix}\gamma_{11}^2 & 0\\ 0 & \gamma_{22}^2\end{pmatrix} = \begin{pmatrix}\alpha & 0\\ 0 & \alpha\end{pmatrix}, \quad \alpha = 0, 1, 10.$$

This implies that

$$\gamma_{11} = \gamma_{22} = \gamma = \left(\frac{\alpha \cdot q}{n}\right)^{1/2}.$$

Here instruments are weak for both β_1 and β_2 if $\alpha < 10$. The following table summarizes the values of γ for $q = 2, 5, 20$ and $n = 100$:

q/α	0	0.25	1
2	0	0.0707	0.1414
5	0	0.1118	0.2236
20	0	0.2236	0.4472 .

- Weak Instrument Case II: $\gamma_{12} = \gamma_{21} = 0$. Set γ_{11} and γ_{22} such that

$$\underline{\boldsymbol{\Lambda}}'\underline{\boldsymbol{\Lambda}}/q = \left(\frac{n}{q}\right)\begin{pmatrix}\gamma_{11}^2 & 0\\ 0 & \gamma_{22}^2\end{pmatrix} = \begin{pmatrix}\alpha & 0\\ 0 & 25\end{pmatrix}, \quad \alpha = 0, 1, 10$$

This implies that

$$\gamma_{11} = \left(\frac{\alpha \cdot q}{n}\right)^{1/2}, \quad \gamma_{22} = \left(\frac{25 \cdot q}{n}\right)^{1/2}.$$

Here instruments are weak for β_1 if $\alpha < 10$ and the instruments are always good for β_2. The following table summarizes the values of γ_{11} for $q = 2, 5, 20$ and $n = 100$:

q/α	0	1	10
2	0	0.1414	0.4472
5	0	0.2236	0.7071
20	0	0.4472	1.4142

Table 5.2 *Weak Instrument Case I: Empirical Rejection Frequency of 5-Percent Tests*

Design				Test Statistics for $H_0 : \beta_1 = 1$							
q	α	ρ_1	ρ_2	IV t	LIML t	AR_{IV}	AR_{LIML}	AR_{proj}	K	LR_1	S_1
2	0	.5	.5	.014	.013	.024	.004	.000	.004	.004	.024
2	1	.5	.5	.013	.013	.030	.007	.000	.007	.007	.030
2	10	.5	.5	.020	.020	.046	.015	.002	.015	.015	.046
2	0	.1	.99	.036	.036	.024	.004	.000	.004	.004	.024
2	1	.1	.99	.014	.014	.269	.045	.014	.045	.045	.269
2	10	.1	.99	.005	.005	.208	.048	.011	.048	.049	.208
2	0	.99	.1	.616	.616	.024	.004	.000	.004	.004	.024
2	1	.99	.1	.221	.221	.029	.006	.001	.006	.006	.029
2	10	.99	.1	.110	.110	.035	.013	.001	.013	.013	.035
5	0	.5	.5	.152	.066	.035	.003	.001	.012	.061	.069
5	1	.5	.5	.157	.060	.046	.007	.002	.015	.075	.062
5	10	.5	.5	.125	.052	.064	.023	.008	.031	.085	.054
5	0	.1	.99	.331	.144	.033	.002	.001	.011	.060	.108
5	1	.1	.99	.138	.018	.549	.052	.027	.057	.196	.076
5	10	.1	.99	.056	.011	.352	.056	.024	.054	.140	.044
5	0	.99	.1	.992	.735	.034	.002	.001	.011	.060	.326
5	1	.99	.1	.826	.183	.035	.004	.002	.012	.020	.228
5	10	.99	.1	.516	.090	.042	.016	.005	.022	.030	.121
20	0	.5	.5	.818	.226	.056	.003	.002	.038	.347	.453
20	1	.5	.5	.716	.159	.089	.011	.005	.048	.302	.373
20	10	.5	.5	.480	.090	.115	.052	.034	.056	.172	.242
20	0	.1	.99	.996	.320	.064	.004	.003	.039	.351	.721
20	1	.1	.99	.354	.040	.882	.079	.057	.082	.412	.122
20	10	.1	.99	.122	.058	.603	.082	.058	.066	.223	.050
20	0	.99	.1	1.00	.801	.063	.004	.003	.039	.351	1.00
20	1	.99	.1	1.00	.111	.066	.008	.006	.028	.042	.981
20	10	.99	.1	.981	.063	.072	.041	.029	.038	.043	.812

The values of γ_{22} for $q = 2, 5$, and 20 are 0.7071, 1.1180, and 2.2361, respectively.

5.8.2 Results

There are 27 different designs for each of the weak instrument cases. For each design, 10,000 simulations are performed, and the Monte Carlo experiments for each design use the same random numbers to eliminate simulation noise between experiments. We compute the unrestricted IV and LIML estimates as well as the corresponding estimates that impose the restriction $\beta_i = 1$. We also compute the IV and LIML t-statistics, the concentrated AR statistics using the restricted IV and LIML estimates (21), the concentrated K statistic (22),

Table 5.3 *Weak Instrument Case II: Empirical Rejection Frequency of 5-Percent Tests*

Design				Test Statistics for $H_0 : \beta_1 = 1$									
q	α	ρ_1	ρ_2	IV t	LIML t	AR_{IV}	AR_{LIML}	AR_{proj}	K	LR_1	LR_{q-1}	S_1	S^2_{q-1}
2	0	.5	.5	.016	.016	.050	.047	.013	.047	.047	.047	.024	.050
2	1	.5	.5	.028	.028	.050	.047	.014	.047	.047	.047	.050	.050
2	10	.5	.5	.036	.036	.050	.047	.013	.047	.047	.047	.050	.050
2	0	.1	.99	.000	.000	.057	.048	.015	.048	.048	.048	.057	.057
2	1	.1	.99	.002	.002	.057	.048	.014	.048	.048	.048	.057	.057
2	10	.1	.99	.021	.021	.057	.048	.014	.048	.048	.048	.057	.057
2	0	.99	.1	.620	.620	.048	.047	.013	.047	.047	.047	.048	.048
2	1	.99	.1	.131	.131	.048	.047	.013	.047	.047	.047	.048	.048
2	10	.99	.1	.064	.064	.048	.047	.012	.047	.047	.047	.048	.048
5	0	.5	.5	.147	.087	.058	.054	.028	.058	.228	.023	.078	.004
5	1	.5	.5	.117	.070	.058	.054	.028	.054	.124	.012	.050	.003
5	10	.5	.5	.058	.044	.058	.054	.030	.051	.056	.002	.046	.002
5	0	.1	.99	.008	.006	.072	.055	.030	.058	.232	.024	.022	.001
5	1	.1	.99	.017	.017	.072	.055	.029	.057	.143	.013	.029	.002
5	10	.1	.99	.040	.043	.072	.055	.031	.051	.057	.003	.045	.002
5	0	.99	.1	.989	.740	.055	.054	.027	.059	.227	.023	.419	.052
5	1	.99	.1	.512	.098	.055	.054	.027	.048	.049	.002	.139	.011
5	10	.99	.1	.107	.050	.055	.054	.029	.048	.047	.002	.055	.004
20	0	.5	.5	.693	.272	.086	.082	.065	.085	.531	.004	.346	.000
20	1	.5	.5	.402	.106	.086	.082	.065	.059	.179	.000	.206	.000
20	10	.5	.5	.105	.054	.086	.082	.066	.052	.058	.000	.083	.000
20	0	.1	.99	.066	.086	.103	.083	.065	.085	.533	.004	.018	.000
20	1	.1	.99	.053	.099	.103	.083	.065	.066	.221	.000	.025	.000
20	10	.1	.99	.048	.059	.103	.083	.067	.053	.062	.000	.039	.000
20	0	.99	.1	1.00	.799	.082	.082	.061	.086	.528	.004	1.00	.071
20	1	.99	.1	.981	.070	.082	.082	.066	.049	.049	.000	.812	.002
20	10	.99	.1	.228	.048	.082	.082	.066	.047	.049	.000	.203	.000

the projection-based confidence sets based on the joint AR statistic, and the S statistic[11] (17) for testing the individual hypothesis

$$H_0 : \beta_i = 1, \ i = 1, 2.$$

The results of a subset of the experiments are summarized in Tables 5.2–5.4 and described below. Power results are only reported for a subset of weak instrument case II designs.

5.8.2.1 Weak Instrument Case I. In this design, the instruments are weak for both β_1 and β_2 in a symmetric way, and so results are only presented for tests on β_1. The asymptotic results indicate that none of the tests considered are

[11] The results for the S statistic and the modified t-statistics (20) are almost identical, and so we only show the results for the S statistic.

Table 5.4 *Weak Instrument Case II: Empirical Rejection Frequency of 5-Percent Tests*

Design				Test Statistics for $H_0 : \beta_2 = 1$									
q	α	ρ_1	ρ_2	IV t	LIML t	AR_{IV}	AR_{LIML}	AR_{proj}	K	LR_1	LR_{q-1}	S_1	S^2_{q-1}
2	0	.5	.5	.007	.007	.023	.044	.000	.004	.004	.004	.023	.023
2	1	.5	.5	.018	.018	.046	.044	.002	.014	.014	.014	.046	.046
2	10	.5	.5	.038	.038	.056	.045	.022	.049	.049	.049	.056	.056
2	0	.1	.99	.013	.013	.025	.053	.001	.004	.004	.004	.025	.025
2	1	.1	.99	.029	.029	.030	.049	.002	.012	.012	.012	.030	.030
2	10	.1	.99	.051	.051	.049	.051	.024	.047	.047	.047	.049	.049
2	0	.99	.1	.011	.011	.028	.047	.000	.004	.004	.004	.028	.028
2	1	.99	.1	.003	.003	.227	.046	.006	.054	.054	.054	.227	.227
2	10	.99	.1	.022	.022	.080	.049	.028	.055	.055	.055	.080	.080
5	0	.5	.5	.033	.014	.034	.049	.001	.009	.015	.000	.028	.001
5	1	.5	.5	.045	.023	.063	.048	.004	.022	.030	.000	.040	.001
5	10	.5	.5	.057	.048	.063	.043	.033	.054	.057	.002	.056	.002
5	0	.1	.99	.048	.017	.034	.060	.000	.009	.015	.000	.028	.001
5	1	.1	.99	.061	.031	.039	.056	.004	.019	.025	.000	.043	.001
5	10	.1	.99	.071	.051	.053	.044	.031	.052	.053	.002	.056	.002
5	0	.99	.1	.037	.017	.036	.050	.001	.009	.014	.000	.026	.003
5	1	.99	.1	.018	.008	.386	.049	.024	.055	.058	.002	.050	.005
5	10	.99	.1	.043	.043	.102	.048	.037	.055	.058	.002	.060	.004
20	0	.5	.5	.080	.019	.059	.053	.002	.023	.038	.000	.062	.000
20	1	.5	.5	.082	.041	.111	.045	.016	.043	.050	.000	.070	.000
20	10	.5	.5	.076	.057	.089	.019	.029	.055	.057	.000	.066	.000
20	0	.1	.99	.132	.020	.062	.091	.001	.021	.036	.000	.097	.000
20	1	.1	.99	.135	.043	.069	.063	.014	.037	.044	.000	.104	.000
20	10	.1	.99	.135	.054	.076	.016	.026	.054	.055	.000	.108	.000
20	0	.99	.1	.097	.024	.061	.054	.002	.022	.038	.000	.071	.000
20	1	.99	.1	.040	.030	.657	.048	.027	.058	.061	.000	.058	.000
20	10	.99	.1	.055	.058	.149	.030	.028	.058	.061	.000	.056	.000

asymptotically pivotal. The empirical sizes of the tests for individual coefficients are summarized in Table 5.2. For the just-identified models, the IV and LIML t-statistics for β_i $(i = 1, 2)$ have size distortions that increase with ρ_i. The LR, AR_{LIML}, and K statistics for β_i are well behaved and appear to be very close numerically. This result was also noted by Kleibergen (2000). The S and AR_{IV} statistics for β_i are nearly identical and are slightly oversized when $\rho_{\tilde{i}}$ is large. The tests for β_i based on the projected AR confidence sets are very conservative. Most of the confidence sets are unbounded – even for moderately strong instruments.

For the overidentified models, the IV t-statistics and the S-statistics can be severely size distorted using standard normal critical values – especially for highly overidentified models with very weak instruments and $\rho_i \approx 1$. The LIML-t, LR, and AR_{IV} statistics are also size distorted but to a lesser degree. Interestingly, the size distortions of $AR_{IV}(\beta_i^0)$ and $LR(\beta_i^0)$ are more sensitive to the degree of endogeneity of $X_{\tilde{i}}$ than the degree of endogeneity of X_i. In contrast, there is surprisingly little size distortion in the AR_{LIML} and K statistics for β_i $(i = 1, 2)$. As with the AR_{IV} and LR statistics, the size distortions of $AR_{LIML}(\beta_i^0)$ and $K(\beta_i^0)$ are larger for higher values of ρ_i. The tests for β_i based on the projected AR confidence sets are again very conservative when instruments are very weak but are nearly correctly sized when instruments become stronger. For instruments of moderate strength, roughly 35 percent of the confidence sets are closed.

5.8.2.2 Weak Instrument Case II: Size. In this design, the instruments are weak for β_1 but not for β_2. The asymptotic results indicate that the S^2, LR, AR, and K statistics for testing $\beta_1 = \beta_1^0$ have asymptotically pivotal or boundedly pivotal distributions in this case. The empirical sizes for the individual coefficient tests are summarized in Table 5.3. For the just-identified models, the IV and LIML t-statistics are sized distorted for β_1 when ρ_1 is high. The remaining statistics for β_1 are properly sized, as predicted by theory. Interestingly, when instruments are very weak, most of the test statistics for β_2 are undersized. However, $S(\beta_2^0)$ and $AR_{IV}(\beta_2^0)$ are slightly oversized when $\rho_1 \approx 1$ and β_1 is weakly identified.

For the overidentified models, the IV and LIML t-statistics, S-statistic, and LR statistic for β_1 can be severely size-distorted using the $\chi^2(1)$ critical value. The S^2 and LR statistics become size-controlled, although conservative, when using the $\chi^2(q-1)$ critical value as predicted by theory. The AR_{LIML} and K statistics for β_1 have stable sizes, as predicted by theory. However, $AR_{IV}(\beta_2^0)$ is oversized when $\rho_1 \approx 1$ and β_1 is weakly identified.

The tests for β_i $(i = 1, 2)$ based on the projected AR confidence sets are conservative, and the tests for β_2 are much more conservative than the tests for β_1. The empirical size of the tests for β_1 does not vary with the quality of the instruments, whereas the empirical size of the tests for β_2 becomes closer to the nominal size as the instruments for β_1 improve. When instruments are weak for β_1, most of the confidence sets for β_1 and β_2 are unbounded. When instruments become moderately strong for β_1, the percentage of closed confidence sets approaches the nominal coverage rates.

5.8.2.3 Weak Instrument Case II: Power. Three sets of power experiments are run to evaluate the tests for individual coefficients. In the first two sets, nominal 5-percent tests for the null hypothesis $\beta_1 = 1$ against the alternatives $\beta_1 = 1 + \delta$, for selected values of δ, are computed for designs in which instruments are moderately strong for β_1 and for designs in which instruments are weak for β_1. In the third set, 5-percent tests for the null hypothesis $\beta_2 = 1$ against the alternatives $\beta_2 = 1 + \delta$ are computed in designs for which instruments are weak for β_1. In all cases, size-adjusted power is computed using the finite sample critical values based on the Monte Carlo experiments under the appropriate null hypothesis.

Figure 5.2 shows the power results for tests on β_1 for the designs in which instruments are good $(\alpha = 10)$ and endogeneity is moderate for both variables

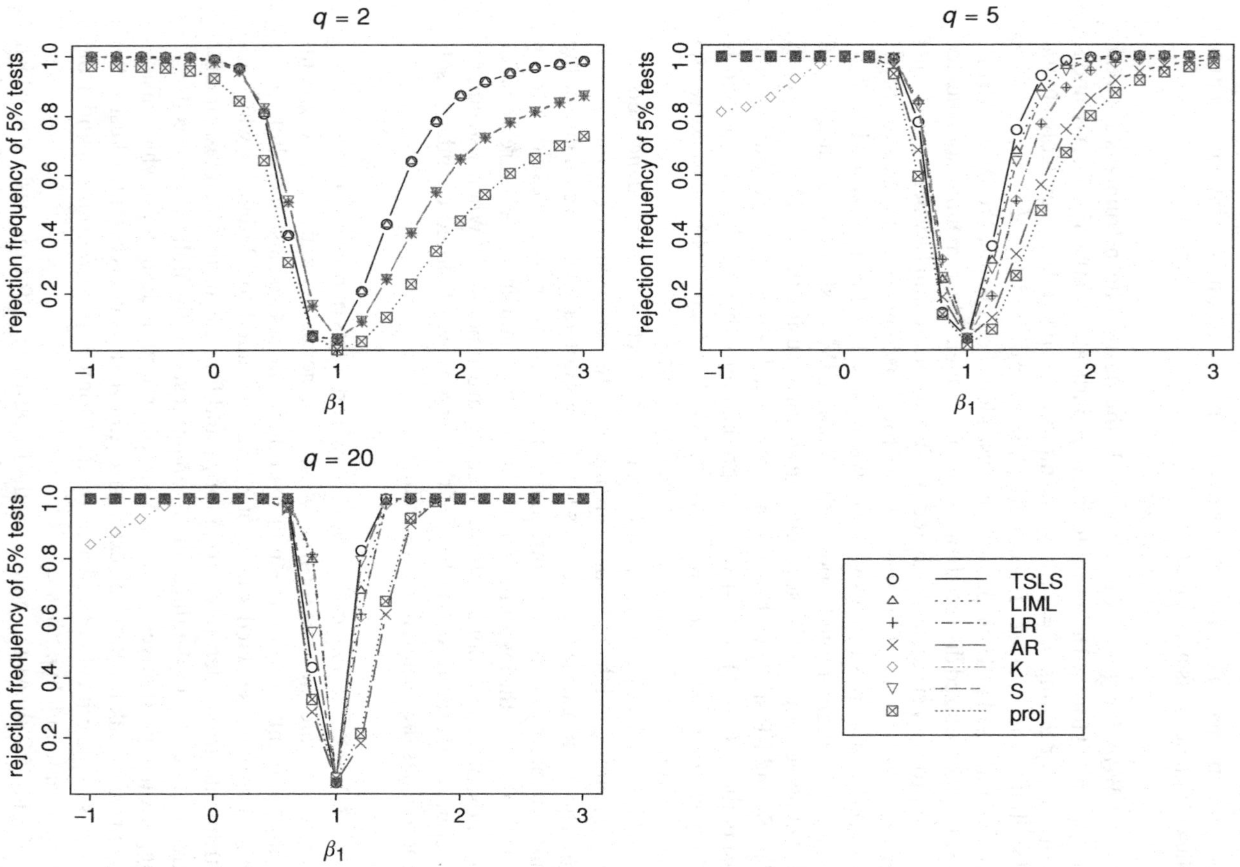

Figure 5.2. Size-adjusted power of various test statistics. Weak instrument case II; moderate instruments for X_1.

($\rho_1 = \rho_2 = 0.5$). In these designs all of the test statistics have sizes close to nominal size.[12] For $q = 2$, the power of the IV and LIML t-statistics is almost identical, and the powers of the LR, AR_{LIML}, K, and S statistics are almost identical. The IV and LIML t-statistics have higher power for $\delta > 0$ and the LR, AR_{LIML}, K, and S statistics have slightly higher power for $\delta < 0$. The power of the projected *AR* confidence set is uniformly below the power of the other test statistics. For $q > 2$, the powers of the IV and LIML t-statistics differ slightly, and the LR, K, and S statistics have very similar power. Owing to the larger critical values, the AR_{LIML} statistic loses power relative to the other statistics and is close to the power of the projected AR confidence set. Interestingly, the power of the K statistic is not monotonic for $\delta < 0$. The IV t-statistic has the best power for $\delta > 0$, and the S statistic has the best overall power for $\delta < 0$.

Figure 5.3 gives the power results for the tests on β_1 for designs in which instruments are weak ($\alpha = 1$) and endogeneity is moderate for both variables. In these designs, the IV and LIML t-statistics and LR statistics are moderately oversized, whereas the other statistics are size controlled. In general, the size-adjusted power of the IV and LIML t-statistics dominates the power of the other statistics. However, this result is somewhat misleading because size adjustment is not possible in empirical applications. When $q = 2$, the power of the AR_{LIML}, K, LR, and S statistics is identical and never exceeds 0.4. When $q > 2$, the powers of the AR_{LIML}, K, LR, and S statistics diverge, and the S statistic generally dominates in terms of power. The shapes of the LR, AR_{LIML}, and projected AR power curves are very similar to the ranking LR > AR_{LIML} > projected AR. Contrary to the results of Kleibergen (2000), the K statistic often has lower power than the AR_{LIML} statistic and the projected AR statistic.

Figure 5.4 gives the power results for the tests on β_2 for designs in which instruments are weak for β_1 ($\alpha = 1$) and endogeneity is moderate for both variables ($\rho_1 = \rho_2 = 0.5$). In these designs, all of the tests for β_2 are generally undersized. When $q = 2$, the powers of the IV and LIML t-statistics are similar and dominate the power of the other statistics. The power curves for AR_{LIML}, K, LR, and S are similar in shape and flatten out for large values of $|\delta|$, suggesting that they are inconsistent tests. The power of the projected AR confidence set is uniformly the lowest and never rises above about 17%. For $q > 2$, all statistics exhibit higher power than when $q = 2$. The IV and LIML t-statistics and the S statistic are very similar and exhibit the highest power followed by the LR, AR_{LIML}, and projected AR statistics. For highly

12 For all plots, size-adjusted power based on the $\chi^2(1)$ critical value is used for the S and LR statistics because these statistics have size close to the nominal size of 5 percent based on using the $\chi^2(1)$ critical value. The power results for the modified t-statistics are almost identical to those for the S statistic and therefore are omitted. Similarly, the power results for the AR_{LIML} and AR_{IV} statistics are almost identical, and so the results for AR_{IV} are omitted.

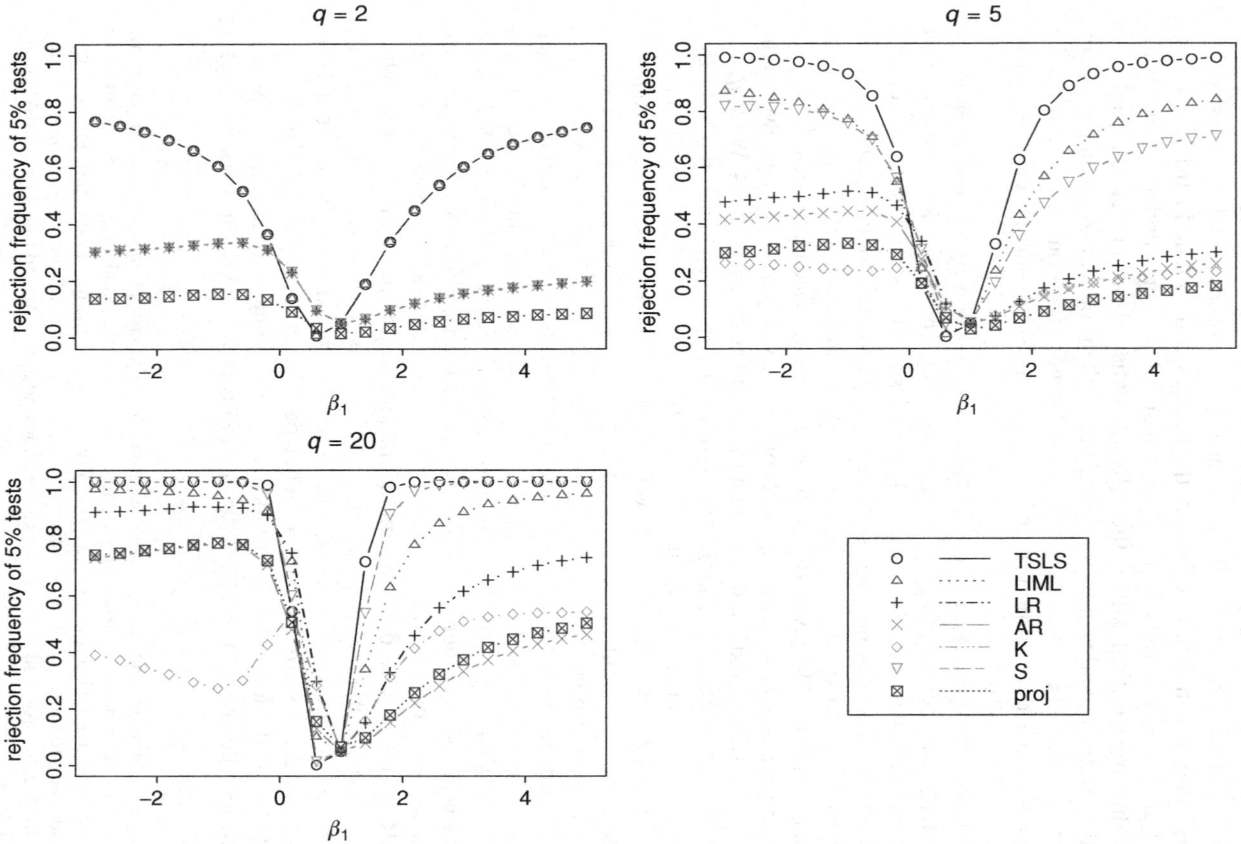

Figure 5.3. Size-adjusted power for various test statistics. Weak instrument case II; weak instruments for X_1.

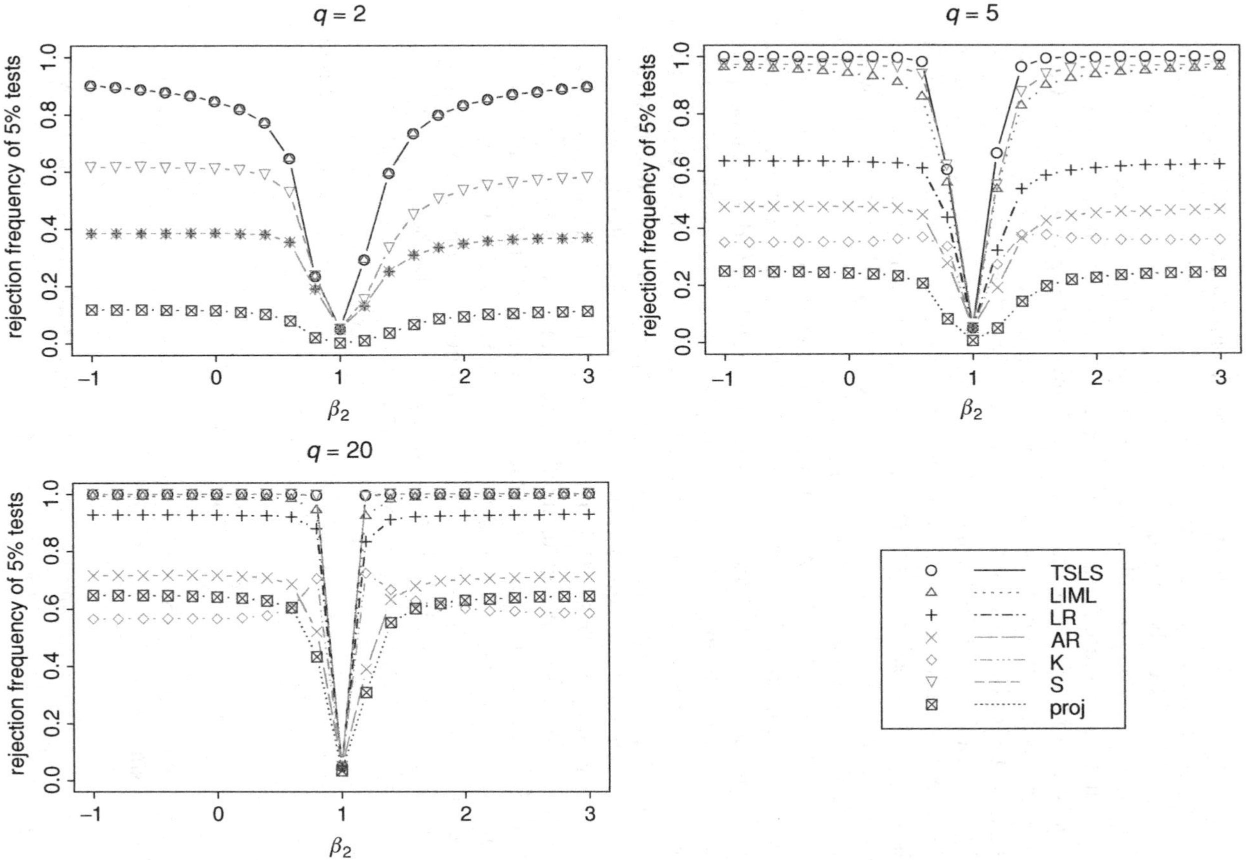

Figure 5.4. Size-adjusted power for various test statistics. Weak instrument case II; Weak instruments for X_1.

overidentified models, the power of the K statistic is nonmonotonic in $|\delta|$ and is lower than the power of the projected AR confidence set.

5.9 CONCLUSION

For inference on individual structural coefficients in IV regression models with weak instruments, we make the following observations. Valid inference is available for weakly identified coefficients using a variety of statistics as long as the remaining coefficients are well identified. The asymptotic results show that valid inference on well-identified coefficients in the presence of some weakly identified coefficients is problematic. However, the Monte Carlo experiments reveal that tests on the well-identified coefficient based on all of the statistics except the IV t-statistic are generally undersized. The only asymptotically valid tests for individual coefficients regardless of the quality of the instruments are based on projections of asymptotically valid tests for all coefficients. Most of the statistics perform as well as the IV t-statistic when instruments are good and generally much better than the IV t-statistic when instruments are weak. The concentrated K and AR_{LIML} statistics have the most stable size across the Monte Carlo experiments – even in situations for which the asymptotic theory shows the statistics to be nonpivotal. Tests based on the projected AR confidence sets are also well behaved but can be quite conservative if instruments are moderately weak for some or all of the right-hand-side endogenous variables. Interestingly, none of the statistics dominate in terms of power. The best statistic to use depends on the characteristics of the data-generating process, which are unobservable in real data.

The current practice for IV estimation in commercial software is that estimated coefficients are accompanied by the estimated asymptotic standard error. This allows for trivial computation of confidence intervals and tests of point hypotheses. However, if instruments are weak, then these confidence intervals may be highly misleading. For IV models with multiple right-hand-side endogenous variables, if instruments are suspected of being weak for one variable but not the others, then we recommend that confidence intervals be formed by inverting either the K, AR, S, or modified-t statistics. If instruments are suspected of being weak for all variables, the confidence intervals based on the projected joint AR statistic should be computed.

APPENDIX A

The proofs of Theorems 5.1 and 5.2 follow from straightforward manipulations of the results in the following lemmas.

Lemma A.1 Under Assumption 5.1 and weak instrument case I, the following results hold jointly as $n \to \infty$ *for* $i = 1, 2$*:*

1. $n^{-1}\mathbf{Z}'\mathbf{X}_i \xrightarrow{p} \mathbf{0}$
2. $n^{-1/2}\mathbf{Z}'\mathbf{X}_i \Rightarrow \sigma_{ii}^{1/2}\mathbf{M}^{1/2}(\boldsymbol{\lambda}_i + \mathbf{z}_i)$
3. $\mathbf{X}_i'\mathbf{P}_Z\mathbf{X}_i = \hat{\boldsymbol{\Gamma}}_i'\mathbf{Z}'\mathbf{Z}\hat{\boldsymbol{\Gamma}}_i \Rightarrow \sigma_{ii}(\boldsymbol{\lambda}_i + \mathbf{z}_i)'(\boldsymbol{\lambda}_i + \mathbf{z}_i) = \sigma_{ii}\eta_i$
4. $\mathbf{X}_i'\mathbf{P}_Z\mathbf{X}_{-i} = \hat{\boldsymbol{\Gamma}}_i'\mathbf{Z}'\mathbf{Z}\hat{\boldsymbol{\Gamma}}_{-i} \Rightarrow (\sigma_{ii}\sigma_{\bar{i}\bar{i}})^{1/2}(\boldsymbol{\lambda}_i + \mathbf{z}_i)'(\boldsymbol{\lambda}_{-i} + \mathbf{z}_{-i})$
5. $\mathbf{X}_i'\mathbf{P}_Z\mathbf{u} = \hat{\boldsymbol{\Gamma}}_i'\mathbf{Z}'\mathbf{u} \Rightarrow (\sigma_{ii}\sigma_{uu})^{1/2}(\boldsymbol{\lambda}_i + \mathbf{z}_i)'\mathbf{z}_u = (\sigma_{ii}\sigma_{uu})^{1/2}\xi_i$

Lemma A.2 *Under Assumption 5.1 and weak instrument case II, the following results hold jointly as $n \to \infty$:*

1. $n^{-1}\mathbf{X}_1'\mathbf{X}_1 \Rightarrow \sigma_{11}$
2. $n^{-1}\mathbf{X}_1'\mathbf{u} \Rightarrow \sigma_{u1}$
3. $n^{-1}\mathbf{Z}'\mathbf{X}_1 \xrightarrow{p} \mathbf{0}$
4. $n^{-1/2}\mathbf{Z}'\mathbf{X}_1 \Rightarrow \sigma_{11}^{1/2}\mathbf{M}^{1/2}(\boldsymbol{\lambda}_1 + \mathbf{z}_1)$
5. $n^{-1}\mathbf{Z}'\mathbf{X}_2 \xrightarrow{p} \mathbf{M}\boldsymbol{\Gamma}_2$
6. $\mathbf{X}_1'\mathbf{P}_Z\mathbf{X}_1 = \hat{\boldsymbol{\Gamma}}_1'\mathbf{Z}'\mathbf{Z}\hat{\boldsymbol{\Gamma}}_1 \Rightarrow \sigma_{11}(\boldsymbol{\lambda}_1 + \mathbf{z}_1)'(\boldsymbol{\lambda}_1 + \mathbf{z}_1)$
7. $n^{-1/2}\mathbf{X}_1'\mathbf{P}_Z\mathbf{X}_2 = n^{-1/2}\hat{\boldsymbol{\Gamma}}_1'\mathbf{Z}'\mathbf{Z}\hat{\boldsymbol{\Gamma}}_2 \Rightarrow \left(\sigma_{11}^{1/2}\mathbf{M}^{1/2}(\boldsymbol{\lambda}_1 + \mathbf{z}_1)\right)'\boldsymbol{\Gamma}_2$
8. $n^{-1}\mathbf{X}_2\mathbf{P}_Z\mathbf{X}_2 = n^{-1}\hat{\boldsymbol{\Gamma}}_2'\mathbf{Z}'\mathbf{Z}\hat{\boldsymbol{\Gamma}}_2 \xrightarrow{p} \boldsymbol{\Gamma}_2'\mathbf{M}\boldsymbol{\Gamma}_2$
9. $\mathbf{X}_1'\mathbf{P}_Z\mathbf{u} = \hat{\boldsymbol{\Gamma}}_1'\mathbf{Z}'\mathbf{u} \Rightarrow (\sigma_{11}\sigma_{uu})^{1/2}(\boldsymbol{\lambda}_1 + \mathbf{z}_1)'\mathbf{z}_u$
10. $n^{-1/2}\mathbf{X}_2'\mathbf{P}_Z\mathbf{u} = n^{-1/2}\hat{\boldsymbol{\Gamma}}_2'\mathbf{Z}'\mathbf{u} \Rightarrow \sigma_{uu}{}^{1/2}\boldsymbol{\Gamma}_2'\mathbf{M}^{1/2}\mathbf{z}_u$

Proof of Theorem 5.1. Under $H_0 : \beta_1 = \beta_1^0$, $\mathbf{y} - \mathbf{X}_1\beta_1^0 = \mathbf{X}_2\beta_2 + \mathbf{u}$, and thus

$$\tilde{\beta}_2(\beta_1^0) - \beta_2 = (\mathbf{X}_2'\mathbf{P_Z}\mathbf{X}_2)^{-1}\mathbf{X}_2'\mathbf{P_Z}\mathbf{u}. \tag{27}$$

Using results 3 and 5 of Lemma A.1, we find that

$$\tilde{\beta}_2(\beta_1^0) - \beta_2 \Rightarrow \left(\frac{\sigma_{uu}}{\sigma_{22}}\right)^{1/2} \eta_2^{-1}\boldsymbol{\xi}_2.$$

By definition $\tilde{\sigma}_{uu}(\beta_1^0) = n^{-1}\tilde{\mathbf{u}}(\beta_1^0)'\tilde{\mathbf{u}}(\beta_1^0)$, where

$$\tilde{\mathbf{u}}(\beta_1^0) = y - \mathbf{X}_1\beta_1^0 - \mathbf{X}_2\tilde{\beta}_2(\beta_1^0) = \left[\mathbf{I}_n - \mathbf{X}_2(\mathbf{X}_2'\mathbf{P_Z}\mathbf{X}_2)^{-1}\mathbf{X}_2'\mathbf{P_Z}\right]\mathbf{u}. \tag{28}$$

After some algebra and results of Lemma A.1, it can be shown that

$$\begin{aligned} n^{-1}\tilde{\mathbf{u}}(\beta_1^0)'\tilde{\mathbf{u}}(\beta_1^0) &= n^{-1}\mathbf{u}'\mathbf{u} - 2n^{-1}\mathbf{u}'\mathbf{X}_2(\mathbf{X}_2'\mathbf{P_Z}\mathbf{X}_2)^{-1}\mathbf{X}_2'\mathbf{P_Z}\mathbf{u} \\ &\quad + \mathbf{u}'\mathbf{P_Z}\mathbf{X}_2(\mathbf{X}_2'\mathbf{P_Z}\mathbf{X}_2)^{-1}n^{-1}\mathbf{X}_2'\mathbf{X}_2(\mathbf{X}_2'\mathbf{P_Z}\mathbf{X}_2)^{-1}\mathbf{X}_2'\mathbf{P_Z}\mathbf{u} \\ &\Rightarrow \sigma_{uu}\left\{1 - 2\frac{\sigma_{u2}}{(\sigma_{22}\sigma_{uu})^{1/2}}\left(\frac{\xi_2}{\eta_2}\right) + \left(\frac{\xi_2}{\eta_2}\right)^2\right\} \\ &= \sigma_{uu}\left\{1 + \omega_2^*(\beta_1^0)\right\}, \end{aligned}$$

where $\omega_2^* = \left(\frac{\xi_2}{\eta_2}\right)^2 - 2\rho_{u2}\left(\frac{\xi_2}{\eta_2}\right)$.

Proof of Theorem 5.2. First consider the Part 1 results. From the formula for the partitioned IV estimate of β_i, it follows that

$$\hat{\beta}_{i,\text{IV}} - \beta_i = (\hat{\mathbf{X}}_i'\hat{\mathbf{Q}}_{\neg i}\hat{\mathbf{X}}_i)^{-1}\hat{\mathbf{X}}_i'\hat{\mathbf{Q}}_{\neg i}\mathbf{u},\ i = 1, 2.$$

Using the results of Lemma A.2, we obtain

$$\begin{aligned}
\hat{\mathbf{X}}_1'\hat{\mathbf{Q}}_2\hat{\mathbf{X}}_1 &= \hat{\boldsymbol{\Gamma}}_1'\mathbf{Z}'\mathbf{Z}\hat{\boldsymbol{\Gamma}}_1 - \frac{\hat{\boldsymbol{\Gamma}}_1'\mathbf{Z}'\mathbf{Z}\hat{\boldsymbol{\Gamma}}_2}{\sqrt{n}}\left(\frac{\hat{\boldsymbol{\Gamma}}_2'\mathbf{Z}'\mathbf{Z}\hat{\boldsymbol{\Gamma}}_2}{n}\right)^{-1}\frac{\hat{\boldsymbol{\Gamma}}_2'\mathbf{Z}'\mathbf{Z}\hat{\boldsymbol{\Gamma}}_1}{\sqrt{n}}\\
&\Rightarrow \sigma_{11}(\boldsymbol{\lambda}_1 + \mathbf{z}_1)'\left[\mathbf{I}_q - \mathbf{M}^{1/2}\boldsymbol{\Gamma}_2(\boldsymbol{\Gamma}_2'\mathbf{M}\boldsymbol{\Gamma}_2)^{-1}\boldsymbol{\Gamma}_2'\mathbf{M}^{1/2\prime}\right](\boldsymbol{\lambda}_1 + \mathbf{z}_1)\\
&= \sigma_{11}(\boldsymbol{\lambda}_1 + \mathbf{z}_1)'\mathbf{Q}_{\mathbf{M}^{1/2}\boldsymbol{\Gamma}_2}(\boldsymbol{\lambda}_1 + \mathbf{z}_1)\\
\hat{\mathbf{X}}_1'\hat{\mathbf{Q}}_2\mathbf{u} &= \hat{\boldsymbol{\Gamma}}_1'\mathbf{Z}'\mathbf{u} - \frac{\hat{\boldsymbol{\Gamma}}_1'\mathbf{Z}'\mathbf{Z}\hat{\boldsymbol{\Gamma}}_2}{\sqrt{n}}\left(\frac{\hat{\boldsymbol{\Gamma}}_2'\mathbf{Z}'\mathbf{Z}\hat{\boldsymbol{\Gamma}}_2}{n}\right)^{-1}\frac{\hat{\boldsymbol{\Gamma}}_2'\mathbf{Z}'\mathbf{u}}{\sqrt{n}}\\
&\Rightarrow (\sigma_{11}\sigma_{uu})^{1/2}(\boldsymbol{\lambda}_1 + \mathbf{z}_1)'\left[\mathbf{I}_q - \mathbf{M}^{1/2}\boldsymbol{\Gamma}_2(\boldsymbol{\Gamma}_2'\mathbf{M}\boldsymbol{\Gamma}_2)^{-1}\boldsymbol{\Gamma}_2'\mathbf{M}^{1/2\prime}\right]\mathbf{z}_u\\
&= (\sigma_{11}\sigma_{uu})^{1/2}(\boldsymbol{\lambda}_1 + \mathbf{z}_1)'\mathbf{Q}_{\mathbf{M}^{1/2}\boldsymbol{\Gamma}_2}\mathbf{z}_u,
\end{aligned}$$

where $\mathbf{Q}_{\mathbf{M}^{1/2}\boldsymbol{\Gamma}_2} = \mathbf{I}_q - \mathbf{M}^{1/2}\boldsymbol{\Gamma}_2(\boldsymbol{\Gamma}_2'\mathbf{M}\boldsymbol{\Gamma}_2)^{-1}\boldsymbol{\Gamma}_2'\mathbf{M}^{1/2\prime}$ is an idempotent matrix of rank $q-1$. Therefore,

$$\hat{\beta}_{1,\text{IV}} - \beta_1 \Rightarrow \left(\frac{\sigma_{uu}}{\sigma_{11}}\right)^{1/2}\frac{(\boldsymbol{\lambda}_1 + \mathbf{z}_1)'\mathbf{Q}_{\mathbf{M}^{1/2}\boldsymbol{\Gamma}_2}\mathbf{z}_u}{(\boldsymbol{\lambda}_1 + \mathbf{z}_1)'\mathbf{Q}_{\mathbf{M}^{1/2}\boldsymbol{\Gamma}_2}(\boldsymbol{\lambda}_1 + \mathbf{z}_1)} = \beta_1^{\dagger}.$$

Similarly, results of Lemma A.2 imply

$$\begin{aligned}
n^{-1}\hat{\mathbf{X}}_2'\hat{\mathbf{Q}}_1\hat{\mathbf{X}}_2 &= n^{-1}\hat{\boldsymbol{\Gamma}}_2'\mathbf{Z}'\mathbf{Z}\hat{\boldsymbol{\Gamma}}_2 - n^{-1/2}\hat{\boldsymbol{\Gamma}}_2'\mathbf{Z}'\mathbf{Z}\hat{\boldsymbol{\Gamma}}_1\left(\hat{\boldsymbol{\Gamma}}_1'\mathbf{Z}'\mathbf{Z}\hat{\boldsymbol{\Gamma}}_1\right)n^{-1/2}\hat{\boldsymbol{\Gamma}}_1'\mathbf{Z}'\mathbf{Z}\hat{\boldsymbol{\Gamma}}_2\\
&\Rightarrow \boldsymbol{\Gamma}_2'\mathbf{M}^{1/2\prime}\left\{\mathbf{I}_q - (\boldsymbol{\lambda}_1 + \mathbf{z}_1)'\left[(\boldsymbol{\lambda}_1 + \mathbf{z}_1)'(\boldsymbol{\lambda}_1 + \mathbf{z}_1)\right]^{-1}\right.\\
&\quad \left.\times(\boldsymbol{\lambda}_1 + \mathbf{z}_1)'\right\}\mathbf{M}^{1/2}\boldsymbol{\Gamma}_2\\
&= \boldsymbol{\Gamma}_2'\mathbf{M}^{1/2\prime}\mathbf{Q}_{\boldsymbol{\lambda}_1+\mathbf{z}_1}\mathbf{M}^{1/2}\boldsymbol{\Gamma}_2\\
n^{-1}\hat{\mathbf{X}}_2'\hat{\mathbf{Q}}_1\mathbf{u} &= n^{-1}\hat{\boldsymbol{\Gamma}}_2'\mathbf{Z}'\mathbf{u} - n^{-1/2}\hat{\boldsymbol{\Gamma}}_2'\mathbf{Z}'\mathbf{Z}\hat{\boldsymbol{\Gamma}}_1\left(\hat{\boldsymbol{\Gamma}}_1'\mathbf{Z}'\mathbf{Z}\hat{\boldsymbol{\Gamma}}_1\right)^{-1}n^{-1/2}\hat{\boldsymbol{\Gamma}}_1'\mathbf{Z}'\mathbf{u}\\
&\Rightarrow 0,
\end{aligned}$$

and thus

$$\hat{\beta}_{2,\text{IV}} - \beta_2 \Rightarrow 0$$

and $\hat{\beta}_{2,\text{IV}}$ is consistent for β_2. Furthermore, using Lemma A.2 again gives

$$\begin{aligned}
&n^{-1/2}\hat{\mathbf{X}}_2'\hat{\mathbf{Q}}_1\mathbf{u}\\
&\quad = n^{-1/2}\hat{\boldsymbol{\Gamma}}_2'\mathbf{Z}'\mathbf{u} - n^{-1/2}\hat{\boldsymbol{\Gamma}}_2'\mathbf{Z}'\mathbf{Z}\hat{\boldsymbol{\Gamma}}_1\left(\hat{\boldsymbol{\Gamma}}_1'\mathbf{Z}'\mathbf{Z}\hat{\boldsymbol{\Gamma}}_1\right)^{-1}\hat{\boldsymbol{\Gamma}}_1'\mathbf{Z}'\mathbf{u}\\
&\quad \Rightarrow \sigma_{uu}^{1/2}\boldsymbol{\Gamma}_2'\mathbf{M}^{1/2\prime}\left\{\mathbf{I}_q - (\boldsymbol{\lambda}_1 + \mathbf{z}_1)'\left[(\boldsymbol{\lambda}_1 + \mathbf{z}_1)'(\boldsymbol{\lambda}_1 + \mathbf{z}_1)\right]^{-1}(\boldsymbol{\lambda}_1 + \mathbf{z}_1)'\right\}\mathbf{z}_u\\
&\quad = \sigma_{uu}^{1/2}\boldsymbol{\Gamma}_2'\mathbf{M}^{1/2\prime}Q_{\boldsymbol{\lambda}_1+\mathbf{z}_1}\mathbf{z}_u.
\end{aligned}$$

Therefore,

$$\sqrt{n}\left(\hat{\beta}_{2,\text{IV}} - \beta_2\right) \Rightarrow \sigma_{uu}^{1/2} \cdot \frac{\mathbf{\Gamma}_2' \mathbf{M}^{1/2\prime} \mathbf{Q}_{\boldsymbol{\lambda}_1 + \mathbf{z}_1} \mathbf{z}_u}{\mathbf{\Gamma}_2' \mathbf{M}^{1/2\prime} \mathbf{Q}_{\boldsymbol{\lambda}_1 + \mathbf{z}_1} \mathbf{M}^{1/2} \mathbf{\Gamma}_2}.$$

Finally, consider $\hat{\sigma}_{uu,\text{IV}} = n^{-1}\hat{\mathbf{u}}_{\text{IV}}'\hat{\mathbf{u}}_{\text{IV}}$, where

$$\begin{aligned}\hat{\mathbf{u}}_{\text{IV}} &= \mathbf{y} - \mathbf{X}_1\hat{\beta}_{1,\text{IV}} - \mathbf{X}_2\hat{\beta}_{2,\text{IV}} \\ &= \mathbf{u} - \mathbf{X}_1(\hat{\beta}_{1,\text{IV}} - \beta_1) + \mathbf{X}_2(\hat{\beta}_{2,\text{IV}} - \beta_2).\end{aligned}$$

Now, using the results of Lemma A.2, we find that

$$\begin{aligned}n^{-1}\hat{\mathbf{u}}_{\text{IV}}'\hat{\mathbf{u}}_{\text{IV}} &= n^{-1}\mathbf{u}'\mathbf{u} - 2n^{-1}\mathbf{u}'\mathbf{X}_1(\hat{\beta}_{1,\text{IV}} - \beta_1) - 2n^{-1}\mathbf{u}'\mathbf{X}_2(\hat{\beta}_{2,\text{IV}} - \beta_2) \\ &\quad + n^{-1}\mathbf{X}_1'\mathbf{X}_1(\hat{\beta}_{1,\text{IV}} - \beta_1)^2 + 2n^{-1}\mathbf{X}_1'\mathbf{X}_2(\hat{\beta}_{1,\text{IV}} - \beta_1)(\hat{\beta}_{2,\text{IV}} - \beta_2) \\ &\quad + n^{-1}\mathbf{X}_2'\mathbf{X}_2(\hat{\beta}_{2,\text{IV}} - \beta_2)^2 \\ &\Rightarrow \sigma_{uu} - 2\sigma_{u1}\beta_1^{\dagger} + \sigma_{11}\left(\beta_1^{\dagger}\right)^2 \\ &= \sigma_{uu}\left\{1 + \omega_1^{\dagger}\right\},\end{aligned}$$

where $\omega_1^{\dagger} = \left(\beta_1^{\dagger}\right)^2 \frac{\sigma_{11}}{\sigma_{uu}} - 2\beta_1^{\dagger}\frac{\sigma_{u1}}{\sigma_{uu}}$.

Next, consider the Part 2 results. For (d), using the results of Part 1, we find that

$$\begin{aligned}t_{\text{IV}}(\beta_1^0)^2 &= \frac{(\beta_{1,\text{IV}} - \beta_1^0)^2}{\hat{\sigma}_{uu,\text{IV}}\hat{\mathbf{X}}_1'\hat{\mathbf{Q}}_2\hat{\mathbf{X}}_1} \Rightarrow \frac{[(\boldsymbol{\lambda}_1 + \mathbf{z}_1)'\mathbf{Q}_{\mathbf{M}^{1/2}\mathbf{\Gamma}_2}\mathbf{z}_u]^2}{\left\{1 + \omega_1^{\dagger}\right\}(\boldsymbol{\lambda}_1 + \mathbf{z}_1)'\mathbf{Q}_{\mathbf{M}^{1/2}\mathbf{\Gamma}_2}(\boldsymbol{\lambda}_1 + \mathbf{z}_1)} \\ &= \frac{\mathbf{z}_u'\mathbf{P}_{\mathbf{A}}\mathbf{z}_u}{\left\{1 + \omega_1^{\dagger}\right\}},\end{aligned}$$

where $\mathbf{A} = \mathbf{Q}_{\mathbf{M}^{1/2}\mathbf{\Gamma}_2}(\boldsymbol{\lambda}_1 + \mathbf{z}_1)$.

Parts (e), (f), and (g) follow from standard asymptotic arguments, given Assumption 5.1, because, under $H_0 : \beta_1 = \beta_1^0$, the restricted model

$$\mathbf{y} - \mathbf{X}_1\beta_1^0 = \mathbf{X}_2\beta_2 + \mathbf{u}$$

is a well-identified IV regression model.

For part (h), first note that when $q = 2$

$$\text{LR}(\beta_1^0) = n\ln[\tilde{k}_{\text{LIML}}(\beta_1^0)]$$

because $\hat{k}_{\text{LIML}} = 1$. Using the same arguments as in Wang and Zivot (1998), it follows that

$$\text{LR}(\beta_1^0) \Rightarrow \mathbf{z}_u'\mathbf{Q}_{\mathbf{M}^{1/2}\mathbf{\Gamma}_2}\mathbf{z}_u \sim \chi^2(1)$$

because $\mathbf{Q}_{\mathbf{M}^{1/2}\mathbf{\Gamma}_2}$ is an idempotent matrix with rank 1. When $q > 2$, $\hat{k}_{\text{LIML}} \neq 1$ but, as shown by Wang and Zivot, $n(\hat{k}_{\text{LIML}} - 1) \Rightarrow \xi$, where ξ is a random variable that only takes on positive values. It follows that

$$\mathrm{LR}(\beta_1^0) \Rightarrow \mathbf{z}_u'\mathbf{Q}_{\mathbf{M}^{1/2}\Gamma_2}\mathbf{z}_u - \xi < \mathbf{z}_u'\mathbf{Q}_{\mathbf{M}^{1/2}\Gamma_2}\mathbf{z}_u \sim \chi^2(q-1)$$

because $\mathbf{Q}_{\mathbf{M}^{1/2}\Gamma_2}$ is an idempotent matrix with rank $q-1$.

To prove part (i), first consider the numerator of $S(\beta_1^0)^2$:

$$\begin{aligned}\hat{\Psi}_1^2 &= (\hat{\mathbf{X}}_1'\hat{\mathbf{Q}}_2\hat{\mathbf{X}}_1)[(\hat{\mathbf{X}}_1'\hat{\mathbf{Q}}_2\hat{\mathbf{X}}_1)^{-1}\hat{\mathbf{X}}_1'\hat{\mathbf{Q}}_2\mathbf{u}]^2 \\ &= (\hat{\mathbf{X}}_1'\hat{\mathbf{Q}}_2\hat{\mathbf{X}}_1)^{-1}\left(\hat{\mathbf{X}}_1'\hat{\mathbf{Q}}_2\mathbf{u}\right)^2.\end{aligned}$$

From the results for part (a), it follows that

$$\begin{aligned}\hat{\Psi}_1^2 &\Rightarrow \sigma_{uu}(\boldsymbol{\lambda}_1+\mathbf{z}_1)'\mathbf{Q}_{\mathbf{M}^{1/2}\Gamma_2}(\boldsymbol{\lambda}_1+\mathbf{z}_1)\left((\boldsymbol{\lambda}_1+\mathbf{z}_1)'\mathbf{Q}_{\mathbf{M}^{1/2}\Gamma_2}\mathbf{z}_u\right)^2 \\ &= \sigma_{uu}\mathbf{z}_u'\mathbf{P}_{\mathbf{A}}\mathbf{z}_u,\end{aligned}$$

where $\mathbf{A} = \mathbf{Q}_{\mathbf{M}^{1/2}\Gamma_2}(\boldsymbol{\lambda}_1+\mathbf{z}_1)$. Provided $\hat{\sigma}^2_{\hat{\Psi}_i} \Rightarrow \sigma_{uu}$, it follows that

$$\mathrm{S}(\beta_1^0) \Rightarrow \mathbf{z}_u'\mathbf{P}_{\mathbf{A}}\mathbf{z}_u.$$

Moreover, because $\mathbf{Q}_{\mathbf{M}^{1/2}\Gamma_2}$ and $\mathbf{P}_{\mathbf{A}}$ are idempotent

$$\begin{aligned}\mathbf{z}_u'\mathbf{P}_{\mathbf{A}}\mathbf{z}_u &= \mathbf{z}_u'\mathbf{Q}_{\mathbf{M}^{1/2}\Gamma_2}(\boldsymbol{\lambda}_1+\mathbf{z}_1)\left[(\boldsymbol{\lambda}_1+\mathbf{z}_1)'\mathbf{Q}_{\mathbf{M}^{1/2}\Gamma_2}(\boldsymbol{\lambda}_1+\mathbf{z}_1)\right]^{-1}(\boldsymbol{\lambda}_1+\mathbf{z}_1)'\mathbf{Q}_{\mathbf{M}^{1/2}\Gamma_2}\mathbf{z}_u \\ &= (\mathbf{Q}_{\mathbf{M}^{1/2}\Gamma_2}\mathbf{z}_u)'\,\mathbf{P}_{\mathbf{A}}\,(\mathbf{Q}_{\mathbf{M}^{1/2}\Gamma_2}\mathbf{z}_u) < \mathbf{z}_u'\mathbf{Q}_{\mathbf{M}^{1/2}\Gamma_2}\mathbf{z}_u \sim \chi^2(q-1).\end{aligned}$$

The proof for $\tilde{t}_{\mathrm{IV}}(\beta_1^0)^2$ is identical given that $\tilde{\sigma}_{uu,\mathrm{IV}}(\beta_1^0) \Rightarrow \sigma_{uu}$.

For part (j), note that under $H_0: \beta_1 = \beta_1^0$, $\tilde{\beta}_2(\beta_1^0) - \beta_2$ is given by (27) and $\tilde{\mathbf{u}}(\beta_1^0)$ is given by (28). The numerator of $\mathrm{AR}_{\mathrm{IV}}(\beta_1^0)$ may then be expressed as

$$\begin{aligned}\tilde{u}(\beta_1^0)'\mathbf{P}_{\mathbf{Z}}\tilde{u}(\beta_1^0) &= \mathbf{u}'\left[\mathbf{I}_n - \mathbf{X}_2(\mathbf{X}_2'\mathbf{P}_{\mathbf{Z}}\mathbf{X}_2)^{-1}\mathbf{X}_2'\mathbf{P}_{\mathbf{Z}}\right]\mathbf{P}_{\mathbf{Z}} \\ &\quad\times\left[\mathbf{I}_n - \mathbf{X}_2(\mathbf{X}_2'\mathbf{P}_{\mathbf{Z}}\mathbf{X}_2)^{-1}\mathbf{X}_2'\mathbf{P}_{\mathbf{Z}}\right]\mathbf{u} \\ &= \mathbf{u}'\left\{\mathbf{P}_{\mathbf{Z}}\left[\mathbf{I}_n - \mathbf{X}_2(\mathbf{X}_2'\mathbf{P}_{\mathbf{Z}}\mathbf{X}_2)^{-1}\mathbf{X}_2'\mathbf{P}_{\mathbf{Z}}\right]\right\}\mathbf{P}_{\mathbf{Z}} \\ &\quad\times\left\{\mathbf{P}_{\mathbf{Z}}\left[\mathbf{I}_n - \mathbf{X}_2(\mathbf{X}_2'\mathbf{P}_{\mathbf{Z}}\mathbf{X}_2)^{-1}\mathbf{X}_2'\mathbf{P}_{\mathbf{Z}}\right]\right\}\mathbf{u}.\end{aligned}$$

Next, observe that

$$\mathbf{P}_{\mathbf{Z}}\left[\mathbf{I}_n - \mathbf{X}_2(\mathbf{X}_2'\mathbf{P}_{\mathbf{Z}}\mathbf{X}_2)^{-1}\mathbf{X}_2'\mathbf{P}_{\mathbf{Z}}\right]\mathbf{u} = (\mathbf{P}_{\mathbf{Z}} - \mathbf{P}_{\hat{\mathbf{X}}_2})\mathbf{u},$$

where $\mathbf{P}_{\mathbf{Z}} - \mathbf{P}_{\hat{\mathbf{X}}_2}$ is idempotent. Therefore, the numerator of $\mathrm{AR}_{\mathrm{IV}}(\beta_1^0)$ is

$$\mathbf{u}'(\mathbf{P}_{\mathbf{Z}} - \mathbf{P}_{\hat{\mathbf{X}}_2})\mathbf{u} = \mathbf{u}'\mathbf{P}_{\mathbf{Z}}\mathbf{u} - \mathbf{u}'\mathbf{P}_{\hat{\mathbf{X}}_2}\mathbf{u}.$$

Using the results of Lemma A.2, we obtain

$$\mathbf{u}'\mathbf{P}_{\mathbf{Z}}\mathbf{u} = \frac{\mathbf{u}'\mathbf{Z}}{\sqrt{n}}\left(\frac{\mathbf{Z}'\mathbf{Z}}{n}\right)^{-1}\frac{\mathbf{Z}'\mathbf{u}}{\sqrt{n}} \Rightarrow \boldsymbol{\Psi}_{Zu}'\mathbf{M}^{-1}\boldsymbol{\Psi}_{Zu} = \sigma_{uu}\mathbf{z}_u'\mathbf{z}_u$$

$$\mathbf{u}'\mathbf{P}_{\hat{\mathbf{X}}_2}\mathbf{u} = \frac{\mathbf{u}'\hat{\mathbf{X}}_2}{\sqrt{n}}\left(\frac{\hat{\mathbf{X}}_2'\hat{\mathbf{X}}_2}{n}\right)^{-1}\frac{\hat{\mathbf{X}}_2'\mathbf{u}}{\sqrt{n}} \Rightarrow \boldsymbol{\Psi}'_{Zu}\boldsymbol{\Gamma}_2'(\boldsymbol{\Gamma}_2'\mathbf{M}\boldsymbol{\Gamma}_2)^{-1}\boldsymbol{\Gamma}_2'\boldsymbol{\Psi}_{Zu}$$
$$= \sigma_{uu}\mathbf{z}_u'\mathbf{P}_{\mathbf{M}^{1/2'}\boldsymbol{\Gamma}_2}\mathbf{z}_u,$$

where $\mathbf{P}_{\mathbf{M}^{1/2'}\boldsymbol{\Gamma}_2}$ is an idempotent matrix of rank 1. It follows that

$$\tilde{\mathbf{u}}(\beta_1^0)'\mathbf{P_Z}\tilde{\mathbf{u}}(\beta_1^0) = \mathbf{u}'(\mathbf{P}_Z - \mathbf{P}_{\hat{\mathbf{X}}_2})\mathbf{u} \Rightarrow \sigma_{uu}\mathbf{z}_u'(\mathbf{I}_q - \mathbf{P}_{\mathbf{M}^{1/2'}\boldsymbol{\Gamma}_2})\mathbf{z}_u,$$

where $\mathbf{I}_q - \mathbf{P}_{\mathbf{M}^{1/2'}\boldsymbol{\Gamma}_2}$ is an idempotent matrix of rank $q-1$.

The denominator of $\mathrm{AR}_{\mathrm{IV}}(\beta_1^0)$ is

$$\begin{aligned}
&n^{-1}\tilde{\mathbf{u}}(\beta_1^0)'\mathbf{Q_Z}\tilde{\mathbf{u}}(\beta_1^0)\\
&= n^{-1}u'\left[\mathbf{I}_n - \mathbf{X}_2(\mathbf{X}_2'\mathbf{P_Z}\mathbf{X}_2)^{-1}\mathbf{X}_2'\mathbf{P_Z}\right]\mathbf{Q_Z}\left[\mathbf{I}_n - \mathbf{X}_2(\mathbf{X}_2'\mathbf{P_Z}\mathbf{X}_2)^{-1}\mathbf{X}_2'\mathbf{P_Z}\right]\mathbf{u}\\
&= n^{-1}\mathbf{u}'\left[\mathbf{I}_n - \mathbf{X}_2(\mathbf{X}_2'\mathbf{P_Z}\mathbf{X}_2)^{-1}\mathbf{X}_2'\mathbf{P}_Z\right]'\left[\mathbf{I}_n - \mathbf{X}_2(\mathbf{X}_2'\mathbf{P_Z}\mathbf{X}_2)^{-1}\mathbf{X}_2'\mathbf{P}_Z\right]\mathbf{u}\\
&\quad - n^{-1}\mathbf{u}'(\mathbf{P_Z} - \mathbf{P}_{\hat{\mathbf{X}}_2})\mathbf{u}\\
&= n^{-1}\mathbf{u}'\left[\mathbf{I}_n - \mathbf{X}_2(\mathbf{X}_2'\mathbf{P_Z}\mathbf{X}_2)^{-1}\mathbf{X}_2'\mathbf{P_Z}\right]'\left[\mathbf{I}_n - \mathbf{X}_2(\mathbf{X}_2'\mathbf{P_Z}\mathbf{X}_2)^{-1}\mathbf{X}_2'\mathbf{P_Z}\right]\mathbf{u} + o_p(1).
\end{aligned}$$

Now, using the results of Lemma A.2, we find that

$$\begin{aligned}
&n^{-1}\mathbf{u}'\left[\mathbf{I}_n - \mathbf{X}_2(\mathbf{X}_2'\mathbf{P_Z}\mathbf{X}_2)^{-1}\mathbf{X}_2'\mathbf{P_Z}\right]'\left[\mathbf{I}_n - \mathbf{X}_2(\mathbf{X}_2'\mathbf{P_Z}\mathbf{X}_2)^{-1}\mathbf{X}_2'\mathbf{P_Z}\right]\mathbf{u}\\
&= \frac{\mathbf{u}'\mathbf{u}}{n} - \frac{\mathbf{u}'\mathbf{X}_2}{n}\left(\frac{\hat{\mathbf{X}}_2'\hat{\mathbf{X}}_2}{n}\right)^{-1}\frac{\hat{\mathbf{X}}_2'\mathbf{u}}{n} - \frac{\mathbf{u}'\hat{\mathbf{X}}_2}{n}\left(\frac{\hat{\mathbf{X}}_2'\hat{\mathbf{X}}_2}{n}\right)^{-1}\frac{\hat{\mathbf{X}}_2'\mathbf{u}}{n}\\
&\quad + \frac{\mathbf{u}'\hat{\mathbf{X}}_2}{n}\left(\frac{\hat{\mathbf{X}}_2'\hat{\mathbf{X}}_2}{n}\right)^{-1}\frac{\mathbf{X}_2'\mathbf{X}_2}{n}\left(\frac{\hat{\mathbf{X}}_2'\hat{\mathbf{X}}_2}{n}\right)^{-1}\frac{\hat{\mathbf{X}}_2'\mathbf{u}}{n}\\
&= \sigma_{uu} + o_p(1) \Rightarrow \sigma_{uu}.
\end{aligned}$$

Therefore,

$$n^{-1}\tilde{\mathbf{u}}(\beta_1^0)'\mathbf{Q_Z}\tilde{\mathbf{u}}(\beta_1^0) \Rightarrow \sigma_{uu}.$$

It follows that

$$\mathrm{AR}_{\mathrm{IV}}(\beta_1^0) = \frac{\tilde{\mathbf{u}}(\beta_1^0)'\mathbf{P_Z}\tilde{\mathbf{u}}(\beta_1^0)}{n^{-1}\tilde{\mathbf{u}}(\beta_1^0)'\mathbf{Q_Z}\tilde{\mathbf{u}}(\beta_1^0)} \Rightarrow \mathbf{z}_u'(\mathbf{I}_q - \mathbf{P}_{\mathbf{M}^{1/2'}\boldsymbol{\Gamma}_2})\mathbf{z}_u \sim \chi^2(q-1).$$

Given that $\tilde{\beta}_{2,\mathrm{LIML}}(\beta_1^0)$ is consistent for β_2, similar arguments may be used to show that $\mathrm{AR}_{\mathrm{LIML}}(\beta_1^0) \Rightarrow \mathbf{z}_u'(\mathbf{I}_q - \mathbf{P}_{\mathbf{M}^{1/2'}\boldsymbol{\Gamma}_2})\mathbf{z}_u \sim \chi^2(q-1)$.

Part (k) follows directly from the results in Kleibergen (2001).

APPENDIX B

In this appendix, we follow Zivot et al. (1998) and show how to compute AR_{IV} and S confidence regions in closed form that are asymptotically valid under weak instrument case II. As stated in Section 5.7, analytic confidence intervals may be obtained if the nonrejection region of the test statistic in question may be expressed as the quadratic inequality (26). For the statistic $\text{AR}_{\text{IV}}(\beta_i)$, the $(1-\alpha)\cdot 100\%$ confidence region (35) is determined by those values of β_1^0 such that

$$\frac{(\mathbf{y}-\mathbf{X}_i\beta_1^0-\mathbf{X}_{\text{-}i}\tilde{\beta}_{\text{-}i,\text{IV}}(\beta_i^0))'\mathbf{P_Z}(\mathbf{y}-\mathbf{X}_i\beta_i^0-\mathbf{X}_{\text{-}i}\tilde{\beta}_{\text{-}i,\text{IV}}(\beta_i^0))}{(\mathbf{y}-\mathbf{X}_{\text{-}i}\beta_i^0-\mathbf{X}_{\text{-}i}\tilde{\beta}_{\text{-}i,\text{IV}}(\beta_i^0))'\mathbf{Q_Z}(\mathbf{y}-\mathbf{X}_i\beta_i^0-\mathbf{X}_{\text{-}i}\tilde{\beta}_{\text{-}i,\text{IV}}(\beta_i^0))/(n-k)} \leq \chi_\alpha^2(q-1), \tag{29}$$

where $\chi_\alpha^2(q-1)$ denotes the right tail α percent quantile of the chi-square distribution with $q-1$ degrees of freedom. Because $\tilde{\beta}_{\text{-}i,\text{IV}}(\beta_i^0) = (\mathbf{X}_{\text{-}i}'\mathbf{P_Z}\mathbf{X}_{\text{-}i})^{-1}\mathbf{X}_{\text{-}i}'\mathbf{P_Z}(\mathbf{y}-\mathbf{X}_i\beta_i^0)$, (29) may be rewritten as

$$(\mathbf{y}-\mathbf{X}_i\beta_i^0)'\mathbf{D}(\mathbf{y}-\mathbf{X}_i\beta_i^0) \leq 0, \tag{30}$$

where $\mathbf{D}=\mathbf{B}'\mathbf{A}\mathbf{B}$ with $\mathbf{B}=\mathbf{I}_n-\mathbf{X}_{\text{-}i}(\mathbf{X}_{\text{-}i}'\mathbf{P_Z}\mathbf{X}_{\text{-}i})^{-1}\mathbf{X}_{\text{-}i}'\mathbf{P_Z}$ and $\mathbf{A}=\mathbf{P_Z}-\left(\frac{\chi_\alpha^2(q-1)}{n-k}\right)\mathbf{Q_Z}$. The inequality (30) may be put in the form (26) with $a=\mathbf{y}'\mathbf{D}\mathbf{y}$, $b=-2\mathbf{y}'\mathbf{D}\mathbf{X}_i$, and $c=\mathbf{X}_i'\mathbf{D}\mathbf{X}_i$.

To derive analytic expressions for the S-confidence region, it is more convenient to find those values of β_i^0 that satisfy $S_i^2 \leq c_\alpha^2$, which implies $\Psi_i^2 \leq \hat{\sigma}_{\hat{\Psi}_i}^2 c_\alpha^2$. For a conservative confidence set, use $c_\alpha^2=\chi_\alpha^2(q-1)$. However, as illustrated in Section 5.8, the critical value $c_\alpha^2=\chi_\alpha^2(1)$ is often appropriate. To compute analytic confidence intervals, it is useful to define $\hat{\phi}_i \equiv \hat{\Delta}_i\hat{\beta}_{i,\text{IV}}$ and then note[13]

$$\hat{\Psi}_i^2 = \hat{\Delta}_i^2\beta_i^{0^2} - 2\hat{\Delta}_i\hat{\phi}_i\beta_i^0 + \hat{\phi}_i^2 \tag{31}$$

$$\hat{\sigma}_{\hat{\Psi}_i}^2 = \text{var}(\hat{\Psi}_i) = \beta_i^{0^2}\text{var}(\hat{\Delta}_i) - 2\beta_i^0\text{cov}(\hat{\Delta}_i,\hat{\phi}_i) + \text{var}(\hat{\phi}_i). \tag{32}$$

From eqs. (31) and (32), the condition $\Psi_i^2 < \hat{\sigma}_{\hat{\Psi}_i}^2 c_\alpha^2$ gives the confidence region defined by the quadratic inequality

$$\left[\hat{\Delta}_i^2 - c_\alpha^2\text{var}(\hat{\Delta}_i)\right]\beta_i^{0^2} + 2\left[-\hat{\Delta}_i\hat{\phi}_i + c_\alpha^2\text{cov}(\hat{\Delta}_i,\hat{\phi}_i)\right]\beta_i^0 + \left[\hat{\phi}_i^2 - c_\alpha^2\text{var}(\hat{\phi}_i)\right] \leq 0, \tag{33}$$

which is in the form (26) with $a=\hat{\Delta}_i^2 - c_\alpha^2\text{var}(\hat{\Delta}_i)$, $b=2\left[-\hat{\Delta}_i\hat{\phi}_i + c_\alpha^2\text{cov}(\hat{\Delta}_i,\hat{\phi}_i)\right]$, and $c=\hat{\phi}_i^2 - c_\alpha^2\text{var}(\hat{\phi}_i)$.

The nonrejection regions based on the AR_{LIML}, LR, and K statistics cannot be expressed as the simple quadratic inequality (26) because the restricted LIML estimate $\tilde{\beta}_{\text{-}i,\text{LIML}}(\beta_i^0)$ is a complicated nonlinear function of β_i^0.

[13] Computationally we estimate $\text{var}(\hat{\Delta}_i) = \frac{\partial\hat{\Delta}_i}{\partial\hat{\lambda}'}\text{var}(\hat{\lambda})\frac{\partial\hat{\Delta}_i}{\partial\hat{\lambda}}$ and $\text{cov}(\hat{\Delta}_i,\hat{\phi}_i) = \frac{\partial\hat{\Delta}_i}{\partial\hat{\lambda}'}\text{var}(\hat{\lambda})\frac{\partial\hat{\phi}_i}{\partial\hat{\lambda}}$, where the vector of partial derivatives is computed numerically.

The S-confidence region is defined by the roots of eq. (33). Let

$$R = \sqrt{\left(-\hat{\Delta}_i\hat{\phi}_i + c_\alpha^2 \text{cov}(\hat{\Delta}_i, \hat{\phi}_i)\right)^2 - \left(\hat{\Delta}_i^2 - c_\alpha^2 \text{var}(\hat{\Delta}_i)\right)\left(\hat{\phi}_i^2 - c_\alpha^2 \text{var}(\hat{\phi}_i)\right)} \tag{34}$$

$$\{\beta_i^L, \beta_i^H\} = \frac{(\hat{\Delta}_i\hat{\phi}_i - c_\alpha^2 \text{cov}(\hat{\Delta}_i, \hat{\phi}_i)) \pm R}{\hat{\Delta}_i^2 - c_\alpha^2 \text{var}(\hat{\Delta}_i)}. \tag{35}$$

If $\hat{\Delta}_i^2/\text{var}(\hat{\Delta}_i^2) > c_\alpha^2$, then the confidence region from inverting S_i^2 is the connected interval $(\beta_i^{\text{L}}, \beta_i^{\text{H}})$. For higher critical values, if $\hat{\Delta}_i^2/\text{var}(\hat{\Delta}_i^2) < c_\alpha^2$, the S-region is the union of two rays defined by $(-\infty, \beta_i^{\text{L}}) \cup (\beta_i^{\text{H}}, \infty)$ if R in (34) is real and the entire real line otherwise. The corresponding confidence region is the entire real line when the argument to the root in (34) is negative, which occurs for critical values above c^*, where

$$c^* = \sqrt{\frac{\hat{\Delta}_i^2 \text{var}(\hat{\phi}_i) + \hat{\phi}_i^2 \text{var}(\hat{\Delta}_i) - 2\hat{\Delta}_i\hat{\phi}_i \text{cov}(\hat{\Delta}_i, \hat{\phi}_i)}{\text{var}(\hat{\Delta}_i)\text{var}(\hat{\phi}_i) - \text{cov}(\hat{\Delta}_i, \hat{\phi}_i)^2}}.$$

In sufficiently well-identified models the uncertainty about $\hat{\Delta}_i$ is negligible, and so $\text{var}(\hat{\Delta}_i) << \hat{\Delta}_i^2$, $\text{cov}(\hat{\Delta}_i, \hat{\phi}_i) << \hat{\Delta}_i\hat{\phi}_i$, and $\text{var}(\hat{\phi}_i) \approx \hat{\Delta}_i^2 \text{var}(\hat{\beta}_{i,IV})$. Equations (33) through (35) reduce to

$$\left(\hat{\Delta}_i^2\right)\beta_i^{02} + 2\left(-\hat{\Delta}_i\hat{\beta}_{i,\text{IV}}\right)\beta_i^0 + \hat{\Delta}_i^2\left(\hat{\beta}_{i,\text{IV}}^2 - c_\alpha^2 \text{var}(\hat{\beta}_{i,\text{IV}})\right) < 0$$

$$R = \sqrt{\left(-\hat{\Delta}_i\hat{\beta}_{i,\text{IV}}\right)^2 - \left(\hat{\Delta}_i^2\right)^2\left(\hat{\beta}_{i,\text{IV}}^2 - c_\alpha^2 \text{var}(\hat{\beta}_{i,\text{IV}})\right)} = \hat{\Delta}_i^2 c_\alpha^2 \sqrt{\text{var}(\hat{\beta}_{i,\text{IV}})}$$

$$\{\beta_i^{\text{L}}, \beta_i^{\text{H}}\} = \hat{\beta}_{i,\text{IV}} \pm c_{\alpha/2}\sqrt{\text{var}(\hat{\beta}_{i,\text{IV}})}.$$

This establishes that S-regions approach the intervals based on the usual IV t-statistic as identification becomes certain. Evaluating the ratio of $\hat{\Psi}_i^2$ to $\hat{\sigma}_{\hat{\Psi}_i}^2$ as $\beta_i^0 \to \pm\infty$, it follows immediately that $\lim_{\beta_i^0 \to \pm\infty} S_i^2 = \hat{\Delta}_i^2/\text{var}(\hat{\Delta}_i^2)$. Therefore, the S-region is unbounded if the "Wald statistic" for identification of β_i is not significantly different from zero, for in this case S_i^2 asymptotically approaches a value less than c_α^2. Said differently, if $\hat{\Delta}_i^2/\text{var}(\hat{\Delta}_i^2) < c_\alpha^2$, then $S_i^2 < c_\alpha^2$ for large values of $|\beta_i^0|$; thus, extreme values of β_i^0 are not rejected. It follows that the S-region asymptotically satisfies Dufour's (1997) condition requiring, in the case of a near nonidentification, that a $(1-\alpha)\cdot 100\%$ confidence region be unbounded at least $1-\alpha$ percent of the time for the regions to attain coverage probability $1-\alpha$.

References

Anderson, T. W. and H. Rubin (1949). "Estimation of the parameters of a single equation in a complete system of stochastic equations," *Annals of Mathematical Statistics*, 20, 46–63.

Bekker, P. A. (1994). "Alternative approximations to the distributions of the instrumental variables estimators," *Econometrica*, 62, 657–681.

Blomquist, S. and M. Dahlberg (1999). "Small sample properties of LIML and jackknife IV estimators: experiments with weak instruments," *Journal of Applied Econometrics*, 14(1), 69–88.

Bound, J., D. A. Jaeger, and Baker R. M. (1995). "Problems with instrumental variables estimation when the correlation between the instruments and the endogenous explanatory variable is weak," *Journal of the American Statistical Association*, 90, 443–450.

Chamberlain, G. and G. Imbens (2004). "Random effects estimators with many instrumental variables," *Econometrica*, 72, 295–306.

Choi, I. and P. C. B. Phillips (1992). "Asymptotic and finite sample distribution theory for IV estimators and tests in partially identified structural equations," *Journal of Econometrics*, 51, 113–150.

Davidson, R. and J. G. MacKinnon (1993). *Estimation and Inference in Econometrics*, New York: Oxford University Press.

Dufour, J.-M. (1997). "Some impossibility theorems in econometrics with applications to structural and dynamic models," *Econometrica*, 65, 1365–88.

Dufour, J.-M. and J. Jasiak (2001). "Finite sample limited information inference methods for structural equations and models with unobserved and generated regressors," *International Economic Review*, 42, 815–843.

Dufour, J.-M. and L. Khalaf (1997). "Simulation based finite and large sample inference methods in simultaneous equations," unpublished manuscript, Université de Montréal.

Dufour, J.-M. and M. Taamouti (2003). "Projection-based statistical inference in linear structural models with possibly weak instruments," unpublished manuscript, Department of Economics, Université de Montréal.

Flores-Lagunes, A. (2000). "Estimation methods robust to weak instruments," unpublished manuscript, Department of Economics, Ohio State University.

Hall, A. R., G. D. Rudebusch and D. W. Wilcox (1996). "Judging instrument relevance in instrumental variables estimation," *International Economic Review*, 37, 283–289.

Hahn, J. and J. A. Hausman (2002), "A new specification test for the validity of instrumental variables," *Econometrica*, 70, 163–189.

Hahn, J. and A. Inoue (2002). "A Monte Carlo comparison of various asymptotic approximations to the distribution of instrumental variables estimators," *Econometric Reviews*, 21, 309–336.

Kleibergen, F. (2000). "Pivotal statistics for testing subsets of structural parameters in the IV regression model," Tinbergen Institute Discussion Paper 2000-88/4, University of Amsterdam.

Kleibergen, F. (2002). "Pivotal statistics for testing structural parameters in instrumental variables regression," *Econometrica*, 70, 1781–1803.

Kleibergen, F. and E. Zivot (2003). "Bayesian and classical approaches to instrumental variables regression," *Journal of Econometrics*, 114, 29–72.

Maddala, G. S. and J. Jeong (1992). "On the exact small sample distribution of the IV estimator," *Econometrica*, 60, 181–83.

Moreira, M. (2003). "A conditional likelihood ratio test for structural models," *Econometrica*, 71, 1027–1048.

Nelson, C. R. and R. Startz (1990a). "Some further results on the exact small sample properties of the instrumental variables estimator," *Econometrica*, 58, 967–976.

Nelson, C. R. and R. Startz (1990b): "The distribution of the instrumental variables estimator and its *t*-ratio when the instrument is a poor one," *Journal of Business*, 63, S125–S140.

Phillips, P. C. B. (1989). "Partially identified econometric models," *Econometric Theory*, 5, 181–240.

Shea, J. (1997). "Instrument relevance in multivariate linear models: A simple measure," *The Review of Economics and Statistics*, Vol. LXXIX, No. 2, 348–352.

Staiger, D. and J. H. Stock (1997): "Instrumental variables regressions with weak instruments," *Econometrica*, 65, 557–586.

Stock, J. H. and J. Wright (2000), "GMM with weak identification," *Econometrica*, 68, 1055–1096.

Stock, J. H., J. Wright. and M. Yogo (2002). "A survey of weak instruments and weak identification in generalized method of moments," *Journal of Business and Economic Statistics*, 20, 518–529.

Stock, J. H. and M. Yogo (2004). "Testing for Weak Instruments in Linear IV Regression," in D. W. K. Andrews and J. H. Stock, eds., *Identification and Inference in Econometric Models: Essays in Honor of Thomas J. Rothenberg*, Cambridge: Cambridge University Press.

Taamouti, M. (2001). "Techniques d'inférence exact dans les modèles structurels avec applications macroéconomiques," Ph.D. thesis, Departemente de sciences économiques, Université de Montréal.

Wang, J. and E. Zivot (1998): "Inference on structural parameters in instrumental variables regressions with weak instruments," *Econometrica* , Vol. 66, No. 6, 1389–1404.

Wong, K.-F. (1999). "A simulation comparison of inference for instrumental variable estimators," unpublished manuscript, Department of Economics, Chinese University of Hong Kong.

Zivot, E., R. Startz, and C. R. Nelson (1998). "Valid confidence intervals and inference in the presence of weak instruments," *International Economic Review*, Vol. 39, No. 4, pp. 1119–1144.

PART THREE

NONSTATIONARITY

SIX

Extracting Cycles from Nonstationary Data

Dean Corbae and Sam Ouliaris

6.1 INTRODUCTION

At least since Burns and Mitchell (1946), economists have been interested in developing methods for extracting "business cycle" components from the level of a time series. One important practical issue, for example, is how to extract the cyclical component from real gross domestic product (GDP). Modern approaches to this problem include removal of polynomial functions of time, first differencing, and applying the Hodrick–Prescott[1] (1980) filter, among others. Given the proliferation of these time-domain techniques to extracting the cyclical component, one might want to know which approach, if any, is optimal. If one accepts Burns and Mitchell's definition that the business cycle is fluctuations of real GDP with a specific periodicity (between 6 and 32 quarters), the answer is relatively clear using frequency-domain techniques. The problem arises in trying to map this approach back to the time domain. In particular, the exact bandpass filter is a moving average of infinite order in the time domain. For this reason, Baxter and King (1999), as well as Christiano and Fitzgerald (1999), construct a time-domain approximation to the exact filter that satisfies a particular set of criteria.

Here we wish to avoid the "time-domain" approximation error by approaching the problem in the frequency domain. One of the important drawbacks to frequency-domain filtering, noted by Baxter and King (1999, p. 580), is that, because most economic time series are likely to have nonstationary components, it is necessary to filter the series before taking its Fourier transform. The problem is that such prefiltering can be distortionary.[2] The main contribution of this chapter, which draws heavily on asymptotic results in Corbae, Ouliaris, and Phillips (2002), is to suggest a new frequency-domain

[1] See Prescott (1986) for a description of this filter.

[2] A second objection to frequency-domain methods suggested by Baxter and King has to do with ease of computation. In particular, frequency-domain methods have to be recomputed if the sample data changes.

methodology for extracting specific components that does not require any prefiltering in the time domain. Our approach yields an approximation to the ideal bandpass filter that is $\sqrt{n}$-consistent in the presence of deterministic and stochastic trends. As this chapter will show, it also has extremely good properties for samples the size of post-WWII data.

Corbae, Ouliaris, and Phillips (2002) provided an asymptotic analysis of frequency-domain regression with trending data for the two cases of stationary and cointegrated nonstationary data. They considered both semi-parametric and fully nonparametric formulations of the standard regression model. In dealing with the nonstationary case, the paper introduced some new methods for obtaining a limit theory for discrete Fourier transforms of integrated time series. This work extended and simplified some earlier asymptotic theory given in Phillips (1991) and developed a theory for spectral estimates in the nonstationary case. In particular, it was shown that the discrete Fourier transform of an *I(1)* process generates frequency responses that are necessarily spatially (i.e., frequency-wise) dependent across all the fundamental frequencies, even in the limit as the sample size $n \to \infty$, owing to leakage from the zero-frequency component. This leakage is strong enough to ensure that smoothed periodogram estimates of the spectrum away from the origin are inconsistent at all frequencies $\omega \neq 0$. In this chapter, we show that the techniques and results given in Corbae, Ouliaris, and Phillips (2002) can be utilized to avoid the pitfalls of frequency-domain filtering.

This chapter is organized as follows. In Section 6.2, we discuss in depth the potential problems associated with bandpass filters. In Section 6.3, we show how our techniques can be applied to remedy these problems. In Section 6.4, we conduct some Monte Carlo experiments to assess the small sample properties of our suggested approach. In Section 6.5, we apply our results to two empirical studies: the extraction of business cycles and the cyclical relationship between output and prices. Section 6.6 provides concluding remarks.

6.2 PITFALLS IN EXTRACTING BUSINESS CYCLES

As discussed in the introduction, if one accepts the Burns and Mitchell (1946) definition of the business cycle as all fluctuations in the *level* of a series within a specified range of periodicities, the ideal filter is simply the bandpass filter that extracts components of the time series with periodic fluctuations between 6 and 32 quarters. It can be shown that the exact band-pass filter is a double-sided moving average of the original series of infinite order with known weights. It follows that if we want to estimate the filter starting from the time domain, an approximation to the correct result is necessary.

The objective of Baxter and King (1999) is to generate the best approximation subject to certain constraints.[3] One constraint is that the filter should

[3] The constraints elucidated by Baxter and King are: (1) the filter should extract a specified range of periodicities and leave the properties of this extracted component unaffected, (2) the

eliminate nonstationary (deterministic or stochastic) trends. Baxter and King show that if a symmetric moving average has weights that sum to zero, then it will render stationary any series containing quadratic trends or stochastic trends of the I(1) or I(2) variety. Another constraint is that an approximation to the ideal filter should minimize a quadratic loss function of discrepancies between the exact and approximate filter. Because the ideal low-pass symmetric filter is of the form $b(L) = \sum_{h=-\infty}^{\infty} b_h L^h$, where $b_0 = \underline{\lambda}/\pi$, $b_h = \sin(h\underline{\lambda})/h\pi$ for $h = 1, 2, \ldots$ and $\underline{\lambda}$ denotes the endpoint of the symmetric band, Baxter and King prove an important result; the optimal finite approximating filter for given maximum lag length K is in fact simply a truncation of the ideal filter's weights b_h at lag K.[4] They also show that there is a trade-off in choosing K; although the approximation is improved by higher K, one loses K observations at either end of the series.

Given the approximation error associated with their time-domain filter, why then not go to the frequency domain where the ideal filter lies? Baxter and King list potential violations of two of their six critieria. First, they argue that one must prefilter the data to eliminate deterministic or stochastic trends before using discrete Fourier transforms, which indeed is the approach taken in practice (see Rush, Li, and Zhu 1997). They suggest this is a serious problem because one is forced to choose a detrending method. Second, they argue that the finite-sample results of the frequency-domain approach are not invariant to sample size. This is because frequency responses will be computed at different fundamental frequencies $\left(\lambda_s = \frac{2\pi s}{n} : s = 0, 1, \ldots, n-1\right)$ as the sample size n increases. In contrast, provided the time-series observation does not fall in the left or right truncation range, the Baxter and King approximation will not change with the sample size. This is because the moving average window involves a fixed, known set of weights that do not depend on the sample size. Although this particular characteristic of the Baxter–King filter may be desirable under some conditions, it does, however, render the approach statistically inconsistent given that its approximation error will not converge to zero as $n \to \infty$.

6.3 AN ALTERNATIVE APPROACH

In this section, we address the first criticism of frequency-domain methods leveled by Baxter and King (1999); namely, problems dealing with nonstationarity of macroeconomic data. In particular, we show how to avoid this pitfall and develop a $\sqrt{n}$-consistent estimator of the ideal bandpass filter that does not

filter should not introduce phase shift, (3) an approximation to the ideal filter should minimize a quadratic loss function of discrepancies between the exact and approximate filter, (4) the filter should result in a stationary series even when applied to trending data, (5) the filter should yield components unrelated to the length of the sample, and (6) the filter should be operational.

4 That is, in the finite-order approximation $a(L) = \sum_{h=-K}^{K} a_h L^h$, they show $a_h = b_h$.

involve a loss of K observations at either end of the time series. We remark that our alternative approach can easily be applied to stationary data as well.

Assume that x_t $(t = 1, \ldots, n)$ is an observable time series (e.g., real GDP) generated by[5]

$$x_t = \Pi_2' z_t + \widetilde{x}_t, \tag{1}$$

where z_t is a $p+1$-dimensional deterministic sequence and $\widetilde{x}_t$ is a zero mean time series. The series x_t therefore has both a deterministic component involving the sequence z_t and a stochastic (latent) component $\widetilde{x}_t$. In developing our approach to estimating ideal bandpass filters, we will make the following assumptions about z_t and $\widetilde{x}_t$.

Assumption 6.1 $z_t = (1, t, \ldots, t^p)'$ is a pth order polynomial in time.

Assumption 6.2 $\widetilde{x}_t$ is an I(1) process satisfying $\Delta\widetilde{x}_t = v_t$ initialized at $t = 0$ by any $O_p(1)$ random variable. We assume that v_t has a Wold representation $v_t = \sum_{j=0}^{\infty} c_j \xi_{t-j}$, where $\xi_t = iid\left(0, \sigma^2\right)$ with finite fourth moments and coefficients c_j satisfying $\sum_{j=0}^{\infty} j^{\frac{1}{2}} |c_j| < \infty$. The spectral density of v_t is $f_{vv}(\lambda) > 0$, $\forall\lambda$.

Assumption 6.2 suffices for partial sums of v_t to satisfy the functional law $n^{-1/2} \sum_{t=1}^{[nr]} v_t \xrightarrow{d} B(r) = BM(\sigma^2)$, a univariate Brownian motion with variance $\sigma^2 = 2\pi f_{vv}(0)$ (e.g., Phillips and Solo 1992, Theorem 3.4) and where $\xrightarrow{d}$ is used to denote weak convergence of the associated probability measures as the sample size $n \to \infty$.

We now state the result that motivates our filtering procedure.

Lemma B (Corbae, Ouliaris, and Phillips 2002) *Let $\widetilde{x}_t$ be an $I(1)$ process satisfying Assumption 6.2. Then, the discrete Fourier transform of $\widetilde{x}_t$ for $\lambda_s \neq 0$ is given by*

$$w_{\widetilde{x}}(\lambda_s) = \frac{1}{1 - e^{i\lambda_s}} w_v(\lambda_s) - \frac{e^{i\lambda_s}}{1 - e^{i\lambda_s}} \frac{[\widetilde{x}_n - \widetilde{x}_0]}{n^{1/2}}, \tag{2}$$

where the discrete Fourier transform (dft) of $\{a_t; t = 1, \ldots, n\}$ is written $w_a(\lambda) = \frac{1}{\sqrt{n}} \sum_{t=1}^{n} a_t e^{i\lambda t}$ and $\{\lambda_s = \frac{2\pi s}{n}, s = 0, 1, \ldots, n-1\}$ are the fundamental frequencies.

Equation (2) shows that the discrete Fourier transforms of an *I(1)* process are not asymptotically independent across fundamental frequencies. Indeed, they are frequency-wise dependent by virtue of the component $n^{-1/2}\widetilde{x}_n$, which

[5] In what follows, *I(1)* signifies an integrated process of order one, and $BM(\Omega)$ denotes a univariate Brownian motion with variance Ω. The discrete Fourier transform (dft) of $\{a_t; t = 1, \ldots, n\}$ is written $w_a(\lambda) = \frac{1}{\sqrt{n}} \sum_{t=1}^{n} a_t e^{i\lambda t}$, where $\{\lambda_s = \frac{2\pi s}{n}, s = 0, 1, \ldots, n-1\}$ are the fundamental frequencies.

produces a common leakage into all frequencies $\lambda_s \neq 0$ even in the limit as $n \to \infty$. The paper goes on to show (in Lemma C(f) of Corbae, Ouliaris, and Phillips 2002) that the leakage is still manifest when the data are first detrended in the time domain. These results on leakage show that, in the presence of I(1) variables, any frequency-domain estimate of the "cyclical" component of a series (e.g., real GDP) will be badly distorted.

There is, however, a frequency domain fix. To see it, note that the second expression in (2) can be rewritten using

$$w_{\left(\frac{t}{n}\right)}(\lambda_s) = \frac{-1}{\sqrt{n}}\left(\frac{e^{i\lambda_s}}{1 - e^{i\lambda_s}}\right)$$

by Lemma A of Corbae, Ouliaris, and Phillips (2002). Thus, even for the case in which there is no deterministic trend in (1), it is clear from the second term in (2), which is a deterministic trend in the frequency domain with a random coefficient $[\widetilde{x}_n - \widetilde{x}_0]/\sqrt{n}$, that we need to detrend in the frequency domain to remove the leakage from the low frequency. That is, frequency-domain detrending (i.e., using residuals from regressions of the frequency-domain data on $w_{\left(\frac{t}{n}\right)}(\lambda_s)$) will estimate the second term of (2), leaving an unbiased estimate of $\frac{1}{1 - e^{i\lambda_s}} w_v(\lambda_s)$. It follows that applying the indicator function $\beta(\lambda_s)$ for λ_s in a given frequency band to $w_{\widetilde{x}}$ will yield an unbiased estimate of the filtered data.

Using Lemma A of Corbae, Ouliaris, and Phillips (2002), one can show that Hannan's (1970) frequency-domain estimator of $[\widetilde{x}_n - \widetilde{x}_0]/\sqrt{n}$ in (2) will be $\sqrt{n}$ consistent. In particular,

$$\sqrt{n}\left(\widehat{\beta}^{f}_{w\left(\frac{t}{n}\right)} - \frac{[\widetilde{x}_n - \widetilde{x}_0]}{\sqrt{n}}\right) \xrightarrow{d} N\left(0, \varphi^2\right), \tag{3}$$

where $\varphi^2 = \frac{(2\pi)^2 \int_{B_A^c} f_1(\omega) f_{vv}(\omega) f_1(\omega)^* d\omega}{\left(\int_{B_A^c} f_1(\omega) f_1(\omega)^* d\omega\right)^2}$ and $f_1(\omega) = \frac{e^{i\omega}}{e^{i\omega}-1}$. Given that $\widetilde{x}_n$ is an $I(1)$ process, the frequency-domain estimator $\widehat{\beta}^{f}_{w\left(\frac{t}{n}\right)}$ converges to $[\widetilde{x}_n - \widetilde{x}_0]/\sqrt{n}$ at the rate $\sqrt{n}$, which is a feature clearly evident in the Monte Carlo evidence presented in the following section. We remark that if $\widetilde{x}$ is a stationary process, then $\widehat{\beta}^{f}_{w\left(\frac{t}{n}\right)} \xrightarrow{p} 0$, and $(\widetilde{x}_n - \widetilde{x}_0)$ will diverge as $n \to \infty$, yielding a simple frequency-domain test of the unit-root hypothesis.

If one is willing to sacrifice a single observation at the beginning of the series, an alternative estimator of the filtered series can be proposed: simply impose the coefficient $[\widetilde{x}_n - \widetilde{x}_0]$ in (2) using the actual value of $\widetilde{x}_n$ and $\widetilde{x}_1$ as the initial value. The resulting estimate of the filtered series will not have any finite sampling error for $t = 2, 3, \ldots, n$. It may therefore have superior endpoint properties to the approach developed above because any errors in estimating $(\widetilde{x}_n - \widetilde{x}_0)$ will not eliminate the leakage from the zero frequency completely.

It can be shown that such errors will manifest themselves particularly at the endpoints of the filtered series, which is likely to be a serious issue if the goal is to obtain early warning of turning points.

Note that imposing this adjustment on a detrended stationary series will introduce a distortionary trend component unless $\widetilde{x}_n = \widetilde{x}_1$. It is therefore essential to verify that the original series is an integrated process before using this approach, and (3) is likely to be useful for this purpose.

Lastly, we remark that the proposed frequency-domain filter has an important advantage over the Baxter and King (1999) and Hodrick–Prescott (1980) filters in that it does not require the investigator to set any parameters except the business cycle range.

6.4 MONTE CARLO RESULTS

Here we design a Monte Carlo experiment to assess how well the Hodrick–Prescott (HP) and Baxter–King (BK) time-domain filters work relative to our frequency-domain method (FD). In particular, we consider an ARI(1,1) data-generation process for real output estimated from U.S. data. We evaluate the filters by computing the root-mean-squared error of the difference between the filtered data and the "true" cycle.

Letting $\widetilde{x}_t$ denote the latent stochastic component of log real GDP and $g_t = (1 - L)\widetilde{x}_t$ denote its growth rate, we take the data-generation process to be

$$g_t = \alpha g_{t-1} + \varepsilon_t,$$

where $\widetilde{x}_0 = 0$ and ε_t is drawn from $N(0, 1)$. The value we use for $\alpha = 0.34$ is estimated from an autoregression of actual real GDP over the sample period 1947:1 to 2000:4, which comprises $n = 216$ observations.[6] Then, to construct the level of real GDP, we simply form $\widetilde{x}_t = \sum_{j=1}^{t} g_t$. To construct the "true" cycle, denoted $\widetilde{x}_t^*$, we first take the dft of g_t, which we denote $w_g(\lambda_s)$. Then we construct

$$\beta(\lambda_s) w_g(\lambda_s)/(1 - e^{i\lambda_s}) \tag{4}$$

and finally inverse Fourier transform (4) to get $\widetilde{x}_t^{*}$[7]. To obtain the filtered data, denoted $\widetilde{x}_t^f$ where $f \in \{\text{HP, BK, FD}\}$, we simply apply the associated time- or frequency-domain filter to the level of the simulated data. We calculate the sample mean-squared error as $\text{MSE}^f = n^{-1} \sum_{t=1}^{n} \left(\widetilde{x}_t^f - \widetilde{x}_t^*\right)^2$. We also calculate a sample correlation (CORR^f) between the filtered data $\widetilde{x}_t^f$ and the "true" cycle $\widetilde{x}_t^*$.

[6] The GDP (1996 Chained $) data were taken from the Bureau of Economic Analysis Web site.

[7] Note that there is no reduction in the sample size because $\widetilde{x}_0$ is known in the simulations.

Table 6.1 *Summary Statistics for Simulated Data*

	HP	BK	FD	$\widetilde{x}_t^*$
Stdev	0.49664	0.47323	0.52553	0.53591
Skew	0.00582	0.00892	0.00481	0.00187
Kurtosis	−0.1968	−0.2442	−0.2620	−0.2802

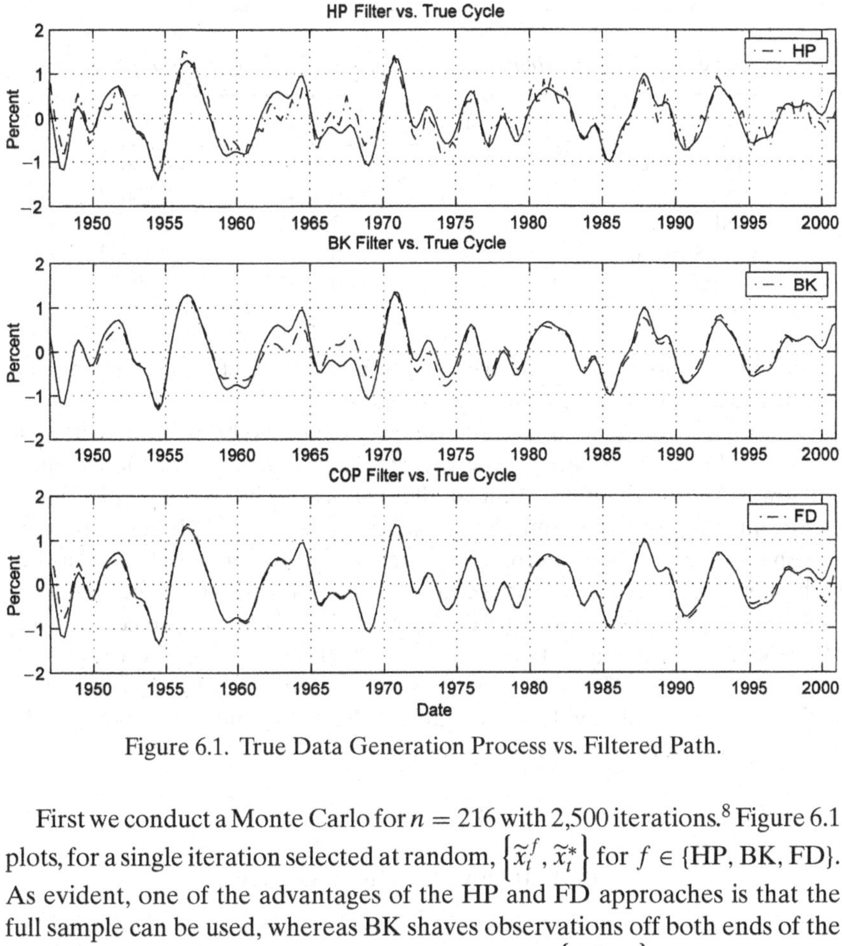

Figure 6.1. True Data Generation Process vs. Filtered Path.

First we conduct a Monte Carlo for $n = 216$ with 2,500 iterations.[8] Figure 6.1 plots, for a single iteration selected at random, $\left\{\widetilde{x}_t^f, \widetilde{x}_t^*\right\}$ for $f \in \{\text{HP, BK, FD}\}$. As evident, one of the advantages of the HP and FD approaches is that the full sample can be used, whereas BK shaves observations off both ends of the series. An estimate of the true summary statistics for $\left\{\widetilde{x}_t^f, \widetilde{x}_t^*\right\}$ for $f \in \{\text{HP, BK, FD}\}$ from this Monte Carlo is presented in Table 6.1.

[8] We backfilled ε_t using 100 observations. This is to ensure that the innovation sequence is consistent with the AR(1) generating mechanism. The HP cycle was calculated using $\lambda = 1600$.

Table 6.2 *Moment Measures of Goodness of Fit (Short Sample)*

$n = 216$	HP	BK	FD
MSE mean	0.06369	0.05121	0.01126
MSE stdev	0.02202	0.02247	0.01594
$\text{MSE}^f/\text{MSE}^{FD}$	5.6543	4.5479	1
CORR mean	0.8842	0.9107	0.98111
CORR stdev	0.03789	0.03547	0.02476

Table 6.3 *Moment Measures of Goodness of Fit (Long Sample)*

$n = 10{,}000$	HP	BK	FD
MSE mean	0.07164	0.05149	0.00017
MSE stdev	0.00411	0.00315	0.00024
$\text{MSE}^f/\text{MSE}^{FD}$	421.418	302.824	1
CORR mean	0.85288	0.88594	0.99963
CORR stdev	0.00817	0.00688	0.00053

Taking the moments of the true series as the correct moments, one can clearly see that the FD filter performs best.

In Table 6.2, we provide an assessment of the goodness of fit of the alternative filtering approaches. The average MSE is highest for the HP filter and lowest for the FD filter.[9] Indeed, there appear to be sizable reductions in mean-square error from using the FD approach relative to HP and BK; over five and four times smaller error, respectively. The FD approach also has the highest average correlation between the filtered data and the "true" data.

To assess the $\sqrt{n}$-consistency result for the FD approach, we conduct another Monte Carlo simulation using $n = 10{,}000$ iterations. The results are shown in Table 6.3. Not surprisingly, the improvement in FD as the sample size increases is quite evident. In contrast, the performance of both the HP and BK filters does not improve with n.

6.5 APPLICATIONS

6.5.1 Extracting the Business Cycle

Here we apply our techniques, as well as the HP and BK filters, to extract the business cycle for U.S. data discussed in the previous section. The standard deviation, skewness, and kurtosis of the business cycle extracted by each filter are given in Table 6.4.[10]

[9] We note that the BK approach shaves data points off the beginning and end of the sample. The MSE and CORR calculations under BK are for the smaller sample.

[10] These are the same moments considered by Canova (1998).

Table 6.4 *Summary Statistics for U.S. Business Cycle*

	HP	BK	FD
Stdev	1.7420	1.6466	1.7288
Skew	−0.4445	−0.3747	−0.6369
Kurtosis	0.48842	−0.1350	0.64598

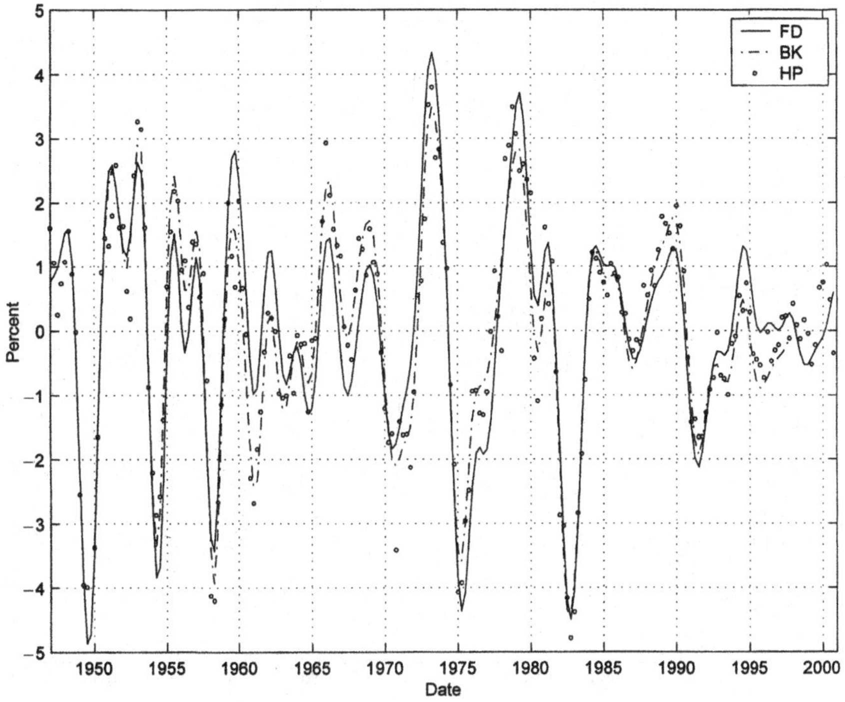

Figure 6.2. HP, BK, and FD filtered quarterly real GDP.

We plot the filtered data employing the three different methods in Figure 6.2. It is clear from the diagram that the HP filter has more of the irregular or "high-frequency" component of the series; however, all the filtered series identify "significant" turning points at much the same time.

6.5.2 The Cyclical Relationship between Output and Prices

To illustrate the effects of filtering on the cyclical properties of a given variable, we consider the cross correlation of filtered output and price level data. Various studies, starting with Burns and Mitchell (1946), have examined this issue. Burns and Mitchell (1946, Table 22, p. 101), considering a sample period from

Table 6.5 *Summary Statistics for U.S. GDP deflator*

	HP	BK	FD
Stdev	1.0355	0.9967	1.0049
Skew	−0.1072	−0.1174	−0.0178
Kurtosis	1.4022	1.0073	0.8211
Corr with $\tilde{x}^f$	−0.2577	−0.3204	−0.2651

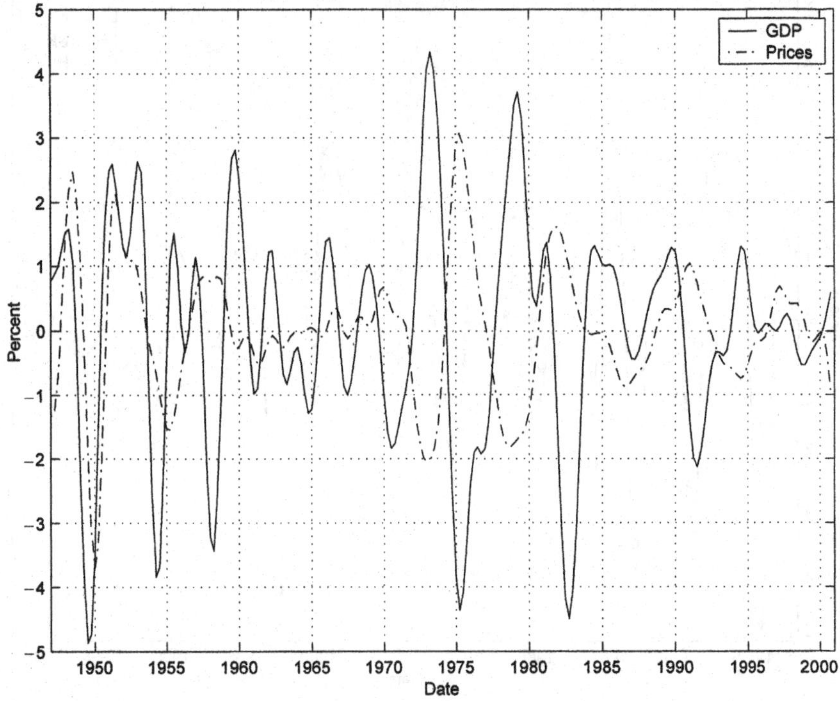

Figure 6.3. Cyclical component of real GDP and the price level.

1854 to 1933, found the wholesale price level to be procyclical based on reference dates. Employing the HP filter on postwar data from 1959:1 to 1989:4, Kydland and Prescott (1990) found the price level to be countercyclical. Here we use the log GDP deflator for the sample period 1947:1 to 2000:4.[11]

Table 6.5 provides the standard deviation, skewness, and kurtosis of the price level for each filter as well as the cross correlation with output using each filtering procedure.

We plot the filtered data for real output and prices employing the FD method in Figure 6.3. The relationship between real GDP and the price level is countercyclical for the entire sample period. However, if we truncate the

[11] The Implicit Price deflator was taken from the Bureau of Economic Analysis Web site.

sample period at 1973:4, the relationship between output and prices becomes procyclical, albeit with a small correlation of 0.07.

6.6 CONCLUSIONS

We have proposed a new frequency-domain filter for extracting the cyclical component of a time series from the level of a time series that easily handles stochastic and deterministic trends but also works for stationary series. Our approach yields a statistically consistent estimator of the ideal bandpass filter. Using a series of Monte Carlo exeriments, we have shown that our approach has much lower mean-squared error than popular time-domain filters for a data-generation process similar to that of the growth rate of U.S. real output.

References

Baxter, M. and R. King (1999). "Measuring business cycles: Approximate band-pass filters for economic time series," *Review of Economics and Statistics*, 81, 575–593.

Burns, A. and W. Mitchell (1946). *Measuring Business Cycles.* New York: National Bureau of Economic Research.

Canova, F. (1998) "Detrending and business cycle facts," *Journal of Monetary Economics*, 41:475–512.

Christiano, L. and T. Fitzgerald (1999). "The band pass filter," mimeograph, Federal Reserve Bank of Cleveland.

Corbae, D., S. Ouliaris, and P. C. B. Phillips (2002). "Band spectral regression with trending data," *Econometrica*, 70, 1067–1109.

Hannan, E. J. (1970). *Multiple Times Series*, New York: Wiley.

Hodrick, R. J. and E. C. Prescott (1980). "Post-War U.S. business cycles: An empirical investigation." Discussion Paper 451, Carnegie-Mellon University.

Kwiatkowsi, D., P. C. B. Phillips, P. Schmidt, and Y. Shin (1992). "Testing the null hypothesis of stationarity against the alternative of a unit root: How sure are we that economic time series have a unit root?," *Journal of Econometrics*, 54, 159–178.

Kydland, F. and E. Prescott (1990). "Business Cycles: Real Facts and a Monetary Myth," *Quarterly Review*, Federal Reserve Bank of Minneapolis, 3–18.

Phillips, P. C. B. (1991). "Spectral regression for co-integrated time series," in W. Barnett, J. Powell, and G. Tauchen, eds., *Nonparametric and Semiparametric Methods in Economics and Statistics.* Cambridge: Cambridge University Press.

Phillips, P. C. B. and V. Solo (1992). "Asymptotics for linear processes," *Annals of Statistics*, 20: 971–1001.

Prescott, E. (1986). "Theory ahead of business cycle measurement," *Carnegie–Rochester Conference Series on Public Policy*, 25:11–66.

Rush, M. Y. Li and L. Zhu (1997). "Filtering methodology and fit in dynamic business cycle models," University of Florida working paper.

SEVEN

Nonstationary Nonlinearity

*An Outlook for New Opportunities**

Joon Y. Park

7.1 INTRODUCTION

It has long been recognized that many economic and financial time series data exhibit nonstationarity that can be reasonably well modeled as integrated processes. Integrated processes have stochastic trends, which allow us to build their relationships using the notion of cointegration. As is well known, cointegration refers to the presence of a linear relationship among multiple integrated processes that holds up to stationary and mean-reverting residuals, and it has thus been widely used to describe various long-run economic equilibria. Although the concept of cointegration has been received enthusiastically by many applied researchers, its practical implementation appears not to have been entirely successful. In particular, we have not witnessed many meaningful empirical findings on the subject despite the numerous attempts that have been made by many practitioners for the past two decades. Most of them seem to have found nothing beyond our common sense.

Both integration and cointegration, respectively, as a means of modeling observed individual time series and describing relationships among them, often appear to be too restrictive to be very useful in practical applications. For instance, many time series observed in reality are bounded yet locally nonstationary and behave like integrated processes. Clearly, such time series cannot be effectively modeled as integrated processes that should necessarily be unbounded. It is also apparent that any time series taking only nonnegative values cannot be generated by an integrated process. Moreover, in many cases it seems extremely unrealistic to assume that a simple linear relationship persists among integrated processes over a long period of time,

* This chapter is a revised and extended version of an invited lecture delivered at the 2001 Econometric Society Australasian Meeting, which was held in Auckland, New Zealand. The research reported is based on my earlier works with several coauthors. In particular, the joint work with Peter Phillips provides the essential theoretical background for this research. I thank Yoosoon Chang for her support as well as many helpful discussions and comments.

which is implied by the presence of cointegration. Undoubtedly, there are many economic problems and phenomena that the concepts of integration and cointegration, both of which are very linear, appear to be too simple to deal with effectively.

This chapter considers the nonlinear models with integrated time series. The relevant theory has been developed in recent papers by Park and Phillips (1998, 1999, 2000, 2001, 2003); Chang, Park and Phillips (2001); Park (2002, 2003); Phillips and Park (1997) and several others that are still in progress. We concentrate on the positive side of the theory and seek new research opportunities, rather than pitfalls, in nonstationary nonlinearity. The outlook for the new opportunities is explored in three different directions: in data generation, in mean, and in volatility. Presented are various possibilities that can come out of nonstationary nonlinearity in data generations, in regressions, and in models for conditional variance. They are given in a unified framework. We also introduce the basic tools to deal effectively with nonstationary nonlinearity and subsequently develop some fundamental nonstationary, nonlinear asymptotics.

First, we consider the nonstationary nonlinearity in data generation. Here we look for the possibility that integrated time series undergo a nonlinear transformation before our final observation. The transformation may come as a result of policy or market intervention, as in the case of the exchange rate regime with a target zone, or simply from taking variable transformations such as logs, ratios, or both. To investigate the effect of a nonlinear transformation, we examine the time series properties of the transformed integrated processes. Quite a few interesting results are obtained here. It is shown, for instance, that the nonlinear transformation of an integrated time series may yield bounded nonstationarity, long memory, or both. Leptokurticity, thick tails, or both can also be generated by the nonstationary nonlinearity in data generation. Moreover, we demonstrate that the nonlinear transformation may or may not preserve the unit root, depending on the transformation function.

Second, the nonlinear relationships between integrated time series are discussed. We consider both the parametric nonlinear least-squares regression and the nonparametric kernel regression, which are useful to make inference on the nonlinear and nonparametric cointegration models. As shown in Park and Phillips (2001), the usual nonlinear least squares yields consistent estimates for the nonlinear cointegrating regression. Also, we may use the standard kernel method to consistently estimate a cointegrating relationship nonparametrically. The nonparametric method, however, reduces the convergence rate dramatically – especially when the regression function is increasing at infinity. We suggest as a practical solution to this problem the partial parametric approach, which in the first step models and estimates the dominant component parametrically. The residual component can be estimated nonparametrically in the second step.

Third, we look at a stochastic volatility model with conditional variance given by a nonlinear function of a random walk. The model, referred to as *nonstationary nonlinear heteroskedasticity*, was introduced and investigated earlier by Park (2002). Here we clearly demonstrate that the nonstationary nonlinearity can also play an important role in modeling volatility. In particular, it is shown that the nonstationary nonlinearity in volatility may generate samples with volatility clustering and leptokurticity, which are observed commonly for many economic and financial time series data. There appear to be many potential examples for such time series. For instance, the volatility of a stock return may well be positively related to the level of interest rate, transactions quantity, or both which are believed by many to be integrated.

All our subsequent discussions are heuristic. This is to focus effectively on the main theme we want to deliver in this chapter: new research opportunities from nonstationary nonlinearity. The assumptions made here are far from being necessary to obtain the stated results. Also, the results are not proved rigorously. Readers are referred to other existing literature for the minimal conditions and rigorous proofs. The standard notations are used without specific references. In particular, $=_d$ signifies the equivalence in distribution, and $\to_d$ denotes the convergence in distribution. Likewise, we use $\to_{a.s}$ and $\to_p$, respectively, to signify almost sure convergence and convergence in probability. The stochastic order symbols o_p and O_p are also used, and **MN** stands for mixed normal distribution.

The rest of the chapter is organized as follows. Section 7.2 introduces the technical preliminaries necessary to understand the subsequent development of our theory. Basic tools to deal with nonstationary nonlinearity are introduced, and some fundamental nonstationary nonlinear asymptotics are also developed. In Sections 7.3 to 7.5, various new opportunities from nonstationary nonlinearity are proposed. Section 7.3 lays out the statistical properties of nonlinear transformations of integrated processes. The nonlinear relationships for nonstationary processes are considered in Section 7.4. Here we develop their asymptotics, and discuss how they can be properly formulated and effectively estimated. In Section 7.5, we introduce nonstationary nonlinear heteroskedasticity as a volatility model and compare it with other competing models. Section 7.6 concludes the chapter.

7.2 THEORETICAL BACKGROUND

We consider an integrated time series (x_t) given by

$$x_t = x_{t-1} + v_t, \tag{1}$$

where (v_t) is an independent and identically distributed sequence of random variables with mean zero and variance ω^2. It is assumed that (v_t) has continous-type distribution. Some of our subsequent results require the existence of higher moments for (v_t), that is., $\mathbf{E}|v_t|^r < \infty$ for some $r > 2$. The assumption made here is far from being necessary for most of our subsequent results. Many of the results derived in the chapter are applicable to more general integrated processes driven by linear processes or mixing sequences. In those cases, we may obtain similar results using higher moment conditions on innovations sequences, stronger assumptions on nonlinear transformation functions, or both. As we move along, we will indicate what types of extensions are possible and where to find more general results.

Our primary objective is to investigate the probabilistic and statistical properties of an integrated process, such as (x_t) introduced in (1), under a transformation. The transformation is presumed, though not restricted, to be nonlinear. In general, the asymptotics for integrated time series under the nonlinear transformation depend crucially on the type of transformation involved. This was clearly demonstrated by Park and Phillips (1999). They indeed introduced three different classes of transformation functions – integrable functions, asymptotically homogeneous functions and exponential functions – to characterize the asymptotics for the nonlinear transformations of integrated processes. Of the three classes, we consider only the first two. The integrated processes have stochastic trends, and their exponential transformations appear to be too explosive to be useful for practical applications.

Obviously, the transformations like $T(x) = 1\{a \leq x \leq b\}$, with some constants a and b, and $T(x) = e^{-x^2}$ are integrable. Asymptotically homogeneous functions are roughly the functions that behave asymptotically as homogeneous functions. In short, the transformation T is asymptotically homogeneous if we have

$$T(\lambda x) \approx \nu(\lambda)S(x) \tag{2}$$

for all large λ and for all x on any bounded interval. We will call ν and S, respectively, the *asymptotic order* and the *limit homogeneous function* of T. The class of asymptotically homogeneous transformations includes a wide variety of functions. It includes, for instance, constant functions, all distribution function-like functions, logarithmic functions, and all functions that behave asymptotically as polynomials.

The transformation given by $T(x) = |x|^k$ is homogeneous and is certainly asymptotically homogeneous with asymptotic order $\nu(\lambda) = \lambda^k$ and limit homogeneous function $S(x) = |x|^k$. The logarithmic transformation $T(x) = \log|x|$ is also asymptotically homogeneous with asymptotic order $\nu(\lambda) = \log\lambda$ and limit homogeneous function $S(x) = 1$. Note that $\log|\lambda x| = \log\lambda + \log|x| \approx \log\lambda$ for all large λ and for all x on any bounded interval. The logistic transformation $T(x) = e^x/(1+e^x)$ can be decomposed as $T(x) = S(x) + R(x)$, where $S(x) = 1\{x \geq 0\}$ is homogeneous and $R(x) = 1\{x < 0\}e^x/(1+e^x) - 1\{x \geq 0\}1/(1+e^x)$ is integrable. However, it follows that $S(\lambda x) = S(x)$ for all λ and for all x, and $R(\lambda x) \to 0$ as $\lambda \to \infty$ for all x on any bounded interval. We thus have $T(\lambda x) \approx 1\{x \geq 0\}$ for all large λ and for all x on a bounded interval. Consequently, it has asymptotic order $\nu(\lambda) = 1$ and limit homogeneous function $S(x) = 1\{x \geq 0\}$. The same result applies to any distribution function-like transformation.

7.2.1 Statistical Tools

The classical Donsker's theorem applies to (v_t). Therefore, if we let $[nr]$ be the integral part of nr for $r \in [0, 1]$ and define

$$V_n(r) = \frac{1}{\sqrt{n}} \sum_{t=1}^{[nr]} v_t, \tag{3}$$

it follows that

$$V_n \to_d V, \tag{4}$$

where V is the Brownian motion with variance ω^2 on the unit interval $[0, 1]$. The invariance principle (4) holds under conditions that are much weaker than those we impose here. We may, for example, obtain this principle for, linear processes driven by martingale difference sequences satisfying some mild summability and moment conditions. See Hall and Heyde (1980) and Phillips and Solo (1992) for technical details.

Our subsequent asymptotic theory is presented using various functionals of the limit Brownian motion V introduced above in (4). It also involves the local time L of the Brownian motion V. The Brownian local time L is a stochastic process with two parameters, t and s, for instance, which can be defined as

$$L(t, s) = \lim_{\epsilon \to 0} \frac{1}{2\epsilon} \int_0^t 1\{|V(r) - s| < \epsilon\}\, dr. \tag{5}$$

Roughly, it may be interpreted as the time, measured as an instantaneous rate, spent by V in an immediate neighborhood of s up to time t.[1] Refer to Chung and Williams (1990) for an elementary introduction to the concept of local time.

The Brownian local time is known to have a version continuous both in t and s, and so we may assume L is given as such. For each t, $L(t, \cdot)$ has a compact support a.s. This should be obvious because Brownian motion has continuous sample path a.s. Some of our asymptotics, in particular, include the Brownian local time at $t = 1$ and $s = 0$, that is, $L(1, 0)$. It is well known that $L(1, 0)$ has the same distribution as $|V(1)|$, that is, the modulus of the normal variate with mean zero and variance ω^2. This follows immediately from the fact that the local time of standard Brownian motion has distribution given by the truncated

[1] The local time is defined for a broader class of semimartingales. Also, it is more customary to measure the time in the unit of the quadratic variation of the underlying process. Our local time L in (5) may thus be defined more conventionally using $d[V](r) = \omega^2 dr$ in place of dr. However, it is more convenient to use our definition (5) for the subsequent asymptotics on nonstationary nonlinearity.

standard normal supported on the positive half of **R** (see, e.g., Revuz and Yor, 1994, Proposition 3.7, p. 100 and Theorem 2.3, p. 230). Note that the local time L of V at time and spatial parameters t and s has the same value with $1/\omega$ times of the local time of W at t and s/ω. This can easily be deduced from our defition in (5).

The local time yields the formula

$$\int_0^t T(V(r))\,dr = \int_{-\infty}^{\infty} T(s)L(t,s)\,ds \tag{6}$$

for any T locally integrable. The relationship (6) is commonly referred to as the *occupation times formula*. For each fixed t, it allows us to evaluate the integral of any locally integrable transformation of a Brownian motion with respect to time as the integral of the function itself weighted by the local time. In this sense, we may legitimately interpret the local time as a function of its spatial parameter – as the spatial density of the values that the underlying Brownian motion takes. The interpretation of the local time as the spatial density is illustrated in Figure 7.1. There we present a simulated Brownian sample path with its estimated local time, which shows the relative frequencies for the realized values of the underlying Brownian motion.

7.2.2 Basic Asymptotics

Now we are ready to derive some basic asymptotics for the nonlinear models with integrated time series. To develop the covariance asymptotics, as well as the mean asymptotics, we introduce (u_t) in addition to (x_t) defined in (1). In what follows, we assume that $(u_t, \mathcal{F}_t)$ is a martingale difference sequence, where $(\mathcal{F}_t)$ is a filtration such that (x_t) is adapted to $(\mathcal{F}_{t-1})$. We let

$$\sigma^2 = \mathbf{E}(u_t^2|\mathcal{F}_{t-1})$$

and $\mathbf{E}(|u_t|^r|\mathcal{F}_{t-1}) < \infty$ a.s. for some $r > 2$. Moreover, we define a partial sum process U_n on $[0,1]$ from (u_t), as is done for V_n in (3) constructed from (v_t), and denote by U the limit Brownian motion of U_n. Clearly, U is a Brownian motion with variance σ^2 and is allowed to be dependent with the limit Brownian motion V of V_n. We may indeed permit U and V to be perfectly correlated and identical.

We let $T_n : \mathbf{R} \to \mathbf{R}$ and consider the asymptotic behaviors of

$$\sum_{t=1}^n T_n(x_t) \quad \text{and} \quad \sum_{t=1}^n T_n(x_t)\,u_t$$

under appropriate normalizations. Under suitable conditions, we may expect

$$\frac{1}{n}\sum_{t=1}^n T_n(x_t) = \int_0^1 T_n(\sqrt{n}V_n(r))\,dr \approx \int_0^1 T_n(\sqrt{n}V(r))\,dr \tag{7}$$

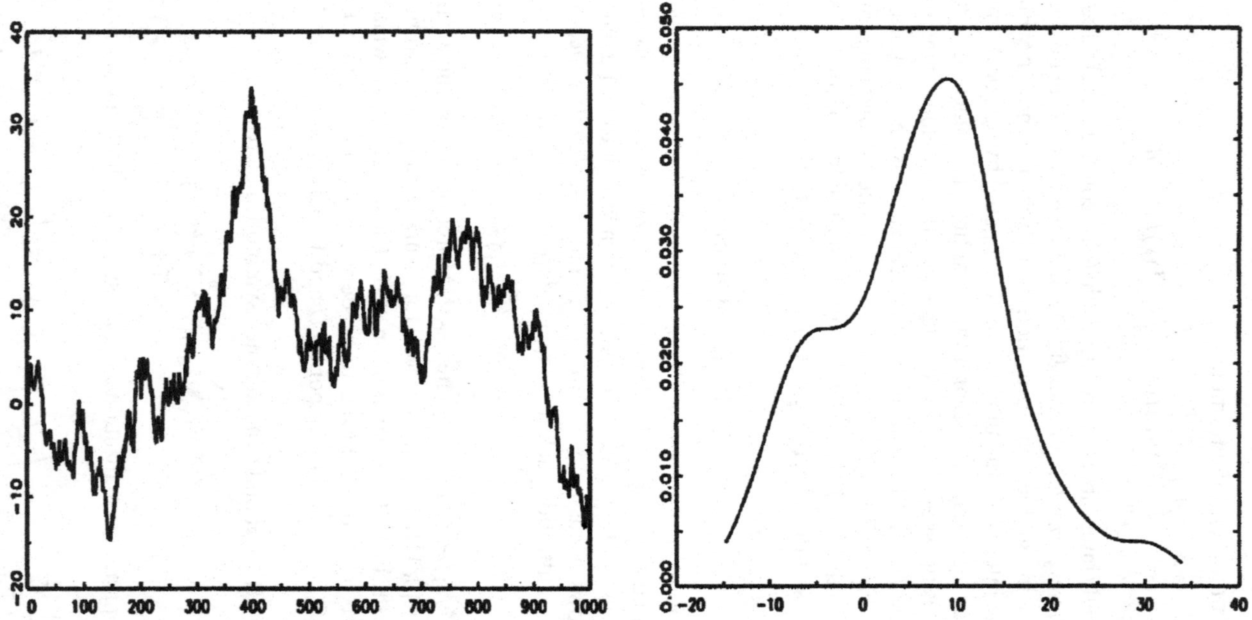

Figure 7.1. Sample Path and Local Time of Brownian Motion.

$$\frac{1}{\sqrt{n}}\sum_{t=1}^{n} T_n(x_t)\,u_t = \int_0^1 T_n(\sqrt{n}V_n(r))\,dU_n(r) \approx \int_0^1 T_n(\sqrt{n}V(r))\,dU(r) \quad (8)$$

for large n.

If, for instance, T_n is given by

$$T_n(x) = T\left(\frac{x}{\sqrt{n}}\right)$$

for some locally integrable T, both the mean and covariance asymptotics follow immediately from (7) and (8). It is indeed easy to see that (7) and (8) imply in this case

$$\frac{1}{n}\sum_{t=1}^{n} T\left(\frac{x_t}{\sqrt{n}}\right) \to_d \int_0^1 T(V(r))\,dr \quad (9)$$

$$\frac{1}{\sqrt{n}}\sum_{t=1}^{n} T\left(\frac{x_t}{\sqrt{n}}\right) u_t \to_d \int_0^1 T(V(r))\,dU(r) \quad (10)$$

as $n \to \infty$.

If, on the other hand, we let $T_n = T$ for all n, the asymptotics become crucially dependent on the type of function T. If T is asymptotically homogeneous and given as in (2), the relevant asymptotics follow somewhat similarly, as in (9) and (10). We only need different normalizations. Indeed, because

$$T(x_t) \approx \nu(\sqrt{n})S\left(\frac{x_t}{\sqrt{n}}\right)$$

in this case, we may readily deduce that

$$\frac{1}{n}\nu^{-1}(\sqrt{n})\sum_{t=1}^{n} T(x_t) \to_d \int_0^1 S(V(r))\,dr \quad (11)$$

$$\frac{1}{\sqrt{n}}\nu^{-1}(\sqrt{n})\sum_{t=1}^{n} T(x_t)\,u_t \to_d \int_0^1 S(V(r))\,dU(r) \quad (12)$$

as $n \to \infty$.

The asymptotics for $T_n = T$ with an integrable T are more intriguing. To obtain the mean asymptotics in this case, we need to note that

$$\begin{aligned}\sqrt{n}\int_0^1 T(\sqrt{n}V(r))\,dr &= \sqrt{n}\int_{-\infty}^{\infty} T(\sqrt{n}s)L(1,s)\,ds \\ &= \int_{-\infty}^{\infty} T(s)L\left(1,\frac{s}{\sqrt{n}}\right)\,ds \\ &\to_{a.s.} L(1,0)\int_{-\infty}^{\infty} T(s)\,ds \quad (13)\end{aligned}$$

as $n \to \infty$. This follows from the successive applications of occupation times formula, change of variables, and dominated convergence. Consequently, we may obtain the mean asymptotics

$$\frac{1}{\sqrt{n}}\sum_{t=1}^{n} T(x_t) \to_d L(1,0)\int_{-\infty}^{\infty} T(s)\,ds \tag{14}$$

as $n \to \infty$ on the basis of (7) and (13).

The covariance asymptotics are more difficult to obtain. From the representation theorem of continuous martingale by time-changed Brownian motion (see, e.g., Revuz and Yor, 1994, Theorem 1.6, p. 173), we may regard for each n a continuous martingale

$$M_n(t) = \sqrt[4]{n}\int_0^t T(\sqrt{n}V(r))\,dU(r)$$

as Brownian motion – for instance, W_n evaluated at time

$$[M_n](t) = \sigma^2\sqrt{n}\int_0^t T^2(\sqrt{n}V(r))\,dr,$$

where $[M_n]$ is the quadratic variation of M_n. That is, $M_n(t) = W_n([M_n](t))$, where W_n is often referred to as Dambis–Dubins–Schwarz (DDS) Brownian motion. It is obvious that we may write

$$M_n(t) =_d W([M_n](t)) \text{ a.s.}$$

for all n.

Now we obtain the limit distribution of $M_n(1)$ using its representation as the DDS Brownian motion. We have exactly, as in (13),

$$[M_n](1) \to_{\text{a.s.}} \sigma^2 L(1,0)\int_{-\infty}^{\infty} T^2(s)\,ds$$

and, as a result,

$$M_n(1) \to_d W\left(\sigma^2 L(1,0)\int_{-\infty}^{\infty} T^2(s)\,ds\right)$$

as $n \to \infty$, where W is the standard Brownian motion. Moreover, if we denote by $[M_n, V]$ the quadratic covariation of M_n and V, then

$$[M_n, V](t) = \sqrt[4]{n}\int_0^t T(\sqrt{n}V(r))\,d[U,V](r) \to_{\text{a.s.}} 0$$

for all $t \geq 0$. Therefore, M_n is asymptotically independent of V, and hence of L, which is the local time of V. This, however, implies in turn that L is independent of W because it is the distributional equivalence of the DDS Brownian motion of M_n. Consequently, it follows that

$$W\left(\sigma^2 L(1,0)\int_{-\infty}^{\infty} T^2(s)\,ds\right) =_d \mathbf{MN}\left(0, \sigma^2 L(1,0)\int_{-\infty}^{\infty} T^2(s)\,ds\right)$$

(see, e.g., Revuz and Yor, 1994, Chapter XIII for a more detailed derivation). The covariance asymptotics for $T_n = T$ with integrable T now follow immediately and are given by

$$\frac{1}{\sqrt[4]{n}} \sum_{t=1}^{n} T(x_t)\, u_t \to_d \mathbf{MN}\left(0, \sigma^2 L(1,0) \int_{-\infty}^{\infty} T^2(s)\, ds\right) \tag{15}$$

as $n \to \infty$ due to (8).

The asymptotics for more general T_n can be obtained in a completely analogous manner once the approximations in (7) and (8) are validated. Refer to Akonom (1993), Borodin and Ibragimov (1995), and Park (2003) for the precise conditions and the exact orders of approximation errors. The asymptotics derived here hold for much more general time series than are assumed here. The asymptotics for integrable transformation in (14) and (15) hold for general integrated processes driven by linear processes with independent and identically distributed (iid) innovations satisfying some mild regularity conditions. The asymptotics in (9) and (10) for normalized transformations, and those in (11) and (12) for asymptotically homogeneous transformations, are obtainable under even much weaker conditions. For these results, the invariance principle (4) is virtually all that is required. See Park (2003) for the exact conditions and technical details.

7.3 NONSTATIONARY NONLINEARITY IN DATA GENERATION

In this section we look at the time series (y_t) given by

$$y_t = F(x_t)$$

and consider its time series properties. Such a time series (y_t) may be generated in reality owing to the presence of institutional restriction, barrier or policy intervention, or all of these factors, in which case (x_t) would represent the corresponding economic fundamentals. A prime example for (y_t) would be the observed exchange rates in the presence of target zone. In this example, F is given by a bounded and S-shaped nonlinear function, which is shown in Figure 7.2. The resulting time series (y_t) may exhibit very different characteristics depending on the type of function F. If F is integrable, then (y_t) would look more like a stationary process. If F is asymptotically homogeneous, then (y_t) would behave like an integrated process having a unit root. The time series (y_t) itself of course becomes an integrated process when F is the identity. In Figure 7.3, the sample paths of the transformed time series are simulated for $F(x) = e^{-x^2}$ and $F(x) = e^x/(1+e^x)$.

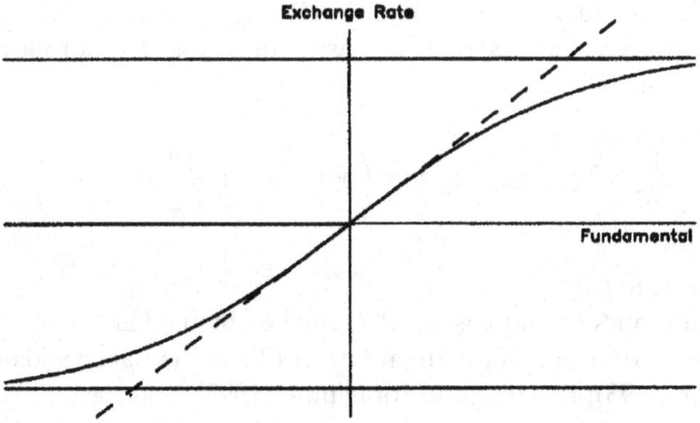

Figure 7.2. Target Zone Exchange Rate Model.

To investigate the statistical properties of the transformed series (y_t), we define the sample autocorrelation for (y_t) by

$$R_{nk} = \frac{\sum_{t=k+1}^{n} (y_t - \bar{y}_n)(y_{t-k} - \bar{y}_n)}{\sum_{t=1}^{n} (y_t - \bar{y}_n)^2},$$

where $\bar{y}_n$ denotes the sample mean of (y_t). We also look at the sample variance of (y_t) given by

$$S_n^2 = \frac{1}{n}\sum_{t=1}^{n}(y_t - \bar{y})^2$$

and the sample kurtosis

$$K_n^4 = \frac{\frac{1}{n}\sum_{t=1}^{n}(y_t - \bar{y})^4}{\left(\frac{1}{n}\sum_{t=1}^{n}(y_t - \bar{y})^2\right)^2},$$

which will be analyzed subsequently for both integrable and asymptotically homogeneous transformations.

7.3.1 Integrable Transformations

We assume that F is bounded and integrable. Then it follows from (14) that

$$\frac{1}{\sqrt{n}}\sum_{t=1}^{n} F^p(x_t) \to_d L(1,0)\int_{-\infty}^{\infty} F^p(x)\,dx \tag{16}$$

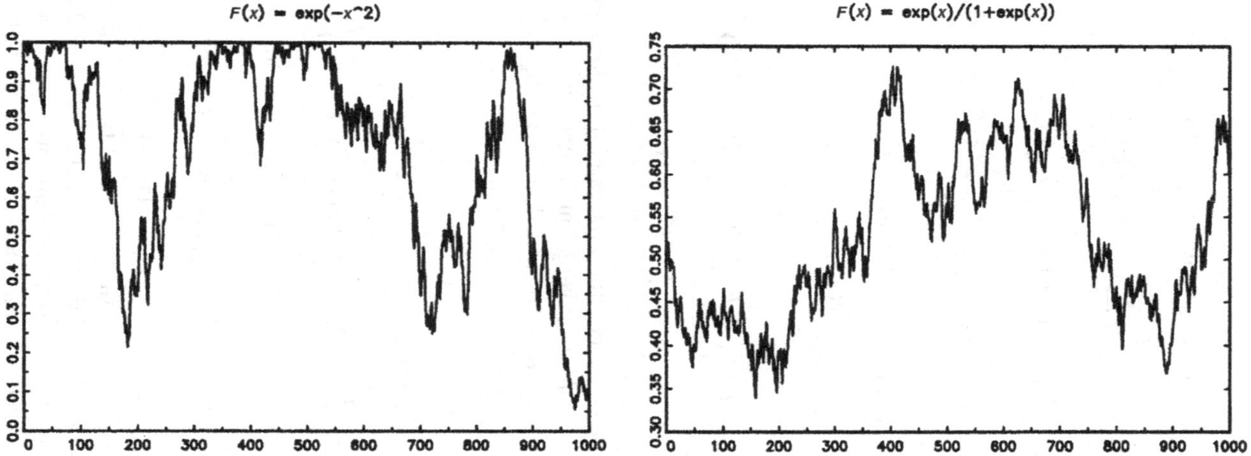

Figure 7.3. Simulated Sample Paths.

for $p = 1, 2, \ldots,$ as $n \to \infty$. Moreover, if we denote by D_k the density of $(x_t - x_{t-k})$ that is assumed to be independent of (x_{t-k}) for $k = 1, 2, \ldots,$ then we have $\mathbf{E}(F(x_t)|\mathcal{F}_{t-k}) = G(x_{t-k})$ with an integrable function G given by

$$G(x) = \int_{-\infty}^{\infty} F(x+y) D_k(y)\, dy. \tag{17}$$

We may therefore deduce under suitable regularity conditions that

$$\begin{aligned}\frac{1}{\sqrt{n}} \sum_{t=1}^{n} F(x_t)F(x_{t-k}) &= \frac{1}{\sqrt{n}} \sum_{t=1}^{n} (GF)(x_{t-k}) + o_p(1) \\ &\to_d L(1,0) \int_{-\infty}^{\infty} (GF)(x)\, dx \\ &= L(1,0) \int_{-\infty}^{\infty} \int_{-\infty}^{\infty} F(x)F(x+y)D_k(y)\, dx\, dy \qquad (18)\end{aligned}$$

as $n \to \infty$.

We may now easily deduce from (16) and (18) that

$$R_{nk} \to_p R_k,$$

where

$$R_k = \frac{\int_{-\infty}^{\infty} \int_{-\infty}^{\infty} F(x)F(x+y)D_k(y)\, dx\, dy}{\int_{-\infty}^{\infty} F^2(x)\, dx}$$

for $k = 1, 2, \ldots,$ as $n \to \infty$. For the integrable transformation, the sample autocorrelation R_{nk} therefore converges in probability to a nonrandom limit. Of course, the limit R_k may be regarded as its asymptotic autocorrelation function.

We have

$$\begin{aligned}\int_{-\infty}^{\infty} G^2(x)\, dx &= \int_{-\infty}^{\infty} \left(\int_{-\infty}^{\infty} F(x+y) D_k(y) dy \right)^2 dx \\ &< \int_{-\infty}^{\infty} dx \int_{-\infty}^{\infty} dy\, D_k(y) F^2(x+y) = \int_{-\infty}^{\infty} F^2(x)\, dx\end{aligned}$$

from which, together with the Cauchy–Schwarz inequality

$$\left| \int_{-\infty}^{\infty} (GF)(x)\, dx \right| < \left(\int_{-\infty}^{\infty} G^2(x)\, dx \right)^{1/2} \left(\int_{-\infty}^{\infty} F^2(x)\, dx \right)^{1/2},$$

it follows that $R_k < 1$ for all $k = 1, 2, \ldots$. This implies, in particular, that the first-order autoregression run with the integral transformation of a random walk would asymptotically yield the coefficient strictly less than unity. Hence, the unit root disappears under integrable transformations. The actual values of the asymptotic autocorrelation function R_k are determined by the distribution of (v_t) as well as the transformation function.

It is important to investigate the behavior of the asymptotic autocorrelation R_k as a function of k. This is to find the degree of persistency for the integral transformation of a random walk. If (v_t) are normally distributed, then $x_t - x_{t-k} =_d k^{1/2} v_t$. We therefore have $D_k(x) = k^{-1/2} D(k^{-1/2}x)$, where D is the density of (v_t). Consequently, we may deduce that

$$k^{1/2} R_k = \frac{\int_{-\infty}^{\infty}\int_{-\infty}^{\infty} F(x)F(x+y)D(k^{-1/2}y)\,dx\,dy}{\int_{-\infty}^{\infty} F^2(x)\,dx}$$

$$\to D(0)\frac{\left(\int_{-\infty}^{\infty} F(x)\,dx\right)^2}{\int_{-\infty}^{\infty} F^2(x)\,dx}$$

as $k \to \infty$ owing to dominated convergence. The transformation function $F(x) = e^{-x^2}$ actually yields the asymptotic autocorrelation function $R_k = 1/\sqrt{k+1}$ for $k = 1, 2, \ldots$.

It is interesting to note that the autocorrelation function of the integrable transformation of a random walk decays, as in the stationary time series. The decaying rate, however, is much slower and is given by

$$R_k = c\,k^{-1/2}$$

for some constant $c > 0$. The integral transformations of random walks would thus be expected to show considerable persistency in memory. The rate of decay for their autocorrelations is indeed comparable to that of the stationary long-memory processes. For the I(d) process with $0 < d < 1/2$, the autocorrelation function is given by $R_k = c\,k^{2d-1}$ for some constant $c > 0$ (see, e.g., Beran, 1994, p. 63). The autocorrelation function of the integrable transformation of a random walk has therefore the same rate of decay as that of the I(d) process with $d = 1/4$. Stationary long memory can thus be generated by nonstationary nonlinearity.

The asymptotics of the sample variance and kurtosis for the integrable transformations of random walks can also be easily obtained. Indeed, it follows immediately from (16) and (18) that

$$\sqrt{n}S_n^2 \to_d L(1,0)\int_{-\infty}^{\infty} F^2(x)\,dx$$

$$\frac{1}{\sqrt{n}}K_n^4 \to_d \frac{\int_{-\infty}^{\infty} F^4(x)\,dx}{L(1,0)\left(\int_{-\infty}^{\infty} F^2(x)\,dx\right)^2}$$

as $n \to \infty$.

The sample variance of the integral transformation of a random walk is thus expected to decrease at the rate of $n^{-1/2}$. Roughly, this implies that the second-order variations of the integral transformations of random walks are increasing but not as fast as the sample size. On the other hand, the sample kurtosis of the integral transformation of a random walk increases at an $n^{1/2}$ rate as the sample size gets large. We may thus expect the sample kurtosis to be large for the integral transformations of random walks. The leptokurticity, along with the aforementioned long-memory property, is frequently observed in many macroeconomic and financial time series.

All of our results derived in this section apply to the transformations that can be defined as the constant shifts of integrable functions as well as the integrable functions themselves. This is so because the statistics, sample autocorrelation, sample variance, and sample kurtosis considered here are all invariant with respect to the constant shift. More precisely, all the previous results hold also for the function F, which can be written as

$$F(x) = c + G(x), \tag{19}$$

where c is some constant and G is an integrable function that has been considered thus far. The function F in (19) is, of course, not integrable. It is indeed asymptotically homogeneous with the unit asymptotic order and the constant-limit homogeneous function. The analysis for general asymptotically homogeneous functions with nonconstant limit homogeneous functions will follow in the next section.

7.3.2 Asymptotically Homogeneous Transformations

We now let F be an asymptotically homogeneous function with asymptotic order κ and limit homogeneous function H. Under very mild regularity conditions that are satisfied by virtually all asymptotically homogeneous functions used in practical applications, F^p would also be asymptotically homogeneous with asymptotic order κ^p and limit homogeneous function H^p, that is

$$F^p(\lambda x) \approx \kappa^p(\lambda) H^p(x)$$

for $p = 1, 2 \ldots$. This will be assumed in what follows. Then it follows immediately from (11) that

$$\frac{1}{n}\kappa^{-p}(\sqrt{n}) \sum_{t=1}^{n} F^p(x_t) \to_d \int_0^1 H^p(V(r))\, dr \tag{20}$$

as $n \to \infty$.

Moreover, if we let G be defined as in (17), then we may expect

$$\begin{aligned} G(\lambda x) &= \int_{-\infty}^{\infty} F(\lambda x + y) D_k(y)\,dy \\ &\approx \kappa(\lambda) \int_{-\infty}^{\infty} H\Big(x + \frac{y}{\lambda}\Big)\, D_k(y)\,dy \\ &\approx \kappa(\lambda) H(x) \end{aligned}$$

for all large λ and for all x on any bounded interval. That is, G is asymptotically homogeneous with asymptotic order κ and limit homogeneous function H exactly as for F. As a result, we have

$$(GF)(\lambda x) \approx \kappa^2(\lambda) H^2(x)$$

for all large λ and for all x on any bounded interval. We may therefore establish that

$$\begin{aligned} \frac{1}{n}\kappa^{-2}(\sqrt{n}) \sum_{t=1}^{n} F(x_t)F(x_{t-k}) &= \frac{1}{n}\kappa^{-2}(\sqrt{n}) \sum_{t=1}^{n} (GF)(x_{t-k}) + o_p(1) \\ &\to_d \int_0^1 H^2(V(r))\,dr \end{aligned} \tag{21}$$

as $n \to \infty$ under suitable technical assumptions.

Here we assume that the limit homogeneous function H of F is nonconstant. The case in which H is a constant yields quite different results and has already been considered. The asymptotically homogeneous function will be called *nontrivial* if it has a nonconstant limit homogeneous function. Otherwise, it will be called *trivial*. For the nontrivial asymptotically homogeneous function F, it only requires some simple algebra to deduce from (20) and (21) that

$$R_{nk} \to_p 1$$

as $n \to \infty$ for every $k = 1, 2, \ldots$. The asymptotic autocorrelations for the nontrivial asymptotically homogeneous transformation of a random walk are therefore unity at all lags just like those of untransformed random walks. In particular, the asymptotic first-order autocorrelation remains as unity. The nontrivial asymptotically homogeneous transformation would thus preserve the unit root, that is, the transformed time series continue to have unit roots if the nontrivial asymptotically homogeneous function is used. This is in sharp constrast to the integrable or trivial asymptotically homogeneous functions for which the unit root disappears upon transformations.

Once again, we let F be a nontrivial, asymptotically homogeneous function with asymptotic order κ and limit homogeneous function H. It is straightforward to derive

$$\kappa^{-2}(\sqrt{n})S_n^2 \to_d \int_0^1 \left(H(V) - \int_0^1 H(V) \right)$$

$$K_n^4 \to_d \frac{\int_0^1 \left(H(V) - \int_0^1 H(V) \right)^2}{\int_0^1 \left(H(V) - \int_0^1 H(V) \right)^4}$$

as $n \to \infty$, using the results in (20) and (21). Note that we use the shorthand notation for the integrals to simplify the exposition. This convention will be followed also in the subsequent presentation of our results whenever they become lengthy and require simplifications in expressions.

The sample variance of the nontrivial asymptotically homogeneous transformation of a random walk may diverge or converge, depending on its asymptotic order. If $\kappa(\lambda) \to 0$ as $\lambda \to \infty$, as in the case of the power function with a negative power, then $S_n^2 \to_p 0$ as $n \to \infty$. On the other hand, $S_n^2 \to_p \infty$ as $n \to \infty$ for all power functions with positive powers and any other functions with diverging asymptotes, including the logarithmic function, because for them $\kappa(\lambda) \to \infty$ as $\lambda \to \infty$. For the bounded asymptotically homogeneous functions such as the logistic function or any other distribution function-like functions, we have $\kappa(\lambda) = 1$, and the sample variance would be stochastically bounded although it remains to be random in the limit. Indeed, the sample variance in this case has a well-defined limit distribution represented by a functional of the limit homogeneous transformation of Brownian motion.

In contrast, the sample kurtosis has a random limit in all cases. As long as the underlying asymptotically homogeneous transformation is nontrivial, the sample kurtosis has the limit distribution given as a functional of the limit homogeneous transformation of Brownian motion. The sample kurtosis, just as the sample variance in the case of the asymptotically homogeneous transformations that are nontrivial and bounded, is expected to be given randomly with distribution depending on the limit homogeneous function of the underlying transformation. The limit distributions for the sample variance and sample kurtosis can easily be simulated for any asymptotically homogeneous transformation, if its limit homogeneous function is given.

7.4 NONSTATIONARY NONLINEARITY IN MEAN

In this section, we statistically analyze the nonlinear relationships between nonstationary time series. We consider the regression model

$$y_t = F(x_t) + u_t, \tag{22}$$

where (x_t) is an integrated regressor, as specified earlier in (1), and (u_t) is a stationary error. We assume the regression function F to be either integrable or asymptotically homogeneous. The regressand (y_t) can therefore have characteristics of both stationary and integrated time series as determined by F. Our results in the previous section imply that the process (y_t) would behave like a stationary time series if F were integrable, whereas it would look more like an integrated time series if F were asymptotically homogeneous.

Assume that (u_t) satisfies the conditions introduced in Section 7.2. Then we have in particular

$$\mathbf{E}(y_t|\mathcal{F}_{t-1}) = F(x_t),$$

as in the usual regression model. However, our regression involves integrated time series and would thus have different interpretations. If the regression function F is asymptotically homogeneous, the regression model specifies a nonlinear cointegrating relationship, that is, a long-run nonlinear equilibrium relationship between (y_t) and (x_t). On the other hand, the integrable regression function F would remove the stochastic trend in (x_t), and therefore the model specifies a usual stationary relationship between (y_t) and $(F(x_t))$. We may leave the regression function F completely unrestricted or further parametrize it using some appropriate family of functions. We consider both cases here, and they will be analyzed below.

7.4.1 Nonlinear Regressions with Integrated Processes

The model (22) becomes, and may be analyzed as a nonlinear regression if we further specify F as

$$F(x) = G(x, \theta_0),$$

where $G(\cdot, \theta)$ with $\theta \in \Theta$ represents a parametric family of functions. The function G is assumed to be known, whereas the true parameter value θ_0 is regarded as being unknown. The family of functions should, of course, be chosen so that the regresion is *balanced*, that is, we should choose an integrable family if the regressand (y_t) behaves like a stationary process. If the regressand is closer to an integrated process, an asymptotically homogeneous family should be more appropriate. The linear cointegrating regression can be considered as a special case with $G(x, \theta) = x\theta$.

The nonlinear regression

$$y_t = G(x_t, \theta_0) + u_t \tag{23}$$

can be estimated by the nonlinear least squares (NLLS), in which case the estimator $\hat{\theta}_n$ can be obtained by

$$\hat{\theta}_n = \underset{\theta \in \Theta}{\operatorname{argmin}} \sum_{t=1}^{n} (y_t - G(x_t, \theta))^2.$$

It is shown by Park and Phillips (2001) that the estimator $\hat{\theta}_n$ of θ in nonlinear regression (23) is asymptotically equivalent to the usual least-squares (LS) estimator of θ in the linear regression

$$y_t = \dot{G}(x_t, \theta_0)'\theta + u_t, \tag{24}$$

where $\dot{G}$ denotes the partial derivative of G with respect to θ. The asymptotic equivalence of (23) and (24) is well established and long known for the standard stationary regressions.

The asymptotic distribution of $\hat{\theta}_n$ can readily be obtained from the asymptotic equivalence of (23) and (24), using the basic nonstationary nonlinear asymptotics introduced earlier. Note that the aforementioned asymptotic equivalence implies

$$\begin{aligned}\hat{\theta}_n &\approx \left(\sum_{t=1}^n \dot{G}(x_t, \theta_0)\dot{G}(x_t, \theta_0)'\right)^{-1} \sum_{t=1}^n \dot{G}(x_t, \theta_0) y_t \\ &= \theta_0 + \left(\sum_{t=1}^n \dot{G}(x_t, \theta_0)\dot{G}(x_t, \theta_0)'\right)^{-1} \sum_{t=1}^n \dot{G}(x_t, \theta_0) u_t \end{aligned} \tag{25}$$

for large n. The asymptotic distribution of $\hat{\theta}_n$ may therefore be derived from our mean and covariance asymptotics developed in Section 7.2.

If $\dot{G}(\cdot, \theta_0)$ is integrable, we may deduce from (14) and (15) that

$$\sqrt[4]{n}(\hat{\theta}_n - \theta_0) \to_d \mathbf{MN}\left(0, \sigma^2 \left(L(1,0) \int_{-\infty}^{\infty} \dot{G}(s, \theta_0)\dot{G}(s, \theta_0)' ds\right)^{-1}\right) \tag{26}$$

as $n \to \infty$. Moreover, if $\dot{G}(\cdot, \theta_0)$ is asymptotically homogeneous with asymptotic order $\dot{\kappa}(\cdot)$ and limit homogeneous function $\dot{H}(\cdot, \theta_0)$, then we have, owing to (11) and (12),

$$\sqrt{n}\dot{\kappa}(\sqrt{n})(\hat{\theta}_n - \theta_0) \to_d \left(\int_0^1 \dot{H}(V, \theta_0)\dot{H}(V, \theta_0)'\right)^{-1} \int_0^1 \dot{H}(V, \theta_0)\, dU \tag{27}$$

as $n \to \infty$.

The NLLS estimator $\hat{\theta}_n$ in both cases is consistent. The convergence rate, however, is different as determined by the regression function. If $\dot{G}(\cdot, \theta_0)$ is integrable, $\hat{\theta}_n$ converges at the $\sqrt[4]{n}$ rate, which is of an order of magnitude slower than the standard linear stationary case. For asymptotically homogeneous $\dot{G}(\cdot, \theta_0)$, the actual convergence rate is dependent on its asymptotic order $\dot{\kappa}$ and is given by $\sqrt{n}\dot{\kappa}(\sqrt{n})$. The rate becomes n for the linear cointegrating regression because $\dot{\kappa}(\lambda) = \lambda$ in this case. The distribution of $\hat{\theta}_n$ is asymptotically mixed normal when $\dot{G}(\cdot, \theta_0)$ is integrable. If it is asymptotically homogeneous, however, the limiting distribution is generally non-Gaussian. We have the Gaussianity only under strict exogeneity, that is the case in which the regressors are uncorrelated with the regression errors in all leads and lags. This is unrealistic.

To obtain our results in (26) and (27), we need to require some obvious identifiability assumptions as well as technical regularity conditions. In particular, we should have $\int_{-\infty}^{\infty} \dot{G}(s, \theta_0)\dot{G}(s, \theta_0)' ds > 0$ for $\dot{G}(\cdot, \theta_0)$ integrable. Likewise, asymptotically homogeneous $\dot{G}(\cdot, \theta_0)$ must have limit homogeneous function $\dot{H}$ satisfying $\int_0^1 \dot{H}(V, \theta_0)\dot{H}(V, \theta_0)' > 0$ a.s. If these conditions fail, then our results here are obviously no longer valid. This, however, does not imply that such an identifiability assumption is absolutely necessary. It is often the case that the failure of the identifiability condition simply results in asymptotic multicollinearity, which can be avoided by an appropriate reparametrization.

For instance, if we let $\theta = (\alpha, \beta)'$ and let

$$G(x, \alpha, \beta) = \alpha + \beta \log |x|,$$

because $\log |x|$ is asymptotically homogeneous with asymptotic order $\log \lambda$ and limit homogeneous function 1, $\dot{H}$ becomes $(1, 1)'$ and the identifiability condition does not hold. We may nevertheless reformulate the regression as

$$\begin{aligned} y_t &= \alpha + \beta \log |x_t| + u_t \\ &= (\alpha + \beta \log \sqrt{n}) + \beta \log \frac{|x_t|}{\sqrt{n}} + u_t \end{aligned}$$

to obtain the proper asymptotics. After some simple algebra, we may obtain

$$\sqrt{n}\begin{pmatrix} 1 & \log \sqrt{n} \\ 0 & 1 \end{pmatrix}(\hat{\theta}_n - \theta_0) \to_d \begin{pmatrix} 1 & \int_0^1 \log |V| \\ \int_0^1 \log |V| & \int_0^1 \log^2 |V| \end{pmatrix}^{-1} \begin{pmatrix} \int_0^1 dU \\ \int_0^1 dU \log |V| \end{pmatrix}$$

as $n \to \infty$. Similar reformulations are possible for other cases having asymptotic multicollinearities.

The detailed statistical theory of the NLLS estimator for the nonlinear regression with integrated time series is developed in Park and Phillips (2001) and Chang et al. (2001). The rigorous foundation of the formal asymptotics for the models with a single regressor is develped in the former. In the latter, the theory is extended for more realistic models having multiple integrated regressors that are additively nonlinear as well as other stationary and deterministic regressors. Efficient estimation and chi-square testing procedures are also proposed there. Park and Phillips (2000) consider the binary choice model with integrated explanatory variables, and derive the asymptotic distributions of the maximum likelihood estimator. Chang and Park (2003) investigate the index-type model such as the neural network and the smooth transition regression in which the multiple integrated regressors are included in an index form. They develop the relevant statistical theory for the efficient estimators and the chi-square testing procedures.

The nonlinear regression with general nonadditive regression function having multiple regressors yields the results that are drastically different from those in the single regressor or additively separable multiple regressors case. Roughly, this is because integrated processes are represented in the limit by Brownian motions, and a vector Brownian motion has a recurrence property that is very distinctive from that of an univariate Brownian motion. As can be shown using the asymptotic results obtained in Chang et al. (2001), the NLLS estimator is consistent but yet converges very slowly at a logarithmic rate. This is so as long as we have more than two regressors that are integrated. We thus have very severe *curse of dimensionality* in this case. The curse of dimensionality, however, does not get exacerbated along with the increase in the number of integrated regressors. At any rate, the general nonlinear regression with multiple integrated regressors does not seem to be a reasonable choice in practical applications.

7.4.2 Nonparametric Regressions with Integrated Processes

The nonparametric estimation of the regression function F in (22) is also possible. To estimate F nonparametrically, we customarily use the Nadaraya–Watson estimator defined as

$$\hat{F}_n(x) = \frac{\sum_{t=1}^{n} K\left(\frac{x_t - x}{h_n}\right) y_t}{\sum_{t=1}^{n} K\left(\frac{x_t - x}{h_n}\right)},$$

where K is the kernel function and h_n is the bandwidth parameter. We assume in particular that $\int_{-\infty}^{\infty} K(s)\,ds = 1$, $\int_{-\infty}^{\infty} sK(s)\,ds = 0$, and $\int_{-\infty}^{\infty} s^2 K(s)\,ds \neq 0$ (i.e., K is a second-order kernel) and that $h_n \to 0$ as $n \to \infty$. We let F be twice continuously differentiable.

We decompose

$$\hat{F}_n(x) = \hat{F}_n^A(x) + \hat{F}_n^B(x),$$

where

$$\hat{F}_n^A(x) = \frac{\sum_{t=1}^{n} K\left(\frac{x_t - x}{h_n}\right) F(x_t)}{\sum_{t=1}^{n} K\left(\frac{x_t - x}{h_n}\right)}, \quad \hat{F}_n^B(x) = \frac{\sum_{t=1}^{n} K\left(\frac{x_t - x}{h_n}\right) u_t}{\sum_{t=1}^{n} K\left(\frac{x_t - x}{h_n}\right)}.$$

The two components $\hat{F}_n^A(x)$ and $\hat{F}_n^B(x)$ represent, respectively, the conditional mean and variance parts of $\hat{F}_n(x)$. In our context, the decomposition may be viewed as the discrete analogue of the representation of a continuous semimartingale as the sum of a bounded variation process and a continuous martingale.

Under suitable regularity conditions, we have

$$\frac{1}{\sqrt{nh_n^2}}\sum_{t=1}^{n}K\left(\frac{x_t-x}{h_n}\right)=\frac{\sqrt{n}}{h_n}\int_0^1 K\left(\frac{\sqrt{n}V_n(r)-x}{h_n}\right)dr$$
$$=\frac{\sqrt{n}}{h_n}\int_0^1 K\left(\frac{\sqrt{n}V(r)-x}{h_n}\right)dr+o_p(1)$$

and may deduce as in (13) that

$$\int_0^1 K\left(\frac{\sqrt{n}V(r)-x}{h_n}\right)dr \to_{\text{a.s.}} L(1,0)$$

as $n\to\infty$. Consequently, we have

$$\frac{1}{\sqrt{nh_n^2}}\sum_{t=1}^{n}K\left(\frac{x_t-x}{h_n}\right)\to_d L(1,0) \tag{28}$$

as $n\to\infty$.

We also have

$$\frac{1}{\sqrt{nh_n^2}}\sum_{t=1}^{n}K\left(\frac{x_t-x}{h_n}\right)F(x_t)$$
$$=\frac{\sqrt{n}}{h_n}\int_0^1 K\left(\frac{\sqrt{n}V_n(r)-x}{h_n}\right)F(\sqrt{n}V_n(r))\,dr$$
$$=\frac{\sqrt{n}}{h_n}\int_0^1 K\left(\frac{\sqrt{n}V(r)-x}{h_n}\right)F(\sqrt{n}V(r))\,dr+o_p(1) \tag{29}$$

and may derive, as in (13), that

$$\frac{\sqrt{n}}{h_n}\int_0^1 K\left(\frac{\sqrt{n}V(r)-x}{h_n}\right)F(\sqrt{n}V(r))\,dr$$
$$=\frac{\sqrt{n}}{h_n}\int_{-\infty}^{\infty}K\left(\frac{\sqrt{n}s-x}{h_n}\right)F(\sqrt{n}s)L(1,s)\,ds$$
$$=\int_{-\infty}^{\infty}K(s)F(x+h_ns)L\left(1,\frac{1}{\sqrt{n}}(x+h_ns)\right)ds$$
$$=L(1,0)\left(F(x)+\frac{1}{2}h_n^2F''(x)\int_{-\infty}^{\infty}s^2K(s)\,ds\right)+o(h_n^2)\text{ a.s.}$$

for large n. It follows that

$$\frac{1}{\sqrt{nh_n^2}}\sum_{t=1}^{n}K\left(\frac{x_t-x}{h_n}\right)F(x_t)$$
$$=_d L(1,0)\left(F(x)+\frac{1}{2}h_n^2F''(x)\int_{-\infty}^{\infty}s^2K(s)\,ds\right)+o_p(h_n^2) \tag{30}$$

as $n \to \infty$ as long as the approximation error in (29) is small enough. We now have from (28) and (30) that

$$\hat{F}_n^A(x) = F(x) + \frac{1}{2}h_n^2 F''(x) \int_{-\infty}^{\infty} s^2 K(s)\, ds + o_p(h_n^2)$$

for large n.

On the other hand, because

$$\frac{1}{\sqrt{nh_n^2}} \sum_{t=1}^{n} K^2\left(\frac{x_t - x}{h_n}\right) = \frac{\sqrt{n}}{h_n} \int_0^1 K^2\left(\frac{\sqrt{n}V_n(r) - x}{h_n}\right) dr$$
$$= \frac{\sqrt{n}}{h_n} \int_0^1 K^2\left(\frac{\sqrt{n}V(r) - x}{h_n}\right) dr + o_p(1)$$

and we may show, as in (13), that

$$\int_0^1 K^2\left(\frac{\sqrt{n}V(r) - x}{h_n}\right) dr \to_{\text{a.s.}} L(1,0) \int_{-\infty}^{\infty} K^2(s)\, ds$$

as $n \to \infty$, it follows that

$$\frac{1}{\sqrt{nh_n^2}} \sum_{t=1}^{n} K^2\left(\frac{x_t - x}{h_n}\right) \to_d L(1,0) \int_{-\infty}^{\infty} K^2(s)\, ds$$

as $n \to \infty$. We may therefore show as in (15) that

$$\frac{1}{\sqrt[4]{nh_n^2}} \sum_{t=1}^{n} K\left(\frac{x_t - x}{h_n}\right) u_t \to_d \mathbf{MN}\left(0,\, L(1,0) \int_{-\infty}^{\infty} K^2(s)\, ds\right) \qquad (31)$$

as $n \to \infty$. Consequently, it follows from (28) and (31) that

$$\sqrt[4]{nh_n^2}\, \hat{F}_n^B(x) \to_d \mathbf{MN}\left(0,\, L(1,0)^{-1} \int_{-\infty}^{\infty} K^2(s)\, ds\right) \qquad (32)$$

as $n \to \infty$.

We now have from (30) and (32) that the optimal bandwidth is given by

$$h_n = n^{-1/10}, \qquad (33)$$

which balances off the bias and variance terms. The rate here suggests a bandwidth wider than the usual stationary case, for which the optimal bandwidth is given by $h_n = n^{-1/5}$. This is because an integrated regressor has a stochastic trend and is observed more scarcely around any fixed spatial point. We therefore need a wider bandwidth to have a sufficient number of observations to balance off the bias and variance terms. The bandwidth optimal for the stationary regressor would make the variance term dominate the bias term in our case.

Table 7.1 *Rates of Convergence*

		Parametric Approach	Nonparametric Approach
Stationary Regressor		$n^{1/2}$	$n^{2/5} \sim n^{1/2}$
Nonstationary Regressor	H-regular	$n^{1/2}\dot{\kappa}(n^{1/2})$	$n^{1/5} \sim n^{1/4}$
	I-regular	$n^{1/4}$	

With the choice of the optimal bandwidth given in (33), we have

$$\hat{F}_n(x) = F(x) + O_p(n^{-1/5})$$

for each $x \in \mathbf{R}$. The Nadaraya–Watson estimator for the regression function thus converges at rate $n^{1/5}$ when the regressor is an integrated time series. We may obtain faster convergence rates if we use a higher-order kernel, that is the kernel function K such that $\int_{-\infty}^{\infty} s^k K(s)\, ds = 0$ for some integer $k \geq 2$. It is possible, at least theoretically, that we may make the convergence rate arbitrarily close to $n^{1/4}$ by using higher-order kernels. Note that this convergence rate applies to any regression function F, in particular, for both asymptotically homogeneous and integrable functions. This is in sharp contrast to the nonlinear regression, for which the convergence rate is dependent on the type of regression function.

It is interesting to compare the convergence rates of the parametric and nonparametric regressions for the regression with an integrated regressor. The comparison is made explicitly in Table 7.1 and contrasted with the standard stationary regression. The rates for the nonparametric approach depend on the choice of kernels and therefore are given by the ranges. In general, the nonparametric approach yields slower rates of convergence for both stationary and nonstationary regressions. This might be considered as a price to be paid for using unrestrictive and flexible specification for the regression function. The reduction in the convergence rates can, however, be recovered for stationary regression if we rely on higher order kernels, which reduce the order of bias term. This is also true for nonstationary regression if the regression function is integrable, though the convergence rates are overall smaller for both parametric and nonparametric approaches.

For the nonstationary regression with asymptotically homogeneous regression function, a quite different picture emerges. In this case, nonparametric approach yields a drastic reduction in convergence rates that cannot be recovered simply by the use of higher order kernels. For instance, the convergence rate in the parametric linear cointegrating regression is given by n in comparison with the maximal rate $n^{1/4}$ for the nonparametric regression. These differing convergence rates come from the presence of a stochastic trend in the regressor. For the parametric approach, the stochastic trend amplifies the signal if the regression function is increasing, and we may say that the convergence rate is given by the behavior of the function at infinity. This is not so for the nonparametric approach, which essentially estimates the regression function locally at each given point. The nonparametric method thus would not utilize the effect of magnifying signals made by an integrated regressor for the regression function increasing at infinity.

The usual nonparametric approach is thus not very attractive for the estimation of nonlinear relationships between integrated time series. An obviously better method is given by the *partial parametric* approach. Suppose that the regression function F can be decomposed as $F = H + G$, where H is homogeneous and G is integrable. We may then specify H parametrically as

$$H(x, \theta) = \alpha |x|^{\beta} \quad \text{or} \quad \alpha_1 |x|^{\beta_1} 1\{x \geq 0\} + \alpha_2 |x|^{\beta_2} 1\{x < 0\},$$

with parameter $\theta = (\alpha, \beta)'$ or $\theta = (\alpha_1, \alpha_2, \beta_1, \beta_2)'$, while we leave G unrestricted and estimate it nonparametrically.

The partial parametric model can be estimated consistently in two steps. In the first step, we run the parametric NLLS regression

$$y_t = H(x_t, \theta_0) + w_t,$$

where (w_t) is the regression error newly defined by $w_t = u_t + G(x_t)$. This first-step NLLS regression yields a consistent estimator $\hat{\theta}_n$, for instance, for θ_0. It is indeed not difficult to show that the NLLS estimator $\hat{\theta}_n$ of θ here has the same limiting distribution as in the regression having error (u_t). The asymptotic behavior of the NLLS estimator $\hat{\theta}_n$ of θ in this regression is thus given by our earlier results. In the second step, we estimate G nonparametrically from the regression

$$y_t - H(x_t, \theta_0) = G(x_t) + u_t.$$

The limit theory is not affected by using $H(x_t, \hat{\theta}_n)$ in place of $H(x_t, \theta_0)$ in the second-step regression. The asymptotics for the second-step regression are therefore identical to our theories for nonparametric regression given earlier in this section.

7.5 NONSTATIONARY NONLINEARITY IN VOLATILITY

The nonstationary nonlinearity can also be used in modeling volatilities. If we let

$$y_t = \sigma_t \varepsilon_t, \tag{34}$$

where (ε_t) is a sequence of independent and identically distributed random variables with mean zero and unit variance and (σ_t) signifies the conditional variance at time t given information up to time $t-1$, which is represented by the filtration $(\mathcal{F}_{t-1})$. We thus have $\mathbf{E}(y_t^2|\mathcal{F}_{t-1}) = \sigma_t^2$. Furthermore, we let

$$\sigma_t^2 = F(x_t), \tag{35}$$

where (x_t) is an integrated time series, as we specified earlier, which is assumed to be $(\mathcal{F}_{t-1})$ measurable and independent of (ε_t).

The model given by (34) and (35) can be regarded as a stochastic volatility model in which the conditional heterogeneity is generated by a nonlinear function of an integrated process. It is investigated by Park (2002) and referred to as *nonstationary nonlinear heteroskedasticity* (NNH). The function F in (35), which should necessarily be nonlinear to ensure nonnegativity of the conditional variance, is called the heterogeneity generating function (HGF). If (x_t) in (35) is stationary, it is said that we have *stationary nonlinear heteroskedasticity*. Instead of modeling the conditional variance σ_t^2 in (34) explicitly as a function of some explanatory variable, the autoregressive conditional heteroskedasticity (ARCH) or the generalized autoregressive conditional heteroskedasticity (GARCH) model assumes that the conditional variance is given by the past values of the squared process (y_t^2).

It appears that there are many potential examples for which volatilities may reasonably be specified as functions of integrated processes. For instance, the volatility of the return from a stock may well be given as a function of interest rate or transaction quantity, which are both considered by many to be well approximated by integrated processes. We may likewise specify the volatility in the nominal interest rate differentials as a function of inflation, which is also commonly believed to have a unit root. It may also seem reasonable to model the volatility of the spread between forward and spot rates as a function of the level of the spot rate, as is demonstrated in Park (2002).

Using the asymptotics developed in Section 7.2, we may readily derive various statistical properties of the NNH model. Here we consider the limiting behavior of the sample autocorrelations for the squared process (y_t^2), which is defined as

$$R_{nk}^2 = \frac{\sum_{t=k+1}^{n} (y_t^2 - \bar{y}_n^2)(y_{t-k}^2 - \bar{y}_n^2)}{\sum_{t=1}^{n} (y_t^2 - \bar{y}_n^2)^2},$$

where $\bar{y}_n^2$ denotes the sample mean of (y_t^2). Moreover, we investigate the asymptotics for the sample kurtosis

$$K_n^4 = \frac{\frac{1}{n}\sum_{t=1}^{n} y_t^4}{\left(\frac{1}{n}\sum_{t=1}^{n} y_t^2\right)^2}.$$

Other sample statistics, of course, can be analyzed similarly, though we do not report the details here.

Two prominent characteristics are revealed by many time series observations in economics and finance: volatility clustering and leptokurticity. For any volatility model to be useful in describing data having such properties, it should be able to predict the persistency in the autocorrelations of the squared process and the large values of the sample kurtosis. The asymptotics for R^2_{nk} and K^4_n can be obtained as in Section 7.3 because

$$\begin{aligned} y_t^p &= F^{p/2}(x_t)\,\varepsilon_t^p \\ &= \left(\mathbf{E}\varepsilon_t^p\right) F^{p/2}(x_t) + F^{p/2}(x_t)\left(\varepsilon_t^p - \mathbf{E}\varepsilon_t^p\right), \end{aligned} \tag{36}$$

and, for all $k = 1, 2, \ldots,$

$$\begin{aligned} y_t^2 y_{t-k}^2 &= F(x_t)F(x_{t-k})\,\varepsilon_t^2\varepsilon_{t-k}^2 \\ &= F(x_t)F(x_{t-k}) + F(x_t)F(x_{t-k})\left(\varepsilon_t^2\varepsilon_{t-k}^2 - 1\right) \end{aligned} \tag{37}$$

and their first terms dominate.

7.5.1 NNH with Integrable HGF

We first consider the NNH model with integrable HGF. Let the HGF F be bounded and integrable. Then we may easily deduce from (36) and our earlier result (16) in Section 7.3 that

$$\begin{aligned} \frac{1}{\sqrt{n}}\sum_{t=1}^n y_t^p &= \left(\mathbf{E}\varepsilon_t^p\right)\frac{1}{\sqrt{n}}\sum_{t=1}^n F^{p/2}(x_t) + o_p(1) \\ &\to_d \left(\mathbf{E}\varepsilon_t^p\right) L(1,0)\int_{-\infty}^{\infty} F^{p/2}(x)\,dx \end{aligned} \tag{38}$$

as $n \to \infty$. Note that

$$\sum_{t=1}^n F^{p/2}(x_t)\left(\varepsilon_t^p - \mathbf{E}\varepsilon_t^p\right) = O_p(n^{1/4})$$

for all large n on the basis of (15).

Moreover, it follows from (37) and (18) in Section 7.3 that

$$\begin{aligned} \frac{1}{\sqrt{n}}\sum_{t=1}^n y_t^2 y_{t-k}^2 &= \frac{1}{\sqrt{n}}\sum_{t=1}^n F(x_t)F(x_{t-k}) + o_p(1) \\ &\to_d L(1,0)\int_{-\infty}^{\infty}\int_{-\infty}^{\infty} F(x)F(x+y)D_k(y)\,dx\,dy \end{aligned} \tag{39}$$

as $n \to \infty$. Similarly, as above,

$$\sum_{t=1}^n F(x_t)F(x_{t-k})\left(\varepsilon_t^2\varepsilon_{t-k}^2 - 1\right) = O_p(n^{1/4})$$

for all large n.

We may now readily deduce from (38) and (39) that

$$R^2_{nk} \to_p R^2_k,$$

where

$$R^2_k = \frac{\displaystyle\int_{-\infty}^{\infty}\int_{-\infty}^{\infty} F(x)F(x+y)D_k(y)\,dx\,dy}{\displaystyle\mathbf{E}\varepsilon_t^4 \int_{-\infty}^{\infty} F^2(x)\,dx}.$$

As in Section 7.3, D_k, $k = 1, 2, \ldots$, denotes the density of $(x_t - x_{t-k})$. If the HGF F is integrable, the sample autocorrelation R^2_{nk} of the squared process has a nonrandom probability limit R^2_k for each $k = 1, 2, \ldots$, which we may regard as the asymptotic autocorrelation function of the squared process.

The asymptotic autocorrelation function R^2_k of the squared process can be analyzed as in Section 7.3. First, we may easily show that

$$R^2_k < 1/\mathbf{E}\varepsilon_t^4$$

at all lags $k = 1, 2, \ldots$. Note that $\mathbf{E}\varepsilon_t^4 > 1$. The autocorrelations of the squared NNH process with integrable HGF are therefore expected to be strictly less than unity. In particular, if the distribution of (ε_t) has thick tails and large kurtosis, the autocorrelations should be small at all lags $k = 1, 2, \ldots$. Under Gaussianity, we have $\mathbf{E}\varepsilon_t^4 = 3$, and therefore, $R^2_k < 1/3$ for all lags $k = 1, 2, \ldots$. Moreover, it follows as in Section 7.3 that

$$k^{1/2} R^2_k \to D(0)\frac{\left(\displaystyle\int_{-\infty}^{\infty} F(x)\,dx\right)^2}{\displaystyle\mathbf{E}\varepsilon_t^4 \int_{-\infty}^{\infty} F^2(x)\,dx}$$

as $k \to \infty$. The autocorrelations of the squared NNH process with integrable HGF therefore decay slowly at the rate of $k^{-1/2}$, yielding persistency in memory, that is, long memory. The NNH model may thus generate long memory in volatility if an integrable HGF is used.

Now we consider the asymptotic behavior of the sample kurtosis for the NNH model with integrable HGF. Once again, it may easily be deduced from (36) that

$$\frac{1}{\sqrt{n}} K_n^4 \to_d \frac{\displaystyle\mathbf{E}\varepsilon_t^4 \int_{-\infty}^{\infty} F^2(x)\,dx}{\displaystyle L(1,0)\left(\int_{-\infty}^{\infty} F(x)\,dx\right)^2}$$

as $n \to \infty$. For the NNH model with integrable HGF, the sample kurtosis K_n^4 diverges as $n \to \infty$. It is therefore expected to have larger values as the sample size increases, which provides an explanation for the leptokurticity observed in many economic and financial data.

The asymptotics for the sample autocorrelations R^2_{nk} of the squared process obtained here for the NNH model with integrable HGF are applicable also for the NNH model with trivial asymptotically homogeneous HGF. That is, if F is an asymptotically homogeneous function given by a constant shift of an integrable function as in (19), R^2_{nk} asymptotically behaves exactly the same as in the case of an integrable function. This is an obvious consequence of the definition of R^2_{nk}, which is invariant with respect to the constant shift of (y_t^2). Contrarily, such invariance does not hold for our definition of the sample kurtosis K_n^4.[2] The results here for K_n^4 therefore do not extend to the NNH model with any asymptotically homogeneous HGF.

7.5.2 NNH with Asymptotically Homogeneous HGF

We now investigate the NNH model with asymptotically homogeneous HGF. If the HGF F is an asymptotically homogeneous function with asymptotic order κ and limit homogeneous function H, we may easily derive that

$$\begin{aligned}\frac{1}{n}\kappa^{-p/2}(\sqrt{n})\sum_{t=1}^{n} y_t^p &= \left(\mathbf{E}\varepsilon_t^p\right)\frac{1}{n}\kappa^{-p/2}(\sqrt{n})\sum_{t=1}^{n} F^{p/2}(x_t) + o_p(1)\\ &\to_d \mathbf{E}\varepsilon_t^p \int_0^1 H^{p/2}(V(r))\,dr \qquad (40)\end{aligned}$$

as $n \to \infty$ from (36), our earlier result (20) in Section 7.3, and because

$$\kappa^{-p/2}(\sqrt{n})\sum_{t=1}^{n} F^{p/2}(x_t)\left(\varepsilon_t^p - \mathbf{E}\varepsilon_t^p\right) = O_p(n^{1/2})$$

for all large n on the basis of (12).

Moreover, it follows from (37), (21) in Section 7.3, and

$$\kappa^{-2}(\sqrt{n})\sum_{t=1}^{n} F(x_t)F(x_{t-k})\left(\varepsilon_t^2\varepsilon_{t-k}^2 - 1\right) = O_p(n^{1/2})$$

for all large n, which follows as above, that

$$\begin{aligned}\frac{1}{n}\kappa^{-2}(\sqrt{n})\sum_{t=1}^{n} y_t^2 y_{t-k}^2 &= \frac{1}{n}\kappa^{-2}(\sqrt{n})\sum_{t=1}^{n} F(x_t)F(x_{t-k}) + o_p(1)\\ &\to_d \int_0^1 H^2(V(r))\,dr \qquad (41)\end{aligned}$$

as $n \to \infty$.

We assume that the asymptotically homogeneous HGF is nontrivial – that is, it has nonconstant limit homogeneous function H. Then we may easily deduce

[2] Recall that we assume $\mathbf{E}y_t = 0$ is known to define the sample kurtosis K_n^4.

from (40) and (41) that

$$R_{nk}^2 \to_d R^2,$$

where

$$R^2 = \frac{\displaystyle\int_0^1 H^2(V) - \left(\int_0^1 H(V)\right)^2}{\displaystyle\mathbf{E}\varepsilon_t^4 \int_0^1 H^2(V) - \left(\int_0^1 H(V)\right)^2}$$

as $n \to \infty$.

It is important to note that the limit R^2 of R_{nk}^2 is *random* and *independent of k*. The squared NNH process with nontrivial asymptotically homogeneous HGF therefore has a random asymptotic correlation function that is identical for all lags. It is thus expected that their sample autocorrelations are given randomly and independently of the lag order even when the sample size is fairly large. The distribution of the asymptotic correlation R^2, of course, depends on the fourth moment of (ε_t) and the limit homogeneous function H of the HGF F. It is obtained through simulation in Park (2002) for the Gaussian NNH model with asymptotically homogeneous HGF having limit homogeneous function $H(x) = 1\{x \geq 0\}$ and $H(x) = |x|$. The distribution of R^2 may vary substantially across different H's. For the models with $H(x) = 1\{x \geq 0\}$, R^2 is likely to take values that could be either very small or very large. In contrast, if $H(x) = |x|$, R^2 is most likely to have moderate values. For the former, the sample paths may show either little or heavy volatility clusterings. The latter in most cases will generate samples with moderate volatility clusterings.

We may also easily obtain from (40) that

$$K_n^4 \to_d \frac{\displaystyle\mathbf{E}\varepsilon_t^4 \int_0^1 H^2(V)}{\displaystyle\left(\int_0^1 H(V)\right)^2}$$

as $n \to \infty$. The sample kurtosis continues to be random in the limit for the NNH process with asymptotically homogeneous HGF. Its limit distribution depends on the limit homogeneous function of the HGF. However, for all NNH processes with asymptotically homogeneous HGFs, the limit distribution of the sample kurtosis has support truncated on the left by the kurtosis $\mathbf{E}\varepsilon_t^4$ of the innovations (ε_t). To see this, note that

$$\left(\int_0^1 H(V)\right)^2 \leq \int_0^1 H^2(V) \text{ a.s.,}$$

Table 7.2 *Sample Autocorrelations of Squared Stock Returns*

	Daily		Weekly		Monthly	
k	DJ	SP500	DJ	SP500	DJ	SP500
1	.0931	.1167	.1258	.2431	.0190	.0880
2	.1466	.1532	.0852	.1378	.0259	.0673
3	.0736	.0852	.0571	.1256	.0394	.0720
4	.0199	.0305	.0491	.1310	.0166	.0095
5	.1098	.1412	.0862	.0582	−.0069	−.0045
10	.0119	.0203	.0837	.0774	.0206	.0365
100	.0008	.0026	−.0110	.0094	−.0529	−.0705

which holds for all H on the basis of the Cauchy–Schwarz inequality. The inequality is strict unless H is a constant function. The leptokurticity is therefore naturally expected for the NNH processes with asymptotically homogeneous HGFs.

The limit distribution of the sample kurtosis for the NNH model with asymptotically homogeneous HGF is given in Park (2002) for the choices of the limit homogeneous function H, $H(x) = 1\{x \geq 0\}$ and $H(x) = |x|$. For the former, the limit density has the peak at the left boundary of its support. For the latter, the limit distribution is unimodal, though substantially skewed to the right. We may indeed obtain the limit distribution analytically for the former. As is well known, $\int_0^1 1\{V \geq 0\}$ has arcsine law with density $1/(\pi\sqrt{x(1-x)})$ on the unit interval $(0, 1)$. The limit distribution in this case is therefore given by a constant multiple of the reciprocal of arcsine law, which has the density $1/(\pi x\sqrt{x-1})$ over the support $(1, \infty)$.

7.5.3 Comparisons with SNH and GARCH Models

It is illuminating to compare the properties of the NNH processes with those of the stationary nonlinear heteroskedasticity (SNH) and the GARCH models. In particular, the comparison is made with respect to their ability to explain the commonly observed patterns of the sample autocorrelations for the squared processes. In Table 7.2[3] we present the sample autocorrelations of the squared returns for Dow–Jones Industrial Averages (DJ) and Standard & Poor's 500 (SP500) stock indices at three different frequencies, that is, daily, weekly, and monthly.

Although we have different outcomes for different indices and frequencies, the sample autocorrelations have some common features. First, they are

[3] The data were obtained for the period of 1970.1.1–2003.3.3, and the returns were calculated as the first differences of logged stock price indices.

quite persistent. Sometimes they do not decay at all. If they decay, they do so very slowly. Second, they are far below unity at all lags. Even at the first lag, they are usually pretty small, though they do not seem negligible. The patterns are quite consistent with those predicted by the NNH models. Recall that the autocorrelations for the NNH processes decay very slowly or are given randomly, depending on whether the HGF is integrable (or trivial asymptotically homogeneous) or nontrivial asymptotically homogeneous.

Of the ARCH–GARCH class of models, we consider the simple but most popular GARCH(1,1) model given by

$$\sigma_t^2 = \omega + \alpha y_{t-1}^2 + \beta \sigma_{t-1}^2,$$

where ω, α, and β are parameters assumed to be nonnegative. For the usual GARCH model, we have $\alpha + \beta < 1$. If $\alpha + \beta = 1$, it becomes the so-called integrated GARCH (IGARCH).

For the usual GARCH model with $0 < \alpha + \beta < 1$, the theoretical autocorrelation of the squared process decreases at a geometric rate. Indeed, one may easily see that the sample autocorrelation of the squared process has probability limit given by

$$(\alpha + \beta)^{k-1} \frac{\alpha + \alpha\beta^2 + \beta^3}{1 - \alpha\beta},$$

which is just the kth autocorrelation of the stationary process (y_t^2). When $\alpha + \beta = 1$, as is the case for IGARCH, the process (y_t^2) becomes an integrated process and R_{nk}^2 converges in probability to unity at all values of k. It is very clear that the observed patterns of the sample autocorrelations are consistent with neither GARCH nor IGARCH. They neither decay at geometric rates nor are close to unity at any lag.

The SNH models are also inconsistent with the patterns we observe in Table 7.2. Under SNH, the sample autocorrelations of the squared process are expected to decrease as the number of lags increases. To see this more explicitly, we let (x_t) be generated as

$$x_t = \alpha x_{t-1} + v_t$$

with $|\alpha| < 1$. Also, we denote by D and D_k, respectively, the densities of (x_t) and (x_t^k), where $x_t^k = v_t + \alpha v_{t-1} + \cdots + \alpha^{k-1} v_{t-k+1}$, and assume that $\mathbf{E} F^2(x_t) < \infty$ and $\mathbf{E} F^2(x_t^k) < \infty$ for all values of k. Then we have

$$R_{nk}^2 \to_p \frac{\mathbf{E} y_t^2 y_{t-k}^2 - \left(\mathbf{E} y_t^2\right)^2}{\mathbf{E} y_t^4 - \left(\mathbf{E} y_t^2\right)^2},$$

where $\mathbf{E}y_t^2 = \mathbf{E}F(x_t) = \int_{-\infty}^{\infty} F(x)D(x)\,dx$, $\mathbf{E}y_t^4 = \mathbf{E}\varepsilon_t^4\,\mathbf{E}F^2(x_t) = \mathbf{E}\varepsilon_t^4 \times \int_{-\infty}^{\infty} F^2(x)D(x)\,dx$, and

$$\begin{aligned}\mathbf{E}\, y_t^2 y_{t-k}^2 &= \mathbf{E}\, F(x_t)F(x_{t-k}) \\ &= \int_{-\infty}^{\infty}\int_{-\infty}^{\infty} F(\alpha^k x + y)F(x)D(x)D_k(y)\,dx\,dy.\end{aligned}$$

Let F be differentiable with derivative F' so that we have

$$F(\alpha^k x + y) \approx F(y) + \alpha^k x F'(y)$$

for large k. Then we may easily deduce, under suitable technical conditions, that for large k

$$R_{nk}^2 = c\,|\alpha|^k$$

with some constant $c > 0$. It is thus clear that the sample autocorrelations of the squared SNH processes decrease at a geometric rate as the order k of lags increases up to infinity. This is comparable to the usual GARCH process and inconsistent with what we observe in Table 7.2.

7.6 CONCLUDING REMARK

This chapter has presented a unified theory for nonstationary nonlinearity and laid out new research possibilities in several directions. One direction was omitted in our exposition: nonstationary nonlinearity in statistical inference. Nonstationary nonlinearity can also be used as testing instruments. Nonlinear transformations of integrated time series have some important statistical properties that can be exploited to develop tests with some desirable characteristics. Phillips et al. (2004) and Chang (2002) have demonstrated this possibility very well. The asymptotic theory for unit root models is intrinsically non-Gaussian, rendering standard tests relying on Gaussian limiting distribution not applicable. The limiting Gaussianity of some nonlinear transformations of integrated time series, however, allows us to use the nonlinear IV method to test for a unit root using the normal table. Moreover, nonlinear transformations of integrated processes are asymptotically orthogonal as long as they are not cointegrated. Chang (2002) use this property to develop panel unit root tests that are robust with respect to the cross-sectional dependency.

References

Akonom, J. (1993). "Comportement asymptotique du temps d'occupation du processus des sommes partielles." *Annales de l'Institut Henri Poincaré*, 29, 57–81.

Beran, J. (1994). *Statistics for Long-Memory Processes*. New York: Chapman & Hall.

Borodin, A. N. and I. A. Ibragimov (1995). *Limit Theorems for Functionals of Random Walks*, Proceedings of the Steklov Institute of Mathematics, Vol. 195. American Mathematical Soceity.

Chang, Y. (2002). "Nonlinear IV unit root tests in panels with cross-sectional dependency," *Journal of Econometrics*, 110, 261–292.

Chang, Y. and J. Y. Park (2003). "Index models with integrated time series," *Journal of Econometrics*, 114, 73–106.

Chang, Y., J. Y. Park, and P. C. B. Phillips (2001). "Nonlinear econometric models with cointegrated and deterministically trending regressors," *Econometrics Journal*, 4, 1–36.

Chung, K. L. and R. J. Williams (1990). *Introduction to Stochastic Integration*, 2nd ed. Boston: Birkhäuser.

Hall, P. and C. C. Heyde (1980). *Martingale Limit Theory and Its Application*. New York: Academic Press.

Park, J. Y. (2002). "Nonlinear nonstationary heteroskedasticity," *Journal of Econometrics*, 110, 383–415.

Park, J. Y. (2003). "Strong approximations for nonlinear transformations of integrated time series," mimeograph, Department of Economics, Rice University.

Park, J. Y. and P. C. B. Phillips (1998). "Unit roots in nonlinear transformations of integrated time series," mimeograph, Department of Economics, Rice University.

Park, J. Y. and P. C. B. Phillips (1999). "Asymptotics for nonlinear transformations of integrated time series," *Econometric Theory*, 15, 269–298.

Park, J. Y. and P. C. B. Phillips (2000). "Nonstationary binary choice," *Econometrica*, 68, 1249–1280.

Park, J. Y. and P. C. B. Phillips (2001). "Nonlinear regressions with integrated time series," *Econometrica*, 69, 1452–1498.

Park, J. Y. and P. C. B. Phillips (2003). "Nonparametric cointegrating regression," mimeograph, Department of Economics, Rice University.

Phillips, P. C. B. and J. Y. Park (1997). "Nonstationary density estimation and kernel autoregression," mimeograph, Cowles Foundation for Research in Economics, Yale University.

Phillips, P. C. B., J. Y. Park, and Y. Chang (2004). "Nonlinear instrumental variable estimation of an autoregression," *Journal of Econometrics*, 118, 219–246.

Phillips, P. C. B. and V. Solo (1992). "Asymptotics for linear processes," *Annals of Statistics*, 20, 971–1001.

Revuz, D. and M. Yor (1994). *Continuous Martingale and Brownian Motion*. New York: Springer–Verlag.

EIGHT

Multiple Structural Change Models

*A Simulation Analysis**

Jushan Bai and Pierre Perron

8.1 INTRODUCTION

Both the statistics and econometrics literature contain a vast amount of work on issues related to structural change, most of it specifically designed for the case of a single change. The problem of multiple structural changes, however, has received considerably less attention. Recently, Bai and Perron (1998, 2003a) provided a comprehensive treatment of various issues in the context of multiple structural change models: consistency of estimates of the break dates, tests for structural changes, confidence intervals for the break dates, methods to select the number of breaks, and efficient algorithms to compute the estimates. Their results are solely asymptotic, however, and the adequacy in finite samples remains to be investigated. This chapter is intended to fill this gap partially.

We present simulation results pertaining to the behavior of the estimators and tests in finite samples. We consider the problem of forming confidence intervals for the break dates under various hypotheses about the structure of the data and errors across segments. In particular, we may allow the data and errors to have different distributions across segments or impose a common structure. The issue of testing for structural changes is also considered under very general conditions on the data and the errors and the properties of tests – both in the data-generating processes and in the specification of the tests. We also address the issue of estimating the number of breaks. To that effect, we discuss methods based on information criteria and a method based on a sequential testing procedure, as suggested in Bai and Perron (1998).

The rest of this chapter is structured as follows. Section 8.2 presents the model and the estimator. Section 8.3 summarizes the relevant asymptotic

* Jushan Bai acknowledges financial support from the National Science Foundation under grant SBR9709508.

results about the construction of confidence intervals for the break dates, the tests for multiple structural changes, and methods to estimate the number of breaks. It describes the exact nature of the various tests and procedures on various specifications about the nature of the errors and data across segments. Section 8.4 presents the results of simulations analyzing the adequacy of the asymptotic approximations in finite samples, the size and power of the various tests, and the relative merits of several methods to estimate the number of structural changes. Some concluding remarks and practical recommendations are presented in Section 8.5.

8.2 THE MODEL AND ESTIMATORS

For the purpose of the simulation study, we consider the following multiple linear regression with m breaks ($m+1$ regimes):

$$y_t = z_t'\delta_j + u_t, \qquad t = T_{j-1}+1, \ldots, T_j \tag{1}$$

for $j = 1, \ldots, m+1$. This is a special case of the general model considered in Bai and Perron (1998) corresponding to a pure structural change model. Here, y_t is the observed dependent variable at time t, z_t $(q \times 1)$ is a vector of covariates, δ_j $(j = 1, \ldots, m+1)$ is the corresponding vector of coefficients, and u_t is the disturbance at time t. The indices $(T_1, \ldots, T_m)$, or the break points, are explicitly treated as unknown (we use the convention that $T_0 = 0$ and $T_{m+1} = T$). The purpose is to estimate the unknown regression coefficients together with the break points when T observations on (y_t, z_t) are available.

The method of estimation considered is that based on the least-squares principle. For each m-partition $(T_1, \ldots, T_m)$, the associated least-squares estimates of δ_j are obtained by minimizing the sum of squared residuals

$$S_T(T_1, \ldots, T_m) = \sum_{i=1}^{m+1} \sum_{t=T_{i-1}+1}^{T_i} [y_t - z_t'\delta_i]^2.$$

Let $\hat{\delta}(\{T_j\})$ signify the resulting estimates based on the given m-partition $(T_1, \ldots, T_m)$ denoted $\{T_j\}$. Substituting these estimates in the objective function, the estimated break points $(\hat{T}_1, \ldots, \hat{T}_m)$ are such that

$$(\hat{T}_1, \ldots, \hat{T}_m) = \text{argmin}_{\text{T}_1,\ldots,\text{T}_\text{m}} S_T(T_1, \ldots, T_m), \tag{2}$$

where the minimization is taken over all partitions $(T_1, \ldots, T_m)$ such that $T_i - T_{i-1} \geq h \geq q$. Thus, the break point estimators are global minimizers of the objective function. Finally, the regression parameter estimates are obtained using the associated least-squares estimates at the estimated m-partition $\{\hat{T}_j\}$, that is, $\hat{\delta} = \hat{\delta}(\{\hat{T}_j\})$. An efficient algorithm, based on the principle of dynamic programming, for obtaining global minimizers of the sum of squared residuals is presented in Bai and Perron (2003a).

Note that, in general, h need not be set to q. Indeed, in many instances the choice of the trimming is made independently of the number of regressors. This is the case, in particular, when obtaining estimates for the purpose of constructing test statistics (see Section 8.3.2).

A central result derived in Bai and Perron (1998) concerns the convergence of the break fractions $\hat{\lambda}_i = \hat{T}_i/T$ and the rate of convergence. The results obtained show not only that $\hat{\lambda}_i$ converges to its true value λ_i^0 but that it does so at the fast rate T, that is, $T(\hat{\lambda}_i - \lambda_i^0) = O_p(1)$ for all i. This convergence result is obtained under a very general set of assumptions and thus allows a wide variety of models. It, however, precludes integrated variables (with an autoregressive unit root) but permits trending regressors; for example, with a trend of the form $g_t = a + b(t/T)$. The assumptions concerning the nature of the errors in relation to the regressors $\{z_t\}$ are of two kinds. First, when no lagged dependent variable is allowed in $\{z_t\}$, the conditions on the residuals are quite general and allow substantial correlation and heteroskedasticity. The second case allows lagged dependent variables as regressors, but then, of course, no serial correlation is permitted in the errors $\{u_t\}$. In both cases, the assumptions are general enough to allow different distributions for both the regressors and the errors across segments.

8.3 SUMMARY OF RELEVANT ASYMPTOTIC RESULTS

8.3.1 Constructing Confidence Intervals

To obtain an asymptotic distribution for the break dates, we consider the strategy of adopting an asymptotic framework in which the magnitudes of the shifts converge to zero as the sample size increases. The resulting limiting distribution is then independent of the specific distribution of the pair $\{z_t, u_t\}$. To describe the relevant distributional result, we need to define some notations. For $i = 1, \ldots, m$, and $\Delta T_i^0 = T_i^0 - T_{i-1}^0$, let

$$\Delta_i = \delta_{i+1}^0 - \delta_i^0,$$

$$Q_i = \lim(\Delta T_i^0)^{-1} \sum_{t=T_{i-1}^0+1}^{T_i^0} E(z_t z_t'), \text{ and}$$

$$\Omega_i = \lim(\Delta T_i^0)^{-1} \sum_{r=T_{i-1}^0+1}^{T_i^0} \sum_{t=T_{i-1}^0+1}^{T_i^0} E(z_r z_t' u_r u_t).$$

In the case in which the data are nontrending, we have, under various assumptions[1] stated in Bai and Perron (1998), the following limiting distribution of

[1] The important ones are as follows: the magnitude of the shifts decreases at a suitable rate as the sample size increases, a functional central limit theorem holds for the partial sums of the

the break dates:

$$\frac{(\Delta_i' Q_i \Delta_i)^2}{(\Delta_i' \Omega_i \Delta_i)}(\hat{T}_i - T_i^0) \Rightarrow \arg\max_s V^{(i)}(s), \quad (i = 1, \dots, m), \tag{3}$$

where

$$V^{(i)}(s) = \begin{cases} W_1^{(i)}(-s) - |s|/2, & \text{if } s \leq 0, \\ \sqrt{\xi_i}(\phi_{i,2}/\phi_{i,1}) W_2^{(i)}(s) - \xi_i |s|/2, & \text{if } s > 0, \end{cases} \tag{4}$$

and

$$\begin{aligned} \xi_i &= \Delta_i' Q_{i+1} \Delta_i / \Delta_i' Q_i \Delta_i, \\ \phi_{i,1}^2 &= \Delta_i' \Omega_i \Delta_i / \Delta_i' Q_i \Delta_i, \\ \phi_{i,2}^2 &= \Delta_i' \Omega_{i+1} \Delta_i / \Delta_i' Q_{i+1} \Delta_i. \end{aligned}$$

Also, $W_1^{(i)}(s)$ and $W_2^{(i)}(s)$ are independent, standard Weiner processes defined on $[0, \infty)$, starting at the origin when $s = 0$. These processes are also independent across i.

The cumulative distribution function of $\text{argmax}_s V^{(i)}(s)$ is derived in Bai (1997a), and only estimates of Δ_i, Q_i, and Ω_i are needed to compute the relevant critical values. These are given by

$$\begin{aligned} \hat{\Delta}_i &= \hat{\delta}_{i+1} - \hat{\delta}_i, \\ \hat{Q}_i &= (\Delta \hat{T}_i)^{-1} \sum_{t=\hat{T}_{i-1}+1}^{\hat{T}_i} z_t z_t', \end{aligned}$$

and an estimate of Ω_i can be constructed using the covariance matrix estimator of Andrews (1991) applied to the vector $\{z_t \hat{u}_t\}$ and using data over segment i only. We use the quadratic spectral kernel with an AR(1) approximation for each element of the vector $\{z_t \hat{u}_t\}$ to construct the optimal bandwidth (henceforth referred to as a heteroskedasticity and autocorrelation consistent [HAC] estimator). The pre-whitening device suggested by Andrews and Monahan (1992) can also be used.

In practice, one may want to impose some constraints on this general framework related to the distribution of the errors and regressors across segments. For ease of reference, especially with the simulation results presented later, we adopt the following notation. We denote by $cor\_u = 1$ the case in which the errors are allowed to be correlated and by $cor\_u = 0$ the case in which no correction for serial correlation is made. Similarly, $het\_z = 1$ denotes the case in which the regressors are allowed to have heterogenous distributions across segments and $het\_z = 0$ the case in which the distributions are assumed

variables $\{z_t u_t\}$, and $\lim(\Delta T_i^0)^{-1} \sum_{t=T_{i-1}^0+1}^{T_{i-1}^0+[s\Delta T_i^0]} E(z_t z_t') = s Q_i$ is assumed to exist with Q_i a fixed matrix. The latter precludes trending regressors.

to be homogenous across segments. Finally, $het\_u = 1$ permits heterogenous variances of the residuals across segments, and $het\_u = 0$ imposes the same variance throughout. We have the following cases when adding restrictions:

- The regressors z_t are identically distributed across segments ($cor\_u = 1$, $het\_z = 0$, $het\_u = 1$). Then $Q_i = Q_{i+1} = Q$, which can consistently be estimated by $\hat{Q} = T^{-1}\sum_{t=1}^{T} z_t z_t'$. In this case, the limiting result states that

$$\frac{(\hat{\Delta}_i'\hat{Q}\hat{\Delta}_i)^2}{(\hat{\Delta}_i'\hat{\Omega}_i\hat{\Delta}_i)}(\hat{T}_i - T_i^0) \Rightarrow \arg\max_s V^{(i)}(s)$$

  with $\xi_i = 1$.
- The errors are identically distributed across segments ($cor\_u = 1, het\_z = 1$, $het\_u = 0$). Then $\Omega_i = \Omega_{i+1} = \Omega$, which can consistently be estimated using an HAC estimator applied to the variable $\{z_t\hat{u}_t\}$ using data over the whole sample.
- The errors and the data are identically distributed across segments ($cor\_u = 1$, $het\_z = 0$, $het\_u = 0$). Here, we have $\xi_i = 1$ and $\phi_{i,1} = \phi_{i,2}$, and the limiting distribution reduces to

$$\frac{(\hat{\Delta}_i'\hat{Q}\hat{\Delta}_i)^2}{(\hat{\Delta}_i'\hat{\Omega}\hat{\Delta}_i)}(\hat{T}_i - T_i^0) \Rightarrow \arg\max_s\{W^{(i)}(s) - |s|/2\},$$

  which has a density function symmetric about the origin.
- The errors are serially uncorrelated ($cor\_u = 0$, $het\_z = 1$, $het\_u = 1$). In this case $\Omega_i = \sigma_i^2 Q_i$ and $\phi_{i,1}^2 = \phi_{i,2}^2 = \sigma_i^2$, which can be estimated using $\hat{\sigma}_i^2 = (\Delta\hat{T}_i)^{-1}\sum_{t=\hat{T}_{i-1}+1}^{\hat{T}_i}\hat{u}_t^2$. The confidence intervals can then be constructed from the approximation

$$\frac{(\hat{\Delta}_i'\hat{Q}_i\hat{\Delta}_i)}{\hat{\sigma}_i^2}(\hat{T}_i - T_i^0) \Rightarrow \arg\max_s V^{(i)}(s). \tag{5}$$

- The errors are serially uncorrelated, and the regressors are identically distributed across segments ($cor\_u = 0$, $het\_z = 0$, $het\_u = 1$). Here $\phi_{i,1}^2 = \phi_{i,2}^2 = \sigma_i^2$ and $\xi_i = 1$. The confidence intervals can then be constructed from the approximation

$$\frac{(\hat{\Delta}_i'\hat{Q}\hat{\Delta}_i)}{\hat{\sigma}_i^2}(\hat{T}_i - T_i^0) \Rightarrow \arg\max_s\{W^{(i)}(s) - |s|/2\}. \tag{6}$$

- The errors are serially uncorrelated and identically distributed across segments ($cor\_u = 0$, $het\_z = 1$, $het\_u = 0$). The approximation is the same as (5) with $\hat{\sigma}^2 = T^{-1}\sum_{t=1}^{T}\hat{u}_t^2$ instead of $\hat{\sigma}_i^2$.
- The errors are serially uncorrelated, and both the data and the errors are identically distributed across segments ($cor\_u = 0$, $het\_z = 0$, $het\_u = 0$). The approximation is the same as (6) with $\hat{\sigma}^2$ instead of $\hat{\sigma}_i^2$.

Because the break dates are integer valued, we consider confidence intervals that are likewise integer valued by using the highest smaller integer for the lower bound and the smallest higher integer for the upper bound.

8.3.2 Test Statistics for Multiple Breaks

8.3.2.1 A Test of No Break versus a Fixed Number of Breaks. We consider the sup$F$-type test of no structural break ($m = 0$) versus the alternative hypothesis that there are $m = k$ breaks. Let $(T_1, \ldots, T_k)$ be a partition such that $T_i = [T\lambda_i]$ $(i = 1, \ldots, k)$. Let R be the conventional matrix such that $(R\delta)' = (\delta_1' - \delta_2', \ldots, \delta_k' - \delta_{k+1}')$. Define

$$F_T^*(\lambda_1, \ldots, \lambda_k; q) = \frac{1}{T}\left[\frac{T - (k+1)q}{kq}\right] \hat{\delta}' R'[R\hat{V}(\hat{\delta})R']^{-1} R\hat{\delta}, \qquad (7)$$

where $\hat{V}(\hat{\delta})$ is an estimate of the variance covariance matrix of $\hat{\delta}$ robust to serial correlation and heteroskedasticity, such that

$$T\hat{V}(\hat{\delta}) \rightarrow p\lim T(\overline{Z}'\overline{Z})^{-1}\overline{Z}'\Omega\overline{Z}(\overline{Z}'\overline{Z})^{-1} \equiv \hat{V}(\hat{\delta}). \qquad (8)$$

The statistic F_T^* is simply the conventional F-statistic for testing $\delta_1 = \cdots = \delta_{k+1}$ against $\delta_i \neq \delta_{i+1}$ for some i given the partition $(T_1, \ldots, T_k)$. The sup$F$-type test statistic is then defined as

$$\sup F_T^*(k; q) = \sup_{(\lambda_1, \ldots, \lambda_k) \in \Lambda_\epsilon} F_T^*(\lambda_1, \ldots, \lambda_k; q),$$

where

$$\Lambda_\epsilon = \{(\lambda_1, \ldots, \lambda_k); |\lambda_{i+1} - \lambda_i| \geq \epsilon, \lambda_1 \geq \epsilon, \lambda_k \leq 1 - \epsilon\}$$

for some arbitrary positive number ϵ. In this general case, if one allows for serial correlation in the errors, the sup$F_T^*(k; q)$ may be rather cumbersome to compute. However, one can obtain a much simpler, yet asymptotically equivalent, version by using the estimates of the break dates obtained from the global minimization of the sum of squared residuals. If these estimates are denoted by $\hat{\lambda}_i = \hat{T}_i / T$ for $i = 1, \ldots, k$, the test is then

$$\sup F_T(k; q) = F_T^*(\hat{\lambda}_1, \ldots, \hat{\lambda}_k; q).$$

The estimates $\hat{\lambda}_1, \ldots, \hat{\lambda}_k$ are equivalently the arguments that maximize the following F-statistic:

$$F_T(\lambda_1, \ldots, \lambda_k; q) = \left[\frac{T - (k+1)q}{kq}\right] \hat{\delta}' R'[RT\tilde{V}(\hat{\delta})R']^{-1} R\hat{\delta}$$

and

$$\tilde{V}(\hat{\delta}) = \hat{\sigma}^2(\overline{Z}'\overline{Z})^{-1},$$

the covariance matrix of $\hat{\delta}$ assuming spherical errors. This procedure is asymptotically equivalent because the break dates are consistent even in the presence of serial correlation. The asymptotic distribution still depends on the specification of the set Λ_ϵ via the imposition of the minimal length h of a segment. Hence, $\epsilon = h/T$.

Various versions of the tests can be obtained depending on the assumptions made with respect to the distribution of the data and the errors across segments. These variations relate to different specifications in the construction of the estimate of the limiting covariance matrix $V(\hat{\delta})$ given by (8). They are as follows:

- No serial correlation, different distributions for the data, and identical distribution for the errors across segments ($cor\_u = 0$, $het\_z = 1$, $het\_u = 0$). In this base case, the estimate is

$$\hat{V}(\hat{\delta}) = \hat{\sigma}^2(\overline{Z}'\overline{Z})^{-1}.$$

- No serial correlation in the errors, different variances of the errors, and different distributions of the data across segments ($cor\_u = 0$, $het\_z = 1$, $het\_u = 1$). In this case,

$$\hat{V}(\hat{\delta}) = \text{diag}[\hat{V}(\hat{\delta}_1), \ldots, \hat{V}(\hat{\delta}_{m+1})],$$

  where $\hat{V}(\hat{\delta}_i)$ is the covariance matrix of the estimate $\hat{\delta}_i$ using only data from segment i, that is, $\hat{V}(\hat{\delta}_i) = \hat{\sigma}_i^2[\sum_{t=\hat{T}_{i-1}+1}^{\hat{T}_i} z_t z_t']^{-1}$ with $\hat{\sigma}_i^2 = (\Delta\hat{T}_i)^{-1}\sum_{t=\hat{T}_{i-1}+1}^{\hat{T}_i} \hat{u}_t^2$. These are simply the ordinary least squares (OLS) estimates obtained using data from each segment separately.
- Serial correlation in the errors and different distributions for the data and the errors across segments ($cor\_u = 1$, $het\_z = 1$, $het\_u = 1$). Here, we make use of the fact that the errors in different segments are asymptotically independent. Hence, the limiting variance is given by

$$V(\hat{\delta}) = \text{diag}[V(\hat{\delta}_1), \ldots, V(\hat{\delta}_{m+1})],$$

  where, for $i = 1, \ldots, m+1$,

$$V(\hat{\delta}_i) = p\lim(\Delta T_i)(Z_i'Z_i)^{-1}Z_i'\Omega_i Z_i(Z_i'Z_i)^{-1}.$$

  This can be consistently estimated, segment by segment, with an HAC estimator of $V(\hat{\delta}_i)$ using only data from segment i.
- Serial correlation in the errors and the same distribution for the errors across segments ($cor\_u = 1$, $het\_z = 1$, $het\_u = 0$). In this case the limiting covariance matrix is

$$V(\hat{\delta}) = p\lim T(\overline{Z}'\overline{Z})^{-1}(\Lambda \otimes (Z'\Omega Z))(\overline{Z}'\overline{Z})^{-1},$$

where (using the convention that $\lambda_0 = 0$ and $\lambda_{m+1} = 1$)

$$\Lambda = \begin{pmatrix} \lambda_1 - \lambda_0 & & & \\ & \lambda_2 - \lambda_1 & & \\ & & \ddots & \\ & & & \lambda_{m+1} - \lambda_m \end{pmatrix}.$$

This can consistently be estimated using $\hat{\lambda}_i = \hat{T}_i/T$ and an HAC estimator based on the pair $\{z_t\hat{u}_t\}$ constructed from the full sample. Note that we have an implicit assumption that the regressors z_t have the same distribution across segments because the consistent estimate of $p\lim Z'\Omega Z/T$ is constructed using the full sample. For reasons discussed next we do not impose that restriction when evaluating $p\lim \overline{Z}'\overline{Z}/T$. That is, we still use $\overline{Z}'\overline{Z}/T$ instead of an estimate of $(\Lambda \otimes Q)$ obtained using $\hat{Q} = T^{-1}\sum_{t=1}^{T} z_t z_t'$ based on the full sample.

In the construction of the tests we do not consider imposing the restriction that the distribution of the regressors z_t be the same across segments even if they are (except as they enter in the construction of an HAC estimate involving the pair $\{z_t\hat{u}_t\}$). This might at first sight seem surprising because imposing a valid restriction should lead to a more precise estimate. This is, however, not true. Consider the case with no serial correlation in the errors and the same distribution for the errors across segments ($cor\_u = 0$, $het\_u = 0$). Imposing the restriction $het\_z = 0$ leads to the asymptotic covariance matrix

$$V(\hat{\delta}) = \sigma^2(\Lambda \otimes Q)^{-1},$$

where $Q = \lim_{T\to\infty} T^{-1}\sum_{t=1}^{T} E(z_t z_t')$. Note that a consistent estimate can be obtained using $\hat{Q} = T^{-1}\sum_{t=1}^{T} z_t z_t'$, $\hat{\sigma}^2 = T^{-1}\sum_{t=1}^{T} \hat{u}_t^2$ and $\hat{\Lambda}$ constructed using $\hat{\lambda}_i = \hat{T}_i/T$ $(i = 1, \ldots, m)$. Suppose that the z's are exogenous and the errors have the same variance across segments. Then, for a given partition $(T_1, \ldots, T_m)$, the exact variance of the estimated coefficients $\hat{\delta}$ is

$$V(\hat{\delta}) = \sigma^2 \left(\frac{\overline{Z}'\overline{Z}}{T}\right)^{-1}.$$

Using the asymptotic version $V(\hat{\delta}) = \sigma^2(\Lambda \otimes Q)^{-1}$ may imply an inaccurate approximation to the exact distribution. This would occur especially if small segments were allowed, in which case the exact moment matrix of the regressors might deviate substantially from its full sample analog.

The same problem occurs in the case with no serial correlation in the errors and different variance for the residuals across segments ($cor\_u = 0$, $het\_u = 1$). Imposing $het\_z = 0$ gives the limiting variance

$$V(\hat{\delta}) = (\Lambda^* \otimes Q)^{-1},$$

where

$$\Lambda^* = \begin{pmatrix} \sigma_1^2(\lambda_1 - \lambda_0) & & & \\ & \sigma_2^2(\lambda_2 - \lambda_1) & & \\ & & \ddots & \\ & & & \sigma_{m+1}^2(\lambda_{m+1} - \lambda_m) \end{pmatrix},$$

which can consistently be estimated using $\hat{Q}$, $\hat{\lambda}_i = \hat{T}_i/T$, and $\hat{\sigma}_i^2 = (\Delta\hat{T}_i)^{-1}\sum_{t=\hat{T}_{i-1}+1}^{\hat{T}_i} \hat{u}_t^2$. Again, in finite samples, imposing the constraint that $Z_i'Z_i/(\Delta\hat{T}_i)$ be approximated by $\hat{Q}$ over all segments may imply a poor approximation in finite samples. We have found, in these two cases, that imposing a common distribution for the regressors across segments leads to tests with worse properties even when the data indeed have an invariant distribution. These distortions becomes less important, however, when the sample size is large, the trimming ϵ is large, or both.

The relevant asymptotic distribution has been derived in Bai and Perron (1998), and critical values can be found in Bai and Perron (1998) for a trimming $\epsilon = .05$ and values of k from 1 to 9 and values of q from 1 to 10. As the simulation experiments will show, a trimming as small as 5% of the total sample can lead to tests with substantial size distortions when allowing different variances of the errors across segments or when serial correlation is permitted. This is because one is then trying to estimate various quantities using very few observations; for example, if $T = 100$ and $\epsilon = .05$, one ends up estimating, for some segments, quantities like the variance of the residuals using only five observations. Similarly, with serial correlation, an HAC estimator would need to be applied to very short samples. The estimates are then highly imprecise, and the tests accordingly show size distortions. When allowing different variances across segments or serial correlation, a higher value of ϵ should be used.

Hence, the case ($cor\_u = 0$, $het\_z = 1$, $het\_u = 0$) should be considered the base case in which the tests can be constructed using an arbitrary small trimming ϵ. For all other cases, care should be exercised in the choice of ϵ and larger values should be considered. Critical values for trimming parameter $\epsilon = .10, .15, .20$, and $.25$ can be found in Bai and Perron (2003b). Note that when $\epsilon = .10$ the maximum number of breaks considered is eight because allowing nine breaks imposes the estimates to be exactly $\hat{\lambda}_1 = .1$, $\hat{\lambda}_2 = .2$ up to $\hat{\lambda}_9 = .9$. For similar reasons, the maximum number of breaks allowed is five when $\epsilon = .15$, three when $\epsilon = .20$, and two when $\epsilon = .25$.

8.3.2.2 Double Maximum Tests. Often, an investigator does not wish to prespecify a particular number of breaks to make inference. To allow this, Bai and Perron (1998) have introduced two tests of the null hypothesis of no structural break against an unknown number of breaks given some upper bound M. These are called the *double maximum tests.* The first is an equal-weighted version defined by

$$UD\max F_T^*(M, q) = \max_{1 \le m \le M} \sup_{(\lambda_1,\ldots,\lambda_m)\in\Lambda_\epsilon} F_T^*(\lambda_1, \ldots, \lambda_m; q).$$

We use the asymptotically equivalent version

$$UD\max F_T(M, q) = \max_{1 \le m \le M} F_T(\hat{\lambda}_1, \ldots, \hat{\lambda}_m; q),$$

where $\hat{\lambda}_j = \hat{T}_j / T\,(j = 1, \ldots, m)$ are the estimates of the break points obtained using the global minimization of the sum of squared residuals.

The second test applies weights to the individual tests such that the marginal p-values are equal across values of m. This implies weights that depend on q and the significance level of the test – for instance α. To be more precise, let $c(q, \alpha, m)$ be the asymptotic critical value of the test $\sup_{(\lambda_1,\ldots,\lambda_m)\in\Lambda_\epsilon} F_T(\lambda_1, \ldots, \lambda_m; q)$ for a significance level α. The weights are then defined as $a_1 = 1$, and for $m > 1$ as $a_m = c(q, \alpha, 1)/c(q, \alpha, m)$. This version is denoted by

$$WD\max F_T^*(M, q) = \max_{1 \le m \le M} \frac{c(q, \alpha, 1)}{c(q, \alpha, m)} \sup_{(\lambda_1,\ldots,\lambda_m)\in\Lambda_\epsilon} F_T^*(\lambda_1, \ldots, \lambda_m; q). \quad (9)$$

Again, we use the asymptotically equivalent version

$$WD\max F_T(M, q) = \max_{1 \le m \le M} \frac{c(q, \alpha, 1)}{c(q, \alpha, m)} F_T(\hat{\lambda}_1, \ldots, \hat{\lambda}_m; q).$$

Note that, unlike the $UD\max F_T(M, q)$ test, the value of the $WD\max$ $F_T(M, q)$ depends on the significance level chosen because the weights themselves depend on α. Critical values can be found in Bai and Perron (1998, 2003b) for $\epsilon = .05$ $(M = 5)$, $\epsilon = .10$ $(M = 5)$, .15 $(M = 5)$, .20 $(M = 3)$, and .25 $(M = 2)$.

8.3.2.3 A Test of ℓ versus $\ell + 1$ Breaks. Bai and Perron (1998) proposed a test for ℓ versus $\ell + 1$ breaks. This test is labeled $\sup F_T(\ell + 1|\ell)$. The method amounts to the application of $(\ell + 1)$ tests of the null hypothesis of no structural change versus the alternative hypothesis of a single change. The test is applied to each segment containing the observations $\hat{T}_{i-1}$ to $\hat{T}_i$ $(i = 1, \ldots, \ell + 1)$. The estimates $\hat{T}_i$ need not be the global minimizers of the sum of squared residuals; all that is required is that the break fractions $\hat{\lambda}_i = \hat{T}_i / T$ converge to their true value at rate T. We conclude for a rejection in favor of a model with $(\ell + 1)$ breaks if the overall minimal value of the sum of squared residuals (over all segments for which an additional break is included) is sufficiently smaller than the sum of squared residuals from the ℓ breaks model. The break date thus selected is the one associated with this overall minimum.

Asymptotic critical values were provided by Bai and Perron (1998, 2003b) for q ranging from 1 to 10 and for trimming values ε of .05, .10, .15, .20, and .25.

Of course, all the same options are available as for the previous tests concerning the potential specifications of the nature of the distributions for the errors and the data across segments.

8.3.3 Estimating the Number of Breaks

A common procedure for selecting the dimension of a model is to consider an information criterion. Yao (1988) suggests the use of the Bayesian information criterion (BIC) defined as

$$\mathrm{BIC}(m) = \ln \hat{\sigma}^2(m) + p^* \ln(T)/T,$$

where $p^* = (m+1)q + m + p$, and $\hat{\sigma}^2(m) = T^{-1} S_T(\hat{T}_1, \ldots, \hat{T}_m)$. He showed that the number of breaks can be consistently estimated (at least for a normal sequence of random variables with shifts in mean). An alternative proposed by Liu, Wu, and Zidek (1997), which is denoted as LWZ, is a modified Schwarz criterion that takes the form

$$\mathrm{LWZ}(m) = \ln(S_T(\hat{T}_1, \ldots, \hat{T}_m)/(T - p^*)) + (p^*/T)c_0(\ln(T))^{2+\delta_0}.$$

They suggest using $\delta_0 = 0.1$ and $c_0 = 0.299$. Perron (1997) presented a simulation study of the behavior of these two information criteria and of the Akaike information criterion AIC in the context of estimating the number of changes in the trend function of a series in the presence of serial correlation. The results first showed the AIC to perform very badly and, hence, this criterion will not be considered any further. The BIC and LWZ perform reasonably well when no serial correlation in the errors is present but imply choosing a number of breaks much higher than the true value when serial correlation is present. When no serial correlation is present in the errors but a lagged dependent variable is present, the BIC performs badly when the coefficient on the lagged dependent variable is large (and more so as it approaches unity). In such cases, the LWZ performs better under the null of no break but underestimates the number of breaks when some are present.

The method suggested by Bai and Perron (1998) is based on the sequential application of the $\sup F_T(\ell+1|\ell)$ test. The procedure for estimating the number of breaks is the following. Start by estimating a model with a small number of breaks that are thought to be necessary (or start with no break). Then perform parameter-constancy tests for each subsample (those obtained by cutting off at the estimated breaks), adding a break to a subsample associated with a rejection by using the test $\sup F_T(\ell+1|\ell)$. This process is repeated, increasing ℓ sequentially until the test $\sup F_T(\ell+1|\ell)$ fails to reject the null hypothesis of no additional structural changes. The limiting distribution of the test is the same when using global minimizers for the estimates of the break dates or sequential one-at-a-time estimates because both imply break fractions that converge at rate T (see Bai 1997b). The final number of breaks is thus equal to the number of rejections obtained with the parameter-constancy tests plus the number of breaks used in the initial round.

A distinct advantage of model selection procedures based on hypothesis testing is that, unlike information criteria, they can directly take into account the possible presence of serial correlation in the errors and nonhomogeneous variances across segments.

8.4 SIMULATION EXPERIMENTS

In this section, we present the results of simulation experiments to analyze the size and power of the tests, the coverage rates of the confidence intervals for the break dates, and the adequacy of the various methods to select the number of structural changes. We consider a wide variety of data-generating processes, allowing different variances for the residuals and different distributions for the regressors across segments as well as serial correlation. All computations are performed in GAUSS using a computer program that is available on request for nonprofit academic use (see Bai and Perron 2003a for a thorough description of the features of this program).

8.4.1 The Case with No Break

We start with the case in which the data-generating processes exhibit no structural change and, hence, analyze the size of the tests and how well the methods to select the number of break points actually select none. Throughout, $\{e_t\}$ denotes a sequence of i.i.d. $N(0, 1)$ random variables, and $\{\Psi_t\}$ is a sequence of i.i.d. $N(1, 1)$ random variables uncorrelated with $\{e_t\}$. We use sample sizes of $T = 120$ and $T = 240$. The values of the trimming ϵ and the maximum number of breaks (M) considered are $\epsilon = .05$ and $M = 5$, $\epsilon = .10$ and $M = 5$, $\epsilon = .15$ and $M = 5$, $\epsilon = .20$ and $M = 3$, and $\epsilon = .25$ and $M = 2$. In all cases, 2,000 replications are used.

The data-generating processes and the corresponding regressors used are

- DGP-1: $y_t = e_t$ and $z_t = \{1\}$ $(q = 1)$;
- DGP-2: $y_t = \Psi_t + e_t$ and $z_t = \{1, \Psi_t\}$ $(q = 2)$;
- DGP-3: $y_t = 0.5y_{t-1} + e_t$ and $z_t = \{1, y_{t-1}\}$ $(q = 2)$;
- DGP-4: $y_t = v_t$ with $v_t = 0.5v_{t-1} + e_t$ and $z_t = \{1\}$ $(q = 1)$;
- DGP-5: $y_t = v_t$ with $v_t = e_t + 0.5e_{t-1}$ and $z_t = \{1\}$ $(q = 1)$;
- DGP-6: $y_t = v_t$ with $v_t = e_t - 0.3e_{t-1}$ and $z_t = \{1\}$ $(q = 1)$.

The DGP-1 with i.i.d. data is a base case to assess the basic properties of the tests and methods to select the number of breaks. It is useful to assess the effect of allowing different variances of the errors across segments, serial correlation, or both when these features are not present. The DGP-2 is a variation that includes an exogenous regressor. DGP-3 is a variation in which serial correlation is taken into account parametrically. DGPs 4 to 6 are used to assess the effect of serial correlation in the errors and how well the corrections for its presence leads to tests with adequate sizes.

Table 8.1 *Size of the Tests and Probabilities of Selecting Breaks*

	DGP-1					DGP-2					DGP-3				
ϵ	.05	.10	.15	.20	.25	.05	.10	.15	.20	.25	.05	.10	.15	.20	.25
$cor\_u = 0, het\_u = 0$															
sup$F(1)$	.05	.04	.05	.04	.04	.05	.04	.05	.05	.05	.05	.06	.07	.05	.06
sup$F(2)$	.05	.05	.05	.04	.04	.04	.04	.04	.05	.05	.06	.07	.08	.07	.06
sup$F(3)$	.05	.05	.04	.03		.05	.05	.04	.05		.09	.09	.08	.07	
sup$F(4)$	.06	.05	.04			.07	.06	.04			.12	.11	.08		
sup$F(5)$	.06	.05	.04			.08	.07	.03			.15	.12	.07		
UDMax	.05	.04	.05	.04	.04	.05	.04	.05	.05	.05	.06	.06	.07	.06	.07
WDMax	.06	.05	.04	.04	.04	.06	.05	.05	.05	.05	.10	.09	.09	.07	.06
Sequa $- Pr[m = 0]$	.95	.96	.95	.96	.96	.95	.96	.95	.95	.95	.95	.95	.94	.95	.94
Sequa $- Pr[m = 1]$	.05	.04	.05	.04	.04	.05	.04	.05	.05	.05	.05	.05	.06	.05	.06
Sequa $- Pr[m = 2]$	.00	.00	.00	.00	.00	.00	.00	.00	.00	.00	.00	.00	.00	.00	.00
$cor\_u = 0, het\_u = 1$															
sup$F(1)$	.10	.06	.06	.05	.04	.16	.08	.07	.06	.05	.18	.10	.10	.07	.07
sup$F(2)$	.24	.11	.08	.06	.06	.35	.14	.09	.06	.06	.40	.22	.14	.10	.08
sup$F(3)$	.24	.11	.07	.05		.42	.17	.08	.07		.49	.26	.14	.11	
sup$F(4)$	.29	.11	.07			.48	.19	.08			.59	.29	.15		
sup$F(5)$	.31	.12	.06			.53	.18	.07			.65	.30	.13		
UDMax	.27	.10	.06	.05	.04	.46	.14	.08	.06	.06	.51	.17	.13	.09	.08
WDMax	.33	.12	.07	.06	.05	.57	.19	.10	.07	.06	.66	.27	.16	.10	.08
Sequa $- Pr[m = 0]$	.90	.94	.94	.95	.96	.85	.92	.93	.94	.95	.82	.90	.90	.93	.93
Sequa $- Pr[m = 1]$	.09	.06	.06	.05	.04	.14	.08	.07	.06	.05	.16	.09	.09	.07	.07
Sequa $- Pr[m = 2]$	.01	.00	.00	.00	.00	.01	.00	.00	.00	.00	.02	.01	.01	.00	.00
$cor\_u = 1, het\_u = 0$															
sup$F(1)$	.06	.06	.06	.05	.05	.08	.06	.06	.07	.07					
sup$F(2)$	.08	.08	.07	.06	.06	.10	.09	.09	.08	.08					
sup$F(3)$	.11	.10	.08	.05		.14	.12	.10	.08						
sup$F(4)$	.15	.12	.08			.18	.16	.10							
sup$F(5)$	.21	.14	.07			.23	.20	.10							
UDMax	.08	.07	.07	.06	.05	.12	.09	.08	.08	.07					
WDMax	.14	.11	.08	.06	.05	.21	.17	.11	.09	.07					
Sequa $- Pr[m = 0]$	.94	.95	.94	.95	.95	.92	.94	.93	.93	.93					
Sequa $- Pr[m = 1]$	.06	.05	.06	.05	.05	.07	.06	.07	.07	.07					
Sequa $- Pr[m = 2]$	.00	.00	.00	.00	.00	.01	.00	.00	.00	.00					
$cor\_u = 1, het\_u = 1$															
sup$F(1)$	.12	.08	.07	.05	.05	.25	.14	.11	.10	.08					
sup$F(2)$	.29	.14	.10	.07	.07	.54	.31	.19	.13	.10					
sup$F(3)$	.32	.15	.10	.07		.65	.39	.22	.15						
sup$F(4)$	.37	.16	.09			.75	.44	.25							
sup$F(5)$	.39	.16	.09			.81	.48	.24							
UDMax	.36	.14	.09	.07	.05	.77	.35	.18	.12	.09					
WDMax	.43	.17	.10	.07	.06	.86	.49	.24	.15	.10					
Sequa $- Pr[m = 0]$	.88	.92	.93	.95	.95	.75	.86	.89	.90	.92					
Sequa $- Pr[m = 1]$	.11	.08	.07	.05	.05	.21	.13	.11	.10	.08					
Sequa $- Pr[m = 2]$	.01	.00	.00	.00	.00	.04	.01	.00	.00	.00					
BIC $- Pr[m = 0]$	.94	.96	.97	.98	.98	.97	.98	.99	.99	.99	.97	.98	.98	.98	.99
BIC $- Pr[m = 1]$	.04	.03	.03	.02	.02	.03	.02	.01	.01	.01	.03	.02	.02	.02	.01
BIC $- Pr[m = 2]$	.02	.01	.00	.00	.00	.00	.00	.00	.00	.00	.00	.00	.00	.00	.00
LWZ $- Pr[m = 0]$	1.0	1.0	1.0	1.0	1.0	1.0	1.0	1.0	1.0	1.0	1.0	1.0	1.0	1.0	1.0
LWZ $- Pr[m = 1]$	.00	.00	.00	.00	.00	.00	.00	.00	.00	.00	.00	.00	.00	.00	.00
LWZ $- Pr[m = 2]$	.00	.00	.00	.00	.00	.00	.00	.00	.00	.00	.00	.00	.00	.00	.00

Table 8.1 (*continued*)

	DGP-4					DGP-5					DGP-6				
ϵ	.05	.10	.15	.20	.25	.05	.10	.15	.20	.25	.05	.10	.15	.20	.25
$cor\_u = 0, het\_u = 0$															
sup$F(1)$	.52	.52	.50	.44	.44	.24	.24	.24	.21	.20	.00	.00	.00	.00	.00
sup$F(2)$	.82	.77	.69	.59	.53	.42	.38	.34	.29	.24	.00	.00	.00	.00	.00
sup$F(3)$	.90	.84	.74	.60		.51	.44	.39	.30		.00	.00	.00	.00	
sup$F(4)$	.94	.88	.75			.60	.49	.39			.00	.00	.00		
sup$F(5)$	.95	.89	.71			.67	.53	.36			.00	.00	.00		
UDMax	.81	.73	.64	.53	.49	.38	.33	.31	.25	.23	.00	.00	.00	.00	.00
WDMax	.92	.85	.73	.59	.53	.55	.46	.38	.28	.24	.00	.00	.00	.00	.00
Sequa $- Pr[m = 0]$	.48	.48	.50	.56	.56	.76	.76	.76	.79	.80	1.0	1.0	1.0	1.0	1.0
Sequa $- Pr[m = 1]$	.29	.31	.33	.31	.35	.18	.18	.21	.18	.18	.00	.00	.00	.00	.00
Sequa $- Pr[m = 2]$	.16	.15	.14	.12	.09	.05	.05	.03	.03	.02	.00	.00	.00	.00	.00
$cor\_u = 0, het\_u = 1$															
sup$F(1)$	.61	.58	.52	.46	.44	.35	.30	.28	.22	.21	.01	.00	.00	.00	.00
sup$F(2)$	.92	.84	.72	.62	.56	.70	.51	.41	.31	.27	.04	.00	.00	.00	.00
sup$F(3)$	.96	.89	.77	.64		.76	.57	.45	.33		.02	.00	.00	.00	
sup$F(4)$	.98	.92	.78			.84	.63	.46			.03	.00	.00		
sup$F(5)$	.99	.93	.76			.87	.65	.43			.02	.00	.00		
UDMax	.96	.84	.70	.57	.51	.77	.49	.38	.27	.24	.04	.00	.00	.00	.00
WDMax	.98	.92	.78	.62	.55	.85	.62	.46	.31	.27	.04	.00	.00	.00	.00
Sequa $- Pr[m = 0]$	.39	.42	.48	.55	.56	.65	.70	.73	.78	.79	.99	1.0	1.0	1.0	1.0
Sequa $- Pr[m = 1]$	.27	.32	.33	.32	.35	.23	.23	.23	.19	.19	.01	.00	.00	.00	.00
Sequa $- Pr[m = 2]$	.21	.18	.15	.12	.09	.09	.06	.04	.03	.02	.00	.00	.00	.00	.00
$cor\_u = 1, het\_u = 0$															
sup$F(1)$	.07	.08	.08	.07	.07	.09	.08	.10	.08	.08	.03	.03	.03	.03	.03
sup$F(2)$	.12	.14	.12	.10	.09	.15	.16	.14	.12	.11	.05	.04	.04	.03	.03
sup$F(3)$	.22	.21	.16	.10		.25	.22	.17	.12		.07	.06	.04	.03	
sup$F(4)$	.34	.28	.17			.38	.29	.18			.11	.08	.05		
sup$F(5)$	.46	.32	.15			.47	.32	.17			.15	.09	.04		
UDMax	.18	.14	.11	.08	.08	.18	.14	.12	.10	.08	.04	.03	.03	.03	.03
WDMax	.35	.27	.15	.11	.08	.36	.26	.17	.12	.10	.09	.06	.05	.03	.03
Sequa $- Pr[m = 0]$	.93	.92	.92	.93	.93	.91	.92	.91	.92	.93	.97	.97	.97	.97	.97
Sequa $- Pr[m = 1]$	.06	.08	.08	.06	.07	.08	.08	.09	.08	.07	.03	.03	.03	.03	.03
Sequa $- Pr[m = 2]$	.01	.00	.00	.00	.00	.01	.00	.00	.00	.00	.00	.00	.00	.00	.00
$cor\_u = 1, het\_u = 1$															
sup$F(1)$	.22	.15	.13	.08	.08	.18	.13	.11	.09	.08	.04	.02	.02	.02	.02
sup$F(2)$	.56	.36	.23	.14	.12	.51	.28	.19	.13	.11	.11	.04	.03	.02	.02
sup$F(3)$	.64	.41	.26	.15		.56	.31	.21	.13		.10	.03	.02	.02	
sup$F(4)$	.76	.47	.28			.65	.34	.21			.11	.03	.02		
sup$F(5)$	.82	.51	.28			.70	.37	.19			.10	.03	.02		
UDMax	.75	.39	.24	.11	.09	.62	.26	.17	.11	.09	.11	.03	.02	.02	.02
WDMax	.84	.52	.31	.15	.11	.72	.36	.21	.13	.11	.14	.04	.03	.02	.02
Sequa $- Pr[m = 0]$	.78	.85	.87	.92	.93	.82	.87	.89	.92	.92	.96	.98	.98	.98	.98
Sequa $- Pr[m = 1]$	.17	.14	.12	.08	.07	.15	.12	.11	.08	.08	.04	.02	.02	.02	.02
Sequa $- Pr[m = 2]$	.04	.01	.01	.00	.00	.03	.01	.00	.00	.00	.00	.00	.00	.00	.00
BIC $- Pr[m = 0]$	.21	.33	.45	.58	.63	.62	.71	.77	.84	.87	1.0	1.0	1.0	1.0	1.0
BIC $- Pr[m = 1]$	.11	.20	.25	.23	.26	.13	.13	.15	.12	.11	.00	.00	.00	.00	.00
BIC $- Pr[m = 2]$	.21	.24	.22	.17	.11	.15	.12	.07	.04	.02	.00	.00	.00	.00	.00
LWZ $- Pr[m = 0]$	.82	.84	.87	.90	.92	.97	.98	.98	.98	.99	1.0	1.0	1.0	1.0	1.0
LWZ $- Pr[m = 1]$	.12	.10	.10	.08	.07	.03	.02	.02	.02	.01	.00	.00	.00	.00	.00
LWZ $- Pr[m = 2]$	.05	.05	.03	.01	.01	.00	.00	.00	.00	.00	.00	.00	.00	.00	.00

The results are presented in Table 8.1. Consider first the base case represented by DGP-1 in which the series is white noise. With the specification $cor\_u = 0$ and $het\_u = 0$, all tests have the right size for any value of the trimming ε. As expected, the sequential procedure chooses no break around 95% of the time. The BIC does so between 94 and 98% (depending on ε), and the LWZ 100% of the time. When different variances of the residuals are allowed across segments, we see substantial size distortions if the trimming ϵ is small. These, however, disappear when ε reaches .15 or .20. The sequential procedure is somewhat biased when $\varepsilon = .05$, but this bias disappears quickly as soon as ε reaches .10. Similar size distortions occur when allowing serial correlation in the errors ($cor\_u = 1$). These are somewhat more severe if, in addition, different variances are allowed. When $het\_u = 0$, the sequential procedure shows no size distortion at any values of ε. However, if $het\_u = 1$, the sequential procedure is adequate only if ε is at least .15.

A similar picture emerges for DGP-2 in which a random regressor is included. If $cor\_u = het\_u = 0$, all tests have the right size. However, allowing for either different variances, serial correlation, or both in the residuals induces substantial size distortions unless ε is large. When no serial correlation is allowed, the procedures have the right size if ε is at least .15; when serial correlation is allowed a larger value is needed.

The results for DGP-3, which is an AR(1), shows that if one is testing against a large number of breaks (or using the WD max test) there are some distortions even if $cor\_u = het\_u = 0$ when ε is small. The sequential procedure, however, remains adequate for any values of ε. If different variances are allowed, size distortions occur unless ε is at least .20.

The DGPs 4 to 6 are cases in which serial correlation is present in the residuals. As expected, if $cor\_u = 0$, all procedures show substantial size distortions (with positive correlation the tests are liberal, and with negative correlation they are conservative). It is therefore important to correct for serial correlation. This, however, can be done adequately only if a large trimming is used (.15 or .20 depending on the cases). An interesting feature, however, is that the sequential procedure works very well for any values of ε when the variances are constrained to be the same ($het\_u = 0$). In particular, it performs much better than the information criterion BIC (and also LWZ in the case of positive AR errors).

In summary, if no serial correlation is present and allowed for, all procedures work well for any values of the trimming ε when the specification $cor\_u = het\_u = 0$ is used. If serial correlation is present, a larger value of the trimming is needed when constructing the tests using the specification $cor\_u = 1$. This is also the case if different variances are allowed across segments. Also, the results show the sequential procedure to perform quite well for any values of the trimming provided one is correcting for serial correlation when needed and not correcting for it when it is not needed.

8.4.2 The Case with One Break

The basic data-generating process considered is (Case 1):

$$y_t = \mu_1 + \gamma_1 \Psi_t + e_t, \qquad \text{if } t \le [0.5T],$$
$$y_t = \mu_2 + \gamma_2 \Psi_t + e_t, \qquad \text{if } t > [0.5T],$$

where $\Psi_t \sim$ i.i.d $N(1, 1)$ and $e_t \sim$ i.i.d $N(0, 1)$ and both are uncorrelated. Because, no serial correlation is present in the errors and no change in the distribution of the data or the errors is allowed, we use the specification $cor\_u = het\_u = 0$ and $\varepsilon = .05$. For the tests, we use $het\_z = 1$, and to construct the confidence intervals on the break dates we use $het\_z = 0$. We consider three types of shifts: (a) a change in intercept only ($\gamma_1 = \gamma_2 = 1$), (b) a change in slope only ($\mu_1 = \mu_2 = 0$), and (c) a simultaneous change in slope and intercept.

We also consider a variation without the regressor Ψ_t^* with errors that are serially correlated:

- Case 2: $\gamma_1 = \gamma_2 = 0$ and e_t replaced by $v_t = 0.5v_{t-1} + e_t$. Here $z_t = \{1\}$.

In this second case, we use the specifications $cor\_u = 1$, $het\_u = 0$, and $\varepsilon = .20$. Again, for the tests, we use $het\_z = 1$, and to construct the confidence intervals on the break dates we use $het\_z = 0$. The experiments are performed for $T = 120$ and $T = 240$, and again 2,000 replications are used.

The results are presented in Table 8.2. Row (a) presents a case with a small change in intercept only. Here the power of the test is rather low and the coverage rate of the break date is imprecise. We will use this base case to investigate what increases power. There are, nevertheless, some features of interest. First, the power of the sup$F(k)$ test is decreasing as k increases (more so as k reaches 5; not shown). However, both $D\max$ tests have power as high as the case with $k = 1$ (which gives the highest power). Also, of the three methods to select the number of breaks, the sequential method works best. The criterion LWZ is quite inaccurate because it chooses no break 98% of the time. Row (b) considers the same specifications but doubles the sample size to 240. The power of the tests increases, the sequential method selects one break more often, and the coverage rate is better – but not to a great extent. For comparisons, row (c) keeps $T = 120$ but doubles the size of the shift in intercept. Here power increases greatly, the sequential procedure chooses $m = 1$ 95% of the time, and the exact coverage rate is close to the nominal 95%. Hence, we can conclude that what is important is not the size of the sample but the size of the break.

Row (d) presents the case of a mild change in slope. Again, the power of the sup$F(k)$ decreases as k increases, but the $D\max$ tests have power as high as the sup$F(1)$ test. Also, the sequential procedure is best to select the correct value $m = 1$, whereas the LWZ is very inaccurate. Row (e) considers merging the small shifts in intercept and slope. We see that the simultaneous occurrence of two shifts at the same dates considerably increases the power of the tests

Table 8.2 *Power of the Tests and Break Selection When $m = 1$*

			Tests (Probability of Rejection)							Probability of Selecting k Breaks									Coverage Rate
			$\sup F(k)$			$\sup F(\ell+1\mid\ell)$		$D\max$		Sequa			BIC			LWZ			
Case	Values	Specifications*	1	2	3	2|1	3|2	U	W	0	1	2	0	1	2	0	1	2	95%
a) 1, $\varepsilon = .05$, $T = 120$	$\gamma_1 = \gamma_2 = 1$, $\mu_1 = 0, \mu_2 = .5$	$cor\_u = 0$	.43	.35	.34	.03	.01	.42	.42	.57	.42	.02	.66	.32	.02	.98	.02	.00	.74
b) 1, $\varepsilon = .05$, $T = 240$	$\gamma_1 = \gamma_2 = 1$, $\mu_1 = 0, \mu_2 = .5$	$cor\_u = 0$	.66	.53	.50	.02	.01	.65	.62	.34	.65	.01	.57	.43	.00	.99	.01	.00	.80
c) 1, $\varepsilon = .05$, $T = 120$	$\gamma_1 = \gamma_2 = 1$, $\mu_1 = 0, \mu_2 = 1$	$cor\_u = 0$	.99	.97	.96	.04	.02	.99	.99	.01	.95	.04	.02	.95	.03	.36	.64	.00	.93
d) 1, $\varepsilon = .05$, $T = 120$	$\gamma_1 = 1, \gamma_2 = 1.5$, $\mu_1 = \mu_2 = 0$	$cor\_u = 0$	.79	.69	.66	.03	.01	.78	.77	.21	.77	.02	.28	.68	.03	.87	.13	.00	.83
e) 1, $\varepsilon = .05$, $T = 120$	$\gamma_1 = 1, \gamma_2 = 1.5$, $\mu_1 = 0, \mu_2 = .5$	$cor\_u = 0$	1.0	.99	.98	.04	.02	1.0	1.0	.00	.96	.04	.01	.96	.03	.18	.82	.00	.94
f) 1, $\varepsilon = .05$, $T = 120$	$\gamma_1 = 1, \gamma_2 = 2$, $\mu_1 = \mu_2 = 0$	$cor\_u = 0$	1.0	1.0	1.0	.04	.02	1.0	1.0	.00	.96	.04	.00	.97	.03	.02	.98	.00	.93
g) 1, $\varepsilon = .05$, $T = 120$	$\gamma_1 = 1, \gamma_2 = 2$, $\mu_1 = 0, \mu_2 = 1$	$cor\_u = 0$	1.0	1.0	1.0	.04	.02	1.0	1.0	.00	.96	.04	.00	.97	.03	.00	1.0	.00	.96
h) 2, $\varepsilon = .20$, $T = 120$	$\mu_1 = 0, \mu_2 = .5$	$cor\_u = 1$	.25	.27	.30	.04	.00	.30	.31	.75	.24	.01	.32	.48	.18	.68	.29	.03	.93
i) 2, $\varepsilon = .20$, $T = 240$	$\mu_1 = 0, \mu_2 = .5$	$cor\_u = 1$	.38	.34	.31	.02	.00	.39	.38	.62	.37	.01	.21	.58	.19	.64	.35	.01	.91
j) 2, $\varepsilon = .20$, $T = 120$	$\mu_1 = 0, \mu_2 = 1$	$cor\_u = 1$	.66	.61	.61	.03	.00	.68	.69	.34	.63	.02	.05	.71	.22	.23	.74	.04	.89
k) 2, $\varepsilon = .20$, $T = 240$	$\mu_1 = 0, \mu_2 = 1$	$cor\_u = 1$	.91	.85	.82	.03	.00	.91	.90	.09	.88	.03	.01	.74	.23	.07	.90	.02	.91

Note: *In all cases $het\_u = 0$. When constructing the tests, $het\_z = 1$, and when constructing the confidence intervals $het\_z = 0$.

and the precision of the selected number of breaks as well as the coverage rate of the break date (much more than an increase in sample size). Rows (e) and (f) consider a larger change in slope only and larger simultaneous changes, respectively. Here, the power of the tests is one. In such cases, the coverage rates are accurate, and all methods select the correct number of breaks accurately.

Rows (h) to (k) consider Case 2 of a change in mean with serially correlated errors. We see that the presence of serial correlation decreases the power of the test substantially. Here, for a given shift, doubling the sample size induces a negligible increase in power and in the accuracy of the selection methods or coverage rates. Nevertheless, the coverage rates are quite accurate, which shows that the nonparametric correction for the presence of serial correlation seems to be effective.

8.4.3 The Case with Two Breaks

For Case 1, the basic structure is similar except that now the data-generating process is

$$\begin{aligned} y_t &= \mu_1 + \gamma_1 \Psi_t^* + e_t^*, & &\text{if } 1 < t \leq [T/3], \\ y_t &= \mu_2 + \gamma_2 \Psi_t^* + e_t^*, & &\text{if } [T/3] < t \leq [2T/3], \\ y_t &= \mu_3 + \gamma_3 \Psi_t^* + e_t^*, & &\text{if } [2T/3] < t \leq T, \end{aligned}$$

where

$$\begin{aligned} \Psi_t^* &\sim \text{i.i.d. } N(\varsigma_1, 1), & &\text{if } 1 < t \leq [T/3], \\ \Psi_t^* &\sim \text{i.i.d. } N(\varsigma_2, 1), & &\text{if } [T/3] < t \leq [2T/3], \\ \Psi_t^* &\sim \text{i.i.d. } N(\varsigma_3, 1), & &\text{if } [2T/3] < t \leq T, \end{aligned}$$

and

$$\begin{aligned} e_t^* &\sim \text{i.i.d. } N(0, \sigma_1^2), & &\text{if } 1 < t \leq [T/3], \\ e_t^* &\sim \text{i.i.d. } N(0, \sigma_2^2), & &\text{if } [T/3] < t \leq [2T/3], \\ e_t^* &\sim \text{i.i.d. } N(0, \sigma_3^2), & &\text{if } [2T/3] < t \leq T. \end{aligned}$$

For Case 2, we have only changes in mean with serially correlated errors. That is,

$$\begin{aligned} y_t &= \mu_1 + v_t, & &\text{if } 1 < t \leq [T/3], \\ y_t &= \mu_2 + v_t, & &\text{if } [T/3] < t \leq [2T/3], \\ y_t &= \mu_3 + v_t, & &\text{if } [2T/3] < t \leq T, \end{aligned}$$

where $v_t = 0.5v_{t-1} + e_t$ with $e_t \sim$ i.i.d. $N(0, 1)$.

We first consider Case 1 in which the data and errors are identically distributed across segments, that is, $\sigma_1^2 = \sigma_2^2 = \sigma_3^2$ and $\varsigma_1 = \varsigma_2 = \varsigma_3$. Results are first presented in Table 8.3 for cases in which the shifts involve either only

Table 8.3 *Power of the Tests and Break Selection When $m = 2$. Case 1, $T = 120$, $\varepsilon = .05$, $cor\_u = 0$, $het\_u = 0$*

		Tests (Probability of Rejection)							Probability of Selecting k Breaks									Coverage Rate 95%	
		$\sup F(k)$			$\sup F(\ell+1\mid\ell)$		$D\max$		Sequa			BIC			LWZ				
	Values	1	2	3	2|1	3|2	U	W	0	1	2	0	1	2	0	1	2	#1	#2
a)	$\gamma_1 = \gamma_2 = \gamma_3 = 1$ $\mu_1 = \mu_3 = 0, \mu_2 = .5$	.13	.23	.26	.11	.01	.18	.25	.87	.11	.02	.90	.06	.04	1.0	.00	.00	.51	.49
b)	$\gamma_1 = \gamma_2 = \gamma_3 = 1$ $\mu_1 = \mu_3 = 0, \mu_2 = 1$	.41	.89	.89	.73	.03	.82	.88	.59	.08	.31	.31	.05	.62	.98	.00	.02	.87	.85
c)	$\gamma_1 = \gamma_2 = \gamma_3 = 1$ $\mu_1 = 0, \mu_2 = 1, \mu_3 = 2$	1.0	1.0	1.0	.56	.03	1.0	1.0	.00	.44	.54	.00	.38	.59	.00	.96	.04	.88	.86
d)	$\gamma_1 = \gamma_2 = \gamma_3 = 1$ $\mu_1 = 0, \mu_2 = 1, \mu_3 = -1$	1.0	1.0	1.0	.86	.04	1.0	1.0	.00	.14	.82	.00	.13	.83	.02	.67	.31	.89	.96
f)	$\gamma_1 = \gamma_2 = \gamma_3 = 1$ $\mu_1 = 0, \mu_2 = -1, \mu_3 = 2$	1.0	1.0	1.0	.86	.05	1.0	1.0	.00	.14	.82	.00	.13	.82	.00	.71	.29	.88	.99
g)	$\gamma_1 = \gamma_2 = \gamma_3 = 1$ $\mu_1 = 0, \mu_2 = 1, \mu_3 = 3$	1.0	1.0	1.0	.83	.06	1.0	1.0	.00	.17	.77	.00	.15	.80	.00	.75	.25	.88	.96
h)	$\gamma_1 = \gamma_2 = \gamma_3 = 1$ $\mu_1 = 0, \mu_2 = 2, \mu_3 = -1$	1.0	1.0	1.0	1.0	.05	1.0	1.0	.00	.00	.95	.00	.00	.96	.00	.00	1.0	.98	.99
j)	$\gamma_1 = \gamma_3 = 1, \gamma_2 = 1.5$ $\mu_1 = \mu_2 = \mu_3 = 0$	.22	.49	.52	.28	.03	.40	.50	.78	.14	.07	.75	.08	.16	1.0	.00	.00	.67	.66
k)	$\gamma_1 = \gamma_3 = 1, \gamma_2 = 2$ $\mu_1 = \mu_2 = \mu_3 = 0$	.77	1.0	1.0	.98	.04	.99	.99	.23	.01	.69	.02	.01	.93	.61	.01	.38	.92	.93
l)	$\gamma_1 = 1, \gamma_2 = 1.5, \gamma_3 = 2$ $\mu_1 = \mu_2 = \mu_3 = 0$	1.0	1.0	1.0	.14	.02	1.0	.99	.00	.85	.13	.01	.85	.13	.24	.76	.00	.68	.68
m)	$\gamma_1 = 1, \gamma_2 = 2, \gamma_3 = 3$ $\mu_1 = \mu_2 = \mu_3 = 0$	1.0	1.0	1.0	.97	.05	1.0	1.0	.00	.03	.88	.00	.02	.94	.00	.36	.64	.92	.92
o)	$\gamma_1 = 1, \gamma_2 = .5, \gamma_3 = -.5$ $\mu_1 = \mu_2 = \mu_3 = 0$	1.0	1.0	1.0	.41	.04	1.0	1.0	.00	.59	.39	.00	.57	.40	.00	.98	.02	.72	.87

Note: For the construction of the tests, we use $het\_z = 1$, and for the construction of the confidence intervals of the break dates we use $het\_z = 0$.

the intercept (rows (a) to (h)) or in the slope (rows (j) to (o)). In all cases $T = 120$, $T_1 = 40$, $T_2 = 80$, $\varepsilon = .05$, $cor\_u = 0$, $het\_u = 0$, and $het\_z = 1$ for the construction of the tests, and $het\_z = 0$ for the construction of the confidence intervals for the break dates.

We start with a case in which the detection of the number of breaks is notoriously difficult. Here, the intercept increases by some value at $T_1 = 40$ and goes back to its original value at $T_2 = 80$. Row (a) considers the case in which this change is .5. The power is, indeed, very low, and all methods basically select no break. The case in which the change is 1 (row (b)) is very instructive about the usefulness of the $D\max$ tests and the $\sup F(\ell + 1|\ell)$ test to determine the number of breaks. Here the power of the $\sup F(1)$ test is very low; hence, the sequential procedure selects two breaks only 31% of the time. The $UD\max$ and $WD\max$ tests, however, have high power (82 and 88%, respectively). The sup(2|1) test also has high power (73%). Hence, a useful strategy is to first decide that some break is present based on the $D\max$ test. Then look at the $\sup F(\ell + 1|\ell)$ to see if more than one is present. In the example of row (b) this would lead to selecting two breaks 64% of the time. Another example of the usefulness of this strategy is presented in row (k). Here, there is a change in slope from 1 to 2 then back to 1. The sequential procedure chooses two breaks only 69% of the time. The strategy discussed above, however, would lead to the selection of two breaks almost 100% of the time because the $D\max$ tests have 99% power and the $\sup F(2|1)$ has 98% power.

The case discussed above clearly show the usefulness of considering tests for multiple structural changes. As shown in Andrews (1993), a test for a single change is consistent versus an alternative hypothesis of multiple changes. As shown here, however, in finite samples the power of such a test can be quite low, whereas tests against more than one change can have much higher power. This also suggests that a mechanical application of a specific to general sequential testing procedure to select the number of breaks can be suboptimal. Indeed, in practice it is advisable to look at the double maximum tests first to avoid such cases in which it is difficult to distinguish between no break and a single break but it is easy to distinguish between no break and more than one break.

The other cases of Table 8.3 show various configurations for changes in intercept or slope. The results can be summarized as follows. First, intercept changes of the form $\mu_1 = 0, \mu_2 = 1, \mu_3 = 2$ (increasing steps) are also difficult cases in which most procedures fail to select two breaks (the same is true for slope changes of the same form). In general, when the magnitude of the change is small (or difficult to identify) the coverage rates for the break dates are too small (e.g., rows (a,b,j,l,o)). If the changes are very large (e.g., row (h) or row f, second break) they are too wide. However, in most cases in which the number of breaks is well identified the coverage rates are adequate.

Table 8.4 first considers Case 1 with simultaneous changes in intercept and slope. Row (a) shows that very little gain in power or accuracy of the coverage

Table 8.4 *Power of the Tests and Break Selection When $m = 2$*

Case	Values	Specifications*	Tests (Probability of Rejection)							Probability of Selecting k Breaks									Coverage Rate 95%	
			$\sup F(k)$			$\sup F(\ell+1\mid\ell)$		$D\max$		Sequa			BIC			LWZ				
			1	2	3	2|1	3|2	U	W	0	1	2	0	1	2	0	1	2	#1	#2
a) 1 $\varepsilon = .05$ $T = 120$	$\gamma_1 = 1, \gamma_2 = .5, \gamma_3 = 1$ $\mu_1 = \mu_3 = 0, \mu_2 = .5$	$cor\_u = 0$	.12	.21	.24	.08	.01	.17	.25	.88	.10	.02	.90	.06	.03	1.0	.00	.00	.46	.46
b) 1 $\varepsilon = .05$ $T = 240$	$\gamma_1 = 1, \gamma_2 = 1.5, \gamma_3 = 2$ $\mu_1 = 0, \mu_3 = 1, \mu_2 = 2$	$cor\_u = 0$	1.0	1.0	1.0	1.0	.05	1.0	1.0	.00	.00	.89	.00	.00	.95	.00	.12	.88	.95	.95
c) 1 $\varepsilon = .05$ $T = 120$	$\gamma_1 = 1, \gamma_2 = 2, \gamma_3 = 1$ $\mu_1 = 0, \mu_2 = 1, \mu_3 = 2$	$cor\_u = 0$	1.0	1.0	1.0	.82	.04	1.0	1.0	.00	.19	.78	.00	.17	.79	.00	.72	.28	.95	.85
d) 2 $\varepsilon = .20$ $T = 120$	$\mu_1 = \mu_3 = 0, \mu_2 = .5$	$cor\_u = 1$	.14	.28	.25	.09	.00	.23	.28	.86	.13	.01	.39	.24	.37	.79	.12	.08	.96	.95
e) 2 $\varepsilon = .20$ $T = 240$	$\mu_1 = \mu_3 = 0, \mu_2 = .5$	$cor\_u = 1$	.18	.32	.29	.11	.00	.26	.31	.82	.15	.03	.32	.20	.46	.82	.11	.07	.96	.95
f) 2 $\varepsilon = .20$ $T = 120$	$\mu_1 = \mu_3 = 0, \mu_2 = 1$	$cor\_u = 1$	.25	.58	.53	.29	.00	.48	.55	.75	.15	.09	.13	.12	.73	.51	.12	.36	.94	.94
g) 2 $\varepsilon = .20$ $T = 240$	$\mu_1 = \mu_3 = 0, \mu_2 = 1$	$cor\_u = 1$	.43	.83	.74	.55	.00	.71	.78	.57	.16	.26	.03	.04	.90	.33	.11	.56	.93	.93
h) 2 $\varepsilon = .20$ $T = 120$	$\mu_1 = \mu_3 = 0, \mu_2 = 2$	$cor\_u = 1$	.47	.97	.94	.86	.00	.94	.96	.53	.06	.41	.00	.00	.95	.02	.01	.96	.93	.93
i) 2 $\varepsilon = .20$ $T = 240$	$\mu_1 = \mu_3 = 0, \mu_2 = 2$	$cor\_u = 1$	.91	1.0	1.0	1.0	.00	1.0	1.0	.09	.00	.90	.00	.00	.97	.00	.00	1.0	.95	.94
j) 2 $\varepsilon = .20$ $T = 120$	$\mu_1 = \mu_3 = 0, \mu_2 = 4$	$cor\_u = 1$	.37	1.0	1.0	1.0	.00	1.0	1.0	.63	.00	.37	.00	.00	1.0	.00	.00	1.0	.99	.99
k) 2 $\varepsilon = .20$ $T = 240$	$\mu_1 = \mu_3 = 0, \mu_2 = 4$	$cor\_u = 1$	.96	1.0	1.0	1.0	.00	1.0	1.0	.04	.00	.96	.00	.00	1.0	.00	.00	1.0	.99	.99

Note: *In all cases $het\_u = 0$. When constructing the tests, $het\_z = 1$, and when constructing the confidence intervals $het\_z = 0$.

rates is gained when two shifts that are very difficult to identify individually occur simultaneously. Rows (b) and (c), however, show that important gains can be obtained in other cases (in particular compare row (b) of Table 8.4 with row (c) of Table 8.3).

The other parts of Table 8.4 consider Case 2 with intercept shifts and serially correlated errors with the specification $cor\_u = 1$. Rows (d) to (k) consider the difficult cases in which the mean returns to its old value at the second break. Here power is low when the change is .5 and even 1. Hence, serial correlation induces a loss in power. The coverage rates are adequate, and we conclude that the nonparametric correction for the presence of serial correlation works well. Also, we see that, for given changes in mean, an increase in the sample size has some effect on power – probably because, for given trimming ϵ, a larger number of observations allows more precise estimates of nuisance parameters related to correlation in the residuals. When the change in mean is larger, for instance 2 or 4 (see rows (h) to (k)), the power of the sup$F(1)$ test is low but the powers of the sup$F(2)$ and sup$F(2|1)$ tests are high. A model selection strategy based on these statistics would hence conclude essentially 100% of the time that two breaks are present.

Tables 8.5 and 8.6 consider cases in which the distribution of the errors and the data are heterogenous across segments. The goal is to see if applying the required corrections leads to tests, model selections, and coverage rates that are better. Table 8.5 considers data generated by the two-break model with $\gamma_1 = 1$, $\gamma_2 = 1.5$, $\gamma_3 = 0.5$ and $\mu_1 = 0$, $\mu_2 = 1.5$, $\mu_3 = .5$. Table 8.6 considers data generated by the two-break model with $\gamma_1 = 1$, $\gamma_2 = 1.5$, $\gamma_3 = 2$ and $\mu_1 = 0$, $\mu_2 = .5$, $\mu_3 = 1$. In all cases, $\sigma_1^2 = \sigma_3^2 = 1$, $\varsigma_1 = \varsigma_3 = 1$, and we vary σ_2^2 and ς_2. To ensure tests with adequate sizes, we set $\varepsilon = .15$ for the cases in Table 8.5 and consider $\varepsilon = .20$ for the cases in Table 8.6. We compare the properties of the procedures using the uncorrected versions ($het\_z = 1$ and $het\_u = 0$ in the construction of the tests and $het\_z = het\_u = 0$ in the construction of the confidence intervals) and the corrected versions ($het\_z = het\_u = 1$ in the construction of the tests and in the construction of the confidence intervals). The relevant columns are the sup$F(2|1)$ test, the probabilities of selecting two breaks, and the coverage rates of the break dates (note that for the selection procedures based on the BIC and LWZ, only the uncorrected version is presented because these methods cannot be modified to account for heterogeneity across segments).

The results show that important gains in the power of the tests can be obtained when allowing for different distributions of the errors across segments. In almost all cases, the power of the sup(2|1) test is higher when corrected. For example, in Table 8.6, when the variance of the errors is four times higher in the middle segment (and the mean of the regressors is also four times higher) and $T = 120$ (row(g)), the power of the uncorrected version is .53 whereas it is .78 when allowing for different variances. This also translates into a higher probability of selecting two breaks (76% instead of 52%),

Table 8.5 *Power of the Tests and Break Selection When $m = 2$. Different Distributions for the Errors and Data Across Segments; $cor\_u = 0$, $\varepsilon = .15$. Case 1 with $\gamma_1 = 1, \gamma_2 = 1.5, \gamma_3 = .5$ and $\mu_1 = 0, \mu_2 = .5, \mu_3 = -.5$*

		Tests (Probability of Rejection)					Probability of Selecting k Breaks									Coverage Rate 95%	
		$\sup F(k)$			$\sup F(\ell+1\|\ell)$		Sequa			BIC			LWZ				
Values	Specifications*	1	2	3	2|1	3|2	0	1	2	0	1	2	0	1	2	#1	#2
a) $T = 120$	Uncorrected	1.0	1.0	1.0	.91	.02	.00	.09	.89	.00	.08	.89	.01	.57	.42	.90	.96
$\sigma_1^2 = 1, \sigma_2^2 = 2, \sigma_3^2 = 1$																	
$\varsigma_1 = 1, \varsigma_2 = 2, \varsigma_3 = 1$	Corrected	1.0	1.0	1.0	.94	.01	.00	.06	.92							.89	.96
b) $T = 240$	Uncorrected	1.0	1.0	1.0	1.0	.02	.00	.00	.98	.00	.00	.98	.00	.20	.80	.93	.96
$\sigma_1^2 = 1, \sigma_2^2 = 2, \sigma_3^2 = 1$																	
$\varsigma_1 = 1, \varsigma_2 = 2, \varsigma_3 = 1$	Corrected	1.0	1.0	1.0	1.0	.02	.00	.00	.98							.93	.97
c) $T = 120$	Uncorrected	1.0	1.0	1.0	.78	.02	.00	.22	.77	.00	.21	.76	.01	.75	.23	.83	.94
$\sigma_1^2 = 1, \sigma_2^2 = 2, \sigma_3^2 = 1$																	
$\varsigma_1 = 1, \varsigma_2 = 4, \varsigma_3 = 1$	Corrected	1.0	1.0	1.0	.89	.02	.00	.11	.87							.89	.96
d) $T = 240$	Uncorrected	1.0	1.0	1.0	.99	.02	.00	.01	.98	.00	.02	.97	.00	.44	.56	.87	.97
$\sigma_1^2 = 1, \sigma_2^2 = 2, \sigma_3^2 = 1$																	
$\varsigma_1 = 1, \varsigma_2 = 4, \varsigma_3 = 1$	Corrected	1.0	1.0	1.0	1.0	.01	.00	.00	.99							.92	.98
e) $T = 120$	Uncorrected	1.0	1.0	1.0	.70	.02	.00	.30	.68	.00	.22	.73	.09	.68	.23	.84	.93
$\sigma_1^2 = 1, \sigma_2^2 = 4, \sigma_3^2 = 1$																	
$\varsigma_1 = 1, \varsigma_2 = 2, \varsigma_3 = 1$	Corrected	1.0	1.0	1.0	.76	.02	.00	.24	.75							.87	.94
f) $T = 240$	Uncorrected	1.0	1.0	1.0	.97	.02	.00	.03	.96	.00	.03	.93	.00	.54	.46	.88	.94
$\sigma_1^2 = 1, \sigma_2^2 = 4, \sigma_3^2 = 1$																	
$\varsigma_1 = 1, \varsigma_2 = 2, \varsigma_3 = 1$	Corrected	1.0	1.0	1.0	.98	.02	.00	.02	.97							.90	.96
g) $T = 120$	Uncorrected	1.0	1.0	1.0	.54	.03	.00	.46	.53	.00	.36	.59	.09	.80	.11	.79	.93
$\sigma_1^2 = 1, \sigma_2^2 = 4, \sigma_3^2 = 1$																	
$\varsigma_1 = 1, \varsigma_2 = 4, \varsigma_3 = 1$	Corrected	1.0	1.0	1.0	.80	.04	.00	.19	.79							.86	.94
h) $T = 240$	Uncorrected	1.0	1.0	1.0	.91	.02	.00	.09	.90	.00	.09	.86	.00	.77	.23	.88	.97
$\sigma_1^2 = 1, \sigma_2^2 = 4, \sigma_3^2 = 1$																	
$\varsigma_1 = 1, \varsigma_2 = 4, \varsigma_3 = 1$	Corrected	1.0	1.0	1.0	.98	.03	.00	.01	.96							.90	.97

Note: *Uncorrected means using $het\_z = 1$ and $het\_u = 0$ in the construction of the tests and $het\_z = 0$, $het\_u = 0$ in the construction of the confidence intervals. Corrected means that $het\_z = 1$ and $het\_u = 1$ for the construction of the tests and the confidence intervals.

Table 8.6 *Power of the Tests and Break Selection When $m = 2$. Different Distributions for the Errors and Data Across Segments; $cor\_u = 0$, $\varepsilon = .20$. Case 1 with $\gamma_1 = 1$, $\gamma_2 = 1.5$, $\gamma_3 = 2$ and $\mu_1 = 0$, $\mu_2 = .5$, $\mu_3 = 1$*

		Tests (Probability of Rejection)					Probability of Selecting k Breaks									Coverage Rate 95%	
		$\sup F(k)$			$\sup F(\ell+1\|\ell)$		Sequa			BIC			LWZ				
Values	Specifications*	1	2	3	2|1	3|2	0	1	2	0	1	2	0	1	2	#1	#2
a) $T = 120$, $\sigma_1^2 = 1, \sigma_2^2 = 2, \sigma_3^2 = 1$	Uncorrected	1.0	1.0	1.0	.73	.00	.00	.27	.73	.00	.28	.72	.01	.91	.09	.92	.91
$\varsigma_1 = 1, \varsigma_2 = 2, \varsigma_3 = 1$	Corrected	1.0	1.0	1.0	.78	.00	.00	.22	.77							.91	.90
b) $T = 240$, $\sigma_1^2 = 1, \sigma_2^2 = 2, \sigma_3^2 = 1$	Uncorrected	1.0	1.0	1.0	1.0	.00	.00	.01	.98	.00	.01	.99	.00	.46	.54	.94	.94
$\varsigma_1 = 1, \varsigma_2 = 2, \varsigma_3 = 1$	Corrected	1.0	1.0	1.0	1.0	.00	.00	.00	.98							.94	.94
c) $T = 120$, $\sigma_1^2 = 1, \sigma_2^2 = 2, \sigma_3^2 = 1$	Uncorrected	1.0	1.0	1.0	.63	.00	.00	.37	.63	.00	.39	.61	.00	.95	.05	.83	.85
$\varsigma_1 = 1, \varsigma_2 = 4, \varsigma_3 = 1$	Corrected	1.0	1.0	1.0	.79	.00	.00	.21	.79							.90	.91
d) $T = 240$, $\sigma_1^2 = 1, \sigma_2^2 = 2, \sigma_3^2 = 1$	Uncorrected	1.0	1.0	1.0	.99	.00	.00	.02	.98	.00	.03	.97	.00	.69	.31	.88	.89
$\varsigma_1 = 1, \varsigma_2 = 4, \varsigma_3 = 1$	Corrected	1.0	1.0	1.0	.99	.00	.00	.01	.98							.93	.92
e) $T = 120$, $\sigma_1^2 = 1, \sigma_2^2 = 4, \sigma_3^2 = 1$	Uncorrected	1.0	1.0	1.0	.28	.00	.00	.72	.28	.00	.68	.32	.08	.91	.01	.90	.91
$\varsigma_1 = 1, \varsigma_2 = 2, \varsigma_3 = 1$	Corrected	1.0	1.0	1.0	.40	.02	.00	.60	.40							.92	.92
f) $T = 240$, $\sigma_1^2 = 1, \sigma_2^2 = 4, \sigma_3^2 = 1$	Uncorrected	1.0	1.0	1.0	.87	.00	.00	.13	.87	.00	.15	.85	.00	.94	.06	.92	.91
$\varsigma_1 = 1, \varsigma_2 = 2, \varsigma_3 = 1$	Corrected	1.0	1.0	1.0	.91	.00	.00	.09	.90							.92	.93
g) $T = 120$, $\sigma_1^2 = 1, \sigma_2^2 = 4, \sigma_3^2 = 1$	Uncorrected	1.0	1.0	1.0	.22	.01	.00	.78	.22	.00	.71	.28	.06	.93	.01	.84	.84
$\varsigma_1 = 1, \varsigma_2 = 4, \varsigma_3 = 1$	Corrected	1.0	1.0	1.0	.60	.02	.00	.40	.60							.90	.90
h) $T = 240$, $\sigma_1^2 = 1, \sigma_2^2 = 4, \sigma_3^2 = 1$	Uncorrected	1.0	1.0	1.0	.82	.00	.00	.18	.81	.00	.23	.77	.00	.97	.03	.88	.89
$\varsigma_1 = 1, \varsigma_2 = 4, \varsigma_3 = 1$	Corrected	1.0	1.0	1.0	.98	.01	.00	.02	.96							.91	.91

Note: *Uncorrected means using $het\_z = 1$ and $het\_u = 0$ in the construction of the tests and $het\_z = 0$, $het\_u = 0$ in the construction of the confidence intervals. Corrected means that $het\_z = 1$ and $het\_u = 1$ for the construction of the tests and the confidence intervals.

making the sequential procedure more suitable for selecting the number of breaks than the BIC. Even stronger comparisons obtain with the second case presented in Table 8.6. For example, in row (g) we see an increase in the power of the $\sup F(2|1)$ test, and the probability of choosing two breaks rises from 22 to 60%. The results also show that correcting for heterogeneity in the data improves the coverage rates of the confidence intervals of the break dates.

8.5 SUMMARY AND PRACTICAL RECOMMENDATIONS

The simulations have shown the tests, model selection procedures, and the construction of the confidence intervals for the break dates to be useful tools for analyzing models with multiple breaks. Care must be taken, however, when using particular specifications. We make the following recommendations.

- First, ensure that the specifications are such that the size of the tests are adequate under the hypothesis of no break. If serial correlation, heterogeneity, or both in the data or errors across segments are not allowed in the estimated regression model (and not present in the DGP), using any value of the trimming ε will lead to tests with adequate sizes. If such features are allowed, however, a higher trimming is needed. The simulations show that, with a sample of $T = 120$, $\varepsilon = .15$ should be sufficient for heterogeneity in the errors or the data. If serial correlation is allowed, $\varepsilon = .20$ may be needed. These could be reduced if larger sample sizes were available.
- Overall, selecting the break point using the BIC works well when breaks are present but less so under the null hypothesis – especially if serial correlation is present. The method based on the LWZ criterion works better under the null hypothesis (even with serial correlation) by imposing a higher penalty. This higher penalty, however, translates into very bad performance when breaks are present. Also, model selection procedures based on information criteria cannot take into account potential heterogeneity across segments unlike the sequential method. Overall, the sequential procedure works best in selecting the number of breaks.
- There are important instances in which the performance of the sequential procedure can be improved. A useful strategy is first to look at the $UD\max$ or $WD\max$ tests to see if at least a break is present. Then the number of breaks can be decided based on an examination of the $\sup F(\ell + 1|\ell)$ statistics constructed using estimates of the break dates obtained from a global minimization of the sum of squared residuals. This is, in our opinion, the preferred strategy.
- The power of the $UD\max$ or $WD\max$ tests is almost as high as the power of a test of no change versus an alternative hypothesis that specifies the true number of changes. This provides added justifications for their use in practice.

- The coverage rates for the break dates are adequate unless the break is either too small (so small as not to be detected by the tests) or too big. This is, from a practical point of view, however, an encouraging result. The confidence intervals are inadequate (in that they miss the true break value too often) exactly in those situations in which it would be quite difficult to conclude that a break is present (in which case they would not be used anyway). When the breaks are very large, the confidence intervals do contain the true values but are quite wide, leading to a conservative assessment of the accuracy of the estimates. It was found that correcting for heterogeneity in the data, errors across segments, or both yields improvements over a more straightforward uncorrected interval. Correcting for serial correlation also leads to substantial improvements.
- Correcting for heterogeneity in the distribution of the data or the errors and for serial correlation also improves the power of the tests and the accuracy in the selection of the number of breaks.

References

Andrews, D. W. K. (1991). "Heteroskedasticity and autocorrelation consistent covariance matrix estimation," *Econometrica*, 59, 817–858.

Andrews, D. W. K. (1993). "Tests for parameter instability and structural change with unknown change point," *Econometrica*, 61, 821–856.

Andrews, D. W. K. and J. C. Monahan (1992). "An improved heteroskedasticity and autocorrelation consistent covariance matrix estimator," *Econometrica*, 60, 953–966.

Bai, J. (1997a). "Estimation of a change point in multiple regression models," *Review of Economics and Statistics*, 79, 551–563.

Bai, J. (1997b). "Estimating multiple breaks one at a time," *Econometric Theory*, 13, 315–352.

Bai, J. and P. Perron (1998). "Estimating and testing linear models with multiple structural changes," *Econometrica*, 66, 47–78.

Bai, J. and P. Perron (2003a). "Computation and analysis of multiple structural change models," *Journal of Applied Econometrics*, 18, 1–22.

Bai, J. and P. Perron (2003b). "Critical values for multiple structural change tests," *Econometrics Journal*, 6, 72–78.

Liu, J., S. Wu, and J. V. Zidek (1997). "On segmented multivariate regressions," *Statistica Sinica*, 7, 497–525.

Perron, P. (1997). "L'estimation de modèles avec changements structurels multiples," *Actualité Économique*, 73, 457–505.

Yao, Y-C. (1988). "Estimating the number of change-points via Schwarz' Criterion," *Statistics and Probability Letters*, 6, 181–189.

PART FOUR

LAD AND QUANTILE REGRESSION

NINE

On Efficient, Robust, and Adaptive Estimation in Cointegrated Models

Douglas J. Hodgson*

9.1 INTRODUCTION

One of the many topics in the field of time series econometrics to which Peter Phillips has made contributions of great importance and originality is that of the estimation of cointegrated models. This is one of many areas in which his doctoral students from Yale have also made contributions. To enumerate all the contributions that Phillips and his students have made (and are making) in the area of unit roots and cointegration (not to mention fractionally integrated processes) would take a great deal of time and space; thus, in this introduction we restrict ourselves to highlighting some of the more important papers that Phillips has written on the topic of efficient and robust estimation of cointegrating regressions, position these papers within the larger literature on this topic, and then briefly summarize the contents of this chapter.

Phillips and Durlauf (1986) and Stock (1987) have shown that a cointegrating regression can be superconsistently estimated by ordinary least squares (OLS). However, OLS generally has a nuisance–parameter-dependent asymptotic distribution and is not asymptotically mixed normally distributed. It is also not efficient in the class of estimators of the "triangular" representation of a cointegrated system on which the variables treated as the regressors are conditioned. In other words, OLS is not asymptotically equivalent to the limited information maximum likelihood estimator (LIMLE) of such a system. The fully modified OLS (FM–OLS) estimator of Phillips and Hansen (1990), however, not only has a nuisance–parameter-free, mixed normal asymptotic distribution, but it will be efficient in the sense of having the same asymptotic distribution as the Gaussian LIMLE. Phillips and Loretan (1991) derived an alternative approach to obtaining an asymptotically equivalent estimator, the

* Financial support is acknowledged from the National Science Foundation (SBR-9701959), the Social Sciences and Humanities Research Council of Canada and l'Institut de Finance Mathématique de Montréal.

so-called lags and leads estimator (developed independently by Saikkonen 1991 and Stock and Watson 1993, who term the estimator "dynamic OLS"). A related estimator is the canonical cointegrating regressions estimator of Park (1992). Gaussian full-information maximum likelihood estimators of cointegrated systems specified as error correction models were derived by Johansen (1988) and Ahn and Reinsel (1990). Phillips (1991) has provided a detailed and insightful discussion of efficient Gaussian estimation in cointegrated systems.

Because many of the economic time series likely to contain unit roots are such financial variables as stock prices, interest rates, and exchange rates, it is of interest to investigate the possibilities for robust or efficient estimation in the presence of possibly non-Gaussian disturbances in cointegrating regressions. Since financial variables tend to be characterized by distributions that are considerably thicker-tailed than the normal, estimators that downweight outlying observations provide an attractive alternative to least-squares and Gaussian ML estimators. Robust least absolute deviation (LAD) and M-estimators in cointegrating regressions are analyzed by Phillips (1995), who derives fully modified LAD (FM–LAD) and M-(FM-M) estimators having asymptotic distributions that are free of nuisance parameters and mixed normal. The estimators have been implemented in an empirical analysis of forward and spot exchange rates by Phillips, McFarland, and McMahon (1996). Optimal adaptive estimation in the presence of possibly non-Gaussian disturbances has been considered by Jeganathan (1995) and Hodgson (1998a,b), and this chapter extends this line of investigation.

Jeganathan (1995) developed an adaptive estimator of a single-equation cointegrating regression in which one conditions on the regressors (thus the resulting estimator is asymptotically equivalent to LIML) and the disturbances to the regression are iid, the regressor first differences are independent and identically distributed (iid), and the joint density of the disturbances and regressor first differences are elliptically symmetric but otherwise unknown. Hodgson (1998a) extended Jeganathan's (1995) model by allowing the regression disturbances to follow a general stationary and invertible autoregressive moving average (ARMA) process, but the iid assumption on the regressor first differences is maintained. The FM–OLS estimator of Phillips and Hansen (1990) has the benefit of allowing for general autocorrelation in the disturbances and regressor first differences as well as nonparametric treatment of the autocorrelation while still arriving at an estimator that is equivalent to LIML through the use of a preliminary estimate of the joint long-run covariance matrix of the disturbances and regressor first differences. The robust estimators of Phillips (1995) obtain asymptotic mixed normality through similar means but are not asymptotically efficient. In fact, it seems to the present author that it is not possible to achieve fully efficient estimates in non-Gaussian cointegrated models without parameterically modeling the short-run dynamics through a vector ARMA model or a vector autoregressive (VAR) model. In this chapter we consider efficent estimation in possibly non-Gaussian cointegrated models for which such a vector autoregressive moving average (VARMA) model has been specified. Once such a model has been specified, however, it is actually a simpler matter to compute full-information maximum likelihood (FIML) than it is to compute LIML. Because the former is generally a more efficient estimator than the latter, we concern ourselves only with obtaining FIML estimates.

The Gaussian FIML estimators of Johansen (1988) and Ahn and Reinsel (1990), which consider estimation of the cointegrated error correction representation of a vector autoregression, are extended to allow for a data-generating process in the VARMA class by Yap and Reinsel (1995). Hodgson (1998b), working with Ahn and Reinsel's (1990) specification of the VAR error correction model, has obtained a fully efficient adaptive estimator of the cointegrating parameters under the assumption that the VAR innovations are iid and symmetrically distributed but of otherwise unknown distributional form. This chapter extends Hodgson (1998b) in that we allow the data to follow a general VARMA process analogous to Yap and Reinsel's (1995) extension of Ahn and Reinsel (1990). The resulting adaptive estimator will be asymptotically equivalent to the FIML for this model. Note that the estimators we derive for the triangular and error correction parameterizations of the model will be asymptotically equivalent to the FIML and therefore to each other. The two parameterizations we consider basically represent alternative approaches to parameterizing the transitory dynamics of the system, and thus the parameterization to be used in applied work will depend on the purposes or tastes of the investigator.

In the following section we present the two parameterizations of the model and show how to compute efficient estimators for both models when the short-run dynamics and the distribution of the errors are known. The estimators take the form of one-step iterations for which the existence of a consistent preliminary estimator (such as OLS) is assumed. We then proceed to discuss the issue of relaxing the respective assumptions of known short-run dynamics and known error distribution. The former issue is dealt with through standard model selection and estimation techniques for VARMA models, whereas the latter issue is handled through the application of nonparametric kernel density estimation techniques to the residuals from the estimated VARMA model. We also consider the implications for reducing the dimensionality of the nonparametric density estimation problem of assuming that the errors have an elliptically symmetric distribution (an assumption made by Jeganathan 1995 but not exploited for its dimensionality-reduction possibilities). The assumption made in most of this literature that the dependence in a time series is fully captured through the modeling of its autocorrelations is at variance with the presence of conditional heteroskedasticity in many time series. In Section 9.3, we discuss the implications for the estimators developed in Section 9.2 of the presence of unmodeled conditional heteroskedasticity in the data, obtaining the asymptotic distribution of the parametric one-step iterative estimator but not of the semiparametric iterative "adaptive" estimator. Nevertheless, it is conjectured that the latter will deliver robust estimates by controlling for the thick tails present in the unconditional density of the conditionally heteroskedastic disturbances. This conjecture is evaluated in Section 9.4 through a brief Monte Carlo simulation exercise. An appendix presents detailed discussions of some relevant topics touched on in the main text.

9.2 MAXIMUM LIKELIHOOD ESTIMATION OF COINTEGRATING PARAMETERS

This section introduces the model specifications we are concerned with estimating and derives expressions for fully efficient estimators of the cointegrating parameters in the respective models. In the first part, we analyze the triangular representation, and in the second part we are concerned with the error correction representation. In both cases we derive estimators under the assumption that the remainder of the model is known – in particular that the lag order of the ARMA component of the model is known, that the parameters of the ARMA component are known, and that the distribution function of the errors is known. In the last part, we discuss practical issues of efficient estimation that arise in the more realistic situation in which these "nuisance" components of the model specification are unknown. We focus principally on the problem of unknown error density and its nonparametric estimation.

9.2.1 The Triangular Representation

We assume that the I(1) m_1-vector time series y_t and m_2-vector series x_t are observed for $t = 1, \ldots, n$ and are generated according to the following triangular representation of a cointegrated system:

$$y_t = Cx_t + u_{1t} \tag{1}$$

$$x_t = x_{t-1} + u_{2t}, \tag{2}$$

where C is an $m_1 \times m_2$ matrix of unknown cointegrating coefficients that has $rank = \min(m_1, m_2)$. The stationary m_3-vector process $u_t = \left(u_{1t}^T, u_{2t}^T\right)^T$ is generated by the following vector ARMA(p, q) model (where $m_3 = m_1 + m_2$):

$$u_t = A_1 u_{t-1} + \cdots + A_p u_{t-p} + \varepsilon_t + B_1 \varepsilon_{t-1} + \cdots + B_q \varepsilon_{t-q}.$$

We assume that this process is stationary and invertible (i.e., all roots of the polynomials $|A(z)| = |I - A_1 z - \cdots - A_p z^p| = 0$ and $|B(z)| = |I + B_1 z + \cdots + B_q z^q| = 0$ lie outside the unit circle) and that it is identified[1] (cf. Lutkepohl 1991). We initially assume that the lag orders p and q are known as are the parameters of the ARMA model. These assumptions are obviously unrealistic but facilitate our derivation of the asymptotic theory

[1] Some sufficient conditions for identification are presented in the appendix.

for the maximum likelihood (ML) and adaptive estimators of C because this asymptotic theory is the same whether these quantites are known or not. We will later drop this assumption and discuss practical issues in the estimation of the cointegrating parameters when the stationary component of the model is also unknown.

We assume that the innovations $\{\varepsilon_t\}$ are iid from the absolutely continuous Lebesgue density $f(\varepsilon)$, the negative of whose score we denote by $\psi(\varepsilon) = (\partial f(\varepsilon)/\partial\varepsilon)/f(\varepsilon)$ and whose finite, positive definite information matrix is $\Omega = \int \psi(\varepsilon)\psi(\varepsilon)^T f(\varepsilon)\,d\varepsilon$. Define the $m(=m_1m_2)$-dimensional full-parameter vector $\theta = \text{vec}(C)$ whose true value is θ_0 and which belongs to the parameter space Θ which is taken to be all of R^m except for points at which C is of deficient rank. Assume the existence of initial conditions $\underline{\varepsilon}_0 = (\varepsilon_0, \ldots, \varepsilon_{1-q}, x_0, \ldots, x_{1-p}, y_0, \ldots, y_{1-p})$ with continuous Lebesgue density $f_0(\underline{\varepsilon}_0;\theta)$ which has the property that $f_0(\underline{\varepsilon}_0;\theta_n) - f_0(\underline{\varepsilon}_0;\theta_0) = o_p(1)$ in $P_{\theta_0,n}$ if $\theta_n \to \theta_0$, where the probability measure $P_{\theta_0,n}$ represents the distribution of the sample $(\underline{\varepsilon}_0, x_1, \ldots, x_n, y_1, \ldots, y_n)$.

Note that we can rewrite (1) as

$$y_t = \left(I_{m_1} \otimes x_t^T\right)\theta + u_{1t}. \tag{3}$$

The likelihood function is

$$\mathcal{L}_n(\theta) = f_0(\underline{\varepsilon}_0;\theta) \cdot \prod_{t=1}^{n} f(\varepsilon_t(\theta)).$$

To derive an expression for efficient estimators in this model, we need to obtain an explicit expression for ε_t in terms of observables and unknown parameters. Following Kreiss's (1987) analysis of univariate ARMA models, note that we have

$$(1 + B_1 z + \cdots B_q z^q)^{-1} = \sum_{k=0}^{\infty} \Gamma_k z^k$$

and $\sum_{k=0}^{\infty} \|\Gamma_k\| < \infty$, where $\|\cdot\|$ denotes the matrix norm. We can compute the elements of $\{\Gamma_k\}$ using the following recursive formula:

$$\Gamma_s + B_1\Gamma_{s-1} + \cdots + B_q\Gamma_{s-q} = 0 \ \ \forall s \geq 1,$$

where $\Gamma_k = 0\ \forall k < 0$ and $\Gamma_0 = I$. With this notation, we have the following representation of the innovation vector:

$$\begin{aligned}
\varepsilon_t(\theta) &= \sum_{k=1}^{t-1} \Gamma_{k-1}\left(-\sum_{i=1}^{p} A_i u_{t+1-k-i}\right) + \sum_{s=0}^{q-1} \varepsilon_{-s}\left(\sum_{k=0}^{s} \Gamma_{t+s-k} B_k\right) \\
&= \sum_{k=1}^{t-1} \Gamma_{k-1}\left[-\sum_{i=1}^{p} A_i \begin{pmatrix} y_{t+1-k-i} - \left(I_{m_1} \otimes x_{t+1-k-i}^T\right)\theta \\ x_{t+1-k-i} - x_{t-k-i} \end{pmatrix}\right] \\
&\quad + \sum_{s=0}^{q-1} \varepsilon_{-s}\left(\sum_{k=0}^{s} \Gamma_{t+s-k} B_k\right).
\end{aligned}$$

We can therefore rewrite the likelihood as

$$\mathcal{L}_n(\theta) = f_0(\underline{\varepsilon}_0;\theta)\cdot\prod_{t=1}^{n} f$$

$$\times\left\{\begin{array}{l}\sum_{k=1}^{t-1}\Gamma_{k-1}\left[-\sum_{i=1}^{p}A_i\begin{pmatrix} y_{t+1-k-i}-\left(I_{m_1}\otimes x_{t+1-k-i}^T\right)\theta \\ x_{t+1-k-i}-x_{t-k-i}\end{pmatrix}\right] \\ \quad +\sum_{s=0}^{q-1}\varepsilon_{-s}\left(\sum_{k=0}^{s}\Gamma_{t+s-k}B_k\right)\end{array}\right\}$$

and the log-likelihood as

$$\log\mathcal{L}_n(\theta) = \log f_0(\underline{\varepsilon}_0;\theta) + \sum_{t=1}^{n}\log f$$

$$\times\left\{\begin{array}{l}\sum_{k=1}^{t-1}\Gamma_{k-1}\left[-\sum_{i=1}^{p}A_i\begin{pmatrix} y_{t+1-k-i}-\left(I_{m_1}\otimes x_{t+1-k-i}^T\right)\theta \\ x_{t+1-k-i}-x_{t-k-i}\end{pmatrix}\right] \\ \quad +\sum_{s=0}^{q-1}\varepsilon_{-s}\left(\sum_{k=0}^{s}\Gamma_{t+s-k}B_k\right)\end{array}\right\}.$$

We have the following approximation to the score scaled by n^{-1}:

$$\begin{aligned} W_n(\theta) &= -n^{-1}\sum_{t=1}^{n}\left[\sum_{k=1}^{t-1}\Gamma_{k-1}\sum_{i=1}^{p}A_i\begin{pmatrix} I_{m_1}\otimes x_{t+1-k-i}^T \\ 0_{m_2\times m}\end{pmatrix}\right]^T\psi\left(\varepsilon_t(\theta)\right) \\ &= -n^{-1}\sum_{t=1}^{n}H_{t-1}^T\psi\left(\varepsilon_t(\theta)\right), \end{aligned}$$

and the approximate sample information scaled by n^{-2}:

$$S_n(\theta) = n^{-2}\sum_{t=1}^{n}H_{t-1}^T\Omega H_{t-1}.$$

We denote the local approximation to the parameter vector θ_0 by $\theta_n = \theta_0 + n^{-1}h_n$, where $\{h_n\}$ is a sequence of bounded m-vectors. Our first concern is with the asymptotic behavior of the log-likelihood ratio statistic

$$\Lambda_n(\theta_n,\theta) = \log\left(\frac{dP_{\theta_n,n}}{dP_{\theta_0,n}}\right).$$

We can apply results of Jeganathan (1995) to obtain the following result on the locally asymptotically mixed normal (LAMN) structure of the likelihood ratio:

Proposition 9.1 *The likelihood ratio has the following quadratic approximation in this model:*

$$\Lambda_n(\theta_n,\theta) = h_n^T W_n(\theta) - \left(\frac{1}{2}\right)h_n^T S_n(\theta)h_n + o_p(1) in\ P_{\theta_0,n}.$$

Furthermore, our model falls with the LAMN family, that is, the following convergence result obtains:

$$L(W_n(\theta), S_n(\theta)) \Rightarrow L\left[S(\theta_0)^{-1/2} N(0, I), S(\theta_0)\right],$$

where $S(\theta_0)$ *is the asymptotic information matrix and has the following form:*

$$S(\theta_0) = \int_0^1 (I_{m_1} \otimes B_x, 0_{m \times m_2}) \Upsilon \begin{bmatrix} I_{m_1} \otimes B_x^T \\ 0_{m_2 \times m} \end{bmatrix},$$

where $\Upsilon = \left[\sum_{k=0}^{\infty} \sum_{i=1}^{p} A_i^T \Gamma_k^T\right] \Omega \left[\sum_{k=0}^{\infty} \sum_{i=1}^{p} \Gamma_k A_i\right]$ *and* B_x *is a Brownian motion with variance* $E\left[\Delta x_t \Delta x_t^T\right]$.

With this result on the likelihood, we can obtain a characterization of an asymptotically efficient estimator for our model. Because of our LAMN limit theory, it turns out that an estimator asymptotically mixed normal with an asymptotic covariance matrix equal to the inverse of the asymptotic information is optimal, or asymptotically efficient, according to the locally asymptotically minimax (LAM) criterion. Formally, we have the following definition:

Definition A sequence of estimators $\{\widehat{\theta}_n\}$ of θ_0 is efficient if

$$n\left(\widehat{\theta}_n - \theta_0\right) - S_n^{-1}(\theta_0) W_n(\theta_0) = o_p(1)$$

in $P_{\theta_0,n}$. It follows that

$$L\left[n\left(\widehat{\theta}_n - \theta_0\right)\right] \Rightarrow L\left\{MN\left[0, S(\theta_0)^{-1}\right]\right\}.$$

Now suppose that we have some discretized[2] preliminary estimator θ_n^* having the property that $n(\theta_n^* - \theta_0) = O_p(1)$ in $P_{\theta_0,n}$. Then we can construct the following asymptotically efficient one-step iterative estimator of θ_0:

$$\overline{\theta}_n = \theta_n^* + n^{-1} S_n^{-1}(\theta_n^*) W_n(\theta_n^*).$$

We will discuss the problems of unknown ARMA parameters and unknown innovation density in Section 9.2.3.

9.2.2 The Error Correction Representation

Suppose we observe the m_3-vector of I(1) time series Z_t, $t = 1, \ldots, n$, which are generated by the following partially nonstationary vector ARMA model (cf. Yap and Reinsel (1995)):

$$Z_t = A_1 Z_{t-1} + \cdots + A_p Z_{t-p} + \varepsilon_t + B_1 \varepsilon_{t-1} + \cdots + B_q \varepsilon_{t-q},$$

[2] See the appendix for a discussion of discretization.

where the m_3-vector iid innovation process ε_t has the same properties as in the triangular model. We assume that $\det(I - A_1 z - \cdots - A_p z^p) = 0$ has m_2 roots on the unit circle and $m_1 = m_3 - m_2$ roots outside the unit circle and that all roots of $\det(I + B_1 z + \cdots + B_q z^q) = 0$ lie outside the unit circle. We also assume that conditions for identification of the ARMA parameters are satisfied.[3]

We can write this system in the following error correction format (cf. Yap and Reinsel 1995):

$$\Delta Z_t = AZ_{t-1} + \sum_{j=1}^{p-1} \widetilde{A}_j \Delta Z_{t-j} + \varepsilon_t + \sum_{j=1}^{q} B_j \varepsilon_{t-j}, \tag{4}$$

where $\widetilde{A}_j = -\sum_{k=j+1}^{p} A_k \, \forall j = 1, \ldots, p-1$ and $A = -\left(I - \sum_{j=1}^{p} A_j\right)$. Because the system has only m_2 unit roots, A will have reduced rank equal to m_1, corresponding to the presence in the system of this number of cointegrating relationships. We therefore have the decomposition $A = \alpha_0 \alpha_1^T$, where α_0 and α_1 are $m_3 \times m_1$ matrices of full-column rank, the former containing the error correction coefficients for the model and the latter's columns constituting the cointegrating vectors for the system. Assuming an identified system, we write $\alpha_1^T = [I_{m_1}, -C]$, where C is an $m_1 \times m_2$ matrix of cointegrating parameters and uses the decomposition $Z_t = \left[Y_t^T, X_t^T\right]^T$ in which Y_t is an m_1-vector and X_t is an m_2-vector among whose elements no cointegrating relationships exist (i.e., the process $\{X_t\}$ contains m_2 unit roots). This notation allows us to rewrite (4) as

$$\begin{aligned}\Delta Z_t &= \alpha_0 \left[Y_{t-1} - CX_{t-1}\right] + \sum_{j=1}^{p-1} \widetilde{A}_j \Delta Z_{t-j} + \varepsilon_t + \sum_{j=1}^{q} B_j \varepsilon_{t-j} \\ &= \alpha_0 \left[Y_{t-1} - \left(I_{m_1} \otimes X_{t-1}^T\right)\theta\right] + \sum_{j=1}^{p-1} \widetilde{A}_j \Delta Z_{t-j} + \varepsilon_t + \sum_{j=1}^{q} B_j \varepsilon_{t-j},\end{aligned}$$

where $\theta = \operatorname{vec}(C)$ is the $m (= m_1 m_2)$ $-$vector of cointegrating parameters we wish to estimate. We denote its true value by θ_0. We proceed to describe the construction of efficient and adaptive estimators of this parameter under the assumption that the parameters α_0, $\left\{A_j^*\right\}_{j=1}^{p-1}$, and $\left\{B_j\right\}_{j=1}^{q}$ are known to the investigator. As in the triangular model, this assumption facilitates derivation of the estimators and their asymptotic properties and can be relaxed without affecting our theory.

To derive an expression for the likelihood function of our model, and hence of an efficient iterative estimator, we employ the following closed-form

[3] See the appendix.

solution for ε_t:

$$\varepsilon_t = \sum_{k=1}^{t} \Gamma_{k-1} \left\{ \Delta Z_t - \alpha_0 \left[Y_{t-1} - \left(I_{m_1} \otimes X_{t-1}^T \right) \theta \right] - \sum_{j=1}^{p-1} \widetilde{A}_j \Delta Z_{t-j} \right\} + \sum_{s=0}^{q-1} \varepsilon_{-s} \left(\sum_{k=0}^{s} \Gamma_{t+s-k} B_k \right).$$

This allows us to define the approximate sample score, scaled by n^{-1}, as

$$W_n(\theta) = -n^{-1} \sum_{t=1}^{n} \left[\sum_{k=1}^{t} \Gamma_{k-1} \alpha_0 \left(I_{m_1} \otimes X_{t-1}^T \right) \right]^T \psi(\varepsilon_t)$$
$$= -n^{-1} \sum_{t=1}^{n} H_{t-1}^T \psi(\varepsilon_t),$$

where $H_{t-1} = \left[\sum_{k=1}^{t} \Gamma_{k-1} \alpha_0 \left(I_{m_1} \otimes X_{t-1}^T \right) \right]$. We can also define the approximate sample information, scaled by n^{-2}, as follows:

$$S_n(\theta) = n^{-2} \sum_{t=1}^{n} H_{t-1}^T \Omega H_{t-1}.$$

We can prove a LAMN result in the same way as was done for the triangular model and have the result that $S_n(\theta) \Rightarrow S(\theta_0)$, where $S(\theta_0)$ is the asymptotic information matrix and has the form

$$S(\theta_0) = \int_0^1 \left(I_{m_1} \otimes B_x \right) \Upsilon \left(I_{m_1} \otimes B_x^T \right),$$

where $\Upsilon = \alpha_0^T \left(\sum_{k=1}^{\infty} \Gamma_{k-1}^T \right) \Omega \left(\sum_{k=1}^{\infty} \Gamma_{k-1} \right) \alpha_0$. We can use these expressions for $W_n(\theta)$ and $S_n(\theta)$ to construct one-step iterative estimators $\overline{\theta}_n$ in the manner described at the end of Section 9.2.1 for the triangular model.

9.2.3 Practical Implementation

For both of the parameterizations just discussed, the one-step iterative estimator $\overline{\theta}_n$ will be fully efficient provided that the preliminary estimator θ_n^* is consistent at the rate of n, that the transitory dynamics are well-specified (i.e., that the ARMA orders p and q are correctly chosen), that the parameters of the VARMA process are known, and that the functional form of the innovation density $f(\varepsilon)$, and in particular of its score $\psi(\varepsilon)$, are known. All of these assumptions require some further discussion. First, it is not difficult to find an n-consistent preliminary estimator. Ordinary least squares, for example, will have this property under very general conditions. The remaining assumptions are not so easy to handle in practice, although on theoretical grounds they can be relaxed and dealt with using more or less standard techniques without any loss in asymptotic efficiency.

Define the time series of residuals to the preliminary estimation of the cointegrating regression by

$$u_{1t}^* = Y_t - C_n^* X_t,$$

where C_n^* is the preliminary estimator (OLS, for example). Define the full vector of transitory deviations from the triangular representation of the system by $u_t^* = \left(u_{1t}^{*T}, u_{2t}^T\right)^T$, where $u_{2t} = X_t - X_{t-1}$. Then our problem is to fit lag orders p and q, and then to estimate the parameters, of the following VARMA model:

$$u_t^* = A_1 u_{t-1}^* + \cdots + A_p u_{t-p}^* + \varepsilon_t + B_1 \varepsilon_{t-1} + \cdots + B_q \varepsilon_{t-q}. \tag{5}$$

In the case of the error correction representation, the corresponding model to fit and estimate is

$$\Delta Z_t = \alpha_0 u_{1t}^* + \sum_{j=1}^{p-1} \widetilde{A}_j \Delta Z_{t-j} + \varepsilon_t + \sum_{j=1}^{q} B_j \varepsilon_{t-j}. \tag{6}$$

The issue of order selection and estimation in VARMA models is an involved one and would consume too much space to discuss in any detail here, and so we refer the reader to Lutkepohl (1991) for a discussion of these topics.

Denote by p^* and q^* the VARMA lag orders arrived at by applying a consistent order selection criterion to eqs. (5) or (6). Next, estimate these systems using a $\sqrt{n}$-consistent estimator, such as Gaussian maximum likelihood estimation (MLE) to deliver estimates for (5) of

$$\left(A_1^*, \ldots, A_{p^*}^*, B_1^*, \ldots, B_{q^*}^*\right)$$

and for (6) of

$$\left(\alpha_0^*, \widetilde{A}_1^*, \ldots, \widetilde{A}_{p^*-1}^*, B_1^*, \ldots, B_{q^*}^*\right).$$

Now define the sequence of matrices $\left\{\Gamma_k^*\right\}_{k=0}^{\infty}$ by

$$\left(1 + B_1^* z + \cdots B_{q^*}^* z^{q^*}\right)^{-1} = \sum_{k=0}^{\infty} \Gamma_k^* z^k$$

and define the estimated residuals $\left\{\varepsilon_t^*\right\}$ as follows for the triangular representation:

$$\begin{aligned}
\varepsilon_t^* &= \sum_{k=1}^{t-1} \Gamma_{k-1}^* \left(- \sum_{i=1}^{p^*} A_i^* u_{t+1-k-i}^* \right) + \sum_{s=0}^{q^*-1} \varepsilon_{-s}^* \left(\sum_{k=0}^{s} \Gamma_{t+s-k}^* B_k^* \right) \\
&= \sum_{k=1}^{t-1} \Gamma_{k-1}^* \left\{ - \sum_{i=1}^{p^*} A_i^* \begin{bmatrix} y_{t+1-k-i} - \left(I_{m_1} \otimes x_{t+1-k-i}^T\right) \theta^* \\ x_{t+1-k-i} - x_{t-k-i} \end{bmatrix} \right\}, \\
&\quad + \sum_{s=0}^{q^*-1} \varepsilon_{-s}^* \left(\sum_{k=0}^{s} \Gamma_{t+s-k}^* B_k^* \right);
\end{aligned}$$

for the error correction representation define the estimated residuals by

$$\varepsilon_t^* = \sum_{k=1}^{t} \Gamma_{k-1}^* \left\{ \Delta Z_t - \alpha_0^* \left[Y_{t-1} - \left(I_{m_1} \otimes X_{t-1}^T \right) \theta^* \right] - \sum_{j=1}^{p^*-1} \widetilde{A}_j^* \Delta Z_{t-j} \right\}$$
$$+ \sum_{s=0}^{q^*-1} \varepsilon_{-s}^* \left(\sum_{k=0}^{s} \Gamma_{t+s-k}^* B_k^* \right).$$

Finally, we must contend with the problem that the functional form of the innovation density $f(\varepsilon)$ and its score $\psi(\varepsilon)$ are unknown. We follow the general approach of the literature on adaptive estimation by using nonparametric kernel estimators applied to the estimated residuals $\{\varepsilon_t^*\}$ to estimate these functions nonparametrically. Kernel estimators have been used to deliver adaptive estimators in several modeling contexts (e.g., Stone 1975, Bickel 1982, Kreiss 1987, Steigerwald 1992a, and Linton 1993). Although many possible kernels are available for practical implementation, we focus our attention here on Gaussian kernels and derive density and score estimators under the alternative assumptions of symmetry and elliptical symmetry on the unknown innovation density.

We first consider the case in which the density f is symmetric and thus in which $f(\varepsilon) = f(-\varepsilon)$. We can then estimate the score $\psi(\varepsilon)$ following the method described in Jeganathan (1995) as modified by Hodgson (1998b). We begin by defining the m_3-dimensional Gaussian kernel

$$\pi(z, \sigma_n) = \left(\sigma_n \sqrt{2\pi}\right)^{-m_3} \exp\left(-\frac{z^T z}{2\sigma_n^2}\right),$$

where σ_n is a bandwidth, or smoothing parameter, that converges to zero as sample size goes to infinity. We then have the symmetrized density estimator

$$\widehat{f}_t(z) = \frac{1}{2(n-1)} \sum_{\substack{i=1 \\ i \neq t}}^{n} \left\{ \pi\left(z + \varepsilon_i^*, \sigma_n\right) + \pi\left(z - \varepsilon_i^*, \sigma_n\right) \right\}.$$

Now, for every $j = 1, \ldots, m_3$, define the partial derivative of $\widehat{f}_t(z)$ with respect to the jth element of z by $\widehat{f}_t^j(z)$. Our estimator of the jth element of the score vector ψ is given by

$$\widehat{\psi}_t^j(z) = \begin{cases} \frac{\widehat{f}_t^j(z)}{\widehat{f}_t(z)} & \text{if } \begin{cases} \widehat{f}_t(z) \geq \eta_n \\ \sqrt{z^T z} \leq \beta_n \\ \left|\widehat{f}_t^j(z)\right| \leq \delta_n \widehat{f}_t(z) \end{cases} \\ 0 & \text{otherwise} \end{cases},$$

where the trimming parameters η_n, β_n, and δ_n are chosen such that, as $n \to \infty$, we have $\delta_n \to 0$, $\beta_n \to \infty$, $\eta_n \to 0$, $\sigma_n \delta_n \to 0$, and $n^{-1} \beta_n \sigma_n^{-(4+m_3)} \to 0$. We can then define our score estimator by

$$\widehat{\psi}_t(z) = \left(\widehat{\psi}_t^1(z), \ldots, \widehat{\psi}_t^{m_3}(z)\right)^T.$$

The purpose of the trimming conditions is to omit outlying observations for which the density estimate $\widehat{f}_t(z)$ is so close to zero that the ratio $\frac{\widehat{f}_t^j(z)}{\widehat{f}_t(z)}$ is very high and distorts our overall score estimate. The asymptotic restrictions on the trimming and bandwidth parameters do not of course provide much guidance as to how to select these parameters in practice, and there is little in the way of analytical research into the optimal choice of these parameters in finite samples. A fair amount of Monte Carlo simulation evidence, however, has been compiled in recent years (Hsieh and Manski 1987, Steigerwald 1992b, Hodgson 1998a, 1999, 2000) that allows us to provide some rough guidelines. The basic finding is that point estimates are not too sensitive to trimming parameter variation (although standard error estimation can be) and that good results can be obtained with very little trimming (under 1% of the observations for a sample size of 100 in a bivariate model, for example). There are thicker tailed kernels (for example, the logistic kernel of Schick 1987) for which trimming is completely unnecessary, although the low amount required in practice for the Gaussian kernel indicates that the theoretical trimming requirement is not a major practical shortcoming for this kernel. Results are more sensitive to bandwidth choice, and we are on less firm ground here in offering suggestions, although standard rule-of-thumb bandwidths, such as those described by Silverman (1986) for Gaussian kernel density estimation, have been found in Monte Carlos to perform reasonably well. Note that separate bandwidths for the density and derivative estimations, respectively, may yield better results in practice.

Once we have our score estimator $\widehat{\psi}_t$, it is a simple matter to estimate the information Ω of the density f in the following fashion:

$$\widehat{\Omega}_n = n^{-1} \sum_{t=1}^{n} \widehat{\psi}_t(\varepsilon_t^*) \widehat{\psi}_t^T(\varepsilon_t^*). \tag{7}$$

We can then define our semiparametric score estimator for the model by

$$\widehat{W}_n^* = -n^{-1} \sum_{t=1}^{n} H_{t-1}^{*T} \widehat{\psi}_t(\varepsilon_t^*) \tag{8}$$

and our semiparametric information estimator by

$$\widehat{S}_n^* = n^{-2} \sum_{t=1}^{n} H_{t-1}^{*T} \widehat{\Omega}_n H_{t-1}^*, \tag{9}$$

where, for the triangular representation, we have

$$H_{t-1}^{*} = \sum_{k=1}^{t-1} \Gamma_{k-1}^{*} \sum_{i=1}^{p^{*}} A_i^{*} \begin{pmatrix} I_{m_1} \otimes x_{t+1-k-i}^{T} \\ 0_{m_2 \times m} \end{pmatrix},$$

whereas, for the error correction model we have

$$H_{t-1}^{*} = \sum_{k=1}^{t} \Gamma_{k-1}^{*} \alpha_0^{*} \left(I_{m_1} \otimes X_{t-1}^{T} \right).$$

We then have the fully efficient semiparametric estimator

$$\widetilde{\theta}_n = \theta_n^{*} + n^{-1} \widehat{S}_n^{*-1} \widehat{W}_n^{*}, \tag{10}$$

which has the asymptotic distribution

$$L\left(n\left(\widetilde{\theta}_n - \theta_0\right)\right) \Rightarrow L\left(MN\left(0, S\left(\theta_0\right)^{-1}\right)\right).$$

The asymptotic covariance matrix is consistently estimated by $\widehat{S}_n^{*-1}$, and thus we can compute asymptotically normal t-ratios or asymptotically chi-squared Wald statistics using the fact that

$$L\left(n \widehat{S}_n^{*1/2} \left(\widetilde{\theta}_n - \theta_0\right)\right) \Rightarrow L\left(N(0, I)\right).$$

A problem can arise in implementing this estimator in practice because, when the dimension m_3 of the system is at all large, the nonparametric density estimator $\widehat{f}_t$ and its associated score and information estimators $\widehat{\psi}_t$ and $\widehat{\Omega}_n$ may be highly inaccurate in finite samples owing to the so-called curse of dimensionality, according to which nonparametric estimators of functions with high-dimensional arguments perform poorly in finite samples. An approach that allows us to avert the curse of dimensionality in semiparametric efficient estimation procedures, relying on an assumption of elliptical symmetry of the unknown innovation density, has been developed by Hodgson, Linton, and Vorkink (2002) based on earlier work by Bickel (1982) and Stute and Werner (1991). The innovation vector ε is elliptically symmetrically distributed if its density function can be written as follows:

$$f(\varepsilon) = (\det \Sigma)^{-1/2} g\left(\varepsilon^{T} \Sigma^{-1} \varepsilon\right), \tag{11}$$

where $g(\cdot)$ is a function of unknown form and Σ is a positive definite, symmetric matrix proportional to the covariance matrix of ε (which we denote by Σ_{ε}) and also is proportional to the inverse of the information matrix of f, and thus $\Sigma^{-1} = \text{const} \cdot \Omega$. For a further discussion of the properties of elliptical densities and some examples, see the appendix.

We now describe a method for nonparametrically estimating the score function $\psi(\varepsilon)$ while imposing the restriction of elliptical symmetry. From (11), we can see that imposing such a restriction effectively reduces the dimensionality of our nonparametric density estimation problem from m_3 to one because now the density f is proportional to the one-dimensional function $g(\cdot)$. Note that because the matrix Σ is only identified up to a scalar multiple when $g(\cdot)$ is of unknown functional form, we proceed without loss of generality by choosing the normalization $\det \Sigma = 1$. To compute the score estimator of Hodgson, Linton, and Vorkink (2002), begin by computing the residuals $\{\varepsilon_t^*\}$ as defined earlier in this section. Use these to obtain the covariance matrix estimator

$$\widehat{\Sigma}_\varepsilon = n^{-1} \sum_{t=1}^{n} \varepsilon_t^* \varepsilon_t^{*T}$$

and characteristic matrix estimator

$$\widehat{\Sigma} = \left[\det \widehat{\Sigma}\varepsilon\right]^{-1/m_3} \widehat{\Sigma}\varepsilon.$$

We then have the standardized residuals $e_t^* = \widehat{\Sigma}^{-1/2}\varepsilon_t^*$, the inner product sequence $v_t^* = e_t^{*T} e_t^*$, and the transformed sequence $w_t^* = \tau(v_t^*)$, where $\tau(\cdot)$ is in the family $\tau(v;\varsigma) = \left(v^\varsigma - 1\right)/\varsigma$. Define the density function of the random variable w_t by $\gamma(w)$ and its Gaussian kernel estimator by

$$\widehat{\gamma}_t(z) = \frac{1}{(n-1)} \sum_{\substack{i=1 \\ i \neq t}}^{n} \pi\left(z + w_i^*, \sigma_n\right),$$

where $\pi(z, \sigma_n)$ is the Gaussian kernel defined above and σ_n is a bandwidth parameter. Defining $\widehat{\gamma}_t'(z)$ as the derivative of $\widehat{\gamma}_t(z)$, we can define our score estimator by

$$\widehat{\psi}_t(\varepsilon_t^*) = \begin{cases} \widehat{\Sigma}^{-1/2} e_t^* \left[s(v_t^*) + \tau'(v_t^*) \frac{\widehat{\gamma}_t'}{\widehat{\gamma}_t}(w_t^*) \right] & \text{if} \begin{cases} \widehat{\gamma}_t(w_t^*) \geq \eta_n \\ \left|w_t^*\right| \leq \beta_n \\ \left|\rho^{1/2}(w_t^*)\widehat{\gamma}_t'(w_t^*)\right| \leq \delta_n \widehat{\gamma}_t(w_t^*), \\ \left|\lambda(w_t^*)\right| \leq \varsigma_n \end{cases} \\ 0 & \text{otherwise} \end{cases}$$

where $s(v) = (1 - m_3/2)v^{-1} - \frac{J\tau'}{J\tau}\{\tau(v)\}\tau'(v)$, $J\tau(w) = \left|\partial\tau^{-1}(w)/\partial w\right|$, $\tau^{-1}(w) = v$, $\rho(w) = v\tau'(v) J\tau^{-1}(w)$, $\lambda(w) = (d/dw)^{-1} \rho^{1/2}(w)$, $\delta_n \to \infty$, $\beta_n \to \infty$, $\varsigma_n \to \infty$, $\sigma_n \to 0$, $\eta_n \to 0$, $\sigma_n\delta_n \to 0$, $\beta_n\sigma_n^{-3} = o(n)$, and $\varsigma_n\sigma_n^{-3} = o(n)$. We can then use $\widehat{\psi}_t(\varepsilon_t^*)$ to compute $\widehat{\Omega}_n$, W_n^*, S_n^*, and $\widetilde{\theta}_n$ as in eqs. (7)–(10).

9.3 CONDITIONAL HETEROSKEDASTICITY

The discussion in the foregoing sections assumes that the dependence in a time series can be fully characterized through its autocorrelations. This is, of course, unrealistic owing principally to the presence of conditional heteroskedasticity, although dependence in higher moments than the second may, in principle, also be present. In both of our versions of the model discussed in Section 9.2, we defined a sequence $\{\varepsilon_t\}$ of white noise innovations that also happened to be iid. Under the latter assumption, we derived maximum likelihood and efficient adaptive estimators, the latter allowing for thick tails of unknown form in the density. As is well known, the unconditional density of a sequence of uncorrelated observations will tend to be thicker-tailed than a Gaussian density – even if the observations are conditionally Gaussian – if they possess conditional heteroskedasticity. Thus, it is of interest to analyze the behavior of the estimators derived in the previous section if the uncorrelated innovations $\{\varepsilon_t\}$ possess dependence in higher moments but are incorrectly modeled as being iid. A similar analysis for stationary regression models has been reported in Hodgson (2000), the analysis here being extended to cointegrated models. We replace our assumption of iid innovations with the following:

Assumption We assume that the innovation sequence $\{\varepsilon_t\}$ is a stationary and ergodic martingale difference sequence and is mixing with mixing numbers that decay exponentially and that satisfy the mixing and moment conditions of Hansen (1992). Define the σ-field generated by the observations up to period t by $\mathcal{I}_t = \sigma(Y_t, X_t, Y_{t-1}, X_{t-1}, \ldots)$ and denote the conditional density of ε_t conditional on $\mathcal{I}_{t-1}$ by $f_c(\varepsilon \,|\mathcal{I}_{t-1})$ and the unconditional density by $f(\varepsilon)$. We assume that the conditional density is symmetric in ε, that is, that $f_c(\varepsilon \,|\mathcal{I}_{t-1}) = f_c(-\varepsilon \,|\mathcal{I}_{t-1})$ a.s., from which it follows that the unconditional density is also symmetric.

The conditional symmetry assumption allows for a wide range of conditional heteroskedasticity processes (although the range of conditionally heteroskedastic multivariate processes that satisfy the mixing and stationarity assumptions is not at all well known) and also allows for dependence in fourth moments (conditional heterokurtosis) for example.

We now investigate the behavior of the estimators developed in the preceding sections under these assumptions. We first consider the parametric iterative estimator $\overline{\theta}_n$. Note that the equation:

$$\begin{aligned} n(\overline{\theta}_n - \theta_0) & \qquad\qquad (12) \\ &= n(\theta_n^* - \theta_0) + S_n^{-1}(\theta_n^*)\, W_n(\theta_n^*) \\ &= n(\theta_n^* - \theta_0) + S_n^{-1}(\theta_n^*)\left[W_n(\theta_0) + \frac{\partial}{\partial\theta^T} W_n(\theta_n^+)(\theta_n^* - \theta_0) + o_p(1)\right] \end{aligned}$$

holds using a mean-value expansion of $W_n(\theta_n^*)$ about θ_0, where θ_n^+ is a convex combination of θ_n^* and θ_0. We can work out the asymptotic distribution of the right-hand side of the second equality in (12) by applying the weak convergence results of Hansen (1992) for possibly non-iid data. We have

$$S_n^{-1}(\theta_n^*) \Rightarrow S(\theta_0)^{-1}$$

and

$$L(W_n(\theta_0)) \Rightarrow L(MN(0, S(\theta_0))),$$

where, for our respective parameterizations, we have, as above, that

$$S(\theta_0) = \int_0^1 (I_{m_1} \otimes B_x, 0_{m \times m_2}) \Upsilon \begin{pmatrix} I_{m_1} \otimes B_x^T \\ 0_{m_2 \times m} \end{pmatrix}$$

for the triangular parametrization in which

$$\Upsilon = \left[\sum_{k=0}^{\infty} \sum_{i=1}^{p} A_i^T \Gamma_k^T \right] \Omega \left[\sum_{k=0}^{\infty} \sum_{i=1}^{p} \Gamma_k A_i \right],$$

and, for the error correction model, we have

$$S(\theta_0) = \int_0^1 (I_{m_1} \otimes B_x) \Upsilon \left(I_{m_1} \otimes B_x^T \right),$$

where now

$$\Upsilon = \alpha_0^T \left(\sum_{k=1}^{\infty} \Gamma_{k-1}^T \right) \Omega \left(\sum_{k=1}^{\infty} \Gamma_{k-1} \right) \alpha_0.$$

In both cases, Ω is the information matrix of the *unconditional* density of the innovation vector ε, and thus

$$\Omega = \int f(\varepsilon)^{-1} \frac{\partial f(\varepsilon)}{\partial \varepsilon} \frac{\partial f(\varepsilon)}{\partial \varepsilon^T} d\varepsilon.$$

To complete our analysis of (12), we must consider the term

$$\frac{\partial}{\partial \theta^T} W_n\left(\theta_n^+\right).$$

This can be rewritten as

$$-n^{-1} \sum_{t=1}^{n} \frac{\partial}{\partial \theta^T} H_{t-1}^T \psi\left(\varepsilon_t\left(\theta_n^+\right)\right) = -n^{-1} \sum_{t=1}^{n} H_{t-1}^T \frac{\partial \psi\left(\varepsilon_t\left(\theta_n^+\right)\right)}{\partial \varepsilon^T} H_{t-1}.$$

Note that $(\theta_n^+ - \theta_0) = O_p\left(n^{-1}\right)$, and thus

$$n^{-1} \sum_{t=1}^{n} \frac{\partial \psi\left(\varepsilon_t\left(\theta_n^+\right)\right)}{\partial \varepsilon^T} = E\left[\frac{\partial \psi(\varepsilon)}{\partial \varepsilon^T}\right] + o_p(1) = \Omega + o_p(1),$$

the latter equality just being the usual information matrix equality between the expected outer product of the score and the negative of its expected derivative (recall that $\psi(\varepsilon)$ is the *negative* of the score of $f(\varepsilon)$). We can therefore show that

$$-n^{-2} \sum_{t=1}^{n} H_{t-1}^T \frac{\partial \psi\left(\varepsilon_t\left(\theta_n^+\right)\right)}{\partial \varepsilon^T} H_{t-1} \Rightarrow -S(\theta_0), \tag{13}$$

which, when substituted into (12), yields

$$L\left(n\left(\overline{\theta}_n - \theta_0\right)\right) \Rightarrow L\left(MN\left(0, S(\theta_0)^{-1}\right)\right).$$

In this model, the failure of the information matrix equality that usually occurs in standard stationary models in the presence of misspecification (White 1982) does not occur owing to (13). Note that under the assumption on $\{\varepsilon_t\}$ made at the start of this section, Hodgson (2000) has shown that the symmetrized score estimator $\widehat{\psi}_t(z)$ and the associated information estimator $\widehat{\Omega}$ are consistent estimators of the score and information of the unconditional density of ε – particular that the following results hold in particular,

$$n^{-1/2}\sum_{t=1}^{n}\left(\widehat{\psi}_t\left(\varepsilon_t^*\right)-\psi\left(\varepsilon_t^*\right)\right)=o_p(1)$$

and

$$n^{-1}\sum_{t=1}^{n}\widehat{\psi}_t\left(\varepsilon_t^*\right)\widehat{\psi}_t^T\left(\varepsilon_t^*\right)-\Omega=o_p(1).$$

It is conjectured that similar results can be obtained for the estimators of ψ and Ω constructed under the elliptical symmetry assumption if the unconditional innovation density is indeed elliptically symmetric, although this result has not been formally established.

Hodgson (2000) has shown that semiparametric, one-step, iterative estimators such as $\widetilde{\theta}_n$ will be asymptotically equivalent to their parametric analogues $\overline{\theta}_n$ in stationary regression models with strictly exogenous regressors. Unfortunately, Hodgson (2000) was unable to extend this result to autoregressions, and the method of proof used for the exogenous regressors model is also inapplicable in the presence of cointegration. Nevertheless, Monte Carlo simulation results presented by Hodgson (2000) for the estimation of AR(1) models with a variety of possible conditional heteroskedasticity models generating the disturbances show that the semiparametric estimator is generally more efficient than OLS, which implies that the nonparametric score estimator does control for the thick tails induced in the unconditional density of the disturbances by the conditional heteroskedasticity in a fashion suggested by intuition. We would therefore expect the semiparametric iterative estimator $\widetilde{\theta}_n$ to yield more efficient estimates of the cointegrated model than Gaussian pseudo-MLE techniques in the case in which thick tails in the unconditional distribution are due to conditional heteroskedasticity, although we currently lack analytical results to this effect.

9.4 MONTE CARLO SIMULATIONS

9.4.1 Simulation Setup

We report in this section the results of a simulation exercise in which we evaluate the behavior of the estimators developed in Section 9.2 in the presence of various types of conditional heteroskedasticity. The conditional heteroskasticity models considered are an autoregressive conditional heteroskedasticity

(ARCH) model as well as Markov switching and threshold models similar to those used in Hodgson's (2000) Monte Carlo analysis of semiparametric estimators in stationary autoregressions. We will consider a triangular parameterization of a bivariate model in which the regression disturbances and regressor first differences follow a first-order VAR, although the martingale difference innovations have a time-invariant correlation structure; however, the magnitude of the conditional variances can be time-varying according to one of the aforementioned conditional heteroskedasticity processes. Our specification of the model and our choice of parameter values are entirely arbitrary. They have not been chosen to mimic any particular empirical model, nor have they been calibrated to give "good" simulation results. The data-generating process can be written as follows:

$$y_t = \theta x_t + u_{1t}$$
$$x_t = x_{t-1} + u_{2t},$$

where $t = 1, \ldots, T$, and we set $\theta = 1$ and $T = 300$ (200 initial observations were thrown out in an attempt to eliminate the impact of initial conditions). We ran 3,000 simulations for each model. The disturbance process $u_t = (u_{1t}, u_{2t})$ is generated by the VAR:

$$u_t = Au_{t-1} + \varepsilon_t,$$

where

$$A = \begin{bmatrix} .75 & .25 \\ .25 & .75 \end{bmatrix}$$

and $\{\varepsilon_t\}$ has a conditionally Gaussian mean-zero distribution with conditional covariance matrix given by

$$E\left[\varepsilon_t \varepsilon_t^T \mid \mathcal{I}_{t-1}\right] = h_t \Sigma$$

in which

$$\Sigma = \begin{bmatrix} 1 & .25 \\ .25 & 1 \end{bmatrix}.$$

The scalar process $\{h_t\}$, which is the conditional variance of both ε_{1t} and ε_{2t}, follows one of the following conditional variance models:

(a) ARCH(1) model: The conditional variance is given by

$$h_t = \alpha_0 + \alpha_1 \varepsilon_t^T \varepsilon_t.$$

Setting $(\alpha_0, \alpha_1) = (.3, .45)$ implies $E[h_t] = 3$ and $E\left[\varepsilon_t \varepsilon_t^T\right] = 3\Sigma$.

(b) Threshold model: We now have

$$h_t = \begin{cases} \sigma_A^2 & \text{if } |\varepsilon_{1t}| < \kappa \\ \sigma_B^2 & \text{otherwise} \end{cases},$$

where $\sigma_B^2 > \sigma_A^2$ and κ is the threshold. The unconditional density of ε is

$$\gamma N\left(0, \sigma_A^2 \Sigma\right) + (1-\gamma) N\left(0, \sigma_B^2 \Sigma\right),$$

where

$$\begin{aligned}
\gamma &= \text{prob}\left(|\varepsilon_{1t}| < \kappa\right) = p_B / \left(1 - p_A + p_B\right) \\
p_A &= \text{prob}\left(|\varepsilon_{1t}| < \kappa \left| h_t = \sigma_A^2\right.\right) = \Phi\left(\kappa/\sigma_A\right) - \Phi\left(-\kappa/\sigma_A\right) \\
p_B &= \text{prob}\left(|\varepsilon_{1t}| < \kappa \left| h_t = \sigma_B^2\right.\right) = \Phi\left(\kappa/\sigma_B\right) - \Phi\left(-\kappa/\sigma_B\right),
\end{aligned}$$

and $\Phi(\cdot)$ is the standard Gaussian probability distribution function (PDF). In our simulations, we set

$$\left(\sigma_A^2, \sigma_B^2, \kappa\right) = (1/3, 27, 1.32),$$

and thus $\gamma = 0.9$ and the unconditional covariance matrix is $E\left[\varepsilon_t \varepsilon_t^T\right] = 3\Sigma$.

(c) *Markov Switching Model:* The conditional variance follows an exogenous first-order Markov process with the following transition probabilities (here p_A and p_B are exogenously given constants):

$$\begin{aligned}
\text{prob}\left(h_t = \sigma_A^2 \left| h_{t-1} = \sigma_A^2\right.\right) &= p_A \\
\text{prob}\left(h_t = \sigma_B^2 \left| h_{t-1} = \sigma_A^2\right.\right) &= 1 - p_A \\
\text{prob}\left(h_t = \sigma_A^2 \left| h_{t-1} = \sigma_B^2\right.\right) &= 1 - p_B \\
\text{prob}\left(h_t = \sigma_B^2 \left| h_{t-1} = \sigma_B^2\right.\right) &= p_B,
\end{aligned}$$

where $\sigma_B^2 > \sigma_A^2$ and $p_A > 1 - p_B$. The unconditional density of ε is

$$\gamma N\left(0, \sigma_A^2 \Sigma\right) + (1-\gamma) N\left(0, \sigma_B^2 \Sigma\right),$$

where $\gamma = (1 - p_B)/(2 - p_A - p_B)$. In our simulations, we set

$$\left(\sigma_A^2, \sigma_B^2, p_A, p_B\right) = (1/3, 27, .92, .3),$$

and thus we again have $\gamma = 0.9$ and $E\left[\varepsilon_t \varepsilon_t^T\right] = 3\Sigma$.

(d) *iid Model:* We also estimated a model in which the error process $\{\varepsilon_t\}$ was iid with a density equal to the mixed normal unconditional density that obtains in parts (*b*) and (*c*).

9.4.2 Results

We report mean-squared error (MSE) results for three estimators for each of the four models described immediately above. The estimators considered are OLS, the Gaussian one-step iterative pseudo-MLE, and our semiparametric one-step iterative estimator, which will be adaptive for the special case of iid innovations. In the case of the iterative estimators, OLS is used as the preliminary estimator, and the VAR parameters are estimated by an OLS autoregression of the OLS residuals and regressor first differences on their first

Table 9.1 *Simulation Results: MSE for Different Estimators and Models of Conditional Heteroskedasticity*

Model	MSE(OLS)	MSE(GML)	MSE(SPE)	$\frac{\text{MSE(GML)}}{\text{MSE(OLS)}}$	$\frac{\text{MSE(SPE)}}{\text{MSE(OLS)}}$
ARCH	2.26×10^{-5}	2.39×10^{-5}	2.21×10^{-5}	1.06	0.98
Threshold	2.32×10^{-5}	2.44×10^{-5}	2.20×10^{-5}	1.05	0.95
Markov	2.23×10^{-5}	2.34×10^{-5}	2.12×10^{-5}	1.05	0.95
iid	2.24×10^{-5}	2.36×10^{-5}	2.14×10^{-5}	1.05	0.96

lags. The bandwidth used for the semiparametric estimator is the Silverman (1986) rule-of-thumb, and the trimming parameters are set as in Hodgson (1998a, 2000) and reflect very little trimming. The error density is estimated directly without the elliptical symmetry restriction. The results are contained in Table 9.1, where we report MSE results for each of the estimators (where GML denotes the Gaussian one-step pseudo-MLE and SPE denotes the one-step semiparametric estimator) as well as the ratios of each the MSEs of the iterative estimators with respect to OLS.

The most interesting point to be noticed in these results is that the relative behavior of the estimators seems to depend only on the unconditional distribution of the errors. The threshold, Markov switching, and iid models feature three different types of dependence but have the same unconditional distribution. Also worthy of note is that the semiparametric estimator does account for the thick tails present in this unconditional distribution even when the thick tails are generated by conditional heteroskedasticity in a model that is conditionally Gaussian. This estimator does improve upon the other two, although only to a small extent. More care in choice of bandwidth would likely yield better results here. A somewhat surprising result is the good robustness of OLS in the presence of both conditional heteroskedasticity and autocorrelation in the regression disturbances – in particular that OLS outperforms the Gaussian pseudo-MLE.

APPENDIX

A.1 IDENTIFICATION CONDITIONS FOR A VARMA MODEL

The issue of identification is more complex in the case of VARMA models than in univariate ARMA models. We merely present some sufficient conditions for identification here. For a detailed discussion of these conditions, together with examples, see Lutkepohl (1991, pp. 241–252). Our m_3-dimensional VARMA process u_t is defined by

$$A(L)u_t = B(L)\varepsilon_t,$$

where

$$A(L) = I - \sum_{j=1}^{p} A_j L^j$$

and

$$B(L) = I + \sum_{j=1}^{q} B_j L^j.$$

Now consider some arbitrary polynomial

$$D(L) = I - \sum_{j=1}^{k} D_j L^j.$$

We call the polynomial $D(L)$ *unimodular* if

$$\left|D(L)\right| = \overline{d} \neq 0,$$

where $\overline{d}$ is a real constant that is not a function of L or powers of L. We say that the matrix operator $[A(L), B(L)]$ is *left co-prime* if

$$D(L)\left[\widetilde{A}(L), \widetilde{B}(L)\right] = [A(L), B(L)]$$

for matrix operators $\left\{D(L), \widetilde{A}(L), \widetilde{B}(L)\right\}$ holds only if $D(L)$ is unimodular. If $[A(L), B(L)]$ is indeed left co-prime, and if the iid innovations have a nonsingular covariance matrix $E\left[\varepsilon\varepsilon^T\right]$, then either of the following two sets of conditions is sufficient for identification of the VARMA parameters:

(a) Final Equations Form: The VAR polynomial $A(L)$ has the form

$$A(L) = I - \sum_{j=1}^{p} a_j I,$$

where a_j, $j = 1, \ldots, p$ are scalars and $a_p \neq 0$;

(b) Echelon Form: The AR and moving average (MA) polynomials $A(L) = [a_{i\ell}(L)]_{i,\ell=1,\ldots,m_3}$ and $B(L) = [b_{i\ell}(L)]_{i,\ell=1,\ldots,m_3}$ are such that each of the scalar polynomials in the ith row of each matrix polynomial (i.e., $\left\{a_{i\ell}(L)\right\}_{\ell=1,\ldots,m_3}$ and $\left\{b_{i\ell}(L)\right\}_{\ell=1,\ldots,m_3}$) has the same lag order – for instance p_i. Furthermore, these scalar polynomials have the form

$$a_{ii}(L) = 1 - \sum_{j=1}^{p_i} a_{ii,j} L^j \quad i = 1, \ldots, m_3;$$

$$a_{i\ell}(L) = - \sum_{j=p_i-p_{i\ell}+1}^{p_i} a_{i\ell,j} L^j \quad i \neq \ell;$$

$$b_{ii}(L) = 1 + \sum_{j=1}^{p_i} b_{ii,j} L^j \quad i = 1, \ldots, m_3;$$

and

$$b_{i\ell}(L) = \sum_{j=1}^{p_i} b_{i\ell,j} L^j \quad i \neq \ell.$$

In the polynomial $a_{i\ell}(L)$, we have

$$p_{i\ell} = \begin{cases} \min(p_i + 1, p_\ell) & \text{for } i \geq \ell \\ \min(p_i, p_\ell) & \text{for } i < \ell \end{cases} \quad i, \ell = 1, \ldots, m_3.$$

Of course we have $p = q = \max(p_1, \ldots, p_{m_3})$.

For the two representations presented here, possible approaches to specification of the lag orders and estimation of the parameters are discussed in Lutkepohl (1991).

A.2 DISCRETIZATION

The concept of discretization has been defined and discussed in many places – for example, LeCam (1960) and Jeganathan (1995). We here describe the manner in which one can compute the discretized estimator θ_n^* mentioned in the main text. We must first obtain some preliminary estimator θ_n^{**} of the cointegrating parameter vector θ that is consistent at the rate n (e.g., OLS). Recall that $\theta \in \Theta \subset R^m$. We now partition R^m into cubes whose sides are of length n^{-1}, indexing these cubes as $C_i, i = 1, 2, \ldots$. Within each cube, we define a fixed point $t_i \in C_i \cap \Theta$ (e.g., the central point of the cube). Now, for the cube C_i into which the preliminary estimator θ_n^{**} falls, we define the discretized version of θ_n^{**} by the prespecified fixed point $t_i = \theta_n^*$. Note that θ_n^* will be consistent at rate n.

The "trick" of discretization was introduced by LeCam (1960) and allows us to prove the efficiency of the one-step iterative estimator $\overline{\theta}_n$ without making some of the differentiability and boundedness assumptions on the likelihood function that were traditionally required in efficiency proofs. For practical purposes, Monte Carlo simulation evidence reported in Hodgson (1998a, 1999, 2000) suggests that one-step, iterative, semiparametric estimators will have good performance properties, even if there is no further rounding off of the preliminary OLS estimator beyond that automatically imposed by computational packages such as GAUSS.

A.3 ELLIPTICAL DENSITIES[4]

An m_3-dimensional random vector ε is said to be elliptically distributed about the origin if its density can be written as

$$f(\varepsilon) = (\det \Sigma)^{-1/2} g\left(\varepsilon^T \Sigma^{-1} \varepsilon\right),$$

[4] See Fang, Kotz, and Ng (1990) and Owen and Rabinovitch (1983) for further discussion.

where Σ is a positive definite, symmetric matrix that is proportional to the covariance matrix of ε (when a finite covariance matrix exists) and is also proportional to the inverse of the information matrix of f. The characteristic function of ε is

$$\lambda(s) = E\left[\exp\left(is^T\varepsilon\right)\right] = \phi\left(s^T\Sigma s\right)$$

for some function $\phi(\cdot)$. The standardized m_3-vector $e = \Sigma^{-1/2}\varepsilon$ is said to be spherically symmetric with density

$$f(e) = g\left(e^T e\right).$$

Note that the isoprobability contours of the density of the elliptical random variable ε will be elliptical, and those of the spherical random variable e will be spherical (circular in the case of $m_3 = 2$).

Some examples of spherical densities are as follows:

(a) the Gaussian,

$$g(\cdot) = \text{const} \cdot \exp\left(-\frac{e^T e}{2}\right);$$

(b) the Student's t with τ degrees of freedom,

$$g(\cdot) = \text{const} \cdot \left(1 + \frac{e^T e}{\tau}\right)^{-(m_3+\tau)/2};$$

(c) the Cauchy,

$$g(\cdot) = \text{const} \cdot \left(1 + e^T e\right)^{-(m_3+1)/2};$$

(d) the logistic,

$$g(\cdot) = \text{const} \cdot \exp\left(-e^T e\right) / \left[1 + \exp\left(-e^T e\right)\right]^2;$$

(e) and the scale mixed normal,

$$g(\cdot) = \text{const} \cdot \int_0^\infty s^{-m_3/2} \exp\left(-\frac{e^T e}{2s}\right) dF(s)$$

for some cdf $F(\cdot)$. Note that all the non-Gaussian densities listed here feature thick tails, and some of them are popular candidates for modeling tail thickness in empirical work that takes a fully parametric tack.

Elliptical distributions have a few properties that are of interest. First, define the norm $\|e\| = \sqrt{e^T e}$. The random variables $\frac{e}{\|e\|}$ and $\|e\|$ are independent of one another. Furthermore, the random variable $\frac{e}{\|e\|}$ has a uniform distribution on the $(m_3 - 1)$-dimensional unit hypersphere. These two features of elliptical distributions form the basis for Beran's (1979) test for elliptical symmetry.

Define the $m^* \times m_3$ matrix Φ of rank $m^* \leq m_3$. Then the m^*-dimensional random variable $\Phi\varepsilon$ is elliptically and symmetrically distributed with characteristic matrix of $\Phi\Sigma\Phi^T$. Define the partition $\varepsilon = \left(\varepsilon_1^T, \varepsilon_2^T\right)^T$ and partition Σ conformably as

$$\begin{bmatrix} \Sigma_{11} & \Sigma_{12} \\ \Sigma_{21} & \Sigma_{22} \end{bmatrix}.$$

Then the marginal densities of ε_1 and ε_2 are of the same form as the joint density of ε with respective characteristic matrices of Σ_{11} and Σ_{22}. The conditional mean can be written as

$$E\left[\varepsilon_i \left|\varepsilon_j\right.\right] = \Sigma_{ij}\Sigma_{jj}^{-1}\varepsilon_j.$$

Furthermore, the density of ε_i conditional on ε_j will be elliptically symmetric with a characteristic matrix of $\Sigma_{ii} - \Sigma_{ij}\Sigma_{jj}^{-1}\Sigma_{ji}$.

References

Ahn, S. K. and G. C. Reinsel (1990). "Estimation for partially nonstationary multivariate autoregressive models," *Journal of the American Statistical Association*, 85, 813–823.

Beran, R. (1979). "Testing for ellipsoidal symmetry of a multivariate density," *Annals of Statistics*, 7, 150–162.

Bickel, P. J. (1982). "On adaptive estimation," *Annals of Statistics*, 10, 647–671.

Fang, K., S. Kotz, and K. Ng (1990). *Symmetric Multivariate and Related Distributions.* London: Chapman and Hall.

Hansen, B. E. (1992). "Convergence to stochastic integrals for dependent heterogenous processes," *Econometric Theory*, 8, 489–500.

Hodgson, D. J. (1998a). "Adaptive estimation of cointegrating regressions with ARMA errors," *Journal of Econometrics*, 85, 231–267.

Hodgson, D. J. (1998b). "Adaptive estimation of error correction models," *Econometric Theory*, 14, 44–69.

Hodgson, D. J. (1999). "Adaptive estimation of cointegrated models: Simulation evidence and an application to the forward exchange market," *Journal of Applied Econometrics*, 14, 627–650.

Hodgson, D. J. (2000). "Unconditional pseudo-maximum likelihood estimation in the presence of conditional heteroskedasticity of unknown form," *Econometric Reviews*, 19, 175–206.

Hodgson, D. J., O. Linton, and K. Vorkink (2002). "Testing the capital asset pricing model efficiently under elliptical symmetry: A semiparametric approach," *Journal of Applied Econometrics*, 17, 617–639.

Hsieh, D. A. and C. F. Manski (1987). "Monte Carlo evidence on adaptive maximum likelihood estimation of a regression," *Annals of Statistics*, 15, 541–551.

Jeganathan, P. (1995). "Some aspects of asymptotic theory with applications to time series models," *Econometric Theory*, 11, 818–887.

Johansen, S. (1988). "Stochastic analysis of cointegration vectors," *Journal of Economic Dynamics and Control*, 12, 231–254.

Kreiss, J.-P. (1987). "On adaptive estimation in stationary ARMA processes," *Annals of Statistics*, 15, 112–133.

LeCam, L. (1960). Locally asymptotically normal families of distributions. *University of California Publications in Statistics*, 3, 37–98.

Linton, O. (1993). "Adaptive estimation in ARCH models," *Econometric Theory*, 9, 539–569.

Lutkepohl, H. (1991). *Introduction to Multiple Time Series Analysis.* Berlin: Springer–Verlag.

Owen, J. and R. Rabinovitch (1983). "On the class of elliptical distributions and their applications to the theory of portfolio choice," *Journal of Finance*, 38, 745–752.

Park, J. Y. (1992). "Canonical cointegrating regressions," *Econometrica*, 60, 119–143.

Phillips, P. C. B. (1991). "Optimal inference in cointegrated systems," *Econometrica*, 59, 283–306.

Phillips, P. C. B. (1995). "Robust nonstationary regression," *Econometric Theory*, 11, 912–951.

Phillips, P. C. B. and S. N. Durlauf (1986). "Multiple time series regression with integrated processes," *Review of Economic Studies*, 53, 473–495.

Phillips, P. C. B., and B. E. Hansen (1990). "Statistical inference in instrumental variables regression with I(1) processes," *Review of Economic Studies*, 57, 99–125.

Phillips, P. C. B. and M. Loretan (1991). "Estimating long-run economic equilibria," *Review of Economic Studies*, 58, 407–436.

Phillips, P. C. B., J. W. McFarland, and P. C. McMahon (1996). "Robust tests of forward exchange market efficiency with empirical evidence from the 1920's," *Journal of Applied Econometrics*, 11, 1–22.

Saikkonen, P. (1991). "Asymptotically efficient estimation of cointegrating regressions," *Econometric Theory*, 7, 1–21.

Schick, A. (1987). "A note on the construction of asymptotically linear estimators," *Journal of Statistical Planning and Inference*, 16, 89–105.

Silverman, B. (1986). *Density Estimation for Statistics and Data Analysis.* London: Chapman and Hall.

Steigerwald, D. (1992a). "Adaptive estimation in time series regression models," *Journal of Econometrics*, 54, 251–276.

Steigerwald, D. (1992b). "On the finite sample behavior of adaptive estimators," *Journal of Econometrics*, 54, 371–400.

Stock, J. H. (1987). "Asymptotic properties of least squares estimators of cointegrating vectors," *Econometrica*, 55, 1035–1056.

Stock, J. H. and M. W. Watson (1993). "A simple estimator of cointegrating vectors in higher order cointegrated systems," *Econometrica*, 61, 783–820.

Stone, C. (1975). "Adaptive maximum likelihood estimation of a location parameter," *Annals of Statistics*, 3, 267–284.

Stute, W. and U. Werner (1991). "Nonparametric estimation of elliptically contoured densities," In G. Roussas, ed., *Nonparametric Functional Estimation and Related Topics,* pp. 173–190, Amsterdam: Kluwer Academic Publishers.

White, H. (1982). "Maximum likelihood estimation of misspecified models," *Econometrica*, 50, 1–25.

Yap, S. F. and G. C. Reinsel (1995). "Estimation and testing for unit roots in a partially nonstationary vector autoregressive moving average model." *Journal of the American Statistical Association*, 90, 253–67.

TEN

Testing Stationarity Using M-Estimation*

Roger Koenker and Zhijie Xiao

10.1 INTRODUCTION

There is a large body of literature in time series econometrics on the debate over whether economic time series are best characterized as trend stationary processes or difference stationary processes. Since the influential article by Nelson and Plosser (1982), hundreds of economic time series have been examined by unit root tests (against a stationary alternative) or stationarity tests (against a unit root alternative). Refer to Meese and Singleton (1982); Perron (1989); Schotman and van Dijk (1991); Phillips (1991); Zivot and Andrews (1992); Gil-Alana and Robinson (1997) among others. Despite the large body of literature on unit root tests, there have been several attempts at testing (trend) stationarity (Park 1988; Park and Choi 1988; Rudebusch 1988; Kwiatkowski et al. 1992; Leybourne and McCabe 1994; Fukushige, Hatanaka, and Koto 1994). In particular, Kwiatkowski et al. (1992) (hereafter KPSS) considered a time series model that can be decomposed as the sum of a deterministic trend, a random walk, and a stationary error, and they proposed Lagrange multiplier (LM) test for the null hypothesis of stationarity. Leybourne and McCabe (1994) suggested a similar test that differs from the KPSS test in its treatment of autocorrelation and applies when the null hypothesis is an AR(k) process.

The primary purpose of this chapter is to propose a unified view for testing stationarity. Our test is general and has power against a wide range of alternatives that are of possible econometric interest. The proposed test naturally extends to a generalized residual-based test for cointegration.

Although there are several important papers on the study of unit root tests based on M-estimation (see, among others Cox and Llatas 1991, Phillips 1995, Lucas 1995, Rothenberg and Stock 1997, and Juhl 2001), the existing

* We thank Dean Corbae for helpful comments on an early version of this chapter. The research was partially supported by NSF under Grant No. SBR-9617206 and the Hong Kong Research Grants Council under Grant No. CUHK 4078/98.

procedures for testing stationarity are all based on least-squares detrending and there is no study in the literature on tests of stationarity based on M-estimation detrending. In empirical analysis, many applications in time series involve financial data such as exchange rates whose distributions are heavy-tailed. It is therefore of interest to consider estimation and testing procedures that are robust to departures from Gaussianity. A second purpose of this chapter is to develop a stationarity test based on M-estimation. Unlike the least-square detrending case, the limiting distribution of the partial sum process of the detrended time series based on M-estimation is dependent on a nuisance parameter related to the criterion function, and the conventional methods in the previous literature can not remove this nuisance parameter. To construct an asymptotically distribution-free test in this case, we propose a martingale transformation originally studied by Khmaladze (1981) on the partial sum process and construct an asymptotically valid test based on the martingalized process. This test provides a useful complement to the M-estimation-based unit root tests and the existing stationarity tests.

A famous phenomenon in the theory of trend-stationarity tests and unit root tests is that the removal of deterministic trends is not negligible even asymptotically. Even for least-squares-based methods, the effect of detrending enters the limiting distributions of these tests. Consequently, critical values are dependent on the limiting functions of the deterministic trend and have to be generated by Monte Carlo experiments given the choice of deterministic trend and the method of detrending. The martingale transformation approach we use here addresses this issue. In particular, the martingale transformation eliminates the part that is dependent on the trending function but preserves the Brownian motion (in transformed time). As a result, the proposed tests based on the martingalization are independent of the limiting trend function and other nuisance parameters.

The chapter is organized as follows: The motivation and general principle of testing stationarity is discussed in Section 10.2. Section 10.3 gives a generalized test for trend stationarity based on martingalization. Consistency of the test is discussed in Section 10.4 and, Section 10.5 discusses implementations of the test. A Monte Carlo experiment was conducted, and the results are reported in Section 10.6. Section 10.7 contains an empirical example, and Section 10.8 is the conclusion. Proofs are provided in the appendix. For notation, we use "$\Rightarrow$" to signify weak convergence, L for lag operator, and $[nr]$ to signify the integer part of nr.

10.2 THE MODEL

We consider an observed time series y_t that can be written as the sum of a deterministic trend d_t and a stochastic component y_t^s:

$$y_t = d_t + y_t^s, \ t = 1, \ldots, n. \tag{1}$$

The deterministic trend d_t depends on unknown parameters and is specified as $d_t = \gamma' x_t$, where $\gamma = (\gamma_0, \ldots, \gamma_p)'$ is a vector of trend coefficient and x_t is a deterministic trend of known form – for example, $x_t = (1, t, \ldots, t^p)'$. We want to test whether y_t is stationary around the deterministic trend d_t. The leading case of the deterministic component is a linear time trend $x_t = (1, t)'$. The trend function d_t may be more complex than a simple time polynomial. For example, time polynomials with sinusoidal factors and piecewise time polynomials may be used. The latter corresponds to a class of models with structural breaks in the deterministic trend.

Our purpose is to test whether y_t is stationary around the deterministic trend $\gamma' x_t$. Precisely, we are interested in testing the hypothesis H_0: y_t^s is an I(0) process whose partial sum process satisfies an invariance principle so that $n^{-1/2} \sum_{t=1}^{[nr]} y_t^s \Rightarrow B_y(r)$, where the limiting process $B_y(r)$ is a Brownian motion with variance ω_y^2. We consider alternative hypotheses under which the time series has an unstable or explosive trajectory.

If y_t^s is a stationary time series, it has a fixed mean and finite variance and consequently cannot grow indefinitely. An unstable (unit root) or explosive process, however, has unbounded variance and grows over a long period. As a result, the fluctuation of a unit root or explosive process is much larger than that of a stationary process. Under H_0, the fluctuation in y_t^s is stable and the partial sum process is of order $n^{1/2}$. Under H_1, however, the fluctuation in y_t^s will have a much larger order of magnitude. This suggests that we can test whether y_t^s is stationary by looking at the fluctuation in the time series. If a time series displays too much fluctuation, we should reject the null hypothesis of stationarity. As will be clear later, the general principle of the proposed test applies to a wide range of models and has power against various alternatives, including the popular unit root alternative and explosive alternative, and so on.

In the past 10 years, the attention of time series econometrics has been focused on the test for unit root nonstationarity versus trend stationarity. For this reason, and also for convenience of exposition, we consider the following model, which has attracted considerable attention in econometric applications:

$$y_t^s = \alpha y_{t-1}^s + u_t, \; t = 1, \ldots, n, \tag{2}$$

where α is the largest autoregressive root. The residual term u_t is a general $I(0)$ process whose partial sum process satisfies an invariance principle. For convenience in deriving asymptotic theory, we assume that the disturbances u_t follow a general linear process (Phillips and Solo 1992) whose coefficients satisfy the summability conditions given in the following assumption.

Assumption L (Linear Process) $u_t = C(L)\varepsilon_t$, where ε_t is a white noise process with zero mean and $E(\varepsilon_t^2) = \sigma\varepsilon^2 < \infty$, $C(L) = \sum_{j=0}^{\infty} c_j L^j$, $C(1) \neq 0$, and $\sum_{j=1}^{\infty} j^2 c_j^2 < \infty$.

This assumption ensures that the partial sum process of u_t satisfies an invariance principle: $n^{-1/2}\sum_{t=1}^{[nr]} u_t \Rightarrow B_u(r), 0 \leq r \leq 1$, where $B_u(r)$ is a Brownian motion with variance ω^2. Similar results could be obtained under strong mixing conditions (e.g., Phillips and Perron 1988), which also ensure invariance principles for the partial sums of u_t. Notice that the asymptotic analysis of linear processes holds under a variety of conditions, and the limiting results of our test can also be generalized to different classes of time series innovations. With a strengthening of the moment and the summability condition, our results can be generalized to time series with stationary martingale difference sequence innovations.

Assumption L_2 $u_t = C(L)\varepsilon_t$, where ε_t is a stationary martingale difference sequence with respect to the natural filtration, $E(\varepsilon_t^{2+\eta}) < \infty$ for some $\eta > 0$, and $C(L) = \sum_{j=0}^{\infty} c_j L^j$ with $C(1) \neq 0$ and $\sum_{j=1}^{\infty} j \left|c_j\right| < \infty$.

These linear processes include quite general classes of time series models, including the autoregressive moving average (ARMA) processes. Assumptions L and L_2 ensure that u_t is covariance stationary and has positive spectral density at the origin.

If $|\alpha| < 1$, y_t^s is a stationary process; when $\alpha = 1$, y_t^s is unstable and has an autoregressive unit root; when $\alpha > 1$, y_t^s is an explosive process. We consider the null hypothesis that y_t^s is stationary, that is, $H_0 : |\alpha| < 1$, against the alternative $H_1 : \alpha = 1$, or, more generally, $\alpha \geq 1$. Under H_0 and Assumption L, $n^{-1/2}\sum_{t=1}^{[nr]} y_t^s \Rightarrow B_y(r) = (1-\alpha)^{-1}B_u(r)$. The limiting process $B_y(r)$ is a Brownian motion with variance $\omega_y^2 = \omega^2/(1-\alpha)^2$. Under the alternative hypothesis, however, the asymptotic behavior of time series y_t^s will be different in orders of magnitude. For example, under the unit root alternative hypothesis, y_t^s is an integrated process such that $y_t^s = \sum_{j=1}^{t} u_j + O_p(1)$ and $n^{-1/2}y_{[nr]}^s \Rightarrow B_u(r)$.

Remark The general approach of this chapter can easily be extended to a wide range of time series models beyond model (2). For example, it can be applied to the following time series model with nonlinearity. Consider, for instance, time series y_t with a nonlinear component $g(\cdot)$,

$$y_t = \alpha y_{t-1} + g(y_{t-1}) + u_t, \qquad (3)$$

where $g(\cdot)$ is a bounded, Lipschitz continuous, and differentiable function, and the residual process u_t *is* $I(0)$. Nonlinear time series models have received increasing attention in recent years (see Tong 1990, and Granger and Terasvirta 1993, among others), and models of type (3) have been studied by many researchers (see, e.g., Corradi, Swanson, and White 2000). In particular, when u_t is iid, y_t is a first-order, nonlinear Markov process. When $|\alpha| < 1$, y_t is a geometric ergodic (stationary) process with invariant probability measure absolutely continuous with respect to the Lebesgue measure. When $\alpha = 1$, the time series y_t is no longer a unit root process (in the sense that its first difference is stationary) in the presence of a nonlinear component. The time series y_t, however, is nonstationary and has an explosive trajectory.

If y_t^s were known, a natural way to look at the fluctuation in the data would be to consider the empirical process (or partial sum process)

$$Y_n(r) = \frac{1}{\omega_y \sqrt{n}} \sum_{t=1}^{[nr]} y_t^s, \tag{4}$$

where ω_y^2 is the long-run variance of y_t^s. Under the null hypothesis, it converges weakly to a standard Brownian motion $W(r)$. Consider a continuous functional $h(\cdot)$ (whose property will be further specified for subsequent analysis; also see Section 10.5 for implementations of the test) that measures the fluctuation of $Y_n(r)$, we can use $h(Y_n(r))$ as a test statistic for stationarity. By the continuous mapping theorem, under regularity conditions and the null of stationarity,

$$h(Y_n(r)) \Rightarrow h(W(r)).$$

Notice that in practical analysis the long-run variance parameter ω_y is unknown, and thus (4) can not be used directly for testing stationarity. Fortunately, ω_y^2 can be consistently estimated by nonparametric methods (see, among others, and Andrews 1991). We consider the nonparametric kernel estimator

$$\widehat{\omega}_y^2 = \sum_{h=-M}^{M} k(\frac{h}{M}) C_{yy}(h) \tag{5}$$

for ω_y^2 and construct the following partial sum process:

$$\widehat{Y}_n(r) = \frac{1}{\widehat{\omega}_y \sqrt{n}} \sum_{t=1}^{[nr]} y_t^s.$$

The expression $\widehat{\omega}_y^2$ is the conventional spectral density estimator. In formula (5), $C_{yy}(h)$ is the sample variance defined as $n^{-1} \sum' \widehat{y}_t \widehat{y}_{t+h}$, where $\sum'$ signifies summation over $1 \leq t, t+h \leq n$, $k(\cdot)$ is the lag window defined on $[-1, 1]$ with $k(0) = 1$, and M is the bandwidth parameter satisfying the property that $M \to \infty$ and $M/n \to 0$ as the sample size $n \to \infty$. Then, $\widehat{\omega}_y^2$ is a consistent estimator of ω_y^2 under H_0. Under $H_1, \widehat{\omega}_y^2 = o_p(n^2)$. Candidate kernel functions can be found in standard texts (e.g., Hannan 1970, and Priestley 1981). For example, when we use $k(x) = 1 - |x|$, we obtain the Bartlett estimator.

It will be convenient in what follows to make the following assumptions about the functional $h(\cdot)$.

Assumption H: h is continuous and $h(\theta\lambda(r)) = \theta^\tau h(\lambda(r))$ for some $\tau > 0$.

Thus, given the choice of functional $h(\cdot)$, $h(\widehat{Y}_n(r))$ can be used in testing stationarity. We summarize the limiting result in the following Theorem.

Theorem 10.1 *Under the null hypothesis and Assumptions L and H, as* $n \to \infty$, $h(\widehat{Y}_n(r)) \Rightarrow h(W(r))$.

In applications, y_t^s is unobservable since the deterministic component $\gamma' x_t$ is unknown. In order to test H_0, we need to estimate γ (and thus y_t^s) first and then test stationarity by looking at the fluctuation in the detrended data. In the next section we extend our analysis to testing stationarity around a deterministic trend.

10.3 TESTING TREND STATIONARITY BASED ON M-ESTIMATION

10.3.1 M-Estimation of the Deterministic Trend

Evidence has accumulated that many financial and macroeconomic time series are usually heavy-tailed and thus not normally distributed. For this reason, it is useful to consider estimation based on a more robust method. Following the idea of Huber (1964) for the location problem, to obtain more robust estimators, Relles (1968) and Huber (1973) introduced a class of the so-called M estimators that generally have good properties over a wide range of distributions.

In the simple case that $\{u_t, t = 1, \ldots, n\}$ are unobserved i.i.d. errors with mean zero and log density $-\rho(u)$, $y_1 = 0$, if α were known, the conditional log density of y_t would be given as follows:

$$-\rho\left(\Delta_\alpha y_t - \gamma' \Delta_\alpha x_t\right),$$

where $\Delta_\alpha = 1 - \alpha L$ and L is the lag operator, and thus $\Delta_\alpha y_t = y_t - \alpha y_{t-1}$. The log likelihood function of the random sample is

$$\mathcal{L}(\gamma) = \sum_{t=2}^{n} \rho\left(\Delta_\alpha y_t - \gamma' \Delta_\alpha x_t\right). \tag{6}$$

The M estimator of γ can then be found by minimizing $\mathcal{L}(\gamma)$ with respect to γ. In practice, α is unknown and has to be estimated. In this case, the estimator involves a nonlinear regression. Combining (1) and (2) gives a nonlinear regression model

$$y_t = \gamma' \Delta x_t + (1 - \alpha)\gamma' x_{t-1} + \alpha y_{t-1} + u_t; \tag{7}$$

thus, a joint estimation of γ and α is needed. Under the null hypothesis, the estimator of γ is asymptotically equivalent to the following analogue of (6) based on

$$\min_{\gamma} \sum_{t=2}^{n} \rho\left(\Delta_{\widehat{\alpha}} y_t - \gamma' \Delta_{\widehat{\alpha}} x_t\right), \tag{8}$$

where $\widehat{\alpha}$ is a preliminary root-n consistent estimator of α. The asymptotic behavior of these two estimators, however, is different under the unit root alternative. Under regularity conditions, it can been shown that the limiting distributions of the nonlinear estimators (7) are jointly determined by a nonlinear equation system of Brownian motions and the limiting trending functions. However, the limiting distribution of (8) has an analytical solution. Both estimators (7) and (8) can be used in the stationarity test proposed in this chapter. For clarity of exposition and without loss of generality, we use estimator (8) in the following analysis.

Generally, if we consider some criterion function ρ, the so-called M estimator of γ is obtained from a similar optimization problem:

$$\widehat{\gamma} = \arg\min_{\gamma} \sum_{t=2}^{n} \rho\left(\Delta_{\widehat{\alpha}} y_t - \gamma' \Delta_{\widehat{\alpha}} x_t\right). \tag{9}$$

We may also extend the preceding estimation to the case that u_t is an I(0) process satisfying Assumption L or L_2. In this case, the regression (9) takes into account the major source of serial correlation in y_t^s coming from the largest root α.

Under regularity conditions, the M estimator may also be defined as a solution of the first-order condition of the extremum problem. The following assumptions are standard conditions in M-estimation asymptotic analysis. In practice, even if these conditions do not hold, as long as the data have distributional properties similar to the function ρ described, Monte Carlo evidence indicates that the M estimation still has good sampling properties.

Assumption MM $\rho(\cdot)$ possesses derivatives ψ and ψ'. $[u, \psi(u)]$ has kth moments for some $k > 2$, $E[\psi(u_t)] = 0$, and ψ' is Lipschitz continuous.

The moment conditions on u and $\psi(u)$ are needed to establish the weak convergence results. We may also replace the moment condition on $\psi(u)$ by boundedness conditions of the derivatives of ρ because the latter and the moment condition on u_t imply the corresponding condition on ψ.

The limiting distributions of $\widehat{\gamma}$ will be dependent on the weak limit of the partial sums of $\psi(u)$. Under Assumption L, as n goes to ∞, $n^{-1/2}\sum_1^{[nr]} u_t$ converges weakly to a standard Brownian motion $B_u(r)$. If we let $\omega_\psi^2 = lrvar[\psi(u_t)]$, then $n^{-1/2}\sum_1^{[nr]}\psi(u_t) \Rightarrow B_\psi(r) = \omega_\psi W_\psi(r)$, where W_ψ is a standard Brownian motion.

The convergence (or divergence) rate of $\widehat{\gamma}$ is generally dependent on the integration order of y_t and thus will be different under H_0 and H_1. In general, for a wide range of detrending procedures, $\sqrt{n}D_n(\widehat{\gamma} - \gamma) = O_p(1)$ under the null hypothesis. Different regularity conditions may be made for asymptotic analysis of $\widehat{\gamma}$. To cover a wide range of models, we simply assume that the following conditions hold.

Assumption B Under H_0, $n^{1/2}D_n(\widehat{\gamma}-\gamma)=o_p(n^{1/4})$, whereas under H_1, $n^{-1/2}D_n(\widehat{\gamma}-\gamma)=o_p(n^{1/4})$.

Assumptions similar to B are standard in the development of M-estimator asymptotics. They are similar to Assumption (b) in Theorem 5.1 of Phillips (1995) and the assumption on $\widetilde{\varepsilon}_t-\varepsilon_t$ in Theorem 1 of Lucas (1995). For asymptotic analysis of the deterministic trend, we assume that there are standardizing matrices D_n such that $D_n^{-1}x_{[nr]}\to X(r)$ and $nD_n^{-1}\Delta x_{[nr]}\to g(r)$, as $n\to\infty$, uniformly in $r\in[0,1]$. In the case of a linear trend, $D_n=\text{diag}[1,n]$ and $X(r)=(1,r)'$. If x_t is a general pth order polynomial trend, $D_n=\text{diag}[1,n,\ldots,n^p]$ and $X(r)=(1,r,\ldots,r^p)$.

Theorem 10.2 *Under the null hypothesis and Assumptions L, MM, and B, the limiting distribution of the M estimators (9) $\widehat{\gamma}$ is*

$$\sqrt{n}D_n(\widehat{\gamma}-\gamma)\Rightarrow\left[\int X(r)X(r)'dr\right]^{-1}\int X(r)dB_\delta(r),$$

where

$$B_\delta(r)=\frac{\omega_\psi}{\delta(1-\alpha)}W_\psi(r),\ \delta=-E[\psi'(u_t)].$$

If we denote the detrended time series as $\widehat{y}_t=y_t-\widehat{\gamma}'x_t$, under H_0 the partial sum of the detrended time series converges to the following limiting process:

$$n^{-1/2}\sum_{t=1}^{[nr]}\widehat{y}_t\Rightarrow B_y(r)-\int_0^1 dB_\delta(s)X(s)'\left[\int_0^1 X(s)X(s)'ds\right]^{-1}\int_0^r X(s)ds.$$

Notice that $B_y(r)$ and $B_\delta(r)$ are correlated Brownian motions and thus nuisance parameters enter the limit of the partial sum process.

Remark If we consider the M estimator of γ based on the regression $y_t=\gamma'x_t+y_t^s$, we minimize an objective function of the form

$$\sum_{t=1}^{n}\rho\left(y_t-\gamma'x_t\right)$$

for some criterion function ρ. The property of this estimator and stationarity tests based on it can be analyzed similarly. In particular, under the null hypothesis and regularity conditions, we can show that

$$\sqrt{n}D_n(\widehat{\gamma}-\gamma)\Rightarrow\left[\int X(r)X(r)'dr\right]^{-1}\int X(r)dB\eta(r),$$

where $B\eta(r)=\omega\psi W\psi(r)/\delta$. In the special case in which $\rho(u)=u^2$, we obtain the least-squares estimator.

10.3.2 A Generalized Test for Trend Stationarity

We want to examine the fluctuation of y_t using the partial sum process of the detrended time series

$$\widetilde{Y}_n(r) = \frac{1}{\widehat{\omega}_y\sqrt{n}}\sum_{t=1}^{[nr]}\widehat{y}_t. \tag{10}$$

Under H_0, the partial sum of the detrended time series converges to the limiting process

$$\widetilde{Y}_n(r) \Rightarrow \widetilde{W}_X(r) = W(r) - g(r)^\top\xi(W_\eta, X),$$

where

$$g(r) = \int_0^r X(s)ds,\ \xi(W_\eta, X) = \int_0^1 dW_\delta(s)X(s)'\left[\int_0^1 X(s)X(s)'ds\right]^{-1}$$

and $W_\delta(s) = \omega_y^{-1}B_\delta(s)$. The limiting variate of the trend estimator is generally a functional of $X(r)$ and, more importantly, the Brownian motion $W_\delta(r)$. Thus, the limiting process $\widetilde{W}_X(r)$ is dependent on nuisance parameters that reflect the correlation between $W_\delta(r)$ and $W(r)$. Consequently, $h(\widehat{Y}_n(r))$ can not be used as test statistics.

To obtain an asymptotically distributional free test, we apply a martingale transformation suggested by Khmaladze (1981) to the process $\widehat{Y}_n(r)$. Such a transformation eliminates the nuisance parameters and the deterministic trend components from $\widetilde{W}_X(r)$ but preserves the Brownian motion component (in transformed time), and thus asymptotically distributional free tests can be constructed based on the transformed process.

Although the idea of martingale transformation dates back to 1981, the expansion of this approach to a wide variety of statistical models is a recent event. In particular, the approach has played an important role in work on regression diagnostics by Stute, Thies, and Zhu (1998); Koul and Stute (1999); and Bai (2004). In a recent paper, Koenker and Xiao (2002) studied inference on the quantile regression process using this approach.

Khmaladze's general approach can be motivated as a natural elaboration of the Doob–Meyer decomposition for the partial sum process. Doob–Meyer decompose an empirical process into two parts: a martingale component and a compensator. Intuitively, the transformation maps the process into its martingale part, which converges to a Brownian motion in transformed time. Applying Khmaladze's idea in our problem, we may construct a linear operator $\mathcal{K}$ for $\widetilde{Y}_n(r)$ so that the transformation will annihilate the $g(r)^\top\xi$ contribution; consequently, the transformed process will have a limiting distribution independent of the trend function $X(r)$ and the preliminary estimation. Thus, the proposed stationarity test has the form $h(\mathcal{K}\widehat{Y}_n(r))$, where $\mathcal{K}$ is a linear operator that annihilates the trend function but preserves the Brownian motion.

To construct the transformation $\mathcal{K}$, notice that

$$\widetilde{W}_X(r) = W(r) - g(r)^\top \xi(W_\delta, X),$$

where $\xi(W_\delta, X)$ is dependent on both the Brownian motion W_δ and the trending function X. If x_t is a polynomial trend, then $X(r) = (1, r, \ldots, r^p)$ and $g(r) = (r, r^2, \ldots, r^{p+1})$. Consider the linear transformation $\mathcal{K}$ on process $V(r)$,

$$\mathcal{K}V(r) = V(r) - \int_0^r \left[X(s)'C(s)^{-1} \int_s^1 X(t)dV(t) \right] ds,$$

where

$$C(s) = \int_s^1 X(t)X(t)'dt.$$

This transformation has the following important properties: (i) for a standard Brownian motion $W(r)$, $W^*(r) = \mathcal{K}W(r)$ is also a standard Brownian motion (in transformed time) (Khmaladze 1981), (ii) for any function $h(r)$ in the space spanned by $g(r)$, $\mathcal{K}h(r) = 0$.

If we apply the transformation $\mathcal{K}$ to $\widetilde{W}_X(r)$ (notice that this is a linear transformation, and the component $g(r)^\top \xi(W_\delta, X)$, which is dependent on the trend function, is filtered out because $\mathcal{K}g(r) = 0$), we obtain a standard Brownian motion in transformed time:

$$\mathcal{K}\widetilde{W}_X(r) = \mathcal{K}W(r) - \mathcal{K}g(r)^\top \xi(W_\delta, X) = \mathcal{K}W(r) = W^*(r).$$

Thus, $h(\mathcal{K}\widetilde{W}_X(r)) = h(W^*(r))$. In addition,

$$\mathcal{K}\widehat{Y}_n(r) = \mathcal{K}\widetilde{W}_X(r) + o_p(1).$$

The result (12) therefore follows immediately.

Roughly speaking, notice that $\widehat{\beta} = \left[\int_s^1 X(t)X(t)'dt\right]^{-1} \int_s^1 X(t)dV(t)$ may be obtained from the continuous time regression

$$dV(t) = \beta'\dot{g}(t)dt + dW(t) \tag{11}$$

over time $t \in [s, 1]$,

$$\int_0^r \left[X(s)'C(s)^{-1} \int_s^1 X(t)dV(t) \right] ds$$

may be viewed as a prediction of $V(r)$ based on the recursive regression (11), and $\mathcal{K}V(r)$ is the recursive (nonorthogonal) prediction error.

Theorem 10.3 *Under the null hypothesis and Assumptions L, H, MM, and B, as $n \to \infty$,*

$$h(\mathcal{K}\widehat{Y}_n(r)) \Rightarrow h(W^*(r)), \tag{12}$$

where $W^*(r)$ is a standard Brownian motion.

Remark When $\varphi(u) = u^2$, least-squares detrending is used, and W_δ is the same Brownian motion as $W(r)$. In particular, we have

$$n^{-1/2}\sum_{t=1}^{[nr]}\widehat{y}_t$$
$$\Rightarrow \omega_y\left\{W(r) - \left[\int_0^1 dW(s)X(s)'\right]\left[\int_0^1 X(s)X(s)'ds\right]^{-1}\int_0^r X(s)ds\right\}$$
$$= \omega_y W_X(r),$$

where $W_X(r) = W(r) - \left[\int_0^1 dW(s)X(s)'\right]\left[\int_0^1 X(s)X(s)'ds\right]^{-1}\int_0^r X(s)ds$. The limiting process, $W_X(r)$, is a generalized Brownian bridge process depending on the limiting trend function $X(r)$. We could accept the presence of the deterministic trend function $X(r)$ in the limiting distribution of $\widetilde{W}_X(r)$ and still use $h(\widetilde{Y}_n(r))$ in testing stationarity. Critical values of these tests then have to be generated by Monte Carlo methods given different choice of $X(r)$ and detrending methods. Even in this case, however, the proposed test $h(\mathcal{K}\widehat{Y}_n(r))$ still provides an interesting complement whose limiting distribution is independent of the limiting trend function.

10.4 CONSISTENCY

In this section, we consider the asymptotic behavior of the proposed test under the unit root alternative. Our analysis can easily be modified to accommodate other alternatives under which the process has unstable or explosive trajectories.

Under the unit root alternative hypothesis, $n^{-1/2}y_{[nr]} \Rightarrow B_u(r)$ and the M estimator of γ has the following asymptotic behavior.

Theorem 10.4 *Under the unit root alternative and Assumptions L, H, MM, and B, the limiting distribution of the M estimators (9) $\widehat{\gamma}$ is*

$$n^{-1/2}D_n(\widehat{\gamma} - \gamma) \Rightarrow \left[\int X_\eta(r)X_\eta(r)'dr\right]^{-1}\int X_\eta(r)dB_\eta(r),$$

where

$$B_\eta(r) = \frac{1}{-\delta}B_\psi(r) + \eta\int_0^r B_u.$$

The detrended time series then has limit

$$n^{-1/2}\widehat{y}_{[nr]} \Rightarrow B_{u,X}(r) = B_u(r) - \xi' X(r),$$

and $n^{-1}\sum_{t=1}^{[nr]}(\widehat{y}_t/\sqrt{n}) \Rightarrow \int_0^r B_{u,X}(s)ds$. *Thus,* $\sum_{t=1}^{[nr]}(\widehat{y}_t/\sqrt{n})$ *diverges at rate n under* H_1.

Under H_1, the nonparametric spectral density estimate $\widehat{\omega}_y$ diverges as well. To show the consistency of the test, we need that $\widehat{\omega}_y$ diverges at a slower rate. Under H_1 and Assumption L_1 (or L_2), it can be shown that, as $n \to \infty$,

$$\frac{1}{nM}\widehat{\omega}_y^2 \Rightarrow 2\pi K(0) \int_0^1 B_{u,X}(r)^2 dr,$$

where $B_{u,X}(r) = B_u(r) - \left[\int_0^1 B_\eta(s)X(s)'ds\right]\left[\int_0^1 X(s)X(s)'ds\right]^{-1} X(r)$ is a detrended Brownian motion and $K(\lambda) = \frac{1}{2\pi}\int_{-\infty}^{\infty} k(x)e^{-i\lambda x}dx$ is the spectral window. Thus, the kernel estimator diverges at rate $\sqrt{nM} = o(n)$. By assumptions H and B, we obtain the consistency of the test.

10.5 IMPLEMENTATION OF THE TEST

The previous sections give an analysis on the general test for stationarity. We now discuss some important implementations of this general test. In principle, any metric that measures the fluctuation in $\widehat{Y}_n(r)$ is a natural candidate for the functional h. The classical Kolmogoroff–Smirnoff-type or Cramer–von Mises-type measures are of particular interest. In this section, we use $W(r)$ to denote a standard Brownian motion.

10.5.1 The CUSUM (Cumulative Sum) Test

The CUSUM- or MOSUM-type statistics based on the classical Kolmogoroff–Smirnoff measure are natural choices of functional h. The original CUSUM test was introduced by Brown, Durbin, and Evans (1975) based on cumulated sums of recursive residuals. Motivated by the idea that the true disturbances can be better approximated by the OLS residuals, Ploberger and Kramer (1992) proposed a CUSUM test based on cumulated sums of least-squares residuals. To test the hypothesis of trend stationarity, we may consider the following CUSUM test based on the transformed cumulated sum process (also see Sen 1980 and Ploberger, Kramer and Kortrus 1989 for related discussions on the recursive-estimates statistic)

$$h(\mathcal{K}\widehat{Y}_n(r)) = \sup_{r\in R} \left|\mathcal{K}\widehat{Y}_n(r)\right|, \tag{13}$$

where $R \subseteq [0, 1]$. Usually we take $R = [0, 1]$ or $R = [\delta, 1-\delta]$ for some small fixed δ. Under H_0,

$$\sup_{r\in R} \left|\mathcal{K}\widehat{Y}_n(r)\right| \Rightarrow \sup_{r\in R} \left|W(r)\right|.$$

10.5.2 The MOSUM Test

As a complement of the CUSUM tests, Bauer and Hackl (1978) proposed testing structural changes based on moving sums of residuals and introduced the recursive MOSUM test. This test has been further studied and extended to the case with OLS residuals by Hornik and Kuan (1995). We may consider the following MOSUM statistic for testing stationarity:

$$h(\mathcal{K}\widehat{Y}_n(r)) = \sup_{r\in R(\theta)} \left|\mathcal{K}\widehat{Y}_n(r+\theta) - \mathcal{K}\widehat{Y}_n(r)\right|, \tag{14}$$

where $0 < \theta < 1$ is a prespecified bandwidth parameter of moving windows indicating the proportion of $\widehat{y}_t$ used to construct the moving sum. $R(\theta) \subseteq [0, 1]$ is an interval such that $r, r+\theta \in [0, 1]$ when $r \in R(\theta)$. Usually we choose $R(\theta) = [0, 1-\theta]$ or $R(\theta) = [\delta, 1-\theta-\delta]$. Under H_0,

$$\sup_{r\in R(\theta)} \left|\mathcal{K}\widehat{Y}_n(r+\theta) - \mathcal{K}\widehat{Y}_n(r)\right| \Rightarrow \sup_{r\in R(\theta)} \left|W(r+\theta) - W(r)\right|.$$

10.5.3 The Cramer–von Mises Test

Another functional frequently used in measuring the fluctuation of $\widehat{Y}_n(r)$ is the Cramer–von Mises-type metric. For a suitably chosen weight function $w(r)$, we can construct the following Cramer–von Mises-type test for stationarity:

$$h(\mathcal{K}\widehat{Y}_n(r)) = \int_{r\in R} w(r)[\mathcal{K}\widehat{Y}_n(r)]^2 dr,$$

where $w(r)$ is a weighting function. Under the null,

$$\int_{r\in R} w(r)[\mathcal{K}\widehat{Y}_n(r)]^2 dr \Rightarrow \int_{r\in R} w(r)W(r)^2 dr.$$

In particular, choosing $w(r) = 1$, we obtain a stationarity test with the conventional limiting distribution

$$h(\widehat{Y}_n(r)) = \int_{r\in R} \widehat{Y}_n(r)^2 dr \Rightarrow \int_{r\in R} W(r)^2 dr. \tag{15}$$

Notice that the well-known KPSS test could be viewed as a Cramer–von Mises-type test based on the OLS detrended time series $\widehat{y}_t$ and a constant weighting function $w(r) = 1$:

$$\text{KPSS} = \int_0^1 [\widehat{Y}_n(r)]^2 dr.$$

The test (15) may be treated as a KPSS-type test based on the martingalized time series.

10.5.4 The Range Test

The fourth functional that we consider in measuring fluctuations in a process $\widehat{Y}_n(r)$ is the range functional based on the difference between the maximum and the minimum values of the empirical process. This functional was first considered by Feller (1951) and later used in many applications (e.g., Kuan and Hornik 1995). We may consider the following stationarity test based on the range functional:

$$h(\mathcal{K}\widehat{Y}_n(r)) = \sup_{r\in R} \left|\mathcal{K}\widehat{Y}_n(r)\right| - \inf_{r\in R} \left|\mathcal{K}\widehat{Y}_n(r)\right|, \tag{16}$$

where $R \subseteq [0, 1]$. Under H_0,

$$\sup_{r\in R} \left|\widehat{Y}_n(r)\right| - \inf_{r\in R} \left|\widehat{Y}_n(r)\right| \Rightarrow \sup_{r\in R} \left|W(r)\right| - \inf_{r\in R} \left|W(r)\right|.$$

The asymptotic distribution of this test is well known and can be found in the existing literature (e.g., Shorack and Wellner 1986, p. 142).

10.6 MONTE CARLO RESULTS

We conducted some limited Monte Carlo experiments to examine the finite sample performance of the proposed testing procedures. In particular, we examined the size and power properties of the tests based on the martingale transformation and compared them with the conventional stationarity tests. The sample size considered in our experiment was $n = 100$ (different sample sizes were also examined and quantitatively similar results were obtained). The data-generation process is

$$y_t = \alpha y_{t-1} + u_t,$$

where u_t are iid random variables. The following error distributions were considered: standard normal and Student's t distribution with degrees of freedom 3, 4, 5. For the M-estimation of deterministic trend, we used the log-density of student-t distribution with 3 degrees of freedom. We considered three Kolmogorov-type testing procedures: the test (13) that uses the detrending procedure (9) and the martingale transformation (denoted as KSMG), and the test based on OLS detrending and martingale transformation (denoted as KSMLS), and the test based on OLS detrending and critical values calculated based on Monte Carlo experiments (denoted as KSOLS). For comparison, we also calculated the empirical size and power of the KPSS test (denoted as KPSS) because this is the best known stationarity test in the econometrics literature.

We considered the leading cases in which the deterministic component is a linear time trend. From the construction of these test statistics, the finite sample performance of these tests depends on the bandwidth parameter M used to calculate $\widehat{\omega}_y^2$. Thus, special attention was paid to the effects of the bandwidth and sample sizes on the performance of these tests. Two bandwidth choices were considered: the first bandwidth value, $M1 = 1$, is small and fixed, whereas the second bandwidth, $M2 = [6(n/100)^{1/4}]$, is a function of the sample sizes and increases with n. These bandwidth values were used because

Table 10.1 *Gaussian Error*

		$M1$	$M2$			$M1$	$M2$
$\alpha = 0$	KSMG	0.068	0.072	$\alpha = 0.6$	KSMG	0.150	0.070
	KSMLS	0.078	0.081		KSMLS	0.164	0.085
	KSOLS	0.021	0.015		KSOLS	0.145	0.017
	KPSS	0.054	0.045		KPSS	0.263	0.112
$\alpha = 0.7$	KSMG	0.201	0.069	$\alpha = 0.95$	KSMG	0.456	0.113
	KSMLS	0.211	0.093		KSMLS	0.559	0.278
	KSOLS	0.255	0.023		KSOLS	0.770	0.185
	KPSS	0.384	0.143		KPSS	0.897	0.584
$\alpha = 0.8$	KSMG	0.266	0.074	$\alpha = 1$	KSMG	0.645	0.296
	KSMLS	0.289	0.122		KSMLS	0.670	0.372
	KSOLS	0.406	0.039		KSOLS	0.844	0.305
	KPSS	0.562	0.237		KPSS	0.923	0.686
$\alpha = 0.9$	KSMG	0.406	0.138	$\alpha = 1.1$	KSMG	1.000	1.000
	KSMLS	0.423	0.189		KSMLS	1.000	1.000
	KSOLS	0.641	0.106		KSOLS	1.000	0.998
	KPSS	0.796	0.424		KPSS	1.000	1.000

similar choices had been made in Kwiatkowski et al. (1992), and other simulations. In the presence of serial correlation, we need the bandwidth to increase with n in estimating the long-run variance. Thus, we expected that small, fixed bandwidth would have relatively better effect for the iid case and $M2$ would work better for cases with high serial correlation. All experiments used 5,000

Table 10.2 $t(2)$ *Error*

		$M1$	$M2$			$M1$	$M2$
$\alpha = 0$	KSMG	0.060	0.066	$\alpha = 0.6$	KSMG	0.155	0.070
	KSMLS	0.072	0.079		KSMLS	0.173	0.094
	KSOLS	0.014	0.018		KSOLS	0.163	0.020
	KPSS	0.043	0.034		KPSS	0.266	0.093
$\alpha = 0.7$	KSMG	0.212	0.079	$\alpha = 0.95$	KSMG	0.510	0.169
	KSMLS	0.243	0.096		KSMLS	0.578	0.266
	KSOLS	0.272	0.027		KSOLS	0.829	0.264
	KPSS	0.404	0.139		KPSS	0.893	0.601
$\alpha = 0.8$	KSMG	0.301	0.086	$\alpha = 1$	KSMG	0.599	0.226
	KSMLS	0.336	0.119		KSMLS	0.700	0.368
	KSOLS	0.444	0.056		KSOLS	0.890	0.387
	KPSS	0.584	0.221		KPSS	0.944	0.737
$\alpha = 0.9$	KSMG	0.413	0.102	$\alpha = 1.1$	KSMG	1.000	1.000
	KSMLS	0.472	0.182		KSMLS	1.000	1.000
	KSOLS	0.699	0.127		KSOLS	1.000	1.000
	KPSS	0.806	0.429		KPSS	1.000	1.000

Table 10.3 $t(3)$ *Error*

		$M1$	$M2$			$M1$	$M2$
$\alpha = 0$	KSMG	0.063	0.069	$\alpha = 0.6$	KSMG	0.148	0.069
	KSMLS	0.069	0.074		KSMLS	0.158	0.085
	KSOLS	0.015	0.014		KSOLS	0.157	0.017
	KPSS	0.058	0.045		KPSS	0.265	0.102
$\alpha = 0.7$	KSMG	0.189	0.072	$\alpha = 0.95$	KSMG	0.525	0.199
	KSMLS	0.212	0.093		KSMLS	0.579	0.278
	KSOLS	0.254	0.023		KSOLS	0.795	0.185
	KPSS	0.393	0.143		KPSS	0.893	0.584
$\alpha = 0.8$	KSMG	0.289	0.089	$\alpha = 1$	KSMG	0.615	0.286
	KSMLS	0.306	0.122		KSMLS	0.675	0.372
	KSOLS	0.420	0.039		KSOLS	0.868	0.305
	KPSS	0.553	0.237		KPSS	0.942	0.706
$\alpha = 0.9$	KSMG	0.412	0.140	$\alpha = 1.1$	KSMG	1.000	1.000
	KSMLS	0.472	0.189		KSMLS	1.000	1.000
	KSOLS	0.674	0.106		KSOLS	1.000	0.998
	KPSS	0.804	0.424		KPSS	1.000	1.000

replications. For the kernel function in estimating the long-run variance, following Kwiatkowski et al. (1992), we used the Bartlett window $k(x) = 1 - |x|$ so that the nonnegativity of $\widehat{\omega}_y^2$ was guaranteed.

For comparison, in each iteration all tests were calculated based on the same data. In this model, the autoregressive (AR) coefficient α is a convenient nuisance parameter to investigate. It measures the distance from the null to the alternative. As α approaches unity, y_t behaves more and more like a random walk. In consequence, it is anticipated that the tests will overreject the null hypothesis for positive α and that, as α increases, the empirical rejection rate of these tests will also increase depending on how close α is to unity. We examined the empirical rejection rates for cases with $\alpha = 0, 0.6, 0.7, 0.8, 0.9,$ $0.95, 1, 1.1.,$ and 1.2. Our choices of α put a particular emphasis on those values close to unity because many macroeconomic time series contain a large autoregressive root. The values 0.95, 0.9, and 0.8 are typically used in the "unit root" Monte Carlo experiments in the literature.

Notice that the bandwidth parameter M corresponds to the number of lags used to calculate $\widehat{\omega}_y^2$. Intuitively, for $\alpha > 0$, the larger α is, the longer the lags we need. In the case that $\alpha = 0$, y_t is an independent sequence and the long-run variance of y_t equals the variance of y_t. Thus, for small α, we expect that a small bandwidth value can provide reasonably good finite sample performance. As α increases, we need a larger M to estimate ω_y^2. This is confirmed in the simulation. In cases of large α values the problem of overrejection is severe for all these tests when M is small ($M = M1 = 1$) because, according to the asymptotic theory, the validity of the tests requires M to increase with

Table 10.4 $t(4)$ *Error*

		*M*1	*M*2			*M*1	*M*2
$\alpha = 0$	KSMG	0.063	0.062	$\alpha = 0.6$	KSMG	0.158	0.070
	KSMLS	0.069	0.075		KSMLS	0.163	0.094
	KSOLS	0.016	0.018		KSOLS	0.162	0.020
	KPSS	0.047	0.034		KPSS	0.272	0.091
$\alpha = 0.7$	KSMG	0.216	0.075	$\alpha = 0.95$	KSMG	0.543	0.169
	KSMLS	0.228	0.096		KSMLS	0.581	0.266
	KSOLS	0.253	0.027		KSOLS	0.803	0.264
	KPSS	0.385	0.139		KPSS	0.889	0.601
$\alpha = 0.8$	KSMG	0.279	0.086	$\alpha = 1$	KSMG	0.630	0.286
	KSMLS	0.299	0.119		KSMLS	0.683	0.368
	KSOLS	0.416	0.056		KSOLS	0.854	0.387
	KPSS	0.554	0.221		KPSS	0.925	0.737
$\alpha = 0.9$	KSMG	0.424	0.112	$\alpha = 1.1$	KSMG	1.000	1.000
	KSMLS	0.463	0.182		KSMLS	1.000	1.000
	KSOLS	0.675	0.127		KSOLS	1.000	1.000
	KPSS	0.807	0.429		KPSS	1.000	1.000

n in this circumstance. As will become clear in Tables 10.1 to 10.4, however, larger bandwidth *M*2 reduces the power of these tests and a trade-off has to be made.

The Monte Carlo results indicate that the tests based on martingalized time series have reasonably good sampling performance. In particular, they have relatively better size properties. Because these tests are designed based on the same general principle, it is expected that similarities exist among them. Given the advantage that the proposed tests are independent of the limiting trend function, they provide a useful complement to the existing procedures.

10.7 AN EMPIRICAL APPLICATION

We applied the proposed tests to U.S. historical time series. In particular, we re-visited the famous Nelson–Plosser data and examined trend stationarity of the 14 macroeconomic time series. Comparison was made with the classical KPSS stationarity test.

The original time series data of Nelson and Plosser (1982) are annual observations. The starting dates for the series vary from 1860 for industrial production and consumer prices to 1909 for GNP. All series terminate in 1970 in the original Nelson–Plosser data. Schotman and Van Dijk (1991) extended all these 14 series to 1988. In their original study, Nelson and Plosser conducted the ADF_t unit root test on these series and could not reject the unit root hypothesis at the 5% level of significance for all of the series except the unemployment rates. Perron (1988) arrived at similar conclusions using Z-tests.

Table 10.5 *Empirical Application*

Series	KSMG		KSMLS		KSOLS		KPSS	
	*M*1	*M*2	*M*1	*M*2	*M*1	*M*2	*M*1	*M*2
CPI	4.904	3.350[a]	4.973	3.386[a]	1.366	0.93[a]	0.818	0.379[a]
GNP Def.	3.155	2.443[a]	3.205	2.472[a]	0.935	0.713	0.284	0.165[a]
Ind. Prod.	1.936	1.446	1.95	1.447	1.048	0.782	0.301	0.167[a]
Money	2.614	1.874	2.615	1.877	1.085	0.778	0.212	0.109
Nom. GNP	2.846	2.123	2.842	2.122	1.320	0.985[a]	0.439	0.244[a]
Stock Price	4.180	2.944[a]	4.208	2.973[a]	1.466	1.036[a]	0.698	0.348[a]
Velocity	4.436	3.075[a]	4.523	3.086[a]	1.391	0.948[a]	0.891	0.414[a]
Employment	1.297	1.018	1.291	1.018	0.882	0.692	0.179	0.110
GNP/Cap.	1.666	1.349	1.679	1.343	0.793	0.642	0.176	0.115
Interest Rate	3.029	2.218[a]	3.717	2.729[a]	1.214	0.891	0.582	0.313[a]
Real GNP	1.804	1.448	1.811	1.451	0.899	0.722	0.207	0.133
Real Wage	3.238	2.465[a]	3.243	2.472[a]	1.029	0.784	0.294	0.171[a]
Unemployment	1.009	0.842	1.011	0.843	0.723	0.603	0.079	0.055
Nominal wage	2.953	2.210[a]	2.959	2.215[a]	1.232	0.922[a]	0.413	0.231[a]

[a] Values are smaller than the 5% level critical values.

We considered the null hypothesis that the variables are trend stationary processes versus the difference stationary alternatives. We applied the four tests examined in the Monte Carlo experiment, that is, the KSMG (Kolmogoroff-type test based on M estimation with Student's t density [degrees of freedom = 3] and martingalization), KSMLS, KSOLS, and KPSS tests, to these series. The critical values at the 5% level of significance for these tests are 2.21(KSMG, KSMLS), 0.901(KSOLS), and 0.146(KPSS), respectively.

Table 10.5 reports the calculated tests. Again, we used the two bandwidth choices that had been used in the Monte Carlo.

It is clear from Table 10.5 that the test statistics decline as M increases. Because these series are obviously temporally dependent, serial dependence should be taken into account when we estimate the long-run variance. For

Table 10.6 ADF_t *Tests*

Series	$\hat{\alpha}$	ADF_t	Series	$\hat{\alpha}$	ADF_t
CPI	0.998	−1.4	Employment	0.854	−3.28
GNP Def.	0.967	−1.63	GNP/Cap.	0.81	−3.59*
Ind. Prod.	0.818	−3.68*	Interest rate	0.94	−1.69
Money	0.936	−2.89	Real GNP	0.812	−3.05
Nom. GNP	0.938	−2.03	Real wage	0.927	−1.73
Stock price	0.916	−2.42	Unemployment	0.772	−3.94*
Velocity	0.964	−1.44	Nominal wage	0.933	−2.43

* Values are smaller than the 5% level critical values.

bandwidth choices *M2*, we find that we cannot reject the null hypothesis of trend stationarity at the 5% level for the series of Industrial Production, Money, Employment, GNP per capita, and Unemployment, but we can reject trend stationarity in the other three series.

To compare our results with the unit root tests, Table 10.5 gives the classical ADF *t*-ratio test for these series. For the choice of lag length, we use the Bayesian information criterion (BIC) criterion of Schwarz (1978) and Rissanen (1978) in selecting the appropriate lag length of the autoregression. Combining these results with the stationarity tests, we may conclude that the series of industrial production, GNP per capita, and unemployment are trend stationary. CPI, GNP deflator, interest rate, velocity, real wage, and nominal wage have a unit root.

APPENDIX

For discussions and analysis about the martingale transformation, refer to Khmaladze (1981) and Koenker and Xiao (2002).

Proof of Theorem 10.2: The first-order condition corresponding to M estimation (9) is given by the following equation system:

$$\sum_{t=2}^{n} \psi\left(\Delta_{\widehat{\alpha}} y_t - \widehat{\gamma}' \Delta_{\widehat{\alpha}} x_t\right) \Delta_{\widehat{\alpha}} x_t = 0. \tag{17}$$

For simplicity, we write

$$\widehat{u}_t = \Delta_{\widehat{\alpha}} y_t - \widehat{\gamma}' \Delta_{\widehat{\alpha}} x_t;$$

then,

$$\widehat{u}_t = u_t - (\widehat{\alpha} - \alpha) y_{t-1}^s - (\widehat{\gamma} - \gamma)' \Delta_\alpha x_t + (\widehat{\alpha} - \alpha)(\widehat{\gamma} - \gamma)' x_{t-1}).$$

Under Assumptions M and B, for all c in a compact set, the left-hand side of eq. (17) is asymptotically equivalent to

$$\sum_{t=1}^{n} \psi(u_t) \Delta_{\widehat{\alpha}} x_t + \sum_{t=1}^{n} \psi'(u_t) \left[(\widehat{\alpha} - \alpha)(\widehat{\gamma} - \gamma)' x_{t-1} \right.$$
$$\left. - (\widehat{\alpha} - \alpha) y_{t-1}^s - (\widehat{\gamma} - \gamma)' \Delta_\alpha x_t \right] \Delta_{\widehat{\alpha}} x_t.$$

Under the assumptions of Theorem 10.2, it can be shown that the following asymptotics hold:

$$\frac{1}{\sqrt{n}} \sum_{t=1}^{n} \psi(u_t) \Delta_{\widehat{\alpha}} x_t D_n^{-1} \Rightarrow (1 - \alpha) \int_0^1 dB_\psi(r) X(r) \tag{18}$$

$$\frac{1}{\sqrt{n}}\sum_{t=1}^{n}\psi'(u_t)(\widehat{\alpha}-\alpha)y^s_{t-1}\Delta_{\widehat{\alpha}}x_t D_n^{-1} = O_p(\frac{1}{\sqrt{n}}) \tag{19}$$

$$\frac{1}{\sqrt{n}}\sum_{t=1}^{n}\psi'(u_t)(\widehat{\alpha}-\alpha)(\widehat{\gamma}-\gamma)'x_{t-1}\Delta_{\widehat{\alpha}}x_t D_n^{-1} = O_p(\frac{1}{\sqrt{n}}) \tag{20}$$

$$\frac{1}{n}\sum_{t=1}^{n}\psi'(u_t)D_n^{-1}\Delta_{\alpha}x_t\Delta_{\widehat{\alpha}}x_t' D_n^{-1} \Rightarrow \delta(1-\alpha)^2\int_0^1 X(r)X(r)dr; \tag{21}$$

thus, we have

$$\sqrt{n}D_n(\widehat{\gamma}-\gamma) \Rightarrow \left[\int X(r)X(r)'dr\right]^{-1}\int X(r)dB_\eta(r),$$

where

$$B_\eta(r) = \frac{\omega_\psi}{\delta(1-\alpha)}W_\psi(r), \delta = -E[\psi'(u_t)]. \quad \blacksquare$$

Proof of Theorem 10.4: The proof is similar to that of Theorem 10.2. Notice that under the alternative hypothesis and Assumptions M and B, for all c in a compact set the left-hand side of eq. (17) is asymptotically equivalent to

$$\sum_{t=1}^{n}\psi(u_t)\Delta_{\widehat{\alpha}}x_t + \sum_{t=1}^{n}\psi'(u_t)\left[-(\widehat{\alpha}-\alpha)y^s_{t-1}-(\widehat{\gamma}-\gamma)'\Delta_{\widehat{\alpha}}x_t\right]\Delta_{\widehat{\alpha}}x_t.$$

The following asymptotics hold:

$$n(\widehat{\alpha}-1) \Rightarrow \eta$$
$$F_n^{-1}\Delta_{\widehat{\alpha}}x_{[nr]} \Rightarrow g(r)-\eta X(r) = X_\eta(r).$$

It can be verified that

$$\frac{1}{\sqrt{n}}\sum_{t=1}^{n}\psi(u_t)\Delta_{\widehat{\alpha}}x_t F_n^{-1} \Rightarrow \int_0^1 dB_\psi X_\eta \tag{22}$$

$$\frac{1}{\sqrt{n}}\sum_{t=1}^{n}\psi'(u_t)(\widehat{\alpha}-\alpha)y^s_{t-1}\Delta_{\widehat{\alpha}}x_t F_n^{-1} \Rightarrow -\delta\eta\int B_u X_\eta \tag{23}$$

$$\frac{1}{n}\sum_{t=1}^{n}\psi'(u_t)F_n^{-1}\Delta_{\widehat{\alpha}}x_t\Delta_{\widehat{\alpha}}x_t' F_n^{-1} \Rightarrow -\delta\int X_\eta X_\eta; \tag{24}$$

thus, we have

$$n^{-1/2}D_n(\widehat{\gamma}-\gamma) \Rightarrow \left[\int X_\eta(r)X_\eta(r)'dr\right]^{-1}\int X_\eta(r)dB_\eta(r),$$

where

$$B_\eta(r) = \frac{1}{-\delta}B_\psi(r) + \eta\int_0^r B_u. \quad \blacksquare$$

References

Andrews, D. W. K. (1991). "Heteroskedasticity and autocorrelation consistent covariance matrix estimation," *Econometrica*, 59, 817–858.

Bai, J. (2004). "Testing parametric conditional distribution of dynamic models.," Forthcoming in Review of Economics and Statistics.

Bierens, H. (1981). Robust methods and asymptotic theory in nonlinear econometrics, Lecture notes in economics and mathematical systems No. 192, Berlin: Springer–Verlag.

Chu, C., K. Hornik, and C. M. Kuan (1995). "The moving-estimates tests for parameter stability," *Econometric Theory*, 11, 699–720.

Corradi, V., N. R. Swanson, and H. White (2000). "Testing for stationarity ergodicity and for comovements between nonlinear discrete-time Markov processes," *Journal of Econometrics*, 96, 39–73.

Cox, D. and Llatas, I. (1991). "Maximum likelihood type estimation for nearly nonstationary autoregressive time series," *Annals of Statistics* 19, 1109–1128.

Feller, W. (1951). "The asymptotic distribution of the range of sums of independent random variables," *Annals of Mathematical Statistics*, 22, 427–432.

Granger, C. and T. Terasvirta (1993). Modeling Nonlinear Economic Relationships. New York: Oxford.

Grenander, U. and M. Rosenblatt (1957). Statistical Analysis of Stationary Time Series. New York: John Wiley.

Hannan, E. J. (1970). *Multiple Time Series*. New York: John Wiley.

Huber, P. J. (1964). "Robust estimation of a location parameter," *Annals of Mathematical Statistics*, 35, 73–101.

Huber, P. J. (1973). "Robust regression: asymptotics, conjectures, and Monte Carlo," *Annals of Statistics*, 1, 799–821.

Juhl, T. (2001). "Testing for cointegration using M estimators, preprint cointegration analysis using M-Estimators," *Economics Letters*, 71, 149–154.

Khmaladze, E. V. (1981). "Martingale approach in the theory of goodness-of-fit tests," *Theory of Probability and Its Applications*, 26, 240–257.

Koenker, R. (1982). "Robust methods in econometrics," *Econometric Reviews*, 1, 213–236.

Koenker, R. and Z. Xiao (2002). "Inference on the quantile regression process," *Econometrica*, V70, 1583–1612.

Koul, H. and W. Stute (1999). "Nonparametric model checks for time series," *Annals of Statistics*, 27, 204–236.

Kuan, C. M. and K. Hornik (1995). "The generalized fluctuation test: A unifying view," *Econometric Reviews*, 14, 135–161.

Kwiatkowski, D., P. C. B. Phillips, P. Schmidt, and Y. Shin (1992). "Testing the null hypothesis of stationarity against the alternative of a unit root: How sure are we that economic time series have a unit root?"*Journal of Econometrics*, 54, 159–178.

Leybourne S. J. and B. P. M. McCabe (1994). "A consistent test for a unit root," *Journal of Business and Economic Statistics*, 12, 157–166.

Lucas, A. (1995). "Unit root tests based on M estimators," *Econometric Theory*, 11, 331–346.

MacNeill, I. B. (1978). "Properties of sequences of partial sums of polynomial regression residuals with applications to tests for change of regression at unknown times," *Annals of Statistics*, 6, 422–433.

Meese, R. A. and K. J. Singleton (1982). "On unit roots and the empirical modeling of exchange rate," *Journal of Finance*, 37, 1029–1035.

Nelson, C. R. and C. Plosser (1982). "Trends and random walks in macro-economic time series: Some evidence and implications," *Journal of Monetary Economics*, 10, 139–162.

Perron, P. (1988). "Trend and random walks in macro economic time series: Further evidence from a new approach,"*Journal of Economic Dynamics and Control*, 12, 297–332.

Perron, P. (1989). "The great crash, the oil price shock and the unit root hypothesis," *Econometrica*, 57, 1361–1401.

Phillips, P. C. B. (1991). "Spectral regression for cointegrated time series," In Nonparametric and Semiparametric Methods in Economics and Statistics, eds. W. Barnett, J. Powell, and G. Tauchen, New York: Cambridge University Press.

Phillips, P. C. B. (1995). "Robust nonstationary regression," *Econometric Theory*, 12, 912–951.

Phillips, P. C. B. and P. Perron (1988). "Testing for unit roots in time series regression," *Biometrika*, 75, 335–346.

Phillips, P. C. B. and V. Solo (1992). "Asymptotics for linear processes," *Annals of Statistics*, 20, 971–1001.

Ploberger, W. and W. Kramer (1992) "The CUSUM Te with OLS Residuals," Econometrica, 60, 271–280.

Ploberger, W., W. Kramer, and K. Kontrus (1989). "A new test for structural stability in the linear regression model," *Journal of Econometrics*, 40, 307–318.

Priestley, M. B. (1981). *Spectral Analysis and Time Series*. New York: Academic Press.

Relles, D. (1968). *Robust Regression by Modified Least Squares*. New Haven: Yale University Press.

Rothenberg, T. and J. Stock (1997). "Inference in a nearly integrated autoregressive model with nonnormal innovations," *Journal of Econometrics*, 80, 269–286.

Schotman, P. and H. K. van Dijk (1991). "A Bayesian analysis of the unit root in real exchange rates," *Journal of Econometrics*, 49, 195–238.

Schwarz, G. (1978). "Estimating the dimension of a model," *Annals of Statistics*, 6, 461–464.

Sen, P. K. (1980). "Asymptotic theory of some tests for a possible change in regression slope occurring at an unknown time point," *Zeitschrift für Wahrscheinlichkeitstheorie und Verwandte Gebiete*, 52, 203–218.

Shorack, G. R. and J. A. Wellner, (1986). *Empirical Processes with Applications to Statistics*, New York: Wiley.

Stute, W., H. Thies, and L. X. Zhu (1998). "Model checks for regression: An innovation process approach," *Annals of Statistics*, 26, 1916–1934.

Tanaka, K. (1990). "Testing for a moving average unit root," *Econometric Theory*, 6, 445–458.

Tong, H. *Nonlinear Time Series: A Dynamical System Approach*. Oxford: Oxford University Press.

White, H. and I. Domowitz (1984). "Nonlinear regression with dependent observations," *Econometrica*, 52, 143–161.

ELEVEN

Consistent Specification Testing for Quantile Regression Models

Yoon-Jae Whang*

11.1 INTRODUCTION

This chapter considers specification testing for a linear quantile regression model. The null hypothesis of interest is that the linear quantile regression function is correctly specified. The alternative hypothesis is the negation of the null hypothesis – that is, that the quantile regression function is not linear.

The tests we consider are generalizations of the Kolmogorov–Smirnov and Cramer–von Mises tests of goodness of fit. The tests can be applied to time series as well as cross-sectional contexts. The main characteristics of our tests are that they (i) are consistent against all alternatives to the null hypothesis, (ii) are powerful against $1/\sqrt{N}$ alternatives, (iii) do not depend on any smoothing parameters, (iv) allow for data dependence, and (v) are simple to compute.

The quantile regression models have been increasingly popular in econometric applications in recent years. Examples include Chamberlain (1994), Buchinsky (1994, 1998), Poterba and Rueben (1994), Koenker and Geling (2001), Engle and Manganelli (2002), and Chernozhukov and Umantsev (2001). See also Koenker and Hallock (2001) for a recent survey and the special issue of *Empirical Economics* (2001, vol. 26). In contrast to mean regression models, quantile regression models impose less restrictions on the data, are robust to outliers in the data, and provide more complete information on conditional distributions of dependent variables.

Despite the large body of literature on testing functional forms in parametric *mean* regression models,[1] there has been little research in the

* This research was supported by the Korea Research Foundation Grant. I owe special thanks to Joel Horowitz and Atsushi Inoue for kindly providing the codes they used in their papers. I also thank Don Andrews and Peter Phillips for helpful comments at an earlier stage of this research.

[1] Examples of the existing tests of parametric mean regression models against nonparametric alternatives include Aït-Sahalia, Bickel, and Stoker (2001); Bierens (1982, 1990); Bierens and Ploberger (1997); De Jong (1996); Eubank and Spiegelman (1990); Fan and Li (1996); Gozalo (1993); Härdle and Mammen (1993); Hart (1997); Hong and White (1995); Horowitz and Spokoiny (2000); Li and Wang (1998); Stinchcombe and White (1998); Whang (2000); Whang and Andrews (1993); Wooldridge (1992); Yatchew (1992); and Zheng (1996).

econometrics literature on the related testing problem in parametric *quantile* regression models. Also, most of the existing results assume independent observations. For example, Zheng (1998) proposes a quantile regression specification test that requires a certain nonparametric estimate. His test has an asymptotically normal limit null distribution, but it is not consistent against $1/\sqrt{N}$ local alternatives and is dependent on a bandwidth parameter. Bierens and Ginther (2001) apply the idea of the integrated conditional moment test of Bierens (1982) and Bierens and Ploberger (1997) to the quantile regression context. Their test is consistent against $1/\sqrt{N}$ alternatives, but it has a case-dependent asymptotic null distribution and relies on an upper bound on the asymptotic critical value, which might be too conservative. Also, they do not take into account uncertainty due to parameter estimation. Horowitz and Spokoiny (2001) have developed a median regression specification test that is uniformly consistent against alternatives whose distance from the linear model converges to zero at the fastest possible rate but one that is slower than $1/\sqrt{N}$. Their test statistic depends on a nonparametric estimate and has a case-dependent asymptotic null distribution, but the suggested bootstrap procedure to calculate the critical value might be computationally burdensome in practice.

To the best of our knowledge, only Koul and Stute (1999) and Inoue (1999) have addressed the problem of consistent testing in quantile regression models accounting for data dependence. Koul and Stute (1999) confine their attention to first-order autoregressive models and suggest a specification test of the hypothesis that the first-order autoregressive median function is AR(1) over a certain interval. They use a martingale transformation that makes its asymptotic null distribution case independent (see also Khmaladze 1988, 1993), but they do not provide local power results. Inoue (1999) generalizes the test of Bierens and Ploberger (1997) to the quantile regression models with time series observations. As is true with Bierens and Ginther (2001), his bound test based on the law of the iterated logarithm might be too conservative. Furthermore, the finite sample performance of this integrated conditional–moment-type test might be sensitive to the choice of the nuisance parameter space over which the integration is calculated (see Whang 2000, Section 7), for details.

Our tests proposed here are applicable to both dependent and independent observations. The asymptotic null distributions are case dependent, but we suggest a subsampling procedure to calculate the critical values. Subsampling is a very powerful resampling tool that allows an asymptotically valid inference under very general sampling schemes (e.g., Politis and Romano 1994 and Politis, Romano, and Wolf 1999). The main idea of subsampling is that each subsample of a given size b taken *without* replacement from the original data is indeed a sample of size b from the true model. Therefore, in contrast to the standard bootstrap, we do not have to impose the null restrictions (which generally depends on the true data-generating process) in our resampling procedure to mimic the asymptotic null distributions.

The remainder of the chapter is organized as follows: Section 11.2 defines the main test statistics and establishes their asymptotic null distributions. Section 11.3 introduces a subsampling procedure for obtaining critical values and justifies the procedure asymptotically. Section 11.5 establishes consistency of the tests and determines the power of the proposed tests against $1/\sqrt{N}$ local alternatives. Section 11.6 summarizes the results from Monte Carlo experiments. Finally, an appendix presents proofs of results stated in the text.

11.2 THE TEST STATISTICS AND ASYMPTOTIC NULL DISTRIBUTIONS

In this section, we define our test statistics and derive their asymptotic distributions under the null hypothesis of interest.

We first introduce the hypotheses of our interest. Let $\{W_i = (Y_i, X_i', Z_i')' : i = 1, \ldots, N\}$ denote an observed sample, where $Y \in \mathbb{R}$, $X_i \in \mathbb{R}^P$ and $Z_i \in \mathbb{R}^K$. We are interested in testing the null hypothesis

$$H_0 : P[Y_i \leq X_i'\theta_0 | Z_i] = q \text{ a.s. for some } \theta_0 \in \Theta \ \forall i \geq 1, \tag{1}$$

where $0 < q < 1$, Θ is a bounded subset of $\mathbb{R}^P$and X_i is measurable with respect to $\sigma(Z_i)$, the σ-field generated by Z_i. The alternative hypothesis is the negation of H_0, that is,

$$H_1 : P[Y_i \leq X_i'\theta | Z_i] \neq q \text{ with positive probability for all } \theta \in \Theta \ \forall i \geq 1. \tag{2}$$

To motivate our test statistics, consider

$$g(W_i, \theta, z) = [(Y_i \leq X_i'\theta) - q](Z_i \leq z), \tag{3}$$

where $(\cdot)$ denotes the indicator function of the event.[2] Note that, under the null hypothesis, we have $E[g(W_i, \theta_0, z)] = 0 \ \forall z \in \mathbb{R}^K$ for some $\theta_0 \in \Theta$. Under the alternative hypothesis, however, we have $E[g(W_i, \theta, z)] \neq 0$ for some $z \in \mathbb{R}^K$ for all $\theta \in \Theta$. This suggests that we can take the sample analogue of the latter population moment as the basis of our test statistics. Let $\widehat{\theta}$ be an estimator of θ_0 (that satisfies Assumption 11.2). We consider the following Kolmogorov–Smirnov- and Cramer–von Mises-type test statistics:

$$KS_N = \sqrt{N} \sup_{z \in \mathcal{Z}} |\overline{g}_N(z, \widehat{\theta})| ; \ CM_N = \sum_{i=1}^{N} [\overline{g}_N(Z_i, \widehat{\theta})]^2, \tag{4}$$

[2] In the multivariate case $K > 1$ with, for example, $Z_i = (Z_{i1}, \ldots, Z_{iK})'$ and $z = (z_1, \ldots, z_K)'$, we define $(Z_i \leq z) = \Pi_{m=1}^{K}(Z_{im} \leq z_m)$.

where

$$\overline{g}_N(z,\theta) = \frac{1}{N}\sum_{i=1}^{N} g(W_i, \theta, z);$$

$\mathcal{Z}$ denotes the support of Z_i. We assume that $\mathcal{Z}$ is bounded subset of $\mathbb{R}^K$.[3]

We need the following assumptions to analyze the asymptotic behavior of our test statistics:

Assumption 11.1

(i) $\{W_i = (Y_i, X_i', Z_i')' : i = 1, \ldots, N\}$ is a strictly stationary and α-mixing sequence with $\alpha(m) = O(m^{-A})$ for some $A > \max\{(Q-1)(1+Q/2), 1+2/\delta\}$, where Q is an even integer that satisfies $Q > 2(P+K)$ and δ is a positive constant that also appears in Assumption 11.2(ii).

(ii) $E\|X_i\|^2 < \infty \, \forall i \geq 1$.

(iii) The conditional distribution $H(y|z)$ of Y_i given $Z_i = z$ has uniformly bounded first- and second-order derivatives with respect to $y \in \mathbb{R}$ a.s., and the distribution $J(z)$ of Z_i is absolutely continuous with respect to Lebesgue measure $\forall i \geq 1$.

Assumption 11.2

(i) $\sqrt{N}\left(\widehat{\theta} - \theta_0\right) = \sqrt{N}\Gamma_0\overline{\psi}_N(\theta_0) + o_p(1)$,where Γ_0 is a nonstochastic matrix that may depend on θ_0 and $\overline{\psi}_N(\theta) = \frac{1}{N}\sum_{i=1}^{N}\psi(W_i,\theta)$.

(ii) $\psi(w,\theta) : \mathbb{R}^{P+K+1} \times \Theta \to \mathbb{R}^P$ is a measurable function that satisfies (a) $E\psi(W_i,\theta_0) = 0$ and (b) $E\left\|\psi(W_i,\theta_0)\right\|^{2+\delta} < \infty$ for some $\delta > 0 \, \forall i \geq 1$.

Remark 1. The strict stationarity in Assumption 11.1 (i) is assumed just for simplicity. In fact, it is not difficult to relax this assumption and to show that our results below hold for non-identically distributed observations, see Linton, Maasoumi and Whang (2003, Theorem 4) for a related result.

2. Assumption 11.2 is very general and can be verified for many estimators that are $\sqrt{N}$-consistent and asymptotically normal using the results in the literature. For example, consider a quantile regression estimator of θ_0 that minimizes

$$\min_{\theta\in\Theta}\sum_{i=1}^{N}[Y_i - X_i'\theta]\,[q - (Y_i \leq X_i'\theta)]\,.$$

This estimator is originally suggested by Koenker and Bassett (1978, 1982). The estimator includes as a special case the least absolute deviation (LAD)

[3] The boundedness assumption is made just for simplicity. If needed, this assumption can be avoided using the reparametrization argument; see, for example, Billingsley (1968, Theorem 16.4).

estimator. Under regularity conditions, Assumption 11.2 holds for this estimator with

$$\Gamma_0 = [E(f(X_i'\theta_0|X_i)X_iX_i')]^{-1}$$
$$\psi(W_i,\theta) = X_i[(Y_i \le X_i'\theta) - q],$$

where $f(y|z) = \partial H(y|z)/\partial y$; see, for example, Weiss (1991).

Let

$$\nu_N^*(z,\theta) = \frac{1}{\sqrt{N}}\sum_{i=1}^{N}[g(W_i,\theta,z) - Eg(W_i,\theta,z)]$$
$$\overline{\psi}_N^*(\theta) = \frac{1}{N}\sum_{i=1}^{N}[\psi(W_i,\theta) - E\psi(W_i,\theta)]$$
$$\Delta_0(z) = Ef(X_i'\theta_0|Z_i)(Z_i \le z)X_i.$$

We show that the asymptotic null distributions of our test statistics are functionals of a mean zero Gaussian process $(\nu(\cdot), \nu_0')'$ with covariance function given by

$$C(z_1,z_2,\theta_0) = \lim_{N\to\infty} E\begin{pmatrix}\nu_N^*(z_1,\theta_0)\\ \sqrt{N}\overline{\psi}_N^*(\theta_0)\end{pmatrix}\begin{pmatrix}\nu_N^*(z_2,\theta_0)\\ \sqrt{N}\overline{\psi}_N^*(\theta_0)\end{pmatrix}'. \tag{5}$$

Theorem 11.1 *If Assumptions 11.1–11.2 hold under the null, then*

$$(a)\ KS_N \Rightarrow \sup_{z\in\mathcal{Z}}\left|\nu(z) + \Delta_0(z)'\Gamma_0\nu_0\right|$$
$$(b)\ CM_N \Rightarrow \int (\nu(z) + \Delta_0(z)'\Gamma_0\nu_0)^2\, dJ(z).$$

The asymptotic null distributions of KS_N and CM_N depend on the "true" parameter θ_0 and distribution function $G(\cdot)$. The latter implies that the asymptotic critical values for KS_N and CM_N can not be tabulated. A subsampling procedure (described below), however, can be used to approximate the null distributions.

11.3 SUBSAMPLING APPROXIMATION

In this section, we use a subsampling to approximate the null distributions of our test statistics.

We first define the subsampling procedure for the test KS_N. (The argument for the test CM_N is similar.) With some abuse of notation, we write the test statistic KS_N as a function of the data $\{W_i : i = 1,\ldots,N\}$:

$$KS_N = \sqrt{N}g_N(W_1,\ldots,W_N),$$

where

$$g_N(W_1,\ldots,W_N)=\sup_{z\in\mathcal{Z}}\left|\overline{g}_N(z,\widehat{\theta})\right|. \tag{6}$$

Let

$$G_N(w)=P\left(\sqrt{N}g_N(W_1,\ldots,W_N)\le w\right) \tag{7}$$

denote the distribution function of g_N. Let $g_{N,b,i}$ be equal to the statistic g_b evaluated at the subsample $\{W_i,\ldots,W_{i+b-1}\}$ of size b:

$$g_{N,b,i}=g_b(W_i,W_{i+1},\ldots,W_{i+b-1})\quad \text{for } i=1,\ldots,N-b+1.$$

We note that each subsample of size b (taken *without* replacement from the original data) is indeed a sample of size b from the true sampling distribution of the original data. Hence, it is clear that one can approximate the sampling distribution of KS_N using the distribution of the values of $g_{N,b,i}$ computed over $N-b+1$ different subsamples of size b. That is, we approximate the sampling distribution G_N of KS_N by

$$\widehat{G}_{N,b}(w)=\frac{1}{N-b+1}\sum_{i=1}^{N-b+1}1\left(\sqrt{b}g_{N,b,i}\le w\right).$$

Let $g_{N,b}^{KS}(1-\alpha)$ denote the $(1-\alpha)$-th sample quantile of $\widehat{G}_{N,b}(\cdot)$, that is,

$$g_{N,b}^{KS}(1-\alpha)=\inf\left\{w:\widehat{G}_{N,b}(w)\ge 1-\alpha\right\}.$$

We call it the *subsample critical value* of significance level α. Thus, we reject the null hypothesis at the significance level α if $KS_N>g_{N,b}^{KS}(1-\alpha)$.

Let $g^{KS}(1-\alpha)$ denote the $(1-\alpha)$-th quantile of the asymptotic null distribution of KS_N (given in Theorem 11.1(a)). We now justify the preceding subsampling procedure (define $g_{N,b}^{CM}(1-\alpha)$ and $g^{CM}(1-\alpha)$ analogously for the test CM_N):

Theorem 11.2 *Suppose Assumptions 1-2 hold. Assume $b/N\to 0$ and $b\to\infty$ as $N\to\infty$. Then, under the null hypothesis, we have: as $N\to\infty$,*

(a) $g_{N,b}^{KS}(1-\alpha)\xrightarrow{p}g^{KS}(1-\alpha)$ *and* $g_{N,b}^{CM}(1-\alpha)\xrightarrow{p}g^{CM}(1-\alpha)$

(b) $P\left(KS_N>g_{N,b}^{KS}(1-\alpha)\right)\to\alpha$ *and* $P\left(CM_N>g_{N,b}^{CM}(1-\alpha)\right)\to\alpha$

Remark 1. The assumptions on b are very weak and just require that the size of the subsamples goes to infinity at a rate slower than the total sample size. In practice, however, the choice of b is rather difficult. The main problem is that the b that is good for size distortion is not good for power and vice a versa. Politis et al. (1999) discuss various methods for selecting b. We can also allow b to be data-dependent as in Linton, Maasoumi, Whang (2005). In Section 11.5, we carefully investigate the robustness of our finding to the choice of b and find that our test has fairly good finite-sample size and power performance for a wide range of b.

2. If the true data generating process is known to be i.i.d., then one can recompute the test statistic over all $\binom{N}{b}$ subsamples of size b to approximate the asymptotic null distribution. However, this procedure can be computationally very demanding if N is large, while our method still works for independent as well as dependent observations.

11.4 POWER PROPERTIES

In this section, we investigate power properties of our tests. To help the reader understand why the subsampling test has non-trivial power against fixed and local alternatives, we first discuss a simple testing problem: Let $\{W_1, \ldots, W_N\}$ be a random sample from $N(\mu, 1)$ and the null and alternative hypotheses of interest are given by $\mathbf{H}_0 : \mu = 0$ and $\mathbf{H}_1 : \mu > 0$ respectively. Consider the t-test statistic $T_N = \sqrt{N}\,\overline{W}_N$, which satisfies $T_N \Rightarrow N(0, 1)$ as $N \to \infty$ under $\mathbf{H}_0$. Let $g_{N,b}(1-\alpha)$ be the subsample critical value, i.e., the $(1-\alpha)$-th quantile of the subsampling distribution of $T_b = \sqrt{b}\,\overline{W}_b$, where b denotes the subsample size (that satisfies $b \to \infty$ and $b/N \to 0$ as $N \to \infty$). Note that $T_b \Rightarrow N(0, 1)$ as $b \to \infty$ under $\mathbf{H}_0$. Clearly, the test (that rejects $\mathbf{H}_0$ if $T_N > g_{N,b}(1-\alpha)$) has asymptotically correct size α. Now, suppose that the alternative hypothesis $\mathbf{H}_1$ is true. Then, both T_N and $g_{N,b}(1-\alpha)$ diverge (in probability) to ∞ but the latter diverges at a slower rate than the former, so that the test would reject $\mathbf{H}_0$ with high probability for N large. More specifically, note that, under $\mathbf{H}_1$, both $\overline{W}_N$ and $\overline{W}_b$ converges (in probability) to μ (> 0) as $N, b \to \infty$ and hence

$$
\begin{aligned}
P(T_N > g_{N,b}(1-\alpha)) &= P\left(\sqrt{N/b}\,\overline{W}_N > g_{N,b}(1-\alpha)/\sqrt{b}\right) \\
&= P\left(\sqrt{N/b}\mu > \mu\right) + o(1) \to 1,
\end{aligned}
$$

where the latter convergence holds since $\underline{\lim}_{N\to\infty}(N/b) > 1$. This establishes that the subsampling test is consistent against $\mathbf{H}_1$. On the other hand, consider a sequence of local alternatives $\mathbf{H}_a : \mu (= \mu_N) = \delta/\sqrt{N}$, where $\delta > 0$. Under $\mathbf{H}_a$, we have $T_N \Rightarrow N(\delta, 1)$, while $T_b = \sqrt{b}(\overline{W}_b - \mu_N) + (b/N)^{1/2}\,\delta \Rightarrow N(0, 1)$ since $b/N \to 0$. This implies that

$$
P(T_N > g_{N,b}(1-\alpha)) \to P(N(\delta, 1) > z_{1-\alpha}) > \alpha,
$$

where $z_{1-\alpha}$ denotes the $(1-\alpha)$-th quantile of the standard normal distribution. This establishes that the test has the same first order non-trivial local power as the test based on the normal critical values, and is asymptotically locally unbiased as desired.

We now formally establish that our tests KS_N and CM_N are consistent against the fixed alternative hypothesis H_1:

Theorem 11.3 *Suppose Assumption 11.1 holds and* $\widehat{\theta} \xrightarrow{p} \theta_1$ *for some* $\theta_1 \in \Theta$. *Assume* $b/N \to 0$ *and* $b \to \infty$ *as* $N \to \infty$. *Then, under the alternative hypothesis*

H_1, we have

$$(a)\ P\left(KS_N > g_{N,b}^{KS}(1-\alpha)\right) \to 1$$
$$(b)\ P\left(CM_N > g_{N,b}^{CM}(1-\alpha)\right) \to 1$$

as $N \to \infty$.

Next, we consider the power properties of our tests against a sequence of contiguous alternatives converging to the null at the rate $N^{-1/2}$, i.e.,

$$H_a : P\left[Y_i \leq X_i'\theta_0 + N^{-1/2}d(X_i) \mid Z_i\right] = q \text{ a.s.,} \tag{8}$$

where $d(\cdot) : \mathbb{R}^P \to \mathbb{R}$ is a non-zero function with $Ed^2(X_i) < \infty \forall i \geq 1$[4].

To analyze the asymptotic behavior of the tests under H_a, we need to modify Assumption 11.2. That is, we assume that the estimator $\widehat{\theta}$ satisfies

Assumption 11.2* Assumption 11.2 holds with (ii)(a) replaced by

$$\sqrt{N}E\psi(W_i, \theta_0) \to \xi(\theta_0) \text{ as } N \to \infty.$$

This assumption implies that the mean of the asymptotic distribution of $\sqrt{N}(\widehat{\theta} - \theta_0)$ might be nonzero under H_a.

Let $(v(\cdot), v_0')'$ be a mean-zero Gaussian process with covariance function given by (5) and

$$\delta(z) = \Delta_0'(z)\xi(\theta_0) + \eta(\theta_0), \text{ where}$$
$$\eta_0(z) = -Ef(X_i'\theta_0|Z_i)(Z_i \leq z)d(X_i).$$

Then, the asymptotic distributions of KS_N and CM_N under the local alternatives H_a are given by

Theorem 11.4 *Suppose Assumptions 11.1 and 11.2* hold under H_a. Then we have*

$$(a)\ KS_N \Rightarrow M_1 \equiv \sup_{z \in \mathcal{Z}} \left|\nu(z) + \Delta_0(z)'\Gamma_0\nu_0 + \delta(z)\right|$$

$$(b)\ CM_N \Rightarrow M_2 \equiv \int \left(\nu(z) + \Delta_0(z)'\Gamma_0\nu_0 + \delta(z)\right)^2 dJ(z).$$

This result implies that asymptotic local power of our tests against H_a is given by

[4] Bierens and Ginther (2001) consider the local power of their test only for the special case that θ_0 is known. Our approach, however, does not impose such assumption and allows θ_0 to be estimated.

Corollary 11.1 *Suppose Assumptions 11.1 and 11.2* hold. Assume $b/N \to 0$ and $b \to \infty$ as $N \to \infty$. Then, under H_a, we have:*

$$(a)\ P\left[KS_N > g_{N,b}^{KS}(1-\alpha)\right] \to P\left[M_1 > g^{KS}(1-\alpha)\right]$$
$$(b)\ P\left[CM_N > g_{N,b}^{CM}(1-\alpha)\right] \to P\left[M_2 > g^{CM}(1-\alpha)\right]$$

11.5 MONTE CARLO EXPERIMENTS

In this section, we present the results of Monte Carlo experiments that illustrate the finite sample performance of the KS_N and CM_N tests. We compare the performance of our tests with that found by Zheng (1978).[5]

We consider two data-generating processes: The first one is similar to the design considered by Zheng (1998): For $i = 1, \ldots, N$,

$$\text{DGP1}: Y_i = 1 + X_{1i} + X_{2i} + c_1\left(X_{1i}^2 + X_{1i}X_{2i} + X_{2i}^2\right)^{3/2} + u_{1i}.$$

Here X_{1i} and X_{2i} are sampled independently from $N(0,1)$ and $u_{1i} + \exp[\Phi^{-1}(q)]$ has the standard lognormal distribution; thus, $P(u_{1i} \le 0) = q$ for $0 < q < 1$, where $\Phi(\cdot)$ denotes the cdf of the standard normal distribution. The null-hypothesis model corresponds to $c_1 = 0$. Therefore, under H_0, (1) holds with $X_i = (1, X_{1i}, X_{2i})'$, $\theta_0 = (1,1,1)'$, and $Z_i = (X_{1i}, X_{2i})'$.

The second design is a time series model: For $i = 1, \ldots, N$,

$$\text{DGP2}: Y_i = 1 + 0.9Y_{i-1} + X_i + c_2 X_i^2 + u_{2i},$$

where $X_i = 0.5X_{i-1} + \varepsilon_i$, u_{2i} and ε_i are sampled independently from $N(0,1)$ and $Y_0 = X_0 = 0$. Here, the null-hypothesis model corresponds to $c_2 = 0$. Under H_0, (1) holds with $X_i = (1, Y_{i-1}, X_i)'$, $\theta_0 = (1, 0.9, 1)'$, and $Z_i = (Y_{i-1}, X_i)'$.

We consider three sample sizes $N \in (100, 200, 300)$ and quantile probabilities $q \in (0.5, 0.90, 0.99)$. As the number of subsamples, we take $b = \left[N^\delta\right]$ for $\delta \in (0.7, 0.8, 0.9)$, where $[a]$ denotes the integer part of a. We set the number of Monte Carlo repetitions to be 1,000. The values of θ_0 are estimated by the linear quantile regression estimator of Koenker and Bassett (1978). The kernel used for the Zheng's (1998) test is $K(u) = (15/16)(1-u^2)^2 1(|u| \le 1)$. As suggested by Zheng (1998), the bandwidth parameter for the latter test is chosen by minimizing the generalized cross-validation criterion. In all experiments, the nominal probability of rejecting a correct null hypothesis is 0.05.

[5] We did not consider the tests of Koul and Stute (1999) and Inoue (1999) in our experiments because the Koul and Stute (1999) test is applicable to only nonlinear AR(1) processes, whereas our tests apply to general linear time series models. Also, Inoue's (1999) test can not be directly compared with our tests because his hypotheses assume that the entire history is given, whereas our tests allow for dynamic misspecification under both the null and alternative hypotheses.

Table 11.1 *Rejection Probabilities (DGP1)*

c_1	q	N	*KS*			*CM*			Zheng
			$\delta = .7$	$\delta = .8$	$\delta = .9$	$\delta = .7$	$\delta = .8$	$\delta = .9$	
0.0	0.50	100	**.059**	**.064**	.086	.003	.019	**.042**	.035
		200	**.064**	.071	.091	.010	.025	**.053**	.020
		300	**.052**	.072	.099	.011	.017	**.048**	.015
	0.90	100	.020	**.044**	.074	.005	.018	**.047**	.026
		200	.030	**.047**	.082	.000	.014	**.050**	.020
		300	.032	**.049**	.070	.002	.010	.035	.014
	0.95	100	**.048**	**.059**	.111	.016	.034	**.078**	.019
		200	.030	**.042**	.086	.007	.018	**.059**	.016
		300	.025	**.048**	.078	.006	.024	**.058**	.011
1.0	0.50	100	*.792*	*.711*	.444	.803	.831	*.652*	.997
		200	*.998*	.979	.835	1.00	1.00	*.985*	1.00
		300	*1.00*	1.00	.949	1.00	1.00	*1.00*	1.00
	0.90	100	.179	*.358*	.273	.078	.339	*.310*	.233
		200	.871	*.801*	.601	.838	.814	*.676*	.555
		300	.990	*.972*	.812	.990	.973	.879	.786
	0.95	100	*.154*	*.157*	.230	.099	.109	*.206*	.058
		200	.413	*.460*	.430	.290	.368	*.429*	.220
		300	.675	*.734*	.579	.552	.683	*.553*	.424

Table 11.1 provides the rejection probabilities of the tests for DGP1. When $c_1 = 0$, the results show that the size performance of the KS_N and CM_N tests is reasonably good with a suitable choice of subsamples. (The numbers in boldface in Table 11.1 [in Table 11.2 as well] correspond to the case in which the difference between the nominal and empirical rejection probabilities is not significantly different from zero at the 0.05 level.) Zheng's test, on the other hand, often underrejects the true null hypothesis. When $c_1 = 1$, the results show the power performance of the tests. The rejection probabilities increase as N increases, showing that the tests are consistent against the fixed alternative. We can also see that the power depends on the choice of δ and that it generally increases as δ gets smaller at a fixed N. The latter is to be expected because the power is proportional to N/b for N sufficiently large (see eq. (A.20) in the appendix). To compare the power performance of the tests, we indicate in Table 11.2 (in Table 11.2 as well) the rejection probabilities in italics when they are computed with δ, which yields the empirical probability of rejecting the correct null hypothesis contained in a 95% confidence interval around the nominal rejection probability. In this i.i.d. scenario, as expected, Zheng's test was more powerful in small samples than ours in the case of median regression ($q = 0.5$). Surprisingly, however, in the case of near-extreme quantile regressions ($q = 0.9$ and 0.95), our tests significantly dominate Zheng's test. We conjecture that the latter result might be due to the well-known problem of kernel estimators in estimating tails when data are sparse.

Table 11.2 *Rejection Probabilities (DGP2)*

c_2	q	N	KS			CM			Zheng
			$\delta = .7$	$\delta = .8$	$\delta = .9$	$\delta = .7$	$\delta = .8$	$\delta = .9$	
0.0	0.50	100	**.043**	**.057**	.083	.001	.015	**.038**	**.037**
		200	**.056**	.077	.082	.006	.023	**.049**	**.040**
		300	**.059**	.075	.072	.016	.024	**.050**	.025
	0.90	100	.008	**.039**	**.061**	.003	.012	**.041**	.013
		200	.013	**.040**	**.063**	.002	.014	**.039**	.022
		300	.013	**.040**	**.051**	.003	.014	.028	**.036**
	0.95	100	.035	**.039**	.071	.012	.012	**.053**	.010
		200	.013	.025	**.063**	.002	.007	**.039**	.016
		300	.011	.032	**.062**	.004	.016	**.042**	.029
1.0	0.50	100	*.617*	*.576*	.352	.455	.385	*.385*	*.371*
		200	*.985*	.944	.750	.974	.846	*.846*	*.954*
		300	*.999*	.992	.935	.998	.968	*.968*	1.00
	0.90	100	.484	*.568*	*.353*	.165	.302	*.302*	.095
		200	.995	*.946*	*.749*	.946	.800	*.800*	.251
		300	1.00	*.999*	*.944*	.997	.960	.960	*.416*
	0.95	100	.256	*.191*	.281	.078	.132	*.132*	.029
		200	.873	.679	*.480*	.285	.397	*.397*	.114
		300	.989	.954	*.733*	.745	.707	*.707*	.154

Table 11.2 gives the corresponding results for DGP2. With time series data, as expected, our tests generally had better power performance compared with Zheng's test. In particular, the power of the KS_N test dominates that of the other tests for all values of q considered.

To summarize, we find that the KS_N test generally has the best performance in our experiments with dependent observations. This is also true with independent observations – especially when we are concerned with near-extreme events (i.e., q close to 1).

APPENDIX

We let C_j for some integer $j \geq 1$ denote a generic constant. (It is not meant to be equal in any two places it appears.) In verifying the asymptotic validity of the subsampling procedure, we rely heavily on the arguments used by Politis et al. (1999).

Lemma A.1 *Suppose Assumption 11.1 holds. Then, for each* $\varepsilon > 0$ *there exists* $\delta > 0$ *such that*

$$\overline{\lim_{n\to\infty}} \left\| \sup_{\rho^*((z_1,\theta_1),(z_2,\theta_2))<\delta} \left| \nu_N^*(z_1, \theta_1) - \nu_N^*(z_2, \theta_2) \right| \right\|_Q < \varepsilon, \tag{A.1}$$

where

$$\rho^*[(z_1,\theta_1),(z_2,\theta_2)] = \left\{E\{[(Y_i \le X_i'\theta_1) - q](Z_i \le z_1) - [(Y_i \le X_i'\theta_2) - q](Z_i \le z_2)\}^2\right\}^{1/2} \quad \text{(A.2)}$$

Proof of Lemma A.1: The result follows from Theorem 2.2 of Andrews and Pollard (1994) if we verify the mixing and bracketing conditions in the theorem. The mixing condition is implied by Assumption 11.1(i). The bracketing condition also holds by the following argument:
Let

$$\mathcal{F} = \left\{[(Y_i \le X_i'\theta) - q](Z_i \le z) : (z,\theta) \in \mathcal{Z} \times \Theta\right\}. \quad \text{(A.3)}$$

$\mathcal{F}$ is a class of uniformly bounded functions satisfying the L^2-continuity condition because we have

$$\begin{aligned}
&\sup_{i\ge1} E \sup_{\substack{(z^*,\theta^*)\in\mathcal{Z}\times\Theta:\\ |z^*-z|\le r_1,\|\theta^*-\theta\|\le r_2,\sqrt{r_1^2+r_2^2}\le r}} \Big|[(Y_i \le X_i'\theta^*) - q](Z_i \le z^*) \\
&\quad - [(Y_i \le X_i'\theta) - q](Z_i \le z)\Big|^2 \\
&= E \sup_{\substack{(z^*,\theta^*)\in\mathcal{Z}\times\Theta:\\ |z^*-z|\le r_1,\|\theta^*-\theta\|\le r_2,\sqrt{r_1^2+r_2^2}\le r}} \Big|[(Y_i \le X_i'\theta^*)(Z_i \le z^*) - (Y_i \le X_i'\theta)(Z_i \le z)] \\
&\quad - q[(Z_i \le z^*) - (Z_i \le z)]\Big|^2 \\
&\le E \sup_{\substack{(z^*,\theta^*)\in\mathcal{Z}\times\Theta:\\ |z^*-z|\le r_1,\|\theta^*-\theta\|\le r_2,\sqrt{r_1^2+r_2^2}\le r}} \Big\{4\left|(Y_i \le X_i'\theta^*) - (Y_i \le X_i'\theta)\right|^2 \\
&\quad + (4+2q^2)\left|(Z_i \le z^*) - (Z_i \le z)\right|^2\Big\} \\
&\le C_1 E\|X_i\| r_2 + C_2 r_1 \\
&\le C_3 r,
\end{aligned}$$

where the first inequality holds by the Cauchy–Schwartz inequality, the second inequality holds by Assumption 11.1(iii), and $C_3 = \sqrt{2}(C_1 E\|Z_i\| \vee C_2)$ is finite by Assumption 11.1(ii). Now the desired bracketing condition holds because the L^2-continuity condition implies that the bracketing number satisfies

$$N(\varepsilon, \mathcal{F}) \le C_4 \left(\frac{1}{\varepsilon}\right)^{P+K} \quad \text{(A.4)}$$

(see Andrews and Pollard 1994, p. 121). ■

Lemma A.2 *Suppose Assumptions 1 and 2 (or 2*) hold. Then, we have*

$$\sup_{z\in\mathcal{Z}} \left|\nu_N^*(z,\widehat{\theta}) - \nu_N^*(z,\theta_0)\right| \xrightarrow{p} 0. \tag{A.5}$$

Proof of Lemma A.2: Consider the pseudometric (A.2). We have

$$\begin{aligned}
&\sup_{z\in\mathcal{Z}} \rho^* \left[\left(z,\widehat{\theta}\right), \left(z,\theta_0\right)\right]^2 \\
&\quad = \sup_{z\in\mathcal{Z}} E\left[(Y_i \le X_i'\theta) - (Y_i \le X_i'\theta_0)\right]^2 (Z_i \le z)\Big|_{\theta=\widehat{\theta}} \\
&\quad \le \iint \left[(y \le x'\widehat{\theta}) - (y \le x'\theta_0)\right]^2 dH(y|z)dJ(z) \qquad \text{(A.6)} \\
&\quad \le \int \left|H(x'\widehat{\theta}|z) - H(x'\theta_0|z)\right| dJ(z) \\
&\quad \le CE\left\|X_i\right\| \left\|\widehat{\theta} - \theta\right\| \xrightarrow{p} 0,
\end{aligned}$$

where the last inequality holds by Assumption 11.1(iii) and a one-term Taylor expansion and the last convergence to zero holds by Assumptions 11.1(ii) and 11.2. Now, (A.5) holds because we have $\forall\varepsilon > 0$, $\forall\eta > 0$, $\exists\delta > 0$ such that

$$\begin{aligned}
&\overline{\lim_{N\to\infty}}\, P\left\{\sup_{z\in\mathcal{Z}} \left|\nu_N^*(z,\widehat{\theta}) - \nu_N^*(z,\theta_0)\right| > \eta\right\} \\
&\quad \le \overline{\lim_{N\to\infty}}\, P\left\{\sup_{z\in\mathcal{Z}} \left|\nu_N^*(z,\widehat{\theta}) - \nu_N^*(z,\theta_0)\right| > \eta,\ \sup_{z\in\mathcal{Z}} \rho^*\left[\left(z,\widehat{\theta}\right), \left(z,\theta_0\right)\right] < \delta\right\} \\
&\qquad + \overline{\lim_{N\to\infty}}\, P\left\{\sup_{z\in\mathcal{Z}} \rho^*\left[\left(z,\widehat{\theta}\right), \left(z,\theta_0\right)\right] \ge \delta\right\} \qquad \text{(A.7)} \\
&\quad \le \overline{\lim_{N\to\infty}}\, P^*\left\{\sup_{\rho^*[(z_1,\theta_1),(z_2,\theta_2)]\le\delta} \left|\nu_N^*(z_1,\theta_1) - \nu_N^*(z_2,\theta_2)\right| > \eta\right\} \\
&\quad < \frac{\varepsilon}{\eta},
\end{aligned}$$

where the last term on the right-hand-side (rhs) of the first inequality is zero by (A.6) and the last inequality holds by the stochastic equicontinuity result (A.1). Because $\varepsilon/\eta > 0$ is arbitrary, (A.5) follows.

Lemma A.3 *Suppose Assumptions 11.1 and 11.2 (or 11.2*) hold. Then, we have*

$$\begin{pmatrix} \nu_N^*(\cdot,\theta_0) \\ \sqrt{N}\psi_N^*(\theta_0) \end{pmatrix} \Rightarrow \begin{pmatrix} \nu(\cdot) \\ \nu_0 \end{pmatrix},$$

and the sample paths of $\nu(\cdot)$ are uniformly continuous with respect to pseudometric ρ_d on $\mathcal{Z}$ with probability one, where

$$\begin{aligned}
\rho_d(z_1,z_2) &= \rho^*\left[(z_1,\theta_0), (z_2,\theta_0)\right] \\
&= \left\{E\left[(Y_i \le X_i'\theta_0) - q\right]^2 \left[(Z_i \le z_1) - (Z_i \le z_2)\right]^2\right\}^{1/2}.
\end{aligned}$$

Proof of Lemma A.3: By Theorem 10.2 of Pollard (1990), the result of Lemma A.3 holds if we have (i) total boundedness of pseudometric space $(\mathcal{Z}, \rho_d)$, (ii) stochastic equicontinuity of $\{\nu_N^*(\cdot, \theta_0) : N \geq 1\}$, and (iii) finite dimensional (fidi) convergence. Conditions (i) and (ii) follow from Lemma 11.1. We now verify condition (iii). We need to show that $[\nu_N^*(z_1, \theta_0), \ldots, \nu_N^*(z_J, \theta_0), \sqrt{N}\overline{\psi}_N^*(\theta_0)']'$ converges in distribution to $[\nu(z_1), \ldots, \nu(z_J), , \nu_0']'$ $\forall z_j \in \mathcal{Z}$, $\forall j \leq J, \forall J \geq 1$. This result holds by the Cramer–Wold device and a CLT for bounded random variables (see, e.g., Hall and Heyde, 1980, Corollary 5.1, p. 132) because the underlying random sequence $\{W_i : i = 1, \ldots, N\}$ is strictly stationary and α-mixing with the mixing coefficients satisfying $\sum_{m=1}^{\infty} \alpha(m) < \infty$ by Assumption 11.1, and we have $\left|[(Y_i \leq X_i'\theta_0) - q](Z_i \leq z)\right| \leq 2 < \infty\ \forall z \in \mathbb{R}$. This now establishes Lemma A.3. ∎

Proof of Theorem 11.1: We have

$$
\begin{aligned}
\sqrt{N}\,\overline{g}_N(z, \widehat{\theta}) &= \frac{1}{\sqrt{N}} \sum_{i=1}^{N} [(Y_i \leq X_i'\widehat{\theta}) - q](Z_i \leq z) \\
&= \nu_N^*(z, \widehat{\theta}) + \sqrt{N} E\,[(Y_i \leq X_i'\theta) - q](Z_i \leq z)\big|_{\theta=\widehat{\theta}} \\
&= \nu_N^*(z, \theta_0) + \sqrt{N} E\,[(Y_i \leq X_i'\theta) - q](Z_i \leq z)\big|_{\theta=\widehat{\theta}} + o_p(1)
\end{aligned}
\tag{A.8}
$$

uniformly in $z \in \mathcal{Z}$, where the second equality holds by rearranging terms and the last equality holds by Lemma A.2. By a mean value expansion, we also have

$$
\begin{aligned}
&\sqrt{N} E\,[(Y_i \leq X_i'\theta) - q](Z_i \leq z)\big|_{\theta=\widehat{\theta}} \\
&= \frac{\partial}{\partial \theta'} E\,[(Y_i \leq X_i'\theta) - q](Z_i \leq z)\big|_{\theta=\theta^*(z)} \cdot \sqrt{N}(\widehat{\theta} - \theta_0),
\end{aligned}
\tag{A.9}
$$

where $\theta^*(z)$ lies between $\widehat{\theta}$ and θ_0. By Assumption 11.2, we have $\sqrt{N}(\widehat{\theta} - \theta_0) = O_p(1)$. This implies that there exists a sequence of constants $\{\xi_N : N \geq 1\}$ such that $\xi_N \to 0$ and $P\left(\sup_{z \in \mathcal{Z}} \left\|\theta^*(z) - \theta_0\right\| \leq \xi_N\right) \to 1$. We have

$$
\begin{aligned}
&\sup_{z \in \mathcal{Z}} \left\| \frac{\partial}{\partial \theta} E\,[(Y_i \leq X_i'\theta) - q](Z_i \leq z)\big|_{\theta=\theta^*(z)} - \Delta_0(z) \right\| \\
&\leq \sup_{z \in \mathcal{Z}} \sup_{\theta : \|\theta - \theta_0\| \leq \xi_N} \left\| E f(X_i'\theta | Z_i)(Z_i \leq z) X_i - \Delta_0(z) \right\| \\
&\leq \sup_{\theta : \|\theta - \theta_0\| \leq \xi_N} E\left| f(X_i'\theta | Z_i) - f(X_i'\theta_0 | Z_i)\right| \|X_i\| \\
&\leq C_1 E \|X_i\|^2 \xi_N \to 0,
\end{aligned}
\tag{A.10}
$$

where the first inequality holds with probability $\to 1$ and the last inequality holds by Assumptions 11.1 (ii) and (iii). Now, combining (A.8)–(A.10) and using Assumption 11.2, we have, uniformly in $z \in \mathcal{Z}$,

$$\sqrt{N}\,\bar{g}_N(z,\widehat{\theta}) = \nu_N^*(z,\theta_0) + \Delta_0'(z)\sqrt{N}\,\Gamma_0\overline{\psi}_N^*(\theta_0) + o_p(1). \tag{A.11}$$

Therefore, the result (A.11) and Lemma 11.3 give the results of Theorem 11.1 using the continuous mapping theorem (see Pollard 1984, Theorem IV.12, p. 70) as desired.

Proof of Theorem 11.2: Consider the KS_N test. (The proof of Theorem 11.2 for the CM_N test is analogous and is therefore omitted.) Let

$$k_\infty^* = \sup_{z\in\mathcal{Z}} \left|\nu(z) + \Delta_0(z)'\Gamma_0\nu_0\right|.$$

Let the asymptotic null distribution of KS_N be given by $G(w) \equiv P(k_\infty^* \le w)$. This distribution is absolutely continuous because it is a functional of a Gaussian process whose covariance function is nonsingular (see Lifshits 1982). Therefore, part (a) of Theorem 11.2 holds if we establish

$$\widehat{G}_{N,b}(w) \xrightarrow{p} G(w) \;\; \forall w \in \mathbb{R}. \tag{A.12}$$

Let

$$\begin{aligned} G_b(w) &= P\left(\sqrt{b}g_{N,b,i} \le w\right) \\ &= P\left(\sqrt{b}g_b(W_i,\ldots,W_{i+b-1}) \le w\right) \\ &= P\left(\sqrt{b}g_b(W_1,\ldots,W_b) \le w\right). \end{aligned}$$

By Theorem 11.1(a), we have $\lim_{b\to\infty} G_b(w) = G(w)$, where w is a continuity point of $G(\cdot)$. Therefore, to establish (A.12), it suffices to verify

$$\widehat{G}_{N,b}(w) - G_b(w) \xrightarrow{p} 0 \;\; \forall w \in \mathbb{R}. \tag{A.13}$$

We now verify (A.13). Note first that

$$E\widehat{G}_{N,b}(w) = G_b(w). \tag{A.14}$$

Let

$$I_i = 1\left(\sqrt{b}g_b(W_i,\ldots,W_{i+b-1}) \le w\right)$$

for $i = 1,\ldots,N$. We have

$$\begin{aligned} \mathrm{Var}\left[\widehat{G}_{N,b}(w)\right] &= \mathrm{Var}\left(\frac{1}{N-b+1}\sum_{i=1}^{N-b+1} I_i\right) \\ &= \frac{1}{N-b+1}\left(S_{N-b+1,0} + 2\sum_{m=1}^{b-1} S_{N-b+1,m} + 2\sum_{m=b}^{N-b} S_{N-b+1,m}\right) \\ &\equiv A_1 + A_2 + A_3\,, \text{ for instance,} \end{aligned}$$

where

$$S_{N-b+1,m} = \frac{1}{N-b+1} \sum_{i=1}^{N-b+1-m} \mathrm{Cov}\,(I_i, I_{i+m}).$$

Note that

$$|A_1 + A_2| \leq O(\frac{b}{N}) = o(1). \tag{A.15}$$

Also, we have

$$\begin{aligned} |A_3| &= \left| \frac{2}{N-b+1} \sum_{m=b}^{N-b} \left[\frac{1}{N-b+1} \sum_{i=1}^{N-b+1-m} \mathrm{Cov}\,(I_i, I_{i+m}) \right] \right| \\ &\leq \frac{8}{(N-b+1)^2} \sum_{m=b}^{N-b} \sum_{i=1}^{N-b+1-m} \alpha_X(m-b+1) \\ &\leq \frac{8}{N-b+1} \sum_{m=1}^{N-2b+1} \alpha_X(m) \\ &\to 0 \text{ as } N \to \infty, \end{aligned} \tag{A.16}$$

where the first inequality holds by Theorem A.5 of Hall and Heyde (1980) and the last convergence to zero holds by Assumption 11.1(i). Now the desired result (A.13) follows immediately from (A.14)–(A.16). This establishes part (a) of Theorem 11.2. Given this result, part (b) of Theorem 11.2 holds because we have

$$P\left[KS_N > g_{N,b}^{KS}(1-\alpha)\right] = P\left[KS_N > g^{KS}(1-\alpha) + o_p(1)\right] \to \alpha$$

as $N \to \infty$.

Proof of Theorem 11.3: We have

$$\begin{aligned} &\sup_{z \in \mathcal{Z}} \left| \overline{g}_N(z, \widehat{\theta}) - Eg(W_i, \theta_1, z) \right| \\ &\quad \leq \sup_{z \in \mathcal{Z}} \left| \overline{g}_N(z, \widehat{\theta}) - Eg(W_i, \theta, z)\big|_{\theta=\widehat{\theta}} \right| \\ &\quad + \sup_{z \in \mathcal{Z}} \left| Eg(W_i, \theta, z)\big|_{\theta=\widehat{\theta}} - Eg(W_i, \theta_1, z) \right| \\ &\quad \xrightarrow{p} 0, \end{aligned} \tag{A.17}$$

where the first term on the rhs of (A.17) is $o_p(1)$ by an argument similar to the proof of Lemmas A.2, and A.3, and the second term vanishes by mean value theorem (using an argument similar to (A.10)) using Assumption 11.1 (ii)–(iii). Therefore, under H_1, we have

$$\frac{1}{\sqrt{N}} KS_N = \sup_{z\in\mathcal{Z}} \left|\bar{g}_N(z,\widehat{\theta})\right| \xrightarrow{p} \sup_{z\in\mathcal{Z}} \left|Eg(W_i,\theta_1,z)\right| \equiv g^* > 0 \tag{A.18}$$

$$\frac{1}{N} CM_N = \frac{1}{N}\sum\left[\bar{g}_N(Z_i,\widehat{\theta})\right]^2 \xrightarrow{p} \int \left[Eg(W_i,\theta_1,z)\right]^2 dJ(z) > 0. \tag{A.19}$$

We now verify part (a) of Theorem 11.3. Recall definition (6). Then, consider the empirical distribution of $g_{N,b,i} = g_b(W_i,\ldots,W_{i+b-1})$:

$$\widehat{G}^0_{N,b}(w) = \frac{1}{N-b+1}\sum_{i=1}^{N-b+1} 1\left(g_{N,b,i} \le w\right) = \widehat{G}_{N,b}\left(\sqrt{b}w\right).$$

Let

$$G^0_b(w) = P\left(g_b(W_1,\ldots,W_b) \le w\right).$$

By an argument analogous to those used to verify (A.13), we have

$$\widehat{G}^0_{N,b}(w) - G^0_b(w) \xrightarrow{p} 0\,.$$

Because $g_b(W_1,\ldots,W_b) \xrightarrow{p} g^*$, $\widehat{G}^0_{N,b}(\cdot)$ converges in distribution to a point mass at g^*. It also follows that

$$g^0_{N,b}(1-\alpha) = \inf\left\{w : \widehat{G}^0_{N,b}(w) \ge 1-\alpha\right\} \xrightarrow{p} g^*.$$

Therefore, we have

$$\begin{aligned}
P\left(KS_N > g^{KS}_{N,b}(1-\alpha)\right) &= P\left[\sqrt{N}g_N(W_1,\ldots,W_N) > \sqrt{b}g^0_{N,b}(1-\alpha)\right] \\
&= P\left[\sqrt{\frac{N}{b}}g_N(W_1,\ldots,W_N) > g^0_{N,b}(1-\alpha)\right] \\
&= P\left[\sqrt{\frac{N}{b}}g_N(W_1,\ldots,W_N) > g^* + o_p(1)\right] \\
&= P\left[\sqrt{\frac{N}{b}}g_N(W_1,\ldots,W_N) > g^*\right] + o(1) \\
&\to 1,
\end{aligned} \tag{A.20}$$

where the last convergence holds because $\underline{\lim}_{N\to\infty}\left(\frac{N}{b}\right) > 1$ and $g_N(W_1,\ldots,W_N) \xrightarrow{p} g^* > 0$, as desired. Proof of Theorem 11.3(b) is similar. ■

Proof of Theorem 11.4: The proof of Theorem 11.4 is similar to that of Theorem 11.1: We just describe the main differences. Consider the expression

(A.8), which is still valid under Assumptions 11.1 and 11.2*. By a mean value expansion, we now have

$$\begin{aligned}
&\sqrt{N}E\left[(Y_i \le X_i'\theta) - q\right](Z_i \le z)\big|_{\theta=\widehat{\theta}} \\
&\quad = \sqrt{N}E[(Y_i \le X_i'\theta_0) - q](Z_i \le z) \\
&\qquad + \frac{\partial}{\partial\theta'}E\left[(Y_i \le X_i'\theta) - q\right](Z_i \le z)\big|_{\theta=\theta^*(z)} \cdot \sqrt{N}(\widehat{\theta} - \theta_0), \qquad \text{(A.21)}
\end{aligned}$$

where $\theta^*(z)$ lies between $\widehat{\theta}$ and θ_0. Consider the first term on the rhs of (A.21). We have

$$\begin{aligned}
&\sup_{z\in\mathcal{Z}}\left|\sqrt{N}E[(Y_i \le X_i'\theta_0) - q](Z_i \le z) - \eta(\theta_0)\right| \\
&\quad = \sup_{z\in\mathcal{Z}}\left|\sqrt{N}E\left[(Y_i \le X_i'\theta_0) - \left(Y_i \le X_i'\theta_0 + N^{-1/2}d(X_i)\right)\right](Z_i \le z) - \eta(\theta_0)\right| \\
&\quad = \sup_{z\in\mathcal{Z}}\Big|E\Big[\sqrt{N}\left\{H(X_i'\theta_0 + N^{-1/2}d(X_i)|Z_i) - H(X_i'\theta_0|Z_i)\right\} \\
&\qquad - f(X_i'\theta_0|Z_i)d(X_i)\Big](Z_i \le z)\Big| \\
&\quad \le \frac{C}{\sqrt{N}}E\left|d(X_i)\right|^2 \to 0, \qquad \text{(A.22)}
\end{aligned}$$

where the first equality holds by (8), the second inequality holds by rearranging terms, and the last inequality holds by a mean value expansion.

Next, consider the second term on the rhs of (A.21). Because $\sqrt{N}(\widehat{\theta} - \theta_0) = O_p(1)$ under Assumption 11.2*, we have

$$\sup_{z\in\mathcal{Z}}\left\|\frac{\partial}{\partial\theta}E\left[(Y_i \le X_i'\theta) - q\right](Z_i \le z)\big|_{\theta=\theta^*(z)} - \Delta_0(z)\right\| \xrightarrow{p} 0 \qquad \text{(A.23)}$$

using an argument similar to (A.10).

Now, combining (A.8)–(A.10) and using Assumption 11.2*, we have, uniformly in $z \in \mathcal{Z}$,

$$\sqrt{N}\overline{g}_N(z, \widehat{\theta}) = v_N^*(z, \theta_0) + \Delta_0'(z)\sqrt{N}\Gamma_0\,\overline{\psi}_N^*(\theta_0) + \delta(z) + o_p(1). \qquad \text{(A.24)}$$

Therefore, the result (A.24) and Lemma 11.3 give the desired results of Theorem 11.4. ■

Proof of Corollary 11.1: We know that $g_{N,b}^{KS}(1-\alpha) \xrightarrow{p} g^{KS}(1-\alpha)$ and $g_{N,b}^{CM}(1-\alpha) \xrightarrow{p} g^{CM}(1-\alpha)$ under H_0. By contiguity, we have $g_{N,b}^{KS}(1-\alpha) \xrightarrow{p} g^{KS}(1-\alpha)$ and $g_{N,b}^{CM}(1-\alpha) \xrightarrow{p} g^{CM}(1-\alpha)$ under H_a. The results of Corollary 11.1 now follow immediately from Theorem 11.4.

References

Aït-Sahalia, Y., P. J. Bickel, and T. M. Stoker (2001). "Goodness-of-fit tests for kernel regression with an application to option implied volatilities," *Journal of Econometrics* 105, 363–412.

Andrews, D. W. K. and D. Pollard (1994). "An introduction to functional central limit theorems for dependent stochastic processes," *International Statistical Review*, 62, 119–132.

Bierens, H. J. (1982). "Consistent conditional moment test of functional form," *Journal of Econometrics*, 20, 105–134.

Bierens, H. J. (1990). "A consistent conditional moment test of functional form," *Econometrica*, 58, 1443–1458.

Bierens, H. J. and D. K. Ginther (2001). "Integrated conditional moment testing of quantile regression models," *Empirical Economics*, 26, 307–324.

Bierens, H. J. and W. Ploberger (1997). "Asymptotic theory of integrated conditional moment tests," *Econometrica*, 65, 1129–1151.

Billingsley, P. (1968). *Convergence of Probability Measures*. New York: Wiley.

Buchinsky, M. (1994). "Changes in the U. S. wage structure 1963–1987: Application of quantile regression," *Econometrica*, 65, 1129–1151.

Buchinsky, M. (1998). "Recent advances in quantile regression models," *Journal of Human Resources*, 33, 88–126.

Chamberlain, G. (1994). Quantile regression, censoring and the structure of wages, in *Advances in Econometrics*. Christopher Sims, ed., New York: Elsevier, 171–209.

Chernozhukov, V. and L. Umantsev (2001). "Conditional value-at-risk: Aspects of modeling and estimation," *Empirical Economics* 26, 271–292.

De Jong, R. M. (1996). "The Bierens test under data dependence," *Journal of Econometrics* 72, 1–32.

Engle R. F. and S. Manganelli (2002). CAViaR: Conditional autoregressive value at risk by regression quantiles, forthcoming in *Journal of Business and Economic Statistics*.

Eubank, R. and S. Spiegelman (1990). "Testing the goodness of fit of a linear model via nonparametric regression techniques," *Journal of the American Statistical Association* 85, 387–392.

Fan, Y. and Q. Li (1996). "Consistent model specification tests: Omitted variables and semiparametric functional forms," *Econometrica*, 64, 865–890.

Gozalo, P. L. (1993). "A consistent model specification test for nonparametric estimation of regression function models," *Econometric Theory*, 9, 451–477.

Hall, P. and C. C. Heyde (1980). *Martingale Limit Theory and Its Applications*, New York: Academic Press.

Härdle, W. and E. Mammen (1993). Comparing nonparametric versus parametric regression fits, *Annals of Statistics*, 21, 1926–1947.

Hart, J. D. (1997). *Nonparametric Smoothing and Lack-of-Fit Tests*, New York: Springer–Verlag.

Hong, Y. and H. White (1996). "Consistent specification testing via nonparametric series regressions," *Econometrica*, 63, 1133–1160.

Horowitz, J. L. and V. G. Spokoiny (2001). "An adaptive, rate-optimal test of a parametric mean regression model against a nonparametric alternative," *Econometrica*, 69, 599–631.

Inoue, A. (1999). A conditional goodness-of-fit test for time series, unpublished manuscript, North Carolina State University.

Khmaladze, E. V. (1988). "An innovation approach to goodness-of-fit tests in $\mathbb{R}^m$," *Annals of Statistics*, 16, 1503–1516.

Khmaladze, E. V. (1993). "Goodness-of-fit problem and scanning innovation martingales," *Annals of Statistics*, 21, 798–829.

Koenker, R. and G. Bassett (1978). "Regression quantiles," *Econometrica*, 46, 33–50.

Koenker, R. and G. Bassett (1982). "Robust test for heteroscedasticity based on regression quantiles," *Econometrica*, 50, 43–61.

Koenker, R. and O. Geling (2001). "Reappraising medfly longevity: A quantile regression survival analysis," *Journal of the American Statistical Association* 96, 458–468.

Koenker, R. and K. F. Hallock (2001). "Quantile regression," *Journal of Economic Perspectives*, 15, 143–156.

Koul, H. L. and W. Stute (1999). "Nonparametric model checks for time series," *Annals of Statistics*, 27, 204–236.

Li, Q. and S. Wang (1998). "A simple consistent test for a parametric regression function," *Journal of Econometrics*, 87, 145–165.

Lifshits, M. A. (1982). "On the absolute continuity of distributions of functionals of random processes," *Theory of Probability and Its Applications* 27, 600–607.

Linton, O., E. Maasoumi, and Y.-J. Whang (2005). Consistent testing for stochastic dominance under general sampling schemes, in *Review of Economic Studies*, 72, 735–765.

Politis, D. N. and J. P. Romano (1994). "Large sample confidence regions based on subsamples under minimal assumptions," *Annals of Statistics*, 22, 2031–2050.

Politis, D. N., J. P. Romano, and M. Wolf (1999). *Subsampling*. New York: Springer–Verlag.

Pollard, D. (1984). *Convergence of Stochastic Processes,* New York: Springer–Verlag.

Pollard, D. (1990). *Empirical Processes: Theory and Applications*, CBMS Conference Series in Probability and Statistics, Vol. 2. Institute of Mathematical Statistics, Hayward.

Poterba, J. M. and K. S. Rueben (1994). The distribution of public sector wage premia: New evidence using quantile regression methods, NBER Working Paper No. 4734.

Stinchcombe, M. B. and H. White (1998). "Consistent specification testing with nuisance parameters present only under the alternative," *Econometric Theory* 14, 295–325.

Stute, W. (1997). "Nonparametric model checks for regression," Annals of statistics, 25, 613–41.

Weiss. A. (1991). "Estimating nonlinear dynamic models using least absolute error estimation," *Econometric Theory*, 7, 46–68.

Whang, Y. -J. (2000). "Consistent bootstrap tests of parametric regression functions," *Journal of Econometrics*, 98, 27–46.

Whang, Y. -J. (2001). "Consistent specification testing for conditional moment restrictions," *Economics Letters*, 71, 299–306.

Whang, Y. -J. and D. W. K. Andrews (1993). "Tests of specification for parametric and semiparametric models," *Journal of Econometrics*, 57, 277–318.

Wooldridge, J. M. (1992). "A test for functional form against nonparametric alternatives," *Econometric Theory*, 8, 452–475.

Yatchew, A. J. (1992). "Nonparametric regression tests based on least squares," *Econometric Theory*, 8, 435–451.

Zheng, J. X. (1996). "A consistent test of functional form via nonparametric estimation techniques," *Journal of Econometrics*, 75, 263–289.

Zheng, J. X. (1998). "A consistent nonparametric test of parametric regression models under conditional quantile restrictions," *Econometric Theory*, 14, 123–138.

PART FIVE

NONSTATIONARY PANELS

TWELVE

Combination Unit Root Tests for Cross-Sectionally Correlated Panels*

In Choi

12.1 INTRODUCTION

There have been several approaches to testing for a unit root in panel data. These include Quah (1994); Levin and Lin (1992);[1] Im, Pesaran, and Shin (2003); and Choi (2001). All of these tests assume cross-sectional independence, although Im et al. (1995) consider a simple form of cross-sectional correlation using time-specific effects. It may be more appropriate, however, to assume cross-sectional correlation for some cross-country data sets because comovements of economies are often observed (e.g., Backus and Kehoe 1992) and cross-sectional correlation may affect the finite-sample properties of panel unit root tests as studied in O'Connell (1998).

In response to the need for panel unit root tests allowing cross-sectional correlation, researchers have devised various methods. Maddala and Wu (1999) bootstrap the critical values of Levin and Lin's (1992), Im et al.'s (2003), and Fisher's (1932) tests. Taylor and Sarno (1998) study the multivariate augmented Dickey–Fuller test. O'Connell (1998) considers a generalized least squares (GLS)-based unit root test for homogeneous panels. Chang (2000) applies bootstrap methods to Taylor and Sarno's multivariate augmented Dickey–Fuller and other related tests. All of these methods assume cross-sectional correlation in the innovation terms (e_{it} in this chapter) driving the autoregressive processes in their models.

Here we propose unit root tests for cross-sectionally correlated error-component models. Unlike previous studies, the cross-sectional correlation stems from error components, not from the innovation terms of autoregressive processes. This is a conventional method of modeling cross-sectional

[1] Levin, Lin, and Chu (2002) improve on this by allowing heterogeneous panels.

* Part of this chapter was written while the author was visiting the Cowles Foundation for Research in Economics, Yale University. He thanks the faculty and staff of the Cowles Foundation – especially Don Andrews, John Geanakoplos, David Pearce, Peter Phillips, and Nora Wiedenbach for their support and hospitality.

correlation in panel data. It is difficult to judge a priori which modeling – the one in this chapter or the one incorporating cross-sectional correlation via innovation terms – is more appropriate for panel data. The judgement should depend on the purpose and nature of each application. In this sense, the two approaches are complementary. The cross-sectional covariance structure in our error-component models, however, can be more complicated than those assumed in the aforementioned articles. An example of economic variables suitable for our modeling is real gross domestic product (GDP), as discussed in Section 12.2.

The test statistics we propose are formulated by combining p-values from the augmented Dickey–Fuller test applied to each time series whose non-stochastic trend components and cross-sectional correlations are eliminated by Elliott, Rothenberg, and Stock's (1996, ERS hereafter) GLS-based detrending[2] and the conventional cross-sectional demeaning for panel data. We will call these tests combination tests. Such tests have a standard normal limiting distribution. These results are obtained under the sequential asymptotics $T \to \infty$ and $N \to \infty$, where T and N are the numbers of time series and cross-sectional observations, respectively.

Using p-values to devise tests has a long history in meta-analysis.[3] In econometrics, test statistics incorporating p-values have been used for test synthesis in Choi (1999) and for panel unit root tests in Maddala and Wu (1999) and Choi (2001).

We also report simulation results for the combination tests. The results indicate that the tests have reasonably good size and power properties and that they are not quite sensitive to cross-sectionally correlated innovation terms. In addition, the combinations tests are applied to the annual real GDP data of 23 OECD nations for the sampling period 1960–1992. The results support the presence of a unit root in the GDP data.

Panel unit roots have been used in various applications. Applications to the purchasing power parity hypothesis are found in Frankel and Rose (1996), Oh (1996), Lothian (1997), MacDonald (1996), Taylor (1996), Wu (1996), Coakley and Fuertes (1997), and Papell (1997). Other applications include Culver and Papell (1997), Song and Wu (1998), and McCoskey and Selden (1998).

The remainder of this chapter is organized as follows. Section 12.2 introduces the models, hypotheses, and assumptions. Section 12.3 develops panel unit root test statistics and studies their asymptotic properties. Section 12.4 reports simulation results for our combination unit root tests. Section 12.5 applies the combination unit root tests to real GDP data of 23 OECD nations.

[2] ERS show that the Dickey–Fuller tests using ERS's GLS detrending have better finite sample properties than other existing unit root tests.

[3] Meta analysis is concerned with quantitative methods for combining statistical evidence across independent studies. See Hedges and Olkin (1985) for an introduction to meta-analysis.

Section 12.6 presents concluding remarks. Technical discussions are relegated to Appendixes A and B.

12.2 THE MODELS, HYPOTHESES, AND ASSUMPTIONS

We are concerned with the two-way error-component model

$$y_{it} = \beta_0 + x_{it}, (i = 1, \ldots, N; t = 1, \ldots, T), \tag{1}$$

where

$$x_{it} = \mu_i + \lambda_t + v_{it}; \tag{2}$$

$$v_{it} = \sum_{l=1}^{p_i} \alpha_{il} v_{i(t-l)} + e_{it}; \tag{3}$$

the index i denotes households, individuals, countries, and so on; and the index t, time. We may allow the number of time series observations T to be different across cross-sectional units. But allowing this is so trivial that we retain the model specification of the same number of time series observations for the sake of simplicity.

In model (1), β_0 is the common mean for all i. In eq. (2), μ_i is the unobservable individual effect, λ_t denotes the unobservable time effect, and v_{it} is the remaining random component that follows the autoregressive process of order p_i.

Specification (2) appears to imply that all cross-sectional units are equally affected by the time effect variable λ_t. Because this may not be the case, some authors (e.g., Phillips and Sul 2003) use a dynamic factor model, the simplest form of which is

$$x_{it} = \mu_i \lambda_t + v_{it}, \tag{4}$$

where λ_t is assumed to be stationary. We prefer working with specification (2) for the following two reasons. First, when a logarithm is taken of the data, as in most applications, λ_t affects the cross-sectional unit differently even in specification (2). That is, if $x_{it} = \ln(h_{it})$, $\partial h_{it}/\partial \lambda_t$ depends on μ_i. Second, it is straightforward, as will be discussed in Section 12.3.3, to check the assumption of stationary λ_t for specification (2).

Unlike in conventional error-component models, we allow heterogeneity in v_{it} in the sense that they are autoregressive processes with different coefficient values and orders across i. We assume that initial variables $v_{i0}, \ldots, v_{i(1-p_i)}$ are all stochastically bounded and that the true order p_i's are known. In practice, the true order can be estimated by model selection criteria or sequential testing. Alternatively, we may assume ARMA processes of unknown order for v_{it} and follow Said and Dickey's (1984) long-autoregression procedure. Because the resulting test statistics are practically no different from the augmented Dickey–Fuller tests that we will use, we retain the assumption of the autoregressive process of known order for the sake of simplicity. It is assumed, moreover, that all the roots of the equation

$$1 - \sum_{l=1}^{p_i} \alpha_{il} z_i^l = 0 \tag{5}$$

lie outside the unit circle with the possible exception of one root taking value one.

We assume the following for $i, j = 1, \ldots, N$ and $t, s = 1, \ldots, T$:

Assumption 12.1

(i) $E(\mu_i) = E(\lambda_t) = 0.$
(ii) $E(\mu_i \lambda_t) = E(\mu_i v_{jt}) = E(\lambda_t v_{it}) = 0.$
(iii) $E(\mu_i^2) = \sigma_\mu^2 < \infty; E(\mu_i \mu_j) = 0 \; (i \neq j).$
(iv) λ_t is a weakly stationary process with $E(\lambda_t \lambda_s) = \sigma_\lambda(| t - s |) < \infty.$
(v) For fixed i, $e_{it} \sim \text{iid}(0, \sigma_{e_i}^2)$, $\sigma_{e_i}^2 < \infty.$
(vi) $\{e_{11}, \ldots, e_{1T}\}, \ldots, \{e_{N1}, \ldots, e_{NT}\}$ are independent.

Parts (i), (ii), and (iii) of Assumption 12.1 are standard assumptions in error-component models (e.g., Hsiao 1986). In more conventional settings, λ_t are assumed to be independent across t. But we allow them to be dependent here, as in Part (iv), to introduce cross-sectional and serial correlations among y_{it}. In practice, one may be interested in checking part (iv) of Assumption 12.1 – particularly when the null hypothesis of a unit root in v_{it} (see eq. (8)) is rejected. Checking this assumption is straightforward and will be discussed in Section 12.3.3. Part (vi) makes v_{it} independent across i.

Under Assumption 12.1,

$$\text{Cov}(y_{it}, y_{js}) = \sigma_\lambda(| t - s |) < \infty \text{ for all } i, j, t \text{ and } s \text{ with } i \neq j, \tag{6}$$

$$\text{Cov}(y_{it}, y_{is}) = \sigma_\mu^2 + \sigma_\lambda(| t - s |) + E(v_{it} v_{is}). \tag{7}$$

Relation (6) shows that y_{it} is cross-sectionally correlated. Relation (7) indicates that y_{it} is temporally dependent and that y_{it} has trending variance only when v_{it} does.

The null hypothesis we are interested in is the presence of a unit root in the polynomial equation (5). That is,

$$H_0 : \sum_{l=1}^{p_i} \alpha_{il} = 1 \text{ for all } i. \tag{8}$$

The alternative hypothesis we consider is

$$H_1 : \sum_{l=1}^{p_i} \alpha_{il} < 1 \text{ for some } i\text{'s}. \tag{9}$$

Letting N_k be the number of countries satisfying the alternative hypothesis (9), we assume

Assumption 12.2 As $N \to \infty$, $N_k/N \to k$, where k is a positive constant.

Under this assumption, tests we will propose are consistent against the alternative hypothesis (9).

Many macroeconomic and financial variables appear to contain a linear time trend component in addition to a stochastic component (cf. Nelson and Plosser 1982). Moreover, some economic theories predict the presence of a linear time trend in economic variables.[4] Thus, it is necessary to extend model (1) to include a linear time trend. The extended model can be written as

$$y_{it} = \beta_0 + \beta_1 t + x_{it}, (i = 1, \ldots, N; t = 1, \ldots, T), \tag{10}$$

where

$$x_{it} = \mu_i + \lambda_t + \gamma_i t + v_{it} \tag{11}$$

and v_{it} is as specified in eq. (3). The random variable γ_i signifies the individual trend effect. For example, if y_{it} is a real per capita GDP, μ_i may be considered the country-specific conditions such as endowments of natural resources, technology level, and political system; λ_t as worldwide shocks such as wars and oil embargoes; and γ_i as a country-specific technological progress rate, as in the Solow growth model.[5] One may consider including a term like $\zeta_t t$ in eq. (11) to denote the world-wide trend effect. But the term can be merged into λ_t, and so we do not put it in eq. (11).

Regarding γ_i, assume the following for $i, j = 1, \ldots, N$ and $t = 1, \ldots, T$:

Assumption 12.3

(i) $E(\gamma_i) = 0$.

(ii) $E(\gamma_i^2) = \sigma_\gamma^2 < \infty$; $E(\gamma_i \gamma_j) = 0 \; (i \neq j)$.

(iii) $E(\mu_i \gamma_j) = E(\lambda_t \gamma_i) = E(v_{jt} \gamma_i) = 0$.

Under Assumption 12.3, γ_i is cross-sectionally correlated and uncorrelated with other error components. Under Assumptions 12.1 and 12.3,

$$\text{Cov}(y_{it}, y_{js}) = \sigma_\lambda(\mid t - s \mid) < \infty \text{ for all } i, j, t \text{ and } s \text{ with } i \neq j, \tag{12}$$

$$\text{Cov}(y_{it}, y_{is}) = \sigma_\mu^2 + \sigma_\lambda(\mid t - s \mid) + \sigma_\gamma^2 ts + E(v_{it} v_{is}).$$

Thus, y_{it} is cross-sectionally and temporally dependent.

[4] For example, Solow's (1956) economic growth model predicts the presence of linear time trend in per capita income under steady states (see eq. (6) in Mankiw, Romer, and Weil 1992).

[5] See Romer (1996) for details on this textbook Solow model.

The null and alternative hypotheses for model (10) are the same as those for model (1).

12.3 PANEL UNIT ROOT TESTS

12.3.1 GLS Demeaning and Detrending[6]

To test null hypothesis (8), we need to eliminate the constant term and all error components except v_{it} from the observed panel data y_{it}. When v_{it} is stationary, OLS provides a fully efficient estimator of the constant term, as shown in Grenander and Rosenblatt (1957). When v_{it} is nearly $I(1)$ or $I(1)$, however, ERS show that using GLS to estimate the constant term provides unit root tests with better finite sample properties.

Assuming that the largest root of v_{it} is $(1+\frac{c}{T})$ for all i, we regress $[y_{i1}, y_{i2} - (1+\frac{c}{T})y_{i1}, \ldots, y_{iT} - (1+\frac{c}{T})y_{i(T-1)}]'$ on $[1, 1-(1+\frac{c}{T}), \ldots, 1-(1+\frac{c}{T})]'$ to obtain the GLS estimator of parameter β_0 in model (1), as in ERS. We follow ERS in setting $c = -7$ for all i. Denoting the GLS estimator of β_0 using sample $[y_{i1}, \ldots, y_{iT}]'$ as $\hat{\beta}_{0i}$, we can write the demeaned series for large T as

$$y_{it} - \hat{\beta}_{0i} \simeq \lambda_t - \lambda_1 + v_{it} - v_{i1}. \tag{13}$$

Note that relation (13) holds either when v_{it} has a unit root or when v_{it} is stationary. Relations (13) and (15) are proven in Appendix A.

Demeaning $y_{it} - \hat{\beta}_{0i}$ cross-sectionally gives, for large T,

$$z_{it} = y_{it} - \hat{\beta}_{0i} - \frac{1}{N}\sum_{i=1}^{N}(y_{it} - \hat{\beta}_{0i}) \simeq v_{it} - v_{i1} - \bar{v}_{.t} + \bar{v}_{.1}, \tag{14}$$

where $\frac{1}{N}\sum_{i=1}^{N} q_{ia} = \bar{q}_{.a}$. We find from relation (14) that β_0, μ_i, and λ_t were eliminated from y_{it} by the time series and cross-sectional demeanings. Relation (14) also shows that, z_{it} are independent across i for large T and N because $\bar{v}_{.t}$ and $\bar{v}_{.1}$ converge to zero in probability as $N \to \infty$ for any T. Note that the law of large numbers for $\bar{v}_{.t}$ and $\bar{v}_{.1}$ holds even when v_{it} has infinite variance owing to the presence of a unit root in v_{it} (see Feller 1950, p. 246).

One may also run OLS for each sample $[y_{i1}, \ldots, y_{iT}]'$ and do cross-sectional demeaning to obtain $y_{it} - \bar{y}_{i.} - \bar{y}_{.t} + \bar{y}_{..}$, which is cross-sectionally independent for large T and N. Unreported simulation results indicate, however, that the Dickey–Fuller test adopting this method is inferior to that using the GLS demeaning in terms of finite sample size and power. In addition, we may use the

[6] Leybourne, Kim, and Newbold (2002) report that Leybourne's (1995) MAX tests improve on the Dickey–Fuller–GLS tests in finite samples. For the purpose of comparison, we also used the MAX tests for our combination tests in this section but find that they do not improve on the Dickey–Fuller–GLS tests in finite samples – at least within our experimental design of Section 12.5 – though they seem to be as good as the Dickey–Fuller–GLS tests. Thus, we focus only on the Dickey–Fuller–GLS tests.

pooled data to estimate parameter β_0 (either by GLS as above or by OLS) and then eliminate the terms involving μ_i and λ_t by time series and cross-sectional demeanings. But this is asymptotically equivalent to using $y_{it} - \bar{y}_{i.} - \bar{y}_{.t} + \bar{y}_{..}$ and hence is not recommended.

For model (10), regress $[y_{i1}, y_{i2} - (1+\frac{c}{T})y_{i1}, \ldots, y_{iT} - (1+\frac{c}{T})y_{i(T-1)}]'$ on $[1, 1-(1+\frac{c}{T}), \ldots, 1-(1+\frac{c}{T})]'$ and $[1, 1-\frac{c}{T}, \ldots, 1-\frac{c(T-1)}{T}]'$ to obtain the GLS estimators of parameters β_0 and β_1 (denoted as $\tilde{\beta}_{0i}$ and $\tilde{\beta}_{1i}$). Then, for large T

$$\begin{aligned} y_{it} &- \tilde{\beta}_{0i} - \tilde{\beta}_{1i}t \\ &\simeq \lambda_t - \lambda_1 - \left(\eta\lambda_T + \frac{\mu_i(1-c+c^2/2)}{1-c+c^2/3}\right)\frac{t}{T} - \gamma_i\left(1-c+\frac{c^2}{2}\right) + v_{it} - v_{i1} \\ &- \left[\left(1-\frac{(T-1)c}{T}\right)v_{iT} + \frac{c^2}{T^2}\sum_{t=2}^{T}(t-1)v_{i(t-1)}\right]\frac{t}{T(1-c+c^2/3)}, \end{aligned} \tag{15}$$

and

$$\begin{aligned} w_{it} &= y_{it} - \tilde{\beta}_{0i} - \tilde{\beta}_{1i}t - \frac{1}{N}\sum_{i=1}^{N}(y_{it} - \tilde{\beta}_{0i} - \tilde{\beta}_{1i}t) \\ &\simeq -\mu_i\frac{1-c+c^2/2}{1-c+c^2/3}\frac{t}{T} - \gamma_i\left(1-c+\frac{c^2}{2}\right) + v_{it} - v_{i1} \\ &- \left[\left(1-\frac{(T-1)c}{T}\right)v_{iT} + \frac{c^2}{T^2}\sum_{t=2}^{T}(t-1)v_{i(t-1)}\right]\frac{t}{T(1-c+c^2/3)} \\ &+ \left(\frac{1}{N}\sum_{i=1}^{N}\mu_i\right)\frac{1-c+c^2/2}{1-c+c^2/3}\frac{t}{T} + \left(\frac{1}{N}\sum_{i=1}^{N}\gamma_i\right)\left(1-c+\frac{c^2}{2}\right) - \bar{v}_{.t} + \bar{v}_{.1} \\ &+ \left[\left(1-\frac{(T-1)c}{T}\right)\bar{v}_{.T} + \frac{c^2}{T^2}\sum_{t=2}^{T}(t-1)\bar{v}_{.(t-1)}\right]\frac{t}{T(1-c+c^2/3)}, \end{aligned} \tag{16}$$

where $\eta = (1-c)/(1-c+c^2/3)$. Unlike in relation (14), there are terms involving μ_i and γ_i in w_{it}. These terms, however, do not affect the limiting null distribution of the unit root test we will use; hence, the unit root tests using w_{it} are independent across i for large T and N. As for relation (13), relation (16) holds either when v_{it} has a unit root or when v_{it} is stationary. We follow ERS in setting $c = -13.5$ for all i.

12.3.2 Panel Unit Root Tests

The panel unit root tests we employ are combination tests developed independently by Maddala and Wu (1999) and Choi (2001). The main idea of the tests is to combine p-values from a unit root test applied to each time series. Using

p-values to devise tests has a long history in meta-analysis, which is concerned with quantitative methods for combining statistical evidence across independent studies. See Hedges and Olkin (1985) for an introduction to meta-analysis.

To formulate the combination tests, we apply the augmented Dickey–Fuller test to each detrended time series and calculate p-values. The augmented Dickey–Fuller test using z_{it} defined in eq. (14) is the t-ratio for coefficient estimate $\hat{\rho}_0$ (t-test in Dickey and Fuller 1979) from the regression

$$\Delta z_{it} = \hat{\rho}_0 z_{i(t-1)} + \sum_{l=1}^{p_i-1} \hat{\rho}_l \Delta z_{i(t-l)} + \hat{u}_{it}.$$

This test is called the Dickey–Fuller-GLS$^{\mu}$ test. As shown in Appendix B, the Dickey–Fuller–GLS$^{\mu}$ test has the Dickey–Fuller t-distribution (see Fuller 1976, p. 373) without time trends as $T \to \infty$ and $N \to \infty$.

In the same manner, we apply the augmented Dickey–Fuller test to w_{it} defined in (16). This test, called the Dickey–Fuller–GLS$^{\tau}$ test, has the distribution tabulated in ERS (Table I C, p. 825), as shown in Appendix B.

Let p_i be the asymptotic p-value of one of the Dickey–Fuller–GLS tests for country i. The test statistics we will consider are

$$P_m = -\frac{1}{\sqrt{N}} \sum_{i=1}^{N} (\ln(p_i) + 1),$$

$$Z = \frac{1}{\sqrt{N}} \sum_{i=1}^{N} \Phi^{-1}(p_i),$$

where $\Phi(\cdot)$ is the standard normal cumulative distribution function, and

$$L^* = \frac{1}{\sqrt{\pi^2 N/3}} \sum_{i=1}^{N} \ln(\frac{p_i}{1-p_i}).$$

The P_m test is a modification of Fisher's (1932) inverse chi-square test. The modification was made to make it have a standard normal distribution as $N \to \infty$. The Z test, proposed by Stouffer et al. (1949) is called the inverse normal test. It has a standard normal distribution for any N as long as p_i has a uniform distribution over the interval [0, 1], but we still require for this test that N approach infinity because the p-values of the Dickey–Fuller–GLS tests are calculated under the assumption that N goes to infinity. The L^* test modifies George's (1977) logit test such that it has a standard normal distribution as $N \to \infty$.

To calculate asymptotic p-values of the Dickey–Fuller–GLS tests that are used to compute the preceding tests, we need to know about their distribution functions. Because the analytic expressions of their distribution functions are hard to obtain, however, we obtained their percentiles through simulation. The method for this will be explained in Section 12.4.

Under the null hypothesis (8), we have $p_i \sim \text{iid}U[0, 1]$ as $T \to \infty$ and $N \to \infty$. Thus, $-2\ln(p_i) \sim \text{iid}\chi^2(2)$, $\Phi^{-1}(p_i) \sim \text{iid}N(0, 1)$ and $\ln(\frac{p_i}{1-p_i})$ have the logistic distribution with mean 0 and variance $\frac{\pi^2}{3}$ as $T \to \infty$ and $N \to \infty$. These give, as $T \to \infty$ and $N \to \infty$,

$$P_m, Z, L^* \Rightarrow N(0, 1).$$

Under the alternative hypothesis (9) and Assumption 12.2 as $T \to \infty$ and $N \to \infty$, we have

$$P_m \to_p \infty,$$

and

$$Z, L^* \to_p -\infty,$$

as shown in Choi (2001, p. 256). These relations imply that the P_m, Z, and L^* tests are consistent when appropriate decision rules are used. As discussed in Choi (2001, p. 256), however, when $N_k/N \to 0$, unlike in Assumption 12.2, the P_m, Z, and L^* tests do not diverge in probability.

Therefore, the decision rule for each test is to

Reject the null hypothesis (8) against the alternative hypothesis (9) at the significance level α for each test when the following corresponding inequality holds:

$$P_m > c_{p\alpha},$$

where $c_{p\alpha}$ is from the upper tail of the standard normal distribution;

$$Z < c_{z\alpha}$$

$$L^* < c_{l\alpha},$$

where $c_{z\alpha}$ and $c_{l\alpha}$ are from the lower tail of the standard normal distribution.

12.3.3 Testing for a Unit Root in Time Effect Variables

When the null hypothesis (8) is rejected, the observed time series y_{it} may still be nonstationary if the weak stationarity assumption for the time effect variable λ_t (part (v) of Assumption 12.1) is violated. Thus, one may be interested in checking this assumption. Fortunately, this problem is relatively straightforward. For model (1), when T and N are large,

$$r_t = \frac{1}{N}\sum_{i=1}^{N}(y_{it} - \hat{\beta}_{0i}) \simeq \lambda_t - \lambda_1 + \frac{1}{N}\sum_{i=1}^{N}(v_{it} - v_{i1}) \simeq \lambda_t - \lambda_1.$$

Recall that the law of large numbers for $\frac{1}{N}\sum_{i=1}^{N}(v_{it} - v_{i1})$ holds even when v_{it} has infinite variance owing to the presence of a unit root in v_{it}. Thus, we may apply a unit root test using demeaned series (e.g., Dickey–Fuller–GLS$^{\mu}$ test) to r_t to check part (v) of Assumption 12.1.

In the same manner, for model (10), we have for large T and N

$$s_t = \frac{1}{N}\sum_{i=1}^{N}(y_{it} - \tilde{\beta}_{0i} - \tilde{\beta}_{1i}t)$$
$$\simeq \lambda_t - \lambda_1 - \eta\lambda_T\frac{t}{T}$$

with additional assumptions that $\frac{1}{N}\sum_{i=1}^{N}\mu_i \to 0$ and $\frac{1}{N}\sum_{i=1}^{N}\gamma_i \to 0$ as $N \to \infty$. Thus, part (v) of Assumption 12.1 can be checked by applying a unit root test using demeaned and detrended series (e.g., Dickey–Fuller–GLS$^\tau$ test) to s_t.

12.4 CALCULATION OF P-VALUES

It is important to calculate p-values of the Dickey–Fuller–GLS tests accurately for the combination tests. If the p-values are subject to sizable errors, they will add up to lead to poor size properties of the combination tests. To calculate the percentiles of the Dickey–Fuller–GLS tests that are used for their p-values, we followed the simulation method of MacKinnon (1994). Data for the simulation were generated according to

$$x_t = x_{(t-1)} + u_t,\, x_0 = 0,\, u_t \sim \text{iid}N(0,1),\ (t = 1, \ldots, T + 30), \qquad (17)$$

and the last T data points were used. The following steps summarize the method we used.

Step 1: Generate $\{x_t\}$ I times at $T = 30, 50, 75, 100, 250, 500, 1000$ and calculate 399 equally spaced percentiles of the Dickey–Fuller–GLS$^\mu$ (or Dickey–Fuller–GLS$^\tau$) test. We used $I = 50{,}000$ at $T = 30, 50, 75, 100$; $I = 30{,}000$ at $T = 250, 500$, and $I = 20{,}000$ at $T = 1{,}000$.

Step 2: Repeat Step 1 50 times and record the percentiles. This gives a 7×50 by 399 matrix (denoted as $[q_j^p(T_k)]$ for $j = 1, \ldots, 350$ and $p = 0.0025, 0.0050, \ldots, 0.9975$). The first 50 rows of this matrix (corresponding to $k = 1$) are the percentiles at $T = 30$, for example.

Step 3: Estimate the regression equation

$$q_j^p(T_k) = \eta_\infty^p + \eta_1^p T_k^{-1} + \eta_2^p T_k^{-2} + \varepsilon_j,\ (j = 1, \ldots, 350) \qquad (18)$$

for each p by using the GLS method that takes account of different variances at each T. This step gives a 399×3 coefficient matrix for eq. (18).

For the Dickey–Fuller–GLS$^\mu$ test, for example, the twentieth row of the coefficient matrix in Step 3 gives

$$\eta_\infty^{0.05} = -1.948;\ \eta_1^{0.05} = -19.36;\ \eta_2^{0.05} = 143.4.$$

Using these, the 5% percentile for the Dickey–Fuller–GLS$^{\mu}$ test at $T = 100$ is calculated as

$$-1.948 - \frac{19.36}{100} + \frac{143.4}{100^2} = -2.1273.$$

Thus, at any T, we may obtain 399 percentiles using the coefficient matrix from Step 3. These percentiles, coupled with interpolation, give p-values of the Dickey–Fuller–GLS tests.

The p-values resulting from the MacKinnon method of this section are based on the normality assumption of the generated data. When T is large, this would not matter much because asymptotics works. When T is small, however, the p-values may not be accurate if the underlying distribution is quite different from normal distributions. Effects of nonnormal errors on the empirical size and power of the combination tests using the p-values of this section will be examined in next section.

12.5 SIMULATION

This section reports simulation results for models (1) and (10). For model (1), data were generated by equations (1), (2) and

$$\mu_i \sim \text{iid}N(0,1); \lambda_t = 0.2\lambda_{t-1} + f_t,\ f_t \sim \text{iid}N(0,1); v_{it} = \alpha v_{i(t-1)} + u_{it}; \quad (19)$$

$$u_{it} = \theta_i u_{i(t-1)} + e_{it},\ e_{it} \sim \text{iid}N(0, \sigma_{e_i}^2). \quad (20)$$

We assumed that the parameter α takes the same value for all i to make it easy to interpret simulation results. The Dickey–Fuller–GLS$^{\mu}$ test with the true autoregressive (AR) order was used as an underlying test. Because this test is invariant to the values of the parameters β_0 and $\sigma_{e_i}^2$, we set $\beta_0 = 0$ and $\sigma_{e_i}^2 = 1$ for all i. The values of θ_i were chosen from a uniform distribution $U[-0.2, 0.2]$ and fixed throughout the iterations. In addition, we set $v_{i0} = 0$ and $u_{i0} = 0$ for simplicity. The size of all the tests will not be affected by this, but the power will be. Last, we set $\lambda_0 = 0$. Simulation results for model (1) are reported in Table 12.1.

For model (10), the data were generated by eqs. (10),

$$x_{it} = \mu_i + \lambda_t + \gamma_i t + v_{it}; \gamma_i \sim \text{iid}N(0,1),$$

(19), and (20). As an underlying test, the Dickey–Fuller–GLS$^{\tau}$ test with the true AR order was used. The values of the parameters β_0 and β_1 were set at zero because these do not affect numerical values of the test. Simulation results for model (10) are reported in Table 12.2.

The simulation results are based on 5,000 iterations at $N = 30, 60, 100$, and we considered two time series spans, $T = 50$ and $T = 100$. Nominal size for the

Table 12.1 *Empirical Size and Power of Panel Unit Root Tests (Intercept only; $e_{it} \sim N(0, 1)$; No cross-sectional correlation in e_{it})*

(i) $T = 50$

		P_m	Z	L^*
Size	$N = 30$	0.051	0.043	0.044
$\alpha = 1.00$	$N = 60$	0.042	0.037	0.039
	$N = 100$	0.037	0.032	0.033
Power	$N = 30$	0.197/0.194	0.277/0.313	0.270/0.301
$\alpha = 0.99$	$N = 60$	0.304/0.339	0.470/0.519	0.461/0.513
	$N = 100$	0.430/0.492	0.673/0.746	0.663/0.731
Power	$N = 30$	0.477/0.472	0.674/0.710	0.654/0.691
$\alpha = 0.98$	$N = 60$	0.747/0.777	0.931/0.948	0.923/0.941
	$N = 100$	0.912/0.935	0.994/0.997	0.993/0.996
Power	$N = 30$	0.765/0.761	0.923/0.938	0.916/0.928
$\alpha = 0.97$	$N = 60$	0.961/0.968	0.997/0.998	0.996/0.998
	$N = 100$	0.999/0.999	1.00/1.00	1.00/1.00

(ii) $T = 100$

		P_m	Z	L^*
Size	$N = 30$	0.058	0.055	0.053
$\alpha = 1.00$	$N = 60$	0.060	0.052	0.052
	$N = 100$	0.058	0.055	0.055
Power	$N = 30$	0.562/0.533	0.773/0.762	0.759/0.743
$\alpha = 0.99$	$N = 60$	0.819/0.801	0.973/0.969	0.968/0.965
	$N = 100$	0.957/0.949	1.00/1.00	1.00/0.999
Power	$N = 30$	0.969/0.964	0.998/0.998	0.998/0.997
$\alpha = 0.98$	$N = 60$	1.00/1.00	1.00/1.00	1.00/1.00
	$N = 100$	1.00/1.00	1.00/1.00	1.00/1.00
Power	$N = 30$	1.00/1.00	1.00/1.00	1.00/1.00
$\alpha = 0.97$	$N = 60$	1.00/1.00	1.00/1.00	1.00/1.00
	$N = 100$	1.00/1.00	1.00/1.00	1.00/1.00

simulation results was set at 0.05. In calculating p-values of the Dickey–Fuller–GLS tests, we used the finite sample percentiles obtained by the MacKinnon method discussed in Section 12.4. Note that the percentiles were obtained by using the AR(1) model, whereas our data were generated by the AR(2) model. To make a fair comparison of the tests, we reported both the size-unadjusted and size-adjusted powers. In the tables, the numbers before the "/" are size-unadjusted, and those after the "/" are size-adjusted. The AR lag is assumed to be known for the results in Tables 12.1 and 12.2. But the tests using the Bayesian information criterion (BIC) lag selection method produced almost identical results, which are not worth reporting here.

Table 12.2 *Empirical Size and Power of Panel Unit Root Tests (Intercept and linear time trend; $e_{it} \sim N(0, 1)$; No cross-sectional correlation in e_{it})*

(i) $T = 50$

		P_m	Z	L^*
Size	$N = 30$	0.052	0.049	0.049
$\alpha = 1.00$	$N = 60$	0.050	0.045	0.044
	$N = 100$	0.044	0.044	0.045
Power	$N = 30$	0.058/0.054	0.055/0.057	0.054/0.054
$\alpha = 0.99$	$N = 60$	0.055/0.055	0.053/0.062	0.052/0.061
	$N = 100$	0.051/0.056	0.052/0.059	0.053/0.059
Power	$N = 30$	0.074/0.070	0.074/0.077	0.075/0.076
$\alpha = 0.98$	$N = 60$	0.078/0.079	0.083/0.098	0.086/0.097
	$N = 100$	0.080/0.087	0.096/0.110	0.101/0.109
Power	$N = 30$	0.106/0.099	0.113/0.118	0.113/0.113
$\alpha = 0.97$	$N = 60$	0.126/0.127	0.156/0.174	0.157/0.174
	$N = 100$	0.141/0.155	0.205/0.226	0.204/0.219

(ii) $T = 100$

		P_m	Z	L^*
Size	$N = 30$	0.053	0.052	0.051
$\alpha = 1.00$	$N = 60$	0.051	0.058	0.055
	$N = 100$	0.049	0.051	0.051
Power	$N = 30$	0.085/0.080	0.087/0.083	0.092/0.090
$\alpha = 0.99$	$N = 60$	0.089/0.087	0.107/0.097	0.108/0.100
	$N = 100$	0.100/0.101	0.135/0.131	0.134/0.132
Power	$N = 30$	0.176/0.168	0.227/0.219	0.223/0.221
$\alpha = 0.98$	$N = 60$	0.249/0.245	0.367/0.344	0.360/0.345
	$N = 100$	0.341/0.343	0.515/0.506	0.510/0.502
Power	$N = 30$	0.375/0.364	0.513/0.503	0.503/0.500
$\alpha = 0.97$	$N = 60$	0.587/0.583	0.786/0.763	0.777/0.760
	$N = 100$	0.774/0.775	0.941/0.938	0.938/0.936

The major findings of our experiments reported in Tables 12.1 and 12.2 can be summarized as follows:

- All the tests keep nominal size quite well. Size properties of the tests tend to improve as T increases.
- All the tests become more powerful as N increases, which justifies the use of panel data.
- In terms of size-adjusted power, the Z and P_m tests seem to be superior to the L^* test.
- When a linear time trend term is included in the model, the power of all the tests decreases.

Table 12.3 *Empirical Size and Power of Panel Unit Root Tests (Intercept only; $e_{it} \sim U[-0.5, 0.5]$; No cross-sectional correlation in e_{it})*

(i) $T = 50$

		P_m	Z	L^*
Size	$N = 30$	0.052	0.042	0.041
$\alpha = 1.00$	$N = 60$	0.052	0.045	0.046
	$N = 100$	0.053	0.043	0.046
Power	$N = 30$	0.207/0.198	0.287/0.321	0.280/0.317
$\alpha = 0.99$	$N = 60$	0.321/0.315	0.481/0.495	0.471/0.489
	$N = 100$	0.457/0.447	0.677/0.701	0.671/0.687
Power	$N = 30$	0.490/0.476	0.671/0.704	0.653/0.688
$\alpha = 0.98$	$N = 60$	0.755/0.746	0.926/0.930	0.921/0.926
	$N = 100$	0.914/0.911	0.995/0.996	0.993/0.994
Power	$N = 30$	0.764/0.752	0.916/0.933	0.906/0.923
$\alpha = 0.97$	$N = 60$	0.962/0.959	0.998/0.999	0.998/0.998
	$N = 100$	0.998/0.998	1.00/1.00	1.00/1.00

(ii) $T = 100$

		P_m	Z	L^*
Size	$N = 30$	0.059	0.049	0.048
$\alpha = 1.00$	$N = 60$	0.063	0.055	0.054
	$N = 100$	0.059	0.059	0.056
Power	$N = 30$	0.573/0.544	0.789/0.790	0.770/0.775
$\alpha = 0.99$	$N = 60$	0.842/0.813	0.978/0.972	0.973/0.969
	$N = 100$	0.962/0.950	0.999/0.999	0.999/0.999
Power	$N = 30$	0.972/0.967	0.999/0.999	0.999/0.999
$\alpha = 0.98$	$N = 60$	1.00/1.00	1.00/1.00	1.00/1.00
	$N = 100$	1.00/1.00	1.00/1.00	1.00/1.00
Power	$N = 30$	1.00/1.00	1.00/1.00	1.00/1.00
$\alpha = 0.97$	$N = 60$	1.00/1.00	1.00/1.00	1.00/1.00
	$N = 100$	1.00/1.00	1.00/1.00	1.00/1.00

- On the basis of size and power, the Z and P_m tests seem to outperform the L^* test and hence are recommended for empirical applications.

One may rightfully argue that Tables 12.1 and 12.2 report good size properties of the tests because both the percentiles used to calculate the p-values of the tests and the data-generating processes for the size and power calculations are based on normal distributions. To assess the robustness of the size and power of the tests to the departure from the assumption of normally distributed errors, we generated $e_{it} \sim U[-0.5, 0.5]$ and performed the same experiments as for Tables 12.1 and 12.2. The results, reported in Tables 12.3 and 12.4, indicate

Table 12.4 *Empirical Size and Power of Panel Unit Root Tests (Intercept and linear time trend; $e_{it} \sim U[-0.5, 0.5]$; No cross-sectional correlation in e_{it})*

(i) $T = 50$

		P_m	Z	L^*
Size	$N = 30$	0.055	0.053	0.052
$\alpha = 1.00$	$N = 60$	0.057	0.049	0.052
	$N = 100$	0.057	0.056	0.059
Power	$N = 30$	0.062/0.057	0.057/0.053	0.058/0.056
$\alpha = 0.99$	$N = 60$	0.064/0.053	0.058/0.061	0.060/0.058
	$N = 100$	0.067/0.061	0.067/0.061	0.069/0.060
Power	$N = 30$	0.079/0.072	0.076/0.072	0.078/0.075
$\alpha = 0.98$	$N = 60$	0.094/0.082	0.095/0.098	0.096/0.092
	$N = 100$	0.103/0.088	0.110/0.099	0.115/0.098
Power	$N = 30$	0.112/0.101	0.114/0.111	0.114/0.109
$\alpha = 0.97$	$N = 60$	0.146/0.132	0.171/0.173	0.170/0.166
	$N = 100$	0.177/0.0157	0.222/0.200	0.224/0.195

(ii) $T = 100$

		P_m	Z	L^*
Size	$N = 30$	0.061	0.054	0.055
$\alpha = 1.00$	$N = 60$	0.063	0.056	0.058
	$N = 100$	0.060	0.059	0.061
Power	$N = 30$	0.089/0.075	0.092/0.087	0.093/0.087
$\alpha = 0.99$	$N = 60$	0.101/0.086	0.111/0.101	0.115/0.100
	$N = 100$	0.120/0.103	0.139/0.125	0.143/0.120
Power	$N = 30$	0.178/0.153	0.225/0.216	0.222/0.210
$\alpha = 0.98$	$N = 60$	0.270/0.240	0.359/0.342	0.360/0.330
	$N = 100$	0.370/0.333	0.525/0.486	0.523/0.479
Power	$N = 30$	0.376/0.338	0.498/0.483	0.489/0.471
$\alpha = 0.97$	$N = 60$	0.590/0.552	0.779/0.763	0.774/0.745
	$N = 100$	0.786/0.758	0.941/0.929	0.938/0.927

that the uniformly distributed errors do not bring any apparent differences in the size and power of the tests. Thus, the conclusions derived from Tables 12.1 and 12.2 also apply to Tables 12.3 and 12.4.

Our models assume that the innovation terms e_{it} are cross-sectionally independent and that cross-sectional correlation is introduced by the time-effect variable λ_t. One may, however, question the validity of such assumptions in economic applications. Indeed, O'Connell (1998) argues that the assumption of independent innovation terms is not appropriate for real exchange rates and demonstrates that Levin and Lin's (1992) test suffers from serious size

Table 12.5 *Empirical Size and Power of Panel Unit Root Tests (Intercept only; Cross-sectional correlation in e_{it} with $\varpi = 0.5$)*

(i) $T = 50$

		P_m	Z	L^*
Size	$N = 30$	0.072	0.050	0.052
$\alpha = 1.00$	$N = 60$	0.050	0.033	0.033
	$N = 100$	0.038	0.025	0.026
Power	$N = 30$	0.264/0.308	0.290/0.414	0.296/0.387
$\alpha = 0.99$	$N = 60$	0.304/0.355	0.398/0.535	0.396/0.512
	$N = 100$	0.385/0.439	0.547/0.682	0.545/0.662
Power	$N = 30$	0.523/0.570	0.631/0.766	0.626/0.737
$\alpha = 0.98$	$N = 60$	0.721/0.768	0.876/0.932	0.870/0.919
	$N = 100$	0.872/0.902	0.971/0.988	0.970/0.985
Power	$N = 30$	0.769/0.810	0.883/0.941	0.876/0.927
$\alpha = 0.97$	$N = 60$	0.943/0.957	0.990/0.995	0.989/0.994
	$N = 100$	0.992/0.994	0.999/1.00	0.999/1.00

(ii) $T = 100$

		P_m	Z	L^*
Size	$N = 30$	0.110	0.084	0.086
$\alpha = 1.00$	$N = 60$	0.080	0.056	0.056
	$N = 100$	0.060	0.042	0.044
Power	$N = 30$	0.653/0.623	0.759/0.783	0.753/0.772
$\alpha = 0.99$	$N = 60$	0.818/0.800	0.933/0.942	0.928/0.936
	$N = 100$	0.929/0.921	0.986/0.989	0.984/0.987
Power	$N = 30$	0.964/0.957	0.990/0.992	0.989/0.991
$\alpha = 0.98$	$N = 60$	0.998/0.997	1.00/1.00	1.00/1.00
	$N = 100$	1.00/1.00	1.00/1.00	1.00/1.00
Power	$N = 30$	0.998/0.998	1.00/1.00	1.00/1.00
$\alpha = 0.97$	$N = 60$	1.00/1.00	1.00/1.00	1.00/1.00
	$N = 100$	1.00/1.00	1.00/1.00	1.00/1.00

distortions when the assumption of independence is violated, whereas his GLS test does not. His test, however, is for homogeneous panels and is not appropriate for the data-generating processes of this study. To gauge the importance of the assumption of independent innovation terms for our tests, we generated the innovation terms as

$$\begin{pmatrix} e_{t1} \\ \vdots \\ e_{tN} \end{pmatrix} \sim \text{iid} N(0, \Omega), \ (t = 1, \ldots, T); \ \Omega = \begin{bmatrix} 1 & \varpi & \cdots & \varpi \\ \varpi & 1 & \cdots & \varpi \\ \vdots & \vdots & \ddots & \vdots \\ \varpi & \varpi & \cdots & 1 \end{bmatrix}; \varpi = 0.5$$

Table 12.6 *Empirical Size and Power of Panel Unit Root Tests (Intercept and Linear time Trend; Cross-sectional correlation in e_{it} with $\varpi = 0.5$)*

(i) $T = 50$

		P_m	Z	L^*
Size	$N = 30$	0.139	0.107	0.111
$\alpha = 1.00$	$N = 60$	0.106	0.085	0.087
	$N = 100$	0.086	0.070	0.071
Power	$N = 30$	0.136/0.084	0.106/0.079	0.110/0.081
$\alpha = 0.99$	$N = 60$	0.113/0.064	0.088/0.063	0.091/0.064
	$N = 100$	0.090/0.053	0.075/0.053	0.079/0.055
Power	$N = 30$	0.158/0.095	0.128/0.096	0.134/0.098
$\alpha = 0.98$	$N = 60$	0.139/0.082	0.123/0.091	0.127/0.090
	$N = 100$	0.129/0.074	0.132/0.090	0.136/0.090
Power	$N = 30$	0.203/0.126	0.178/0.136	0.179/0.136
$\alpha = 0.97$	$N = 60$	0.199/0.124	0.205/0.155	0.204/0.156
	$N = 100$	0.202/0.125	0.235/0.181	0.238/0.180

(ii) $T = 100$

		P_m	Z	L^*
Size	$N = 30$	0.202	0.148	0.156
$\alpha = 1.00$	$N = 60$	0.157	0.116	0.122
	$N = 100$	0.125	0.102	0.106
Power	$N = 30$	0.234/0.124	0.187/0.112	0.190/0.113
$\alpha = 0.99$	$N = 60$	0.204/0.102	0.177/0.100	0.176/0.102
	$N = 100$	0.187/0.085	0.178/0.101	0.183/0.101
Power	$N = 30$	0.367/0.225	0.347/0.231	0.346/0.232
$\alpha = 0.98$	$N = 60$	0.406/0.240	0.434/0.300	0.435/0.300
	$N = 100$	0.464/0.280	0.549/0.403	0.547/0.400
Power	$N = 30$	0.576/0.410	0.598/0.463	0.598/0.460
$\alpha = 0.97$	$N = 60$	0.708/0.539	0.798/0.677	0.796/0.671
	$N = 100$	0.830/0.667	0.926/0.857	0.925/0.848

and performed the same experiments as in Tables 12.1 and 12.2. The results, reported in Tables 12.5 and 12.6, can be summarized as follows:

- The empirical size of the tests is not quite sensitive to the cross-sectional correlation of innovation terms, although we observe higher size distortions for the model with a linear time trend at $T = 100$. By contrast, O'Connell (1998) reports quite severe size distortions of Levin and Lin's (1992) test under a similar circumstance.

- Table 12.6 shows that the empirical size of the tests deteriorates as T increases unlike in Tables 12.1–12.4. This must be due to the violation of the independence assumption.
- Table 12.6 indicates that the tests tend to reject more often under the alternative than in Tables 12.1–12.4 owing most likely to size distortions. Comparing Tables 12.1 and 12.5, we observe no apparent differences in empirical power properties of the tests observed.

12.6 AN APPLICATION

This section applies the panel unit root studied in previous sections to logarithms of the annual real per capita GDP (RGDPCH) data for 23 OECD nations during the sampling period 1960–1992. The data were taken from Summers and Heston's Penn World Table Mark 5.6.[7] Testing for a unit root in real GDP has been an important issue in empirical macroeconomics because real-business-cycle models are considered to be consistent with the presence of a unit root in real GDP (see Nelson and Plosser 1982), although it may also be argued that Keynesian business cycle models do not preclude high persistence of real GDP (see Romer 1996, p. 179). Most previous studies could not reject the null of a unit root in real GDP.

It is well documented in the literature of international business cycles (e.g., Backus and Kehoe 1992, Table 4) that real GDPs are correlated across nations. Thus, it seems appropriate to apply the panel unit root tests of this chapter to the real GDP data because the tests are designed for cross-sectionally correlated panels. Using the Dickey–Fuller–GLS$^\tau$ test with BIC lag selection as an underlying test, we report panel unit root test results in Table 12.7. To calculate p-values of the Dickey–Fuller–GLS$^\tau$ test, we used the percentiles obtained by the simulation method of Section 12.4.

The first row of Table 12.7 reports test results using Choi's (2001) tests for independent panels. These are reported for the purpose of comparison. The second row contains results using the panel unit root tests for cross-sectionally correlated panels. The results show that the null of a unit root in real GDP is not rejected at conventional significance levels when the Z and L^* tests for independent panels are used. The P_m test rejects the null at the 5% level, but this occurs probably because cross-sectional correlation is not properly taken care of. All the combination tests for cross-sectionally correlated panels provide evidence supporting the null of a unit root. We conclude from these results that the presence of a unit root in real GDP is statistically supported.

[7] This is an expanded version of the Mark 5 data set and is described in Summers and Heston (1991). The Penn World Table Mark 5.6 can be obtained online from the National Bureau of Economic Research.

Table 12.7 *Panel Unit Root Test Results for Real GDP of 23 OECD Nations*

	P_m	Z	L^*
No cross-sectional correlation	-2.285^a	3.146	3.049
Cross-sectional correlation	-0.9394	0.7105	0.7227

Notes:

[1] Annual data for the sampling period 1960–1992 were used.

[2] The Dickey–Fuller–GLS$^\tau$ test coupled with BIC lag selection was used as an underlying unit root test for time series.

[a] denotes significance at the 5% level.

12.7 CONCLUDING REMARKS

We have developed unit root tests for cross-sectionally correlated panels modeled by error-component models. The test statistics we propose were formulated by combining p-values from the augmented Dickey–Fuller test applied to each time series whose nonstochastic trend components and cross-sectional correlations were eliminated by Elliott, Rothenberg, and Stock's (1996) GLS-based detrending and the conventional cross-sectional demeaning for panel data. The tests have a standard, normal limiting distribution. Simulation results show that these tests have reasonably good size and power properties and that the Z and L^* tests are promising. Moreover, it is found that the tests are not quite sensitive to cross-sectionally correlated innovations. The combinations tests were applied to the real GDP data of 23 OECD nations. The results support the presence of a unit root in the GDP data.

APPENDIX A: GLS DEMEANING AND DETRENDING

For model (1), we may write

$$\hat{\beta}_{0i} = \beta_0 + \left\{ \mu_i + \lambda_1 + v_{i1} + \frac{c\mu_i}{T} - \frac{c}{T}\sum_{t=2}^{T}\left(\Delta\lambda_t - \frac{c}{T}\lambda_{(t-1)} + \Delta v_{it} - \frac{c}{T}v_{i(t-1)}\right)\right\} \div \left\{1 + \frac{c^2(T-1)}{T^2}\right\}$$
$$= \beta_0 + \mu_i + \lambda_1 + v_{i1} + o_p(1). \tag{A.1}$$

This gives $y_{it} - \hat{\beta}_{0i} = \lambda_t - \lambda_1 + v_{it} - v_{i1} + o_p(1)$. More precisely, the $o_p(1)$ term in (A.1) is $O_p(T^{-1/2})$ when v_{it} has a unit root, and it is $O_p(T^{-1})$ when v_{it} is stationary. Demeaning $y_{it} - \hat{\beta}_{0i}$ cross-sectionally eliminates $\lambda_t - \lambda_1$, and hence relation (14) follows.

For model (10), we have

$$\begin{pmatrix}\tilde{\beta}_{0i}\\ \tilde{\beta}_{1i}\end{pmatrix} = \begin{pmatrix}\beta_0\\ \beta_1\end{pmatrix} + \begin{bmatrix} 1 + \frac{c^2(T-1)}{T^2} & 1 - \frac{c}{T}(T-1-\frac{c(T-1)}{2}) \\ 1 - \frac{c}{T}(T-1-\frac{c(T-1)}{2}) & T - c(T-1) + \frac{c^2(T-1)(2T-1)}{6T}\end{bmatrix}^{-1}$$

$$\begin{bmatrix} \mu_i + \lambda_1 + \gamma_i + v_{i1} - \frac{c}{T}\Big[-\frac{c\mu_i(T-1)}{T} + \gamma_i(T-1) - \frac{c\gamma_i(T-1)}{2} \\ + \sum_{t=2}^{T}\left(\Delta\lambda_t - \frac{c}{T}\lambda_{(t-1)} + \Delta v_{it} - \frac{c}{T}v_{i(t-1)}\right)\Big] \\ \mu_i + \lambda_1 + \gamma_i + v_{i1} + \Big[-\frac{c\mu_i(T-1)}{T} + \gamma_i(T-1) - \frac{c\gamma_i(T-1)}{2} \\ + \sum_{t=2}^{T}\left(\Delta\lambda_t - \frac{c}{T}\lambda_{(t-1)} + \Delta v_{it} - \frac{c}{T}v_{i(t-1)}\right)\Big] \\ -\frac{c}{T}\{-\frac{c\mu_i(T-1)}{2} + \frac{\gamma_i T(T-1)}{2} - \frac{c\gamma_i(T-1)(2T-1)}{6} \\ + \sum_{t=2}^{T}\left[(t-1)\Delta\lambda_t - \frac{c}{T}(t-1)\lambda_{(t-1)} + (t-1)\Delta v_{it} - \frac{c}{T}(t-1)v_{i(t-1)}\right]\} \end{bmatrix}. \tag{A.2}$$

Let $\begin{bmatrix} 1 + \frac{c^2(T-1)}{T^2} & 1 - \frac{c}{T}(T - 1 - \frac{c(T-1)}{2}) \\ 1 - \frac{c}{T}(T - 1 - \frac{c(T-1)}{2}) & T - c(T-1) + \frac{c^2(T-1)(2T-1)}{6T} \end{bmatrix}^{-1} = \begin{bmatrix} P & Q \\ Q & R \end{bmatrix}$.

Because $Q \simeq 0$ for large T, (A.2) gives

$$\begin{aligned} y_{it} - \tilde{\beta}_{0i} - \tilde{\beta}_{1i}t &= \mu_i + \lambda_t + \gamma_i t + v_{it} - (\tilde{\beta}_0 - \beta_0) - (\tilde{\beta}_1 - \beta_1)t \\ &= \mu_i + \lambda_t + \gamma_i t + v_{it} - P\left(\mu_i + \lambda_1 + \gamma_i\left(1 - c + \frac{c^2}{2}\right) + v_{i1}\right) \\ &\quad - R\mu_i\left[1 - \frac{c(T-1)}{T} + \frac{c^2(T-1)}{2T}\right]t \\ &\quad - R\gamma_i\left[1 - c(T-1) + \frac{c^2(T-1)(2T-1)}{6T}\right]t \\ &\quad - R\left[\left(1 - \frac{(T-1)c}{T}\right)v_{iT} + \frac{c^2}{T^2}\sum_{t=2}^{T}(t-1)v_{i(t-1)}\right]t \\ &\quad - R\left[\left(1 - \frac{(T-1)c}{T}\right)\lambda_T\right]t + o_p(1). \end{aligned}$$

For large T, $P \simeq 1$ and $R \simeq 1/(1 - c + \frac{c^2}{3})T$, however. Therefore, we have relation (15) from which relation (16) follows.

APPENDIX B: ASYMPTOTIC NULL DISTRIBUTIONS OF THE DICKEY–FULLER–GLS TESTS

Because asymptotic theory for the Dickey–Fuller t-tests is well known, we will give only a brief sketch of the proof here. In addition, we will use asymptotic theory for integrated processes summarized in Phillips (1988). Relation (14) gives for large T

$$\begin{aligned} z_{it} &- \sum_{l=1}^{p_i}\alpha_{il}z_{i(t-l)} \\ &= (v_{it} - v_{i1} - \bar{v}_{.t} + \bar{v}_{.1}) - \sum_{l=1}^{p_i}\alpha_{il}\left[v_{i(t-l)} - v_{i1} - \bar{v}_{.(t-l)} + \bar{v}_{.1}\right] + o_p(1) \\ &= e_{it} - e_{i1} - \bar{e}_{.t} + \bar{e}_{.1} + o_p(1) \\ &= f_{it} + o_p(1), \text{ for instance.} \end{aligned} \tag{A.3}$$

Therefore, we need to find the asymptotic properties of $\sum_{t=p_i+1}^{T} z_{i(t-1)}^2$, $\sum_{t=p_i+1}^{T} \left(\Delta z_{i(t-j)}\right)^2$, $\sum_{t=p_i+1}^{T} z_{i(t-1)} \Delta z_{i(t-j)}$, $\sum_{t=p_i+1}^{T} \Delta z_{i(t-j)} \Delta z_{i(t-k)}$, $\sum_{t=p_i+1}^{T} z_{i(t-1)} f_{it}$, and $\sum_{t=p_i+1}^{T} \Delta z_{i(t-j)} f_{it}$ $(j, k = 1, \ldots, p_i - 1)$ to find the asymptotic distribution of the Dickey–Fuller–GLS$^\mu$ test. Relation (14) gives as $T \to \infty$ and $N \to \infty$

$$z_{i[Tr]}/\sqrt{T} \Rightarrow \sigma_{\Delta v_i} W_i(r),$$

where $[x]$ denotes the integer part of x, $\sigma_{\Delta v_i}^2$ is the long-run variance of Δv_{it}, and $W_i(r)$ is the standard Brownian motion. Thus, as $T \to \infty$ and $N \to \infty$,

$$\frac{1}{T^2} \sum_{t=p_i+1}^{T} z_{i(t-1)}^2 \Rightarrow \sigma_{\Delta v_i}^2 \int_0^1 W_i(r)^2 dr, \tag{A.4}$$

$$\frac{1}{T} \sum_{t=p_i+1}^{T} z_{i(t-1)} f_{it} \Rightarrow \sigma_{e_i} \sigma_{\Delta v_i} \int_0^1 W_i(r) dW_i(r), \tag{A.5}$$

$$\frac{1}{T} \sum_{t=p_i+1}^{T} \left[\Delta z_{i(t-j)}\right]^2 = O_p(1), \tag{A.6}$$

$$\frac{1}{T^{3/2}} \sum_{t=p_i+1}^{T} z_{i(t-1)} \Delta z_{i(t-j)} = o_p(1), \tag{A.7}$$

$$\frac{1}{T} \sum_{t=p_i+1}^{T} \Delta z_{i(t-j)} \Delta z_{i(t-k)} = O_p(1), \tag{A.8}$$

and

$$\frac{1}{\sqrt{T}} \sum_{t=p_i+1}^{T} \Delta z_{i(t-j)} f_{it} = O_p(1). \tag{A.9}$$

Relations (A.4)–(A.9) show that the limiting distribution of the Dickey–Fuller–GLS$^\mu$ test, when $T \to \infty$ and $N \to \infty$, is $\int_0^1 W_i(r) dW_i(r) / \sqrt{\int_0^1 W_i(r)^2 dr}$, which is the limiting distribution of the Dickey–Fuller t-test for the AR(1) model without time trends.

Using w_{it}, we may obtain an equation similar to (A.3). Note that the terms involving μ_i and γ_i in relation (16) vanish from this equation asymptotically because $\sum_{l=1}^{p_i} \alpha_{il} = 1$ for all i under the null. Moreover, we deduce from relation (16) that, as $T \to \infty$ and $N \to \infty$,

$$w_{i[Tr]}/\sqrt{T} \Rightarrow \sigma_{\Delta v_i} V_i(r),$$

where $V_i(r) = W_i(r) - \left\{\eta W_i(1) + 3(1-\eta) \int_0^1 s W_i(s) ds\right\} r$. Thus, the limiting distribution of the Dickey–Fuller–GLS$^\tau$ test using w_{it} is $\int_0^1 V_i(r) dW_i(r) / \sqrt{\int_0^1 V_i(r)^2 dr}$, percentiles of which are tabulated in ERS (Table I C, p. 825).

References

Backus, D. K. and P. J. Kehoe (1992). "International evidence on the historical properties of business cycles," *American Economic Review*, 82, 864–888.

Chang, Y. (2000). "Bootstrap unit root tests in panels with cross-sectional dependency," *Journal of Econometrics*.

Choi, I. (1999). "Testing the random walk hypothesis for real exchange rates," *Journal of Applied Econometrics*, 14, 293–308.

Choi, I. (2001). "Unit root tests for panel data," *Journal of International Money and Finance*, 20, 249–272.

Coakley, J. and A. M. Fuertes (1997). "New panel unit root tests of PPP," *Economics Letters*, 57, 17–22.

Culver, S. E. and D. H. Papell (1997). "Is there a unit root in the inflation rate? Evidence from sequential break and panel data models," *Journal of Applied Econometrics*, 12, 435–444.

Dickey, D. A. and W. Fuller (1979). "Distribution of the estimators for autoregressive time series with a unit root," *Journal of the American Statistical Association*, 74, 427–431.

Elliott, G., T. J. Rothenberg, and J. H. Stock (1996). "Efficient Tests for an Autoregressive Unit Root," *Econometrica*, 64, 813–836.

Feller, W. (1950). *An Introduction to Probability: Theory and Its Applications*, Vol. I, New York: Wiley.

Fisher, R. A. (1932). *Statistical Methods for Research Workers*. London: Oliver and Boyd.

Frankel, J. A. and A. K. Rose (1996). "A panel project on purchasing power parity: Mean reversion within and between countries," *Journal of International Economics*, 40, 209–224.

Fuller, W. (1976). *Introduction to Statistical Time Series*, New York: John Wiley.

George, E. O. (1977), Combining Independent One-Sided and Two-Sided Statistical Tests – Some Theory and Applications, Doctoral dissertation, University of Rochester.

Grenander, U. and M. Rosenblatt (1957). *Statistical Analysis of Stationary Time Series*, New York: John Wiley.

Hedges, L. V. and I. Olkin (1985). *Statistical Methods for Meta-Analysis*, San Diego: Academic Press.

Hsiao, C. (1986). *Analysis of Panel Data*, New York: Cambridge University Press.

Im, K. S., M. H. Pesaran, and S. Shin (2003) "Testing for unit roots in heterogeneous panels," *Journal of Econometrics*, 115, 53–74.

Leybourne, S. J. (1995). "Testing for unit roots using forward and reverse Dickey–Fuller regressions," *Oxford Bulletin of Economics and Statistics*, 57, 559–571.

Leybourne, S. J., T. Kim, and P. Newbold (2002). "Examination of some more powerful modifications of the Dickey–Fuller test," mimeograph, University of Nottingham.

Levin, A. and C.-F. Lin (1992). "Unit root tests in panel data: Asymptotic and finite-sample properties," University of California, San Diego, Discussion Paper 92–23.

Levin, A., Lin, C.-F., and Chu, C.-S. J. (2002), "Unit root tests in panel data: Asymptotic and finite-sample properties," *Journal of Econometrics*, 108, 1–25.

Lothian, J. R. (1997). "Multi-country evidence on the behavior of purchasing power parity under the current float," *Journal of International Money and Finance*, 16, 19–35.

MacDonald, R. (1996). "Panel unit root tests and real exchange rates," *Economics Letters*, 50, 7–11.

MacKinnon, J. G. (1994). "Approximate asymptotic distribution functions for unit-root and cointegration," *Journal of Business and Economic Statistics*, 12, 167–176.

Maddala, G. S. and S. Wu (1999). "A comparative study of unit root tests with panel data and a new simple test," *Oxford Bulletin of Economics and Statistics*, 61, 631–652.

Mankiw, G., D. Romer, and D. N. Weil (1992). "A contribution to the empirics of economic growth," *Quarterly Journal of Economics*, 107, 407–437.

McCoskey, S. and S. Selden (1998). "Health care expenditures and GDP: Panel data unit root test results," *Journal of Health Economics*, 17, 369–376.

Nelson, C. and C. Plosser (1982). "Trends and random walks in macroeconomic time series," *Journal of Monetary Economics*, 10, 139–162.

O'Connell, P. G. J. (1998). "The overvaluation of purchasing power parity," *Journal of International Economics*, 44, 1–19.

Oh, K.-Y. (1996). "Purchasing power parity and unit root tests using panel data," *Journal of International Money and Finance*, 15, 405–418.

Papell, D. H. (1997). "Searching for stationarity: Purchasing power parity under the current float," *Journal of International Economics*, 43, 313–332.

Phillips, P. C. B. (1988). "Multiple regression with integrated processes," in N. U. Prabhu (ed.), *Contemporary Mathematics*, 80, Providence: American Mathematical Society.

Phillips, P. C. B. and D. Sul (2003). "Dynamic panel estimation and homogeneity testing under cross-section dependence," *Econometrics Journal*, 6, 217–259.

Quah, D. (1994). "Exploiting cross-section variations for unit root inference in dynamic panels," *Economics Letters*, 44, 9–19.

Romer, D. (1996). *Advanced Macroeconomics*, New York: McGraw–Hill.

Said, E. S. and D. A. Dickey (1984). "Testing for unit roots in autoregressive moving average models of unknown order," *Biometrika*, 71, 599–607.

Solow, R. M. (1956). "A contribution to the theory of economic growth," *Quarterly Journal of Economics*, 70, 65–94.

Song, F. M. and Y. Wu (1998). "Hysteresis in unemployment: Evidence from OECD countries," *The Quarterly Review of Economics and Finance*, 38, 181–192.

Stouffer, S. A., E. A. Suchman, L. C. DeVinney, S. A. Star, and R. M. Williams Jr. (1949). *The American Soldier, Volume I. Adjustment During Army Life*. Princeton: Princeton University Press.

Summers, R. and A. Heston (1991). "The Penn World Table (Mark 5): An expanded set of international comparisons, 1950–1988," *Quarterly Journal of Economics*, 106, 327–368.

Taylor, A. M. (1996), "International capital mobility in history: Purchasing power parity in the long-run," NBER Working Paper No. 5742.

Taylor, M. P. and L. Sarno (1998). "The behavior of real exchange rates during the post-Bretton Woods period," *Journal of International Economics*, 46, 281–312.

Wu, Y. (1996). "Are real exchange rates nonstationary? Evidence from a panel-data test," *Journal of Money, Credit and Banking*, 28, 54–63.

THIRTEEN

Nonlinear IV Panel Unit Root Tests

Yoosoon Chang*

13.1 INTRODUCTION

Nonstationary panels have recently drawn much attention in theoretical and empirical research. This is largely due to the availability of panel data sets covering relatively long time periods and the growing use of cross-country and cross-regional data over time to investigate many important economic interrelationships – especially those involving convergence and divergence of economic variables. Various statistics for testing unit roots in panel models have been proposed and frequently used for testing growth theories and purchasing-power-parity hypotheses. Panel models are also used to study the long-run relationships between migration flows and income and unemployment differentials across regions and among macroeconomic and international financial series, including exchange rates and spot and future interest rates. Panel-data-based tests also appeared attractive to many empirical researchers because they offer alternatives to the tests based only on individual time series observations that are known to have low discriminatory power. The earlier contributors in theoretical research on the subject include Levin, Lin, and Chu (2002); Quah (1994); Im, Pesaran, and Shin (2003); and Maddala and Wu (1999). Phillips and Moon (2000) and Baltagi and Kao (2000) provide surveys on the recent developments in testing for unit roots in panels.

In general, panels are intrinsically heterogeneous and dependent across cross-sections, and these very properties contribute to the inferential difficulties in testing for unit roots. The cross-sectional dependency, in particular, is very hard to deal with in nonstationary panels. For instance, in the presence of cross-sectional dependency, the usual Wald-type unit root tests based on the ordinary least squares (OLS) and generalized least squares (GLS) system estimators have limit distributions dependent in a very complicated way on

* I am grateful to Joon Y. Park for helpful discussions and comments. This research was supported by the National Science Foundation under Grant SES-0233940.

various nuisance parameters representing correlations across individual units. As a result, most of the existing panel unit root tests have assumed various homogeneities and spatial independence in order to obtain tractable distribution theories. These assumptions are, however, highly restrictive and thus unrealistic for many economic panels of practical interest. Of course the limit distributions of the tests constructed under such assumptions are no longer valid and become unknown when any of the assumptions are violated. Indeed, Maddala and Wu (1999) show through simulations that the tests based on cross-sectional independence, such as those considered in Levin et al. (2002) and Im et al. (2003), yield biased results and have substantial size distortions when applied to cross-sectionally dependent panels.

This chapter presents the nonlinear instrumental variables (IV) methodology explored in Chang (2002) and Chang and Song (2002) to overcome the inferential difficulties in panel unit root testing that arise from the intrinsic heterogeneities and dependencies of general nonstationary panels. Phillips, Park, and Chang (2004) and Chang (2002) show that some nonlinear transformations of integrated processes have important statistical properties that can be exploited to construct unit root tests having Gaussian limit distributions. This is a striking result given that the limit theories for unit root models are generally non-Gaussian, rendering all standard testing procedures based on Gaussian limit theory invalid. Chang (2002) finds an effective inferential basis for the unit root testing in dependent panels in the marriage of this important statistical property and the asymptotic orthogonalities among the nonlinear transfromations of integrated processes. If the transformations of the lagged levels by an integrable function are used as instruments, the t-ratio based on the usual IV estimator for the autoregressive coefficient in the augmented Dickey–Fuller-type regression yields asymptotically normal unit root tests for each cross section, and, more importantly, the nonlinear IV t-ratios from different cross sections are asymptotically independent even when the cross sections are dependent. The asymptotic orthogonalities follow because the nonlinear transformations of dependent integrated processes are asymptotically independent so long as they are not cointegrated. This means that the panel unit root tests constructed as a simple standardized sum of the individual nonlinear IV t-ratios have a standard normal limiting distribution.

The asymptotic independence and normality of the nonlinear IV t-ratios essentially provide a set of N asymptotically independent and identically distributed (iid) normal random variables, which we may use as a basis for constructing statistics capable of testing various unit root hypotheses in panels. Hence, the hypotheses from economic theories and problems can be tested under more flexible forms of null and alternative hypotheses, which are especially important for heterogeneous panels, using the order statistics based on the nonlinear IV t-ratios whose limit distributions are given by simple functionals of the standard normal distribution functions. Moreover, the nonlinear IV estimation allows for the use of relevant covariates to increase power further without incurring nuisance parameter problems. The nonlinear IV approach to panel unit root testing is explored further in Chang and Song (2002) to deal with cointegration among cross sections, which was excluded in the study of Chang (2002). The presence of cointegration invalidates the tests by Chang (2002) constructed from the nonlinear IV t-ratios based on the instruments generated by a single integrable function for all cross sections because the nonlinear IV t-ratios are no longer asymptotically independent in the presence of cross-sectional cointegrations. Chang and Song (2002) show that we may still obtain asymptotically normal panel unit root tests if the instruments for each of the cross sections are constructed from orthogonal functions even when the cross sections are cointegrated.

The rest of the chapter is organized as follows. Section 13.2 introduces the nonlinear IV methodology in a simple univariate setting. The nonlinear IV t-ratio statistic is defined, and the adaptive demeaning and detrending schemes needed to deal with models having deterministic trends are presented. Section 13.3 discusses various issues in panel unit root testing and introduces the nonlinear IV panel unit root test for panels with cross-sectional dependency induced by cross-correlations among innovations. Section 13.4 presents an improved nonlinear IV method to construct valid tests for cointegrated panels and proposes using nonlinear IV order statistics to test for more flexible forms of unit root hypotheses in panels. Section 13.5 is the conclusion.

13.2 NONLINEAR IV METHODOLOGY

13.2.1 Model and Preliminaries

We consider the following unit root regression

$$y_t = \alpha y_{t-1} + u_t, \tag{1}$$

for $t = 1, \ldots, T$. We are interested in testing the null of a unit root, $\alpha = 1$, against the stationarity alternative, $|\alpha| < 1$. The initial value y_0 does not affect our subsequent asymptotic analysis as long as it is stochastically bounded, and therefore we set it at zero for expositional brevity. The errors (u_t) in the model (1) are serially correlated and specified as an AR(p) process given by

$$\alpha(L)u_t = \varepsilon_t, \tag{2}$$

where L is the usual lag operator and $\alpha(z) = 1 - \sum_{k=1}^{p} \alpha_k z^k$. We assume

Assumption 13.1 $\alpha(z) \neq 0$ for all $|z| \leq 1$.

Assumption 13.2 (ε_t) is an iid $(0, \sigma^2)$ sequence of random variables with $\mathbf{E}|\varepsilon_t|^\ell < \infty$ for some $\ell > 4$, and its distribution is absolutely continuous with respect to the Lebesgue measure and has characteristic function φ such that $\lim_{\lambda\to\infty} \lambda^r \varphi(\lambda) = 0$ for some $r > 0$.

Define a stochastic processes U_T for (ε_t) as

$$U_T(r) = T^{-1/2} \sum_{t=1}^{[Tr]} \varepsilon_t$$

on $[0, 1]$, where $[s]$ denotes the largest integer not exceeding s. The process $U_T(r)$ takes values in the space of cadlag functions on $[0, 1]$. Under Assumption 13.2, an invariance principle holds for U_T, expressed by

$$U_T \to_d U \tag{3}$$

as $T \to \infty$, where U is Brownian motion with variance σ^2. It is also convenient to define $B_T(r)$ from (u_t) in a way similar to the definition of $U_T(r)$. Let $\alpha(1) = 1 - \sum_{k=1}^{p} \alpha_k$ and $\pi(1) = 1/\alpha(1)$. Then we have $B_T(r) = T^{-1/2} \sum_{t=1}^{[Tr]} u_t \to_d B(r)$, where $B = \pi(1)U$, as shown in Phillips and Solo (1992). This implies that the process (y_t), when scaled by $T^{-1/2}$, behaves asymptotically as the Brownian motion B under the null $\alpha = 1$ of unit root.

Our limit theory involves the two-parameter stochastic process called *local time* of Brownian motion.[1] We denote by L the (scaled) local time of U, which is defined by

$$L(t, s) = \lim_{\epsilon\to 0} \frac{1}{2\epsilon} \int_0^t 1\{|U(r) - s| < \epsilon\}\, dr. \tag{4}$$

The local time L is therefore the time that the Brownian motion U spends in the immediate neighborhood of s, up to time t, measured in chronological units. Then we may have an important relationship

$$\int_0^t G(U(r))\, dr = \int_{-\infty}^{\infty} G(s) L(t, s)\, ds,$$

which we refer to as the occupation time formula. The conditions in Assumption 13.2 are required to obtain the convergence and invariance of the sample local time as well as those of the sample Brownian motion for the asymptotics of integrable transformations of integrated time series.

[1] Refer to Chung and Williams (1990) and the references cited in Park and Phillips (1999, 2001) for the concept of local time and its use in the asymptotics for nonlinear models with integrated time series.

13.2.2 IV Estimation and Its Limit Theories

Inserting the serial correlations in the error (u_t) specified in (2) into the model (1) gives

$$y_t = \alpha y_{t-1} + \sum_{k=1}^{p} \alpha_k \Delta y_{t-k} + \varepsilon_t, \tag{5}$$

where Δ is the difference operator, because $\Delta y_t = u_t$ under the unit root null hypothesis. We consider the IV estimation of the augmented autoregression (5), using the instruments

$$(F(y_{t-1}), \Delta y_{t-1}, \ldots, \Delta y_{t-p})', \tag{6}$$

where F is an integrable function. Notice that the instrument we use for the lagged level y_{t-1} is a nonlinear transformation of itself, that is, $F(y_{t-1})$. For the lagged differences $(\Delta y_{t-1}, \ldots, \Delta y_{t-p})$, we use the variables themselves as the instruments. The transformation F is called the *instrument-generating function* (IGF) and is assumed to satisfy

Assumption 13.3 Let F be integrable and satisfy $\int_{-\infty}^{\infty} xF(x)dx \neq 0$.

The condition given in Assumption 13.3 requires that the instrument $F(y_{t-1})$ be correlated with the regressor y_{t-1} that it is instrumenting for. Phillips et al. (2004) show for simple random walk models that IV estimators become inconsistent when the instrument is generated by a regularly integrable function F such that $\int_{-\infty}^{\infty} xF(x)\,dx = 0$. This is analogous to the nonorthogonality (between the instruments and regressors) requirement for the validity of IV estimation in standard stationary regressions. In our nonstationary IV estimation, where an integrable function of an integrated regressor is used as the instrument, such instrument failure occurs when the instrument-generating function is orthogonal to the regression function.

Define $x_t = (\Delta y_{t-1}, \ldots, \Delta y_{t-p})'$ and let y, y_ℓ, and X be the observations on y_t, y_{t-1}, and x_t, respectively. Using this notation, we write the regression (5) in matrix form as

$$y = y_\ell \alpha + X\beta + \varepsilon = Y\gamma + \varepsilon,$$

where $\beta = (\alpha_1, \ldots, \alpha_p)'$, $Y = (y_\ell, X)$, and $\gamma = (\alpha, \beta')'$. Denote by w_t the instrumental variables given in (6), and let $W = (F(y_\ell), X)$ be the matrix of observations on w_t, where $F(y_\ell) = (F(y_p), \ldots, F(y_{T-1}))'$. We consider the following estimator $\hat{\gamma}$ for γ:

$$\hat{\gamma} = \begin{pmatrix} \hat{\alpha} \\ \hat{\beta} \end{pmatrix} = (W'Y)^{-1}W'y = \begin{pmatrix} F(y_\ell)'y_\ell & F(y_\ell)'X \\ X'y_\ell & X'X \end{pmatrix}^{-1} \begin{pmatrix} F(y_\ell)'y \\ X'y \end{pmatrix}, \tag{7}$$

which is the usual IV estimator of γ using the instruments w_t. The IV estimator $\hat{\alpha}$ for the AR coefficient α corresponds to the first element of $\hat{\gamma}$ and is given by

$$\hat{\alpha} - 1 = B_T^{-1} A_T \tag{8}$$

under the null, where

$$A_T = \sum_{t=1}^T F(y_{t-1})\varepsilon_t - \sum_{t=1}^T F(y_{t-1})x_t' \left(\sum_{t=1}^T x_t x_t'\right)^{-1} \sum_{t=1}^T x_t \varepsilon_t$$

$$B_T = \sum_{t=1}^T F(y_{t-1})y_{t-1} - \sum_{t=1}^T F(y_{t-1})x_t' \left(\sum_{t=1}^T x_t x_t'\right)^{-1} \sum_{t=1}^T x_t y_{t-1}.$$

The variance of A_T is given by

$$\sigma^2 \mathbf{E} C_T$$

under Assumption 13.2, where

$$C_T = \sum_{t=1}^T F^2(y_{t-1}) - \sum_{t=1}^T F(y_{t-1})x_t' \left(\sum_{t=1}^T x_t x_t'\right)^{-1} \sum_{t=1}^T x_t F(y_{t-1}).$$

For testing the unit root hypothesis $\alpha = 1$, we construct the t-ratio statistic from the nonlinear IV estimator $\hat{\alpha}$ defined in (8) as

$$\tau = \frac{\hat{\alpha} - 1}{s(\hat{\alpha})}, \tag{9}$$

where $s(\hat{\alpha})$ is the standard error of the IV estimator $\hat{\alpha}$ given by

$$s^2(\hat{\alpha}) = \hat{\sigma}^2 B_T^{-2} C_T. \tag{10}$$

The $\hat{\sigma}^2$ is the usual variance estimator given by $T^{-1}\sum_{t=1}^T \hat{\varepsilon}_t^2$, where $\hat{\varepsilon}_t$ is the fitted residual from the augmented regression (5), that is, $\hat{\varepsilon}_t = y_t - \hat{\alpha} y_{t-1} - x_t'\hat{\beta}$. It is natural in our context to use the IV estimate $(\hat{\alpha}, \hat{\beta})$ given in (7) to get the fitted residual $\hat{\varepsilon}_t$. However, we may obviously use any other estimator of (α, β) as long as it yields a consistent estimate for the residual error variance. The nonlinear IV t-ratio τ reduces to $\tau = \hat{\sigma}^{-1} A_T C_T^{-1/2}$ owing to (8), (9) and (10).

The following lemma presents the asymptotics for the sample product moments appearing in the definition of τ.

Lemma 13.1 *Under Assumptions 13.1, 13.2, and 13.3, we have*

(a) $T^{-1/4} \sum_{t=1}^T F(y_{t-1})\,\varepsilon_t \ \to_d\ \mathbf{MN}\left(0,\ \sigma^2 \alpha(1)\, L(1,0) \int_{-\infty}^{\infty} F^2(s)ds\right)$

(b) $T^{-1/2} \sum_{t=1}^T F^2(y_{t-1}) \ \to_d\ \alpha(1)\, L(1,0) \int_{-\infty}^{\infty} F^2(s)ds$

$$(c)\ T^{-3/4}\sum_{t=1}^{T} F(y_{t-1})\Delta y_{t-k} \to_p 0, \text{ for } k = 1, \ldots, p,$$

as $T \to \infty$.

Parts (a) and (b) can easily be obtained, as in Park and Phillips (1999, 2001), using the recent extension made by Park (2003a).[2] Part (c) is shown in Chang (2002).

The result in Part (a) shows that the covariance asymptotics of the integrable F yields a mixed normal limiting distribution with a mixing variate depending upon the local time L of the limit Brownian motion U as well as the integral of the square of the instrument-generating function F. It is indeed an intriguing result, which will lead to the normal limit theory for the nonlinear IV t-ratio. It is very useful to note that

$$T^{-1/4}\sum_{t=1}^{T} F(y_{t-1})\varepsilon_t \approx_d \sqrt[4]{T}\int_0^1 F(\sqrt{T}B(r))dU(r)$$
$$T^{-1/2}\sum_{t=1}^{T} F^2(y_{t-1}) \approx_d \sqrt{T}\int_0^1 F^2(\sqrt{T}B(r))dr,$$

from which we may easily deduce the results in parts (a) and (b) using the theory of continuous martingales and the relationship $B = \pi(1)U$ with $\pi(1) = 1/\alpha(1)$. Refer to Park (2003b) for a heuristic of the results in parts (a) and (b) along this line.

The result in part (c) implies that the lagged differences $\Delta y_{t-k}, k = 1, \ldots, p$, and the nonlinear instrument $F(y_{t-1})$ are asymptotically independent. This in turn implies that the presence of the stationary lagged differences in our base regression (5) does not affect the limit theory of the nonlinear IV estimator for the coefficient on the lagged level, which is an integrated process under the null. The rate $T^{3/4}$ at which the sample moment vanishes is obtained in Chang, Park, and Phillips (2001). The asymptotic orthogonalities here are analogous to the familiar asymptotic orthogonalities between the stationary and integrated regressors we have seen in the usual cointegrating regressions shown earlier in Park and Phillips (1988).

The limit null distribution of the IV t-ratio statistic τ now follows readily from the results in Lemma 13.1, as in Phillips et al. (2004) and Chang (2002).

Theorem 13.1 *Under Assumptions 13.1, 13.2, and 13.3, we have*

$$\tau \to_d \mathbf{N}(0, 1)$$

as $T \to \infty$.

[2] Park and Phillips (1999, 2001) impose piecewise higher order Lipschitz conditions on F to derive the asymptotics here. Such conditions, however, are shown to be unnecessary in Park (2003a).

The limiting distribution of τ for testing $\alpha = 1$ is standard normal if a regularly integrable function is used to generate the instrument. The limit theory here is fundamentally different from the asymptotics for the usual linear unit root tests such as those by Phillips (1987) and Phillips and Perron (1988). The use of nonlinear IV is essential for our Gaussian limit theory, which is obtained from the local time asymptotics and mixed normality result given in Lemma 13.1.

The nonlinear IV t-ratio statistic is a consistent test for testing the null of unit root. To see this, consider the limit behavior of the IV t-ratio τ given in (9) under the alternative of stationarity, that is, $\alpha = \alpha_0 < 1$. We may express τ as

$$\tau = \tau(\alpha_0) + \frac{\sqrt{T}(\alpha_0 - 1)}{\sqrt{T}\,s(\hat{\alpha})}, \tag{11}$$

where

$$\tau(\alpha_0) = \frac{\hat{\alpha} - \alpha_0}{s(\hat{\alpha})}, \tag{12}$$

which is the IV t-ratio for testing $\alpha = \alpha_0 < 1$. Under the alternative, we may expect that $\tau(\alpha_0) \to_d \mathbf{N}(0, 1)$ if the usual mixing conditions for (y_t) are assumed to hold. Moreover, if we let $B_0 = \text{plim}_{T\to\infty} T^{-1} B_T$ and $C_0 = \text{plim}_{T\to\infty} T^{-1} C_T$ exist under suitable mixing conditions for (y_t), then the second term in the right-hand side of eq. (11) diverges to $-\infty$ at the rate of $\sqrt{T}$ under the alternative of stationarity. This is because $\sqrt{T}(\alpha_0 - 1) \to -\infty$ and $\sqrt{T}\,s(\hat{\alpha}) \to_p \nu$, as $T \to \infty$, where $\nu^2 = \sigma^2 B_0^{-2} C_0 > 0$. Hence, under the alternative

$$\tau \to_p -\infty$$

at $\sqrt{T}$-rate, implying that the IV t-ratio τ is $\sqrt{T}$-consistent just as in the case of the usual OLS-based t-type unit root tests such as the augmented Dickey–Fuller test.

We note that the IV t-ratios constructed from integrable IGFs are asymptotically normal, for all $|\alpha| \leq 1$, which makes a drastic contrast with the limit theory of the standard t-statistic based on the ordinary least squares estimator. The continuity of the limit distribution of the t-ratio in (12) across all values of α including the unity, in particular, allows us to construct the confidence intervals for α from the nonlinear IV estimator $\hat{\alpha}$ given in (8). We may construct $100\,(1 - \lambda)$ % asymptotic confidence interval for α as

$$\left[\hat{\alpha} - z_{\lambda/2}\, s(\hat{\alpha}),\quad \hat{\alpha} + z_{\lambda/2}\, s(\hat{\alpha})\right],$$

where $z_{\lambda/2}$ is the $(1 - \lambda/2)$-percentile from the standard normal distribution. This is another important advantage of using the nonlinear IV method. The OLS-based standard t-ratio, such as the augmented Dickey–Fuller (ADF) test, has non-Gaussian limiting null distribution called Dickey–Fuller (DF) distribution. The DF distribution is tabulated in Fuller (1996) and known to be asymmetric and skewed to the left, rendering it impossible to construct a confidence interval valid for all $|\alpha| \leq 1$ from the standard OLS-based t-ratios.

13.2.3 IV Estimation for Models with Deterministic Trends

The models with deterministic components can be analyzed as was done in the previous section if properly demeaned or detrended data are used. A proper demeaning or detrending scheme must be able to remove the nonzero mean or time trend successfully but maintain the orthogonality of the demeaned or detrended series with the error term, which is essential in retaining the martingale property of the error and ultimately the Gaussian limit theory of the covariance asymptotics for the nonlinear instrument. To meet the needs described above, Chang (2002) devised *adaptive demeaning* and *detrending*, which we introduce now.

For a time series (z_t) with a nonzero mean given by

$$z_t = \mu + y_t, \tag{13}$$

where the stochastic component (y_t) is generated as in (1), we may test for a unit root in (y_t) from the regression

$$y_t^{\mu} = \alpha y_{t-1}^{\mu} + \sum_{k=1}^{p} \alpha_k \Delta y_{t-k}^{\mu} + \varepsilon_t, \tag{14}$$

where y_t^{μ} and y_{t-1}^{μ} are, respectively, the *adaptively demeaned* series of z_t and z_{t-1} defined as

$$y_t^{\mu} = z_t - \frac{1}{t-1}\sum_{k=1}^{t-1} z_k$$

$$y_{t-1}^{\mu} = z_{t-1} - \frac{1}{t-1}\sum_{k=1}^{t-1} z_k$$

$$\Delta y_{t-k}^{\mu} = \Delta z_{t-k}, \quad k = 1, \ldots, p.$$

The term $(t-1)^{-1}\sum_{k=1}^{t-1} z_k$ appearing in the preceding definitions is the least-squares estimator of μ obtained from the preliminary regression

$$z_k = \mu + y_k, \quad \text{for } k = 1, \ldots, t-1.$$

We note that the mean μ is estimated from the model (13) using the observations up to time $(t-1)$ only rather than the full sample. This leads to demeaning based on the partial sum of the data up to $(t-1)$, and for this reason the demeaning scheme just described is considered adaptive. Notice that, even for the tth observation z_t, we use $(t-1)$-adaptive demeaning to maintain the martingale property. The lagged differences Δz_{t-k}, $k = 1, \ldots, p$, need no further demeaning because the differencing has already removed the mean.

We may then construct the nonlinear IV t-ratio τ^μ to test for unit root in (y_t) based on the nonlinear IV estimator for α from the regression (14) just as in (9). The adaptively demeaned lagged level y_{t-1}^μ is orthogonal to the error ε_t, which ensures the predictability of the nonlinear instrument $F(y_{t-1}^\mu)$, thereby retaining the martingale property of the error. Consequently, the sample moment $T^{-1/4}\sum_{t=1}^T F(y_{t-1}^\mu)\varepsilon_t$ has mixed normal limit theory, as in the models with no deterministic trends given in Lemma 13.1 (a), leading to the normal distribution theory for the IV t-ratio τ^μ for the models with nonzero mean.

We may also test for a unit root in the stochastic component of the time series with linear time trend using the nonlinear IV t-ratio τ^τ constructed in a similar way using *adaptively detrended* data. For a time series with a linear time trend given by

$$z_t = \mu + \delta t + y_t, \tag{15}$$

where (y_t) is generated as in (1), we may use the following regression as the basis for testing unit root in the stochastic component (y_t):

$$y_t^\tau = \alpha y_{t-1}^\tau + \sum_{k=1}^p \alpha_k \Delta y_{t-k}^\tau + e_t, \tag{16}$$

where y_t^τ, y_{t-1}^τ, and Δy_{t-k}^τ are adaptively detrended series of z_t, z_{t-1}, and Δz_{t-k}, $k = 1, \ldots, p$, given as

$$y_t^\tau = z_t + \frac{2}{t-1}\sum_{k=1}^{t-1} z_k - \frac{6}{t(t-1)}\sum_{k=1}^{t-1} kz_k - \frac{1}{T}z_T$$

$$y_{t-1}^\tau = z_{t-1} + \frac{2}{t-1}\sum_{k=1}^{t-1} z_k - \frac{6}{t(t-1)}\sum_{k=1}^{t-1} kz_k$$

$$\Delta y_{t-k}^\tau = \Delta z_{t-k} - \frac{1}{T}z_T, \quad k = 1, \ldots, p,$$

and (e_t) signifies the regression errors. The variables z_t and z_{t-1} are detrended using the least-squares estimators of the drift and trend coefficients, μ and δ, from the model (15) using again the observations up to time $(t-1)$ only, that is,

$$z_k = \mu + \delta k + y_k, \quad \text{for } k = 1, \ldots, t-1.$$

The term $T^{-1}z_T$ appearing in the definitions of y_t^τ and Δy_{t-k}^τ, $k = 1, \ldots, p$ is the grand sample mean of Δz_t, that is, $T^{-1}\sum_{k=1}^T \Delta z_k$. The grand sample mean is needed for y_t^τ to eliminate the remaining drift term of $z_t + 2(t-1)^{-1}\sum_{k=1}^{t-1} z_k - 6(t(t-1))^{-1}\sum_{k=1}^{t-1} kz_k$ and for Δy_{t-k}^τ to remove the nonzero mean of Δz_{t-k} for $k = 1, \ldots, p$.

The nonlinear IV t-ratio τ^τ is then defined as in (9) from the nonlinear IV estimator for α from the regression (16) with the detrended data. The adaptive detrending of the data given above also preserves the predictability of the instrument $F(y_{t-1}^{\tau})$, and the martingale property of the error e_t is also retained in this case, as shown in Chang (2002). These characteristics ensure the mixed normal limit theory of the the sample moment $T^{-1/4}\sum_{t=1}^{T}F(y_{t-1}^{\tau})e_t$ and the normal limit theory for the IV t-ratio τ^{τ}. For the actual derivation of the limit theories for the statistics τ^{μ} and τ^{τ}, we need to characterize the limit processes of the adaptively demeaned and detrended series (y_t^{μ}) and (y_t^{τ}). When scaled by $T^{-1/2}$, (y_t^{μ}) and (y_t^{τ}) converge in distribution to the constant $\pi(1)$ multiple of the adaptively demeanded Brownian motion U^{μ} and the adaptively detrended Brownian motion U^{τ}, respectively. More explicitly, the *adaptively demeaned* Brownian is defined as

$$U^{\mu}(r) = U(r) - \frac{1}{r}\int_0^r U(s)ds,$$

and similarly, the *adaptively detrended* Brownian motion as

$$U^{\tau}(r) = U(r) + \frac{2}{r}\int_0^r U(s)ds - \frac{6}{r^2}\int_0^r sU(s)ds.$$

If we let $U^{\mu}(0) = 0$ and $U^{\tau}(0) = 0$, then both processes have well-defined, continuous versions on $[0, \infty)$, as shown in Chang (2002).

The asymptotic results given in Lemma 13.1 extend easily to the models with nonzero means and deterministic trends if we replace the lagged level y_{t-1} with the lagged detrended series y_{t-1}^{μ} and y_{t-1}^{τ}. They are indeed given similarly with the local times L^{μ} and L^{τ} of the adaptively demeaned and detrended Brownian motions U^{μ} and U^{τ} in the place of the local time L of the Brownian motion U. Then the limit theories for the nonlinear IV t-ratio statistics τ^{μ} and τ^{τ} for the models with nonzero means and deterministic trends follow immediately, as shown in Chang (2002), and are given in

Corollary 13.1 *Under Assumptions 13.1, 13.2, and 13.3, we have*

$$\tau^{\mu},\ \tau^{\tau}\ \to_d \mathbf{N}(0, 1)$$

as $T \to \infty$.

The standard normal limit theory of the nonlinear IV t-ratio for the models with no deterministic trends given in Theorem 13.1, therefore, continues to hold for the models with nonzero mean and linear time trend.

13.3 PANEL UNIT ROOT TESTS

13.3.1 Issues in Panel Unit Root Testing

Several unit root tests for panel data have been developed in the recent literature, including, most notably, those by Levin et al. (2002) and Im et al. (2003).

They all have some important drawbacks and limitations, however. The test proposed by Levin et al. (2002) is applicable only for homogeneous panels, where the AR coefficients for unit roots are in particular assumed to be the same across cross sections. Their tests are based on the pooled OLS estimator for the unit root coefficient and therefore cannot be used for heterogeneous panels with different individual unit root AR coefficients. In addition, they assume cross-sectional independence. Im et al. (2003) allow for the heterogeneous panels and propose the unit root tests, which are based on the average of the individual unit root tests, t-statistics, and LM statistics computed from each individual unit. The validity of their tests, however, also requires cross-sectional independence. Needless to say, cross-sectional independence and homogeneity are quite restrictive assumptions for most of the economic panel data we encounter.

Chang (2002) explores the nonlinear IV methodology introduced in the previous section to solve the inferential difficulties in the panel unit root testing arising from the instrinsic heterogeneities and dependencies of panel models. For each cross section, the t-statistic for testing the unit root is constructed from the IV estimator of the autoregressive coefficient obtained from using an integrable transformation of the lagged level as instrument. As expected from our earlier results, each individual nonlinear IV t-ratio statistic constructed as such has standard normal limit null distribution. What is more important, however, is that the individual IV t-ratio statistics are asymptotically independent even across dependent cross-sectional units. This is indeed an intriguing result and follows from the asymptotic orthogonality results established in Chang et al. (2001) for the nonlinear transformations of integrated processes by an integrable function.

The most important implication of the asymptotic normality and orthogonalities of the individual nonlinear IV t-ratios is that we now have a set of N asymptotically independent standard normal random variables to construct the unit root test for panels with N cross-sections. Of course, a simple average, defined as a standardized sum, of the individual IV t-ratios is a valid statistic for testing joint unit root null hypothesis for the entire panel. Chang (2002) shows that such a normalized sum of the individual IV t-ratios also has standard normal limit distribution as long as the number of observations in each individual unit is large and the panel is asymptotically balanced in a weak sense. The standard limit theory is thus obtained without having to require the sequential asymptotics[3] upon which most of the available asymptotic theories for panel unit root models heavily rely. As a result, we may allow the number of cross-sectional units N to be arbitrarily small as well as large. The asymptotics presented here are T-asymptotics, and we assume throughout the chapter that N is fixed.

[3] The usual sequential asymptotics is carried out by first passing T to infinity with N fixed and subsequently letting N go to infinity–usually under cross-sectional independence.

However, three important issues remain to be addressed. First, the presence of cointegration across cross-sectional units has never been allowed. It appears that there is a high potential for such possibilities in many panels of practical interest. Yet none of the existing tests, including the nonlinear IV panel unit root test by Chang (2002) discussed in the last paragraph, is applicable to such panels. Second, there is the issue of using covariates. As demonstrated by Hansen (1995) and Chang, Sickles, and Song (2001), the inclusion of covariates can dramatically increase the power of the tests. Nevertheless, the potential has never been investigated in the context of panels. Third, the issue of formulating the panel unit root hypothesis remains largely unresolved. We often need to consider the null and alternative hypotheses that some, not all, of the cross-sectional units have unit roots. Though no one has seriously considered such hypotheses, they seem to be more relevant for many practical applications. The nonlinear IV methodology can be extended to resolve all these issues, as shown in Chang and Song (2002).

The improved IV methodology introduced in Chang and Song (2002) is based on the ADF regression further augmented by stationary covariates and uses the instruments generated by a set of orthogonal functions. The use of orthogonal instrument-generating functions is crucial for retaining the Gaussian limit theory and asymptotic orthogonalities of the nonlinear IV t-ratios in cointegrated panels. With these properties, the nonlinear IV t-ratios computed from N cross sections continue to serve as the basis for N asymptotically independent and identically distributed standard normal random variables, which can be used to construct various unit root tests. In particular, we may use the order statistics, minimum or maximum, of the nonlinear IV t-ratios to test for or against the existence of the unit roots in only a fraction of the cross-sectional units. The limit distributions of the order statistics computed from the nonlinear IV t-ratios are nuisance parameter-free and given by simple functionals of the standard normal distribution functions, as shown in Chang and Song (2002). This implies, in particular, that the critical values of the tests can be obtained from the standard normal table.

The nonlinear IV-based panel unit root testing is indeed very general and applicable to a wide class of panel models. The nonlinear IV methodology, more specifically, the asymptotic independence and normality of the individual nonlinear IV t-ratios, allow us to derive simple Gaussian limit theories for the panel unit root tests in panels with cross-sectional dependency at all levels. We may allow for cross-correlations of the innovations, cross-sectional dynamics in the short run or both and also for the comovements of the individual stochastic trends in the long run. The nonlinear IV approach, moreover, allows us to formulate hypotheses in a much sharper form, which in turn makes it possible to test for and against the existence of unit roots in a subgroup of the cross-sections. Such general results are not entertained in other existing testing procedures because their results require either cross-sectional independence or rely on a specific form of cross-sectional correlation structure, which may have limited applicability in practice.

In what follows we first present the nonlinear IV unit root test for the dependent panels with no cointegration among cross sections in Section 13.3.2 and in Section 13.4.1 introduce the improved IV methodology for cointegrated panels. In Section 13.4.2 the issue of properly formulating the unit root hypotheses in panels is discussed, and nonlinear IV-order statistics are then presented as vehicles to conduct testing for more flexibly formulated hypotheses.

13.3.2 Nonlinear IV Panel Unit Root Tests

We consider a panel unit root model given by

$$y_{it} = \alpha_i y_{i,t-1} + u_{it}, \quad i = 1, \ldots, N; \; t = 1, \ldots, T. \tag{17}$$

As usual, the index i denotes individual cross-sectional units such as individuals, households, industries, or countries, and the index t denotes time periods. The cross-sectional dimension N is fixed, but not restricted and is allowed to take a large or small value. For expositional simplicity, the cross sections are assumed to have the same T number of observations; however, the results here easily extend to unbalanced panels, as we discuss later in this section. The error terms (u_{it}) are allowed to have serial correlations, which we specify by an AR process of order p_i, that is, $\alpha^i(L)u_{it} = \varepsilon_{it}$, where $\alpha^i(z) = 1 - \sum_{k=1}^{p_i} \alpha_{ik} z^k$, for $i = 1, \ldots, N$. Note that we let $\alpha^i(z)$ and p_i vary across i, thereby allowing heterogeneity in individual short-run dynamic structures. The cross sections are allowed to be dependent via cross-sectional dependency of the innovations (ε_{it}), $i = 1, \ldots, N$, that generate the errors (u_{it}). To be more explicit about the cross-sectional dependency we allow here, let us define $(\varepsilon_t)_{t=1}^T$ by

$$\varepsilon_t = (\varepsilon_{1t}, \ldots, \varepsilon_{Nt})'. \tag{18}$$

We allow the N-dimensional innovation process (ε_t) to have covariance matrix Σ, which is unrestricted except for being positive definite.

We are interested in testing whether the series (y_{it}) generated as in (17) has a unit root in all cross sections $i = 1, \ldots, N$ against the alternative that (y_{it}) are stationary in some cross-section i. The null hypothesis is therefore formulated as $H_0 : \alpha_i = 1$ for all i and tested against the stationarity alternative $H_1 : |\alpha_i| < 1$ for some i. The test statistic we first consider for testing the panel unit root hypothesis is a simple average of the individual nonlinear IV t-ratio statistics for testing the unity of the AR coefficient computed from each cross-sectional unit. Under the AR(p_i) specification of the error u_{it}, the model (17) is written as

$$y_{it} = \alpha_i y_{i,t-1} + \sum_{k=1}^{p_i} \alpha_{ik} \Delta y_{i,t-k} + \varepsilon_{it}, \quad i = 1, \ldots, N; \; t = 1, \ldots, T, \tag{19}$$

which is identical, at each cross-sectional level, to the regression (5) used in the previous section to derive the univariate nonlinear IV t-ratio given in (9). For each cross section i, we therefore instrument the lagged level $y_{i,t-1}$, using an integrable transformation of itself, $F(y_{i,t-1})$, and accordingly define the nonlinear IV t-ratio τ_i for testing $\alpha_i = 1$ as

$$\tau_i = \frac{\hat{\alpha}_i - 1}{s(\hat{\alpha}_i)},$$

where $\hat{\alpha}_i$ and $s(\hat{\alpha}_i)$ are, respectively, the nonlinear IV estimator of α_i and its standard error defined as in (8) and (10). The limit theories for each individual IV t-ratio τ_i follow exactly in the same manner as for the univariate nonlinear IV t-ratio given in Lemma 13.1 and Theorem 13.1, under the same set of conditions modified for our panel setting here. Let $|\cdot|$ denote the Euclidean norm: for a vector $x = (x_i)$, $|x|^2 = \sum_i x_i^2$, and for a matrix $A = (a_{ij})$, $|A| = \sum_{i,j} a_{ij}^2$. We assume

Assumption 13.4 For $i = 1, \ldots, N$, $\alpha^i(z) \neq 0$ for all $|z| \leq 1$.

Assumption 13.5 (ε_t) is an iid $(0, \Sigma)$ sequence of random vectors with $\mathbf{E}|\varepsilon_t|^\ell < \infty$ for some $\ell > 4$, and its distribution is absolutely continuous with respect to Lebesgue measure and has characteristic function φ such that $\lim_{\lambda \to \infty} |\lambda|^r \varphi(\lambda) = 0$ for some $r > 0$.

Under Assumption 13.5, an invariance principle holds for the partial sum process U_T of the N-vector innovations (ε_t) – that is, $U_T \to_d U$ as $T \to \infty$, where $U = (U_1, \ldots, U_N)'$ is an N-dimensional vector Brownian motion with covariance matrix Σ. It is also convenient to define $B_T(r)$ from $u_t = (u_{1t}, \ldots, u_{Nt})'$ in much the same way as was done for $U_T(r)$. Let $\alpha^i(1) = 1 - \sum_{k=1}^{p_i} \alpha_{ik}$ and $\pi_i(1) = 1/\alpha^i(1)$. Then under Assumptions 13.4 and 13.5 we have $B_T \to_d B$, where $B = (B_1, \ldots, B_N)'$ and $B_i = \pi_i(1) U_i$ for $i = 1, \ldots, N$. The local times that appear in our limit theory are L_i and are (scaled) local times of U_i, for $i = 1, \ldots, N$. As shown in Chang (2002), we have

Theorem 13.2 *Under Assumptions 13.3–13.5, we have*

$$\tau_i \to_d \mathbf{N}(0, 1)$$

as $T \to \infty$ for all $i = 1, \ldots, N$, and

$$\tau_i, \tau_j \sim \textit{asymptotically independent}$$

for all $i \neq j = 1, \ldots, N$.

The standard normal limit theory of the univariate nonlinear IV t-ratio τ given in Theorem 13.1 continues to apply for each individual IV t-ratio τ_i for $i = 1, \ldots, N$. Moreover, the nonlinear IV t-ratios from different cross sections are asymptotically independent even under cross-sectional dependency. The asymptotic orthogonalities of the nonlinear IV t-ratios play a crucial role in developing our panel unit root test because these, along with the Gaussianity of the individual IV t-ratios, provide a basis of N asymptotically iid normal random variates for us to work with.

Before we proceed to define our panel unit root test, we provide some heuristics to understand the important asymptotic orthogonalities. We have the following distributional equivalences in the limit for the sample moments determining the limit theories of the IV t-ratios τ_i and τ_j from the cross sections i and j:

$$T^{-1/4}\sum_{t=1}^{T} F(y_{i,t-1})\varepsilon_{it} \approx_d \sqrt[4]{T}\int_0^1 F(\sqrt{T}B_i(r))dU_i(r)$$
$$T^{-1/4}\sum_{t=1}^{T} F(y_{j,t-1})\varepsilon_{jt} \approx_d \sqrt[4]{T}\int_0^1 F(\sqrt{T}B_j(r))dU_j(r).$$

It is well known that the two right-hand-side stochastic processes become asymptotically independent if their quadratic covariation

$$\sigma_{ij}\sqrt{T}\int_0^1 F(\sqrt{T}B_i(r))F(\sqrt{T}B_j(r))dr \tag{20}$$

converges almost surely to zero, where σ_{ij} denotes the covariance between U_i and U_j. The order of the integral $\int_0^1 F(\sqrt{T}B_i(r))F(\sqrt{T}B_j(r))dr$ in eq. (20) is known to be $O_p(T^{-1}\log(T))$ a.s. (Kasahara and Kotani 1979), which in turn implies that the quadratic covariation (20) vanishes almost surely, regardless of the value of σ_{ij}. The reasons why the integral is of such a small order are twofold. The first is that the instrument-generating function F is an integrable function that assigns a nontrivial value only when the argument takes a small value; the second is that each of the arguments $\sqrt{T}B_i$ and $\sqrt{T}B_j$ takes a large value with increasing probability as T grows owing to the stochastic trends in the Brownian motions B_i and B_j. As a result, the product $F(\sqrt{T}B_i)F(\sqrt{T}B_j)$ takes a nontrivial value only with a small probability, making the preceding integral of such a small order.

Notice that U_i and U_j are the limit Brownian motions of the innovations (ε_{it}) and (ε_{jt}) generating the (y_{it}) and (y_{jt}). The result above therefore shows that the nonlinear instruments $F(y_{i,t-1})$ and $F(y_{j,t-1})$ from different cross-sectional units i and j are asymptotically uncorrelated – even when the variables (y_{it}) and (y_{jt}) generating the instruments are correlated. This then implies that the individual IV t-ratio statistics τ_i and τ_j constructed from the nonlinear instruments $F(y_{i,t-1})$ and $F(y_{j,t-1})$ are asymptotically independent. Hence, we may naturally consider an average of such asymptotically normal and independent nonlinear IV t-ratios to test for the joint unit root null hypothesis $H_0 : \alpha_i = 1$ for all $i = 1, \ldots, N$. The test is defined by

$$S = \frac{1}{\sqrt{N}} \sum_{i=1}^{N} \tau_i, \tag{21}$$

and the limit theory for S follows immediately from Theorem 13.2 as

Theorem 13.3 *We have*

$$S \to_d \mathbf{N}(0, 1)$$

as $T \to \infty$ under Assumptions 13.3–13.5.

Our limit theories derived here for the balanced panels continue to hold for the unbalanced panels, where each cross section i may have a different number T_i of observations, as shown in Chang (2002). To deal with the unbalanced nature of the data, we only need to ensure that the panel is asymptotically balanced in a weak sense. Specifically, it is required that $T_i \to \infty$ for all i and $T_{\min}^{-3/4} T_{\max}^{1/4} \log(T_{\max}) \to 0$, where $T_{\min}$ and $T_{\max}$ denote, repectively, the minimum and the maximum of T_i, $i = 1, \ldots, N$. Note that our limit theory is derived using T-asymptotics only, and the factor $N^{-1/2}$ in the definition of the test statistic S in (21) is used just as a normalization factor because S is based on the sum of N independent random variables. This implies the dimension of the cross-sectional units N may take any value, small as well as large. Our results also extend to the panels with heterogeneous deterministic components such as individual fixed effects and linear time trends. The asymptotic results established here for the models without deterministic components continue to hold for those with nonzero means and linear trends if the nonlinear IV estimation in each cross section is based on the properly detrended data, using the adaptive demeaning or detrending scheme introduced in Section 13.2.3. The standard normal theory for our nonlinear IV panel unit root test, therefore continues to hold for the panels with heterogeneous fixed effects and time trends.

The normal limit theory is also obtained for the existing panel unit root tests, such as the pooled OLS test by Levin et al. (2002) and the group mean t-bar statistic by Im et al. (2003); however, their theory holds only under cross-sectional independence and is obtained only through sequential asymptotics. More recently, several authors have made serious attempts to allow for cross-sectional dependencies. Chang (2004) allows for dependencies of unrestricted form, but her bootstrap procedure requires the dimension of time series T to be substantially larger than that of the cross section N, which is restrictive for many practical applications. On the other hand, the procedures by Choi (2001), Phillips and Sul (2001), Moon and Perron (2001), and Bai and Ng (2004) allow for a specific form of cross-sectional correlation structures that may find little justification in practical applications. In contrast, here we achieve the standard limit theory from the Gaussianity and independence of the limit distributions of the individual IV t-ratios without having to assume independence across cross-sectional units or relying on specific correlation structures. We can now engage in simple inference for panel unit root testing based on the critical values from the standard normal table in dependent panels driven by cross-correlated innovations and with various heterogeneities.

13.4 EXTENSIONS AND GENERALIZATIONS

13.4.1 Cointegrated Panels with Covariates

Our nonlinear IV approach can be extended to allow for the presence of cross-sectional cointegration and the use of relevant stationary covariates. We now let $y_t = (y_{1t}, \ldots, y_{Nt})'$ and assume that there are $N - M$ cointegrating relationships in the unit root process (y_t) represented by the cointegrating vectors (c_j), $j = 1, \ldots, N - M$. The usual vector autoregression and error correction representation allows us to specify the short-run dynamics of (y_t) as

$$\Delta y_{it} = \sum_{j=1}^{N} \sum_{k=1}^{P_{ij}} a_{ij} \Delta y_{j,t-k} + \sum_{j=1}^{N-M} b_{ij} c_j' y_{t-1} + \varepsilon_{it} \tag{22}$$

for each cross-sectional unit, $i = 1, \ldots, N$.

Our unit root tests at individual levels will be based on the regression

$$y_{it} = \alpha_i y_{i,t-1} + \sum_{k=1}^{P_i} \alpha_{ik} \Delta y_{i,t-k} + \sum_{k=1}^{Q_i} \beta_{ik}' w_{i,t-k} + \varepsilon_{it} \tag{23}$$

for $i = 1, \ldots, N$, where we interpret (w_{it}) as the *covariates* added to the augmented DF regression for the ith cross-sectional unit. It is important to note that the vector autoregression and error correction formulation of the cointegrated unit root panels in (22) suggest that we use such covariates. Under the null, we may obviously rewrite (1) and (22) as (23) with the covariates, which may include several lagged differences of other cross-sections and linear combinations of lagged levels of all cross sections. Indeed, in many panels of interest, we naturally expect to have interrelated short-run dynamics, which would make it necessary to include the dynamics of other cross-sections to model the dynamics properly in an individual unit. In the presence of cointegration, we also need to incorporate the long-run trends of other cross-sectional units because the stochastic trends of other cross-sectional units would interfere with the short-run dynamics in an individual unit through the error correction mechanism. Hence, the potential covariates for unit root testing in a cointegrated panel include the lagged differences of other cross sections to account for interactions in short-run dynamics and the linear combinations of cross-sectional levels in the presence of cointegration. Other stationary covariates may also be included to account for idiosyncratic characteristics of individual cross-sectional units.

The idea of using stationary covariates in the unit root regression was first entertained by Hansen (1995) in a univariate context and pursued further by Chang et al. (2001) using a bootstrap method. Both papers clearly demonstrate that the use of meaningful covariates offers a great potential in power gains for the test of a unit root. Given that one of the main motivations to use panels to test for unit roots is to increase the power, we have indeed overlooked this important opportunity in panel unit root testing. Choosing proper covariates can be a difficult issue in univariate applications, and the limit distribution of the standard covariates augmented ADF test by Hansen (1995) involves a nuisance parameter. In a panel context, however, there are many natural candidates for covariates such as those listed in the last paragraph. Moreover, the nonlinear instruments are asymptotically orthogonal to the stationary covariates, as shown in Chang and Song (2002), and therefore the inclusion of the stationary covariates does not incur the nuisance parameter problem for our nonlinear IV tests.

Denote, as before, by $U = (U_1, \ldots, U_N)'$ the limit of the partial sum process constructed from the N-vector innovations $\varepsilon_t = (\varepsilon_{1t}, \ldots, \varepsilon_{Nt})'$, which is assumed to satisfy the conditions in Assumption 13.2, and define $B = (B_1, \ldots, B_N)'$ to be the corresponding limit Brownian motion for $u_t = (u_{1t}, \ldots, u_{Nt})'$. As is well known, the presence of cointegration in (y_t) implies that the vector Brownian motion B is degenerate – that is, some of the individual limit Brownian motions $B_i, i = 1, \ldots, N$, are linearly dependent. This has important consequences for our asymptotic analyses. Most importantly, the asymptotic orthogonalities of the nonlinear IV t-ratios no longer hold. This is because the quadratic covariation given in (20) no longer vanishes in the limit. To see this, suppose $B_i = B_j$ for some i and j. Then the quadratic covariation becomes

$$\begin{aligned}\sigma_{ij}\sqrt{T}\int_0^1 F(\sqrt{T}B_i(r))F(\sqrt{T}B_i(r))dr &= \sigma_{ij}\sqrt{T}\int_0^1 F^2(\sqrt{T}B_i(r))dr \\ &= O_p(1), \text{ a.s.}\end{aligned}$$

because the integral $\int_0^1 F^2(\sqrt{T}B_i(r))dr$ is now of order $O_p(T^{-1/2})$, which is higher than the order for the case with no cointegration given below Theorem 13.2. This is because the integral now involves an integrable function of only one Brownian motion, that is, $F^2(\sqrt{T}B_i)$, which takes a nontrivial value with much larger probability compared with the product $F(\sqrt{T}B_i)F(\sqrt{T}B_j)$.

The presence of cointegration can be dealt with if we use an orthogonal set of functions as instrument generating functions (IGFs). This idea is exploited in

Chang and Song (2002). It is indeed easy to see that the quadratic covariation given in the expression above may vanish in the limit if we use orthogonal functions F_i and F_j to generate the instruments for cross sections i and j. As shown, for example, in Park (2003b),

$$\sqrt{T}\int_0^1 F_i(\sqrt{T}B_i(r))F_j(\sqrt{T}B_i(r))dr \to_{\text{a.s.}} 0$$

if F_i and F_j are orthogonal and $\int_{-\infty}^{\infty} F_i(x)F_j(x)\,dx = 0$.

The Hermite functions of odd orders $k = 2i - 1, i = 1, \dots, N$, for instance, can be used as a valid set of IGFs for the cointegrated panels. The Hermite function G_k of order k, $k = 0, 1, 2, \dots$, is defined as

$$G_k(x) = (2^k k!\sqrt{\pi})^{-1/2} H_k(x)e^{-x^2/2},$$

where H_k is the Hermite polynomial of order k given by

$$H_k(x) = (-1)^k e^{x^2} \frac{d^k}{dx^k} e^{-x^2}.$$

It is well known that the class of Hermite functions just introduced forms an orthonormal basis for $L^2(\mathbf{R})$, that is, the Hilbert space of square integrable functions on $\mathbf{R}$. We thus have

$$\int_{-\infty}^{\infty} G_j(x)G_k(x)dx = \delta_{jk}$$

for all j and k, where δ_{jk} is the Kronecker delta. Moreover, the odd-order Hermite functions satisfy the IGF validity conditions in Assumption 13.3.

The IV estimation for the regression (23) is straightforward given our earlier discussions. To deal with the cross-sectional cointegration, we use the instrument $F_i(y_{i,t-1})$ for the lagged level $y_{i,t-1}$ for each cross-sectional unit $i = 1, \dots, N$, where (F_i) is a set of orthogonal IGFs. For the augmented regressors $x_{it} = (\Delta y_{i,t-1}, \dots, \Delta y_{i,t-P_i}; w_{i,t-1}, \dots, w_{i,t-Q_i})'$, we use the variables themselves as the instruments. Hence the instruments $(F(y_{i,t-1}), x'_{it})'$ are used for the entire regressors $(y_{i,t-1}, x'_{it})'$. As is well expected, our previous asymptotic results also apply in this more general context. In particular, the limit theories in Theorems 13.2 and 13.3 continue to hold for the IV t-ratios τ_i's and also for the panel unit root statistic S in the presence of cointegration and covariates if constructed in the way suggested in the previous paragraph. This is shown in Chang and Song (2002).

13.4.2 Formulations of Hypotheses and Order Statistics

We now turn to the problems of formulating unit root hypotheses in panels, which were considered in Chang and Song (2002). For many practical applications, we are often interested in testing for unit roots collectively for a group of cross-sectional units included in the given panel. In this case, we need to formulate both the null and the alternative hypotheses more precisely. In particular, we may want to test for and against the existence of unit roots in only a fraction of cross-sectional units. Such formulations, however, seem more relevant and appropriate for many interesting empirical applications, including testing for purchasing power parity and growth convergence, among others. Here we lay out three sets of possible hypotheses in panel unit root testing and propose using the order statistics constructed from the nonlinear IV t-ratios to test effectively for such hypotheses.

We consider

Hypothesis (A) $\text{H}_0 : \alpha_i = 1$ for all i versus $\text{H}_1 : \alpha_i < 1$ for all i

Hypothesis (B) $\text{H}_0 : \alpha_i = 1$ for all i versus $\text{H}_1 : \alpha_i < 1$ for some i

Hypothesis (C) $\text{H}_0 : \alpha_i = 1$ for some i versus $\text{H}_1 : \alpha_i < 1$ for all i

Hypotheses (A) and (B) share the same null hypothesis that a unit root is present in all individual units. The null hypothesis, however, competes with different alternative hypotheses. In Hypothesis (A), the null is tested against the alternative hypothesis that all individual units are stationary, whereas in Hypothesis (B) it is tested against the alternative that there are some stationary individual units. On the contrary, the null hypothesis in Hypothesis (C) holds as long as a unit root exists in at least one individual unit and is tested against the alternative hypothesis that all individual units are stationary. The alternative hypotheses in both Hypotheses (B) and (C) are the negations of their respective null hypotheses. This is, however, not the case for Hypothesis (A). Hypothesis (C) has never been considered in the literature. Note that the rejection of H_0 in favor of H_1 in Hypothesis (C) directly implies that all (y_{it})'s are stationary, and, therefore, purchasing power parity or growth convergence holds if we let (y_{it})'s be real exchange rates or differences in growth rates, respectively. No test, however, is available to deal with Hypothesis (C) appropriately.

For the tests for Hypotheses (A)–(C), we define

$$\begin{aligned} S &= \frac{1}{\sqrt{N}} \sum_{i=1}^{N} \tau_i \\ S_{\min} &= \min_{1 \le i \le N} \tau_i \\ S_{\max} &= \max_{1 \le i \le N} \tau_i, \end{aligned}$$

where τ_i is the nonlinear IV t-ratio for the ith cross-sectional unit. The average statistic S is comparable to other existing tests and is proposed for the test of Hypothesis (A). Virtually all of the existing panel unit root tests effectively test for Hypothesis (A). Some recent work, including Im et al. (2003) and Chang (2002), formulate their null and alternative hypotheses as in Hypothesis (B). However, their use of average t-ratios can only be justified for the test of Hypothesis (A). The minimum statistic $S_{\min}$ is more appropriate for the test of Hypothesis (B) than the tests based on the averages. The average statistic S may also be used to test for Hypothesis (B), but the test based on $S_{\min}$ would have more power, especially when only a small fraction of cross-sectional units are stationary under the alternative hypothesis. The maximum statistic $S_{\max}$ can be used to test Hypothesis (C). Obviously, the average statistic S cannot be used to test for Hypothesis (C) because it would have incorrect size.

Let M be $0 \leq M \leq N$, assume $\alpha_i = 1$ for $1 \leq i \leq M$, and set $M = 0$ if $\alpha_i < 1$ for all $1 \leq i \leq N$. It is easy to derive the asymptotic theories for the test statistics defined in the previous paragraph. Recall that the nonlinear IV t-ratios for all individual cross-sections have standard normal limiting distributions and are asymptotically orthogonal to each other. This leaves a set of M random variates τ_i's that are asymptotically independent and identically distributed as standard normal. To obtain the asymptotic critical values for the statistics S, $S_{\min}$, and $S_{\max}$, we let Φ be the distribution function for the standard normal distribution and let λ be the size of the tests. For a given size λ, we define $x_M(\lambda)$ (with $x_1(\lambda) = x(\lambda)$) and $y_N(\lambda)$ by

$$\Phi(x_M(\lambda))^M = \lambda, \quad (1 - \Phi(y_N(\lambda)))^N = 1 - \lambda.$$

These provide the critical values of the statistics S, $S_{\min}$, and $S_{\max}$ for the tests of Hypotheses (A)–(C). The following table shows the tests and critical values that can be used to test each of Hypotheses (A)–(C).

Hypothesis	Test Statistics	Critical Values
Hypothesis (A)	S	$x(\lambda)$
Hypothesis (B)	S	$x(\lambda)$
	$S_{\min}$	$y_N(\lambda)$
Hypothesis (C)	$S_{\max}$	$x(\lambda)$
	$S_{\max}$	$x_M(\lambda)$

It is clear that

$$\lim_{T\to\infty} \mathbf{P}\{S \leq x(\lambda)\} = \lambda$$

$$\lim_{T\to\infty} \mathbf{P}\{S_{\min} \leq y_N(\lambda)\} = \lambda$$

if $M = N$. The tests using statistics S and $S_{\min}$ with critical values $x(\lambda)$ and $y_N(\lambda)$, respectively, have the exact size λ asymptotically under the null hypotheses in Hypotheses (A) and (B).

Moreover, if $1 \leq M \leq N$, then

$$\lim_{T\to\infty} \mathbf{P}\{S_{\max} \leq x_M(\lambda)\} = \lambda, \quad \lim_{T\to\infty} \mathbf{P}\{S_{\max} \leq x(\lambda)\} \leq \lambda.$$

The null hypothesis in Hypothesis (C) is composite, and the rejection probabilities of the test $S_{\max}$ based on the critical value $x(\lambda)$ may not be exactly λ even asymptotically. The size λ in this case is the maximum rejection probabilities that can be obtained under the null hypothesis.

These results imply that the nonlinear IV order statistics suggested here have limit distributions that are nuisance parameter free and are given by simple functions of the standard normal distribution function. The critical values are thus easily derived from those of the standard normal distribution.

13.5 CONCLUSION

This chapter has considered the nonlinear IV approach to testing for unit roots in general panels with dependency and heterogeneity. The nonlinear IV-based tests have many desirable properties. First, the tests permit both short- and long-run cross-sectional dependencies of the most general form. The presence of cointegration, the interrelatedness of short-run dynamics, and the cross-correlations among the errors are all allowed. This is in sharp constrast to other existing tests, which assume complete cross-sectional independence of the errors. Second, various heterogeneities are allowed. Heterogeneities in dynamics, individual fixed effects and trends, and the numbers of individual time series observations are all permitted in our framework. Third, the tests are flexible enough to accommodate the extensions in various directions. In particular, they allow for the use of relevant stationary covariates to increase power without running into nuisance parameter problems. For the standard approach, the use of covariates yields limit distributions including nuisance parameters that are difficult to deal with. They can also be extended to test for cointegration in panels with general dependency, as will be reported in a later work. Finally, our nonlinear IV method makes it possible to formulate the panel unit root hypotheses in more flexible and more precise forms that can be tested by the order statistics. With the tests provided here, the empirical researchers will be able to investigate much more precisely and rigorously a wide variety of important economic issues regarding international and interstate comparisons and interactions, including purchasing power parities and growth convergences and divergences.

References

Bai, J. and S. Ng (2004). "A PANIC attack on unit roots and cointegration," *Econometrica*, 72, 1127–1177.

Baltagi, B. H. and C. Kao (2000). "Nonstationary panels, cointegration in panels and dynamic panels: A survey," mimeograph, Department of Economics, Texas A&M University.

Chang, Y. (2002). "Nonlinear IV unit root tests in panels with cross-sectional dependency," *Journal of Econometrics*, 110, 261–292.

Chang, Y. (2004). "Bootstrap unit root tests in panels with cross-sectional dependency," *Journal of Econometrics*, 120, 263–293.

Chang, Y., J. Y. Park, and P. C. B. Phillips (2001). "Nonlinear econometric models with cointegrated and deterministically trending regressors," *Econometrics Journal*, 4, 1–36.

Chang, Y., R. C. Sickles, and W. Song (2001). "Bootstrapping unit root tests with covariates," mimeograph, Department of Economics, Rice University.

Chang, Y. and W. Song (2002). "Panel Unit Root Tests in the Presence of Cross-Sectional Dependency and Heterogeneity," mimeograph, Department of Economics, Rice University.

Choi, I. (2001). "Unit root tests for cross-sectionally correlated panels," mimeograph, Kukmin University.

Chung, K. L. and Williams, R. J. (1990). *Introduction to Stochastic Integration*, 2nd ed. Boston: Birkhäuser.

Fuller, W. A. (1996). *Introduction to Statistical Time Series*, 2nd ed. New York: Wiley.

Hansen, B. E. (1995). "Rethinking the univariate approach to unit root testing: Using covariates to increase power," *Econometric Theory*, 11, 1148–1171.

Im, K. S., M. H. Pesaran, and Y. Shin (2003). "Testing for unit roots in heterogeneous panels," *Journal of Econometrics*, 115, 53–74.

Kasahara, Y. and S. Kotani (1979). "On limit processes for a class of additive functionals of recurrent diffusion processes," *Z. Wahrscheinlichkeitstheorie verw. Gebiete*, 49, 133–153.

Levin, A., C. F. Lin, and C. S. Chu (2002). "Unit root tests in panel data: Asymptotic and finite sample properties," *Journal of Econometrics*, 108, 1–24.

Maddala, G. S. and S. Wu (1999). "A comparative study of unit root tests with panel data and a new simple test: Evidence from simulations and bootstrap," *Oxford Bulletin of Economics and Statistics*, 61, 631–652.

Moon, H. R. and B. Perron, (2001). "Testing for a unit root in panels with dynamic factors," *Journal of Econometrics*.

Park, J. Y. (2003a). "Strong approximations for nonlinear transformations of integrated time series," mimeograph, Department of Economics, Rice University.

Park, J. Y. (2003b). "Nonstationary nonlinearity: An outlook for new opportunities," mimeograph, Deparment of Economics, Rice University.

Park, J. Y. and P. C. B. Phillips (1988). "Statistical inference in regressions with integrated processes: Part 1," *Econometric Theory*, 5, 468–498.

Park, J. Y. and P. C. B. Phillips (1999). "Asymptotics for nonlinear transformations of integrated time series," *Econometric Theory*, 15, 269–298.

Park, J. Y. and P. C. B. Phillips (2001). "Nonlinear regressions with integrated time series," *Econometrica*, 69, 1452–1498.

Phillips, P. C. B. (1987). "Time series regression with a unit root," *Econometrica*, 55, 277–301.

Phillips, P. C. B. and H. R. Moon (2000). "Nonstationary panel data analysis: An overview of some recent developments," *Econometric Reviews*, 19, 263–286.

Phillips, P. C. B., J. Y. Park, and Y. Chang (2004). "Nonlinear instrumental variable estimation of an autoregression," *Journal of Econometrics*, 118, 219–246.

Phillips, P. C. B. and P. Perron (1988). "Testing for a unit root in time series regression," *Biometrika*, 75, 335–346.

Phillips, P. C. B. and V. Solo (1992). "Asymptotics for linear processes," *Annals of Statistics*, 20, 971–1001.
Phillips, P. C. B. and D. Sul (2001). "Dynamic panel estimation and homogeneity testing under cross section dependence," mimeograph, University of Auckland.
Quah, D. (1994). "Exploiting cross-section variations for unit root inference in dynamic panels," *Economics Letters*, 44, 1–9.

Index